Courage Above All Things

Courage Above All Things

GENERAL JOHN ELLIS WOOL AND THE U.S. MILITARY, 1812–1863

HARWOOD P. HINTON
and
JERRY THOMPSON

UNIVERSITY OF OKLAHOMA PRESS: NORMAN

Publication of this book is made possible through the generous support of Sanchez Oil and Gas and the Office of the Provost and the Office of the Dean, College of Arts and Sciences, at Texas A&M International University.

LIBRARY OF CONGRESS CATALOGING-IN-PUBLICATION DATA
Names: Hinton, Harwood P., 1927– author. | Thompson, Jerry D., author.
Title: Courage Above All Things : General John Ellis Wool and the U.S. Military, 1812–1863 / Harwood P. Hinton and Jerry Thompson.
Other titles: General John Ellis Wool and the U.S. military, 1812–1863
Description: Norman : University of Oklahoma Press, [2020] | Includes bibliographical references and index. | Summary: "Biography of John Ellis Wool a military commander who figured prominently in many critical moments in nineteenth-century U.S. history."—Provided by publisher.
Identifiers: LCCN 2020017602 | ISBN 978-0-8061-6724-4 (hardcover)
Subjects: LCSH: Wool, John Ellis, 1784–1869. | United States. Army—Officers—Biography. | United States. Army—History—19th century. Generals—United States—Biography. | Troy (N.Y.) —Biography.
Classification: LCC E403.1.W8 H56 2020 | DDC 973.6/2092—dc23
LC record available at https://lccn.loc.gov/2020017602

The paper in this book meets the guidelines for permanence and durability of the Committee on Production Guidelines for Book Longevity of the Council on Library Resources, Inc. ∞

1 2 3 4 5 6 7 8 9 10

For Diana Davids Hinton

I must study politics and war that my sons may have liberty and study mathematics and philosophy.

John Adams

CONTENTS

MAPS

PREFACE

For well more than fifty years, Harwood Perry Hinton researched and wrote a definitive biography of Gen. John Ellis Wool, a strikingly significant military figure of nineteenth-century America. Harwood was born into a poor family in a run-down house without indoor plumbing near Irving, Texas, on March 26, 1927. His father, Harwood Perry Hinton Sr., ran a small grocery store at the nearby hamlet of Twin Wells. Harwood could trace his family back to colonial Virginia and the family's migration to North Carolina and then to Alabama. Graduating from Irving High School in suburban Dallas in 1945, Harwood wanted to join the military, but World War II was ending and he was off to the Agricultural and Mechanical College of Texas in College Station. His stay at College Station was cut short by a savage beating received during a freshmen hazing incident. Returning to Irving, he enrolled in courses at what became the University of Texas–Arlington. Hinton was bright, made good grades, and loved history. He was accepted at the University of Texas–Austin, where one of his professors was Walter Prescott Webb, whom Harwood found entertaining but less than inspirational.[1]

Diploma in hand, Harwood took a job teaching junior high school in the oil boomtown of Odessa in the heart of the Permian Basin. Getting off the train with only a suitcase and a typewriter, he soon rented a room in a two-room converted garage next to a "lady whose business kept her very busy at night," he recalled. Harwood loved his time in Odessa but yearned to pursue his growing interest in history. Hoping to obtain a master's degree, in 1950 he enrolled in summer classes at Columbia University in New York City. Hinton had been at Columbia for only a few weeks when the Korean War erupted and he was drafted into the army. After basic training at Fort Riley, Kansas, he was sent to Japan and assigned stenographic work. Hinton rose rapidly to the rank of sergeant and was given a top security clearance. In the land of the rising sun, he traveled extensively, dated, and enjoyed life. Diana Davids Hinton, Harwood's second wife, is sure that it was in Japan that he obtained his love of military history.[2]

Back in the United States, Harwood returned to Odessa to teach and resume his summer classes at Columbia. His thesis at Columbia on John Simpson Chisum, the legendary western cattle baron who was a central player in the bloody Lincoln

County War, was revised and published in three parts by the *New Mexico Historical Review* in 1956 and 1957.[3]

While in Odessa, Harwood met a young librarian named Mary Ann Brookshire from the well-to-do and well-known Brookshire Brothers supermarket family of East Texas, and the two married in June 1956. Three children, John Harwood, Mary Ann, and James R., came of the marriage. By this time, Harwood had been accepted into the PhD program at the University of Wisconsin, and the couple was off to the frigid north country. Using benefits from the GI Bill and working as a teaching assistant, Harwood fell under the influence of Vernon Carstensen, a nationally known specialist in agricultural economics.[4]

At Madison, Hinton's historical focus shifted toward nineteenth-century American military history, especially the Civil War. A lifelong fascination with the war's impact on his paternal ancestors may have propelled him toward General Wool. Wool's years on the western frontier, as well as the general's pivotal role in the conflict between the United States and Mexico, especially the bloody and decisive Battle of Buena Vista, fascinated Hinton. Wool's various assignments during the Civil War, including his command in New York City during the violent draft riots in 1863, also interested Hinton, and he decided to undertake a dissertation on Wool's military career. Consequently, at every opportunity, Harwood spent time at the New York State Archives in Albany, which housed ninety-eight boxes of the voluminous Wool papers.[5] During his fifty-one years in the army, Wool retained every document of significance, including his personal correspondence. When in the field or away from home, he wrote his wife, Sarah, several times a week. Not only did she preserve her husband's letters as well as newspaper clippings highlighting his career, but he preserved her letters as well. Hinton meticulously copied hundreds of Wool's letters in longhand and took thousands of pages of notes. Perusing hundreds of documents from other archives and libraries, and tracking down Wool's relatives, Hinton completed and successfully defended his dissertation on Wool in 1960.

Hinton had several job offers, but on the recommendations of his Wisconsin mentors, he decided to accept an offer from Texas A&M University, despite his bad experience in College Station as a freshman. Besides, Ann and Harwood yearned to return to Texas. There was a downside to Texas A&M, however. The department was chaired by the larger-than-life, dictatorial John Milton Nance, a recognized authority on the Texas Revolution and the Texas Republic. Senior faculty quarreled, and Nance insisted junior faculty teach only the survey classes in American history.[6] A day or two before the end of every month, Nance would visit junior faculty in their office and ask for an accounting of their activities during the previous thirty days. In what seemed an unpardonable intrusion into a faculty's privacy and personal life, every Sunday afternoon after church junior faculty were expected to be at home ready to receive a social visit from either the chairman or senior faculty. Such visits were routine. Outgoing as they were, Harwood and Ann were tolerant, but the enforced entertaining became tiresome and intrusive. At the end of Hinton's first year at A&M, five faculty, including Harwood, found jobs elsewhere. Nance later told Hinton that the exodus led the department to rethink its treatment of junior faculty.

While Hinton was in College Station in the early summer of 1961, he wrote Savoie Lottinville, director and editor of the University of Oklahoma Press, saying he was "preparing a full-length biography of Major General John Ellis Wool, 1784–1869." Only months earlier he had defended his dissertation, a "well-researched" study of Wool's military career, that drew largely from the voluminous Wool papers at the New York State Library. Hinton went to great lengths to impress Lottinville with Wool's distinguished career. For a half century, Hinton pointed out, Wool was "one of America's most illustrious figures—a soldier whose exploits school children of the pre–Civil War generation knew well." Hinton had tentatively entitled his biography "Trojan in Blue: The Biography of John Ellis Wool." The distinguished Rice University historian Frank Vandiver had critiqued the manuscript and recommended several revisions, Hinton explained. Lottinville responded that the University of Oklahoma Press was most interested, and Hinton promised to "get right after it."[7]

Vandiver told Hinton he had learned a lot from the biography, especially the chapter on Wool's role in the expulsion of the Cherokees. There was little doubt Hinton had the makings of a "good book," but Vandiver recommended several revisions. "Line for line" editing was needed and Hinton should look more into the general's personality and private life. "Publishers are a harsh and crass breed who pay lip service to scholarly impediments and then demand that you pare it to the bone," Vandiver went on to say. Lastly, he recommended Hinton not "blow up your man's achievements beyond the power of your sources," but urged him to work on it and "publish it by all means." "I want to cite it!" Vandiver wrote. Always remember, the Rice scholar continued, "all facts are not created equal."[8]

Hinton was at the University of Arizona for thirty years. There he joined John Alexander Carroll, the Pulitzer Prize–winning historian and Pearl Harbor survivor, who had recently established the reputable historical journal *Arizona and the West.* Hinton was a co-editor for the journal. Fresh out of Rice University, one of Vandiver's students, Bruce Dinges, joined Carroll and Hinton. Years later, Dinges remembered Hinton and Carroll as polar opposites. Carroll was easygoing and just as comfortable in the pool hall as in the classroom. Hinton was meticulous and dedicated and spent endless hours mentoring students and attending historical conferences to seek out potential articles for *Arizona and the West.*[9] Decades later, a student in Hinton's graduate symposium recalled some of his words: "If it is easy to write, it is hard to read. If it is hard to write, it is easy to read."[10] Hinton's new duties pressed him hard and there was little time to work on the Wool manuscript.

Along with Ray Allen Billington and others, Hinton was instrumental in establishing the Western History Association (WHA), which met for the first time in Santa Fe in 1961. The association was bound by the belief that the American West was rich in history and deserved further study.[11] Meeting at the first WHA gathering in Santa Fe, Hinton told Lottinville that although his work in Tucson was "unremitting," he planned to spend his summer "recasting and revising Wool."[12] When Hinton finally submitted the manuscript and he saw Lottinville at the WHA in Denver in the fall of 1962, there were no reader reports and Hinton grew anxious. Finally, in October, Lottinville sent Hinton a reader report, most likely from Vandiver, in which the reviewer recommended publication of the manuscript, but only with major revisions.

What sort of a person was Wool? the reviewer asked. Was Wool a "true martinet? A moderately capable soldier serving among fools? A political general?" There should be more on Wool's family life. Moreover, the manuscript still bore the "earmarks of a dissertation." Either Hinton could not make Wool interesting, or the general possessed a "singularly dry personality." Wool was lacking a biographer and was deserving of one, and Hinton was undoubtedly that person, but he needed to "brighten up" the general.[13]

The critique was both "fair and rewarding," Hinton told Lottinville, and he felt entirely confident in revising the manuscript to "delineate Wool's personality and rebuild the story around the man." A week later, Lottinville sent Hinton a contract.[14] Hinton promised to begin revisions immediately and do everything possible to produce a first-class biography that would "reflect the high standards of scholarship your press has long maintained."[15] He hoped to have a final draft to Lottinville by early fall of 1962.

By January 1963, it was Lottinville who grew anxious. He asked Hinton if the manuscript could be completed in three to four months so that the press could publicize the biography for fall publication. Several months later, Hinton wrote to say that he was hoping to "push right along on the work" and planned to get a manuscript to the press "at the earliest possible moment." But Hinton had assumed the editorship of *Arizona and the West* and was working hard to "bolster the sagging fortunes" of the "fine journal." Hinton was proud of his tenure with *Arizona and the West,* and he felt honored that the journal had published the first articles for a number of western historians who had gone on to become leaders in their field.[16] Harwood also loved teaching and he particularly enjoyed mentoring students. Scouting several history conferences a year for potential articles for *Arizona and the West* was also time-consuming. Hinton was hoping for "brighter news" by early winter.

In September 1966, Hinton wrote to apologize for not having a final draft. He had been forced to go back to his notes and rewrite three chapters from scratch. Lottinville was still hoping to have the book out by spring 1967. When Edward A. Shaw became director of the University of Oklahoma Press in 1967, he continued to press Harwood, saying one of the last things Lottinville told him before leaving the press was to expect a "terribly significant manuscript."[17] Hinton responded that the revisions were "going very slowly" but he was hoping to find time for them in the summer.[18]

For the next forty-seven years Hinton continued working on his biography of General Wool, adding a footnote here and there, always revising, rewriting, and editing. Meeting Harwood at a conference was like greeting a tornado. In minutes, the conversation turned to Wool and some aspect of the general's career, whereupon Harwood would deliver an "encyclopedic knowledge of Western history and an amazing capacity to rattle off dates, places, and names of people," one historian recalled.[19] His daughter Mary remembered watching Westerns on TV with her father and being irritated by his constant interruptions to comment on how the saddles were not from the period being depicted, how the hats were also wrong, the clothing too modern, and the mountains just outside Dodge City, Kansas, misplaced. Hinton was always able to uncover a new document or a new piece of scholarship that needed integrating into the manuscript. Frequently the entire manuscript was retyped and, with the computer era, there were time consuming changes from one word processing software to another. Mary remembered her father constantly working on the manuscript. She also colored her father's lecture notes which Harwood found amusing.

After thirty years in Tucson, Harwood retired, and he and Ann moved to Austin. In February 1994, tragic news followed when they learned that their son John was dead at the age of 32 from a heart attack while working at the post office back in Tucson. Neither Harwood, Ann, Mary, or James, ever got over the loss of their son and brother. Sadly, three years later in November 1997, Ann also died suddenly from cardiac arrest while sitting at a desk writing to her brother. As heartbroken as he had been when his son passed away, Harwood sought solace in a major project. He hastened to join Ron Tyler and the staff of the Texas State Historical Association as senior editor on the momentous six-volume *Handbook of Texas*.[20] Harwood was always as meticulous with his editing as he was with his research.

In Tucson and in Austin, Hinton worked to mentor promising young scholars such as Glen Sample Ely, Dawn Moore, Mark Santiago, Andy Masich, and Karen Underhill. Hinton also continued his exhaustive research into the life of John Chisum, a Southwestern cattle baron, hoping to turn his previous work into a book-length manuscript as he had done with Wool. Hinton was close to many well-known historians, and he carried on a lively correspondence with several. Among them was

John P. Wilson, whom Hinton greatly respected and considered the most knowledgeable historian of the Lincoln County War. "I have not done much with Wool in the last few years," Hinton confessed to the Harvard-trained Wilson in March of 2000, "I have a large manuscript, but reduced eyesight—and my time has been focused elsewhere."[21] In August 2007, Harwood wrote Wilson that he was "plugging away" on the Wool biography, "although my eyesight grows dim."[22] Later yet, Hinton wrote that he had been "slicing" on the manuscript "for months—even though my eyesight continues to dim." The "motivation is still there—and I move ahead."[23]

In May 2005, Harwood and Diana Davids Olien were married in Midland. Diana was a Yale PhD and distinguished historian, who continued to teach in Odessa at the University of Texas–Permian Basin. Both enjoyed seeing mutual friends at history conferences. There were lengthy automobile drives across the vast arid expanses of West Texas where Harwood talked about the Battle of Buena Vista and other aspects of General Wool's career, and Diana explained the differences between sweet and sour crude oil. Bruce Dinges would later remark that Harwood had the great luck of being married to two wonderful women. Mary would later say that if she could have designed a perfect partner for her father that person would have been Diana.[24]

While Diana was at work, Harwood spent long hours every day working on edits to his Wool manuscript. In January 2013, he contracted a severe and painful case of the shingles that seemed to settle in his left eye. "I cannot read newspapers or books at the moment and have trouble signing my name. I live on pain pills," he acknowledged to his friend Wilson.[25] He was also taking insulin three times a day to control his diabetes. Hinton was also struggling to organize his Chisum papers, which he had decided to donate to Texas Tech University. Hinton went to seven different eye specialists but there was little they could do. With the help of a bright light and magnifying equipment, Harwood could read, but barely. In fact, Diana had to read to him most of the time. His fifty years of work on the life of Gen. John Ellis Wool was at an end. The loss of his vision was a terrible blow.

In May 2016, Harwood, who never consumed alcohol, was diagnosed with stage four cirrhosis of the liver. Harwood Perry Hinton, historian of the American Southwest, died in Midland on September 6, 2016, at the age of 89 and was laid to rest in Laurel Land Cemetery in Dallas with other members of the Hinton family.[26]

What follows is Hinton's long-awaited biography of Gen. John Ellis Wool, rightfully published by the University of Oklahoma Press. The study has been recast, chapters rewritten, recent scholarship added, information rearranged, and the entire manuscript thoroughly edited. Some information, especially the general's views of race, have been given a new, more critical interpretation. When possible, the general's family life has been incorporated into the study. As Vandiver wanted fifty-eight years ago, Wool has, I hope, been "brightened up."

1

OFF TO WAR WITH THE JOLLY SNORTERS

In a graying dusk on a late-summer afternoon, August 19, 1848, sharp blasts from the *Henrick Hudson* echoed up and down the picturesque Hudson River, signaling the arrival of a group of dignitaries at the river port of Troy, New York. During the afternoon hundreds of people gathered near the wharf, waiting to welcome home a hero from the killing fields of Mexico. As the steamboat eased to the dock, a band struck up a lively martial tune, the crowd cheered and surged forward, all eyes turned to a small, barely five-feet-tall, spare man with a cherubic face, smartly dressed in a blue uniform and wearing the stars of a major general. It was a glorious moment for John Ellis Wool, then sixty one, whose ties to Troy ran back to his childhood. It was here, seven miles up the Hudson from the state capital of Albany, where the general had lived for nearly a decade. Coming ashore, Wool greeted municipal officials, shook hands with hundreds of old friends and dignitaries, and rode in an open carriage up Ferry Street to his residence near the town square. In the weeks that followed, there would be other celebrations of his services in Mexico, but the warm reception John Wool received that day in Troy would remain a cherished memory in his long and distinguished military career.[1]

Long before the nation gained its independence, the Wool family had lived in the Hudson Valley for several generations. The first of the line, Jörgen Woll, a Swede, arrived in the English colony of New York about 1700 from Viborg, in what is today Finland. He worked as a common laborer, and in 1707 married Altje Brouwer, a girl of Dutch parentage living in Brooklyn. At least nine children were born to the union, and, like many immigrant families, Jörgen's offspring broke sharply with the past. The sons changed their surname from Woll to Wool, anglicized Swedish or Dutch given names, and married into Scotch, Scotch-Irish, and Welsh families. Several members of the Wool family became successful craftsmen and prominent citizens in New York City.[2]

James Wool, one of Jörgen's younger sons, who was born in 1719, never learned a trade, and in 1768, had moved his family up the Hudson Valley to a farm on the Hoosic River, near the village of Schaghticoke in Albany (later Rensselaer) County.

Two of his sons, Ellis and John, remained in New York to complete apprenticeships. Ellis Wool became a heelmaker, but his brother John dallied at various trades. About 1772, John Wool married Ann Reliva, the daughter of a cordwainer, and settled near his father on the Hoosic River. At the outbreak of the American Revolution, several of James Wool's sons joined the militia. The British captured Ellis and Robert Wool, and Ellis died on a dreadful New Jersey prison ship. John Wool, the father of the future general, enrolled in John Knickerbocker's Fourteenth Regiment, Albany County Militia, and fought in the battle of Stony Point (July 16, 1779) on the Hudson, south of West Point, but afterwards saw little military service.[3]

With the return of peace in 1781, John Wool moved his wife and five daughters down the Hudson to the village of Newburgh, where the remnants of Gen. George Washington's army remained camped awaiting discharge. Wool rented Martin Weigand's two-story rickety log tavern and frame addition across the street from Washington's headquarters. He sought work as a heelmaker, someone who made the heels of shoes or boots. The tavern received a brief financial boost in the fall of 1782 when Gen. Anthony Wayne set up his headquarters there. The shoe business was brisk, but by mid-November of 1783, the remaining veterans had left for home. The Wools postponed a planned move to New York City, as Ann was expecting a sixth child. On a cold wintry morning, February 29, 1784, she gave birth to a son, and the proud parents named him John Ellis.[4]

By that summer, John Wool had settled at 14 Broad Street in Lower Manhattan. At the time, New York City boasted a population of over 20,000, and extended north some two miles from the old fort or Battery. There being few shoemakers on Broad Street, Wool seemed well located for his trade but failed to prosper. On April 1, 1789, John Wool finally attained "freeman" status, but less than a year later, on July 23, 1790, he died unexpectedly at the age of forty.[5]

With a large family to support, the eldest being seventeen, Ann Wool sent six-year-old John Ellis to live with his grandparents on a farm near Schaghticoke, 171 miles up the Hudson River, just north of Troy. The family included James Wool, sixty-five, his wife Mary and their married son James Jr., who had several children and did most of the farm work. Although frail and small for his age, John was a bright and energetic boy who tackled chores cheerfully and soon learned to ride and care for a horse. But farm life was drab, dull, and the hours were long and demanding. At the local country school, he became an avid reader and became particularly interested in history. By age twelve, John Wool complained of the monotony and laborious farm life to a cousin visiting from New York City. The cousin found a merchant in Troy, ten miles downriver from Schaghticoke, who agreed to employ him as an apprentice. In the early autumn of 1796, James Wool drove his grandson in a wagon to his new home. Wool long remembered this trip, his "little all" tied in a large handkerchief, and the despair of being thrown "upon the world" without fortune or friends at a young age.[6]

In 1796, Troy was a bustling community of 500 inhabitants. The village sat in a cove on the east bank of the Hudson River at the head of sloop navigation. After the revolution, the Jacob D. Vanderheyden family, who had operated farms there, laid out a town in a grove of oak and pine trees on the high ground back from the river. Immigrants, mostly from New England, arrived, and built stores, warehouses, and homes. In January of 1789, the residents named the village Troy, and after the creation of Rensselaer County in February of 1791, Troy became the county seat. The village was not only a river port, but a small industrial center. Poestenkill Creek, fed by the falls from Mt. Ida, furnished power for several small mills and supplied water for a brewery, tanning yards, potash and rope works. Trade and politics dominated village life. Many early settlers and public officials were Federalists, but by the late 1790s the followers of Thomas Jefferson had gained influence and launched a weekly newspaper, *The Farmer's Oracle.*[7]

John Wool began his apprenticeship with a merchant on River Street, bordering the Hudson. In his free time, on clear days he frequently climbed to the 300-foot summit of Mt. Ida, where he could gaze across the river to the Mohawk River as it emptied water from the western lake country into the Hudson. Six miles to the southwest lay Albany, the state capital, with more than six thousand people. There were also visits to the wharves where old men gathered to reminisce about the Revolution and life under the British. Every boy in Troy knew ninety-year-old Col. Donald Campbell, a walking specter, his hair as white as new-fallen snow. Campbell was known for having helped to carry the mortally wounded British Gen. James Wolfe from the Plains of Abraham at Quebec during the French and Indian War. On the Fourth of July, the Declaration of Independence was read to a large public gathering and the local militia paraded on the village green and fired a cannon. In his free time in the evenings, the young apprentice found a schoolmaster who agreed to tutor him. On many a "stilly night," Wool later recalled, he wrestled with arithmetic and elementary bookkeeping.[8]

A break came in 1798, when Wool, then fourteen, met the genial Howard Moulton, one of Troy's leading businessmen. Moulton liked the boy, brought him into his own home, and made him a clerk at his inn. The Moultons were a family of education and refinement. The household consisted of eight children, five daughters and three sons, who ranged from five to eighteen years of age. Sarah and Howard Jr. were near Wool's age. Short and stout, his forehead scarred by a blow from a British sabre, the Connecticut-born Moulton had come to Troy with family money and built several stores, a three-story coffeehouse, and a twenty-two-room inn near the town square. Young Wool found himself in the mainstream of village life.

In many ways, Moulton was a father for the boy. "If I am indebted to any mortal being for my present standing in society," Wool acknowledged three decades later, "it is to my early and first friend, for it is he that first animated me with hope and initiated my desires."[9]

In 1802, with Moulton's financial help, John Wool, aged eighteen, opened a small book shop on Water (formerly River) Street. Three years later, he moved into a store located under the offices of the *Troy Northern Budget*, where he dealt in dry goods and groceries, retail and wholesale. In the *Northern Budget* in June 1805, the young merchant advertised competitive prices, "Fashionable Dry Goods" and "a good assortment of groceries" from New York City. Wool also traded in various properties, and on one occasion advertised a female slave for sale. The chattel was a "Black WOMAN, about 23 years of age, well acquainted with all kinds of kitchen work, and will answer for a gentleman or farmer." At the time, several Trojan families owned black slaves.[10]

Wool realized valuable political contacts could play a critical role in a young man's world and he joined and became active in the Troy branch of the Tammany Society, a national club of Jeffersonian Republicans. At public events, he paraded in Indian regalia with the chapter, whose members carried tomahawks and banners and attached "bucktails" to the sides of their hats. Wool also enlisted in a private militia company, the Troy Invincibles, composed of Jeffersonian Republicans. The company drilled with the Troy Fusiliers (Republicans) and Trojan Greens (Federalists). Despite his short stature, his bearing and enthusiasm quickly won him the coveted position of color bearer.[11]

Since the politics of the time was consistently debated in the streets of Troy, as it was in most of the United States, the young merchant was acutely aware of the troubled times facing the infant nation. On the high seas, the British continued to interfere with American shipping while at the same time New York and New England carried on a growing illicit trade with Canadian markets. In 1808, President Thomas Jefferson imposed an embargo to close American ports and curb border smuggling. The Embargo Act proved ineffective, however. Frontier counties in New York complained of the slackening commerce, but Gov. Daniel D. Tompkins was hesitant to act. On November 15, Jefferson ordered certain state governors (including New York) to raise a brigade of volunteers (infantry, artillery, and cavalry) for federal service. The president lifted the embargo on March 1, 1809, before leaving office, but James Madison, his successor, honored the plans for volunteer brigades. In April, John Wool, with local political support, won the position of quartermaster of cavalry and the rank of ensign in the New York brigade. The arrangement, however, was a paper exercise, and on May 6, Madison cancelled the order. Wool, however, profited from the episode. He had stepped forward and as a result, he gained a degree of military and political recognition and made contacts beyond Troy.[12]

The young Wool became a notable figure in the village of Troy. A small man, standing less than five and a half feet tall with an erect bearing, precise but pleasant manners, he had gained a reputation as a prudent businessman. Wool had dark-brown hair, striking grey eyes, a prominent nose and firm mouth and chin. He was an ambitious, strong-willed young man blessed with energy and perseverance. He strove constantly to improve his education, to put his humble beginnings in the past, to excel and rise in the world and gain financial success and prestige. An active, involved citizen of Troy, the young merchant looked forward to a bright future.[13]

On September 27, 1809, John Wool married Sarah N. Moulton, three years his junior, in the Presbyterian Church in Troy. The couple set up housekeeping in a two-story wooden dwelling at 51 First Street near the village green. To help make ends meet, they rented a room for several years to the Rev. Jonas Coe, the minister who married them. Sarah Wool was a small, slender woman with refined tastes and manners. Affable, dignified, and discreet, she would come to play a major role in shaping her husband's attitudes and advancing his career. She patiently tutored him in the proper social graces, was a willing listener, and shared intimately in his business and professional life. When he traveled, they corresponded regularly, and she dutifully clipped newspaper articles that chronicled his travels. John and Sarah Wool had no children of their own, but they later reared a nephew and niece.[14]

In early December 1809, Wool formed a partnership with Eliphalet King and renamed his small mercantile firm John E. Wool and Company. The two entrepreneurs planned to upgrade their merchandise and broaden their operations, but the expansion never developed. At midnight on March 10, 1810, the clang of a fire bell shattered the wintry silence. Wool rushed into the street, glanced toward the river, and saw flames and smoke billowing from buildings along the waterfront. Men rolled the town's toy-like fire engine to the scene and furiously worked the hand-pumps, while others formed bucket brigades. By dawn, four buildings—including Wool's store—lay in smoldering black ruins.[15] The fire was a crushing financial blow.

Tammany friends came to his aid. John Russell, a local attorney, offered Wool employment as a clerk and began tutoring him in the law. An influential Republican, Russell spent as much time with politics as he did with his law practice. When the spring 1811 elections loomed, Wool wrote letters supporting party candidates and boldly declared his candidacy for sheriff of Rensselaer County. In one of his earliest letters, he asked local publisher Hezekiah Munsell for assistance: "I understand that John Mann, Grand Sachem of the Tammany Society, and William McMannus, Secretary, has [*sic*] written to you and requested your aid in procuring me the office of Sheriff of this County. If you could . . . exercise your influence in my behalf . . . it would . . . be greatly assisting an unfortunate Republican Friend." Wool's race was in vain, but the experience provided valuable insights into the workings and personalities of the political arena. At the same time, he also remained active in the militia. In June 1811, he became an ensign and adjutant in Maj. William S. Parker's battalion of Rensselaer County Riflemen. Like other young men, the law clerk was acutely aware of the nation's drift toward war.[16]

The rush to war with Great Britain in 1812 found the United States divided in sentiment and unprepared for hostilities on land and sea. In New England, the stronghold of the Federalist Party, and other areas affected by European interference with American shipping, many businessmen felt the British were in the process of modifying their maritime policies and that the problems of previous years were being resolved. In the South and West, however, the followers of Jefferson were in the ascendancy and they were beginning to turn anxious eyes south to Spanish-held Florida and north to Canada. War could bring additional land and ports and enhance the prestige of the infant nation.[17]

Congress attempted to bolster the military establishment, but efforts to increase the army before the war largely faltered. Nevertheless, in January 1812, to supplement some 6,000 regulars manning frontier garrisons, lawmakers voted to field thirteen new regular regiments (10 infantry, 2 artillery, and 1 dragoon). In February, Congress authorized President Madison to accept 30,000 volunteers, and in April it empowered him to ask governors to hold 100,000 state militia in readiness. To head the expanding military forces, Madison turned to a group of aging men, most of whom had served as officers during the Revolutionary War. He appointed obese, sixty-one-year-old Henry Dearborn, a former secretary of war, the senior major general.[18]

With news that Congress had funded additional regiments, John Wool sought and received a regular army commission. On April 14, 1812, he was made a captain in the new Thirteenth Infantry Regiment, commanded by Col. Peter Phillip Schuyler. Orders came to enlist one hundred men for Wool's company from the local pool of males aged eighteen to forty-five. To enhance his ability to recruit, Wool promptly had himself fitted with an infantry captain's uniform. The ensemble included a dark blue coat with ten brass buttons, a scarlet high-standing collar and cuffs, white shirt, knee breeches, boots, and a black half-moon chapeau with a white plume. A silver epaulet on the right shoulder denoted a captain's rank. Resplendent in his military finery, Wool rode out into the countryside to post handbills and enroll men.[19]

On June 18, 1812, the United States declared war on Great Britain and the Madison administration immediately made plans to invade Canada. General Dearborn planned two attacks on Upper Canada—one from Detroit by Brig. Gen. William Hull, and one from Lewiston, New York, to protect Buffalo and control the Niagara River. A third invasion would be from the head of Lake Champlain at Plattsburgh toward Montreal, the capital of Lower Canada. The general divided New York into two militia divisions (eight brigades each) under a major general. Benjamin Mooers, at Plattsburgh, would command in the north and Stephen Van Rensselear would assemble an army on the Niagara River.[20]

In late August 1812, Capt. John Wool filled his quota of recruits and rode south six miles from Troy to Cantonment Greenbush, across the Hudson from Albany. Greenbush was the principal military training center in the state. Opened in early July, the cantonment sprawled over 261 acres of farmland, and could accommodate 4,000 soldiers. When Wool arrived, summer rains had turned the camp into a sea of mud. Thirteen wooden buildings, all to be painted white, were under construction, and the ring of carpenter hammers mingled with the shouts of drillmasters, beating of drums, and the cursing cries of teamsters. Hundreds of tents covered the plain. Wool reported to Colonel Schuyler and met the nine other company commanders of the regiment. Wool drew clothing, knapsacks, tents, muskets, bayonets, and cartridge boxes for his Company I. The monotony of army routine began.[21]

The small American army, especially the militia, was poorly armed, poorly trained, and disorganized. In New England and parts of upstate New York, Federalists opposed the war and appeared unpatriotic. The war was at a standstill. On August 9, Dearborn signed a truce with Sir George Prevost, the Governor-General of Canada. At Lewiston, twelve days later, Lt. Col. Solomon Van Rensselaer, a militia officer and Gen. Stephen Van Rensselaer's cousin and chief aide, crossed the Niagara and concluded a truce at Fort George with British Gen. Roger Sheaffe. It was agreed that both British and Americans would have unrestricted travel on Lake Ontario. As Dearborn hurried men and supplies to the Niagara frontier, news reached Greenbush that General Hull had made a feeble and embarrassing invasion of Canada from Fort Detroit and surrendered a large part of his army. Dearborn ordered Van Rensselaer to prepare for action.[22]

By early October, in the changing colors of fall, over 7,000 American soldiers were camped on the Niagara River. Van Rensselaer's forces included 5,800 men (2,650 militia and 3,150 regulars) at or near Lewiston, and thirty-eight miles south, near Buffalo, Brig. Gen. Alexander Smyth commanded 1,650 regulars and 386 militia. Coordinating the two forces was difficult. Smyth argued with General Van Rensselaer, his superior, over crossing sites on the river, and refused to cooperate with his commander. Van Rensselaer planned to cross from Lewiston to Queenston and attack neighboring Fort George. If successful, he could sever British communication with the western lake country and secure winter quarters for his army. British defenses were thought weak. Maj. Gen. Isaac Brock, who had defeated Hull at Detroit, commanded about 1,500 soldiers and 400 Indian allies. He had posted detachments along the river from Queenston south to the British bastion at Fort Erie, across from Buffalo, and held a small reserve at Fort George. Halfway up Queenston Heights, an eighteen-pounder cannon sat in a V-shaped earthen redan to cover the slope and landing below. A few miles north, on Vrooman's Point near Fort George, a twenty-four-pounder carronade also pointed toward the Lewiston riverfront.[23]

In mid-September, Captain Wool received marching orders. On the eighteenth, Company I loaded its baggage wagons at Greenbush, ferried across the Hudson with Schuyler's Thirteenth Infantry, to Albany, and headed west along the Mohawk River. The regiment carried an "elegant" stand of colors and sported the name "Jolly Snorters." On entering each village, the regimental band struck up martial music to entertain—and recruit. Four of Wool's recruits deserted, but he quickly found replacements. While camped in a meadow, near the village of Onondaga, eight miles southwest of Syracuse, Schuyler received orders to split his regiment and send a battalion of five companies to Oswego, on Lake Ontario, to man boats loaded with military stores bound for Lewiston. Schuyler would take the remaining companies to the Niagara. Wool immediately volunteered his company and joined four others, all under Lt. Col. John Chrystie. At Oswego, 350 soldiers climbed into thirty-nine boats and began rowing along the lakeshore. On October 9, at midnight, they landed in a heavy fog at Four Mile Creek, a few miles east of Fort Niagara.[24]

On the tenth, Chrystie reported his arrival to Van Rensselaer's headquarters. Since an attack was planned that night on Queenston by militia Col. Solomon Van Rensselaer, Chrystie hurried his regulars to Lewiston to participate. The operation was canceled, however, when an officer mistakenly rowed away from the wharf in a boat carrying oars for the flotilla. Van Rensselaer pressed Chrystie to serve under him, but the regular officer refused. He preferred to lead an independent command. For two days, the soldiers huddled in a rain-soaked forest without tents or camp equipage. At three o'clock in the morning of October 13, Wool rushed with some 300 regulars to the landing at Lewiston and he and his men piled into boats. The militia followed. The roar of Niagara Falls, several miles to the south, muffled conversation. Thirteen boats with about 600 soldiers pushed off into the chilly, damp darkness. At this point the Niagara was 600 feet wide and filled with dangerous eddies.[25]

At midstream, the men saw a bright flash from a small artillery piece on the enemy shore and heard musket fire. Colonel Van Rensselaer had landed 100 men at the foot of the rapids. The regulars had already pushed ashore a short distance to the north. On the heights above Lewiston, Lt. Col. Winfield Scott, Second Artillery, opened canon fire on the enemy slopes and the Canadian detachment near the landing withdrew to Queenston. The crew with the eighteen-pounder in the redan prepared to target the invaders.[26]

Colonel Van Rensselaer quickly learned that Chrystie's boat had been hit and was drifting downstream. He sent an aide to contact the regulars. Who was in charge, he asked? In response, Captain Wool stepped forward in the mist, stating he was the senior officer present and requested orders. "Storm the heights!" came the colonel's reply. The redan had to be taken and the gun silenced. In the darkness, Wool and his men scrambled up the riverbank and turned facing the village below. A British unit, approaching from the village, fired into Wool's right flank. The captain shouted to his men to reply. Van Rensselaer had also climbed the riverbank with the militia only to receive a deadly volley from the British. The enemy fired another round and retreated. The Americans suffered heavy losses. Two officers lay dead and five wounded, while fifty-five rank-and-file had fallen. Wool suffered a flesh wound in his buttocks, and Van Rensselaer, who was hit four times, was carried down the riverbank to shelter.[27]

The next day dawned cold and wet, with a thick fog covering the river. Wool sought out Van Rensselaer, and asked: "What could be done?" Lying on the ground in an overcoat, the wounded colonel gasped that he did not know. Something had to be done, the captain insisted, or they would all be taken prisoner. When the colonel mumbled that a force might climb the heights and capture the redan, Wool offered to lead the attack. The wounded commander looked up at the impatient wounded captain, whose white breeches were soaked with blood and waved him aside. He was too inexperienced for the task, Van Rensselaer grumbled. But Wool argued and insisted—and finally received a nod of approval.[28]

Wool collected a group of regulars and a few militia and proceeded south into the giant chasm of the roaring Niagara. Here, Lt. John Gansevoort, First Artillery, stationed at nearby Fort Niagara, pointed to a steep, little-known fisherman's path up the heights, which rose 230 feet above the rapids of the river. Wool placed Capt. Peter Ogilvie, Thirteenth Infantry, in the lead and more than two hundred men began to climb the slippery trail. They clutched desperately at low-hanging bushes and leaned on their muskets for leverage as they struggled ever upward. Finally reaching the top they entered a wooded area, where Wool formed a skirmish line, and sent the soldiers rushing down on the enemy-held redan. The men in the earthen redoubt, including General Brock, glanced to their rear to see the onrushing Americans, swiftly spiked their eighteen-pound cannon, and ran down the hill for their lives. The Americans swarmed into the fortification, waving their hats and cheering wildly.[29]

It was 7 A.M., and red-coated soldiers soon started up the slope from Queenston. Seeing an enemy detachment separating and veering to his right near the river, Wool dispatched Ogilvie and fifty regulars to meet the danger. The detachment made contact, but retreated toward the roaring chasm below. Suddenly, an officer hoisted a white handkerchief on a bayonet. Ignoring the stiffness in his legs, Wool ran to the man, angrily snatched down the banner of defeat, and shouted at the men to fire until their powder gave out, then charge with bayonets. Waving his sword, the captain led a counterattack that forced the enemy to retire. A regular then broke rank and started down the hill, and Wool ordered him shot. Hearing the order, the soldier quickly returned to the ranks and the captain limped back to the redan.[30]

In the meantime, the main British column continued to climb the wet grassy slope. General Brock, resplendent in a red and gold uniform, dismounted and leading his horse, exhorted his troops to fight on to victory. In the smoke and confusion of battle, an American soldier stepped from behind a tree, took careful aim and fired. The veteran of the Napoleonic Wars and conqueror of Detroit fell mortally wounded. As the attack faltered, Lt. Col. John McDonell, Brock's aide, took command, but he was also killed. The British retired to the village, carrying the bodies of their dead and wounded.[31]

During the lull that followed, General Van Rensselaer crossed the river to the redan. Brig. Gen. William Wadsworth of the New York militia had preceded him in command and had placed Lt. Col. Winfield Scott in charge of the troops. The Americans learned that Gen. Roger Scheaffe was en route from Fort George with British regulars, Canadian militia, and Indian allies. About two o'clock Scott repulsed a large group of Indians, led by Mohawk chieftain John Brant. At this point, he ordered Wool and other wounded officers taken down to the river and ferried across. At Lewiston, as he boarded an ambulance wagon for the field hospital, Wool passed through a milling throng of nearly 2,000 militia near the landing, watching the returning boats loaded with wounded, many in the last grasp of life. General Van Rensselaer and other senior officers were riding among the men, yelling, shouting, threatening, and pleading. "These were the wretches," one observer wrote, "who at this critical moment could talk of the Constitution, and the right of the militia to refuse to cross the [state] line."[32]

About four in the afternoon, Sheaffe started circling Queenston Heights with nearly 1,000 men, plus a large contingent of Indians. Scott, with less than 300 effectives, had been told to retreat to the river, if necessary, and be ferried across. But when his soldiers hurried down to the river, there were no boats. Panic quickly ensued. There was chaos everywhere. Many feared being scalped and jumped into the water and tried to swim across river. Scott consulted with Wadsworth and it was agreed they would have to surrender. At dust, the Americans stacked their arms and were marched under a heavy guard to Fort George. From every point of view, the battle of Queenston was a humiliating defeat to American arms.[33]

In the late afternoon of October 13, Generals Van Rensselaer and Sheaffe agreed to a three-day armistice that was extended to six days. At sundown three days later, the American artillery at Fort Niagara fired a salute in honor of Brock, buried that day at Fort George. In many ways, the conflict was still a gentleman's war. General Van Rensselaer, his staff, and a militia detachment then rode south to Buffalo, accompanied by wagons carrying Solomon Van Rensselaer, John Wool, and other wounded officers. The party took lodgings at Landon's Hotel and there met the governor of New York, Daniel D. Tompkins, soon to be vice president of the United States, who was touring the Niagara frontier. On October 16, Stephen Van Rensselaer transferred command of the Niagara theatre to Gen. Alexander Smyth. Before departing for Albany, he drafted a short list of junior officers who had distinguished themselves in the assault on Queenston Heights. Capt. John Ellis Wool's name was at the top of the list.[34]

Although winter was at hand, General Smyth began plans to cross the Niagara and attack Fort Erie. He moved the battered regulars at Lewiston to his encampment at Black Rock, a few miles north of Buffalo, and circulated handbills in neighboring counties, calling for short-term volunteers. "Companions in arms!" the general proclaimed on November 11: "the time is at hand when you will cross . . . the Niagara to conquer Canada! It is in your power . . . to cover yourself with glory!" Officers laughed at the pompous language and labeled the general "Alexander the Great," but local militia and volunteers poured into his winter camps and Smyth soon had 4,000 men, and 100 boats and scows ready for an assault. Captain Wool ignored his injury and volunteered for limited duty.[35]

In freezing weather at midnight on November 28, Wool reported to Col. William H. Winder, Fourteenth Infantry, to assist the loading of soldiers into boats on nearby Thirteen Mile Creek. Bad weather, sickness, and sustained British bombardment from Fort Erie and other batteries on the Canadian shore prevented earlier sorties. In a matter of hours, two parties pushed out into the icy Niagara. Capt. William King, Fifth Infantry, with 150 regulars and a few sailors, rushed ashore and captured and spiked three batteries. Lt. Col. Charles G. Boerstler, Fourteenth Infantry, landed over 200 men about the same time lower on the river to destroy a strategic bridge. Lacking axes to complete the assignment, he quickly recrossed the river. King, in the meantime, was in trouble. In a mix up with boats, he sent half of his men back to safety, fought off enemy patrols, and waited for reinforcements. At sunrise, Wool embarked with Winder and 250 men to aid King. After struggling with floating ice and dodging heavy gunfire, Winder abandoned the rescue and King was left to surrender. Smyth, facing mutiny by demoralized soldiers, cancelled further action. He discharged the militia and volunteers, ordered the regulars to build a winter camp, and left for Washington, D.C. Wool headed by sleigh for his home in Troy.[36]

While at Buffalo, Wool sought to clarify his role in the battle of Queenston. The *New York Columbian*, published out of New York City, on October 27, interviewed Capt. Peter Ogilvie, and proclaimed him the hero of the assault on Queenston Heights. Wool immediately sought to correct the record. He wrote several politicians in Albany for support, and on November 3, published a similar request in the *New York Evening Post*. He acknowledged that Ogilvie had led the attack—but the captain pointed out that he was serving under his command. Wool also sent the editor of the *Post* a copy of *Niles' Register* of November 14, 1812, that reprinted a battle account, which Wool may have written, from the *National Intelligencer.* "Captain Wool, the hero of the heights at Queenston," wrote the editor of the *Register,* "is 26 [28] years of age. It is presumed that he will be brevetted or promoted." In a joint statement, several officers branded the Ogilvie reference "totally false." Colonel Chrystie also assured Wool of his singular role in the affair. In late December, Ogilvie admitted in the *Post* that the statement had been inaccurate. He had no wish, he said, to diminish the respect due Wool's senior rank, or claim the "exclusive applause" of the battle. The newspaper exchange had cleared the air.[37]

In late January 1813, at Troy, Wool received orders to help fill the decimated ranks of the Thirteenth Infantry. The search for recruits was urgent because the Madison administration planned another invasion of Canada although the campaign of 1812 had closed on an unhappy note. Soon after the Queenston defeat, Dearborn had marched north from Plattsburgh into Lower Canada in hopes of seizing Montreal, but at La Cole Mill, just north of the Canadian border, a reluctant militia and a confused attack on the British outpost forced him to end the campaign. In February 1813, a new secretary of war, John Armstrong, took office. Armstrong doubted that an American army could capture Montreal, and proposed a more limited operation: a joint land-naval expedition on Lake Ontario. This would include an attack on the town of York (present day Toronto), the capture of Fort George, and an active campaign on the Niagara frontier.[38]

On February 6, 1813, Wool opened recruiting offices at Troy and another at Kingsbury, fifty-three miles to the north in Washington County. In the *Troy Post* on March 23, he exhorted all "Patriotic Young Men" aged fourteen to forty-five to enlist in the army for five years or the duration of the war. According to the young captain, the widow and orphan were crying out that "the blood of the husband and the father . . . shed on our frontier" should be avenged. Recruits received three months' pay in advance and scrip for 160 acres. Applicants must be free from "sore legs, scurvy, scalled heads, ruptures, and other infirmities." By early April, the captain had enlisted and forwarded 110 men to Greenbush for training.[39]

Near Utica, Wool learned he was assigned to the Twenty-ninth Infantry, a training regiment, and promotion to major, effective April 13. The salary for a major was several times the national average, and for a man who had been striving to make his way in retail and who suffered being wiped out from a fire, such a salary helped to launch him into an echelon of society that he had only imagined. A few weeks later, an order arrived to escort 200 recruits to the Niagara. Upset with the assignment, he turned the recruits over to a junior officer and hurried back to Troy where he fired off a testy letter to Secretary of War Armstrong. He had entered the service "to be engaged in actual warfare," he bluntly told the secretary, and not a drillmaster. He badgered Armstrong again on May 18 from Greenbush, saying political friends in

Albany had assured him of active duty. After another exchange of letters with the War Department, the major received temporary duty with the Twenty-third Infantry at Fort George, recently captured by Dearborn's forces.[40]

Wool arrived at Fort George in early June, and for two months, he sought every opportunity to engage the enemy. On June 17, while Officer of the Day, he rushed a detachment of the Twenty-third with a field piece to rescue a foraging party under attack. When the British sent reinforcements, the major masked his gun with infantry, began unleashing grapeshot, and brought down ten of the enemy. But American disasters continued. On June 23, Lt. Col. Charles G. Boerstler, with 575 men, struck a British force with Indian allies in a wooded area near Beaver Dams, eight miles south of Queenston. After exchanging desultory fire, Boerstler surrendered the next day to a British lieutenant![41]

On July 8, General Dearborn appointed Wool as acting colonel of the veteran Fifteenth Infantry. The senior officers of the regiment were either sick or on leave. In his new duties, Wool became better acquainted with Dearborn's staff, particularly Col. Winfield Scott, the tall, imposing, tobacco-chewing adjutant general, who had replaced Chrystie who had died of fever. Scott was a stickler for detail. The prim little New Yorker, who was two years older than Scott, and the towering Virginian would serve in the army for half a century. Wool respected Scott's professional ability, but he never admired him as a person. At noon on July 15, Wool joined the officers at Fort George in bidding farewell to the aging Dearborn, who was reassigned. On August 17, Wool also departed the Niagara for duty with the Twenty-ninth Infantry at Burlington, Vermont.[42]

During the summer, Secretary of War Armstrong revived plans to capture Montreal. He proposed sending two armies—one by boat from Sackett's Harbor, New York, down the St. Lawrence River to join a second force that would march overland from Plattsburgh. He promoted James Wilkinson, the fifty-five-year-old senior brigadier, to major general and brought him from New Orleans to command and coordinate the joint operation. Major General Wade Hampton, a South Carolina aristocrat and former congressman, stationed at Plattsburg, would command the army moving overland. Wilkinson and Hampton despised each other, but Armstrong believed he could somehow reconcile their differences. "Unhappily for the country," one historian wrote, the St. Lawrence campaign "was a monster with three heads, biting and barking at each other with a madness which destroyed them all."[43]

Wool stepped into this madness, arriving at Hampton's headquarters at Burlington, Vermont, in early September of 1813. Before dawn, on September 20, Majors Wool, Josiah Snelling, and John McNeil crossed the border at different points into Canada. At the village of Odelltown, five miles north of the border, Wool captured an enemy picket sleeping in a schoolhouse, but the soldier knew little about British movements in the area. At midmorning, Hampton's advance tramped through the village heading north for Montreal. A few miles out, however, the column halted. Drought had parched the route ahead, and the rivers and streams were dry. The column promptly retraced its steps to Champlain.[44]

On September 22, Hampton started west for the Chateauguay River on an alternate route to the St. Lawrence. Besides his infantry, the column consisted of ten cannon and a long baggage and supply train. At the hamlet of Four Corners, orders came to go into camp. Wilkinson was delayed and for twenty-six days the army waited. Soldiers improved the road back to Plattsburgh, built a supply depot, and patrolled the countryside. Autumn weather brought a light frost and sickness. Officers joked about their haughty commander, quartered at a local tavern with a retinue of black servants. Scouts, however, still bore the brunt of danger. On the afternoon of October 1, Wool's mixed batallion ran into an ambush by British regulars and Indian allies. Fortunately, Major Snelling heard the firing and rushed to his defense. Wool lost two dead and one wounded.[45]

On October 21, Hampton finally broke camp at Four Corners. Wilkinson's flotilla was moving down the St. Lawrence, and he instructed the general to join him at the mouth of the Chateauguay near Montreal. As the troops struck tents, confusion reigned when 1,500 New York militia refused to leave the state. They were left to guard the depot and continue roadwork. Two brigades headed the advance. Col. Robert Purdy, Fourth Infantry, led the first brigade and Brig. Gen. George Izard the second. With Wool and Snelling scouting ahead, Izard followed the river into Canada, protecting the work crews clearing a path for wagon use. At Spears's Farm near Ormstown, the Americans captured a blockhouse and camped. The next day, Snelling crossed the river to reconnoiter, and Wool continued scouting on the east bank. Open country lay ahead, ending in a dense forest. Izard was less than fifty miles from Montreal. The weather suddenly changed, and freezing rain slowed military operations.[46]

By October 25, the main army reached Spears's Farm and Hampton quickly learned from scouts that a Canadian force blocked his route. Lt. Col. Charles de Salsbury had gathered some 1,600 troops, mostly militia and Indian allies, and constructed a blockhouse and breastworks at a ford in the river. Outnumbering his opponent four to one, Hampton launched a flanking move that night. In heavy rain, Col. Robert Purdy began crossing 1,500 men to the west bank of the Chateauguay. He was to move eight miles through a forest and swamp, recross the next morning, and attack the enemy rear. On the sound of gunfire, Izard would assault the breastworks. At mid-morning the next day, Major Wool, in charge of camp pickets, reported that Purdy's men were seen resting on the opposite shore, nearly a mile short of their objective. Izard, Wool, and several others went down to the river and shouted for an explanation. Misled by guides, they had wandered most of the night in the swamp and were exhausted. A Canadian detachment suddenly burst from the woods, fired into Purdy's men, then scattered. Some of Purdy's troops fired at each other, and several officers jumped into the river. At two in the afternoon, Izard finally assaulted the breastworks. Discovering a deep ditch in front of the breastworks, he hesitated. Enemy buglers set up a racket, and loud cheering was heard. Hampton stopped the attack. He recalled Izard and Purdy, and ordered a general withdrawal to Plattsburgh to build winter quarters. The battle of Chateauguay had ended. This "battle" Wool later wrote, "was from its inception to termination, a disgrace . . . no officer who had any regard for his own reputation would voluntarily acknowledge . . . being engaged in it."[47]

In early January 1814, after spending the holidays with his family and friends in Troy, Wool, then twenty-nine, returned to Plattsburgh to find General Wilkinson in command. As the general needed a field officer acquainted with the locale for a temporary aide-de-camp, Wool volunteered and received the appointment. For six weeks, Wool walked in the shadow of the round-faced, stocky general, who at age fifty-seven was one of the most famous—and infamous—men in America. Wilkinson had held prestigious staff positions during the Revolutionary War, but later, on the Louisiana frontier, there had been intrigues and the onus of a court-martial. He had arrived on the New York frontier a tarnished warrior. Yet Wilkinson was a fascinating individual. He was courtly and charming, and easily cultivated friendships with influential people. Beneath the glamorous veneer, however, was a restless, partisan mind. General Wilkinson, Wool later stated, had the "most equivocal" character of any man he had ever known, but his "merit as a soldier was never effaced." Wilkinson's habits "were convivial," the major admitted, but the general was never "incapable of business." For the ambitious young officer, Wilkinson would be both a model and a warning for a successful military career.[48]

Wool's role at headquarters did not go unnoticed. In a confidential letter in January to Maj. Charles K. Gardner, Twenty-Fifth Infantry, stationed at French Mills in western New York, Col. Henry Atkinson, Wilkinson's adjutant general, gossiped: "What do you think of Wool being the Gen'l's aid [*sic*] . . . [Y]ou know however that W[ilkinson] & Secty of War [Armstrong] are at [sword] points & that Wool & the Secty's son [Henry B. Armstrong] are at outs also." Atkinson despised Wool's "fauning [*sic*] so much" around the general and considered the little major "a white livered being." Serving Wilkinson, who is thought by many to be one of the worst generals in American history, was no bed of roses. In early February 1814, Wool accompanied Wilkinson and a detachment by sleigh through deep snow to French Mills where soldiers broke up the winter encampment, sank the ice-bound flotilla of over 300 boats in a nearby creek, torched the barracks and huts and departed for new duty stations. Bvt. Maj. Gen. Jacob Brown marched with 2,000 men for Sackett's Harbor, while Brig. Gen. Alexander Macomb brought the remainder, including the sick, about 1,500 men, back to Plattsburgh.[49]

In early March of 1814, Major Wool finally joined the Twenty-ninth Infantry, commanded by Col. Melancthon Smith. The regiment was in shambles. The adjutant was ignorant of his responsibilities, and two captains and four lieutenants had been court-martialed for cowardice. One officer was cashiered, his sword broken over his head in the presence of the regiment, and his name published in the newspapers as a coward. Wool himself became entangled in a personal quarrel.[50]

After the Chateauguay campaign, Colonel Atkinson, regarded by many as a "toady" of Secretary of War Armstrong, had ridiculed Wool's claim to hazardous duty near Ormstown. The major, overly sensitive to any criticism, challenged the colonel to a duel. Atkinson refused to meet him until he had "cleared up" his character. Enraged by the reply, Wool threatened to "post" his adversary—to accuse him of cowardice in the press. Capt. Gabriel H. Manigault, a staff officer with General Izard, intervened. He presented a set of "interrogatives" to Atkinson, and obtained an affidavit stating he had recalled "every observation which he made injurious to the character & reputation of Major Wool." The major accepted the response. But in early March 1814, a rumor circulated that the affair had been mishandled, and Atkinson demanded an explanation. Wool sent the colonel a conciliatory letter and a copy of the affidavit. Atkinson accepted the affidavit but only after Manigault told him Wool had dropped his challenge. His honor questioned, Manigault demanded satisfaction. On May 9, he and Atkinson dueled with pistols in Odletown, Canada, and in the exchange Manigault wounded Atkinson in the leg. Both officers were arrested for dueling, but they were soon released and returned to duty.[51]

In early June, Wool joined his regiment at Plattsburgh. Sarah went along and was able to find lodgings in Burlington. In late July, General Izard received orders to move most of his army to the Niagara frontier, where a British build-up was expected. Izard protested the instructions, since the enemy was also concentrating a large force in his front at Plattsburgh. He had spent the summer building up defensive works to meet the threat, and had asked General Mooers, commanding the militia district, to raise a regiment for support. Vermont authorities agreed to help. On August 29, Izard transferred his command to General Macomb and, as commanded, departed with 4,000 men, not including Wool, to meet the British in western New York.[52]

Macomb inherited about 3,500 soldiers stationed at Plattsburgh and near the villages of Chazy and Champlain, not far from the Canadian border. The camps included remnants of six regular infantry regiments, many filled with recruits, plus assorted detachments. Major Wool's Twenty-ninth Infantry was located on the Little Chazy River, near the village. Nearly 2,000 men were sick or on special duty.

During the summer, Macomb, an engineering graduate of the Military Academy at West Point, spurred work on Izard's projects. Soldiers erected an artillery battery on Cumberland Head on the lake and constructed breastworks at fords on the Saranac River which formed the southern boundary of the village. On the elevated peninsula across the river from the settlement, they built two blockhouses and to the west threw up three earthen redoubts for artillery, protected by deep ditches. They were Fort Scott (Macomb's headquarters near the lake), Fort Moreau (main depot), and Fort Brown at a ford to the west. By late August, the defenses were complete. The officers and men at each fort had orders to defend their works "to the last extremity." Wool's Twenty-ninth Infantry and four companies of the Sixth camped in tents at Fort Moreau. Lt. Col. David Appling commanded the depot while Wool took charge of his rifle corps.[53]

On August 31, British troops, under Gen. Sir Robert Prevost crossed the Canadian border and occupied Champlain, fifteen miles north of Plattsburgh. Macomb alerted the militia in six neighboring counties. Local townsfolk packed their belongings and headed south down the lake for safety. Fearing for her safety, Wool sent Sarah back to Troy. On September 4, Macomb created four corps of observation to scout the roads north. Commanding the fourth corps, Wool was held in reserve. On the evening of the fifth, the British advanced to Sampson's Tavern, eight miles from Plattsburgh, and sent troops to join the column on the Beekmentown Road. A bloody battle was in the offing.[54]

During the afternoon, Wool badgered Macomb for an order to strike the enemy. Appling had encountered British pickets and was slowly withdrawing. The enemy must "know that we intend to give them battle," the major argued. But Macomb wanted no early troop losses and turned Wool away. Several hours later, Wool returned and proposed a swift night sortie to capture pickets who he speculated would have information on the British strength. Again, Macomb said no. About sundown, the general learned the Vermont militia, under General Mooers, were restive and frightened, and he instructed Wool to march against the British at three o'clock the next morning to stiffen their resolve. The major immediately began collecting troops, and shortly after midnight, with about 200 men of the Twenty-ninth plus a small group of volunteers, he crossed the Saranac, and moved in the darkness up the Beekmentown Road. Capt. Luther Leonard, Light Artillery, was to accompany him with two artillery pieces.[55]

Wool reached Mooers's camp before dawn. The British reportedly had halted four miles ahead near the Ira Howe house. At daylight the major rode up the road to a bridge being torn up by the militia. Suddenly, red-coated skirmishers burst from the woods and the work crew fled. Wool raced back at full speed. Shouting orders, he deployed three platoons: one on the road and the others to the flanks. As soon as the British came within musket range, the soldiers on the road opened fire. As they rushed to the rear to reload, a supporting platoon replaced them. This tactical maneuver, similar to "street fighting" sent a fusillade of lead and grape into the head of the British column, creating confusion. Wool ordered Capt. Peter B. Van Buren's company forward, hoping to steady the militia, create a cover for withdrawal, and gain time. As the infantry men stepped out, Wool yelled to the captain: "Shoot down the first man who attempts to run, or I will shoot you!" The regulars advanced, halted and fired, then fell back leaving twenty Redcoats dead or wounded on the road.[56]

Wool began a four-mile retreat toward Plattsburgh. At Culver's Hill he had a bridge ripped apart, and again checked the British column pursuing him. His horse was shot, but he quickly found a second. William Bosworth, his sergeant major, fell wounded in the hip and was hurried to the rear on Wool's crippled horse. Bosworth was a British deserter and would be executed if captured. About eight o'clock in the morning, at Halsey's Corners, Wool met his compatriot Leonard and changed his tactics when he saw Leonard's two six-pounder cannons. At every halt on the road, he masked the guns with infantry, and waited. The British pressed forward, in "a dense column of men," an eyewitness recalled, "with a front equal to the width of the road and extending nearly a half mile in length." When they came into close range, the regulars fired and fell back while the cannons belched smoke and sent round shot plowing breast high into the enemy. With a dozen bugles sounding charge, the Redcoats threw off their knapsacks, levelled bayonets, and moved forward at double quick. Wool again retreated. At the junction of Chazy and Beekmentown roads, Appling and Sproull joined him. As the last soldiers crossed the lower bridge over the Saranac, they ripped up planks under heavy fire to build breastworks on the south bank. By noon, British skirmishers entered the village on the north side of the river, but Macomb's artillery poured shot into the buildings and kept them from crossing over. Wool, the young officer, had conducted a skillful retreat of a large number of men under heavy fire from a column of British troops. "The cool, intrepid and admirable skill and good order displayed by the small detachment of less than three hundred regulars under that excellent officer, Major Wool," Mooers wrote in a letter to his superior, "was highly honorable to themselves, and furnishes an example worthy of our future imitation." The British had lost over 200 killed and wounded, while the American casualties were 45.[57]

A four-day lull followed. British General Prevost's army—8,200 men with 2,000 in reserve—built an encampment on a ridge, north of the Saranac River, and started constructing artillery batteries. Skirmishers daily prowled the riverbanks. Prevost delayed a land attack because of orders to act in concert with a British naval flotilla due to arrive on the lake from the north. Control of Lake Champlain was considered more important than an assault on a small American army. The delay was in

Macomb's favor. He used every device to give an impression of strength. At each guard mount, all available troops paraded, and at night he lit bonfires to brighten the sky and prevent a surprise attack. Spirits rose when 2,500 Vermonters began arriving from across the lake. Macomb also approved sorties, which gave another chance to Major Wool to demonstrate his valor. In a rain storm at midnight on September 9, Major Wool, serving as Officer of the Day, guided Capt. George McGlassin, Fifteenth Infantry, and fifty regulars to the ford near Fort Brown, where they waded across. Within an hour, McGlassin returned and reported they had awakened and driven off a sleeping work crew at the point of their bayonets, and destroyed a mortar battery—all without suffering a casualty.[58]

At eight in the morning, on September 11, sixteen British warships rounded Cumberland Head and headed for Plattsburgh Bay. Commodore Thomas Macdonough, with fourteen American vessels of various sizes, lay at anchor two miles out, blocking the entrance. As the British sailed into the bay, the wind suddenly shifted, and both fleets struggled to gain strategic positions. Macdonough opened fire, initiating a great naval engagement watched by hundreds of soldiers along the shore.[59]

As the first gun on the lake opened fire, General Prevost launched a land offensive. British artillery sent a torrent of metal arching over the Saranac into Macomb's lines. Congreve rockets screamed overhead. American batteries roared back in defiance. At three points on the river, Redcoats with scaling ladders probed the American defenses. They found strong opposition at the lower and upper bridges but weakness near Fort Brown. A British detachment, seeing American militia retreating, penetrated toward Fort Moreau by wading across the river and hiking through a forest before halting near the fort. Before they could spring their attack, however, an American courier on horseback dashed up and shouted that the British fleet had surrendered. The enemy detachment, far behind enemy lines, now hoped for instructions, then sought to withdraw—but were killed or captured by the Vermont militia. The struggle on the lake was over in two hours and twenty minutes, while the artillery duel on land continued until sunset.[60]

Shaken by the defeat on the lake, Prevost ended the invasion. To crush Macomb's army would cost hundreds of lives without giving him a permanent advantage. American militia along Lake Champlain were swarming toward Plattsburgh, and could easily disrupt his supply lines. The battle at Plattsburgh had decided the campaign.[61]

Early on September 12, Wool, Officer of the Day during the battle, received permission to cross the Saranac with Appling's Rifle Corps and reconnoiter. He was hungry for more action. Abandoned baggage and equipment was strewn everywhere, and hundreds of sick and wounded soldiers had been left behind. But the major did not tarry. Wool moved briskly up the Chazy Road toward the village of Champlain. Four miles out, Appling overtook him and demanded command of his men. Wool complied, but grumbled over losing the chance for further "military distinction." Heavy rain ended the scouting.[62]

Later that day, Macomb had the remains of fifteen naval officers, American and British on the damaged ships, brought ashore for burial. Wool volunteered to arrange the proceedings and serve as master of ceremonies. On September 14, soldiers loaded coffins on wagons, and fifteen men with rifles and muffled drums, playing the popular airs "Logan Water" and "Roslin Castle," led a procession of soldiers and civilians to the neighboring Riverside Cemetery. The orders for burial were read, the artillery fired a salute, and the dead were laid to rest. After attending local celebrations for Macomb and Macdonough, Wool, given leave, returned to Troy.[63]

As the nation honored its heroes, Wool sought another promotion. As early as November 8, 1814, General Mooers wrote Governor Tompkins that the major's "active and decisive" role in the retreat to the Saranac, and his "severe check upon the enemy upon his first advance, was perhaps the means of saving this place." He urged the governor to report "the same to the Secretary of War in hopes that he [Wool] may be noticed by the President." Others echoed similar sentiments in letters to Washington. The major's efforts were not in vain. On December 31, 1814, the adjutant general of the army announced that John Ellis Wool had been awarded the brevet of lieutenant colonel for "gallant and meritorious services" at Plattsburgh.[64]

With the war visibly nearing its end, Wool contemplated remaining in the army. He was attracted to the public adulation, display, and pomp of the military, and there also would be opportunities to gain prestige and position. To be a soldier was a noble calling. If he could obtain a respectable appointment in the peacetime army, he would remain in the service. When Congress voted to fund new regular regiments in January 1815 (unaware that a peace treaty had been signed at Ghent, Belgium, on December 24, 1814), Wool placed his name on the list to command a regiment. Col. Melancton Smith, Governor Tompkins, and others supported his petition. But competition was strong, and he was bypassed. In March, when Congress reduced and reorganized the army, Wool accepted the commission of major in the Sixth Infantry.[65]

The War of 1812 was a turning point in John Wool's life. He had exchanged the menial tasks of a law clerk for the responsibilities of an army officer, and had served with distinction through three long years of campaigning. In army circles, the energetic New Yorker had gained a reputation for the training of soldiers, attention to detail, and devotion to duty. These qualities, indeed, made him just the right man for the peacetime military establishment. Wool's decision to remain in the army was the nation's gain, for ahead lay an illustrious career which mirrored not only the development of the military but also the fortunes of the young republic.

2

FEISTY LITTLE COLONEL ON INSPECTION

In the late summer of 1815, Maj. John Wool arrived at Fort Columbus, a red sandstone bastion on Governors Island in New York Harbor, with several companies of the Sixth Infantry. His stay was relatively brief, for within a year he was appointed inspector general of the Northern Division of the army, which required annual visits to garrisons and arsenals and armories from Maine to Michigan Territory. He strove to provide a more precise definition and enhanced prestige to an unpopular staff. Wool gave himself an arduous challenge but proved equal to it, and during his tenure as inspector, first of a division, then for the entire army, he played a prominent role in reforming and elevating the status of the military establishment. These were formative years for John Wool, years that placed a permanent stamp on both his character and career.[1]

After the War of 1812, the army began to reduce its size. On March 3, 1815, Congress cut the enlisted regular personnel from a wartime peak of more than 30,000 to 11,709 enlisted men and 674 officers. A board of six officers—Major Generals Jacob Brown and Andrew Jackson and Brigadier Generals Edmund P. Gaines, Alexander Macomb, Eleazer W. Ripley and Winfield Scott—worked out the details for the reduction. The army offered commissions only to men with distinguished war records, high moral character, and competency to "engage the enemy in battle." The board divided the nation into Northern and Southern Military Divisions, the line of demarcation running west along the southern boundary of Pennsylvania and the Ohio River to the Mississippi. Jacob Brown took command of the garrisons in the Northern Division and Andrew Jackson those in the South.[2]

On May 17, 1815, General Brown reorganized the wartime regiments within his division. Major Wool moved the veteran Twenty-ninth Infantry from Plattsburgh to Cantonment Greenbush, a 400-acre tract of land a few miles southeast of Albany near the village of Greenbush, and there merged it with the remnants of five other regular regiments to form the Sixth Infantry. Col. Henry Atkinson and Lt. Col. Josiah Snelling commanded the new regiment. With Snelling detained in Buffalo, however, Wool, the regimental adjutant, performed most of the labor of combining rosters, weeding out misfits, and perfecting company arrangement. By late summer, the Sixth Infantry sailed down the Hudson to garrison the forts in New York Harbor. Wool's headquarters was the brick and masonry fortress of Fort Columbus on Governors Island, half a mile from the southern tip of Manhattan. Wool and his wife, Sarah, rented lodgings in the city, set up housekeeping, and settled into army routine.[3]

But Wool grew restless. In early February 1816, when Congress considered a bill to restructure the army staff in each division, he expressed interest in two positions in the Northern Division—quartermaster and inspector general. Each carried the rank and pay of a colonel of infantry. With General Brown's permission, Wool made a trip to Washington to press his case. Having obtained an audience with Secretary of War William H. Crawford, Wool told him his war record and emphasized his desire for a staff appointment. On Capitol Hill he secured nineteen signatures from the New York congressional delegation and friends on a petition to become a quartermaster. On April 6, he told New York congressman John W. Taylor he needed a pay increase to provide for his wife and family dependents. Brown favored Wool for the inspectorship, while Macomb and other officers promised their support for either appointment. The major was anxious for a decision, because the Sixth Infantry had orders to move to Plattsburgh in mid-April. Energy and politics paid off. Within a week, Wool learned that he would be appointed inspector general of the Northern Division, and he arranged to move Sarah back to Troy. On May 1, Wool reported for duty at division headquarters at Brownville, New York, a village of 1,800 people four miles up the Black River from Watertown, on Lake Ontario.[4]

Colonel Wool had met General Jacob Jennings Brown during the war, but he had never served under him. Brown had emerged from the war as one of the heroes as a result of his successes on the northern frontier. He was a man of vigorous and cultivated intellect, and Wool found him a genial fellow, easily approachable, and with an air of calm authority. The general had established his headquarters in a two-story mansion of blue limestone, on eight acres at the edge of the village. Brown's military family included two aides-de-camp and several staff officers who lived in the village. Most citizens labored on wheat farms, while others worked at the local sawmill or distillery, or ran taverns, hotels, and stores.[5]

Wool's responsibilities as an inspector general were stupendous. Brown's Northern Division contained five military departments, for all of which Wool was responsible. They ran from upstate New York and Vermont (the First department), up to New England (the Second), down through lower New York and New Jersey (the Third), west to Pennsylvania, Ohio, and Indiana (the Fourth), and further west into Michigan and Illinois territories (the Fifth). Throughout these departments were scattered approximately five thousand troops in garrisons. Artillery units garrisoned the coastal fortifications, while two infantry regiments guarded the border with Canada. Traditionally, the inspector general played a critical role in the discipline and health of the army. During the American Revolution, Maj. Gen. Friedrich W. A. von Steuben gave the position prestige and influence, declaring inspectors "the instructors and censors" of the army. After 1783, the office was abolished, but in July of 1812, the War Department reinstituted it and appointed to it Alexander Smyth, an attorney, but given the rank of brigadier general. The department sent him to Cantonment Greenbush to supervise the muster and training of the troops, and one year later, Smyth brought formality and stability to the office when he issued regulations that remained in use for nearly a decade.[6]

Wool considered the peacetime duties of the inspector ill-defined and cumbersome. The War Department required semi-annual reports on a multitude of topics. To prepare these, Wool was constantly on the road, and he became dependent on assistant inspectors, Maj. Gabriel H. Manigault in New York City, and Maj. Francis S. Belton in Detroit, to collect and forward regimental and post returns, muster rolls, and special surveys. From these documents and notes, Wool would draft a division report for Brown's approval, then mail the document and supporting papers to the Adjutant & Inspector Gen. Daniel Parker at the War Department in Washington. The secretary of war prepared an annual report to the president by gathering information from Wool and from his counterpart in the Southern Division, Col. Arthur P. Hayne. The reporting channels were simple, but relying on assistants in distant areas to gather records often proved frustrating.[7]

Not only was Colonel Wool forced to dash around the Empire State and posts on the American frontier, his job entailed keeping track of scintilla of details. In late May 1816, Colonel Wool left Brownville on his first inspection tour, which would focus on the garrisons in New York State, and carried instructions to check on troop discipline, officer performance, food rations, forage, hospital supplies, court martial proceedings, as well as equipment, arms, and ammunition. His first stop was at Madison Barracks, near Sackets Harbor, on Lake Ontario. Here Col. Hugh Brady of the Second Infantry opened his ledgers and paraded the troops for the inspector. Always on a deadline, Wool then sailed down Lake Ontario to Fort Niagara and watched the artillery company perform. He then hurried back east to Troy, and a few days later went north to visit the Sixth Infantry at Plattsburgh. Turning south, he headed for New York City. Wool's communications with commanding officers show clarity and deference, considerations of protocol. "If it will not interfere with previous arrangements," the colonel informed the troop commander in the harbor, "I will commence inspecting the troops under your command . . . on Sunday next, the 16th [June] instant, at 8 o'clock A.M., commencing with Capt. [Nathaniel N.] Hall's company on Governors Island." On the appointed day, Wool arrived promptly, examined the company books, walked through the barracks, asking questions and scribbling notes, and reviewed the troops at drill. That evening he dined with the officers. The inspector did not record "errors of minor import" and discreetly advised the commander to make corrections before his next visit. On July 24, Wool sent a bundle of papers from division headquarters to Adjutant General Parker in Washington. The bureaucrat complimented the inspector, saying he "never received papers in finer order."[8]

After that successful first tour, Wool embarked on wider circuits. He took his first trip west when in August 1816, he sailed from Black Rock, near Buffalo, for Detroit to visit Alexander Macomb's sprawling Fifth Department. British intrigues with Native Americans and interference with the American fur trade had caused Brown to send the Third and Fifth Infantry regiments to build and garrison new forts in the region. At Detroit, Wool handed Macomb a letter from Brown, in which the general explained Wool's mission, adding, "so far as I have had an opportunity of knowing Colonel Wool in his official capacity, I am much pleased with him." Macomb took Wool to old Fort Shelby in town and later introduced him to Lewis Cass, governor of Michigan Territory. A large, stout man with dark, shaggy eyebrows, Cass had been a militia general during the war, practiced law in Ohio, and as governor was urging the federal government to open the Old Northwest to settlement. The straight-laced little colonel liked Cass, finding in his simple manners and tastes, colorful conversation and jovial disposition, a refreshing change from the formal atmosphere of army officialdom.[9] The department in Cass's territory, however, was inadequate, according to Wool's report to Adjutant General Parker. Most troops were detailed to roadwork and other improvements in the countryside, and many officers were on furlough. The few pieces of ordnance at Shelby were rusting and useless. Macomb was aware of these conditions. "Colonel Wool will give you a detailed account of our situation," he wrote Brown, "but I fear it will fall far short of your expectations." Back east, in October, Wool headed north to artillery posts in the Second Department. He sailed from New York City up the Atlantic Coast to inspect Fort Preble at Portland, Maine, then returned south to Forts Constitution at Portsmouth, New Hampshire, Sewall at Marblehead, Massachusetts, Independence and Warren at Boston, Wolcott and Adams at Newport, Rhode Island, and Trumbull at New London, Connecticut. At each station he examined the cannons and carriages and observed firing practices. By early December of 1816, he had returned to Brownville. In eight months, riding on every kind of land and water conveyance, passing through a hundred towns and hamlets, Wool had traveled 4,500 miles to inspect the eastern and western garrisons in Brown's division.[10]

These travels contributed to Wool's belief that his office required further definition. For example, at Sackets Harbor, Maj. Henry Leavenworth, Second Infantry, had questioned his authority to review the troops. Wool admitted that the 1813 regulations, drawn up by Smyth, gave him no such power, nor did a war department order of February 22, 1815, but added that he merely followed the practices of wartime inspectors. The colonel felt poor definition made his reporting procedures burdensome. Were both semi-annual muster rolls and regimental returns needed? he asked the adjutant general, who explained that he annually bound the muster rolls into books for quick reference to personnel. On another occasion, Colonel Snelling, at Plattsburgh, asked Wool for guidelines to prepare an army discharge. The inspector had none. He drafted a simple form and sent it to Snelling, cautioning that "it may not be strictly correct."[11]

Shortly after his tour of the entire division, Wool discussed his duties with his commanding officer. Keeping records throughout the division was inefficient, disorderly and repetitious. Both general and regimental officers were uninformed regarding inspections. To be effective, Wool asked for special authority conferred by Brown's signature, and the general promptly provided a letter embodying his wishes. Further discussion of the matter ended abruptly, however, on December 21, when Brown's twelve-year-old son, Governeur, fell through the ice and drowned while skating on Black River. As the general mourned the loss of "his promising son," his staff and their families turned to their firesides and the Christmas season.[12]

Improvements in the system came soon. In late March 1817, Brown and his staff attended an elaborate dinner in New York City in honor of Daniel D. Tompkins, wartime governor and newly elected vice president of the United States. Wool again met Stephen Van Rensselaer, of Queenston days, and was introduced to George Croghan, a veteran of the 1812 war, who later also served as inspector general. When Brown's party left for Washington, Wool bid the group adieu and began a tour of garrisons in the First, Third, and Fourth departments. He had improved his note-taking and toyed with the idea of using "mathematical instruments" to make charts for his reports.[13]

While on the road, Wool asked Adjutant General Parker if he could skip the semi-annual report and file an annual statement in the autumn. With troops in transit between stations and in many places employed in the field, he found it impossible to collect the required reports in a six- month period. He also inquired about his per diem and travel allowances. "Every colonel in Division receives double rations, as also several lieutenant colonels, and majors, while their expenses are not so great as mine by considerable sum," Wool wrote. Parker approved the request to omit the June report, but required an annual report by December 1. Indeed, Wool's interest in streamlining his work dovetailed with Parker's interest to protect the army from cost-cutting lawmakers. He urged the inspector to emphasize how the troops had been "usefully employed beyond their regular military duty" during the year, which would enhance the "popularity" of the army in the eyes of a Congress conscious of its budgets and suspicious of standing armies. Parker also approved Wool's claim for extra expenses. Further help came from Brown, who granted Wool an assistant, Second Lt. Richard Douglass, Second Infantry, to help with correspondence and reports.[14]

The colonel chafed at the laxity of his subordinates. For example, Maj. Francis S. Belton, inspector general at Detroit, in July 1816 acknowledged that he was behind with his reports, but blamed this on confusing division orders. General Macomb had instructed him to transmit confidential comments through his local office to the War Department, bypassing division headquarters. Wool grumbled at Macomb's interference. He reminded Belton that a division order dated May 22, 1816, required assistant inspectors to transmit returns "through their [department] commanders to the Inspector General." Only division inspectors reported directly to the War Department. Wool patiently outlined Belton's duties and added a word of encouragement. In late October, a package of papers reached Brownville from Detroit, followed by another batch six weeks later. Wool promptly complimented his assistant on his "zeal, ability and promptitude."[15]

In July of 1817, Wool sailed again for Detroit to begin inspections. A month later, General Brown arrived with a military party escorting President James Monroe on a tour of posts along the Canadian border. On August 14, at a grand review of veterans of the War of 1812, the president presented Macomb an elegant sword, voted by the New York legislature for his wartime services at Plattsburgh. The next day, while discussing his recent inspection with Macomb, Wool was startled by the general's remark on his "fussy procedures." The little colonel took his job seriously, and immediately questioned the general's "singular language" regarding his "official conduct." Several hours later he boldly warned the general: "It remains with you to prevent the unpleasant necessity of my applying for your arrest." Macomb quickly collected three witnesses and in their presence apologized "for any expression he might have made" which reflected upon Wool's "character as an officer."[16]

In his annual report, the inspector described various problems in the Northern Division. The command contained forty forts, eight arsenals, and 4,355 men. During the year, the four infantry regiments had worked 133,654 days on road building and fort construction. There was little time for drill and military training. Several garrisons lacked supplies. At Fort Howard, near Green Bay, Wisconsin, the commander, Lt. Col. Talbot Chambers, Rifle Regiment, had used his personal credit to ration and clothe his men. Wool blamed late and uncertain lake navigation for the problems, and he suggested that quartermaster shipments to the western forts should be made during the summer. In a private note to the adjutant general, Wool said that Brown needed to exercise more energy with his command. On a recent tour, the colonel had demonstrated energetic command. Several times he had suggested that subalterns be court-martialed for neglecting their duties. In other cases he arrested (and released) officers for breaking regulations. How far should he go in disciplining officers? he asked Parker. Was he too rigid? "If so you must inform me and I will govern myself accordingly," he said.[17]

In December of 1817, winds of change began sweeping the army. John C. Calhoun, a South Carolina congressman and only thirty-five years old, became secretary of war. Young and vigorous, Calhoun had taken an interest in military affairs during the War of 1812. As secretary, he moved quickly to renovate and upgrade the War Department, yet his office exercised little influence over the army divisions and had no established policies for war or peace. Writing Brown on the seventeenth, Calhoun emphasized that he intended to give the army the "greatest possible utility and perfection" and requested the support of its ranking officers. In a closing note, which Brown doubtless handed to Wool, the secretary added, "The report of the Inspector General of your Division has afforded me much satisfaction." On April 14, 1818, Congress approved the secretary's request to expand the general staff. Three bureaus—Quartermaster General, Surgeon General, and Commissary General of Subsistence—were added to the three in place: Adjutant & Inspector General, Commissary General of Ordnance, and Paymaster General. The position of inspector general was upgraded to colonel of cavalry (instead of infantry), which gave the two incumbents a slight increase in pay.[18]

In early May of 1818, Colonel and Sarah Wool sailed from Buffalo for Detroit. There they met and dined with General Macomb and Governor Cass. When the colonel left on a western tour, Eliza Spencer Cass insisted that Sarah stay with her. The gubernatorial mansion, Sarah recalled, "was a log house—one story high—with unplastered dormitories under the roof, where Eliza, her numerous children & guests slept." The governor's wife was an exceptional woman. She possessed an extraordinary memory, spoke in a quick, animated fashion, and could entertain for hours with an inexhaustible supply of stories. There were no servants, for Eliza preferred to do her own cooking and household chores. A highlight of Sarah's stay was their trips downtown. The governor had no carriage, so a teamster, on demand, would bring a wagon, spread a carpet on the bed, and place chairs there. In this exalted fashion, the ladies rode through the streets of Detroit, running errands and making calls.[19]

Wool's 1818 tour took him beyond Detroit for the first time. He sailed north on a schooner to Fort Mackinac, and then across Lake Michigan where Maj. Zachary Taylor of the Third Infantry commanded Fort Howard in the Wisconsin Territory. Wool inspected the barracks, scanned company books, and watched the infantry drill. Taylor reported the visit to Brig. Gen. Thomas S. Jesup, recently appointed Quartermaster General of the Army: "It was the first time I ever saw the Colonel [Wool], but am pleased with him, as a gentleman, & think him an honor to his profession." They would meet again in Washington and in Mexico. The inspector headed down the lake by canoe with a small group of civilians to Fort Dearborn, at the village of Chicago. He made a brief inspection then sailed back to Detroit. He joined Sarah, and on July 27 they left for home.[20]

Wool shared Secretary Calhoun's enthusiasm for elevating the character of the army. In August, he wrote the secretary to object to Brown's choice of Judge Advocate Samuel A. Storrow for division adjutant general. "Mr. Storrow may possess some of the qualifications necessary for an Adjutant General," Wool said, "but . . . I think not military." The colonel had no intention of opposing Brown, but considered it "a duty incumbent upon me, and justly due the army," to inform Calhoun of his feelings. Roger Jones, Corps of Artillery, received the assignment of adjutant general on August 10, 1818.[21]

On his inspection trips, Wool kept up with events at Brownville through Lt. John A. Dix, Corps of Artillery, Brown's junior aide. Dix was educated, dignified, and a splendid conversationalist. The inspector even tried to learn French under his tutelage. "Brownville still occupies the same locality and its inhabitants inhale the same atmosphere that surrounded us when you abandoned its premises," Dix wrote in May of 1819. Sarah Wool was well, "as well as all the ladies and gentlemen of the General's domestic and military families." Judge Storrow and his family had departed for Virginia, and Wool could imagine just "how much this migration has detracted from the aggregate beauty and accomplishment" of the village. In closing, Dix inserted a page of French for translation.[22]

In the spring of 1819, Secretary Calhoun appointed Wool to the Board of Visitors for the June examinations at the United States Military Academy at West Point, New York. Established in 1802, the institution was basically an engineering school. The purpose of the visitors—which included three civilians and four army officers—was to report on its status and operation. Wool was familiar with the academy, for he regularly inspected the army's engineer detachment there. When the exams began, six senior cadets filed into a classroom to answer questions posed by the faculty and board. The ordeal lasted about two weeks. In its report on June 5, the board stressed the need to reorganize the administration, broaden the curricula, and add an astronomical observatory. Admission should be lowered to age fourteen and classes started for advance training. Wool also commented on the school in his 1819 annual report. He doubted that a devotion to mathematical science would produce enlightened officers. "The great victories which have called forth the admiration of every age were not achieved by the 'rule and compass' in the measurement of angles," he stated, "but were products of enlarged minds, highly cultivated and improved by a constant and accurate survey of human events." At the end of their second year, students with mathematical talents should focus on language, geography, history, and ethics. Army officers, he observed, would be called on increasingly to play roles in national politics. The call for change at West Point went unheeded.[23]

During the winter of 1819, Wool became involved in Congress's efforts to reduce the army. The nation was reeling from a financial panic, and Secretary of War Calhoun had been instructed to devise a plan to reorganize the administration of the military and cut the number of troops. He turned to division and department commanders and their staff for comments. On February 8, 1820, Wool submitted his views to General Brown. "The great strength and efficiency of every army," he said, "must be looked for in composition of the materials and its organization." Organization was critical. It must not only "preserve the knowledge it has gained," but it must "perfect and perpetuate the art of war." The smaller the army, the more critical its organization. The army also must be "expansible." It should be "capable of furnishing the means, when required, of enlarging itself, according to [an] emergency in the shortest time and at the smallest possible expense to the nation." A staff based on "talent, experience, and permanency" was required to direct the endeavor.[24]

Wool also pointed to a problem that loomed large in the reduction discussion. As early as 1817, he had expressed concern when his name and line rank of major, Sixth Infantry, was omitted from the annual *Army Register.* He had questioned the adjutant general informally about the omission, but received no satisfactory answer. A year later Calhoun stated that officers detached for staff duty should retain their line rank, but said nothing about this being retroactive. With the matter unclear, Wool applied for every vacancy that meant an advancement. In February of 1820, when Brig. Gen. Eleazer W. Ripley resigned his command in the Southern Division, the inspector urged Adjutant General Parker to nominate him for the position. "I can procure as many recommendations civil or military as the Secretary could read in a month," he boasted. The brigadiership (brevet) went to Col. Henry Atkinson, who soon came to head a new Western command, but the scramble underscored the need to resolve the staff-line controversy.[25]

Adjutant General Parker threw a bombshell when, on February 26, 1820, he advised Calhoun that officers selected under an order issued on April 24, 1816, had lost their line rank. In the uproar that followed, Wool scurried around Washington for signatures to a petition for redress and handed it to General Brown, a board member. He reminded the general that the 1816 law guaranteed to staff all privileges granted by the military act of March 3, 1813. The 1813 law specified that such assignments would be made "without prejudice to their rank and promotion in the line." In Wool's opinion, Parker's view of the controversy was ridiculous. On March 30, 1820, the board echoed Wool's argument. The acts of 1813 and 1816 assured all officers their line rank and right to promotion, even though on staff duty. A general order on May 20, 1820, announced that Wool held the lineal rank of lieutenant colonel, retroactive to February 10, 1818.[26]

In January of 1821, Congress began a review of a reduction plan submitted by Calhoun. The secretary showed his political savvy to gain support for his recommendations. He strongly recommended Brown to move troops to certain states in the spring to stimulate local economies and capture political support. He awarded medals to officers from the War of 1812, many of whom were now influential politicians. Calhoun also reminded Congress that he had reduced the army budget by one million dollars and imposed regulations to streamline military administration. But Congress forged ahead. On March 21 Congress and President Madison reduced and centralized the army. The legislation revived the rank of general-in-chief, previously held by George Washington, and recast the army staff. Henceforth there was to be one adjutant general and two inspectors general. Congress kept the seven staff bureaus and engineer corps, but eliminated the ordnance department, assigning its officers to the four artillery regiments. The regular army was trimmed from about 9,000 to 6,000 men. East-West departments replaced the North-South divisions, the demarcation line running from the northwestern corner of Lake Superior to the southern tip of Florida, with a brigadier general commanding each department.[27]

The new legislation was justified. The nation's economy was in disarray, battered by drought, epidemics, and financial disorders. British militancy along the northern frontier had eased. The Rush-Bagot Treaty of 1817 with Great Britain prohibited armed vessels on the Great Lakes, and American forts in the Old Northwest guaranteed national claims there. On the southern border, the friction with Spain over Florida had been settled by occupation and purchase by the Adams-Onís Treaty of 1819. The North-South division had outlived its usefulness, for the nation was marching ever west.[28]

In April of 1821, one month after Congress reformed the army, a board of six generals was appointed to meet in Washington to reshape regiments, make troop assignments, and review officer lists. Wool played an indirect but important role in these deliberations. General Brown had asked him to evaluate each officer in the Northern Division below the rank of lieutenant colonel by submitting to him a confidential list of names, each marked "A.D.Z., that is good, doubtful, bad." A furor arose over the downgrading of the office of adjutant general to the rank of colonel. Brown arranged for incumbent Daniel Parker, who protested mightily, to be made Paymaster General, and urged Bvt. Brig. Gen. Henry Atkinson, who was then commanding the Sixth Infantry, to replace Parker. Wool urged Atkinson to consider the offer, but the western commander preferred his brevet brigadier's rank and pay. The office of adjutant general, then, was staffed temporarily until 1825, when Roger Jones, former adjutant general of the Northern Division, was confirmed for the position. On June 1, Maj. Gen. Jacob Jennings Brown became the general-in-chief of the army, and Scott and Gaines took command of the new Eastern and Western Departments, respectively. Cols. John E. Wool and James Gadsden became roving inspectors, alternating their tours as directed. The debate over army reduction had ended.[29]

In the early winter of 1821, the Wools moved from Brownville to Washington at an anxious time for the army. General Brown had suffered a paralytic stroke in mid-October, which rendered his right arm useless, and it was feared that he would resign from military service. The general, however, ordered his staff to set up army headquarters in the national capital, though it would be nearly a year before he moved there.[30]

The winter in Washington was pleasant. The Wools took lodgings in a fashionable rooming house, and regularly attended parties, balls, and state occasions. "Aunt Wool," a niece later wrote, purchased the latest fashions from New York City and became a "model of taste and elegance." Petite, fair-skinned, with glistening black hair, Sarah possessed both beauty and charm, with "uncommon powers at conversation." She easily made friends and soon joined a social circle that included Floride Bonneau Calhoun, Margaret Lovell, wife of the surgeon general, and other spouses of ranking government officials. Colonel Wool became a familiar, smiling figure on Capitol Hill, exchanging pleasantries, and cultivating acquaintances. He regularly wrote Brown regarding congressional feelings toward the army. On Christmas Day in 1821, he reported that congressmen seemed more interested in the next presidential campaign (1824), than in tampering with the military. "The political cords are already tightened," he observed, and Calhoun, John Quincy Adams, and William H. Crawford "have begun to play their part." Calhoun's friends hoped to divide the South, secure the western states, and carry Pennsylvania and New York. But the political winds could easily shift in the months ahead.[31]

Wool's rooming house contained many interesting guests. Sarah invited her youngest sister, Elizabeth Moulton Deming, an attractive widow of twenty-seven, to join them at the "Metropolis," as Wool often called the capitol, and introduced her to Representative Francis Baylies of Taunton, Massachusetts. A courtship soon developed and Francis and Elizabeth were married the following June at the Moulton home in Nassau, New York. The Wools also befriended Elizabeth Haywood, the daughter of John Haywood, a prominent North Carolinian who spent his winters in Washington. The colonel and his lady, Elizabeth wrote her father, had become a "Brother & Sister" and shown her "every civility & kindness." A coterie formed around the Wools that included Haywood's friends, and Sarah Childress, wife of future president James K. Polk. They attended Sarah's teas and paid calls when her husband was on tour.[32]

In early May of 1822, Wool left Washington on what became the most grueling inspection trip of his career. With army reorganization, Secretary of War Calhoun gave the two inspectors specific assignments each year. Brown directed Wool to visit the major infantry installations on the Great Lakes, travel west to the posts on the Mississippi, Missouri, Arkansas, and Red Rivers, ending the tour at New Orleans. Col. Samuel B. Archer, his counterpart, would inspect the artillery garrisons, arsenals, and foundries along the Atlantic coast. In later years, the inspectors alternated tours. Wool felt his assignment in 1822 was unfair, for he had to cover twice the distance than Archer on a trip that could take nine months.[33]

Wool began his tour at Madison Barracks at Sackets Harbor, New York, where he found Col. Hugh Brady's Second Infantry in transit to construct a fort at Sault Ste. Marie along the Great Lakes. The inspector crossed the St. Lawrence to Kingston, Canada, strolled around the fortifications and shipyards there, then sailed west across Lake Ontario to Fort Niagara. He recrossed into Canada near Queenston. While the driver watered the horses, the colonel guided the passengers up the quiet slope where on a raw October morning, a decade before, he had won renown as a young officer. In a south-bound stage, he rumbled past the battlefields of Lundy's Lane and Chippewa to Fort Erie. Wool then recrossed the Niagara to Black Rock, near Buffalo.[34]

On June 12, the colonel sailed on the steamboat *Superior* for Detroit. He inspected the few troops there, visited with Governor Cass, and took passage for Mackinac. Lake travel could be hazardous. The first day out, the steamboat ran aground in the St. Clair Flats. As the crew rushed to move cargo into two small boats to lighten the vessel, a thunderstorm buffeted operations until after midnight. After brief stops at Forts Mackinac and Howard, the colonel headed into areas where he had never been before. On July 15, he joined a small civilian party traveling southwest on the Fox River in a large birch bark canoe. They paddled across Lake Winnebago, carried the canoe several miles across the portage to the Wisconsin, and descended to Fort Crawford, at the old fur entrepột of Prairie du Chien, on the Mississippi. Here, Wool hired a canoe and crew and ascended the Mississippi to Fort St. Anthony (Snelling) at its junction with the St. Peters (Minnesota) River. The military outpost was under construction high on a bluff. Colonel Snelling, the commander, welcomed his old friend and paraded the garrison of six companies for the visitor. Wool then returned downriver, stopping to inspect Fort Armstrong, at Rock Island.[35]

In mid-August, Wool reached St. Louis and reported to General Atkinson at neighboring Jefferson Barracks. Atkinson's vast western command contained some of the most remote army posts in the nation. Wool's objective was Fort Atkinson, a garrison of more than 500 men of the Sixth Infantry, located 300 miles up the Missouri River, at Council Bluffs (about fifteen miles north of present-day Omaha, Nebraska). The colonel purchased a wagon and team and drove up the Missouri. At

Franklin, he traded his rig for a sturdy saddle horse and two pack animals. On September 5, three men—Maj. Alexander Cummings, Sixth Infantry, a sergeant, and a guide—all bound for Atkinson, joined him. Cummings and the sergeant soon fell ill with fever, forcing Wool and the guide to assume the camp chores. Summer rains created swollen creeks, making each crossing on rafts a nightmare. On the ninth day, the weary party stumbled into Fort Atkinson. Wool rested a few days, inspected the garrison, and headed downriver with a group of travelers on a "Mackinac" boat. It was now late September and he wanted to visit Fort Smith, on the Arkansas River, and Cantonment Jesup, near Natchitoches, Louisiana, before winter.[36]

Wool was exhausted when he landed at Fort Osage, twenty miles upriver from Lexington, Missouri. "For the first time since I was appointed Inspector General," he wrote John Salisbury, "I feel disposed to murmur at my hard fortune. Never was I so wearied of traveling—my long, very long tour appears to have no end either in distance, or fatigue and hardships." The scorching sun, suffocating winds, and wretched mosquitoes, had reduced him to a "mere skeleton." He purchased a horse and pack animals and started south along the Neosho (Grand) River. Stricken with a bilious fever, Wool clung to his saddle and rode on. Four days later, he reached the Dwight Indian Mission, near Chouteau, Indian Territory, and collapsed. Several weeks later the fever subsided, and he struggled to St. Louis where on November 1, he reported his situation to Secretary Calhoun. The weary officer caught a steamboat for New Orleans, then headed east, finally reaching Washington in February of 1823. His ordeal was over.[37]

In late 1823, the Wools moved to the farming village of Nassau, about eighteen miles southeast of Troy, for some tranquility. In previous years, when Wool was on tour, Sarah stayed at Nassau with her sister Abby Moulton Griswold. Upon returning from Detroit in 1823, the Wools learned that Abby had died, leaving two children—Harriette and John, ages ten (b. 1813) and five (b. 1818). The Wools explained their wishes to help rear the children to Abby's husband Chester Griswold, a former school teacher, legislator, and merchant. In the arrangement, the colonel acquired the mortgage to the Griswold house, store, woodlot, and farm. Chester provided the Wools with several rooms in his house as separate living quarters. They could live there inexpensively, after spending winters in Washington. Years later, Harriette Griswold Hart recalled that Uncle Wool and Aunt Wool "did economize" during the fourteen years they lived in Nassau. In time, Chester paid off the mortgage and redeemed his property.[38]

Nassau, or "Old Dutchy," nestled in a pine forest, and a majority of its 2,800 inhabitants worked on farms and had little schooling. "A man could make his mark without knowing how to read and write," Harriette recalled, "and as for Grammar and Geography, I don't suppose the *words* had ever been heard in the farmers' houses." After the glitter and bustle of Washington society, the Wools found village life dull. "Griswold, as usual I presume," Wool wrote Sarah in December 1825 from Charleston, South Carolina, "is engaged in taking care of his pigs, and with the local politics of the county." Life was brighter when the colonel completed his yearly travels and returned home to share his experiences. The Wools also gave receptions and entertained friends from Troy and Albany at Peter Van Valkenburgh's popular tavern in Nassau.[39]

During the Wool's residence at Nassau, the colonel was able to devote more time to his business interests. A dreary, penurious childhood had fixed his determination to gain wealth and independence. His position as inspector general opened avenues for extra pay. In 1816–18, he received $2,048 annually, plus allowances, which was increased to $2,676 by 1821 ($56,196 in 2020). Year after year, he badgered the War Department auditors, secretaries of war, and even presidents for double rations and extra pay for travel and extended duty. At the same time, he invested in local real estate, mortgages, and bank stocks. He also made modest loans to relatives, friends, and even army officers.[40]

Wool kept a tight rein on his personal expenses. In October 1825, when Sarah requested a new stove for her living room, he questioned her closely about other "probable wants" for the winter. He recently had sent her a draft for $1,300 to cover a personal debt in Troy, pay on Griswold's accounts for fire insurance, and support Harriette Griswold's schooling. The remainder of $92, he said, should be enough to purchase "a handsome" stove. He reminded her that the amount was equal to a major's monthly pay. Wool took an active interest in planting and upkeep of the Griswold farm, and hired Hugh Wilson, a local resident, to manage the property. The farming enterprise was not geared for profit, but to raise forage for riding horses and farm animals, and to provide Sarah Wool a coachman.[41]

In February 1825, Wool broached an important matter with Secretary Calhoun. He would complete ten years of staff appointment as colonel in April 1826, and under army regulations, he could be recommended for the rank of brevet brigadier general. Would it be possible to receive the award early? Wool asked. He had received four commissions during the Madison administration and sought association with President Monroe. His request fell on deaf ears. Calhoun was acutely aware that the officer corps had given him little support in his recent bid for the presidency. In fact, Wool, Brown, and others had aligned themselves with New Yorker Martin Van Buren, who was building influence in state politics, and who in 1824, had directed his followers to vote for John Quincy Adams for president.[42]

The colonel decided to make an extended tour that, he hoped, would demonstrate the critical role that army inspectors played in the military establishment—and perhaps enhance his chances for brevet. In the spring of 1825, he swung through the northern garrisons and in the fall headed south. In December, Wool arrived in Charleston, South Carolina. On a visit to Fort Moultrie, across the harbor from Charleston, Wool got so mad at the six drunken artillerists who were acting as oarsmen that he had them thrown in the brig as soon as he reached the fort. In Charleston, he met a German traveler, Karl Bernhard, Duke of Saxe-Weimar Eisenach, who was visiting military installations in the eastern United States. Since army personnel (i.e., paymasters) or civilians often travelled with him for brief periods, the colonel invited the duke to join him on his tour across the southern states to New Orleans. What an experience! On the trip, Bernhard vividly recorded bouts with drunken sailors, erratic steamboat travel, stagecoach breakdowns, trudging along muddy roads for miles, staying in taverns and barns, and dining on plantation fare. In his letters from the South, Wool failed to comment on the cruelties of slavery that was so evident, particularly in Charleston. Armed police patrolled the city looking for errant slaves. At nine P.M. every evening, a bell pealed out after which no slave dared venture into the streets. Any slave caught without a pass was thrown into a blacks-only prison. The owner was notified to retrieve his property the next day and assessed a fine. If he failed to pay the fine, twenty-five lashes were given the slave. Overseers walked around the prison with bull-whips and in the basement there was a medieval rack where disobedient prisoners were tied, hands and feet, and they were flogged unmercifully.[43]

The colonel had originally wanted to go from Charleston to Savannah, but the steamboat service was so irregular, he decided to head for Milledgeville, at the time the capital of Georgia. In a mail stagecoach that proved less than reliable, he and the duke left Charleston on a cold wintry morning five days before Christmas. Across the Ashley River at low tide, slaves busily dug for oysters and clams. The stage turned inland through groves of magnolia, laurel, and live oak trees, rattling past large rice and cotton plantations, many of them so sickly in the summer that the owners fled to Charleston. They saw on one river a plantation owner and his family, in gay holiday attire, being rowed along by six slaves. Across the Salkehatchie and Combahee Rivers in the Carolina low country, on a cold moonlit night, the stage stopped to change horses and then continued into the less settled part of the state where slave gangs cleared pine forests for cotton fields. After ferrying across the Savannah River to Augusta, Georgia, the travelers paused at the fashionable Globe Hotel. In Augusta, Wool decided to pay a visit to William H. Crawford, who had been one of the leading candidates for president in 1824. Of "gigantic stature," Crawford had suffered a paralyzing stroke from medication given him by his physician and he quickly fell out of contention but remained politically powerful. The duke was surprised that Crawford, who had served as secretary of war and secretary of the treasury and who had been the American envoy to Paris during the War of 1812, could not speak French.[44]

Leaving Augusta, the colonel and the duke bounced their way in another moonlit night along a primitive country road over hills and through piney woods with a drunken Irish stage driver at the whip, the eighty-six miles to Milledgeville. They passed several caravans of poor Americans heading west. In one place three families huddled for warmth around a pine log they had set on fire in three places. Entering Milledgeville, the duke noted a gentleman and his lady on horseback followed by a barefooted black slave running behind with a heavy sack of corn for the couple's horses. The pair ferried across the Ocmulgee River to Macon, where they found scant accommodations in a small tavern before continuing on the next morning past the Creek Indian Agency on the left bank of the Flint River at Thlo-no-teas-kal, a small Creek community of twenty log huts and slave quarters. It was the Christmas holidays and at a "grog shop," several drunken Creeks and their slaves were seen "frolicking." Here the duke joyously exchanged a bottle of whiskey for a war dance.[45]

Across the Chattahoochee River on a Creek-operated ferry, the travelers found accommodations in a windowless outbuilding the duke said was little better than a "German barn." At Fort Mitchell, across the river in Alabama, Wool inspected four companies of the Fourth Infantry, commanded by Maj. Sanders Donoho, who was trying, largely in vain, to protect the Creeks from white encroachment on their lands. Here Wool met the controversial Chief Taskanugi Hatke, also known as William McIntosh, who was leading a large faction of the Creeks who were trying to acculturate to European American ways of life. The chief introduced the travelers to his wife and children. The duke noted that the chief also had an Indian wife and seventy slaves. Four months later, after signing yet another treaty with whites that gave away the remaining Creek lands in Georgia, Taskanugi Hatke was seized and executed by his own people.[46]

On January 1, 1826, the travelers awoke to the sounds of drums and fifes and the refrains of "Hail Columbia" and "Yankee Doodle." No sooner had they departed Fort Mitchell than their carriage overturned and the colonel and the duke were forced to walk four miles to the nearest plantation, past Indian huts and Creeks sleeping among their hogs, the duke noted. After a venison dinner, they continued the next day in a cloudless dark blue sky to Montgomery on the Alabama River. Carved out of a pine forest, Montgomery was in the fertile black belt and signs of cotton cultivation were everywhere. Gaining passage on the 170-ton cotton-steamer *Steuvenville,* the travelers headed down the Alabama River for Mobile. On January 6, 1826, the steamer stopped to take on more cotton at Cahawba, the capital of Alabama at the time, although the legislature had just resolved to move the seat of government to Tuscaloosa. Here Wool met Col. Andrew Pickens, an old friend from the War of 1812, a cousin of John C. Calhoun, and former governor of South Carolina, who had become a prominent Alabama politician and planter. Downriver the *Steuvenville* ran aground and everyone on board seemed distraught, although Wool who had acquired through "long experiences" a toleration for such matters, the duke noted, remained quietly on his cot.[47]

Although people feared that the steamer would remain grounded for several days, perhaps weeks, to wait for rain and higher water, the boat was soon freed, and on January 9, the travelers reached Mobile in a thick fog. Here were bananas and oranges from Cuba and summer weather. Wool watched as a volunteer company paraded about, celebrating the anniversary of the Battle of New Orleans. The colonel felt obligated to go to Pensacola to inspect Fort Barrancas and the duke and the colonel caught a tiny thirty-two-ton steamer *Emiline,* the smallest the duke had ever seen, across Mobile Bay, where they hired a two-horse barouche for the sixty-five miles to Pensacola. At Fort Barrancas on the coast, Wool found Col. Duncan Lamont Clinch in command of only two officers and twenty men of the Fourth Infantry, and the inspection was soon over. On their return to Mobile, the travelers came across a runaway slave who graciously helped them across the Perdido River. Spotting his owner, the poor black man disappeared in the woods. When the slave owner requested the two travelers assist him in recovering his "property," the two "unanimously rejected his proposal with disgust" and proceeded on their way. The colonel and the duke were equally repulsed by the gambling houses in Mobile, where half-drunk sailors staggered among "country people who had brought their corn and cotton to market" and were gambling away their money.[48]

On yet another steamer on their way to New Orleans, the two were engulfed by a frightening storm roaring out of the west, which pounded the boat in a cold rain, with loud thunder and spectacular lightening. The furniture on the steamer was tossed about, sky-lights were shattered, most of the passengers became frightened and deathly sick, and the boat was forced to make anchor near the coast out of the storm. At sea again, the steamer ran aground several times but finally navigated past several small islands until the lighthouse at the old Spanish Fort St. John on the south shore of Lake Pontchartrain was spotted, and the steamer anchored safely by. Unable to hire a carriage, the travelers decided to walk the six miles to New Orleans. After several hours along a muddy causeway, the colonel and the duke finally spotted the white spires of St. Louis Cathedral and the masts of ships anchored in the Mississippi River. They were not too tired to make their way to the Mississippi to pay homage to the "father of waters," before finding boarding on Rue de Chartres, only a few blocks from a slave auction house. Here black men and women sat and stood through the day while potential buyers examined them. "The abomination is shocking, and the barbarity and indifference produced by the custom in white men is indescribable," the duke recorded. In his letters to Sarah, Wool expressed no such revulsion. He remained tolerant of an institution that many of his friends and colleagues in Troy found abhorrent. In New Orleans, Wool inspected two companies of the First and Fourth Regiments, commanded by Maj. David. E. Twiggs, eighty men in all, mostly young men from the western states, along with a few German and Irish immigrants who had also enlisted. For more than an hour the young men marched well, but their uniforms were ill-fitted.[49]

In New Orleans on February 1, 1826, Wool bid Bernhard adieu and headed up the Mississippi and then west to Cantonment Jesup in western Louisiana. At Fort Smith, Arkansas, he crossed into Indian Territory to inspect Cantonment Towson on the Red River, and Fort Gibson, on the Grand. Heading back east across the Great Lakes, Wool reached Nassau in the early fall. In eighteen months, the energetic officer had visited thirty-four military posts (several twice) on a tour "greater than had ever been performed in the same period." Brown cited Wool's remarkable exploit in his annual report.[50]

The colonel's wide-ranging travels paid off. In early December, President Adams recommended the Senate approve brigadier brevets for Wool and George Gibson, commissary general of subsistence. Wool's award was backdated to April 29, 1826. He was now forty-two years old and had been in the regular army for fourteen years. The brevet brought no increase in pay, but it enhanced his image and made a permanent promotion more likely.[51]

Basking in his new prestige, the colonel took a more active role in national politics. At parties in Washington in the winter of 1826, hosted by General Brown and his wife Pamela, John and Sarah Wool developed cordial relations with President John Quincy Adams and his family. Wool also cultivated ties with Van Buren's Albany Regency, a political clique within the "Bucktail" Republican Party in New York State, which in 1827 began supporting Andrew Jackson for the presidency. Wool sought to involve his brother-in-law, Francis Baylies, an attorney and former Massachusetts congressman, in the campaign for Jackson. A small, rotund man, well-educated and shrewd, more of an eccentric than a politician, Baylies possessed an able pen and a trenchant wit. Wool and Baylies became as close as brothers, and for nearly thirty years they exchanged opinions about the personalities, politics, and events of their times. By the late 1820s, Baylies had become disillusioned with politics and branded John Quincy Adams "perverse, obstinate, and wrong-headed." Wool encouraged the writer to support Andrew Jackson for high office.[52]

In December 1827, Wool met with members of the regency in Albany. He handed them a lengthy political statement by Baylies that questioned the Whig view that military chieftains were dangerous to the republic. The writer stood ready to prepare other articles, Wool said. The regency accepted his offer, and in the spring of 1828, the *Albany Argus* published commentaries by Baylies, signed "The Military Chieftain," "The Contract," and "Lucius Junius." Pro-Jackson newspapers drew on these articles for publicity. Wool also began a personal letter-writing campaign. "I derived much satisfaction from your account of the political prospects in your own state," William C. Rives, a Virginia politician, wrote on June 9. Information "from one, who is so sagacious an observer as yourself . . . inspires far more confidence than the statements which come to us through other channels," Rives continued. Pennsylvania and seven southern states already were in the Jackson camp, and he presumed that "such magicians as you are in New York can make out 25 more [electoral votes], either in your own state or in other states . . . to elect him." Although the electoral vote in New York was split in the contentious fall election of 1828, Jackson secured twice as many electoral votes as the National Republican, John Quincy Adams, and he easily secured the presidency.[53]

Wool urged Baylies to seek a share in the political spoils. The writer was considered for the collectorship at Boston and at New Bedford, and several other positions without success. Baylies also wrote Jackson a personal letter describing his role in securing votes in New York for the president and asked Wool to deliver it. To buoy Baylies's sagging spirits, the colonel sent comments on foreign affairs and local gossip from Washington. Peggy Eaton, the vivacious wife of John H. Eaton, the new secretary of war, was the center of attention. Peggy's "common" background and "loose" reputation made her unacceptable to cabinet wives, but Jackson included her in his inner circle. The president, Wool wrote Baylies on August 27, 1829, "has been cuped [bled] and for the recovery of his health has gone to the Rip Raps [island near Fortress Monroe] with the Secretary of War and I presume Madam Peggy for Nurse. Pitty [*sic*], he [Jackson] was not a little younger and she might answer a double purpose!" Although troubled waters swirled around Peggy Eaton, the Wools wisely courted the president's favor and were frequent guests at official functions. Aunt Wool, Harriette Hart recalled, "was on social terms at the 'White House,'" and the President "said many things to her, which were more in *his* peculiar style [gossip?], than in the style demanded from his position." Jackson also gave Sarah Wool a lock of his hair, which she treasured for years.[54]

The stiff, formal world of Monroe and Adams gave way to a freer age. Washington society changed as the younger patrons broke with the past. "A certain set of gentlemen & ladies," Wool wrote his friend Isaac Hart, Harriette's husband, "have recently introduced a variety of plays . . . I have been told that they shock very much the modesty of our more holier minded . . . particularly one in the performance of which all the ladies and gentlemen are thrown upon the other pell-mell." The women were especially "delighted with it."[55]

While the nation welcomed a new leader and a far less aristocratic era, the army had also experienced change during Adams's final year in office. On February 24, 1828, Gen. Jacob Brown died in Washington. Although partially crippled for over six years, he had exerted a stabilizing influence on the military establishment, and at his demise, he was planning to modernize the artillery corps. Within a few weeks of Brown's death, the two departmental brigadiers, Winfield Scott and Edmund Gaines, vied to replace him as general-in-chief. They hotly argued over rank, and their bickering quickly spread to the army staff. Amidst this confusion, Wool pressed Secretary of War James Barbour for a regular brigadiership, should Scott or Gaines be promoted. He also asked a friend in the Senate to call for his confidential inspection reports, knowing they could prejudice contending claims for a departmental appointment. President Adams ignored both Scott and Gaines, and nominated Brig. Gen. Alexander Macomb, head of the Engineer Corps, to the position of general-in-chief, with the rank of regular major general. Macomb took command of the army on May 29, 1828.[56]

The new supreme commander quickly announced that he would emphasize order, discipline, and economy in the military. Within a year, he began issuing inspectors special instructions. In orders dated May 16, 1829, to Colonels Wool and George Croghan, who in December 1825 had succeeded Samuel B. Archer, Macomb listed departure times, routes, posts to visit, and objectives. He particularly wanted information on army personnel—both enlisted men and officers. Why was the desertion rate so high? Were rations adequate? Was the whiskey ration injurious to health? What was the condition of the officer corps? Macomb expected "a full disclosure of everything which should be known to the General-in-chief of an army." Annual inspections reports were due in his office by early October.[57]

For many years, Wool had been concerned about personnel problems. He repeatedly stressed the difficulties caused by troop dispersals in one or two company garrisons, where officers, after assigning details, had few men left to train. At larger posts soldiers labored on many projects "to justify continued appropriations" for the army, a program that Calhoun had promoted. During his tenure as war secretary, both infantry and artillery companies regularly worked on fort construction, road building, post gardens, and other types of common labor. In both small and large posts, morale deteriorated, and garrisons became enclaves of unhappy men.[58]

Desertions had soared. As early as July 1818, Brown expressed concern at the desertion rate in his division. Calhoun believed that increasing the daily whiskey ration as a reward for fatigue duty would deter desertions, but the problem grew worse. Guardhouses, Wool reported, were crowded with deserters, and "not one fourth of the guilty have been apprehended." Punishment by "fines, imprisonment, and hard labor with ball and chain" had little effect. Recruiting officers were struggling to keep army ranks "even tolerably well filled." The liquor ration, Wool concluded, should be restricted. "The soldier gets his gill [one-fourth of a pint] in the morning; if he performs extra duty he is allowed another; and if he had been industrious he is permitted to get another, and sometimes two gills." The practice contributed to "drunkenness, idleness, debauchery and every species of depravity." The English gave their soldiers beer, while the French issued cheap wine or brandy. If a substitution was tried in the United States, Wool felt the experiment should begin at the seacoast garrisons.[59]

With complaints from generals, inspectors, and commandants, Secretary of War Eaton decided in December 1830 to replace the daily whiskey ration with money payments. Wool branded the regulation a halfway measure. Sutlers could sell two gills (a half pint) a day to each soldier on the theory that liquor was "necessary to his health or comfort." Such a regulation, the inspector fumed, not only encouraged the purchase of ardent spirits but operated "as a bribe to the sutlers to taint and corrupt the morals of the army." Two years later the War Department ended the money allowance and offered coffee and sugar as a voluntary substitute for whiskey.[60]

The problem of desertion remained. With an estimated 1,251 desertions in 1830, Secretary Eaton tried a new tactic: he rewarded those who stayed in service. Small amounts would be deducted from a soldier's monthly pay during his five-year enlistment, which were forfeited if he deserted. He also allowed soldiers to purchase honorable discharges for twenty-five dollars. Wool scoffed at Eaton's patronizing policies, saying that a majority of the deserters were "indolent, vicious, and dissipated" men, incapable of responding to a reward system. Purchasing discharges was also wrong. The "most prudent, sober and discreet" soldiers, rather than the malcontents, would use this avenue to leave the service. On the other hand, Wool liked Eaton's pay retention program—but suggested that army enlistments be reduced to three years. In December 1831, Secretary of War Lewis Cass, who supported the burgeoning temperance movement, echoed many of the inspector's suggestions in his annual report. The army restored corporal punishment (flogging) for desertion and two years later reduced enlistments from five to three years. Soldiers received a reenlistment bounty, and their monthly pay was increased. The desertion rate dropped, but did not disappear.[61]

Wool also pointed to problems in the officer corps. Many army posts had sick or enfeebled officers. For example, in 1824 at Fort Howard, Wool found that Col. John Miller, commanding the Third Infantry, had been on sick leave for two years. As a result, company commanders developed independent principalities. Each company had "a separate garden, corn and potato field; each a barn and separate plan of deposit for its hay, corn and vegetables; each had its own team, procured its own wood, and materials for building and repairing barracks." This meant a needless duplication of effort and extra expense. At Fort Niagara in 1829, Wool found its commandant, Maj. William Whistler, Second Infantry, under arrest and a captain in command who was ignorant of his duties. Many colonels, lieutenant colonels, and majors, Wool reported in 1831, were "honorable and worthy men," but in the aggregate they sought to please rather than "discover error or advise a correction." Yet the army depended on such officers for discipline and character.[62]

In June 1839 at St. Louis, Wool had the distasteful duty of setting judgment on Col. George Croghan, his fellow inspector general. A hero from the 1812 war, Croghan was serving as postmaster in New Orleans when appointed an inspector in December 1825. The selection of a hopeless alcoholic caused an uproar in the officer corps. Within a year, Croghan's drinking worsened, and he tried to commit suicide. While presiding at the court-martial of Lt. Col. Joshua B. Brant, Quartermaster Corps, Wool had to postpone proceedings when Croghan, a board juror, became intoxicated and was unable to attend. The jury convicted Brant—and condemned Croghan's intemperance. Wool privately asked Secretary of War Joel Poinsett for leniency. The colonel was actually a "noble and generous" person and should not be dismissed. In September, Wool received a pitiful letter from Croghan, requesting help. "I scarcely knew what to say to you in answer," Wool said. "I have done all in my power to save you. . . . [but] it will be out of the power of myself or anyone else to influence the President without reformation, complete and total reformation, on your part." Influential friends in Washington interceded and Croghan remained in service. His problem mirrored the widespread alcoholism in the officer corps in the Old Army.[63]

Wool's efforts to reform the army threatened his job. Secretary of War Eaton had clashed with Macomb's staff over policy. In the spring of 1830, a House resolution instructed the secretary to submit a plan to renovate the war office. In his report, Eaton suggested abolishing several departments, particularly that of the inspectors general. He branded the inspectors as "parasites" whose confidential reports comments grossly violated "the dignity, the feelings, the pride, and character of an officer." Caught up in the political controversy between Jackson and Vice President Calhoun, Eaton resigned on April 7, 1831. Staff renovations were forgotten.[64]

By the spring of 1832, Wool had been an army inspector for sixteen years. He had spent considerable time trying to define his duties and enhance his office, and had traveled great distances to report on an army in motion and scattered to distant horizons. He had also pursued politics with vigor in an effort to expedite his career and gauge the winds of change that regularly influenced the army's mission and swept the nation. With the elevation of Macomb to supreme command, Wool's attention had turned to the problems of the army, to the need to improve its character and health. As his suggestions gained attention, he advanced from reporter to advisor, from inquisitor to seer. The years ahead would be different and difficult. Wool would turn his attention to modernizing the army's weaponry, to creating a viable light artillery corps, and finally to exercising field commands on the nation's frontiers.

3

CASTING ASIDE A COLONIAL PAST

During the early 1830s, Wool played a significant role in modernizing the army artillery corps. As an army inspector he had often raised concerns about the rusting and antiquated ordnance in scattered garrisons, and recommended that unserviceable items be sold and new weapons acquired. Various war secretaries toyed with the matter, but in 1832, Secretary of War Lewis Cass took action. He created an ordnance board to study army needs and sent Wool, who was a board member, to Europe to purchase the latest French and British artillery. The colonel failed to accomplish his goals, but the momentum to modernize resulted in a new army artillery system with enhanced weaponry. Wool resumed his inspection duties, but at the insistence of Cass and Macomb, he soon became a "troubleshooter" with special assignments that extended to trouble with Native Americans and problems on the border.[1]

At the resignation of Secretary Eaton in April 1831, President Jackson appointed Cass, governor of the Michigan Territory, to head the War Department. Cass wrote Wool in October that he looked forward to seeing him in the Washington "metropolis" in the early winter. He also inquired about his daughters, Elizabeth and May Cass, who were visiting the Wools in Nassau. The two girls were in fine spirits, the colonel replied, and diligently studying French four hours a day. They stood ready to comply with whatever wishes Cass had for his daughters. Everyone was excited about the move to the nation's capital, and Sarah Wool planned an extended shopping trip to New York City. The Wools hoped to obtain lodgings in the house where Cass was staying or find rooms nearby. In early December, John and Sarah Wool headed down the Hudson on their journey to the capital.[2]

In earlier conversations, Wool called Cass's attention to the deplorable state of the artillery, which Wool considered the most important branch of the military. He repeatedly urged that the relics of the War of 1812—cannons, howitzers, and mortars—be condemned and sold for scrap. The army's weaponry should be upgraded, he argued. Large sums had been spent building forts to protect the nation's frontiers, but little thought had been given to arming them. In 1818, Calhoun had convened a board to stir aging Col. Decius Wadsworth, who had been in the military since the administration of George Washington, and his small ordnance department (forty-four officers) into action. In a strange reverse, the board, decimated by resignations, ignored Wadsworth's suggestion to adopt new English gun carriage designs, and clung instead to the old French models of Gen. Jean Baptiste de Gribeauval. The 1821 army reduction act abolished the ordnance department and scattered the officers to artillery posts.[3]

In the early 1820s, General Brown gave increasing attention to the ordnance situation. In 1822, he assigned Inspector General Archer to assess ordnance annually in the coastal garrisons. The next year he asked Wool to report on artillery posts, arsenals, and foundries. In October 1824, Wool filed a gloomy report, claiming the Third and Fourth Artillery, stationed south of the Potomac, were in disarray. At Fort Jackson, in fever-ridden Savannah harbor, the majority of the soldiers were on detached duty, in the hospital, or confined in the guardhouse. Barracks, grounds, and storehouses were in disrepair. Post commanders claimed no responsibility for the ordnance. At the arsenal in Augusta, Georgia, Wool found 20,000 stands of arms, principally muskets, still in their boxes and coated with rust. At the Bellona Arsenal, in Richmond, Virginia, the cannons were imperfectly cast and dangerous to fire. At every artillery post, the gun carriages and platforms were dilapidated and needed oil or paint. Powder magazines were inappropriately located and had leaky roofs. North of the Potomac, the situation was better. The men of the First and Second Artillery were neater and better drilled. If dismounted, cannons had protective plugs and sat on skids. Wool urged Brown to have regulations drafted for ordnance care, and he recommended that all unserviceable weapons be sold at public auction. His assessment bore fruit. On March 3, 1825, Congress authorized post commanders to sell defective or antiquated ordnance at public auction. Two years later, at Wool's insistence, Lt. Col. George Bomford, the new ordnance chief, issued a set of regulations for his department. When auctions and sales were completed in 1831, the army had taken in $200,000 and cleared most of its installations of inoperable weaponry.[4]

Secretary of War Calhoun had also tried to upgrade the artillery corps. In April 1824, the army established a School of Practice at Fortress Monroe, Virginia. He planned to send eleven companies there annually from the four artillery regiments for intensive drill and gunnery practice. West Point graduates assigned to the artillery would also spend a year at Fortress Monroe. But the school fared poorly. Wool reported to Brown in November 1827 that the artillery officers at Fortress Monroe exhibited "some knowledge of pyrotechny, of field evolutions, and could point a gun with considerable accuracy and prepare a shell and throw it from a howitzer," but they lacked knowledge in implanting batteries, preparing defensive works, building bridges, or repairing carriages. The following year, John Quincy Adams's secretary of war, Yale graduate Peter B. Porter, cut funding for both Fortress Monroe and the

Infantry School at Jefferson Barracks, near St. Louis, Missouri. Porter branded them the "cherished favorites" of his predecessors.[5]

By 1829, Wool grew increasingly concerned about the ordnance situation. Colonel Bomford, although he was ushering through the sales of unusable artillery, lacked authority to require the production of reliable weaponry. Accidents were common. While observing artillery practice at Fort Columbus on Governors Island, Wool watched in horror as a gun exploded, horribly mangling the hands of two artillerymen. Wool examined the shattered barrel and found that it was poorly cast. The War Department, he stated, must supervise weapon fabrication more closely, and again stressed the need for a board to review designs and conduct tests. Bomford echoed Wool's sentiments. In his annual report in 1830, Bomford related how he was responsible for two federal and nine private armories, four cannon foundries, fourteen arsenals, four ordnance depots, and numerous lead mines. At the same time, he was charged with constructing demonstration weapons, arming the state militia, and storing and protecting vast quantities of munitions. To oversee these tasks, he had a skeleton force in Washington and only four regular ordnance officers, one attached to each artillery regiment. It was an overwhelming responsibility.[6]

In October 1831, Wool pressed Secretary Cass to take action on his ordnance concerns. Bomford's department furnished the army with cannon, muskets, and miscellaneous military equipment, supervised $12 million's worth of property, and annually disbursed $1 million. Yet this crucial office, upon which victory in war could rest, had no "settled system of operations." A board of experienced officers should study ordnance needs and in a workshop construct models, patterns, and drawings, for both cannon and carriages. On November 7, 1831, Cass informed Wool that he was establishing an ordnance board and asked him to serve on it. Without hesitation and with pleasure, Wool accepted the appointment. He also offered to serve Cass in any way possible, saying that in the months ahead, the secretary would have "a great deal to reform in the army." The general staff in Washington could be helpful, but "they may give you unnecessary trouble." He included several pages of "useful hints" for Cass's attention.[7]

On March 28, 1832, Wool met with the ordnance board in Washington for the first time. Macomb presided, while Brig. Gen. Charles Gratiot (chief of engineers), Bvt. Col. Abram Eustis (commandant of the Artillery School at Fortress Monroe), and Bomford and Wool served on it. They focused their attention on gun carriages. The army relied on the Gribeauval, or "split-trail" design, which was made of cast iron and discarded in Europe after Waterloo. In 1818, the War Department sent First Lt. Daniel Tyler, First Artillery, to France to obtain drawings and details of a "stock-trail" design. After Tyler returned with them, the Washington Arsenal built experimental carriages that proved more durable and maneuverable than the "split-trail" that was currently in use. But the army settled with the French design, even after it became obsolete.[8]

After three weeks of meetings, the ordnance board recommended, to no one's surprise, the reestablishment of the ordnance department, and the board compiled a list of officers to staff it. Bomford and Eustis agreed to select weapons for the field artillery, settle the carriage question, and decide whether cannon should be cast in iron or brass. They would also draft a new set of ordnance regulations. To expedite the studies, the board proposed that Inspector General Wool be sent to Europe to purchase examples of the latest cannon for comparison and testing. Secretary of War Cass soon acted on the report, and on April 5, he ordered the ordnance department, after ten years of subservience to the artillery, be placed on an independent footing. The secretary also approved Wool's trip abroad.[9]

The board instructed Wool to visit the major military installations in France and England and examine the latest artillery pieces. In France, he would seek to purchase five weapons: two brass field guns (one four-pounder and one twelve-pounder), a siege mortar (model only), a ten-inch seacoast mortar (model), and a five-and-a-half-inch howitzer—each complete with carriage and caisson. In England, he was to obtain the popular brass six-pounder field gun with block (stock) trail carriage. These items should be crated and shipped home at the earliest opportunity.[10]

Wool spent May preparing for his journey. On the seventh of the month, he requested $1,000 from Quartermaster General Jesup for transportation, food, and quarters while abroad, and received a government warrant for other expenses, negotiable at the Bank of the United States in New York City. Wool also sought letters of introduction from prominent men. At the time, cholera was sweeping France and other parts of Europe, but he was determined to "make the most" of his time. Perhaps he could extend his visit to Holland and Germany. He particularly wanted to see the Dutch troops and their well-equipped cavalry. "I have no doubt I shall be well received by the present commander of the Dutch forces, the Duke of Saxe Weimar." On a previous visit to the United States in 1826, the duke had extended a personal invitation to visit Holland.[11]

On June 6, 1832, Wool arrived in New York City and in his mail at the post office discovered a largesse. Bomford sent orders to sail on the tenth—and a bill of credit for $6,630 on the London banking house of Baring Brothers. The amount included $5,000 for artillery pieces, $1,000 for equipment, and the remainder to cover the difference in monetary exchange. In another letter, Cass forwarded a draft for $1,100 to pay for personal purchases he wanted Wool to make.[12]

Macomb asked Wool to secure patterns for officer uniforms but gave no specifics. Seeking last minute instructions, Wool steamed up the Hudson to West Point, where Macomb was meeting with the board of visitors. He found the general in a classroom, stepped in, and sat beside him. While recitations droned on, he whispered questions about cloth and designs for the uniforms. Back in New York City, he received a farewell letter from Macomb: "In your intercourse with the officers of the different governments," the general wrote, "it will be well to be explicit as to your object, so as to disarm them of all suspicion, assuring them that in every instance our public establishments, particularly those of a military nature, are at all times open to the inspection of friendly powers." Macomb continued: "The present moment, when all the world has got rid in a great measure of its prejudices, and when science is offering the road to general information, we expect with confidence and indulge the hope that every facility will be afforded you in gaining the information obtained in Europe." He also requested a monthly report. Wool went shopping for shirts, nightcaps, flannel sheets, and he prepared to sail for France.[13]

On June 10, 1832, in a hard-driving rain, as the Black Hawk War was exploding on the northwestern frontier, Wool boarded the ocean packet *Charlemagne,* anchored near the Battery on the North River. The vessel was towed to a point off Sandy Hook; the crew raised the sails and set course for Normandy. On board Wool quickly made acquaintances with several "amicable and agreeable" women passengers and continued his study of French. The crossing took twenty-seven days, but the voyage was pleasant. On July 7, a Saturday, he landed at the port of Le Havre, at the mouth of the River Seine on the English Channel, cleared customs, and took lodgings at a hotel. The next day, the American consul, John Beazeley, arrived for a visit, and in the afternoon, Wool watched the colorful National Guard parade in the city. Wool then boarded a large, clumsy stagecoach, called a *Diligence*, with fifteen passengers, and was soon jolting and bouncing across the countryside toward the French capital.[14]

The skies were overcast and gloomy when Wool reached Paris. He secured a room at the Hotel des Premier, and, feeling ill, he took a little brandy, laced with a few drops of peppermint and laudanum, and rested. At that time, Paris boasted 750,000 inhabitants, nearly four times the population of New York City. An air of decay and poverty clung to its streets. Thankfully, the dreaded cholera morbus, which had recently swept the city and carried away thousands, was now subsiding.[15]

On June 11, Wool located William Cabell Rives, the American minister, a genial Virginian he had known for several years. Rives had studied law with Thomas Jefferson at Monticello and became a leading Jacksonian Democrat, although he later became a Whig. Wool explained the purpose of his tour and asked for assistance in making the proper contacts. Rives urged him to put his request in writing and promised to deliver it to the French government as soon as possible. Wool sought an introduction to Louis Philippe, the self-styled "Citizen King" of the constitutional monarchy, and Rives agreed to arrange an audience. Leader of the Orléanist Party, Louis was proclaimed king following the 1830 July Revolution that swept his cousin,

Charles X, from power. Two days after arriving in Paris, Wool handed the minister a formal letter stating his mission both to purchase from the French government (or privately, if necessary) models and specimens used by the artillery, infantry, and cavalry, and to visit French arsenals, foundries, and armories. Unofficially, he also hoped to collect samples of officer uniforms, including caps and belts. Rives promptly presented the American officer's petition to the French government, and Wool and Rives were punctually invited to dine at court a few days later.[16]

Wool hurried to prepare himself properly for his reception at court. Strangely, he had brought no dress uniform to Europe with him, so he sat down with pen and paper to design a coat and trappings. With a French dictionary he listed the materials needed and, then, searched for a tailor. Explaining his wishes to tailors was exasperating. "I was almost compelled to turn Taylor, Hatter, blousemaker, button maker & almost everything else," he wrote Cass. His uniform cost 750 francs (about $350), which made him hesitate to have other uniforms made in Paris. At Rives's hotel, the American minister, whose simple dress reflected prevailing French customs, was astonished at the splendor of Wool's elaborate uniform.[17]

Wool made a grand entrance in the audience chamber of the king's Château de Saint-Cloud, overlooking the Seine about three miles west of Paris. Introduced as "the Inspector General of all the Armies of the United States," the little officer, attired in a bright blue uniform glittering with epaulets and colorful sash, and carrying a hat adorned with feathers, strutted into the room with an air of pomp and dignity. The king and queen then appeared, and Rives introduced Wool to the French monarchs who received him with "great frankness and freedom," the inspector confided to his diary. Fifty-seven-year-old Louis Philippe, tall and affable, was cosmopolitan: he had traveled widely in Europe, had lived in England for eight years, and had even lived in the United States for three years, during which time he visited George Washington. Fluent in English, he questioned Wool at length about America. The inspector ranged widely in his responses, then shifted the conversation to his mission. He expressed his interest in touring the military arsenals in France, and without hesitation, Louis Philippe promised to make the arrangements.[18]

Wool visited frequently at the French court, although he always felt uncomfortable because he knew so little French. For example, on July 24, he entered the crowded reception room at Saint-Cloud in an "undress uniform," as the king requested, and sat quietly. No interpreter was on hand. When the queen appeared, he arose and smiled, but knew she spoke no English. The king then arrived by carriage, dinner was announced, and a lady of the court escorted the inspector to a seat at the table. The king placed Wool at his left and drank a toast to his health. The dinner service was plain—Wool recorded—and the food was terrible. On July 29, mounted on a beautiful horse and dressed in his exquisite uniform, he rode with a group of French generals in a massive parade through Paris to celebrate the king's rise to power. Later, he sat in the royal stands amid cheering crowds and watched the National Guards and troops of the line—a colorful and unending stream of 70,000 men and 100 pieces of artillery—pass in review as a dozen bands blared martial music. That evening he dined with the king and a host of civil and military dignitaries.[19]

Early on July 30, 1832, Wool boarded a coach back to Le Havre. At the advice of Judith Page Rives, wife of the minister, Wool spent several days shopping for relatives and friends. For Cass he purchased an elegant silver dinner service, for Macomb a set of dinner plates, and for his wife expensive dresses, handkerchiefs, and gloves. Distrusting the French mails, Wool personally accompanied several large packages to the seaport and watched as they were placed aboard the *Charlemagne.* Returning to Paris on August 3, he learned the French government had given formal permission for his tour of its military installations.[20]

A rumored outbreak of cholera in the city delayed his tour. Fussy about his health, he carefully avoided exertions that might prostrate him and bring on the plague. "I can . . . truly say," Wool wrote Bomford, "I have not been well a single day since I arrived in Paris, and part of the time as much so as to keep my room. The cholera is by no means a pleasant companion." Yet, while waiting for the sickness to subside, the inspector was certainly no recluse. He visited the celebrated galleries and gardens on the right bank of the Seine at the Tuileries Palace, the imperial residence of most French monarchs until it was burned by the Paris Commune in 1871, went on carriage rides with Judith and William Rives, and studied French with a tutor. He also dined with a General Barnard on several occasions, seeking a friendly channel to the military. He hired a civilian, J. Cartier Letamendi, to serve as interpreter and clerk. On August 13, 1832, Wool learned that the celebrated American hero, the Marquis de Lafayette, was in Paris and he rushed off to see him. A man of "inexhaustible vanity," the seventy-five-year-old Lafayette was friendly, but had little time to visit. He was working with a political committee supporting liberal causes.[21]

On August 18, Wool visited the "depots of ordnance and artillery" in and around Paris. At the Depot of War, Lt. Gen. Jean J. G. Pelet gave him a tour of the grounds and promised to share a six-volume work on the depots. The next day, Wool visited the ordnance shops and artillery garrisons in the vicinity. He had planned to go to the military post at Vincennes, four miles outside of Paris, but cancelled the visit on hearing that the commander had suddenly died of cholera. At the *chasse d'artilleries,* he examined and made notes on the muskets, cannons, carriages, and other equipment on display.[22]

On August 29, Wool made a formal report to General Bomford of his tour. He had been impressed by the new French howitzer, a long, cumbersome weapon that could fire a twenty-four-pound ball, grape, or spherical case shot with the accuracy of a twelve-pounder field cannon. The French considered the weapon the backbone of their artillery. But Wool believed French field carriages were no better than those built at the Washington Arsenal. American muskets and swords also equaled the French. Wool had handed Rives a list of five weapons that he wished to purchase. The howitzer was the key purchase. French generals had recommended that he acquire models of the artillery pieces, but Wool emphasized that he wanted actual weapons.[23]

On September 2, the inspector general and Letamendi left in a mail coach for the military school at Strasbourg on the Rhine River, three hundred miles east of Paris, where the French army was holding field maneuvers. Here Wool witnessed a morning firing practice, then toured the arsenal, foundry, laboratory, and classroom facilities. The commandant gave him a set of manuals, drawings, and other printed information pertinent to the artillery. Wool then crossed the Rhine with a group of French officers to observe a mock assault and siege operation. While an infantry division of six thousand men maneuvered in the field, six artillery battalions gave a demonstration of mortars, howitzers, and field guns. Then came the finale. An engineer corps, working with great speed, threw three bridges across the river in forty minutes, each bridge strong enough to support the heaviest cannon and carriages. Soldiers laid one bridge on barrels and timbers and a second on a line of boats. A third, called a "flying bridge," was a raft 250-feet-long which carried 300 men across the river in less than three minutes. Wool himself rode across on it. The maneuvers at Strasbourg were an exciting and impressive highlight of Wool's European trip.[24]

With no word on the ordnance purchases, Wool obtained an official letter from the French war office to visit Belgium. On September 16, he and Hugh S. Legaré, a dwarfish man who was the American chargé d'affaires in Belgium, headed north for Brussels in a rented stage. The trip was a nightmare. A tire fell off one wheel and was improperly repaired. At the fortified town of Cambrai, where so much blood was shed in 1917, Wool found the city gates closed for the night and was at first refused entrance. He presented his official letter and paid an "insolent and unmannerly rascal" five francs to enter. Two days later, at Douai, he toured a French arsenal and foundry and watched the casting of brass howitzers. Legaré acted as interpreter for Wool's "bawling voice."[25]

The weary travelers crossed into Belgium on September 22. The country was in a precarious situation. It had revolted in 1830 against the hegemony of Holland, and with French and English help was trying to drive the Dutch from its soil. The Belgian army, under King Leopold I, had reclaimed five towns and was preparing to lay siege to the fortified Dutch garrison at Antwerp. In Brussels, Wool and Legaré found lodgings in the Hotel Belvue, contacted the minister of state, and requested an audience with the king. Leopold dispensed with formalities and invited the Americans to dine with him that evening at the palace. Early the next day, Wool expressed a desire to see the Belgian troops, and he accompanied the royal entourage to the encampment at Denderleeuw, twenty miles outside of the city. Here eight thousand soldiers, commanded largely by French officers, passed in review. These troops, Wool wrote Jesup, "performed a few evolutions of the line, but so slow, and so indifferently that if they had been troops of the United States, I should have censured them."[26]

The tempo of the tour increased. On September 29, Wool had difficulty in joining Leopold's party bound for Antwerp. Confusion over teams occurred, and the animals he was finally able to obtain balked on the road. After other delays, he finally caught up with the king at lunch and suffered through an extended display of local formalities. In mid-afternoon, the entourage rolled into Antwerp on the River Scheldt, passing along streets lined with soldiers. The next day, Wool toured the battle line by carriage, visited the American consulate, and stood with the king in a soaking rain at a military review. On October 1, Wool started back to Paris, stopping to sightsee along the way.[27]

Wool had spent a rewarding week in Belgium as a distinguished guest. Leopold had discussed with him in a frank manner the problems he faced in establishing a stable government. Wool's inspection of Antwerp provided insight into Old World defense systems and convinced him that walled citadels could no longer be defended against powerful artillery. On a personal note, he confided to his diary his disgust over outrageous prices and the poor quality of meals and lodgings—and particularly the habit of tipping to secure services. Wool also regretted that he did not have one or two young officers traveling with him. "What an opportunity for instruction!" Wool wrote Macomb. Both France and Belgium were beautiful, he told Jesup, but "they are bound to the earth with hard and unceasing labor." In comparison, the United States was a divine land. "I become every day, nay every hour, every moment, more and more attached to my happy, happy country," he wrote. [28]

Returning to the Hotel des Premier, "the most extravagant House in Paris," Wool found things had changed. Rives had resigned his post and left France to reenter politics in the United States. There was more bad news. The French minister of war notified him that government regulations prohibited the sale of artillery pieces from the military depots to a foreign power. General Pelet also wrote that the war ministry would not permit drawings of the new howitzer. Wool was stunned. "From what the King, as well as the Minister of War, said to me," he informed Macomb, "I did not suppose that any objections existed against taking models or drawings of every description of arms in France. It appears I was mistaken." In a confidential letter to Cass, Wool blamed French officers, particularly "a certain general officer" for the rejection of his requests—but mentioned no names. This officer thought the new howitzer "would not answer for our country—that it was entirely too heavy." To make his trip fruitful, Wool now turned more attention to gathering military journals, regulations, service handbooks, and engravings pertaining to the French army. To acquire journals carrying specific ordnance information, he often had to purchase entire sets. Then, with a French dictionary at hand, Wool sat in his hotel room night after night, marking appropriate pages for the ordnance board, before boxing the collection for shipment to the United States.[29]

Wool believed he had collected useful information. Many French ordnance regulations were broad, covering such topics as arms manufacture, foundries, forging, arsenal operations, and military schools. The *Aide Memoire d'Artillerie* was especially valuable, and once translated, should be distributed to every American artillery and ordnance officer. In a letter to Jesup, Wool praised the printed materials. If "properly examined and studied," the ordnance department should find "all the information requisite to making the artillery of the United States equal to that of any other power." In a personal note, Wool spoke with some bitterness about his trip. His travels in France had been "very awkward" because of his linguistic limitations and his expenses that had soared beyond reason. French staff officers complicated his gathering of military information by refusing to advise him on the books and manuals he sent to America. Perhaps the British would be more helpful.[30]

On October 20, Wool traveled by mail coach to the French seaport of Calais on the English Channel. Here he secured a passport, grudgingly paid a gratuity, and sailed on the *Lord Melville* for England. Two men squabbling over a berth kept him awake all night. Arriving at Dover and then making his way to London in a stage in a thick fog, the inspector located the office of Thomas Aspinwall, the American consul, a fellow New Yorker and friend. Aspinwall helped him find a room complete with firewood and candles on Hanover Square in a fashionable residential part of the city. Together they went to the Baring Brothers bank to open an account for Wool's use. The colonel called on Aaron Vail, chargé d'affaires in London, and asked him to seek permission for a tour of British military establishments. He had requested Aspinwall to inquire into the plausibility of procuring the new brass six-pounder cannon, with caisson and ten rounds of ammunition, for the United States army. Vail promised to take care of the matter.[31]

In London on October 24, Wool met with Sir James Kempt, the master general of ordnance. Sir James received him cordially, inquired about his mission, and granted permission to inspect whatever Wool desired. He recommended that Wool start his excursion at Woolwich, a naval base on the south bank of the Thames, in the southeast part of the city. The purchase of British ordnance was another matter. Within a week, Kempt reported that government policy precluded the release or sale of weapons from its arsenals, but he had no objection to Wool's arranging a contract with the British to manufacture a set of guns for the United States. Wool was disappointed. This was the second time he was refused artillery pieces. Was something wrong in his approach to the French and English? he wondered. Perhaps diplomatic channels would be more appropriate in purchasing the ordnance. Sir James rallied Wool's spirits by giving a dinner in his honor, with several members of the House of Lords in attendance.[32]

On October 31, Wool was finally able to visit Woolwich, the only government facility in England for manufacturing cannon. After a briefing on the nature and purpose of the depot, he was guided through the plant and shown how weapons were cast and shells were packed. From this plant, the American officer went to the nearby school of artillery practice, where the army tested new guns and equipment and trained officers in their use. He was impressed with the British artillery, writing Macomb that it excelled everything he had seen in France and Belgium. The Europeans did not necessarily have better weapons than the Americans, but their constant practice made them superior. This was due to the constant danger of war. In Europe, the enemy was always on the "move, and they must be prepared to defend themselves or they will be conquered." Wool later compared the French and British systems and said that the French siege cannon were superior, but the British had the best light field artillery in the world.[33]

Unable to purchase weapons, Wool inquired about ordnance manuals. Again, he encountered difficulties. The British army, he learned, had no printed rules for the "interior management" of its ordnance department, foundries, and arsenals, or its artillery corps. When a new design or alteration was approved, the weapon was fabricated and tested at Woolwich. British officers were trained in using the weapon, and, upon assignment to regular duty, they carried a small manual, either the *British Gunner* or the *Pocket Gunner*, for field reference. Wool obtained copies of both manuals, plus a book for battery exercises. The board of ordnance, he believed, after studying the French and British publications closely, should be able to develop an artillery branch equal to anything in Europe. In fact, Wool felt that he himself could establish an artillery school superior to Woolwich, and "nearly equal" to the one at Strasbourg, but it would cost more than the government would be willing to pay.[34]

Practically every packet ship leaving London for America in November and December 1832 carried articles that Wool had purchased for the American army. One shipment contained five sets of British uniforms as patterns for the quartermaster department. Another included nine dress swords and other items ordered by ordnance chief Bomford, who wished to adopt a new American design. Wool obtained eight swords in London at Salters Widdowson & Tate, with specific purposes in mind: two for cavalry use, one for medical or paymaster corps, four to illustrate different hilts, and one for the ordnance department. The ninth sword, from a different manufacturer, was of the same quality and design, but cost less. Sword prices ranged from ten to fifteen dollars each. Wool also shipped boxes packed with assorted infantry, cavalry, and artillery equipment. He was greatly chagrined over his failure to satisfy his instructions and he badly wanted to make his trip worthwhile.[35]

While observing artillery exercises at Woolwich, Wool contracted a violent cold that confined him to his hotel room in London for a week. The climate was damp and the sun seldom shone. On November 12, he told Macomb that the fog was so thick that "we are obliged to light our candles in the middle of the day." He fretted about his expenses, calculating that, in less than four months, he had spent the $2,500 set aside for his use. He regretted his failure to obtain "the principal objects" of his European mission but stressed that the information he had sent should provide the ordnance board all it needed for modernizing the artillery. Expensive experiments would be required, but the United States must assume the responsibility to place itself on a footing with other nations.[36]

During his stay in London, Wool combined business with pleasure. He engaged a "taylor" to alter his French-made uniform to fit the new United States army regulations, and, at Macomb's request, had an elaborate uniform made for the general. On November 19, the new suit and trappings were ready. The bill for clothing, epaulets, sashes, gloves, vest, plumes, and spurs ran to over $400. Wool was an avid tourist. He visited the Tower of London, the zoological gardens where he saw a "jiraff," Westminster Abbey, and other historical sites. Having no further need to stay in London, he sailed for France on November 20.[37]

With the French Armée du Nord under Marshal Étierre Maurice Gérard ready to begin a siege of the Dutch garrison in the Antwerp citadel, Wool hurried north to observe the battle. Charles Barnett, son of the new American consul in Paris, Isaac C. Barnett, traveled with him. On December 3, they reached Brussels, where Wool learned that ten days of heavy rains had delayed the French operations. He obtained permission from King Leopold to visit the front, and, on December 5, he entered the French line. The artillery commander bristled and refused to permit him to go to a forward observer's post, but Wool refused to leave. He and Barnett climbed onto a housetop within three hundred yards of the walled bastion to watch the bombardment. "It was an awfully sublime sight," Wool recorded. Over one hundred cannon and mortars roared through the afternoon, pouring "a constant shower of shot and shell" into the stone fortress. At dusk he and Barnett left, but at eight the next morning they climbed back to their perch. The Dutch were refusing to surrender. The French had destroyed several buildings in the fortress, but they had disabled only a few guns and suffered heavy casualties during the assault. The Dutch were making "a brilliant defense," Wool wrote Macomb. If the French failed to reduce the citadel within a week, the coming of winter would decide the issue. On December 7, Wool and Barnett headed back to Paris.[38]

The last few weeks Wool spent on the continent were eventful. On November 22, he attended a gala dinner at the fashionable Paris home of a fellow New Yorker, James Fenimore Cooper, the celebrated American writer of historical romances of frontier and Native American life. Guests included Lafayette, his son George, and a group associated with Cooper and Lafayette in Polish relief work. After dinner, other distinguished people arrived, including the aging Sir John Vanderleur, the British cavalry commander at Waterloo. During the evening, Cooper presented a medal to Lafayette sent by officers of the Twenty-seventh New York Artillery Regiment. The medal commemorated the Frenchman's association with Gen. George Washington and helped to celebrate the centenary year of the illustrious Virginian's birth. Lafayette acknowledged the handsome gift in a short speech. Five days later, Wool accompanied Lafayette to a celebration in Paris commemorating Polish independence. Within days, his thoughts turned toward home.[39]

With winter rapidly approaching, Wool was anxious to return to New York. On December 10, he began farewell calls in Paris. Lafayette embraced the inspector, kissed him on both cheeks, and asked that he be remembered to all his friends in America. Wool thanked the French king and queen for their many courtesies; the queen sent a warm greeting to the Rives family. Wool also paid his respects to Cooper and others he had befriended in the city and on December 18, he bid a cold and damp Paris adieu. At Le Havre, while waiting for the weather to clear, Wool learned that the French had finally battered the Dutch garrison at Antwerp into submission on December 23. The defense "was not equal to my expectation," Wool recorded. Two days after Christmas, he sailed on the packet *Erie* for America.[40]

On February 13, 1833, after six weeks of blustery winds, the *Erie* streamed into New York Harbor. A few days later, Wool was in Washington. Both Cass and Macomb received him warmly and President Jackson invited him to dinner. Wool described at length his overseas trip. Although he had been well received and given free access to military establishments, international tensions and a reluctance to sell weaponry had crippled his mission. Yet his trip had a positive side. It announced an increased desire by the United States to shake its colonial image, and militarily join the ranks of the ruling powers of Europe. Wool's discreet dealing with the various government officials also promoted goodwill and enhanced the status of the United States abroad. Above all, his trip reaffirmed that ordnance development in America was in step with other nations of the world. At the conclusion of the conferences, Wool left for Nassau and reached home, where he was greeted by Sarah on February 28. Soon afterwards, the colonel resumed his inspection duties.[41]

Wool remained on the ordnance board for several years. In early November 1833, at Macomb's call, he joined the members to discuss plans for new weaponry. Ordnance officers presented drawings of artillery pieces, and the government issued contracts for demonstration models. Two years later, on September 7, 1835, Wool accompanied the board to Watervliet Arsenal, across the Hudson River from Troy, to witness tests. Three weeks later, the officers submitted a report that endorsed the adoption of the stock-trail carriage, provided a list of cannon for manufacture, and strongly recommended that all guns be made of brass. On July 8, 1836, the War Department approved the recommendations, which influenced guidelines for artillery development until the Civil War.[42]

For twelve years, Wool had directed his energies toward upgrading army weaponry. He had joined others in urging a careful inventory of the ordnance in coastal garrisons and interior arsenals, and that the antiquated and unserviceable pieces be sold or discarded. He had also stressed the need for a board to study ordnance modernization. He was pleased when Secretary of War Cass created such a group in December 1831 and appointed him a member. During the four years that followed, the ordnance department became an independent entity, and its staff took positive steps to improve the production of weapons. Wool could view with pride his efforts to make the army's "stepchild" a viable military branch.

Wool's last ordnance assignment was dealing with labor problems at the federal armory at Springfield, Massachusetts. Earlier, he had twice investigated the armory at the picture book town of Harpers Ferry, Virginia, at the confluence of the Shenandoah and Potomac Rivers, seventy miles above Washington. Like Springfield, the armory at Harpers Ferry was under the army but operated by civilians and mismanaged for years. Sensitive to the politics of civilian management, Wool in 1827 and 1829 submitted reports that were vague and sidestepped specific reforms, but clearly showed that James Stubblefield, the superintendent, had neglected his duties. Stubblefield resigned, ending a twenty-two-year reign at Harpers Ferry. Springfield was praised for its management and quality of operation, but, in June 1833, Secretary of War Cass ordered Wool to inspect the armory and resolve pay demands there.[43]

As industrial wages rose in the East during the early 1830s, Springfield's skilled civilian armorers had requested a pay raise, claiming that their real income was below that in private armories. Unlike other employees, the armorers depended solely on government salaries. They did not engage in such side work as farming, as less skilled workers did. The armorers also faced the threat of increased mechanization. In the past, Superintendent Roswell Lee had resolved wage problems, but in 1832, he became ill and production at Springfield deteriorated. Cass had convened a board to study pay scales, but its recommendations caused an outcry. The armorers protested that the mean of the scale was too low, while the unskilled laborers denounced the idea of reducing the work force. Cass sent Wool to investigate and mediate.[44]

On June 14, 1833, Wool arrived by stage at Springfield, on the Connecticut River, and took lodgings at a tavern. He carried wide-ranging powers. The inspector could suspend the wage schedule, correct all "errors & abuses" that interfered with the "interests of the public or the Armory," and discharge employees "guilty of misconduct, except those appointed by the President." Wool wasted no time. The next day he crossed the river to the armory, a collection of buildings and shops sitting on an elevated section of land, and presented his instructions to Superintendent Lee. As soon as possible, he wanted to examine the books and accounts of the superintendent, master armorer, paymaster, and military storekeeper. He also wanted an inventory of the public property and a list of items deemed unserviceable. Wool asked to see the reports for the last two years of condemned gun barrels and bayonets, items sold at auction, and review the rent paid on the buildings housing workers. While the management collected records, Wool suspended the wage scale proposed for the armory.[45]

The inspector spent a week examining ledgers and interviewing personnel, and came to realize that he was involved in a "delicate" assignment. "Of all the difficult duties which I have ever had to perform," he wrote Macomb on June 24, "the one I am now engaged in is the most difficult and the most troublesome." The entire labor force at Springfield, 220 skilled and unskilled employees, had appealed to him as an arbiter. Many said that they worked hard to support their families and educate their children, but because of low wages, they had been unable to set anything aside for old age. The government's proposed wage adjustment was unjust, Wool believed. The board should not have considered the lower pay scales at private armories and applied them to a federal armory. Government agencies could not be operated with the same economy as private enterprises. Wool attributed much of the trouble at Springfield to lax supervision. Colonel Bomford, the ordnance chief, was "kind and amiable," Wool told Macomb, but he yielded to his juniors, "who take but a superficial view of things, and who by their advice keep him in a state of doubt and uncertainty." The colonel was "always willing and always doing," but never pursued a "prompt and straightforward course.[46]

The investigation became complicated. Employees complained that certain fellow workers received better wages—but they refused to give names. The officers particularly seemed "to be more or less afraid of the men." Wool wrote John Robb, acting secretary of war, that the operations were carried on "loosely and without any system." Men worked by the piece at all hours from 4 A.M. to 7 P.M., and came and went as they pleased. Some spent three hours a day at the shops; others labored twelve or fourteen. This produced a great difference in pace and pay. Armory inspectors kept no record of hours worked, which made it difficult to determine a just pay for a reasonable day's labor. When the more industrious skilled workers received higher wages for fewer hours, their associates cried favoritism. Furthermore, the armory lacked leadership. Superintendent Lee was so prostrated that Wool often had to write letters for him and serve as acting superintendent.[47]

On June 28, Wool placed Joseph Weatherford, master armorer, temporarily in charge of the installation, and handed him a new wage scale. He told Weatherford to assemble the officers and have them examine and discuss the proposition while he made a short trip to visit his family at Nassau. The pay scale was similar to the one recently in use, but Wool had tried to equalize pay for those working by the piece. The men who worked the hardest, all things being equal, should have the highest pay, although he thought character, skill, and workmanship equally important. The schedule set the regular workday at ten hours and eliminated extra allowances to armorers for making and repairing tools. Wool returned to Springfield on July 5. He reviewed the suggestions received, talked with the workers, and sought a consensus on the matter. A week later, the inspector posted a new schedule retroactive to July 1. Each employee had twenty-four hours to accept it or resign. The rates varied little from the old scale. Few left. [48]

Wool turned next to armory housekeeping. He examined statements of expenses and debts, materials on hand, musket production by month and year, weapons condemned, and projections for the next six months. He compared shop reports showing how many men lacked regular work. Wool required all inspectors leaving the armory during the day to sign out and each shop to record daily absentees. Branch foremen were to synchronize their programs and bring production forward to keep all men actively employed.[49]

The armory also needed a head. Lt. Col. George Talcott, of the ordnance department, abhorred his assignment as government overseer at the armory. He declared he wanted nothing to do with the place, and left before Wool arrived. Certain ordnance officers expressed strong feelings about Wool's interference at Springfield. On July 27, Talcott's replacement, Maj. Henry K. Craig, arrived, and a rumor started that the ordnance department planned its own investigation of the armory. Wool realized it was time to leave. Even though a new superintendent had not been named, the inspector had raised the pay scale slightly, defused much of the discontent at the armory, and suggested new operating procedures. He left the last week of July for home.[50]

Discontent in the army during these years was widespread. In September 1834, Wool reported a rising wave of hostility in the officer corps against General Macomb who had entered office in 1828 amid controversy. The ambitious Winfield Scott, piqued at being bypassed, refused for several months to recognize the former chief engineer as the new general-in-chief. Once this matter was settled, Macomb had proceeded cautiously, but positively, to build vigor and prestige into his position. His predecessor, Jacob Brown, partially paralyzed through his seven-year tenure, had acted primarily as a military advisor to the secretary of war and president, doing little to define his responsibilities or extend his influence over the army. The secretary of war dominated the command structure, with the commanding general, bureau chiefs, and departmental commanders answering to him. In contrast to Brown, Alexander Macomb developed definite views regarding his duties, and early sought to subordinate the various army branches and bureaus to his personal control.[51]

In 1831 Macomb had instructed the two inspector generals, who were officially attached to his office, to extend their routine to the corps of engineers, commanded by Gen. Charles Gratiot. The engineers were the most prestigious branch of the army, reporting directly to the secretary of war and standing separate from the regular army command. Hostility to Macomb's trespass was immediate. When Wool arrived at West Point on May 25, Superintendent Sylvanus Thayer coldly informed him that the academy was under the engineer corps and outside the inspector's jurisdiction. Smarting from his reception, Wool sent the superintendent a stiff letter, dispatched a copy to Macomb, and made an inspection anyway. Thayer complained to Gratiot who promptly wrote to Macomb. In a tersely worded reply, the general-in-chief attacked the idea of independent staff departments, and gave the chief engineer "a full view" of the duties of the inspector general. The battle was joined.[52]

Belligerence within the engineer corps increased. Secretary Cass fanned feelings by allowing Macomb considerable latitude in his drive to centralize army administration. The engineers enjoyed privileged contacts through their work on internal improvements, and remonstrated both inside and outside army channels against Macomb's dictatorial actions. At garrison level, the engineers lived and messed with line officers, but were not subject to the commandant, which also caused friction. Adding tension to the matter was the perennial threat from Congress to reduce expenses in the military establishment. A crisis soon developed.[53]

In mid-July 1834, Wool left Washington on a tour of the coastal fortifications. He carried orders from both Macomb and Cass. Macomb asked him to focus his attention on engineer construction, while Cass instructed the inspector to examine "the whole system of operations of fortifications," with a view of cutting expenses. Wool reached Fortress Monroe, Virginia, on July 24. At the wharf, he met Second Lt. Robert E. Lee, an engineer officer in charge of work on the Rip Raps, a rocky shoal at the entrance to Hampton Roads. Here, the engineer corps was filling in the shoal, located about a mile south of Fortress Monroe, with stone to form a base for mounting artillery. This was the second inspection that week. Macomb and Cass already had visited—and the dapper young Virginian was vexed. Lee's superior, Capt. Andrew Talcott, who supervised construction in Hampton Roads, was away, so Lee escorted Wool on his rounds. The visit was brief. The morning following his arrival, Wool informed Lee before breakfast of his instructions, but, after questioning him about Macomb's inspection, he decided to cut his visit short. He expressed an interest, however, in seeing the Rip Raps, so in the blistering July sun Lee rowed him out to the rocky shoal. The heated granite soon satisfied Wool's "punctilio," Lee snidely recorded, and they returned to the fort. The next morning the inspector embarked to continue his patrol.[54]

In describing the episode to Talcott, Lee said the inspector was tireless, rising early in the morning and retiring late at night. During their conversation, he had made "several wise queries" regarding the engineers having quarters at the fort, which suggested that changes were in the wind. The inspector was never in the office or saw "a paper or book during his stay," Lee said. The lieutenant's premonition proved correct. On July 31, Macomb peremptorily moved the engineers at Monroe to the Rip Raps, and placed a line officer in charge of local construction. He also suspended the rest of Wool's inspection tour. In the howl of protest that followed, Lee, on October 1, wrote Talcott that he was ready to help "cook up Macomb" that winter, allowing him only "one stir in the pot."[55]

"The times certainly are not propitious to discipline," Wool wrote privately to Macomb. The army was becoming "quite republican if not democratic." Bold action was necessary. "We must turn over a new leaf or we shall be turned out of doors." Officers were speaking to their superiors with a freedom that would not be tolerated in other countries. A clique was forming to legislate Macomb out of office, and he warned that "they will try what they can do with Congress on that subject next winter." Wool expressed his views more fully to Cass. His inspection of the engineers had been difficult because of a lack of communication between the War Department and Chief Engineer Gratiot. Also, there were too many conflicting orders emanating from Washington. He knew Cass was besieged with paperwork, with six or seven departments and bureaus reporting to him, but as secretary of war, Wool frankly advised, "you are the responsible person and not the multitude." Cass must exercise greater care in issuing orders.[56]

The "rebellion" against Macomb did not materialize. In his annual report in 1834, Wool carefully avoided criticizing the engineer corps. Wherever he visited coastal fortifications, the engineer officers had been respectful and cooperative, explaining their assignments in a thorough manner. But the duty had not been pleasant. In a diplomatic move, Cass assigned Lee to Gratiot's office in Washington. On November 21, the secretary held a cabinet dinner and invited Wool, Croghan, Jesup, and several engineer officers to attend. But this was not enough. On December 9, 1834, the House of Representatives passed a resolution requesting information on the expediency of abolishing the office of commanding general. Cass immediately rose to the occasion. In a strong statement of support, he argued effectively for the value and need for the office, and the matter was dropped.[57]

During the 1830s the War Department occasionally asked for Wool's views regarding the western frontier. He had toured remote garrisons for nearly twenty years and was well aware of problems and needs there. Cass especially solicited his advice.

For example, during a congressional debate in 1831 over the need for mounted troops along the Santa Fe Trail to combat fast-moving Plains Indians, Wool urged the creation of a regular cavalry corps. He considered Missouri senator Thomas H. Benton's bill to organize a mounted infantry only a halfway measure. Mounted infantry possessed "none of the stimulants" or character of a regular unit, and would be neither infantry nor cavalry. They would quickly become "little less than a marauding party." Regular cavalry could not only protect trading caravans, but also become "an indispensable auxiliary to an army in the field." In 1833, after experimenting briefly with a mounted ranger battalion, Congress authorized the organization of a dragoon regiment.[58]

Cass also asked Wool for comments on western forts. The government was removing Indians beyond the Mississippi, and the problem of preserving order was critical. Wool spent considerable time reviewing reports from western commanders, examining maps, and studying the logistical and tactical aspects. In April 1833, he filed a report. To preserve peace among the Indians, he recommended that three new posts be located as far west as possible. A fort should be built west of Fort Towson, on the Red River near the False Washita River, one on the Canadian River near the Cross Timbers, and one on the Arkansas, three hundred miles above Cantonment Gibson. At each post, the army should station four infantry companies, with two dragoon companies at the site on the upper Arkansas. These posts would preserve peace among the neighboring tribes and "restrain those occupying the country farther west." But Indian troubles in Florida, economic depression in the nation, and scattered border disturbances, caused the army to drop its extended plan and construct western forts one by one as funds were available.[59]

In 1836, having served as inspector general for twenty years, John E. Wool had seen as much of the young nation as anyone. An energetic, precise person with a hardy constitution and total devotion to duty, he was particularly fitted for the office. His extensive travels and regular visits to dozens of garrisons gave him an intimate and unique knowledge of the military establishment, and made him probably the best-informed officer of his day on its nature and character. Wool spoke frankly in his reports about personnel and materiel and provided information and advice that vitally influenced policy. He focused his attention on ordnance matters and played a singular role in its modernization. By the mid-1830s, however, Wool's duties began to change. The army assumed new tasks on the frontier—tasks relating to the unsavory duty of Indian removals—and sent general officers from their desks in Washington to field commands. Wool was among those tapped to help expedite the removal of American Indians to lands west of the Mississippi.

4

NO RESTING PLACE WHERE WHITE MEN TREAD

In late June 1836, Wool received orders from Secretary of War Lewis Cass to suspend his inspector's duties and begin a special assignment. Several weeks before, the Senate had ratified the Treaty of New Echota, and was preparing to remove the Cherokee Indians from their ancestral homelands in Alabama, Georgia, North Carolina, and Tennessee to new homelands west of the Mississippi River. Wool was instructed to act as a federal policeman to keep order, while Indian commissioners processed claims, debts, and property disputes. The colonel's responsibilities were clear: he was to maintain order and to encourage the Cherokees to prepare to move west within the next two years, but not interfere with federal and state government operations. It was Wool's first field command of volunteer units during peacetime. He would enjoy the rank and pay of a brevet brigadier general. The federal program soon bogged down, however, and Wool found himself battling federal and state bureaucracies and tribal factionalism. It was an instructive chapter in the inspector's career.[1]

Census takers in 1835 reported that 16,542 Cherokees claimed ten million acres in the southern Appalachian Mountains as their homeland. This country, blessed with scenic valleys, cool forests, rich soil, and bountiful streams, stretched from western North Carolina across southeastern Tennessee and northern Georgia into northeastern Alabama. Here the Cherokees had lived for generations. They had opened farms, created a government patterned after that of the United States, perfected an alphabet, and started a newspaper. Under the leadership of educated mixed bloods, they prospered and lived in peace. In the early 1830s, however, the state of Georgia had disturbed the Cherokee world. Spurred by frontiersmen and speculators seeking land and gold (which had been discovered near Dahlonega in 1829), and feeling empowered by the Federal Removal Act of 1830, the state legislature extended its legal and political jurisdiction over the Cherokee country in the state. It had the area surveyed and held a land lottery. Georgia authorities also seized the tribal printing press, prohibited Cherokee meetings, voided all council enactments, and denied them access to equity courts.[2]

The Cherokee leadership split into two factions. Wealthy John Ross, son of a Scottish emigrant and a part-Cherokee mother, headed the propertied faction. Ross had led the drive in 1827 for a separate Cherokee constitution and emerged the principal chief. Most of the delegations the tribal council sent to Washington reflected his influence. In 1832 at a tribal meeting at Red Clay, near Chattanooga, Tennessee, an insurgent group, led by Major Ridge, his son John Ridge, and Elias Boudinot, challenged Ross's policies. They resented Ross's stalling with the federal government over removal plans, and took a strong stand for negotiation. On December 29, 1835, in Washington, the Ridge faction signed a removal treaty on behalf of the Cherokee Nation. The Senate approved the document. The tribal council meeting on May 23, 1835, at the Cherokee "capital" at New Echota (near present Rome, Georgia), voted for it. By this agreement, Congress would provide $5,000,000 to settle Indian land and spoliation claims, establish pension and school funds, and defray the expenses of removal to the west. Within a few years, the Ridges and Boudinot were assassinated by Cherokees from Ross's faction. The federal government divided the Cherokee country into seven districts, appointed assessors of Indian farms, plantations, and ferries, and selected two commissioners, William Lumpkin and William Carroll, ex-governors of Georgia and Tennessee, respectively, to review and settle claims and start the removal process. The secretary of war also sent John Wool, an experienced army officer, to keep order and protect the Indians in their rights and possessions during their removal.[3]

On June 20, the day he received his orders, Wool left Washington with Lt. Abner R. Hetzel, Second Infantry, for the Cherokee Nation. They traveled night and day by stage, and nine days later reached Knoxville, the capital of Tennessee. Here they met Lt. Chileab S. Howe, Fourth Infantry, who arranged contracts for 1,250 Tennessee volunteers due to assemble near Athens, about sixty-five miles south of Knoxville. No word had come from the federal arsenal near Pittsburgh regarding the delivery of 1,500 muskets and 89,000 ball cartridges, plus brushes, picks, and bayonets. Hetzel would have to purchase powder and lead for 40,000 cartridges. Because too many volunteers, it was reported, were coming to the rendezvous, additional supplies would be needed. Obtaining forage was difficult, because farmers had sold most of their crops by mid-summer. To estimate the possible needs of indigent Cherokees, Wool hired several "suitable persons" to visit the Cherokee settlements and make a rough count of the Indian population. On July 2, Wool, Hetzel, and Howe departed Knoxville for Athens, Tennessee.[4]

Far more men than Wool expected arrived and were camped in tents at Fort Cass, near Athens, when Wool arrived. On June 6, Tennessee governor Newton Cannon had issued a call for volunteers, with 1,200 men designated for duty in the Cherokee country in the eastern part of the state and surrounding areas. Far more men appeared. On July 9, 2,500 volunteers assembled for inspection and muster into federal service for three months' duty. Wool hesitated to accept the extra men, but Cannon pressed him to reconsider. He said that on June 6, General Gaines, commanding the Western Division, had asked him to raise a mounted brigade for duty on the Louisiana border. The Texas Revolution was still raging, and rumors of Indian troubles in the West came in regularly. The excess men at Fort Cass were likely needed there. The governor assured Wool that if the federal government did not assume the expense for the groups, the State of Tennessee would do so. The volunteers were restless, he warned, and if turned away, they might plunder the countryside on their way home.[5]

On July 4, in General Order 1, Wool created the Army of East Tennessee and the Cherokee Nation. His staff would include Maj. Matthew M. Payne, Fourth Artillery, stationed at Fort Hiwassee, Tennessee, as assistant adjutant and inspector general; Lieutenant Howe, assistant commissary, and Lieutenant Hetzel, assistant quartermaster. The colonel also added Lt. Thomas G. Lyon, a Tennessee volunteer, as an aide-de-camp, and hired Dr. Charles M. Hitchcock to serve as medical officer for his little army. Wool had not commanded troops in twenty years and he knew he faced a challenge. His staff officers would need to purchase tents and cooking utensils and to rent buildings for depots.[6]

Wool acquiesced to Cannon's request. On July 10, "to prevent an excitement," he instructed Major Payne to muster all 2,500 Tennesseans for federal services. Richard G. Dunlap, an ex-Tennessee legislator and militia officer, would command the brigade. Wool asked Dunlap to divide the volunteers into two regiments of ten companies each. Col. Nathaniel Smith commanded one and Col. Joseph Byrd the other. The remaining men were sent home. The extra muster would haunt Wool for weeks to come.[7]

Wool described his situation in the Cherokee Nation in a letter to Winfield Scott, who had recently rounded up hostile Creeks in Alabama and Georgia for removal west. He told Scott that he planned to take mounted troops to the Cherokee settlements in the Great Smoky Mountains in North Carolina as early as possible. The Indians were deemed a full-blood group and hostile to removal. The mission would be expensive because he would have to build roads and haul supplies by wagon up into the mountains. Wool also expected problems with the volunteers, and he asked Scott for several companies of regulars to replace the state troops. He also needed two or three experienced staff officers. Payne was capable, Wool thought, but Hetzel and Howe were young and unequal to the task ahead. He would have to hire civilians as assistants. By the time Wool's letter reached its destination, General Jesup had replaced Scott in the Creek country and he shelved Wool's requests.[8]

By mid-July, Wool was ready to occupy the Cherokee Nation. Howe established three military camps and depots at Ross's Landing (near present-day Chattanooga), near the confluence of Valley River and the Hiwassee in North Carolina, and at New Echota, Georgia, the former capital of the Cherokee Nation. Mounted detachments at these stations would patrol roads, check on Indians, and, if necessary, conduct field operations. Each depot would store thirty days' rations for the troops, and ten thousand rations for issue to needy Cherokees. Civilians handled the rations. Wool sent Colonel Smith with a battalion of three mounted companies and two infantry to clear a road and build a camp in the Valley River district. Colonel Byrd led a mounted battalion of five companies to camp at Ross's Landing near a ferry on the Tennessee River. Capt. Thomas G. Vernon rode south with a mounted company into Georgia and headed for New Echota. Each commander could issue 350 rations a day to needy Cherokee families, recording names as they did so. Officers would hold their men on a tight rein, prohibit whiskey in camp, and avoid collisions with the Indians.[9]

On July 16, at Fort Cass, Tennessee volunteers loaded wagons with provisions and forage and drew arms and ammunition. Wool gave several officers special assignments. He ordered Captain Morrow, an "intelligent, discreet, and vigilant" officer, to make a twenty-day swing from Ross's Landing east up into the Valley River country. He would gauge "the temper and disposition" of the Cherokees regarding the recent treaty and assure them of the peaceful intent of the federal forces. Captain Vernon had a delicate assignment at New Echota. Georgia mounted volunteers had camps at three places in the Cherokee country, and Wool anticipated that Vernon would encounter them. He handed the captain a statement that cited his instructions from the War Department and explained his mission. Each Georgia commander would indicate the authority for his force, its strength, and report any Cherokees held prisoner. As early as July 13, Wool notified Georgia governor William Schley of his instructions and requested his cooperation.[10]

Wool soon experienced problems with the volunteers. The two infantry companies working on thirty miles of a road running east across the Tellico Plains from Athens toward the Great Smoky Mountains were causing trouble. The men grumbled about the back-breaking labor with picks and shovels, and, ignoring orders to avoid contact with the "natives," several soldiers assaulted a Cherokee woman peddling fruits and vegetables in camp. Hearing of the incident, the colonel immediately discharged the responsible parties. If this happened again, he would "post" the men's names in the *Athens Journal.* He hired a civilian to expedite the roadwork. On July 22, Colonel Smith rode out of Fort Cass with a Tennessee battalion for Valley River, escorting fourteen wagons loaded with rations and clothing.[11]

At Athens, Wool talked with A. R. S. Hunter, a planter near Valley Town (near present-day Murphy, North Carolina) about conditions there. Hunter doubted the Cherokee families there would move west or accept federal rations, but he agreed to serve as rations agent at a salary of three dollars a day and personal expenses. He also promised to arrange a council for Wool with the Cherokee headmen near his home. The colonel wanted their views on how best to execute the treaty, and to assure the Cherokees that his primary interest was "to render them such relief as their peculiar situation may require." Writing to Secretary Cass, Wool confidently stated that he could manage the Cherokee "business to the satisfaction of the government and with as little dissatisfaction to the Indians as anyone else." In a second letter on July 19, he added that if necessary, he might use force to induce the Indians to emigrate—a statement he would soon regret.[12]

Before leaving Fort Cass, Wool gave orders to his adjutant, Major Payne, to discharge on July 31 the nine volunteer companies remaining in camp there. After these companies left, Payne would inspect the mounted detachments at Ross's Landing and New Echota, checking arms, equipment, and animals. He would list the rations and forage issued and inventory the amount remaining in the depot. Wool also wanted information on the Georgia troops in the Cherokee Nation, their location, strength, activities.[13]

On July 25, Wool left Fort Cass in a rickety wagon for Valley River. His party included Lieutenant Lyon, his aide, a driver, and an orderly. A young traveler, Kate Hunter, en route to visit her family, accompanied the party. Other wagons carried tents, camp equipage, and provisions. Ten mounted Tennesseans provided an escort. Their objective was the Cherokee settlement near the mouth of Valley River. The location, Wool later said, was "in the midst of the most savage and warlike part of the Cherokee Nation." The site was a few miles up the Hiwassee and twenty miles from the Tennessee River. It began in 1820 as a Baptist mission, and grew slowly over the years. It boasted scattered residences, a gristmill, sawmill, and a small herd of livestock. Smith's battalion camped on Hunter property in tents a few miles from the settlement.[14]

On July 29, Wool met with a group of Cherokee headmen in the yard at Hunter's place. To enhance his image of authority, he wore a full dress uniform and had a sergeant and thirteen soldiers standing nearby. The general opened the meeting by explaining that the president had sent him into the Cherokee Nation to enforce the terms of the New Echota Treaty and to maintain peace. He urged the chiefs to accept the treaty and remain "quietly at their homes" until the time arrived for them to leave. The Creeks had defied federal authority, he reminded his listeners, and the Georgia Guard, a militia unit, was hunting them down like animals. Then, in a kinder tone, Wool added that he was authorized to issue food and clothing to those who would support the treaty. When he finished, the Cherokee leaders arose with sullen faces and walked away. Another fruitless meeting was held the next day. Wool blamed the impasse on the influence of Cherokee leader John Ross and certain whites who resided among the Indians. "We shall have another meeting on Wednesday next the

3d instant," he wrote the adjutant general in Washington, "when it will be determined whether we shall have war or peace." If the Cherokees refused to submit, he would seize them as "prisoners of war." If they consented to abide by the treaty, he would still take hostages to "prevent the shedding of blood."[15]

On August 3, the impasse ended. When no Indians appeared for the announced meeting, Wool sent a Tennessee detachment to bring in several headmen and hold them overnight. The following morning, a group apologized for their conduct and said their people would comply with the treaty. To prove their compliance, the colonel told them to have their young men bring in their arms. The next day, fifty Indians, dressed in white and carrying a flag and reversed muskets, stacked some 120 muskets in Hunter's yard. They made no request, however, for rations or clothing. Wool took a mounted company to the village of Cheloce, thirty miles away, and seized Chief Roman Nose as a hostage. His show of force proved useless, however, and he soon released his prisoner.[16]

In reporting his actions, Wool expressed mixed feelings about the Cherokees in the Valley River region. On August 15, he wrote Cary A. Harris, commissioner of Indian affairs and acting secretary of war, that "ninety-nine out of every hundred" Cherokees in North Carolina opposed the treaty. "It is in vain," Wool informed Macomb, "to reason on this subject with a people who are decided in their conviction that they have made no treaty, and that if they submit to its terms they submit to that which will wrongfully deprive them of their rights." When the removal process began, he added, a firm, prudent officer must be on hand with troops—or there would be bloodshed.[17]

Heavy rains prevented Wool's departure from Valley River settlement. Captain Morrow and his mud-splattered company rode in, having completed a 250-mile circuit through Cherokee country, and reported widespread opposition to the treaty. An express from Athens also arrived, bringing word that the commissary general of the army had deposited $15,000 in Wool's name in the Union Bank of Maryland to purchase additional rations for the volunteers. Wool had advised against sending funds to Knoxville, Tennessee, because the banks there charged a 1.25 percent fee to handle the money. On August 17, after leaving Colonel Smith in command of the Valley Town depot, Wool and his escort returned sixty miles down the mountain and across the plains to Athens, arriving there three days later.[18]

John Ross, the principal Cherokee chief, was waiting when Wool reached Athens. Ross had just returned from an unproductive trip to Washington to pressure the government to reopen treaty negotiations. On August 10, Wool talked with the urbane mixed-blood, a man of "short Scottish stature," who spoke very little Cherokee. Ross said that Wool "expressed great satisfaction that he had come," for he needed "powerful counteracting influences" to cope with the growing hostility in the country. Wool's experience at Valley Town was proof, Ross coolly stated, that the president had made a mistake. Jackson's "determination" could not be changed, Wool responded, and Ross must emphasize this to his followers. The general then lectured the Cherokee leader on the plight of his people. He reminded him that the Creek refugees were being "hunted like wolves and dragged to the emigration camp . . . leaving everything behind them, their houses, lands, horses, cows, and their corn." Ross then broached the real purpose of the meeting. He wanted to hold the fall council early, in mid-September instead of October, at the Red Clay campground about twenty miles east of Chattanooga, Tennessee. Georgia had forbidden all Cherokee meetings. He wanted to report on his recent trip to Washington and explain the provisions of the treaty. Would he have any objections? Wool said he had none—but warned that if the meeting generated hostility toward the treaty, there would be trouble. Wool reported his conference with Ross to President Jackson and requested instructions regarding the gathering. A week later, Ross informed Wool that the council would meet on September 15 at Red Clay. He had invited the Ridge faction and hoped the general would also attend.[19]

While Wool gave room for Cherokee politics to play out, he struggled with his own government over managing the removal. Acting Secretary of War Carey Harris, in several instances, had questioned his proposed use of force at Valley Town and advised him to reread his instructions. The Cherokees must not be coerced to emigrate. Treaty provisions allowed them to remain in their homes for two years—and it could take that long to review and pay their claims. The army was in the Cherokee Nation as a precautionary measure only. Wool was incensed. He wrote to Cass on August 20, "I will never consent to risk my reputation as an officer," he railed to Cass, "with the restrictions embraced in the Acting Secretary's letter." Harris's views were timid and unrealistic. If Wool was "to do nothing" until hostilities commenced, he could not "be recalled too soon" from the command.[20]

On August 21, Wool rode south from Fort Cass with a party to Byrd's camp and depot at Ross's Landing on the Tennessee River. Byrd said that the area was quiet and few Indians had requested provisions. A week later, the travelers crossed the river by ferry into Georgia and continued south to New Echota. The Cherokee "capital" was a collection of weather-beaten wooden buildings and huts in a grove of tall trees. The little settlement included a few stores, a council building, and some residences. Vernon's Tennesseans camped nearby. General Dunlap, whom Wool had sent to prevent encroachments on the Cherokees, had arrived and arranged quarters for the party. The two claims commissioners had yet to arrive.[21]

Wool was restless at New Echota. To gather more information on the Cherokees, he instructed Maj. Charles H. Nelson and his Georgia battalion, sent over by General Jesup from the Creek country, to scout into northwestern Georgia and northeastern

Alabama. Nelson was to look for refugee Creeks and contact the volunteer companies on duty there. If the Georgians were in federal service, they were to report to Wool; if not, Nelson should send them home. The colonel grumbled about the claims commissioners. Cherokee families were collecting at New Echota, and some wanted to settle their affairs and emigrate before winter. Wool also fretted about his muster of unauthorized Tennessee volunteers. In mid-August he had explained to President Jackson the circumstances of his action, and Jackson had promised to ask Congress to provide relief. The War Department, however, refused to recognize the extra companies, and Wool pressed Jackson for attention to the matter. The president resented the pressure, and in a curt letter he criticized Wool for broadly interpreting his instructions. Congress had authorized the raising of 10,000 volunteers for the various Indian campaigns, and quotas had been apportioned among several states. Suppose other commanders had accepted extra troops, the president said. Again, Jackson promised to support a bill to reimburse the men.[22]

The presence of Tennesseans in Georgia created tension. In late July, when Captain Vernon headed south for New Echota, he met the Georgia Guard, commanded by Capt. William Bishop, who were camped at Spring Place, forty miles below the Georgia border. Vernon presented his instructions and was allowed to inspect the Creeks that Bishop was escorting to Gunter's Landing, Alabama, for emigration. Twenty Indians cried out that they were Cherokees, and Vernon demanded an explanation. Bishop hotly denied their claims, words flew, and a collision seemed in the offing. Fortunately, General Dunlap, whom Wool had sent to check on Vernon, rode up and ended the argument. Georgia Governor Schley, hearing of the incident, branded the Tennesseans "invaders," and urged Wool to "calm the troubled waters." In a courteous response, the colonel blamed both parties, saying Dunlap and Bishop misunderstood their duties. On September 8, to promote harmony, he peremptorily ordered Dunlap and his staff discharged from federal service. The few Tennessee troops on duty did not justify a general officer to command them. Dunlap resented the orders, and, upon returning to Athens, he published a complaint in the local newspaper. Soon afterwards, he headed west where he served as secretary of the treasury and minister to the United States in the infant Republic of Texas. Wool turned to other matters.[23]

As the Cherokee council prepared to meet at Red Clay, Wool again asked for instructions. Harris, who had become commissioner of Indian affairs, had restricted, Wool said, his role in the Cherokee country, leaving him with "very little or no discretionary power," except in cases of actual hostilities. Firmness, decision, and promptitude were indispensable in preserving peace. He hoped that many Cherokees could emigrate that fall, particularly those gathered at New Echota. Whites were daily squatting on Indian lands in violation of the treaty. Before sealing the envelope,

Wool inserted one of Ross's handbills announcing the meeting at Red Clay. On September 1, he ordered four Tennessee companies to march to the campground there.[24]

Secretary of War Cass tried to soothe Wool's feelings. He expressed confidence in his old friend's ability to handle delicate situations but gently reminded him that he must use volunteers primarily as police. Should the Cherokees "commence hostilities or pursue such a course as to make their hostile designs manifest," Wool could take action. The secretary also reminded him that the military must not arrest civilians. To reduce friction Wool might further reduce the Tennessee forces. The colonel responded that the conditions in the Cherokee Nation were appalling. "If I could . . . I would remove every Indian tomorrow beyond the reach of white men, who like so many vultures are watching, ready to pounce upon their prey and strip them of everything they have or expect from the government of the United States," he said. The true test of hostility would come when the commissioners began their work.[25]

Commissioner Wilson Lumpkin arrived at New Echota on September 2. President Jackson had chosen Lumpkin, a fifty-three-year-old attorney, planter, and recent governor of Georgia, along with William Carroll, ex-governor of Tennessee, to review and adjudicate Cherokee claims. Lumpkin would meet with the Cherokee Committee, whose five members (all pro-treaty)—Elias Boudinot, John Ridge, William Rogers, John Gunter, and William Chambers—would act as advisors. Ross and members of his faction had been appointed to the committee, but they refused to serve. Ridge's followers had filled their places. As Carroll had not arrived, Lumpkin hesitated to start his work. Government appraisers, the commissioner also learned, had suspended their activities in the New Echota district because of unsettled conditions.[26]

Lumpkin handed Wool copies of the requests he had made to the War Department. He needed two volunteer companies to guard the commissioner's office. He wanted access to the $72,000 Indian account that Wool controlled to pay local businessmen for feeding the "poor and destitute" who had come to New Echota before Wool's arrival. The Indians gathering at New Echota to present their claims also needed subsistence. These requests irritated Wool, who suspected they were attempts to despoil government funds. If he honored the requisitions, the $72,000 appropriation would evaporate within two weeks.[27]

As he prepared to leave for Red Clay, Wool received letters from Cass and Jackson. The secretary of war, writing on September 3, again expressed confidence in his friend. "If the Indians are to be assembled with the fair intention of explaining to them their duty under the treaty, and the necessity of an immediate compliance with its terms, the meeting may perhaps be useful," Cass optimistically wrote. Jackson, on the other hand, lashed out at the general. Wool had a copy of the treaty and War Department instructions before him. No modifications or alterations would be made. John Ross must not use the meeting to stir up opposition to removal. Collisions between Cherokees and whites had been "too long continued for the gratification of himself at the expense of the poor of the nation." Wool rode north, crossed the Tennessee River, and reached Red Clay (thirteen miles south of present-day Cleveland, Tennessee) on September 14. Four Tennessee companies, about three hundred men, had erected tents in a large park between two tree-covered hills. Fresh water gushed from a nearby spring. Wool sent pickets to ride a two-mile perimeter to drive off whiskey peddlers. Smoke from several hundred campfires hung low over the grounds, as nearly three thousand Cherokees gathered for the council. John Ross and other Indian leaders had also arrived.[28]

Wool located his marquee about a quarter mile from the council ground and called Ross in for a talk. He again queried the chief about his intentions at the meeting and warned against the probability of the council rejecting the treaty and voting a new delegation to Washington. Ross admitted this could happen. At a meeting with five other Cherokee leaders, Wool read the president's letter of September 7. If the Cherokees resisted the treaty, he added, they would suffer the fate of the Creeks. Turning to Ross, he asked: Was this what Ross wanted? The chief quietly replied that he would leave "the whole subject to his people and abide [with] the result."[29]

At Red Clay, Wool received estimates from the Cherokee Committee regarding clothing and goods needed for the Indian families desiring to emigrate that fall. He passed this information on to Albert S. Lenoir, the rations agent at New Echota, with a letter of credit and instructions to place orders with the mercantile firm of Larkson & Langdon in New York City. Lenoir would purchase 7,000 Mackinac blankets, 4,000 coarse, well-made shoes of various sizes, 2,000 yards of striped domestic cotton cloth, 2,000 yards of unbleached cotton, and "a due proportion" of thread, buttons, and needles. The goods should be shipped at an early date by sea via Charleston, South Carolina, and hauled by wagon inland to New Echota. Duplicate invoices would be sent to Wool at Athens for payment. A copy of these orders went to Indian Commissioner Harris in Washington.[30]

On Monday, September 19, Ross opened the meeting at Red Clay, with Jesse Bushyhead, a Cherokee Baptist minister, as interpreter. The principal chief spoke little Cherokee and had a limited reading knowledge of the language. Wool and several officers took seats near a long wooden shed which served as a council house. A soldier handed Ross a note, with a request that it be read aloud (and interpreted) to the Cherokees (estimated 2,100 men) sitting among the trees. In a note addressed to "The Cherokee People," Wool spoke briefly of his role in the Cherokee country and reminded the crowd that the president would tolerate no alteration in the New Echota Treaty. The terms were clear and would be faithfully executed. Ross spoke next. He reviewed the treaty, a process that dragged on day after day. In the evenings, his supporters were active. "The mischief was not done in the council-house," an observer said, "it was at night when small groups around their family fires that the poison was imbibed. Those who would elevate themselves at the expense of those poor creatures, were there at work." On September 23, Ross completed his "explanations"—and quickly introduced a new topic. He requested approval of a statement that declared the treaty null and void, authorized a trip to seek support among the Arkansas Cherokees for a new agreement, and the drafting of a memorial to Congress for redress. The statement was approved. Curiously, Wool did not intervene. A week later, on leaving the campground, Ross thanked the general for his "honorable course" during the meeting. Wool saw problems with the Ross statement and he mailed a copy to Cass. On October 19, he left for Athens.[31]

At Red Clay, Wool had received a letter from Lumpkin, bearing recommendations he had made to Jackson concerning the volunteers. To curb the growing hostility to the treaty, he urged that the volunteer force be increased while the Indian claims were being reviewed. Each state should raise and rely on its own soldiers, with Wool mustering and commanding the expanded military presence. Lumpkin believed that certain federal "subordinate officers and agents" in the Cherokee country were encouraging Ross's "mischievous opposition." The message was clear: Georgia wanted the Tennessee volunteers to leave her soil.[32]

Wool returned to New Echota in late October. Two Tennessee companies still remained there. Lumpkin had started processing Cherokee claims alone, but he had no one to make disbursements to those wishing to emigrate. The commissioner resented Wool's complaints about his requests for money. General Wool, Lumpkin wrote Harris, was stubborn and uncommunicative. He was vigilant regarding claims, amounts, and disbursements, but "overlooked the views and consideration to which I attach great importance." Lumpkin wanted to draw on Wool's $72,000 Indian fund, not only to subsist the families gathered at the capital, but also to settle claims. The atmosphere in New Echota grew tense.[33]

Wool soon found himself yoked to Lumpkin. In a terse letter dated October 12, Acting Secretary of War Harris instructed the general to confer with Lumpkin in all matters regarding the Cherokee. He would withdraw Tennessee troops from their outposts in Georgia and Alabama, and call on the governors of those states, if necessary, to furnish fresh levies for federal duty. Future troop assignments would not be made without consulting the commissioners. The general would arrest any federal officer who advised opposition to the treaty and convene a court of inquiry to review his conduct. In conclusion, Harris conveyed Jackson's extreme displeasure over Wool's failure to stop the Red Clay meeting when it degenerated into a protest of the treaty. In a second letter that quickly followed, Harris returned Ross's Cherokee memorial, saying the president was astounded that Wool would transmit "a paper so disrespectful to him." In the future, the general would show the Cherokee commissioners every order he received from the War Office. If a "diversity of opinion arose," he would acquiesce to their views.[34]

Wool grumbled over these decisions but promptly complied with Harris's orders. On October 19, he instructed Smith at Valley Town and Byrd at Ross's Landing, to send three Tennessee companies each to Fort Cass. There they would be relieved of duty, paid, and sent home to await the pleasure of the president. He kept one company (Delaney) for duty at Gunter's Landing in Alabama. As Nelson's Georgians had completed their tour there, the Tennesseans would replace them in early December. Wool requested Georgia Governor Schley to call up and hold in readiness a battalion for twelve months of service. He immediately ordered two mounted companies for duty at New Echota. Then in General Order 74, dated November 3, the general announced to the Cherokees that the president had condemned the proceedings at the Red Clay meeting and ordered him to prohibit all future meetings. He was ready to issue rations to all needy Indians at New Echota.[35]

Wool penned a strident letter to Harris. He described his orders to release volunteers and provide Indian rations and indicated his willingness to consult with Lumpkin. He assured the Washington bureaucrat that he would "discharge every trust confided in me in such a manner as to merit [the president's] high approbation." Harris's censures and restrictions, however, clearly showed that he no longer possessed Jackson's confidence. He "earnestly but respectfully" asked to be recalled from the Cherokee command. Three days later the general reviewed his activities in the Cherokee Nation in a long letter (similar to his "vindication" letter to Macomb on October 12) to Attorney General Benjamin F. Butler, a member of the Albany Regency, who had replaced Harris as acting secretary of war on October 5. Wool hoped to convince the secretary, and the president, that he was not "deserving of censure in any respect whatever."[36]

With winter rapidly approaching, Wool instructed his commanders of the Tennessee companies at Valley River and Ross's Landing to build huts for winter quarters. At Valley Town soldiers also erected a blockhouse "beyond the reach of musquetry." Each man would receive "one pair of good strong shoes, two pairs of winter stockings, two pairs of pantaloons, two shirts, a vest, a close bodied coat or substantial woolen hunting shirt, a blanket, an overcoat, and a decent hat." Regular inspections, guard details, and military courtesy would be observed. With cold weather descending on the mountains, Wool's forces settled into the boredom of camp life.[37]

By November 15, Wool had returned to the Cherokee capitol. There he wrote Secretary of War Butler that he felt like "a ship at sea in a storm without rudder or compass." The destiny of the Cherokees now lay in the commissioner's hands. If the Indians remained submissive, he had no reason to remain there. A field grade officer could handle the responsibilities. The delay in processing claims weighed heavily.

Many Cherokees, he wrote Troy banker Stephen Warren, had sold everything under the impression of leaving soon, but could not get their claims resolved. Cherokees called almost daily on "Oo-wah-nah," the Cherokee word for "wool," the general told Mrs. Stephen Warren. One wanted "his horse restored to him which had just been taken possession of by a white man; another . . . had a horse stolen, another a cow or a hog." Families were being torn apart. A Cherokee lost his wife because she was a Creek by birth and was forced to emigrate; a wife lost her husband, a Creek, when he was sent west. The situation was depressing.[38]

Whites intruded on Cherokee lands everywhere. The most flagrant example was at Ridge's Ferry, on the Coosa River in Alabama. While the Ridge delegation was in Washington in 1835, John H. Garrett, an Alabama militia general, had dispossessed Ridge's tenant, taken over the ferry, and built improvements. In late August 1836, at Ridge's request, Wool had written Garrett, cited the treaty, and ordered him off the property. Major Nelson arrived with his Georgia detachment soon afterward and seized the Ridge ferry. Garrett withdrew, threatening to return with a court order. Wool advised Nelson to surrender the ferry if this occurred. He wanted no trouble with Alabama authorities. Garrett presented a court order granting possession, and Nelson relinquished the ferry. Wool advised Ridge to file a spoliation claim under the treaty in his case.[39]

On November 23, Wilson Lumpkin, in full control of Cherokee affairs, outlined to Wool what he expected from him. In flowery prose the commissioner spoke "of the delicacy, difficulty, and responsibility" of his trust. He hoped that "unity and concert of purpose" would prevail among government agents and officers in the Cherokee country. Lumpkin respected Wool's intentions and believed they could work together. The general held the "power of the sword" and could be useful in coercing "obedience to the legal mandates of the civil authority." He wanted Wool to send volunteer detachments to the Cherokee settlements and urge the Indians to come to New Echota to settle claims and enroll for removal to the west. Lumpkin also asked Wool to scour the woods for refugee Creeks and forward them to emigration authorities. In conclusion, he trusted that his "frank and friendly" remarks would prepare the general's mind for later requests.[40]

Before receiving Lumpkin's letter, Wool placed his case before the public. In mid-November, the *Athens Republican* published a lengthy commentary by "An Observer." The writer (probably Lieutenant Howe) reviewed Wool's course at the Red Clay council and concluded that he had no cause to stop the proceedings because they were peaceful. A week later, on October 23, the newspaper printed Harris's letter from a week earlier that censured Wool, and noted that Emigration Superintendent Benjamin Currey had read parts of the document on the street in Calhoun, and provided a copy to the paper. When he saw this defamatory epistle in the paper, Wool erupted. He clipped the item and sent it to Secretary of War Butler, demanding to know if the War Department had adopted a "new and most extraordinary mode of giving publicity to the censures of the President." The general also mailed clippings to friends for publication in the eastern press. He even sent one to Butler's wife, whom he knew personally, and asked her to place it in the *Washington Globe*. The battle was joined.[41]

On November 25, Wool conveyed his distraught feelings to his friend Senator Tallmadge. Since coming to the Cherokee country, he had overcome a complex and difficult situation. Now Superintendent Currey, "who is detested by all classes, white, red, and black," was trying his patience. Wool would not continue in command under these conditions. To avoid such degradation, he would "sacrifice commission, property, and life itself." "You may say this is bold language," he told Tallmadge. "Be it so. . . . The denunciations of the palace have no terrors for me. I have seen the lightning and heard the thunder of the field of Battle and I was not alarmed."[42]

On November 30, Lumpkin asked Wool to provide an escort to help the disbursing agent, Dr. Philip Minis, bring $100,000 in drafts and specie from Athens to New Echota. The general refused the request. A few days before, Secretary Butler had sent heartening words. The president "directs me to assure you that he has full confidence in your capacity, fidelity, and zeal . . . [and] sees no adequate reason for recalling you from the command." Wool's letters to Tallmadge, Silas Wright, and other members of Congress had proved effective. Furthermore, a fellow New Yorker and friend and Jackson's vice president, Martin Van Buren, had recently been elected president.[43]

Wool's refusal to furnish an escort enraged Lumpkin, and he dashed off a hot note to Washington. The general's refusal to cooperate was "an indirect insult" to the president, the government, and the civil officials seeking to execute the Cherokee treaty. "The General's object," Lumpkin added, "is obviously a childish controversy upon the question, who shall stand at the head of the class." The commissioner was "now growing old, in a long and careworn public service" and was "wholly disinclined to enter upon such boyish controversies." Lumpkin, whom the general branded a "political Jesuit," soon settled their differences. The commissioners apparently made the first move. Lumpkin and John Kennedy, a Tennessee judge who on December 6 replaced the ailing Carroll, assured Wool that they had no wish to exercise authority over him and stressed their need for aid. As the impasse could not continue, the general agreed to honor their requests for guards, escorts, and police details, and to supervise clothing issues. He also agreed to search for refugee Creeks.[44]

In mid-December, Lumpkin tested the compromise. In reviewing claims with the Cherokee Committee, the commissioners decided they needed to consult the tribal records to settle accounts. As the Cherokee Council was scheduled to meet at the home of John Martin, former treasurer of the Cherokee Nation, Lumpkin asked

Wool to borrow or seize these papers. The general promptly dispatched a Georgia mounted detachment on a twenty-mile ride through the night to Martin's house. At dawn they surrounded Martin's home and demanded the files. Martin and other councilmen refused to cooperate and were brought to New Echota. Wool confronted them and threatened to arrest "all the leading men of the nation" if the documents were not delivered. This act produced results. Wool and Lumpkin apparently now had a better working relationship.[45]

"I am doomed to spend the winter in the Cherokee country," Wool wrote a family friend on December 20 from Fort Cass. It was a "cheerless, gloomy, and sad" world. He had been sent to prevent any violence that might arise as a consequence "of real and supposed wrongs by those beings called Cherokees." The Indians were an "oppressed, broken down and dispirited people," but if they were aroused, "the tomahawk and scalping knife might resound through the land." They wanted to "live and die on the lands of their forefathers," Wool said, and they deeply resented the whites' attempts to dispossess them. It was truly "a hard case, but it is the fate of the savage. He can find no resting place where the white man treads."[46]

Despite rainy weather, Cherokee families continued to straggle into New Echota, Georgia, for emigration. They huddled in the woods around campfires, awaiting their turn to present their claims and register for removal. They came from every part of their nation, some riding in buggies or wagons, many on horseback, and others walking. Army agents distributed blankets and shoes and handed out rations. Claim processing proceeded slowly. Accounts, deeds, mortgages, and debts had to be checked, the disbursing agent arrived late, and Currey, the intemperate emigration superintendent, died on December 16. He was replaced by Nathaniel Smith, a militia officer who had served at Valley River under Wool.[47]

Wool reported alarming news to the adjutant general on January 11, 1837. He recently toured his command and not a single Cherokee had started west. This meant that the government must move over 16,000 Indians that fall and winter to meet treaty obligations. An estimated 5,000 Cherokees living in the North Carolina mountains were stubbornly resisting removal. At Valley Town, the focus of the opposition, the destitute would not accept rations or clothing, and headmen were demanding their firearms back. When told they must submit to the treaty to receive them, they walked away in disgust. The region was fast becoming a refuge for discontented Indians. Wool left Athens for New Echota on January 17.[48]

By March 1837, the human disaster that was the Trail of Tears had at long last commenced. Claims of the well-to-do were settled first. This group—about six hundred in separate parties—drew their money and headed west overland by wagon, carriage, and personal conveyance, driving their riding horses and beef cattle. Emigration officials then started a train of wagons from New Echota carrying some five hundred Indians and their luggage north to Ross's Landing where they climbed into eleven flatboats and descended the Tennessee to Gunter's Landing in Alabama. Here they boarded the steamboat *Knoxville* for the West. Moving the emigrants created a brisk business along the river. The same was true at New Echota, where a horde of creditors hovered around the claimant. By March 22, Lumpkin had disbursed $300,000 in vouchers to the Cherokees and urged Indian Commissioner Harris to place an additional $400,000 "within our reach before mid-May." Laying aside the oppression of the Cherokee, the outpouring of federal funds became a blessing to the economies of the southern states in 1837—a year of financial panic and depression in the rest of the nation.[49]

Nearly four thousand Cherokee would die of malnutrition and disease in the course of the 116-day forced march west to the Indian Territory. Federal troops successfully confiscated or destroyed the material basis of Cherokee culture such as sawmills, cotton gins, barns, homes, meetinghouses, and the printing press used to publish the *Cherokee Phoenix,* the first bilingual newspaper in America.

"This is the last day of the reign of Andrew," Wool wrote Miss Warren on March 3, 1837. "I am sure I shall not shed tears. I hope, however, he will be able to live a more mild and tranquil life at the Hermitage than he has for the last four years." Considerable confusion had recently erupted at New Echota. In mid-February, 1,500 Indians met there and argued over who would receive annuities due under former treaties, and 1,269 had voted to commit the funds to George Lowery, a Ross adherent, instead of the Cherokee Committee. After the vote, Wool gave a short speech on horseback, with Bushyhead interpreting. The general reminded his listeners of their plight and assured them that the treaty would be executed, but he made little impression.[50]

Wool sought to expedite the removal process. In a proclamation at New Echota on March 22, he exhorted the Cherokees to look to the West:

> CHEROKEES: . . . The President, as well as Congress, have decreed that you should remove from this country. The people of Georgia, of North Carolina, of Tennessee and of Alabama, have decreed it. Your fate is decided; and if you do not voluntarily get ready and go . . . you will then be forced from this country by the soldiers of the United States.
>
> Hitherto I have been able, in some degree, to protect you from their [white] intrusions; in a short time it will no longer be in my power. If, however, I could protect you, you could not live among them. Your habits, your manners, and your customs are unlike and unsuited to theirs. They have no feelings, no sympathies in common with yourselves . . . remove to the country designated for your new homes. . . . It is a country much better than the one you now occupy; where you can grow more corn, and where game is

> more abundant. . . . Remember, that you have but one summer more to plant corn in this country.[51]

In late March, Wool ordered Georgia companies to search for Creeks hiding among the Cherokees. A year before, when state and federal troops began a roundup, an estimated one thousand Creeks had fled their homes in Georgia, many crossing the Coosa River into Alabama. Others vanished into the mountains of eastern Tennessee and western North Carolina. As the last of the Creek chiefs were deported, these refugees had no leader. The previous fall, soldiers had located small groups and sent them to Gunter's Landing. Wool hoped to ferret out the rest. He placed Lt. Edward Deas, Fourth Artillery, in charge of collecting the fugitives and taking them to Ross's Landing. A Georgia company at New Echota and a Tennessee company at the Cherokee Agency located near Calhoun, Tennessee, began an extended search in the mountains. Each group carried an interpreter and a civilian agent to secure wagons and teams to haul the captives to Ross's Landing. Wool wrote Clement C. Clay, governor of Alabama, explaining his plans and requested his cooperation.[52]

Deas pursued a vigorous course toward the Creeks, employing Cherokees to trail and find the refugees. Cherokees refusing to assist during the operation were seized and taken to the agency at Calhoun for emigration. Commanders tried to separate those who had settled among the Cherokees before the Creek treaty of March 24, 1832. They could emigrate later with the Cherokees. The fugitives, Wool wrote Stephen Warren, were "the most miserable looking creatures" he had ever seen. Many were nearly naked and starving. "The course that had been pursued toward this people will not tell well in history." By mid-May, the volunteers had collected some five hundred Creeks for emigration.[53]

Soon after the Creek roundup began, Wool found himself grappling again with troublesome citizen soldiers. This was his first peacetime experience with volunteers, and he had quickly learned they were lacking in leadership and respect for authority. In sending troops into the Cherokee country earlier, he had tried through instructions and orders to curb drunkenness and depredations and to regulate camp life with drills, inspections, and guard details. In the spring of 1837, however, the Tennessee company at Valley River became unruly. Drunkenness was a serious problem. In mid-April, a group of soldiers burned their bacon rations. Local citizens and Cherokee leaders petitioned North Carolina Governor Edward B. Dudley to curb the misconduct. The governor wrote Joel Poinsett, the new secretary of war, who alerted Wool. The general immediately dispatched a Tennessee company from Ross's Landing to Valley River to restore order, and sent Lieutenant Howe to Raleigh to reassure the governor that peace would prevail. Howe also assured the governor that rumors of arms shipments from Salem, North Carolina, to the Cherokee settlements was unfounded.[54]

Wool had little doubt the whiskey peddler posed the greatest threat to peace in the Cherokee country. Whenever Indians gathered, the peddler appeared and opened his stand. The previous November, at New Echota, Cherokee leaders had complained that their people were "by the frequent potations of whiskey, becoming degraded to brutes." A person could easily obtain a liquor license by paying the local county clerk a small fee. Wool complained to Governor Schley about the situation, and the governor had the Georgia legislature pass a law restricting the licensing of liquor dealers. Suppressing liquor sales at Gunter's Landing was a different matter. In early April 1837, on Wool's orders, Captain Morrow, stationed at neighboring Fort Scott, banned the sale of ardent spirits at the landing. Whiskey dealers petitioned Governor Clay for relief. Clay informed Morrow that Wool could prohibit liquor sales to Indians and soldiers, but he could not halt transactions between white citizens. As the state extended its jurisdiction over the Cherokee lands, Clay asked Secretary of War Poinsett to instruct Wool to modify his ban. Although the general defended his whiskey ban as one of necessity, he did acquiesce and agree to revise his order to fit the governor's wishes.[55]

In late April, Wool learned that Col. William Lindsay, Second Artillery, recently involved in the Florida Indian wars, would replace him on July 1. The federal presence in the Cherokee country was now small, and the War Department wanted an officer of lower rank to oversee the operations there. Several newspapers quickly criticized Wool's dealings with the Cherokees, and Lumpkin joined in the clamor. In a letter to President Van Buren, he censured the general and declared that his actions had been "worse than useless." But all was not gloom. Georgia volunteer officers and civilian friends in Athens and other towns published complimentary letters, and a collation was given at Fort Cass in Wool's honor. On July 1, 1837, in General Orders 39, Wool transferred his command to Lindsay. He expressed "extreme regret and reluctance" at separating from companions who had "so faithfully, so harmoniously and with so much good feeling" toiled through a year of "constant labor, anxiety, and perplexity." In early July, Wool left the Cherokee country for Washington.[56]

But all was not well. Unofficially, the general had heard that Secretary Poinsett, at the urging of John Ross and others, had instructed Lindsay to investigate Wool's acts in the Cherokee Nation. Astonished that he had not been notified of the complaints, Wool demanded a military court of inquiry review his conduct there. By the time Wool reached Washington, the situation worsened. On June 30, the Alabama legislature in a joint resolution charged the general with usurping the rights of its citizens. Specifically, the lawmakers censured Wool for interfering in a land difficulty in Marshall County, an affair that had indirectly caused the death of two persons. Governor Clay forwarded the resolution to Washington and demanded that the government investigate the episode. On instructions from Poinsett, General Macomb ordered a court of inquiry to convene in Knoxville in early September. Wool asked that the inquiry consider his entire stay in Cherokee country, but his request was denied. In late August, he started south by stage.[57]

The court of inquiry convened on September 4. Bvt. Maj. Gen. Winfield Scott presided and joined Colonel Lindsay and Major Payne in forming a tribunal, while Lt. William C. DeHart would serve as judge advocate. Wool had asked five witnesses (including three volunteer officers) to testify on his behalf. Unlike a court martial, the tribunal sat as a grand jury and sought to determine the validity of the charges. Scott recently had stood a review of his command in the Creek country, but this was the first time that Wool had faced such a hearing.[58]

DeHart described his difficulties in the case. He asked Alabama Governor Clay for needed testimony and a list of witnesses, only to learn that Clay had resigned on August 17. The acting governor, Hugh McVay, could find nothing in the executive files to transmit. Under these circumstances, DeHart had to rely on Wool's correspondence and orders, and on officers familiar with the materials. The judge advocate then read the charges in the inquiry. As stated in the Alabama resolutions, the general had: (1) interfered with state civil tribunals; (2) disturbed the peace; and (3) trampled on individual rights. At this point, Wool suddenly rose to declare that there was "not a tittle of evidence" to support the charges. He again asked that his entire conduct in the Cherokee country be considered and again his request was denied.[59]

DeHart focused first on the principal charge: Wool's usurpation of powers in a Gunter's Landing dispute, powers claimed by the Alabama courts. Specifically, the general had adjudicated and determined "the right of possessory ownership of land and improvements thereon," and had used military force to remove one claimant and supplant him with another. Alexander Riddle, sheriff of Jackson County, Alabama, was called to testify. In late March, Riddle, administrator of the John Gunter Sr. estate, asked Wool to remove Nathaniel Steele, a local businessman, from the deceased's home, ferry, and plantation at Gunter's Landing, in Marshall County. The sheriff wanted to sell the property and distribute the proceeds to Gunter's heirs. Gunter's Cherokee wife had owned the land. The critical question was: who owned the improvements? Steele, who was living with John Gunter Jr., had erected buildings and claimed a share in the estate. Wool had instructed Captain Morrow, at nearby Camp Scott, to evict Steele, but the officer hesitated. In early June, Wool visited Gunter's Landing, met the concerned parties and discussed the problem. He cited Article 16 of the treaty, which guaranteed Cherokee property rights, and told Sheriff Riddle to auction the house and plantation—but not the recent improvements.[60]

The auction created more problems. Steele bid $2,540.25 and won the Gunter property and improvements, but refused to pay the full amount. He pointed to certain buildings as his, but had no proof of having paid for the construction. Riddle then reauctioned the property, and Martin Scrimpser, a Gunter relative, bought it for $670. When Scrimpser sought to occupy his purchase, Steele appeared with an armed group, an argument ensued, and two men were killed. Morrow hurried to the scene with soldiers, seized Steele and others, and delivered them to the Alabama authorities.[61]

As the inquiry drew to a close, Wool presented his defense. He had taken command in the Cherokee Nation, he said, with a single purpose in mind: to see that the New Echota treaty was faithfully executed. The assignment had been extremely troublesome. Cherokees complained daily that whites were taking their houses and fields and forcing their families to camp in the forests. The government had pledged protection, and he had made every effort to fulfill that promise. "I have not perplexed myself with the subtle arguments of politicians about the indivisibility of sovereignty, or such like cobwebs of the brain," Wool declared. "I have but obeyed the still small voice of conscience which frequently in the advance of reason, overleaps those barriers with which subtlety and ingenuity sometimes successfully opposes its progress." The general droned on citing in his high-pitched voice, military correspondence, orders, and reports to illustrate and bolster his views. The hearing ended on September 8. A week later the court rendered judgment on only one charge: Wool's interference with state tribunals. In this act Wool had acted within the powers assigned him by Article 16 of the treaty. There was insufficient evidence to render a decision on the other charges.[62].

Wool's command in the Cherokee Nation had been indeed difficult. Ordered to preserve peace while commissioners reviewed and settled Indian claims, he had provoked criticism at every turn. Civilian authorities in Washington had censured him for mustering unneeded volunteers, for threatening to use force against recalcitrant Cherokees at Valley River, and for permitting Ross adherents at Red Clay to reject the New Echota treaty. When the claims commissioners began their work, Wool cooperated fitfully and reluctantly. In dealing with the state authorities, he was careful that he be respectful, yet his increasing sympathy for the displaced Indians generated conflicts with civilians over property. Wool's problems were due largely to administrative changes in the War Department, vague instructions, and his own sense of right and wrong. For the first time, the general saw how a rigid federal Indian policy could cause human misery. His Cherokee assignment was an exasperating experience.

5

DEFENDING THE CANADIAN BORDER

On a cold wintry morning in December 1837, Wool sat at his desk in Nassau and penned a lengthy letter to Edwin Croswell, editor of the *Albany Argus*. He had finished reading President Martin Van Buren's annual message to Congress and was pondering the state of the union. Rumblings of revolution in Canada alarmed him. The Canadians, Wool observed, "have risen with arms in their hands determined no longer to submit to military despotism." A spirit of liberty was abroad, and before the snow melted "in that frosty region," the American frontier could be "lined with the sons of the first blood of the revolution, [ready] to aid the patriots and to establish throughout Canada the principles of freedom and self-government." That result could be a "war with England and war to the *death*." "Will Congress look on and see all this and not prepare for the coming events?" he asked. In the weeks that followed, other important matters claimed Wool's attention, but his assignment to curb Canadian patriot activities along the northern border of New York and Vermont would test his ability to command and compromise.[1]

In the early 1830s, Canadians dissatisfied with British rule had organized a widespread "patriot" movement to obtain political, economic, and social reforms. West of Montreal, in Upper Canada, spokesmen for the growing Scotch-Irish and English farming communities in Ontario demanded liberal land laws and more democracy in the provincial government. To the east, in Quebec and Lower Canada, reform leaders urged the French population to resist the rule of a rising Anglo-Saxon trading class who threatened their traditional social and political structure. By 1837, the unrest became alarming. In Upper Canada, Sir Francis B. Head, the lieutenant governor, purged the assembly of those wanting reform; in Lower Canada a widespread economic depression in the United States spilled over into the St. Lawrence Valley. Banks closed on both sides of the boundary, agricultural and industrial production slackened, and unemployment grew. As the economy and society drifted in limbo, the patriots found fertile ground for their cause.[2]

By early December 1837, the Niagara frontier had become a powder keg. In the Buffalo vicinity, sympathy for the insurgents was strong, and William Lyon

MacKenzie, a patriot organizer, easily drew American recruits to the movement. Rensselaer Van Rensselaer, the twenty-seven-year-old son of Col. Solomon Van Rensselaer, of Albany, joined MacKenzie in setting up a military camp on Navy Island, a Canadian possession in the Niagara River. He hoisted a flag, proclaimed a provisional government based on a constitution that guaranteed equal rights, and provided for a popularly elected governor and legislature. Van Rensselaer promised three hundred Canadian acres to every volunteer who joined the patriot ranks. By Christmas, over five hundred men had gathered on the island. Alarmed by these developments, Lieutenant Governor Head asked New York governor William L. Marcy to halt the flow of supplies to the insurgents. Marcy issued a mild warning but did little else. The situation worsened when the patriots fired a cannon at the Canadian military garrison at Chippewa. They also hired the steamboat *Caroline* to shuttle men and arms from Buffalo to Navy Island. Canadian authorities decided to act.[3]

On the night of December 29, Col. Allan McNab, commanding at Chippewa, sent Commander Andrew Drew, Royal Navy, to destroy the *Caroline.* Drew found the vessel tied to the wharf at old Fort Schlosser, near the village of Black Rock, a few miles from Buffalo. Although in American waters, he and his men fell upon those sleeping on board and killed several individuals including one American, Amos Durfee, of Buffalo. The attackers then towed the vessel out into the river and set her afire. With flames and smoke lighting the frosty night air, the *Caroline* drifted downriver and sank in the rapids just before plunging over Niagara Falls. The next morning, American militia commanders in neighboring Erie and Niagara Counties sounded an alarm and sent expresses hurrying east through heavy snow to the capital at Albany. Governor Marcy rushed the news to Washington.[4]

On the evening of January 4, 1838, just before dinner at the White House, President Van Buren learned about the destruction of the *Caroline.* General Winfield Scott advised that the army could provide little help, as half of its thirteen regiments were in Florida fighting Cherokee, and the rest were scattered in distant garrisons. All available regulars in his department, plus recent recruits, were guarding the federal arsenals near the Canadian border.[5]

Van Buren acted promptly. On January 5, by proclamation, the president warned Americans against violating neutrality laws and endangering amicable relations with Great Britain. He asked Congress to review and update the neutrality legislation. He also asked Congress to grant him powers to prevent American citizens and others inflicting injustices upon neighboring nations by "unlawful acts." Van Buren ordered General Scott to go immediately to the Niagara district, and requested the governors of New York and Vermont to honor his calls for militia support. On passing through Albany, Scott picked up Marcy and hastened across a snowy countryside to Buffalo.[6]

On January 9, at Nassau, Wool received orders to join Scott. He had recently bruised a leg in a stagecoach accident and was hobbling about on crutches, but he and his mulatto servant, James H. Davis, headed west by coach the next day. The destruction of the *Caroline,* the general wrote Sarah on January 14, had caused great excitement, and there was a rising clamor for a "prompt and immediate redress" for the outrage. The patriots had widespread support. In Buffalo, William Lyon MacKenzie had received money, provisions, and supplies from many sources, plus letters "from Ohio, Kentucky, New York, [and] Boston," granting him permission "to draw [money] on site." If kept alive, this sympathy could accomplish exactly what the Canadian patriots desired: a war with England. Van Rensselaer reportedly had 1,500 recruits on Navy Island and was planning to gather more recruits in the United States before attacking the Canadian garrison at neighboring Chippewa.[7]

At Buffalo, Scott, Marcy, and Wool discussed the situation. Scott stressed that Van Rensselaer's force was composed largely of American citizens, and he considered the problem a civil matter. If the insurgents could be persuaded to return to the United States, local authorities could take whatever action they wished. Wool disagreed. These men, he argued passionately, had thrown off "their allegiance to their own country and acknowledge no law and no Government but that of a military despotism." By the law of nations they were "outlaws" and not entitled to the protection or benefit of civil process. If the patriots attempted to use the United States as a base to invade Canada, they should be expelled by military force.[8]

On January 13, General Scott and Governor Marcy went to Navy Island and the general sternly lectured Van Rensselaer on his untenable position. The patriot leader agreed to return to American soil and the next day he transferred his arms and cannon to neighboring Grand Island, an American possession in the Niagara River, and came to Buffalo and surrendered to a United States marshal. Moreover, he posted bail to appear in district court, crossed back into Canada, still hoping to lead a rebellion, and was arrested and jailed there. Wool branded the Navy Island episode a farce. If the government wanted to prevent a collision with Great Britain, he wrote former congressman John W. Taylor, it must arrest the outlaw bands who used the United States as "a highway" for revolutionary operations. To ignore the issue was "preposterous."[9]

General Scott quickly learned that the patriots planned to charter the British steamboat *Barcelona,* moored near Black Rock, to move their arms and supplies from Grand Island to Canadian soil. The British also learned of this plan and stationed three armed schooners in the river near Black Rock. Scott immediately seized the *Barcelona* and the *New England* to intercept any attempt to move patriot arms and supplies. He informed the commander of the British flotilla of his actions, assuring him that the *Barcelona* carried no contraband. On the morning of January 16, Scott,

Marcy, and Wool went to Black Rock. The general placed two field pieces in position to fire if the British battery on the opposite shore opened fire or attempted to board the *Barcelona*. When the steamboat hove into view, Scott resplendent in dress uniform, climbed onto a large oak log near the river, brandished his sword at the British ships at anchor. Wool held the artillerists at ready with lighted matches and loaded cannon. The *Barcelona* passed without incident. The British captain had received conflicting orders, saw Scott pacing along the shore with loaded cannon, and was hesitant to fire. The crisis on the Niagara was over.[10]

General Macomb released Wool from his inspection responsibilities and assigned him to active duty to assist Scott in policing the Canadian border. As in the Cherokee country, Wool enjoyed the rank and pay of a full brigadier. Scott sent his senior aide, Bvt. Lt. Col. William J. Worth, to cooperate with the civil authorities in the Detroit area, and instructed Wool to proceed to Plattsburgh and act in the same capacity there. Insurgent leaders were actively seeking recruits, collecting arms, and making demonstrations in northern New York and Vermont, where there had been clashes with American authorities. In December, a party of some two hundred American and Canadian patriots had crossed the line north of Swanton, Vermont, heading for Montreal. Near Moore's Corners, Canadian militia ambushed the group and sent them scurrying back to the United States. On the last day of 1837, Louis J. Papineau, former speaker of the assembly at Montreal and patriot leader in Lower Canada, boldly addressed a large crown at Middlebury, Vermont, urging militancy.[11]

On January 23, 1838, Wool left Troy by stage for Vermont, traveling with his servant, James and two officers. He carried instructions to confer with Vermont governor Silas H. Jenison regarding American involvement in the border unrest. If needed, Wool could call out a volunteer militia battalion of five companies or less for brief service to preserve neutrality. The Act of 1818, particularly Section 8, made it illegal to organize on American soil a military expedition against any nation at peace with the United States. Scott placed $4,000 at Wool's disposal "for immediate wants." Second Lt. William Smith, Corps of Engineers, would act as Wool's aide-de-camp and adjutant, and First Lt. Morris S. Miller, Third Artillery, would handle quartermaster and commissary duties. Scott advised Jenison that he was sending an officer of "discretion and experience" to Vermont to keep the peace. He urged the governor to cooperate with Wool.[12]

Wool, Smith, and Miller reached Shoreham, Vermont, not far from Lake Champlain, by coach at midnight on a frigid January 23. Here Governor Jenison, as promised, joined them in the growing community. As they rumbled along in the darkness, passing Burlington and heading north for the village of St. Albans, Wool questioned the governor about recent events. He particularly wanted to know what efforts federal civil officials—district attorneys, marshals, customs collectors—had made to curb border excitement. The next day, at St. Albans, less than ten miles south of the Canadian border, Wool and Jenison met briefly with a group of citizens who had requested federal assistance to keep the peace. They boarded a stage, visited the villages of Highgate and Swanton, and decided to call a public meeting in the town hall at St. Albans on January 26.[13]

Local citizens crowded into the meeting. Many were out-spoken. "The warmth with which they expressed themselves of the acts of [pro-British] royalists, the numerous tales of violence and barbarity . . . and the eagerness with which they caught at the least speck that might stain their character," Lieutenant Smith later recalled, "showed them to be either wholly unwilling or incapable of judging their conduct or their actions." The Vermonters had no problem with regular army officers on the frontier, but they did not want them interfering with patriot activities. Wool spoke frankly to the crowd. He doubted that the patriots would succeed in their endeavors. The general lectured his listeners on the nature and value of republican institutions, carefully avoiding all mention of supplying arms. After the meeting, Jenison left for the state capital at Montpelier, but Wool and his aides remained in St. Albans.[14]

Wool wrote Scott that the Vermont border was quiet. Patriot sympathizers in the villages and farms, however, anxiously watched developments in Upper Canada. If the patriots were successful there, leaders and sympathizers in the St. Albans salient planned to gather men and march on Montreal. If it became necessary to arm the militia, Wool notified the federal arsenal at Vergennes, south of Burlington, they should set aside 500 muskets and 20,000 cartridges.[15]

On January 29, the general tested the waters. He opened communication with Capt. James Botham, the British commander of the garrison at Missisquoi Bay, at the head of Lake Champlain. Wool complained that Canadian soldiers and armed civilians were frequently crossing into Vermont to raid and harass the citizens. Such forays must stop. Botham said he had no knowledge of Canadians harassing the American border towns. Moreover, his force at Missisquoi Bay had orders "to prevent or repel" hostile incursions. They were not involved in any act of aggression.[16]

Wool reported to Sarah on his social activities. "Don't be jealous because the old folks are [a] little kind to me during my stay in this Country, I mean the old Ladies, who think I *look remarkably young considering how old I am*," he wrote teasingly. "As for the young girls, you know I don't look at them, however much they look at me. I always turn my back upon their pretty faces." Wool predicted that he would be home within two weeks.[17]

While the Vermont frontier was quiet, Wool attended to public relations. He sent copies of his military correspondence to local editors, believing his statements would soothe citizens' feelings. He also shared information with friends. He mailed Erastus Corning a clip from a Democratic newspaper criticizing Van Buren's neutral stand on the patriot issue and condemning the weak federal presence on the border. Wool thought he could preserve calm without calling up the militia—which could save the government $100,000. "I presume I shall receive no thanks for it," he said.[18]

In early February, the situation suddenly changed. Across Lake Champlain, patriot leaders were active in and around Plattsburgh. Governor Jenison was fearful the insurgents might seize the Vergennes Arsenal in Vermont. An explosion north of the village of Champlain and near the border jangled nerves. Some seventy "roguish boys" pulled a sled with a log "cannon" to Perry's Mills, within a half mile of a Canadian encampment near Odletown. When the soldiers drilled, the boys mocked them. They tramped about, brandished wooden swords and blew tin horns, then set a slow fuse to the gunpowder in the "cannon" and ran. The explosion rocked the village and created an alarm that took hours to settle. Wool informed Governor Marcy that he was investigating every incident and every rumor. Lieutenant Smith had gone to Plattsburgh and Lieutenant Miller to Montpelier to talk with people there, and he had hired "agents" to roam the countryside. Wool had even offered to pay federal marshals and district attorneys in northern New York and Vermont to seek information on suspicious individuals.[19]

By February 9, Wool moved his headquarters from St. Albans back to Plattsburgh. The village had changed little since the desperate days of 1814. The general and his staff took lodgings at an inn and sought out United States Deputy Marshal Hiram Cady and other federal officials residing there. Two patriot leaders, Robert Nelson and Cyrille-Hector-Octave Côté, both physicians and members of the legislative assembly in Lower Canada (Montreal), had been seeking local support and collecting arms and ammunition in and around Plattsburgh for several weeks.[20]

Wool sought out Nelson and advised him to leave Plattsburgh and return to Canada. He warned that organizing and arming a force in that area to invade a friendly country would violate the "law of the land." Treaties and neutrality acts were part of this law, and Wool added that he would draw upon them to prevent hostile expeditions. This meeting and conversation quickly appeared in the Vermont newspapers. The *Middlebury Argus* pronounced Wool's interpretation of the neutrality laws as novel, for he apparently "consulted the spirit of intentions more than the letter of the law." Other papers chimed in. "We are told," said the *Montpelier Patriot,* that the general "has threatened to order or force, all the leading patriots, in a certain quarter, out of the country, and to arrest a distinguished refugee." Would he actually compel "these oppressed exiles to leave this free soil?" Was this the way the federal government protected those who had been "driven from their homes, their property confiscated, and prices set upon their heads, and who have violated none of our laws?" If so, then allegiance to such a government was impossible. Neither Scott, Wool—nor even the president of the United States—could enforce such "tyrannical decrees" in

Vermont. The editor exhorted his readers to join the patriot cause, "cross the line of 45 immediately" and help establish a free government in Lower Canada.[21]

Wool took the offensive against the patriots. He urged his agents to ferret out patriot plans and sent Col. St. John B. L. Skinner of the militia to investigate patriot activities in Ogdensburg, New York, on the St. Lawrence. In Plattsburgh, Wool tried to raise a volunteer company for short-term service, but only a few men came forward. On February 14, he, Marshall Cady, and Daniel Kellogg, the U.S. district attorney for Vermont, spent the day scouring villages and countryside for muskets, ammunition, and a cannon cached in barns.[22]

Wool learned from informants that MacKenzie and Van Rensselaer, the two American patriot leaders, had been in Plattsburgh to confer with Nelson, the Canadian patriot. They planned to collect and arm groups of refugees at French Creek, near Ogdensburg, and attack Kingston, Canada, and also Derby and Troy, Vermont. They were to assemble at Three Rivers, Canada, to join the main thrust from Champlain through Odletown. The conspirators mailed copies of their plans to partisans in Ohio and Michigan, hoping their western supporters might create a diversion. In Plattsburgh, citizens were buying supplies and had starting west for Watertown and Ogdensburg.[23]

The general hunted for more information to plan his next move. He sifted through reports from Sir John Colborne, governor of Lower Canada, from Lieutenant Miller, who recently returned from Watertown, and from citizen informers. The Kingston raid and Troy invasion, Wool believed, were diversions. The main attack would be from the Plattsburgh district. For the moment, he pretended concern about the thrust at Kingston. He informed Colonel Skinner at Watertown of the patriots' plans and told him to urge federal officials in the vicinity—the customs collector, deputy marshal, and district attorney—to break up the operation. If two hundred or more armed patriots assembled, Wool wanted Brig. Gen. James J. Brazelton, commanding the Forty-ninth New York Militia, to call up a battalion and disperse the insurgents.[24]

On February 22, Wool received an alarming letter from Vermont Attorney General George B. Manser. A sleigh had left the Vermont capital at Montpelier for Plattsburgh, carrying two cannons, seventy muskets, and twenty kegs of gunpowder. The muskets had been purchased in stores in Orange County, Vermont, and the gunpowder in Montpelier. Wool moved quickly. Distrusting the local militia, he asked Brig. Gen. Autos I. Bristol, commanding the Forty-second New York Militia Regiment, to recruit two companies of volunteer infantry in the Plattsburgh area. When Bristol had trouble raising men, Wool turned to another regiment and eventually had the required companies.[25]

The delay worked to Wool's advantage. On February 25, 1838, a Sunday, an agent brought him a letter that had been intercepted. Dr. Nelson had written J. B. Ryan, a patriot "captain" at Derby, Vermont, that everything was proceeding as planned. MacKenzie had seized Kingston, and Sir John Colborne was shifting his forces west to that salient. Wool made plans to leave the next day for the St. Lawrence. Nelson assured Ryan that he had abundant "forces and means" at Plattsburgh, and instructed him to move his men from Derby into Canada and join him at Three Rivers. Nelson planned to cross the line on the evening of February 28. Wool doubtless chuckled at the rumor he had started concerning his departure. He now had precise knowledge of Nelson's plans and began assembling a makeshift "army."[26]

Wool sent small mounted patrols with orders to check on the icy roads north to the boundary and stop and search all sleighs. A detachment began combing the countryside for caches of arms and munitions. A band of cavalry rode west along the Chateauguay road to Ransom, while another followed Lake Champlain towards Keeseville. Lieutenant Miller collected sleighs and teams in neighboring villages and farms to transport Wool's forces.[27]

On Monday morning, February 26, the general tightened his grip on the area. The night before, patriots had broken into the state arsenal in Elizabethtown, New York, forty miles south of Plattsburg, and carried off muskets, bayonets, and pistols. To augment his forces, Wool sent Miller across the head of Lake Champlain into Vermont to enroll a volunteer company at the villages of Alburgh and Swanton. Near dusk came a lucky break. At Chazy Landing, New York, a patrol seized Charles G. Bryant, Nelson's artillery leader, and a six-pounder cannon with five loads of powder and shells. Nelson shifted his thrust into Canada, and immediately left Alburgh Springs, Vermont.[28]

On Tuesday, February 27, Wool arrived at Chazy Landing from Plattsburgh with a half dozen sleighs loaded with arms. Along the road, curiosity seekers, many bound for the patriot camp on the border at Alburgh Springs, jeered as his party passed. All Plattsburgh "appeared to have left their homes to see the sport anticipated in Canada," Wool wrote Sarah. Many citizens boasted of "how cleverly I had been deceived, giving great praise to Nelson, Côté, and others for their generalship." They little knew that "I was at that moment preparing to *destroy their prospects and their hopes of another republic*." At Chazy, Wool wrote Secretary of War Poinsett: "I shall make a move this evening. Which I trust will be decisive."[29]

At dusk Wool set his forces in motion. A column of one hundred men picked up muskets, ammunition, and bayonets from boxes on the sleds and climbed into a line of sleighs. Led by Col. J. W. R. Bromley, the forces started for Alburgh Springs, fourteen miles to the east. In Alburgh and Swanton, one company each promised support. Wool and Lieutenant Smith traveled through the glistening snow in a covered rig. After a two-hour ride in the darkness, they saw dozens of campfires in the distance and quickened their pace. The patriots, estimated to number as many as one thousand, had detected Wool's approach and fled. A majority headed for Mauser's

Landing, near Swanton, and for Hog Island on Lake Champlain, leaving a party of three hundred behind with the supplies. Before Wool could organize a pursuit, the New York volunteers with him suddenly halted their teams. The temperature had plunged to twenty degrees below zero—and they were cold, tired, and hungry. They also disliked being in Vermont. The Swanton recruits also refused to proceed. With this impasse, Wool had no alternative but to order the men to return to their respective villages. In the bitter cold, he and Smith rode on to Alburgh.[30]

On the afternoon of February 28, Wool, with a small mounted escort, rode into Nelson's camp at Alburgh Springs. He passed through groups of men huddled around campfires and was directed to a house where Nelson and Côté was staying. The little general demanded entrance and stepped inside a smoke-filled room crowded with heavily armed men. When Nelson appeared, Wool, with an "air, voice, and manner peculiar to him," a relative later wrote, lectured the scowling audience on the illegality of their actions, and advised them to call off their "invasion." Nelson replied in an amiable manner and promised to disperse his men. Upon leaving, the general posted a man to watch the house. Nelson and his followers, almost one-half of them American, departed into the darkness.[31]

Early the next morning—March 1—Wool learned that during the night Nelson had crossed the line to Caldwell Manor with five hundred armed men and several cannons. The general immediately sent express riders racing to his commanders in Champlain, Swanton, and Alburgh and by noon, he had gathered 160 men at Alburgh. With Capt. James Platt's Swanton company in the lead, Wool began moving by sleigh through deep snow for the border. In the distance, he saw smoke from Nelson's camp. Rumors were that the patriot leader had planted a banner proclaiming Lower Canada free and issued a declaration of independence. Nelson's situation, however, was tenuous. Wool had seized most of his ammunition at Alburgh, and British troops, with Canadian militia, was marching for the manor.[32]

Wool sent Nelson an ultimatum. More than a thousand British troops were advancing from three directions on Caldwell Manor, the nearest less than six miles away. Nelson must make a decision. He could surrender to Wool and be delivered to civil authorities—or he could stay and fight the British. If Nelson retreated under arms, Wool would attack him. About two o'clock in the afternoon, Nelson surrendered. A line of an estimated six hundred men began crossing the border into Vermont with their arms. Soon a column of sleighs and sleds carrying those who had surrendered headed for St. Albans. The general placed Nelson and Côté in his covered sleigh and climbed into a nearby rig. Fourteen armed men on horseback rode along as a security guard.[33]

Wool entered St. Albans the next morning, passing small groups of sullen-faced citizens on the streets. In one instance, several bystanders defiantly pointed rifles at the general, but companions pushed their weapons aside. At the courthouse, he turned Nelson and Côté over to civil authorities. Each posted a $3,000 bond to appear in court in May at Windsor to answer charges of neutrality violation, then left for Plattsburgh. With the countryside in an uproar, two British officers arrived in St. Albans to discuss the situation with Wool. When the officers tried to return north, a mob in Swanton attempted to seize their arms and pelted them with snowballs. Wool sent soldiers to escort the visitors to the line. With threats of assassination in the air, he sent the Vermont companies home to await discharge while he and Lieutenant Smith returned to Plattsburgh.[34]

The disposition of the contraband that Wool had collected before the Nelson invasion caused problems. On March 4, an "agitator" in Plattsburgh obtained a court order to reclaim his weapons, and a deputy sheriff attempted to serve a writ of replevin on Wool at his quarters at the inn. When the deputy threatened to arrest the general and his aides, the feisty little officer dared him to try and the civil official left. After nightfall on March 5, Lieutenant Smith left the village of Champlain with several sleds bearing the controversial arms caches, heading south for the Vergennes Arsenal. A citizen party tried to intercept him, but his guard drove them off and the shipment arrived safely.[35]

More excitement came in the border town of Troy, Vermont. A few days after the Nelson debacle, patriots tried to seize a government arms shipment from Montreal to Canadian settlers near the line. In a sharp fight near the village of Potton, they captured six muskets, then fled, leaving one patriot dead. On March 4, Wool dispatched Colonel Bromley and Lieutenants Smith and Sawyer with a Vermont detachment to gauge and calm the feelings in the district of Troy and Derby. On March 16, Bromley returned to Plattsburgh and left Sawyer at Troy to keep watch on the two towns.[36]

To avoid unnecessary expenses, Wool now discharged the volunteers and militia. Unauthorized levies—the problem he faced in the Cherokee country—had occurred again. The day he raced east to break up the patriot camp at Alburgh Springs, Brig. General Bristol, at Plattsburgh, had called out his entire brigade of militia. Within forty-eight hours, Wool cancelled the muster. In Vermont, commanders also called out companies that were not needed and were sent home. This confusion caused Miller, Wool's disbursing officer, numerous headaches in claims for rations, lodgings, teams, sleighs, and wagons. Some of the expenses were extraordinary. For example, in several instances, citizens, perhaps harkening back to the Revolutionary War, had refused to rent barns and sheds to shelter his volunteers, so Wool briefly boarded his men in private residences at $2.50 per week. Despite poor records and a lack of receipts, Miller had by April discharged four of the six New York companies, the two Vermont companies, and furloughed the rest. Wool kept a detachment on duty at Champlain and one at Troy for the time being.[37]

James Platt's Swanton company tried Wool's patience. From the beginning, he had been suspicious of these men when he had been pressured to accept them. Platt had escorted the patriot munitions to Vergennes, and lost a box of ammunition in transit. On March 12, Wool accused him of theft. The captain hotly denied responsibility, saying his orders were to escort the sleighs, not to guard their loading and unloading. "You were as much bound to protect the property until after it had left the sleighs as any other time," the general snapped. If Platt valued his "character and future standing in society," he would find and return the box. There was no response and the troublesome Swanton company was discharged on March 18.[38]

Wool now turned his attention to the Canadian refugees living in American towns along the border. He tackled this problem when twenty French Canadians petitioned for permission to return home. The general presented their case to Governor Sir John Colborne. Nearly one thousand uprooted Canadians, he stated, wanted to return to their farms and families. With no means of support, they were fair prey "to corrupt and designing men who hang upon the borders." Their return home might reduce the continuing friction. Colborne agreed to cooperate. He instructed the civil magistrate at Odletown to interview the refugees, and, if not found objectionable, to furnish passports. But he refused to accept those living at Troy and Derby. Two British officers and a magistrate visited Wool at Champlain to arrange details, and on March 23, refugees began returning to Canada. Wool had opened a door for those displaced persons wishing to resume regular livelihoods.[39]

While the refugee problem headed toward a peaceful solution, the capture of Nelson and Côté stirred a hornet's nest. Wool received scurrilous letters (most of which he burned) from every quarter. Upon hearing of the surrender, the general wrote Sarah that citizens were pouring forth "their hellish feelings . . . threatening me with every species of violence even to assassination." In Plattsburgh, there was a call to burn the general in effigy; at Chazy, a mob smeared the home, ferry, and office of a friend of Wool's with tar and feathers. At Swanton, the cry went up to burn Wool alive "for preventing the establishing of a new Republic." Newspapers in New York fanned the flames. The *Plattsburgh Whig* denounced the general for drawing an "assumed" authority from the neutrality acts and from Van Buren's instructions to stop, search, and arrest peaceful citizens on the public roads. Such actions smacked of martial law.[40]

Wool relished newspaper duels. The friendly *Plattsburgh Republican* declared that the general had exercised authority explicitly granted to him. Under the neutrality acts, the president could empower army officers to raise volunteers to uphold the law, and, in ordering federal officials to prevent foreigners from organizing hostile expeditions on American soil, he conveyed the right to the military to make arrests and detain suspects. Wool sent clips of the *Republican* article, probably written by

Lt. J. C. Moore, a temporary aide, to the Troy and Albany newspapers, the *National Intelligencer*, and the *Army and Navy Chronicle*. When the *Plattsburgh Whig* scolded Moore for supporting Wool, the general cautioned his subordinate to ignore "the article in relation to yourself." A reply "will only tend to add fuel to the flames." The newspaper censure of Wool's actions soon waned.[41]

In late March 1838, Scott extended Wool's military jurisdiction west to Sackets Harbor. The general promptly dispatched Colonel Bromley, his acting inspector general, with a letter to Bvt. Col. Alexander Cummings, Second Infantry, stationed at Sackets. Wool requested Cummings to keep an eye on the towns along the St. Lawrence north to Ogdensburg. On April 2, Bromley reported that William Johnston, a patriot sympathizer, was building boats and collecting arms at French Creek for an attack on Kingston, Canada. Wool instructed Cummings to investigate the activity and, if necessary, call out the county militia to break up the patriot camp.[42]

News of these instructions created a ripple in Washington. Scott endorsed Wool's concern about Johnston, but he questioned the need for militia. Earlier, he had authorized the muster of two battalions in New York, but preferred not to raise militia at random on the frontier. Furthermore, Cummings legally could not break up patriot camps. Congress had just passed a new neutrality act, on March 10, which specifically placed the enforcement of its provisions in civil hands. With Scott's views circulating in the national capital, South Carolina congressman Hugh S. Legaré cautioned Wool. Scott had publicly complimented his subordinate on his energy and vigilance, but he "rather feared" that Wool had "anticipated" additions that had not been incorporated into the new act. "I have done nothing that will not be sustained by the laws of the land," the peppery little general replied, "and if I had violated them not a rascal of those who have so recently trampled underfoot all law would dare to prosecute me." Wool felt the new legislation was defective. Under it, the military could seize arms destined for patriots in Canada, but it could not prevent the enlistment of persons to invade that country. To end the border unrest, Wool agreed that General Macomb should deploy regulars along the New York-Vermont boundary with Canada as soon as possible.[43]

On Sunday, May 19, Wool and three officers arrived by stage in Windsor, Vermont, to attend a United States Circuit Court hearing regarding alleged violation of neutrality laws by Nelson and Côté. The general, apprehensive about the outcome, would serve as a witness. At a recent meeting at St. Albans, a group of patriot leaders—Nelson, Côté, Bryant, Alexander McLeod, and several others—had discussed plans to renew the border warfare. From the beginning of the hearing, it was obvious that witnesses called to testify against Nelson and Côté had been intimidated and threatened. At the hearing, the judge first listed the charges for the jury and reviewed the neutrality legislation. The organization of forces on American soil violated no laws.

There had to be evidence of "a combination within our territory to concentrate" a force on the other side of the line. Wool and others testified at length, but the jury, after a short deliberation, opted for acquittal. Nelson and Côté were joyously free. Disgusted, Wool departed for New York City.[44]

Before the hearing, Nelson told reporters he had been the victim of duplicity. Prior to every move, he had consulted with District Attorney Kellogg about the legality of his actions. Nelson also alleged that Wool had tried to ingratiate himself with the patriots. In fact—said Nelson—the general offered to resign his commission and, at a salary of $25,000, lead the insurgents in their revolution against the British! Upon reading the allegation, Wool quickly penned a denial and mailed copies to newspapers in eastern cities. Nelson subsequently denied that he had made any such accusation.[45]

The hostility sputtered on. At a dinner in Vermont honoring Nelson, the guests raised their glasses and gave a toast: "Brigadier General Wool—more distinguished in the late war with Great Britain as a flogger of American soldiers, than a fearless leader against those of the enemy." When the toast appeared in print, Edwin Croswell, editor of the *Albany Argus*, jumped to Wool's defense. In glowing prose, he reviewed his fellow Trojan's exploits at Queenstown. He soundly condemned those Americans "base enough to mingle in their cups vile slanders of him, while the same cups are quaffed in honor of a renegade who came hither openly and boldly to trample upon our laws."[46]

In late May 1838, General Macomb restored Wool to duty as an inspector general. Bvt. Brig. Gen. Hugh Brady, at Detroit, assumed command along the Canadian border in Scott's Eastern Division. Wool seemed chagrined by the change. He believed a strong federal presence was needed in northern New York and probably hoped to command the Eastern Division while Scott was supervising Cherokee removals. The need for an active commander in northwestern New York soon became apparent. On the evening of May 29, William Johnston and a group of patriots, disguised as Indians, rushed aboard the Canadian steamboat *Sir Robert Peel* when it stopped at Wells' Island on the St. Lawrence to take on firewood for its engine. Shouting "Remember the *Caroline*," they put the passengers ashore and set fire to the vessel and sank it. With the border again in an uproar, Wool returned to Washington to regain his command only to learn that General Macomb, although in ill health, had rushed to Sackets Harbor in the disturbed district. Fortunately, the outcry over the *Peel* affair soon subsided.[47]

Wool was in Washington on June 6, when he dined at the White House with President Van Buren. He wrote Sarah that he had attended "quite a party." Indeed, prominent New York politicians and several foreign ministers attended. A few days later, his visit turned sour. He was already frustrated by an assignment Macomb had given him, in May, to make a detailed reconnaissance of the disputed territory between Maine's northern boundary and Canada. The governor of Maine had badgered the Van Buren administration for this work. Wool argued that not an inspector but the officer "assigned to the command of the Frontier and who is responsible for its defenses" should be given this task. Even worse, he learned in Washington that, contrary to what Macomb promised, he would not draw brigadier's pay while in the field. Stung by the broken promise, Wool drafted a hot letter to two New York congressmen. He had "an enemy in camp," the inspector asserted, and he was the "First Officer of the army." The letter was never sent.[48]

Wool had policed the New York–Vermont border for five months by trying to surveil and dissuade insurgents from breaking neutrality laws. Convinced that a precipitous act was in the making, he called out volunteers, placed the area under de facto martial law, and threatened force to halt potential crimes. His actions provoked a storm of protests, which he largely ignored. Wool had indeed exercised an almost autonomous command, for Secretary of War Poinsett was too sick for regular correspondence and General Scott, though he required reports, gave few instructions. At the border, however, Wool found, for all his command, that he could not resolve the troubles as long as his "argument and address" carried no impression of authority. The inspector now turned his attention to another boundary problem.[49]

Maine's northeastern border had been a bone of contention since the Treaty of Paris in 1783. The state of Maine and province of New Brunswick had clashed over two districts along the St. Johns River: the Aroostook River settlement on the south side of the river, and the Madawaska Valley on the Canadian side, near present-day Edmundston. After statehood in 1820, Maine cast anxious eyes toward both districts. State authorities ordered Canadian timber-cutters out of the Aroostook country in 1825, and several years later tried to attach the Madawaska country to newly formed Penobscot County. The Canadians protested and seized the county census taker. The disputes sputtered along until the British, in early 1838, promised a plan to end the controversy. The Maine legislature agreed to consider it, but before they debated the proposal, Governor Edward Kent requested the federal government make a military reconnaissance of the state boundaries with Canada. Should the deliberations fail and hostilities ensue, Maine wanted an increased federal presence. The Van Buren administration agreed to a survey and to draft a plan to defend the state. Macomb gave Wool the assignment.[50]

In late June 1838, the inspector arrived at the state capital, Augusta. He discussed his instructions with Governor Kent, and met two topographical engineers, who would accompany him on the reconnaissance—Maj. James D. Graham and First Lt. Joseph E. Johnston. Joined by Gen. James Irish, a militia officer who would act as guide, the party traveled by stage through the woods to Bangor. Wool's mission was no secret. "This distinguished officer," the *Portland Advertiser* noted, "has been sent by the War Department . . . for the purpose of making a reconnaissance and selecting the suitable positions for the establishment of posts to protect the boundary of Maine from foreign aggression." The new forts would hopefully "speed the settlement of the boundary dispute." In Bangor, while Graham collected supplies, Wool studied maps of the mountain terrain south of Quebec. "The Maine people are determined to have the whole country or nothing," he wrote friends in Washington on July 2.[51]

Wool's party left Bangor with pack animals on the morning of July 3 for Moosehead Lake, which lay about 120 miles to the northwest, on the east slope of the mountain range dividing Maine from Lower Canada. Reaching the Kennebec River, the party followed a wilderness trace along its banks into a largely uninhabited region with forests of maple, beech, pine, and spruce. The summer days were long, warm, and pleasant, but the nights were cool. A tough campaigner, Wool bedded down using his coat and two or three blankets as cover. Ascending to the headwaters of the Kennebec, they reached Moosehead Lake. This sprawling body of water, Wool wrote home, was dotted with small islands, while moose grazed along the shoreline. Swarms of voracious flies and mosquitoes attacked the men and animals. The travelers circled to the west, then climbed north into the mountains. Fourteen miles from the crest, possibly near present-day Moose River Village, they carefully scanned the countryside with telescopes. They particularly studied the Kennebec or Canada Trace. This pathway left the river about thirty miles below at Three Forks, ran some fifteen miles up the mountains, and descended on the Canadian side for nearly eighty miles to the St. Lawrence River across from Quebec.[52]

The officers discussed strategies for meeting a British invasion from the vicinity of Quebec. Enemy troops must use the Canada Trace, for it was the only practical highway from the St. Lawrence into western Maine. Wool believed the Canada road could be blocked by stationing two infantry companies near their campsite, with an observation post near the crest of the mountain. While exploring the forest north of Moosehead Lake, Graham and Johnston found evidence of work on an alternate trail, but Wool scoffed at the idea of a secondary road being constructed. No commander "who understood his profession," he later reported to Poinsett, would send troops into a great virgin forest where no forage, provisions, or means of transportation were available. The result would be a disaster. Leaving Graham and Johnston to survey and sketch the area, Wool returned with General Irish to Bangor.[53]

On July 16, Wool and Governor Kent set out by stagecoach to visit the sensitive northeastern frontier. After two days travel up the Penobscot, they reached Hancock Barracks, at the border village of Houlton. To the north lay the disputed Aroostook country. Wool considered Houlton strategic to protecting Maine's claims. A major concentration of American troops there would make the British think twice about war. Returning south, he questioned Kent about Maine's eastern boundary, which ran down the St. Croix River to the Atlantic coast. The garrison at Eastport, near the coast and the only post in that sector, had been withdrawn. Back at Augusta, Wool and Kent discussed at length ways to increase the federal presence in Maine. In late July, the inspector sorted his notes and sailed for Boston.[54]

Several weeks later, Wool sent Secretary Poinsett a preliminary report on Maine's frontiers. He regarded three districts as critical in case of a British invasion. In the Moosehead country, the army should station two companies of regulars near Moose River, with a picket near the crest of the "highlands" to watch the Canada road. The "forks" of the Kennebec, down below, was an excellent site to assemble state militia to protect the road. To the northeast, Wool felt the garrison at Houlton should be increased to eight companies—six of infantry and two of artillery. In the southeastern part of Maine, near Calais, the government should build barracks and a large depot to accommodate an infantry regiment and two artillery companies. The site could also serve as a militia rendezvous. Two companies should reoccupy the post at Eastport. A federal arsenal at Bangor, plus fortifications at the entrance to the Penobscot and Kennebec Rivers, completed Wool's defense plan. In November, he received and forwarded a set of sketches and maps prepared by Graham to illustrate the recommendations. The study would prove useful during the negotiations of the Webster-Ashburton Treaty in 1842—and later.[55]

While he was working on the border of Maine, John Wool in August 1838 settled in a much-anticipated home in Troy. Three years before, he had paid a handsome sum of $15,000 for a three-story brick building at the southwest corner of First and Ferry Streets. The residence faced east near the square, and stood within sight of the location of the venerable Moulton Inn. When he bought the house, Wool leased the property until he was ready to move in. In February 1838, Sarah, anxious to leave Nassau for Troy, suggested that her niece Harriette; Harriette's husband, Isaac B. Hart; and Harriette's brother, John A. Griswold, join the Wool household. "I am attached to all, all are favourites, and especially Mrs. Hart," her husband said. "Therefore fix up the house and take them with you as your children." When the inspector returned from Maine in August, he selected a room for a library and installed his small marble statue of Cleopatra as a centerpiece. Officer-like, he handed out chores to the household. He instructed his two black servants, James and Thomas, to weed, cultivate, and keep the flower garden. They regularly must clean and daily sprinkle the front and side streets with water. He also advised Sarah about taxes. If a notice arrived, she must inform the assessor that her husband had no personal property to tax. "Most of my personal property is in bank stock," Wool said, "and what I have exclusive of bank stock does not amount to as much as I owe."[56]

In early January 1839, Wool left Troy for Washington. He was hoping to visit friends and follow a congressional debate on the army bill, introduced by Missouri

Senator Thomas Hart Benton. Benton wanted to enlarge the regular army, which he thought too thinly stretched by disturbances on the Canadian border, the sputtering campaign in Florida, and the expanding needs on the western frontier. Benton would increase the army to 14,000 men, raise soldiers' pay, and restructure the chain of command. Secretary of War Poinsett, a dynamic, reform-minded official, supported the legislation. The discussion also included the creation of a Corps of Topographical Engineers and a rejuvenated Ordnance Department. If the bill passed, certain powers of the aging commanding general of the army, Alexander Macomb, would be diminished and assumed by the secretary of war. Wool was pleased with the bill when he resumed his inspection duties in the spring of 1839.[57]

In early March of that year, Wool received orders to begin his annual tour. He traveled down the Atlantic coast with a small group of young officers (including Lt. Alexander S. Macomb, the general-in-chief's son, as aide-de-camp). They found the conditions of the major fortifications appalling. Rusting cannons sat on dilapidated carriages and platforms, powder magazines had leaky roofs, soldiers were sickly, and garrisons undermanned. At New Orleans, Wool planned a swing through the western posts. By early May, he had steamed up the Mississippi and made side trips to Fort Jesup on the Louisiana-Texas border, and Forts Gibson and Towson in the Indian Territory. At the time, Gibson was the largest post on the western frontier. Nine companies of the Fourth Infantry and four of the elite dragoons were stationed there. When the troops first passed in review, it was obvious there were problems. The dragoons had difficulty controlling their horses, especially during pistol exercises, and the men knew little about the use of the sword. Infantrymen (many recently returned from the Indian campaign in Florida) marched in incomplete uniforms and stumbled in company and battalion drills. From Fort Gibson, Wool went east to Fort Smith, thence back down the Mississippi to the Baton Rouge Arsenal. He again ascended the Mississippi all the way to Fort Snelling in what would become Dakota Territory, on the northern frontier of the old Louisiana Purchase in what would become Minnesota Territory. Continuing his inspection tour, he returned south down the river to Fort Crawford in Prarie du Chien on the east bank of the river in Wisconsin Territory, then Jefferson Barracks below St. Louis at Lemay, Missouri, and then the St. Louis Arsenal.[58]

In late July 1839, Wool made his way by steamer up the Missouri River to Fort Leavenworth, the eastern terminus of the Santa Fe Trail, where he talked at length with Col. Stephen W. Kearny, who had fought with him at Queenstown Heights in 1812. Kearny's dragoons maneuvered and performed carbine drills in expert fashion, but they had no training with the sword. To Wool, the saber was not an ornament—it was a special weapon. "The sword is the legitimate weapon of the cavalry," he observed, and troopers lacking skills with swords were little

Cartography by Carol Zuber-Mallison/ZM Graphics, Inc.

more than mounted infantry. Wool promised he would have a swordmaster sent to Leavenworth.[59]

Wool spoke frankly in his 1839 inspection report. From New Orleans to Maine, the army was in disarray. On the coast the artillerymen had difficulty firing cannon, at the western garrisons many officers were on detached service, and in Florida, nearly four thousand regulars were waging a senseless war with the Seminoles. Wool recommended that troops be given better training, that officers return to their units, and that new policies be tried in Florida. Macomb echoed Wool's comments in his annual report that fall.[60]

In February 1840, Wool left Washington to inspect the Army of the South in Florida and see the Second Seminole War firsthand. For over five years, the federal government had attempted, through treaties, agreements, and force, to remove some eight hundred Seminoles in Florida to a home west of the Mississippi. A succession of commanders—Scott, Gaines, and Jesup—had limited success. In late 1837, Col. Zachary Taylor, Seventh Infantry, who had been serving under Jesup, took command, with headquarters at Fort Brooke on Tampa Bay. Taylor commanded over 2,800 regulars plus several volunteers and militia units. He launched a vicious campaign east of Tampa to hunt down defiant Indians and was promoted to brigadier general in the Army of the South. He then focused his attention on an area west of a line running north from Tampa Bay to St. Augustine. Laid out in twenty-mile-wide squares, each had a small stockade and several huts in the center, each housing twenty men (one-half mounted) and an officer. At the time of Wool's visit, some fifty of these stations were active, escorting travelers, making patrols, protecting soldiers who were building roads, and occasionally scouting for hostiles.[61]

On February 10, 1840, Wool landed at St. Augustine to begin an inspection tour of the military garrisons in the state. He dispatched a letter to Brigadier General Taylor stating the purpose of his mission and saying he was hoping to meet Taylor during his tour. The inspector boarded a stage from St. Augustine west to the small settlement of Garey's Ferry and Fort Heileman, an operations base for the Second Dragoons, commanded by Col. David E, Twiggs. Wool inspected the garrison and the ordnance depot. He also questioned Twiggs about the continuing attempt to round up the Seminoles in Florida for removal west. Scattered in small bands, Seminoles watched army movements and emerged from the swamps to plunder trains and attack travelers. This guerilla warfare seemed to have no end.[62]

Five days later, Wool continued inland to the headwaters of the Suwannee River and then down that stream to its mouth. There he boarded a government revenue cutter made available to Taylor and sailed north to Deadman's Bay, where he fell sick with ague and fever. On March 2, while aboard ship, the weary officer described his adventures to a family friend. Since his arrival in Florida, he had "traveled two hundred miles on horseback in search of troops . . . engaged in hunting . . . Indians, but without success." Daily trips ranged up to thirty miles and were exhausting. Florida was a "sandbank thrown up by the ocean," he said, with swamps, hammocks, lagoons, and ponds. Pestilence was everywhere and Indian removal had been "miserably conducted." It could have been completed at least three times in the past. The principal problem was the lack of "requisite energy; efficiency and enterprise." With five to six thousand regulars, "rightly and effectively directed," the operations could have been over much earlier. A commander was needed to "diffuse the right spirit, especially among the officer corps, to end the struggle."[63]

After nearly a week aboard the revenue cutter at Deadman's Bay, Wool sailed north to the Florida panhandle. At a post near Tallahassee, he inspected infantry and dragoon units recently returned from the "swamps and marshes" to the south. "I never saw a more beggardly looking lot of fellows," he wrote a friend on March 2. Their clothing had been literally "torn off their backs" from chasing Seminoles. Moreover, Taylor's army was sick. Half of the men in the twenty-five companies he inspected were unfit for duty, and at least two thousand would soon be needed to fill depleted ranks. Many of the officers were too old and infirm. Volunteer companies were "dead weight," Wool said.[64]

Crossing the peninsula back to St. Augustine, the inspector sailed down the Atlantic coast, stopping at a few posts, especially Key Biscayne. Entering the Gulf of Mexico and up the west coast, Wool landed at Fort Brooke in Tampa Bay. Here he was unable to see General Taylor, who was ill with fever (malaria) and who had asked for reassignment. Wool inspected the garrison, noting that the ordnance building was cluttered with muskets, swords, and cartridge boxes—all "worthless." Proceeding north, Wool ended his tour up the coast and inland at Fort Fanning on a big bend of the Suwannee River on March 26.[65]

On May 2, 1840, Secretary of War Poinsett replaced Taylor with Brig. Gen. Walker K. Armistead. Most of the artillery regiments in Florida were ordered north to forts on the Canadian border. In line with Wool's advice, Armistead concentrated nine hundred men at Fort King, in north central Florida and divided his forces into nine units to operate independently in the field. But the hostilities dragged on until Col. William J. Worth assumed command and recommended that military operations cease. The expense to round up and deport several hundred Indians was too great. The "war" ended in August 1842.[66]

On June 25, 1841, General Macomb, second commanding general of the United States Army, died of apoplexy. A scramble for his position immediately began, with Bvt. Gen. Winfield Scott, commanding the army's Eastern Division, the most likely contender. Wool was a pallbearer at the Macomb funeral, and remained in Washington to mount a vigorous campaign to capture Scott's command. The appointment carried the pay and allowances of a regular brigadier general. Wool could count on the political influence of the New York congressional delegation, thirty-five strong, but he sought additional support in the Tyler administration and the Senate, which reviewed and confirmed the appointment of general officers. As early as June 29, while Scott's elevation to head of the army was pending, Wool submitted a package of letters to Secretary of War John Bell, supporting his application for division command. Other pledges soon followed. On July 5, with Senate approval, Scott became a regular major general and in charge of the army. Four days later, President Tyler nominated John Wool to succeed Scott.[67]

Nothing was left to chance. In a letter to Secretary Bell, Wool dismissed the claims of Bvt. Brig. Gens. Henry Atkinson and Hugh Brady to the vacant position. They had received their brevets before him, but they could not handle the responsibilities of division command. Atkinson was physically incapacitated, and Brady was seventy-three and partially deaf. Furthermore, both had enjoyed the privileges of department command and the pay and emoluments of regular brigadiers while holding brevet ranks. He had not.[68]

Bvt. Brig. Gen. Nathan Towson, the paymaster general, suddenly threw his hat in the ring. Towson's 1834 brevet had been an "outrage in the army," Wool angrily told Bell. If the paymaster based his claim for division command on his service in the War of 1812, he bristled, "I have some claim on that score myself." Scott entered the fray. He doubted Towson's ability to handle a division command and bluntly told Towson just that. Scott and Jesup both supported Wool, but several army bureau heads and influential politicians did not. Senators Thomas H. Benton and James Buchanan opposed his nomination. Earlier, Wool had chaired the court martial of Col. Joshua Brant, Benton's nephew. Buchanan favored Brady.[69]

Wool grew anxious. More than his career, his manliness seemed at stake. He had to succeed, he wrote to Sarah, "or lose standing and character." Success "makes the man in all things he undertakes, as well in politics as in war." He assured Sarah that he could count on "all Cabinet and cabinet ladies, the most respectable part of the citizens of Washington," along with a host of senators. In late August, Wool won the prize.[70]

On September 1, 1841, the adjutant general announced Wool's appointment as a regular brigadier general (retroactive to June 25) in command of the Eastern Division, with headquarters in Troy. Hugh Brady's Seventh Military Department was transferred to Edmund P. Gaines's Western Division, headquartered in New Orleans. The *New York Military Magazine* branded Wool's appointment an "outrage." He had "fluttered in the avenues of the Capitol decorated with smiles, courting the attention and influence of members of Congress." At Fort Smith, Arkansas, Gen. Zachary Taylor fumed that Wool had been promoted from staff to line "over the heads of several seniors, in violation of every principal of justice and propriety." But he envied the inspector because for over twenty years Wool "had enjoyed stationary domicile, nominal duties, and the opportunity to mass a large fortune." The grumbling within the officer corps, however, soon subsided.[71]

Within weeks of assuming his new responsibilities, Wool was briefly involved in the lingering aftermath of the Canadian border troubles. The patriots had continued their activities after he left the Lake Champlain frontier, but by December 1838, Macomb had stationed regulars in several of the border communities, and the unrest gradually ceased. As the patriot cause languished, state authorities arrested and prosecuted erstwhile leaders. A celebrated case concerned Alexander McLeod, a Canadian deputy sheriff, who allegedly participated in the burning of the *Caroline.* McLeod was apprehended in Lewiston, New York, and jailed at Whitesboro, near Utica. In February 1841, a grand jury indicted him for first degree murder and arson. The British minister protested the action, but Daniel Webster, appointed secretary of state, pronounced the case a local matter and refused to intervene. New York governor William H. Seward assigned Willis Hall, his attorney general, to prosecute McLeod, and asked a member of the state supreme court to preside at the trial, scheduled for Utica in October. Joshua Spencer, a popular New York lawyer, defended McLeod.[72]

In mid-September, Wool received orders to increase the military presence in the Utica vicinity. During the summer, the British had shifted troops along the New York boundary and were building new roads and barracks. With rumors of neutrality violations, Congress on September 4, appropriated $2,250,000 to bolster the defenses on Lake Ontario. With William Mackenzie and a group of patriots attending the trial, Governor Seward asked the Oneida County sheriff to increase the guard at the Whitesboro jail, while he alerted the local militia commander and asked Wool to remain nearby during the proceedings. The general arrived in Utica by train two weeks later with Lt. Horace Brooks of the Second Artillery. Soldiers were ordered to bolster the small force at the federal arsenal at Rome, New York, fifteen miles to the northwest. Wool placed Bvt. Capt. Robert Anderson, his assistant adjutant general in charge and left for his headquarters at Troy.[73]

The McLeod trial opened in Utica on October 4. At the judge's request, Wool had stationed fifty soldiers near town, and arranged with the Oneida County sheriff to take charge of local security. On October 12, after eight days of testimony, the jury deliberated twenty minutes and voted for acquittal. Four days later, the sheriff escorted McLeod to Lake Champlain, where he was placed on a steamer headed north to Plattsburgh. Days later in Montreal he was cheered and celebrated as a hero.[74]

Turning from the McLeod case, Wool faced numerous challenges during the months ahead as an army division commander. Unrest continued to simmer along the Canadian border from Maine to Buffalo, and in the southern climes the Florida "war" sputtered on endlessly without resolution. Wool viewed himself as a "housekeeper," his attention focused on forts, arsenals, military installations, and equipment. The War Department, at Scott's advice, moved troops into and around the Eastern and Western Divisions for campaigns, policing, and training. Inspections and reports required regular attention.

Wool did not shy away from politics. On February 22, 1842, he commented on the state of the nation in a letter to attorney Joshua A. Spencer. "When I reflect upon the conduct of those, who at the present day direct the affairs of our beloved country," he said, "I voluntarily ask myself, is it possible that such a being as [George] Washington . . . could have existed some fifty years since and directed the affairs of this, as it would now seem, doomed Republic?" The men ruling the nation "have lost sight of those great landmarks which should ever be kept steadily in view—virtue and honesty." The nation's commerce was neglected, its business depressed, and its finances unstable. It was no longer a crime to cheat, rob, or plunder. Under such appalling circumstances, how could the twenty-six states continue to exist as a nation?[75]

These had been eventful years. John Wool would not soon forget the anxious hours preceding Robert Nelson's surrender—or the opprobrium heaped upon him by irate newspaper editors. A brigadier sent forth to battle without an army, he had preserved the peace on a remote and unfriendly frontier by enlisting support wherever and whenever he could. The degree to which he succeeded was due to practical decisions and prompt actions, rather than measured policy. As commander of the Eastern Division, Wool now entered upon duties that brought new challenges and a wider perspective on the army. Memories of his days as an inspector and troubleshooter soon faded as he settled into the role of military administrator and looked forward to the honors of a senior command.

6

ACROSS THE RIO GRANDE WITH OLD FUSSY

On Friday, May 15, 1846, Wool abruptly left Troy on the Hudson River Railroad for New York, where he hurried south to Washington. News had reached the capital a few days earlier that Mexican soldiers had ambushed a dragoon detachment of Gen. Zachary Taylor's army on the distant Rio Grande. Reasserting the claim to the Rio Grande as the boundary that came with the annexation of Texas, the president asked Congress on May 11 to declare that a state of war existed, a war that Mexico had already announced, contending that "American blood had been shed on American soil." Three days later, Congress strongly endorsed James K. Polk's request, 174 to 14 in the House of Representatives, and 40 to 2 in the Senate.

In Washington, President Polk, Secretary of War William L. Marcy, and Gen. Winfield Scott immediately began deliberating the best way to prosecute the war. Wool entered into the discussions at the White House on May 17. Polk hoped General Taylor could drive any Mexican forces across the Rio Grande, which he insisted was the international boundary. A smaller column would march west along the Santa Fe Trail to occupy New Mexico before going on to California where a naval squadron would assist in seizing key ports on the Pacific. Polk wanted to seize both provinces and hold as much Mexican territory as possible in negotiating a peace and redrawing the borders between the two countries. Mexico would have no choice but to concede land and conclude that the United States had won the war.

Wool requested an active command, but a decision on his exact role in the forthcoming conflict was delayed. For the time being, Marcy relieved him from command of the Eastern Division and placed him in charge of mustering volunteer regiments in the Ohio Valley and lower Mississippi states for duty on the Rio Grande.[1]

When Congress declared war, it also increased the regular army from 6,562 to 17,812 men, approved Polk's request for 50,000 volunteers for twelve months' service, and appropriated ten million dollars for weapons and supplies. Two days later, the War Department began sending calls and quotas to governors in the midwestern and southern states for volunteer regiments of infantry and cavalry.[2]

While the nation mobilized for "Mr. Polk's war," Wool found himself in the maelstrom of Washington politics. Democrats grumbled about allowing Gen. Winfield Scott to command the army, for not only was he a Whig with presidential ambitions, but he also claimed that it would take several months to organize an expeditionary force. To quell opposition, President Polk supported a bill in Congress that would let him appoint six volunteer generals—two major generals and four brigadiers—and that had a rider to abolish Scott's office at the end of the war. Regular army officers became alarmed. Wool discussed the bill with Marcy and found him equivocal and vague. When he pressed for one of the new major general slots, his old friend hesitated. Wool declared that he would not serve under civilian generals, who sought only pay and political gain, and he left Marcy's office in a huff. Several days later Polk confided to his diary that Scott, Wool, and Adjutant Gen. Roger Jones were trying to defeat the army bill, for which he found their conduct "highly censurable." At their next meeting, Secretary Marcy urged Wool to distance himself from the controversy. Scott also removed himself from the fracas, and the bill quickly passed. Wool now tacked his sails. Influential Democrats urged him to claim Taylor's command since he outranked Taylor, but he backed away. On May 3, the Mexicans opened a barrage of artillery fire on Fort Texas from their positions on the opposite bank of the Rio Grande. With Taylor's victories on the plains at Palo Alto on May 9, 1846, and Resaca de la Palma the next day, he publicly endorsed Taylor's promotion to brevet major general.[3]

In late May, Wool made his way across the Appalachians to the Ohio Valley with instructions to superintend the muster of volunteers in six states—Ohio, Indiana, Illinois, Kentucky, Tennessee, and Mississippi. Inspector Generals George Croghan and Sylvester Churchill would assist him. Both men had experience and political clout. Like Wool, Croghan and Churchill were veterans of the War of 1812. Educated at the College of William and Mary, the Kentucky-born Croghan was a veteran of the 1811 Battle of Tippecanoe. Churchill had published a newspaper, the *Vermont Republican*, at Windsor, before joining the army as a first lieutenant in March 1812.

Wool immediately opened communication with the governors, requested them to select troop rendezvous, and sent requisitions to the army supply departments for drill manuals, equipment, arms, and ammunition. He advertised in state newspapers for subsistence and forage and sought contracts for steamboat transportation. Much of his attention focused on organizing a camp for the Ohio regiments near Cincinnati, while instructing Croghan to oversee the musters at Louisville, Memphis, and Vicksburg. Churchill performed similar duties at New Albany, Indiana, and Alton, Illinois. Quartermaster, commissary, and paymaster officers traveled with the two inspectors to keep records and establish procedures for issuing food and equipment.[4]

Wool regularly visited the state rendezvous. On June 10, at Louisville, he watched Croghan induct two Kentucky regiments, one mounted, into federal service. At Memphis, he learned that 30,000 Tennesseans had responded to the governor's call for 3,000 men. Two infantry regiments had already left for Taylor's army, and a horse unit was forming. On June 13, at Cincinnati, Wool reported to Marcy that the Kentucky and Tennessee cavalry would soon be ready, and the Indiana and Ohio infantry companies were rapidly filling. All regiments should be ready to depart for Texas by the end of June.[5]

The sound of drums echoed daily in the camps, calling men to details, drill, and meals. Uniforms varied in style and color from regiment to regiment, and often from company to company. The Kentucky Cavalry wore broad-brimmed beaver hats looped with gold lace, sported large spurs on red morocco boots, and rode thoroughbred horses. Less picturesque were the Illinois infantry in their short blue or gray coats with red or yellow facings. When not training, the volunteers loafed around their tents, gambled, wrote letters, and performed menial tasks. Camp life was a levelling process. "There is no aristocracy round a camp kettle or a mess chest," one soldier wrote, "and there can be no conventional distinctions on a blanket stretched over an area of mother earth six feet long and eleven inches wide." As the men elected their officers up to the rank of colonel, the daily routine was enhanced by politicking, liquor, and speeches. Toward the end of June, arms and supplies began arriving at the camps and the training for war began in earnest.[6]

On June 30, the Second Kentucky Infantry departed Louisville by steamship as crowds cheered and bands played. During the next ten days, gaily decorated steamboats carrying Ohio and Indiana regiments headed downriver for New Orleans. The First Kentucky Cavalry sailed to Memphis, debarked, and started overland for Texas. By early July, Wool's staff had mustered 12,000 men in fourteen regiments for duty with Taylor, and Wool moved his assistants to St. Louis to induct the Illinois and Mississippi levies. The general was in high spirits with his new field command.[7]

In mid-June, Wool received orders to proceed to San Antonio, Texas, to organize a division for service with Taylor. "The ultimate destination of this force," Marcy informed Taylor, "is Chihuahua, if . . . such an expedition would have a favorable operation in the conduct of the war, but it might be at once used to take and secure the several places on the Rio Grande." Wool's division would include four regiments—the First and Second Illinois Infantry and one regiment each of Arkansas and Texas cavalry—plus a small contingent of regular infantry and artillery. Sylvester Churchill would be his chief staff officer. Wool completed the muster of four Illinois regiments in early July near St. Louis and shifted his attention to Texas.[8]

On July 17, a warm summer day, Wool, his servant James, staff officers, and a detachment of the Second Illinois embarked on the steamboat *Convoy* at Alton.

The general's steamer trunk and riding horses were taken aboard earlier in the day. The rest of the regiment and the First Illinois filed onto the *Hannibal* and *Missouri*. Everyone breathed a sigh of relief. In less than forty days, Wool had been successful in mustering and equipping a small army for the war with Mexico. Everything had to be provided, from six-man tents to camp kettles and nose bags for mules and horses. He had driven his assistants to the point of exhaustion. Several officers requested and received reassignments. Wool had lost twenty pounds and looked emaciated. In St. Louis he purchased extra eyeglasses and other personal needs prior to a relaxing trip down the Mississippi.[9]

On the riverboats the volunteers lolled below deck amid the ceaseless hissings and snortings of massive steam engines bathed in grease. Some went topside only to roast in the July heat and debilitating humidity. In the cabins, the officers played poker and drank excessively. As they passed plantations along the river, the boat captains blew their whistles, and black slave gangs stopped their work to wave. On approaching Baton Rouge, Wool formed the troops on deck. With regimental flags flying and bands playing, they saluted the national colors atop the federal arsenal. On the evening of June 24, the little fleet passed New Orleans and anchored about four miles below the city at the old Chalmette battlefield. The volunteers went ashore and pitched tents in the dark. "The time of picnics had now ceased and the serious life of the warrior was beginning," Wool announced. The general posted guards to keep the men in camp, but within hours, small groups found their way to the thriving fleshpots of the city.[10]

Wool took a suite at the fashionable St. Charles Hotel, styled like a Grecian palace, and began the task of purchasing wagons and teams and hiring teamsters. He needed 200 wagons and over 600 mules, horses, and oxen to move his division from San Antonio into Mexico. Contractors anxious for dollars swarmed his rooms. The general also sent requisitions to the Baton Rouge arsenal for carbines, pistols, and sabers for cavalry, and muskets, cartridges, flints, waist belts, and cartridge boxes for infantry; all to be shipped to Port Lavaca on the Texas coast as soon as possible. Before midnight, on July 27, Wool and his entourage and three Illinois companies went aboard the *Galveston* as a small flotilla cast off and headed south toward the mouth of the Mississippi. The next morning the transports were plowing through the blue waters of the Gulf of Mexico.[11]

After a stopover at Galveston, the flotilla continued down the coast. On July 30, they entered Matagorda Bay in a sweeping rainstorm and made anchor at Port Lavaca, a cluster of wooden shacks housing a dozen or so families. The largest building in the seaside community was a government storehouse recently constructed by the army. On August 2, the troops went ashore and struck out across the flat, rolling prairie. Twelve miles inland at the edge of a grove of timber near Placedo Creek they established Camp Irwin.[12]

As the men pitched tents, Capt. Osborn Cross, Wool's adjutant, posted Order No. 1. Commanders could expect to march for San Antonio within days. Each company of seventy-five men would have a four-horse wagon for baggage. Regular drill began immediately, and problems developed. A few of the men came down with measles and the surgeons began segregating and tending to them.

Wool demanded total subordination from his officers. When Col. John J. Hardin, commanding the First Illinois, arrested a captain for disobedience, the general in an order lectured the volunteers and reminded them that an army lacking subordination was "little better than a mob." The Illinois captain was allowed, nevertheless, to "resume his sword and return to duty."[13]

On August 8, Wool left Camp Irwin with a small party and struck out for San Antonio, 160 miles across the Texas coastal plains to the northwest. The last Illinois detachment had arrived, and the unloading of stores and supplies was proceeding smoothly. Churchill took command at Camp Irwin. Wool also left behind his exuberant aide-de-camp, Ohio-born First Lt. Irvin McDowell of the First Artillery. A large, impulsive man with limitless energy, McDowell had attended the College de Troyes in France before graduating from West Point in 1838. While jumping his horse near camp, he crashed in the mud, badly lacerating his face.

As he rode inland, Wool passed the small settlement of Victoria, perched on a rise on the east bank of the Guadalupe River, before continuing on to Goliad, on the San Antonio River. Horseflies and the heat became unbearable, so the troops began traveling at night. At dawn on August 14, the weary horsemen rode into the historic community of San Antonio de Béxar. Wool reported to Lt. Col. Thomas R. Fauntleroy, Second Dragoons, temporarily commanding the army depot there.[14]

On August 15, Wool took formal command of the troops assembling "at and near" San Antonio. A multitude of problems demanded attention. His immediate concern was to recall Col. William S. Harney, the local commander, from his unauthorized "invasion" of Mexico. In May, Harney, with Taylor's approval, had mustered the Third Texas Mounted Volunteers for frontier duty. In late July, with rumors of a Mexican military buildup at the village of Presidio del Rio Grande, the colonel raced out of San Antonio with a large mounted force—eight volunteer companies, three of dragoons, along with Delaware Indian scouts led by Suck-tum-mah-kway, also known as Black Beaver. Taylor's orders to halt the expedition arrived too late. Wool was so upset by Harney's foray he sent Col. William C. Young and a detachment of Texas cavalry to arrest the colonel and bring him back to San Antonio.[15]

Another problem was the unassigned Texas volunteers who began arriving in San Antonio. Harney asked Governor George Tyler Wood in May to raise seven mounted companies for six months' service, and in late June, he requested five more. Taylor cancelled the second levy, which the Texas governor promptly committed to "ranger" duty. On August 20, Lt. Gov. Albert C. Horton reminded Wool that the War Department quota for Texas was for one mounted regiment and one infantry battalion, and he asked if the five ranger companies could satisfy the battalion levy. Wool agreed to accept the men for federal service providing they enlist for one year. Three of the companies agreed, but the other two preferred to remain as state troops for six months. Wool also dismissed Black Beaver and his Delaware scouts.[16]

On August 21, Wool's engineers staked out Camp Crockett on the east side of the San Antonio River near its headwaters. The site was about two miles north of the old Alamo mission and sprawled over a rolling prairie dotted with mesquite and post oak. Illinois volunteers moved into the camp first and pitched their tents. They were followed by four regular companies—two of the First Dragoons, under Capts. Enoch Steen and William Eustis, and two of the Sixth Infantry, led by Maj. Benjamin L. E. Bonneville. On their heels came Col. Archibald Yell's rowdy regiment of Arkansas Cavalry. Yell was a former congressman and governor of Arkansas, who Wool complained could never control his men. The last contingent to arrive at Camp Crockett was Capt. John Macrae Washington's blue-coated artillerymen, eighty-five strong, towing four six-pounder brass cannons and two twelve-pounder howitzers with caissons. They were accompanied by a small baggage train, a mobile forge, and several extra horses. Their overland trek from Carlisle, Pennsylvania, to Texas had attracted the attention of the national press.[17]

Wool placed Camp Crockett under strict rules. Beginning on August 26, drum beats regulated daily military activities. In the company areas, the rattle of drums also signaled roll calls, drills, inspections, and parades.[18]

San Antonio, a town of about two thousand inhabitants, sprawled along the headwaters of the San Antonio River. Once a Spanish military base and administrative seat, the community had witnessed the changing fortunes of war, with opposing armies clashing at its gates. Only a stone's throw from the banks of the river was the legendary Alamo. Reflecting back to March 1836, the mission ruin was a place of great attention, and soldiers used their pocket knives to dig bullets out of its battered limestone walls. At nightfall, the scene changed. In dozens of "Tiger rooms" filled with candle smoke and pungent odor from perspiring bodies flavored with whiskey, soldiers, teamsters, and gamblers mingled, women danced feverishly, and games of monte and faro abounded. When an enraged Texan shot an Illinois private who was on night patrol, Wool closed down the fandangos and casinos. Men and women moved their drinking and dancing to the main plaza.[19]

The cry of the drillmaster echoed daily across the hillsides at Camp Crockett. Volunteer officers tried to instruct their men, but many had little or no military experience, and the officers frequently drew jeers and catcalls. Many recruits grew restless. Colonel Yell, for all his experience in Congress and as a governor, became "the laughing stock of the men—for as yet he has never undertaken to give an order without making a blunder," an Arkansan wrote. Colonel Churchill bore the burden of training the regiments. The colonel, said one volunteer, was "a very cross, ill-contrived old fellow . . . [who] looks very thunder at all times." At inspections the crusty veteran scolded soldiers and officers alike for dirty weapons, and after each parade or muster, he reportedly washed his hands "with a good Castile soap" to remove the taint of contact with the volunteers.[20]

Wool's greatest cross to bear was the Arkansas cavalry. When Colonel Yell, a short, aggressive little man, arrived in San Antonio and could not find his adjutant who had been sent ahead to locate a camp site, the impatient commander selected his own. Wool's troop assignment officer asked Yell to move, but the colonel refused. Wool let the matter go for three days, then rode to the Arkansas bivouac himself, where he immediately sensed an unmistakable odor and found that no latrines had been dug. Yell was ordered to find another location. Instead of going upriver, the colonel took his men a mile distant to a barren ridge devoid of shade or water, and in the scorching August heat, his men began dropping like flies. Again, Wool intervened and moved the regiment to a better location.[21]

Wool was further miffed when a young recruit climbed the cupola of the 130-year-old Mission Concepción and removed a large cross. The soldier was "an unworthy member of his corps and can have but little respect for religion or morality," Wool decreed. If the march into Mexico was tarnished by "any such outrages on the feelings of the inhabitants of the country through which it may move," that individual was to be severely punished.[22]

Colonel Young returned to San Antonio on August 28 with Harney and most of his command. Young had met the dragoon colonel returning from the Rio Grande and, despite Harney's protest that he was in route back to San Antonio in response to Taylor's order, Young placed him under arrest. Wool sternly lectured the tall, redheaded, impulsive Harney on his misdeeds. Smarting from the rebuke, the high-spirited Harney snapped that he would take the matter to General Taylor. A week later, Texas companies that Harney left on the Rio Grande came straggling into Camp Crockett missing several of their men who had been killed and wounded in a skirmish with the Mexicans. In San Antonio, Wool not only released Harney from arrest but placed him in charge of the impending invasion of Mexico. He needed the officer's knowledge of the border and someone with combat experience.[23]

Wool spared nothing in preparing his division for the field. At Port Lavaca, Maj. Charles Thomas, who had replaced Irwin, paid $600 for a wagon and five yoke of oxen, and Texas newspapers chided him for being "picky." Hauling corn from the coast to San Antonio cost $1.20 per bushel, comparable, it was said, to having shipped it from Iowa. Locally, a group of Texans formed "a combination" to control the market and prices escalated even more. Ranchers demanded nine dollars or more for bony, long-horned Texas cattle, while San Antonio landlords charged $800 a month to rent vacant buildings. With little alternative, Wool overlooked the expenses. The commissariat for his division was "in the finest possible condition," a soldier recalled, with sugar and coffee "of the best quality" a part of the daily ration. Wool also hired several civilian physicians. The only army surgeon on duty, he wrote Sarah, was "entirely broken down and unable to do anything." The civilian doctors were not much better. One had been "on a drunken spree ever since his arrival, another [was] in bed with a wound received in a duel, and another [was] sick at La Vaca."[24]

The shipment of army supplies caused innumerable headaches. Vessels arrived at Port Lavaca with only part of their cargos, the captains having jettisoned both mules and wagons to lighten their ships in rough seas. In other cases, wagon parts were thrown haphazardly into the holds of ships and covered with hundreds of sacks of oats and corn. Assembling a wagon often took days. On August 25, Wool told Major Thomas that he must start forwarding supplies from the coast immediately, and within a week the quartermaster had one hundred wagons and teams running to and from San Antonio.[25]

Wool grew anxious for instructions. Taylor doubted that an army could penetrate the rugged mountainous terrain in Chihuahua with wagons and artillery, but in August 1846, he speculated that an expedition might cross the Rio Grande near Eagle Pass, march south to the town of Monclova, Coahuila, and turn west into Chihuahua. Wool and his staff also studied maps and possible invasion routes. In March, Col. Stephen W. Kearny, commanding at Fort Leavenworth, told Secretary Marcy he was sure an army could easily enter Chihuahua at Presidio del Norte, a village on the upper Rio Grande, which lay on a trail blazed from Fort Smith, Arkansas, across the barren desert of west Texas by merchant caravans. Capt. George W. Hughes, Wool's chief topographical engineer, also suggested the Presidio del Norte crossing, and offered to map a route west from San Antonio to that point. Wool dismissed the idea and on September 15, he informed Taylor that he planned to cross the river at a lower point—Presidio del Rio Grande, a few miles downriver from Eagle Pass, and proceed to Monclova.[26]

Wool readied his division to move. Soldiers loaded a long freight train with rations and enough forage to sustain the column through at least two hundred miles of arid country. Large water barrels were lashed to the sides of the wagons. Wool placed Capt. Robert E. Lee, Corps of Engineers, in charge of a "pioneer" company of twenty-five men, drawn from the Illinois regiments, to accompany the advance to clear the old Camino Real that ran west and then south from San Antonio to the Rio Grande. Lee also tied four wooden boats and a stack of planks onto six wagons to build a flying bridge at the river. Soldiers were busy cooking rations and packing their personal belongings into valises and saddlebags. Wool's division included Washington's artillery of eight guns, two companies of Steen's First Dragoons, three companies of Benjamin L. Beall's Second Dragoons, Bonneville's battalion of regular infantry, Yell's rowdy Arkansas cavalry, the First and Second Illinois infantry, and an independent company of Kentucky infantry. In all, he had about 3,400 men.[27]

On Saturday, September 26, with a regimental band performing a lively tune, Colonel Harney marched out of the plaza in San Antonio with 1,400 men. His command contained dragoons, infantry and artillery regulars, Lee's pioneers, and four Illinois companies. A two-mile-long train of 177 wagons, loaded with subsistence, ammunition, and quartermaster stores, fell into line behind. Captain Hughes rode ahead, checking roads and selecting campsites. Wool left San Antonio with Steen's dragoons three days later, instructing Churchill to follow with the remaining volunteers as wagons became available. Wool caught up with Harney before the lead column reached the Nueces River, a shallow stream swollen by late summer rains. Beyond the Nueces, the column spread out for miles across the desert. On October 6, the advance pitched camp about twelve miles from the Rio Grande. The men had tramped 164 miles from San Antonio in twelve days.[28]

As Wool's little army gazed across the Rio Grande into Mexico at noon on October 8, an unarmed rider appeared on the opposite bank. Carrying a flag of truce, he swam his horse across the river and handed the general a message. The rider was the alcalde of Presidio del Rio Grande, who told Wool the Mexican garrison on the south bank of the river, five miles distant, had fled, and he came to offer friendship. Later in the day, the alcalde visited Wool again to say that after a vicious and bloody, house-to-house, street-to-street battle, General Taylor had captured Monterrey and an eight-week armistice had been declared. He even produced a Mexican newspaper describing the bloodshed. Wool said he had received no word of any armistice and he told the alcalde he planned to move immediately onto Mexican soil. Nevertheless, he was pleased to see the "peaceful intentions" of the local inhabitants and was eager to purchase such supplies as they could spare.[29]

Early the next morning, Wool sent Harney splashing across the Rio Grande with a dragoon detachment to locate a campsite near the ruins of the old presidio. In Order 89, the general cautioned his army:

> Soldiers!
>
> Tomorrow you will cross the Rio Grande, and occupy the territory of our enemies. We have not come to make war upon the people or peasantry of the country, but to compel the government of Mexico to render justice to the United States. The people, therefore, who . . . remain quiet and peaceable at their homes, will not be molested or interfered with, either as regards their

> persons or property; and all those who furnish supplies will be treated kindly, and whatever is received from them will be liberally paid for.
>
> . . . The troops . . . will observe the most rigid discipline and subordination. All depredations on the persons or property of the people of the country are strictly forbidden, and any soldier or follower of the camp, who may so far forget his duty as to violate this injunction will be surely punished.

A word of caution was timely. Captain Lee wrote his wife that there had been "a great whetting of knives, grinding of swords, and sharpening of bayonets." Upon Harney's return in the afternoon, Wool gave a dinner for his officers, and announced that as soon as Churchill arrived with the rest of the column, he would move south across the desert and through the mountains to Monclova.[30]

On October 11, the general crossed the river and met a Mexican lieutenant on horseback with a flag of truce. The officer handed him a protest from the Mexican commander on the Coahuilan frontier, together with a copy of the articles of capitulation at Monterrey. Wool's invasion violated Taylor's armistice, he said. Wool brushed the emissary aside, and with dragoons and several artillery pieces, he rode into the main plaza in Presidio del Rio Grande, a town of about two thousand inhabitants near the old mission and presidio of San Juan Bautista, only to discover that as many as half the town had fled. It was Sunday, and the churchgoers who remained stared at the dusty *yanquis*. After paying respects to the alcalde, Wool rode on to Harney's encampment at a brackish spring, three miles south of town.[31]

The rest of the division forded the Rio Grande during the day. Infantrymen cautiously filed across a bobbing "flying bridge" resting on pontoon boats. Artillerymen drove their teams into four feet of yellowish-gray water, elevated the guns on their carriages, and waded 170 yards on a hard bottom to the opposite shore. Teamsters with the wagon train were leery of the bridge. They halted, repacked and raised the baggage and stores one-foot-high in the beds and drove the wagons across. A lone Texan drowned while attempting to cross the river. On October 13, the remaining eight companies of the First Illinois crossed the river and went into camp just as an unexpected party appeared on the horizon. Brig. Gen. James Shields, traveling with a servant, guide, and four discharged soldiers, came into Wool's camp, having made his way upriver from Camargo. Earlier, Shields, the former commissioner of the General Land Office in Washington, had accompanied Wool to New Orleans, and he had escorted the Third and Fourth Illinois regiments to join Taylor. Shields was hoping for a new assignment after insulting Maj. Gen. Robert Patterson while drunk and leaving Camargo under a cloud of insubordination.[32]

Wool remained near Presidio del Rio Grande for four days. He reorganized his command, placing Shields in charge of the right wing, composed of Bonneville's regulars and the Illinois infantry, and assigned Harney to the left, with the dragoons and the Arkansas cavalry. Harney continued to cause friction. He failed to circulate orders while seeking friends among the volunteer officers. Wool was also aware of another troublemaker in camp. Dr. Josiah Gregg, Santa Fe trader and author of the popular *Commerce on the Prairies*, was traveling with Yell. Gregg, who was well acquainted with northern Mexico, felt snubbed when Wool failed to hire him as an interpreter. In letters to newspapers in the East, Gregg sneered at Wool's interpreters, especially a dark-complexioned chap named Thomas "Ajax" Addicks. Moreover, he questioned the general's competency to command. Any man, Gregg wrote, "with a fair degree of cunning and management, who is abjectly subservient, and will use a sufficiency of flattery, will hardly fail to gain great influence over the general's weak mind." Wool was "petulant and whimsical—decidedly old-womanish," who believed that successful military operations depended on paperwork and ceremonies.[33]

On October 16, the long march into the Mexican interior began. After an infantry company recrossed the river to construct a redoubt on the Texas side to guard the crossing, the army struck their tents at dawn and headed southwest into a sterile desert, with billowing dust clouds marking their progress. Harney's dragoons led the way. Near the middle of the column, Wool and several senior officers jolted along in an army ambulance. That evening the exhausted soldiers reached the village of San Andres de Nava, having traveled twenty-five miles. The alcalde offered hospitality—and corn for sale. That night a howling norther blew down tents and scattered cooking equipment. The next afternoon the column was able to reach San Fernando de Rosas, where Wool turned south and slowly climbed into the foothills of the San José Mountains. On the horizon to the west, the massive Santa Rosa range blocked entry into Chihuahua.[34]

On the evening of October 18, Wool received a letter by courier from General Taylor, who had established his headquarters at Monterrey, 280 miles to the east. The American commander described his capture of the citadel and explained the armistice initiated on September 25. He advised Wool to halt at Monclova and check on possible routes west into Chihuahua. The general called the regimental officers to his tent, read Taylor's letter, and announced that their destination was still Chihuahua. After the meeting, Harney complained of his subordinate role in the campaign, and he asked to be relieved of command in order to join Taylor in Monterrey. Wool promised to draft such an order as soon as the army reached Monclova.[35]

Wool's division crossed the Alamos and Sabinas Rivers, and with flags flying, entered Santa Rosa, a town of 3,500, as a regimental band struck up "Yankee Doodle." Municipal officials gave the American officers a dinner and staged a fandango for the soldiers, with dancing and singing. The Mexicans were Federalists and offered to "pronounce" in favor of the United States, if Wool would sustain and protect them. The general politely declined the offer. The next day Mexican men, women, and children swarmed into camp, Hughes recorded, supplying the soldiers with "all the delicacies of the season."[36]

Resuming their march, the American column began crossing a broad valley where in the distance they could see large flocks of sheep and goats grazing in the foothills. Two days later, the soldiers filed through a pass between the Guachapinas and Lampazos Mountains to see the glistening white buildings of a large hacienda. Miguel Blanco, the manager, rode out to invite Wool to camp on the property. The hacienda at Hermanas was one of many owned by his cousin, Jacobo Sanchez Navarro, who, with his brother Carlos, controlled vast tracts of land in the western part of the Mexican state of Coahuila. For the weary soldiers, the hacienda was a welcome oasis. Wool tarried one day to purchase five hundred bushels of corn.[3736]

As they passed through settled districts, the volunteers grew restless. Wool cautioned his officers to warn their men against "fancied security." He complimented the soldiers on their patience—but stressed that discipline must be maintained to keep the division prepared for the "increased labors and privations and perhaps conflicts with the enemy." Wool tolerated no infractions. Many of the volunteers resented his harsh discipline, and they called him "Old Fussy." Upon learning that Illinois soldiers had wrecked an abandoned house, the general called their commander, Col. John Hardin, to task. Hardin, a small, impulsive man, who had lost an eye in a hunting accident, was quick to argue the matter, while charging that Wool lacked confidence in the volunteer officers and was consistently intimidating them. The general warned against further accusations, and the colonel left. Later that evening he heard Hardin, a veteran of the Black Hawk War who had helped expel the Mormons from Illinois in 1844, dress down his aide, Lieutenant McDowell, and Wool intervened. Hardin again flung forth more allegations, and Wool exploded: "I have a damned sight more confidence in your men than I have in you, or any of your officers. Go, sir, and tell your men so." Wool later regretted his outburst, and he told Hardin that his response referred to conditions in Yell's regiment.[38]

Pvt. Samuel Chamberlain of the First Dragoons recalled in his diary how the volunteers frequently tested Wool's patience. While Chamberlain was on guard duty, he watched as Wool approached a guard post and found the sentry setting on the ground eating beans and tortillas with a young female. The private did not stand up or salute but called out, "Good day, General, hot riding out I reckon." Angered, Wool shouted at the sentry to call the officer of the guard. "Lieutenant Woodson, come here right quick, post nine, for the old General wants you!" the young soldier yelled out. The officer quickly appeared with neither belt or sword, his coat unbuttoned, and a Mexican straw hat on his head. Furiously, Wool ripped into the officer for his sloppy appearance as well as the slovenly conduct of his sentry. In response, the officer turned to the private and barked, "Jake Strout, yer ain't worth shucks. If you don't git up and salute the General, I'll drive your gal away, doggone if I don't." Still sprawled on the ground eating beans and tortillas, the sentry responded that, "if the General wanted saluting the lieutenant might do it, he wasn't going to do anything of the kind." Still furious, General Wool rode away.[39]

On October 30, Wool's division reached the outskirts of Monclova, a town of five thousand and the former capital of Coahuila y Tejas. A Mexican general and twenty soldiers rode to the American camp under a white flag to protest what they perceived as a violation of Taylor's armistice. When Wool learned that most of the local authorities were Centralists, aligned with the government in Mexico City, he decided to make a show of force in the town. The next morning, he and his staff, wearing dress uniforms, rode to the main plaza escorted by two cavalry companies. Wool made a short speech in which he declared the inhabitants subject to American military rule. Moreover, in another sign of force, he had the Stars and Stripes hoisted over the *cabildo.* He also seized one of the better homes in the town as his temporary headquarters and placed soldiers in the stone barracks nearby. In conclusion, the entire division paraded through the city en route to a camp on the Monclova River. Commissary officers, escorted by dragoons, rode into the countryside to secure forage.[40]

Wool now questioned his instructions to invade Chihuahua. He wrote Taylor with news that Kearny had sent a strong column from Santa Fe down the Camino Real into Chihuahua, and believed the force was sufficient to subdue and occupy the Mexican state. Besides, there was a more pressing matter. Rumors were afloat that Gen. Antonio Lopez de Santa Anna was building a large army at San Luis Potosí, 250 miles south of Saltillo, with intentions of moving north to strike Taylor. Wool was certain that Taylor would need help and requested orders to join him. "In making this request," he wrote, "you must not suppose that I am not prepared to carry out all the objects or intentions of the President."[41]

While Wool sat in Monclova awaiting orders, the volunteers continued to test his patience. Churchill's arrival on November 6 with about eight hundred men, mostly companies of Col. William Henry Bissell's Second Illinois, worsened the restlessness. The first incident erupted over food. To conserve flour, the commissary dumped several wagonloads of unshelled Mexican corn in the center of the company areas and issued grinding mills. The soldiers raised an outcry, branded the corn only fit for animals, and refused to touch it. When Wool rode out to investigate, the defiant soldiers brayed like mules and grunted like hogs. A placard on one tent read: "Good accommodations for men and beast. Six ears of corn for a mule, four ears for soldiers, three ears for a hog per day. Rations for officers not known." The corn was replaced with coarse Mexican flour.[42]

Cartography by Carol Zuber-Mallison/ZM Graphics, Inc.

Volunteer officers also became troublesome. Shields, whom Gregg called a pompous "military simpleton," chafed at Wool's indecisions. He sent his aide, Capt. George Turnbull Moore Davis, to Washington to request another assignment. Wool's "sleeping division," an officer wrote home, would never see an enemy. Others shared his feelings. "I have no hopes of doing anything whilst I remain with Genl. Wool," Hardin wrote his law partner back home in Jacksonville, Illinois. The general's orders regarding army attire rankled many of the men. When an Arkansas captain appeared at guard mount in filthy clothing and wearing no tie, the general ordered the entire officer corps to clean up and wear proper uniforms. Misunderstandings produced tensions. On payday, November 15, Arkansan Colonel Yell stormed into the general's tent, demanding to know why his men had received no money. Wool called in Maj. David Hunter, chief paymaster, who stated bluntly that the general had told him not to pay the Arkansans, which Wool emphatically denied. An argument ensued, after which Hunter demanded a court of inquiry, and in fiery rhetoric, was sent to his tent. Wool ordered each Arkansas soldier paid ten dollars and he ignored Hunter's request for a hearing.[43]

By the time Taylor's armistice ended on November 15, Wool had abandoned the idea of invading Chihuahua. Hughes, the topographical engineer, had charted a possible wagon road west from Monclova through a long mountain gorge, via the villages of Pozuelos and Cuatro Cinegas, to the edge of a vast expanse of Chihuahuan desert wasteland called the Bolsón de Mapimi, where no river or stream ran to the sea. Only cavalry with a pack train could cross the sterile Bolsón. Wool announced the division would continue south 162 miles to the town of Parras de la Fuente. Orders came for Harney to join his dragoon regiment at Monterrey and for Shields to return to Matamoros for reassignment. A sigh of relief swept headquarters. Wool had found Shields "a zealous, active, and efficient officer," but he regarded Harney an impossible malcontent.[44]

After sixteen days in Monclova and without orders after three requests, Wool wrote Taylor on November 20 saying he planned to move the army on to Parras. Maj. William B. Warren would remain in the city with four Illinois and three Arkansas companies to control the population and escort army supplies from the Rio Grande. On November 24, the soldiers shook off the morning chill, fell into line, and faced south. Crossing an extensive limestone plain, the movement churned great clouds of dust that caked on perspiring teams and burned men's eyes. Water holes and springs were impregnated with minerals, and hard-hearted teamsters charged twenty-five cents for a drink from a water barrel. Men straggled and dropped to rest, while others climbed into wagons, causing overburdened teams to falter. In the higher elevation the men spotted mule deer, bears, and even wolves. Towering above at times were rugged volcanic mountains of over seven thousand feet. Each evening, wagons loaded with water were sent back to revive and bring in the weakened men who had fallen out.[45] The march was turning into an ordeal.

While laying over to rest his men, Wool received three letters from Taylor. The first two instructed him to abandon the Chihuahua expedition, and the third informed him that Bvt. Maj. Gen. William J. Worth with 1,500 troops was being sent to occupy Saltillo, the capital of Coahuila, about eighty miles east of Parras. Taylor approved Wool's move to Parras, and suggested a plan for a defensive line stretching from Parras east through Saltillo and Monterrey all the way to the gulf. Wool would anchor the western end of the line and create a supply depot capable of supporting five thousand men for four or five months. Moreover, from Parras Wool could move on Chihuahua, Durango, or even San Luis Potosí. If the enemy advanced, Wool would hasten to Saltillo and assume command.[46]

On December 4, the vanguard of the army reached San Lorenzo de Abajo, one of the most picturesque communities the men had seen. Here the army turned south in to the mountains and on December 5, Wool finally reached Parras. The picturesque town of cobblestone streets, with a population of six thousand, was surrounded by extensive vineyards and wheat fields. The oasis of springs and greenery proved a pleasant respite after the exhausting march from Monclova. Wool established his headquarters in the town and placed his men in camp a mile to the east on the road to Saltillo. The general ordered his commissary officers to begin building a supply depot. He turned first to the neighboring hacienda of San Lorenzo de Abajo, owned by the Ibarra family, to make purchases. The Ibarra holdings were gigantic, occupying an area one-fourth the size of the state of Ohio. Over one thousand peons worked on ranches, farms, and in fruit orchards and vineyards. Manuel de Ibarra, the owner, was educated in a Catholic school at Bardstown, Kentucky, and was fluent in English. He had been a classmate of Lt. Col. Henry Clay Jr., third son of the famous Whig statesman, and who was second in his West Point class of 1831 and in command of the Second Kentucky Volunteers. Ibarra not only joyously greeted Clay but graciously opened his doors to the Americans and offered to furnish both beef and flour.[47]

In letters to Taylor, Wool expressed concern with the supply situation at Parras. His immediate concern was finding forage for the three thousand horses and mules that belonged to his cavalry and work teams that pulled his lengthy wagon train. Corn was plentiful, but two English merchants, Edward Chapman and Henry Boultbee, were seeking to control the market and had driven up prices. Wool believed that he could subsist five thousand men for three months on local resources but warned that Santa Anna was also drawing on the same region for his army. Wool questioned Taylor's extended defensive line. With 25,000–30,000 men at San Luis Potosí, the Mexican general might strike north and cut off the American garrisons at Monterrey, Saltillo, and Parras piecemeal.[48]

Taylor ordered Wool to strip the country around Parras of grain, leaving only bare necessities for the inhabitants. This should check enemy efforts to obtain supplies there. As for the speculators, Taylor instructed Wool to confiscate what supplies he needed and pay prices that prevailed before his arrival. Taylor also instructed Wool to move one third of his division east on the Saltillo road to the hacienda of San Francisco de los Patos. He should also send scouting parties south toward San Luis Potosí, Zacatecas, and Durango. Taylor told Wool he was planning to march southeast and occupy Ciudad Victoria, the capital of the Mexican state of Tamaulipas—and was considering continuing on to the port of Tampico. Upon his return to Monterrey, if Santa Anna was determined to move north across the desert from San Luis Potosí, he would hasten west to Saltillo and join Wool. Captain Lee rode east to lay out an encampment near Patos, and Captain Hughes drew up a roster for scouting details.[49]

Taylor's orders came at the right time, for morale in Wool's division was deteriorating rapidly. Volunteers laughed and joked about their commander. They called him "The Big Corporal," "Old Fussy," the "Old Warhorse," and even "Her Ladyship." Camp gossip said the general received visitors "capped, booted, and spurred; that he began business at daybreak, and ate with his sword on; some believed he even slept with his sword." The Arkansans continually tried Wool's patience. A private peered into Wool's tent one day and refused to leave. When the general told his orderly to point a gun at the intruder, the soldier aimed his musket and said: "Old horse, damn your soul, if you give such orders I will shoot you for certain." On another occasion, Wool sent an officer to stop the riotous noise in the Arkansas camp, and was told: "Tell Johnny Wool to kiss our [ass]."[50]

At noonday on December 17, an express rider galloped into Parras with an urgent message from General Worth at Saltillo. Santa Anna was defiantly marching north from San Luis Potosi with a large army. Worth needed help. Maj. Gen. William O. Butler, commanding in Monterrey in Taylor's absence, was hurrying southwest through the mountains with two thousand men to bolster Worth's defenses. Wool dashed out to camp on horseback, assembled his regimental officers, and barked instructions. As drummers furiously beat the long roll, soldiers struck tents, loaded wagons, and fell into line. Within two hours the entire division was in motion. Wool drove his men hard for two days. Imaginations quickened. Spotting a growing dust cloud in the distance, Wool halted the column and sent Colonel Yell and several Arkansas companies to investigate. Through a telescope he watched Yell ride out and wave his sword at the foe, but when the dust cleared a herd of wild mustangs raced into view![51]

On December 19, thirty miles southwest of Saltillo, Wool reached the hacienda at Patos, owned by the wealthy Jacobo Sánchez Navarro. A relative of the Mexican grandee entertained the Yankee general and his officers in a palatial home and promised to sell forage and foodstuffs. "I dined with one of the richest men in Mexico," the general wrote his niece, Harriette Hart. "[T]he *Lady* who did the honors of the table appeared in a costly petticoat, shoes and stockings, and a [shawl]." Wool regarded her as risqué. During the meal she "accidentally exposed her underdress, which consisted of only her chemise which did not cover those attractive parts which the ladies of our common country generally conceal from the vulgar gaze by their dress." After dinner the host and Wool played chess to decide the fate of Mexico. Following a critical move, the hostess exclaimed: "Oh my God . . . there goes our cavalry. You will be ruined, my dear brother." Needless to say, Wool won the game.[52]

Worth now reported that the emergency had passed. He suggested that Wool go into camp at the village of San Juan de la Vaquería, twenty miles outside Saltillo. General Butler concurred. Wool ignored the suggestion, and on December 21, he moved his army beyond San Juan and the rancho of Encantada and continued southeast to the hacienda at Agua Nueva, squarely in Santa Anna's path. The march had been exhausting. Teamsters dragged dozens of dead mules into the desert for the buzzards that circled overhead. Quartermaster officers quickly took over the buildings, forcing over one hundred Mexican civilians to seek refuge in neighboring villages. The weather was cold, and soldiers tore down corrals and fences to build fires. The four-day march from Parras had been exhausting. Twenty miles from Saltillo, Agua Nueva was a strategic outpost, lying near several springs on the edge of a desert that stretched one hundred miles to the south. Wool had Captain Lee and Lt. Phil Kearny scout the mountains on each flank, ordered patrols to check the roads to the south and west, and placed a heavy guard on his wagons, parked five miles north at Encantada.[53]

On the afternoon of December 22, Wool started for Saltillo with several officers and a dragoon escort. The weather continued cold and blustery, and the men wore heavy overcoats and gloves. At dusk, they rode into a drizzling rain and dense fog and often were forced to dismount and reconnoiter the road. By midnight, in the dark and cold, the horsemen finally reached Saltillo and sought General Worth's headquarters. The next morning, Wool met with Butler and Worth, both of whom had suffered battle wounds at Monterrey and hobbled around with discomfort. The three commanders discussed the defense of Saltillo. The city had over 11,000 inhabitants, sat at 5,000 feet elevation, and was surrounded by mountains on three sides. The cathedral was the centerpiece of the city. "As I survey the 'thousand and one' statues, images, candlesticks, crosses & etc. [*sic*], with which its inner walls and domes were ornamented," a dragoon recorded, "I almost began to imagine that I was gazing upon the vast riches of the halls of the ancient Montezumas." The historic capital of Coahuila lay sixty-five miles southwest of Monterrey and was strategic to Taylor's defensive line.[54]

After lunch, the three generals rode to the plain south of the city and discussed the best place and way to meet Santa Anna. Butler, whom Gregg termed an "imbecile," suggested digging rifle pits and building redoubts, saying volunteers would not fight without cover. The courtly Worth stressed bolder action: he would strike an advancing enemy with bayonet and sword. Wool, on the other hand, urged using the narrow pass near the rancho of Buena Vista, five miles to the south, as a defensive position. As the debate waxed hotter, Wool spat out an oath and, according to a dragoon, the veteran lifted a hand and said, "Heaven forgive me for blasphemy." On this discordant note, the meeting ended. Wool and his party started south for Agua Nueva.[55]

When the road dipped below the plain just south of Buena Vista, Wool spurred his large horse upon the plateau to his left. With a telescope, he carefully scanned the terrain in every direction. A tableland extended east for nearly two miles to the southern end of the Sierra Zapaliname, and was cut into islands by arroyos that began in the foothills and became deeper and wider as they ran west to the road. West of the road, a ravine and broken terrain stretched away to another range of mountains. The road through the Angostura Pass narrowed to less than one hundred feet with cliffs on both sides of the roadway. Here a small force with artillery could block an enemy advance, while the yawning arroyos could impede cavalry assaults. The only way to turn a defense line on the plateau would be by the enemy advancing along the rugged base of the mountains to the east. "Mr. Carleton," Wool told Lt. James Henry Carleton of the dragoons, "this is the very spot of all others I have yet seen in Mexico, which I should select for battle, were I obliged with a small army to fight a large one." During the next few days, Churchill, Lee, and other officers carefully scouted the site. Captain Hughes selected a campground near the rancho, a mile and a half north of the pass—just in case.[56]

On a cold Christmas morning, a "stampede" occurred in Wool's camp at Agua Nueva as bugles and drums suddenly called the troops to arms: Santa Anna was advancing with a large army on the San Luis road! The general rushed an Arkansas detachment south to check on the rumor, and dispatched a courier to meet General Butler, who was en route to Agua Nueva. Butler immediately sent a courier to Monterrey for reinforcements. "The troops stood to their arms and I lay on the grass with my sorrel mare saddled by my side and telescope directed to the pass of the mountains through which the road approached," Captain Lee wrote his wife. As the hours passed and no enemy appeared, the men resumed their holiday celebration.[57]

General Butler, the supreme commander at Saltillo, reshuffled his command. He ordered Wool's Illinois infantry back to Encantada and sent Yell's cavalry west to Patos, there to patrol the Parras road. Harney arrived from Monterrey with the Second Dragoons and took station at Agua Nueva, with a picket at San Juan de la Vaquería. On his heels came Brig. Gen. Joseph Lane with the Second and Third

Indiana infantry regiments. Lane camped five miles east of Saltillo and sent scouts east to Palomas Pass and the road through the mountains to Monterrey. Wool ignored Butler's orders and marched to Buena Vista, arguing that he should remain there, before moving to Encantada. At this crucial time in the war, Butler decided to make changes in Wool's division. The general's staff was too large, Butler insisted, and he drew one officer each from the topographical, quartermaster, and ordnance branches for duty in Saltillo. Wool also had too many wagons. He could keep only those sufficient to sustain his men for ten days and send the rest to the depot near Saltillo.[58]

The deployment of pickets caused problems. Soldiers, especially the volunteers, plundered Mexican villages, seizing food and blankets, ripping buildings apart for their campfires, rifled granaries, and slaughtered cattle. Drunken parties broke into rural homes and raped young women. Butler's admonitions did little good, for the officers either ignored him or made little effort to control the men. In contrast, Wool tolerated no lawlessness in his camps. Courts-martial regularly cranked out convictions for drunkenness, theft, mutiny, and desertion. He was lenient with volunteers but harsh with the regulars. Deserters were frequently executed, while the more fortunate received fifty lashes, shaven heads, and a "D" branded on the back of each hand. As drums beat the "Rogues March" at retreat, the deserters were dragged to the edge of camp and dismissed.[59]

On January 2, 1847, Butler notified Wool that the Arkansas cavalry at Patos had killed some Mexican civilians. Wool knew the soldiers there were angry because several of their comrades had been lassoed and robbed. He sent Yell a stiff note, inquiring about the incident. The colonel hotly denied that his men were involved in any murders. He enclosed a statement from the Mexican authorities at Patos to "quiet the indignation" at headquarters. It was later learned that a drunken Texan traveling with an escort for an army train was responsible for the deaths.[60]

Soon after Harney arrived from Monterrey, Wool received a copy of the charges the colonel had filed against him. Harney protested his "illegal" arrest in Texas and his spiteful assignments on the march into Mexico. Moreover, Wool had wasted public money on an abandoned expedition. The general frequently insulted junior officers, saying to one: "Get out of my way, God damn you," or words to that effect. He had also placed Churchill in command positions above his rank, an act subversive of discipline. Finally, Wool's "imbecile, vacillating, and splenetic and undignified course" had alienated the confidence of his men and crippled its effectiveness. Wool wrote Taylor that Harney's charges were absurd and the commanding general paid them little heed. Lt. Samuel C. Ridgely, Taylor's adjutant, concurred. Ridgely saw nothing criminal in the charges, "only an error in judgment," and he doubted that the government would disturb officers "placed in delicate & responsible commands." On

December 31, Harney sent a testy note to Butler demanding reassignment. Butler's adjutant, citing the colonel's uncivil language, referred the request to Wool, saying the officer was his responsibility.[61]

On January 8, 1847, General Butler notified Wool that Winfield Scott had been authorized to organize an expedition to seize the seaport of Vera Cruz and move against Mexico City. Scott, in need of seasoned troops, wanted Worth's division, Harney's dragoons, Bonneville's regular infantry, and the spare artillery. Wool could retain a small regular force—John M. Washington's battery along with Enoch Steen and Daniel H. Rucker's dragoons. Scott also needed engineer officers, including Robert E. Lee. "I regret very much to leave General Wool on many accounts," Lee wrote his wife on January 17, 1847. "He has been exceedingly kind to me in every way, and his letter on my being relieved today is kind and flattering in the extreme." Wool grumbled about the troop withdrawals. Scott's "unholy ambition to be President of the United States," he wrote a friend back in Troy, "would not permit him to make even an inquiry whether any troops, save a few volunteers, would be requisite to defend this line." Scott made himself "the center of all attraction," and believed that Santa Anna "would never think of measuring swords with anyone but he, General Scott, 'six feet six inches high, besides hat and feathers.'"[62]

On January 12, Butler redeployed his forces and withdrew Wool, the two Illinois regiments, and Washington's battery from Encantada back through the pass to the rancho of Buena Vista. The new camp was a welcome change, for strong winter winds had blown down tents, and soldiers complained of the dust. Yell shifted his cavalry from Patos to Encantada, and put patrols on the roads to Palomas Pass, Agua Nueva, and San Juan de la Vaquería. Wool experimented with a series of signals, checking on how far artillery firing at Buena Vista could be heard.[63]

Scouts reported Mexican military activity was increasing to the south. With Santa Anna "hourly expected," Wool fund it disgusting that several officers in the volunteers suddenly applied for sick leave to go to Saltillo. He worried incessantly about the volunteers and continued to fret that General Scott had taken so many of the regulars away. Capt. George T. Howard, a commissary officer scouting with a detachment on the San Luis road, skirmished on January 16 with enemy cavalry near the hacienda of Encarnación, thirty-five miles below Agua Nueva. Butler worried the Americans would be overwhelmed, and he suggested a retreat to Monterrey. Wool dismissed the idea, asserting that if Santa Anna had 12,000 men, as reported, Taylor's 4,000 troops should give battle. A withdrawal from the Saltillo salient would be "utterly ruinous," for it would show a weakness and "rouse against us the whole population from San Luis Potosí to the Rio Grande." Instead of 20,000 Mexicans to contend with, there would be 50,000. The American forces, if besieged in Monterrey, would soon surrender for want of supplies.[64]

Wool exchanged heated words with Butler on January 20. For nearly a month he had tolerated the dismantling of his division and had tried to remain obedient to his superior, but his patience ran out. When Butler came down to Buena Vista one day in his carriage, and asked for wagon mechanics and a traveling forge, Wool sternly protested. His mechanics were repairing a train that just arrived from Monclova, and the Arkansans needed the forge to shoe cavalry horses. The transfers would "seriously embarrass the public service." Butler exploded and, according to Wool, "told me in harsh terms and manner—'that when he gave me orders, I should obey them, [that] I no longer had a Division [but] was merely a commander of a Brigade.'" Butler left in a huff. Two days later, he left for Monterrey to see Taylor.[65]

The evening of the argument, Wool wrote Taylor a long letter. He had marched his troops from San Antonio across nine hundred miles of enemy territory in good order and without incident, but at Saltillo, Butler had crippled his division, undermined his authority, and created a "feeling of insubordination" among his men. He could no longer tolerate these conditions and requested reassignment. "I therefore appeal to you," he concluded, "as General in Chief, either to have me placed in my proper and rightful position or allow me to retire from a command where I can neither do justice to my country or myself." In a letter to Senator Lewis Cass, Wool said that his troubles began when he ignored Worth's suggestion, endorsed by Butler, to halt at San Juan de la Vaquería while marching from Parras. After Worth's "stampede" subsided, he became "an unwelcome visitor" at Butler's headquarters. Butler, who was President Polk's former law partner and the so-called "mustang general," aspired to be president and had come to Mexico "to make political capital," Wool wrote Sarah.[66]

When Butler departed for Monterrey, Wool was placed in temporary command at Saltillo. As Butler had issued few orders for defending the citadel, Wool appointed Gen. Joseph Lane as commandant in the city. Lane was given orders to concentrate the public stores, prepare street barricades, and fortify the cathedral. Capt. Lucien B. Webster placed two twenty-four-pound howitzers on the hill that overlooked a plain to the east. Wool warned local municipal officials about sending information to Santa Anna concerning the American forces and cautioned the troops about molesting citizens. "Old Granny Wool," a volunteer wrote, "will not allow us to impose on them in the least." One Mexican was killed when he refused to give his blanket to one of the volunteers. Three men were drummed out of the service without courts-martial. Two had taken blankets from some Mexicans, while the other had shot at a Mexican dog—"and did not kill him either!"[67]

In late January 1847, south of Saltillo, Mexican cavalry captured two American patrols. Maj. Solon Borland and an Arkansas detachment, scouting on the San Luis road, met Maj. John P. Gaines with a Kentucky unit sent out by Butler. On the night of January 22, they sought shelter by climbing on the roof of a building at

Encarnación. At dawn, they found themselves surrounded by five hundred Mexican lancers under Gen. José Vicente Miñón. The Americans parlayed briefly but then surrendered. Four days later, Capt. William J. Heady and seventeen Kentucky cavalrymen set out to search for Gaines, but they were captured near Encarnación. Heady's men apparently became intoxicated and capitulated to armed Mexican rancheros without firing a shot.[68]

Wool urged Taylor to hurry to Saltillo. There was little doubt the vanguard of the Mexican army, estimated at twelve thousand men, was advancing north out of the desert toward Encarnación. If an attack came, Taylor's "presence, advice, counsel" would be critical. The next day Wool received orders placing him in charge of Saltillo and assigning Butler to command in the Monterrey district.[69]

Wool put his troops on alert. He stationed Hardin's First Illinois at Buena Vista and moved Bissell's Second Illinois and eighteen artillery pieces to a bivouac on high ground south of Saltillo. Each evening at dusk, the men packed everything but tents in wagons and slept with their muskets. Artillerymen at Buena Vista stood ready to fire signals if an enemy approached. Major Warren arrived on January 27 from Monclova with four Illinois companies and a supply train, and Wool put him in charge of the defense of Saltillo. Thinking fighting was imminent, the Mexican population began leaving the city.[70]

On Monday afternoon, February 2, General Taylor and a column of some seven hundred men arrived from Monterrey, and went into camp near Arizpe's flour mills, two miles southeast of town. "Old Rough and Ready," the newspapers labeled Taylor, was short and corpulent, weighing over two hundred pounds and, because of his unusually short legs, appeared toad-like on horseback. His face was leathery and deeply lined, and sharp grey eyes gazed out from under shaggy eyebrows above a hawk-like nose. When he spoke, his left eye twitched. Taylor wore plain attire—an old oilcloth cap, dilapidated frock coat, and nondescript trousers. In army circles, he was regarded as a sober, honest officer of ordinary ability who was slow in decision and lacked both tactical and strategic knowledge. Everyone agreed he was brave and resourceful. Soldiers saw this rough, simply dressed man as an equal, a general who had won great victories in Mexico—and might win more.[71]

Wool met Taylor's officers at a dinner. Bvt. Maj. William W. S. Bliss, adjutant and a former West Point professor, had served in the Florida wars as Taylor's chief of staff. Tactful and shrewd, Bliss handled Taylor's official correspondence, employing his skillful pen to temper his commander's views and correct and polish his grammar. Army officers nicknamed him "Perfect Bliss." Also present was Col. Jefferson Davis, West Pointer and at one time, Taylor's son-in-law. Brave, impetuous, with a deep interest in politics, Davis commanded the First Mississippi Rifles, which had received its baptism of fire at Monterrey. Others included the highly touted dragoon commander Bvt. Col. Charles A. May, described by one officer as looking like a "loafer," and the precise artilleryman Bvt. Maj. Braxton Bragg. Optimism and confidence prevailed as wine flowed and toasts were given.[72]

Taylor ordered his forces south to Agua Nueva. Wool had suggested placing the army near Buena Vista, but Taylor was determined to give the troops space and an opportunity to drill and prepare for battle. At Agua Nueva, the American encampment stretched nearly a mile across a barren plain. The two generals camped apart. Taylor put up his marque at the base of the Sierra Zapaliname on the east with Davis's regiment, May's dragoons, and Bragg and T. W. Sherman's batteries. Wool was to the rear and northeast with the bulk of the army. Here were seven volunteer regiments, a dragoon squadron, and Washington's artillery. The total force numbered over four thousand men. At Taylor's direction, Wool organized a camp of instruction and assigned guards and scouting details. He quickened interest in soldiering by reminding the officers that if they were defeated, Santa Anna would butcher every volunteer because of their depredations on Mexican civilians. Bliss later compared Wool and Taylor as commanders. Wool was "an excellent officer, especially in the way of discipline," but he was "a little too much of a martinet & too nice in trifles" for the volunteers. Taylor believed that the main thing was to keep the men in good health and spirits, teach them a few simple maneuvers, and forget about "niceties."[73]

While camped at Agua Nueva, a group of volunteers committed one of the most barbaric acts of the war. On February 10, a patrol brought in the mutilated body of an Arkansas soldier. Seeing his disfigured corpse, incensed Arkansans from Companies B and G, joined by a few Kentucky cavalrymen, saddled their horses and rode out to seek retribution. At Cantaña, a nearby rancho, they found the carbine sling belonging to the murdered man and demanded an explanation. Receiving none, they opened fire. Men, women, and children fled screaming to a nearby cave, fell on their knees, and while begging for mercy, were indiscriminately shot. Wool dispatched dragoons to stop the massacre and bring the Mexicans into camp for protection.[74]

Wool was furious. He demanded that Yell produce the guilty parties, but the colonel found it impossible to do so. Taylor ordered Companies B and G to prepare for duty on the Rio Grande. Yell pleaded for mercy, saying that banishing the companies to the rear would wreck the morale of his regiment. Wool finally agreed to reconsider, and Taylor suspended his order. Santa Anna's advance claimed his attention—and every American soldier was critical.[75]

Cold winds and snow flurries sent temperatures plunging near freezing as the jockeying for battle continued. "We drill three times daily," an Illinois volunteer complained. "From early morning at five o'clock till eight in the evening the roll of drums is heard." Tensions mounted. One day, when shots were heard near the mountains, Wool sent Lieutenant McDowell to investigate, and the burly officer and an orderly dashed off at a gallop. When a frightful yell was heard, the general called for his horse, buckled on his sword and charged out of camp—only to find the hapless McDowell sitting in a large prickly cactus patch. Wool never seemed to sleep. At night he frequently awoke, crying to the sentinel, "What noise is that?" "What time is it?" "Call Mr. McDowell." In the early dawn, the general mounted his bay horse and with an escort checked the picket lines. He grumbled about Taylor's laxness in army matters, his lack of military knowledge, and particularly his senseless plan to battle a large army on an open plain.[76]

On Saturday morning, February 20, Taylor dispatched two scouting parties to locate the Mexican advance. Colonel May took dragoon and volunteer cavalry units and a section of artillery—four hundred men in all—and moved east between the mountains toward the hacienda of La Hedionda. Wool was concerned Santa Anna would send a force along Taylor's eastern flank to circle through Palomas Pass and attack Saltillo. Maj. Ben McCulloch and his Texas spy company trotted cautiously south toward the hacienda of Encarnación.[77] Santa Anna was indeed marching north. In early January, after three months of preparation, he had collected an army of over twenty thousand men at San Luis Potosí. From a captured American courier, the Mexican general learned that Taylor had sent most of his regulars to Scott, and he was convinced that American volunteers could not withstand a determined Mexican assault. By moving swiftly, perhaps he could defeat Taylor before Scott landed at Vera Cruz. On January 28, with bands playing the popular tune "Adios," Santa Anna's army started north. Four cavalry brigades led the advance, followed by the artillery with twenty-one assorted cannon and a long pack and ammunition train pulled by 450 mules. The infantry, estimated at eighteen thousand men, marched in three divisions under Gens. Francisco Pacheco, Manuel María Lombardini, and José María Ortega. Santa Anna traveled in a carriage protected by a mounted regiment of colorful Hussars. On February 17, at Encarnación, the Napoleon of the West reviewed his army, now reduced to less than fifteen thousand men because of fatigue and desertions. Four days later, he sent General Miñón east and north with his cavalry through Palomas Pass toward Saltillo. A great battle was near, one that might well determine the course of the war and the very history of the two infant republics.[78]

7

TORRENTS OF BLOOD

Shortly before dawn on February 21, 1847, Bvt. Col. Charles A. May, his long hair blowing in the wind, trotted into Gen. Zachary Taylor's camp at Agua Nueva with a dust-begrimed cavalry detachment and two light artillery pieces. The day before, the black-whiskered officer had reached the hacienda at La Hedionda, fifteen miles to the east, and in mid-afternoon sent scouts south to sweep the valley for enemy soldiers. That night, as signal fires glowed on distant mountain peaks, his men brought in a Mexican deserter who said that Santa Anna was at Encarnación and planned to march on Agua Nueva the next day. May rode through the night to report to Taylor. The general listened—but hesitated. Santa Anna had to cross a thirty-mile desert and could not mount a sustained attack that evening.

Excitement in camp reached fever pitch shortly after noon, when Capt. Ben McCulloch and his hard-riding Texas scouts reined up at headquarters. In disguise, McCulloch had managed to prowl around the sprawling Mexican camp at dawn. He estimated the Mexican army numbered as many as twenty thousand men. Taylor sent his orderlies scrambling to call officers to a council. A great battle was in the offing.[1]

At the council Wool, citing reconnaissance reports by engineer officers Maj. Joseph King Fenno Mansfield and First Lt. Henry Washington Benham, fought with Taylor about meeting Santa Anna at Agua Nueva. He reminded the general that together they had reconnoitered both flanks and knew that the enemy, by marching north on roads to their right and left, could turn either flank and cut off Taylor from his depot at Saltillo. Wool urged Taylor to fall back twelve miles to a defensive position at Buena Vista. Here the artillery would be far more effective. Taylor, however, despite the decisiveness of his artillery in the battle at Palo Alto, placed no faith in such weaponry and remained bull-headed. Finally, Wool, his eyes flashing, declared that he would not see the army sacrificed. He would take full responsibility and personally lead the troops back to Buena Vista! Taylor reddened, blistered the air with profanity, and snapped at Bliss to order the army to retire to Buena Vista.[2]

With drums beating and bugles blowing, regiment after regiment struck their tents, packed their baggage, hitched teams, and started north. Yell's Arkansas cavalry was left at the rancho until the military stores there could be collected in wagons scheduled to arrive that night. As the army strung out on the dusty road leading to the pass, Taylor sent Col. William Robertson McKee's Second Kentucky Infantry and a section of artillery to Encantada to assist Yell. At Angostura, the "Narrows," Hardin's First Illinois went into camp to guard the pass. The main force pushed on and bivouacked that afternoon on the plain near Buena Vista.[3]

Taylor and Wool reached the adobe ranch in the late afternoon. In the fading twilight, Wool and a group of officers examined the terrain south of the hacienda. With Wool were Bliss, Davis, and several engineer officers, including Major Mansfield and Lt. John Pope. After nightfall, the wagon train, having discharged its freight, rumbled south with an escort to retrieve the supplies at Agua Nueva. Believing it important to check the defenses at Saltillo, Taylor took May's dragoons, Davis's Mississippi Rifles, along with Sherman's and Bragg's batteries, and headed north at sunset. Before parting, Taylor remarked to Wool, "General, as you have reconnoitered these grounds and I have not, should the enemy arrive before my return, you will select the field of battle, and make such dispositions of the troops as you may deem necessary to meet the opposing force." Candles burned late that night in Wool's tent as he and his staff studied maps and contemplated deployments for battle.[4]

In darkness and bitter cold, soldiers at the Narrows labored with pick and shovel, their area lighted by mesquite-fed bonfires. Here Wool was determined to make a stand. Six Illinois companies scurried up the hill to the east of the road and dug trenches and threw up breastworks; down below and west of the road, other soldiers excavated a trench for two companies and piled up dirt and rocks for protection. Across the dusty road, about twenty paces wide, Washington's artillerymen cut still another ditch, wheeled five guns into position, and formed a movable barricade of wagons loaded with stores, with the wheels locked together with chains. By dawn, Wool was ready.[5]

At four o'clock in the morning, Wool was awakened by the rumble of wagons. Yell had arrived with the train carrying the remaining supplies from Agua Nueva. As Yell's forward picket on the Encarnación road had been driven in about midnight, there had been great alarm in camp. In their panic, the teamsters had started their wagons in haste, many ran into each other and overturned, others became hopelessly locked together. With further loading impossible, the soldiers hurriedly set fire to the rancho and a large stack of wheat, threw great quantities of corn and beans into a nearby stream, and retreated north into the night with the loaded wagons, picking up McKee's infantry on the way. Distant bugles of the Mexican cavalry could be heard in the distance as Yell's column moved hastily along the dark road north. While the American army cooked its breakfast, Wool prepared orders for the various commanders to take up positions on the battle line.[6]

Wool's staff reported to his tent at dawn on February 22. There was no council of war, as was normal, since he regarded such meetings as "shields to bad generalship." During the night, Wool had pondered troop dispositions, and prepared a battle plan. The key position was the pass—about a mile and a half south of the Buena Vista rancho—where the road dropped sixty feet under the western rim of the plateau. A hill overlooked the road on the left, while on the right ran a deep arroyo, a network of treacherous gullies, and broken terrain extending west toward the mountains. At the pass, infantry and artillery hurried into position to block the road. Wool emphasized the importance of the defile because Mexican artillery and cavalry would find it difficult to cross the arroyos on the plateau to the east and move across the gullies to the west. To reach Saltillo, Santa Anna must break through the gap.[7]

Above the pass, a tableland ran southeast for over a mile and a half to steep limestone mountains. Covered by clumps of cactus, the plateau was cut by deep arid arroyos that began in the foothills and stretched like large rugged fingers to the west. These yawning gulches, with steep banks and dry sandy beds, widened as they ran toward the road. Mexican infantry could use them as sheltered passages, but enemy cavalry and horse artillery would find them difficult. One ravine ran all the way from the mountains to the road, debouching just north of the pass. South of this ravine, on a wide strip of plateau, Wool proposed to place his battle line. Here mobile light artillery supported by infantry could sweep enemy infantry marching at the heads of the ravines. To the rear and north of the pass, several arroyos blocked access to the rancho of Buena Vista. One of these reached to the mountains and was a potentially weak point, Wool realized. If Wool had to shorten his line, a Mexican force might move along the foothills, turn his left flank, and strike at Taylor's supply train parked on the road near Buena Vista. All would be lost.[8]

Reports of Santa Anna's advance continued to arrive at Wool's headquarters. At eight o'clock in the morning, Wool rode down to the pass with several officers where he learned that Santa Anna's cavalry was past Encantada and steadily moving north. He sent Capt. George Lincoln, his adjutant, hurrying to bring the regiments onto the field. As the sound of drums echoed along the valley, soldiers packed camp gear in company wagons and checked their ammunition. With banners flying, the regiments wheeled into line and gave a hearty cheer. Bands struck up "Hail Columbia," "Yankee Doodle," and other martial airs as the little army maneuvered into line on the road and moved by columns to the battlefield. It was a bright morning, and the soldiers were in high spirits.[9]

Mounted on his big bay, Wool watched as his small army fell into position. Hardin's First Illinois was already at the pass, overlooking Washington's battery of eight guns. Six companies climbed into trenches on the plateau above the road, while two companies settled behind a breastwork on the right. Hardin's mission was to protect the artillery at the pass. To create a second line, McKee marched his Second Kentucky Infantry to a hill behind Hardin, and Bissell led the Second Illinois to the left of McKee and marched east across the plateau and halted about a half mile from the pass. Marshall's Kentucky Cavalry and Yell's Arkansans trotted east of Bissell toward the foothills with orders to dismount. Meanwhile, Lane's second and third regiments of the Indiana brigade halted on the second ridge behind and to the left of Washington. In the right rear of Bissell sat Steen's First Dragoons and McCullough's Texas spy company. In overview, the two Illinois regiments formed Wool's front line on the plateau, one protecting the pass and the other forming the anchor for the eastern sector. The Indiana brigade, Kentucky infantry, and supporting cavalry were in a position to maneuver and provide support as needed. The line was thin, but Wool planned to fill the half-mile gap when Taylor returned with his troops.[10]

About ten o'clock, General Taylor reached the battlefield from his camp at Saltillo. He glanced at the troop dispositions, and complimented Wool, saying the army was in a position of "remarkable strength." With his staff, Taylor rode east along the line as the soldiers gave a rousing cheer. He had won every battle he had fought against the Mexican army, and his popularity was enormous.[11]

Wool followed in Taylor's wake. In front of each regiment, he made a short spirited speech. In a shrill voice, he reminded the soldiers that it was Washington's birthday and he hoped that "no American soldier would disgrace it." Their protracted and weary marches were over. The enemy "now stood before them in sufficient strength to give them all they could require in the way of combat, and to afford *every* man an opportunity to win all the distinction he could wish." What "great good fortune" it was, Wool declared, to be called upon "to mark the anniversary of a day already hallowed to their country, and one on which no man could be unfaithful to the trust she had confided to him." Wool shouted out, "Memory of Washington!" Cheers again echoed across the plain, with cries of "Washington! Washington!"[12]

In the late morning, a vast, billowing cloud of dust rose along the horizon to the south. As the dust settled, Wool squinted through his spyglass and carefully studied the large body of Mexican cavalry halt about a mile away. Engineers with the group rapidly climbed up the neighboring hills to view the terrain while an unending stream of infantry wheeled off the road toward the American left. The enemy cavalry gradually extended east in a long line with flags and pennants flying. Spirited music from a half dozen Mexican bands drifted up the valley. In the distance, dozens of tiny figures—men and mules—pulled cumbersome cannon toward elevated positions on Taylor's left. Thousands of lances glittered in the bright sunlight. It was a grand, awesome sight.[13]

As Santa Anna deployed his forces, three Mexican horsemen bearing a white flag trotted up the road toward the American lines. Taylor sent three officers and an interpreter to meet them. Handed a message, one horseman dashed back to Taylor. Santa Anna was demanding the Americans surrender. "You are surrounded by twenty thousand men, and cannot in any human probability, avoid suffering a rout and being cut to pieces with your troops," the Mexican general boldly declared. He gave Taylor one hour to save his army from a catastrophe. Taylor bellowed out, "Come and take us!" as he ordered Bliss to compose a proper reply and translate it into Spanish. Bliss's short response read: "Sir: In reply to your note of this date, summoning me to surrender my forces at discretion, I beg leave to say that I decline acceding to your request."[14]

Before noon, Taylor began changing Wool's battle plan. He ordered Bragg's section, McKee's Kentucky Infantry, and Pike's companies of Arkansas Cavalry to cross the road and take a position in the ravine, west of the pass. By this move, nearly one thousand men left the plateau to provide a crossfire if the Mexicans threatened to force the narrow defile guarded by Washington's artillery. American engineers rode out between the lines to count the various units of the Mexican army as bugles blared constantly. About noon, the American engineers reported a large Mexican movement toward the left and Wool gave orders to readjust the battle line. Nearly a mile away, he saw row upon row of infantry heading for the mountain base on his left. At Wool's order, General Lane called Bowles's Second Indiana from reserve and hurried with three guns under Capt. John Paul Jones "Paddy" O'Brien onto the plateau to an advanced defensive position on the left. The infantry would protect O'Brien's "bulldogs," as he called his guns, while he tried to block any enemy attempt to force a flanking passage there. Bissell moved the Second Illinois into the line to fill the gap east of Hardin at the pass and Bowles. Lt. Samuel G. French posted a twelve-inch howitzer on Bissell's left, while Lt. George H. Thomas, later lionized as the "Rock of Chickamauga" in the Civil War, unlimbered a six-pounder cannon to Bissell's right. Behind Washington and Hardin, a line of reserves included McKee's Infantry, Steen's dragoons, McCulloch's Texans, Lane's Third Indiana (behind Bissell), and Davis's Mississippians (behind Bowles). After dark, two dragoon companies rode back to Buena Vista to guard the baggage and supply wagons.[15]

Wool now galloped to the far left of the line, where he positioned Marshall's Kentucky Cavalry and ordered the rifle companies of the Kentuckians and Arkansans to dismount and act as skirmishers. Three hundred yards in their rear, he placed Roane and four dismounted Arkansas companies along with four Indiana companies under Maj. Willis A. Gorman. Colonel Marshall was to command this critical salient. After Wool left, fumbling on the left began immediately. Marshall ordered a battalion of riflemen forward to ascend a prominent spur in the foothills. Mexican infantry was rapidly approaching and the colonel wanted a commanding position.[16]

While the maneuver was underway, Wool spotted an additional enemy force moving toward Marshall that was concealed behind another ridge. He hastily dispatched his quartermaster officer, Capt. William W. Chapman, to alert Marshall. Chapman, however, told the colonel to pull back the skirmishers. When the bugler blew recall, Wool raced up boiling mad and reversed the order, saying Chapman had been confused. Marshall again started the infantrymen toward the spur—but it was too late. Mexican troops under Cuban-born Pedro de Ampudia y Grimaret, veteran of the Siege of the Alamo, San Jacinto, Palo Alto, and Monterrey, had swarmed onto it and opened fire. Marshall extended his line and returned fire.[17]

At 3 P.M., Santa Anna opened the battle by firing a howitzer shell into the American lines. Sporadic cannonading followed, as artillerymen sought to calculate the range. As his infantry scrambled up the mountains on the left, Santa Anna made a feint toward the pass. Earlier, with little knowledge of the terrain near the pass, Taylor became nervous and sent McKee's Second Kentucky foot, Pike's Arkansas cavalry, and Bragg with two guns across the road to the right. After threading two miles of treacherous gullies, they took position in advance of Washington's guns at the pass.[18]

Much to his disgust, Wool found that Taylor had altered his battle plans. "If the General had examined his position and the grounds to the right and front," Wool later told historian Henry Dawson, "he would not have ordered McKee to the right, for a march in his front, extending from the river to the mountains, would not have admitted the passage of the enemy's artillery without great difficulty and loss of time." The shifting of these troops—nearly 750 men—away from the main battlefield was clearly an error. "It was the only instance," Wool said, "in which General Taylor interfered with my order of battle without consulting me. If he had done so in that case, he would not have given the order." The decision "came near to losing us the battle."[19]

The American forces on the plateau watched the ebb and flow of battle in the eastern foothills, cheering whenever their troops gained ground. Fortunately for the Americans, the Mexican infantry consistently fired too high and missed their targets. In the fading twilight, Santa Anna's engineers began moving a long-range twenty-four pounder onto the plateau in the rear of Ampudia's infantry on the mountain slopes. Once in operation, it could enfilade the American line. At dusk Wool instructed Marshall to establish pickets and bring his men down and camp at the base of the mountain.[20]

Believing a night attack unlikely, Taylor took Davis's Mississippi Regiment, May's dragoons, and several engineers and headed north to Saltillo to check on troops posted to protect his supply depot and the city. During the day, Maj. William B. Warren, commanding in the city, had reported that Gen. José Vicente Miñón and twelve hundred lancers had come through Palomas Pass, halted on the plain northeast of Saltillo for several hours, and then retired. It was rumored that one thousand Mexican rancheros had gathered to the north and northwest of the city and were awaiting orders to strike. When Taylor reached the city, he found that Major Warren had concentrated supplies in the cathedral, barricaded the streets, and had sent one of his four Illinois companies to support Webster's battery of twenty-four pounders on the neighboring hill. The general stationed two Mississippi companies and a six-pounder at Arispe's Mills, his supply depot southeast of town. Teamsters parked all available wagons at the mills. Taylor planned to rejoin Wool early next morning.[21]

Wool slept little that night as a light rain swept over the battlefield. After most of the firing ceased at sunset, he sent wagons loaded with food and water lumbering along the line. The regiments had stacked arms and sat huddled in small groups on the cold barren plain. No fires were allowed. The general sent a courier with orders for McKee, Bragg, and Pike to return to the pass. McKee, who had pitched camp, ignored the order. Wool also had teamsters turn the long supply train parked near Buena Vista north toward Saltillo. Moonlight bathed the landscape as dragoons prowled between the lines. Two men took posts at the head of each ravine. As silence fell over the valley, the shouts of thousands of voices could be heard. Santa Anna was haranguing his troops, and the cry "Viva la Republica!" echoed and re-echoed across the landscape. Mexican bands sent strains of music, delicate and sweet, drifting on the night air toward the American lines.[22]

The intense chill of a winter night soon settled over the armies. High on the mountain, pickets exchanged shots. "I sat on my blanket for hours watching the affair on the ridge yonder," one soldier mused. "I couldn't hear the rifles, but the sparkles reminded me of June in Indiana and of fire-flies gleaming across a meadow." Before midnight, the sky became overcast, and a sharp cold wind rushed through the valley, bringing showers of rain. In his tent, Wool pored over battle plans by candle light. The prospects were gloomy. Taylor had removed nearly 1,200 men from the line, leaving him about 3,000 to meet Santa Anna's estimated 12,000 troops.[23]

Throughout the night, the Mexican army worked feverishly. Under the supervision of engineers, long lines of soldiers pulled on ropes to assist mule teams dragging a battery of five eight-pounders up the mountainside to positions from which they could pour a devastating fire into the American left. Mexican infantry, two thousand strong, under Gens. Manuel María Lombardini and Francisco Pacheco, trudged quietly along the broad arroyos fronting the plateau to join Ampudia. Brigades of lancers trotted toward the American left and dismounted to rest their horses. Shortly after midnight, additional infantry pushed their way up the dark slopes toward the summit of the mountain and outflanked the American pickets. On the road, Mexican officers collected troops for a feint at the pass. At dawn, Santa Anna completed plans to hit the American lines at three places—right, left of center, and left. He was highly pleased with his troop dispositions and had little doubt that a great victory was at hand.[24]

After several hours of fitful rest, Wool rose before sunrise on February 23, and summoned his staff. He realized a great battle was at hand, one that might determine the course of the war, and there was much to do. He ordered two veteran regulars, Churchill and Mansfield, to maneuver the companies and regiments on the left and right into battle formation. Staff officers, aides, and civilian assistants would serve as couriers. General Lane would command the troops on the left wing, and Colonel Hardin the units on the right.[25]

As his tiny army was certain to face tidal waves of Mexican infantry, Wool spent much time carefully deploying his artillery. American flintlock muskets had an effective range of 100 yards, but a six-pounder gun could reach 1,500 yards. Pulled by six-horse teams, these highly mobile weapons could move quickly to critical positions to check advancing infantry. Unlike Taylor, who had little faith in artillery, Wool used artillery as anchor points with infantry as support. The Americans would fight a defensive battle. Favored by the terrain, they might with determination, raw courage, and luck, successfully blunt Mexican assaults and hold their positions. If the line collapsed, Wool realized, the American army might be annihilated.[26]

By seven o'clock, Wool began reinforcing the battle line. Skirmishing had resumed on the mountain, so he dispatched Maj. Xerxes Trail with an Illinois rifle battalion and Edward P. Connor with two companies of Texans to strengthen Lane on the left. Wool instructed him to reinforce the skirmishers on the side of the mountain and to hold his position to the last man. The Third Indiana moved to McKee's old position behind the pass while Sherman's battery climbed onto the plateau to reinforce Thomas at the right of Bissell. At the pass, Washington prepared his eight guns for action.[27]

In the crisp morning sunlight on February 23, Santa Anna's army could be seen spread out in colorful array. A cool breeze roused gaudy pennants. With a dozen bands playing anthems, Catholic priests passed along an unending line of kneeling infantry swinging censers, reciting mass, and bestowing blessings. Then, with thunderous "vivas," the Mexican troops rose and marched with banners flying to assigned positions for battle.[28]

At eight o'clock Santa Anna struck both sides of the American line simultaneously. On the road, a heavy column of Mexican cavalry and infantry under Gen. Ignacio Mora y Villamil, with three pieces of artillery providing support, started forward in precise order. Washington sent for Wool, who came immediately to the pass to watch the engagement. At about twelve hundred yards, Washington's guns opened with solid shot. A shower of metal fell on the marching men and horses, tearing gaps in the column. The Mexicans quickly reformed and resumed their advance. A second volley, however, threw the soldiers into confusion, and they rushed to their right off the road into a gorge. There they organized and hurried east along a deep ravine to join the assault on the left.[29]

As the attack on the road collapsed, Wool rushed to bolster his left. He had earlier rushed Mansfield across the road to bring Bragg and McKee from the far right to the battlefield, and sent Churchill galloping off to warn Lane of a major assault. Enemy infantry would emerge from the gorge in his front very soon. At daylight, Mexican forces on the mountain slopes had opened a brisk fire on the dismounted cavalry on the mountains. Lane, posted on the left side of the Second Indiana, hurried eight Kentucky companies and O'Brien's three guns forward to the head of the gorge. As the Americans rushed forward, four thousand blue-coated infantry of Lombardini and Pacheco's divisions and a large body of lancers climbed out of the gorge and burst into view. Forming a column of brigades, they advanced on Lane and opened fire. O'Brien put his guns into action, supported by the well-aimed fire of the Indiana infantry. At the same time, French, Thomas, and Sherman, together with Bissell's six Illinois companies, shifted to the left to provide a crossfire. Nine artillery pieces hurled deadly missiles into the enemy infantry, causing great slaughter. The Guanajuato corps came close to annihilation. As the assault stalled, Mexican officers ordered their men to retire behind a slight rise.[30]

At this point, Wool had just reached the plateau. As he scanned the field with his spyglass, his heart sank. His left flank was crumbling! Hastily calling Lincoln, Churchill, and other officers, he ordered them to race east across the plateau and stop the confusion.[31]

While the Mexican infantry reformed, Lane had decided to alter his position. Bowles's Second Indiana was taking a beating from heavy artillery planted on the neighboring ridge. A brigade of lancers also had appeared. To better engage the enemy infantry organizing at the head of the gorge, Lane ordered O'Brien to move his three guns forward to the head of the next ravine, while sending Bowles word of his decision. Recoiling under heavy fire, the Hoosiers appeared confused. Then came, again and again, Bowles's shrill cry, "Cease fire and retreat!" As the clouds of smoke cleared, the colonel watched as O'Brien brought his teams forward, and having no instructions, somehow assumed the artillery was retreating. In their retreat, the Indiana companies glanced back, saw the dreaded lancers racing forward and started to run for the rear. The flight of the Hoosiers would haunt Wool for years. O'Brien suddenly found himself dangerously exposed. He was in musket range of 3,000 infantry and under fire from the Mexican battery 300 yards to his left. The captain ordered his guns double-shot with canister, fired several salvos, then limbered up and retired, leaving one of his disabled "bulldogs" behind.[32]

The American retreat became a rout. Astonished at the sudden flight to the west of him, Marshall, facing advancing Mexican infantry and cavalry, recalled his Kentuckians from the mountain slopes and joined Yell, with several Arkansas companies, in retreat. Supporting companies under Trail, Gorman, and others scattered into ravines or headed for the rancho—and even Saltillo—in the rear. On the flank, the Second Illinois, less than a quarter mile from the Hoosiers, also wavered, but Churchill, overseeing the American left, galloped into the milling companies and patiently reformed them parallel to the mountain where Mexican troops were streaming along the base. Reinforced by Ampudia's light troops coming down the adjoining slopes, six thousand Mexican infantry and lancers moved in an unending column toward Wool's rear. Simultaneously, the San Patricio Battalion, a group of Irish American deserters who had joined Santa Anna, positioned three pieces of heavy ordnance on a ridge southeast of the battlefield and began to shell the American center. Wool was facing disaster.[33]

He raced to Bissell's position and clamored to bolster the center and check the column on his flank. Churchill shortened the line, wheeled the field guns with the Second Illinois, and began hurling round shot into the enemy. McKee's Kentucky Infantry and Trail's battalion on the right and left of Bissell's position also opened fire. But Wool badly needed reinforcements and more firepower. He sent an aide to hurry Hardin and four companies of the First Illinois from the road onto the plateau. As Hardin hastened east, a Mexican detachment opened fire from a neighboring ravine, and the Americans turned and rushed the foe in the only bayonet charge of the battle.[34]

Where was Bragg? Shortly after 9 A.M., Mansfield brought McKee's Kentuckians, Pike's Arkansas Cavalry, and Bragg's section from the right. Crossing the road, Bragg saw a dust cloud on the road near Buena Vista and, with Mansfield's permission, headed north, thinking the enemy cavalry were advancing. Learning it was Taylor arriving from Saltillo, Bragg turned and, whipping his six-horse teams, climbed directly onto the plateau and prepared the Second Illinois for action. Huge clouds of blue smoke drifted over the battlefield as opposing artillery blasted away.[35]

The concentrated fire of six guns, supported by some one thousand American infantry, partially checked the flow of Mexican troops on the left flank, forcing them back against the mountain, and pinching the column into two bodies. The Mexican advance—several thousand infantry and lancers—found the artillery fire too devastating to face in retreat, so they headed toward Buena Vista. At the same time, the San Patricio Battalion, its green silk flag with its silver cross and golden harp flying in the wind, opened fire on the ridge with two twenty-four-pounders and one sixteen-pounder, hurling canister five hundred yards. The Illinois soldiers were forced to pull back out of range. Wool ordered McKee's Kentuckians into a ravine for shelter and rest. All attention shifted to the Mexican lancers racing for Buena Vista and Taylor's supply train.[36]

Close to ten o'clock in the morning, Wool, who had been dashing around the battlefield rallying his small army for battle, saw Taylor approaching on the Saltillo road with May's Second Dragoons, and Wool galloped north to meet him. Davis's Mississippi infantry were three miles behind. The two generals conversed briefly, Wool explained his troop dispositions and urged that a major effort be made to block the Mexicans moving to his rear. Taylor said that he would ride to the "front" and give directions wherever necessary, but he wanted Wool to continue in charge of the "active duties of the field." With this, they parted. Taylor rode to the pass where he met Bliss, who had remained on the battlefield during the night. "We are whipped," his adjutant cried. "I know it," Taylor responded, "but the volunteers don't know it. Let them alone, and see what they will do."[37]

Wool signaled to May's dragoons and Pike's cavalry to ride to the rancho and join Yell's and Marshall's cavalry. May dallied and never reached the objective. Wool and several officers galloped to the road and again began scouring the ravines for soldiers. With the right collapsing, Lincoln, "noble and gallant," spurred his horse into one of the deep ravines where the Kentucky foot had been compelled to retreat, turned about facing the enemy, and in front of the Kentuckians, waving his saber in the air, shouted out, "Let us draw our sabers and endeavor to rally and lead these men on." Encouraged by "his bold and daring bravery," the men from Kentucky rushed again to the front and poured a devastating fire into the Mexicans. Sensing that he had helped to turn the tide, Lincoln turned about, facing the Kentuckians, and was mortally wounded with a ball in the back of his head. Four men later carried his corpse from the field. Wool's staff officers warned the general against ignoring the dangers. "I overtook Bowles and [James H.] Lane in the deep and broad ravine that bounded our rear," Wool later wrote Sarah. "I asked them why they abandoned their positions. The reply was that the men would not stand the fire of the Mexicans and fled the field." Wool ordered them to return to the plateau and collect their men. Spurring his horse, Wool turned his eye on the Mexicans organizing near the mountain. Once again, he encountered soldiers huddled together and exhorted any officer present to take his men to the battlefield. When the officer refused, the general struck the man with the flat of his sword.[38]

Wool was excited to see Davis's Mississippi infantry advancing in a column of companies—three hundred strong—and he galloped down the road to meet them. Attired in red shirts, white trousers, and black slouch hats, they were a colorful group. He greeted Davis and pointed to the right at the Mexican lancers racing for the rancho. He ordered the colonel to move double-quick to meet them, promising to furnish support. Davis veered to his left and Wool rode south to bring up the Third Indiana and a section of artillery. A major clash of arms was in the offing.[39]

Double-timing his regiment, Davis hurried across a ravine, and moved up a tongue of land toward the mountain and watched. When they came within range of the massed Mexican infantry, the Mississippians, carrying percussion rifles, halted and opened fire. As the enemy foot soldiers stumbled and then fell back, a brigade of eight hundred lancers under Gen. Anastasio Torrejón filed out from behind the infantry and formed in battle order. With bugles blaring, the horsemen thundered toward the rancho. Davis drew his regiment back along the ravine and halted. All eyes turned toward the two hundred supply wagons parked near Buena Vista. American troops scurried to meet the threat. The Third Indiana hurried from its support position to join Davis as Wool signaled Colonel May to move his dragoons and Pike's Arkansas squadron to meet the Mexican onslaught.[40]

Orders and counter-orders flew across the battlefield. Wool advised Taylor to consider plans "to retire" to Saltillo. Taylor agreed and Wool alerted Washington, at the pass, to prepare for such a contingency. When an overanxious subaltern started to "retire" his gun, Taylor quickly ordered Washington to hold his position. Apparently, Wool also alerted the officer in charge of the supply train parked at Buena Vista to start toward Saltillo, but its commander, seeing a Mexican build-up to the east, stopped the train.[41]

At the rancho, Colonels Yell and Marshall rallied some 400 men of their shattered commands and bravely rode out to meet 1,200 Mexican lancers head on, splitting the attacking horsemen into two groups. One group swept by the adobe buildings and corrals under heavy fire by Americans who were inside, then, seeing May approaching, turned and dashed across the road and headed west toward the mountains, eventually regaining the Mexican lines. The second group fell back east toward the Mexican infantry near the mountains and reformed. Although forty-nine-year-old Col. Archibald Yell was killed in the fighting, the brief, determined stand saved the rancho and the train from destruction. May and Pike did not arrive in time to participate in the attack.[42]

It was nearing noon. At the base of the mountain, Mexican officers moved units into formation for yet another attack. Lancers lined up to spearhead the advance. Davis moved his Mississippians east a short distance along the south bank of a large ravine, then filed south to the center of a tongue of land and halted, facing the mountain. He kept his left anchored on the ravine. Wool brought up an Illinois detachment under Bowles, an artillery piece under Lt. Charles L. Kilburn, and James H. Lane's Third Indiana. The Indianans climbed out of a deep arroyo south of Davis's position and, facing north, formed a line along the bank slightly in advance of Davis's right flank to create a crossfire. Kilburn unlimbered on Davis's left. The Hoosiers, their backs to the gorge, formed the right wing of a reentering angle opening toward the enemy. Here was the celebrated "V" that Davis crowed about later, calling it the most critical maneuver of the battle.[43]

At the sound of bugles, some one thousand Mexican lancers trotted forward by squadrons, with the infantry following behind. With their officers yelling for them to hold their fire, the eight hundred American infantry stood silently as the horsemen approached. Suddenly the lancers slowed to a walk, somewhat perplexed at the line stoically arrayed in front of them. When within eighty yards—some said closer—Davis, then Lane, gave the order to fire. The deadly volley crumpled the enemy front ranks—and the horsemen wheeled in a bloody retreat in a cloud of dust. American artillery fired round shot at the Mexican infantry retreating in confusion. Davis and Lane had broken the lancer onslaught—but the enemy was not beaten.[44]

As the artillery fired and pressed forward, Wool noted that his infantry was hesitant. He galloped to a rise, stood in his stirrups, and, waving his cap, cried to the soldiers, "Charge! Charge! Charge!" Only a few could hear or see him amid the thunder and smoke of cannon, so he turned to one of his medical officers, Philadelphia-born Dr. Grayson Mallet-Prevost, who was watching the battle on horseback and yelled out, "Captain, ride quick and order them to charge!" Mallet-Prevost raced down to the infantry and gave a field officer the message. An advance was impossible, came the reply, because of too much disorder in the ranks. In the meantime, Wool sent Addicks to bring up May's dragoons and ordered Bragg to hold his fire until May arrived. Twenty minutes later, the long-haired May rushed up with several volunteer companies and two more guns. With six guns, the general ordered an advance on the retreating Mexicans.[45]

At this point, a cold rare desert rainstorm swept over the battlefield. Lightning lit up the sky, thunder echoed across the mountains, and gale-force winds blew sheets of rain and hail. Great clouds of dust enveloped both armies, who ceased fire and watched in awe as nature displayed its might. In fifteen minutes, it was all over—and the battle resumed. At the center of the plateau, O'Brien and Thomas swung their guns to the left and fired on the drenched masses of Mexicans, who recoiled, then ran for a cove near the mountain base. Josiah Gregg, who was standing near one of the batteries, watched the retreat and predicted an American victory was at hand.[46]

It was now after one o'clock. As Wool watched the artillery roll forward to fire on some two thousand panic-stricken Mexicans huddled near the mountain, a courier rushed up with an order from Taylor who was over half a mile away, to order a cease fire on the left and report to him! Field officers were stunned, for they were sure they were on the verge of crushing a large part of the Mexican army. Whether out of compassion for the trapped enemy or through a ruse perpetuated by an "independent" flag brought onto the field by two Mexicans from the vicinity of the enemy battery at the southeast corner of the battlefield, Taylor rode to the left and halted all firing. The pair claimed Santa Anna had sent the flag bearers to see what Taylor's demands were. Taylor had dispatched a civilian aide, Thomas L. Crittenden, with a flag alone via Bragg's battery to the left to offer surrender terms to the Mexicans trapped in the cove. Ten minutes after he left, Wool rode up, and Taylor asked him to accompany the Mexican emissaries across the field to meet with Santa Anna. In the confusion, Crittenden was captured, but when the Mexicans began scrambling to flee their trap, he managed to escape.[47]

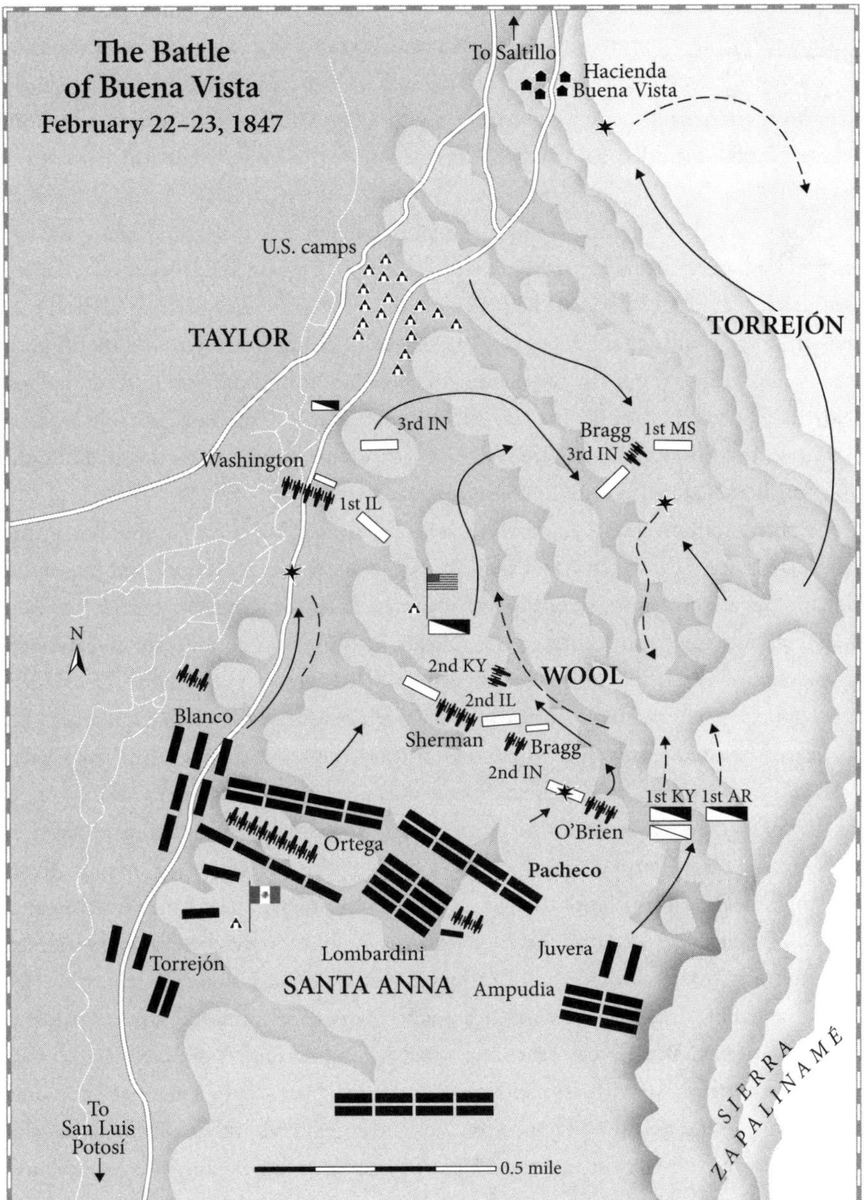

Cartography by Carol Zuber-Mallison/ZM Graphics, Inc.

With a junior officer and an interpreter, Wool galloped across the rocky, arid plateau toward the Mexican lines. Within ten minutes, however, the Mexican battery on the hillside suddenly opened fire, focused on the area around Taylor's position. Wool grew apprehensive—then suspicious. He questioned the Mexicans and they quickly admitted they had no authority to silence the guns—then raced off for their lines. Wool and his party wheeled their horses about and galloped back to safety. In the meantime, the trapped Mexicans began streaming in frenzied haste to rejoin their army. "It seems singular that as judicious an officer as General Taylor should have been entrapped in such an error," Gregg recorded. For years afterward, Wool believed Taylor's sudden compassion "to save human life" nearly cost the Americans the battle.[48]

When Wool reentered the lines, Taylor had left his command post, having ordered Colonel Hardin, near the center of the line, to advance artillery and infantry to attack a Mexican battery on the plateau firing on Wool's forces on the left and rear and strike the flanks of the retreating enemy. O'Brien took two guns to the head of the ravine south of the main gorge, near the position he and the Second Indiana had held that morning. Bissell's Second Illinois moved to O'Brien's right, followed by Hardin's First Illinois and McKee's Second Kentucky foot. George Thomas followed along on Bissell's right with a six-pounder.[49]

With these movements underway, Wool hurried to bring Davis and Bragg forward. The rattle of musketry and booming of cannon had increased, and he sensed that another attack was in the offing on the center. While ordering Bragg and Sherman with their batteries to the center of the plateau, he roused the Mississippi and Indiana regiments from their short respite and personally led them rapidly across the ravines, now slippery from another rainstorm, toward the sound of the guns. Bragg spurred his near-exhausted teams down the gorge toward the road, dropped his heavy caissons, and climbed up on the plateau. It was now after two o'clock in the afternoon.[50]

Taylor's center received a terrific pounding from the enemy artillery. Hardin, McKee, and Bissell moved out ahead of O'Brien's guns to engage the enemy. Then, suddenly, on their right flank, hordes of Mexican soldiers, attired in blue overcoats and tall, tinseled hats, swarmed out of a ravine. Wool thought Santa Anna's soldiers were not only better clothed than the Americans, even the regulars, but were better disciplined. Forming massive lines, they advanced, with mounted lancers trotting along as support. With great exertion, Santa Anna had joined the troops who had escaped from the cove with reserve regiments, creating a force of some five thousand men. In one grand assault, he hoped to crack Taylor's center and decisively defeat the American army. Unfortunately, the Mexicans were nearing exhaustion. Santa Anna was depending on tired, half-starved legions, many of whom had already faced the death-dealing American artillery for several hours.[51]

For the second time in five hours, American volunteer infantry broke and ran. Assailed front and flank, Hardin and a majority of the First Illinois plunged into the nearest ravine on their right, followed by McKee's Kentuckians and some of Bissell's Second Illinois. O'Brien and Thomas pulled back their guns to another ravine. Lancers rode into the ravines and killed at least two hundred Americans. Both Hardin and

McKee lay dead. Stumbling west toward the road, shattered companies suddenly saw more lancers approaching. But when Washington's battery began firing spherical case shot that burst over the horsemen's heads, they turned in retreat. Reaching the road, the Americans, crying and praying, ran toward the safety of Washington's battery at the pass. These men were part of the worst reverse of the entire battle, if not the war.[52]

Commanders now turned their attention to O'Brien's guns on the plateau. With infantry support melting around him, O'Brien and Thomas retired, then went into action again, as Mexican infantry pressed forward, with O'Brien about one hundred years to the right and in advance. Shouting, encouraging his men, O'Brien had one horse shot from under him, then another. Several of his powder-blackened gunners were hit, but they kept working the guns, sending death-dealing salvos at the enemy. Artillery horses fell kicking, some with their entrails hanging from their bodies, convulsing in the dust. Glancing back, O'Brien saw Bragg's artillerymen whipping their teams to bring his three six-pounders onto the plateau. Capt. Thomas "Tim" West Sherman came onto the field with two more guns. "This was the hottest, as well as the most critical, part of the action," Wool told Bliss later. Only about three thousand American troops had been available to meet the onslaught.[53]

Bragg, however, was dallying, taking time to converse with Taylor. According to Bliss, the young artillery officer rode up and expressed apprehension over possibly losing his three guns. "Never mind," Taylor exclaimed. "I'll take the responsibility. You must go into battery where you are." As Bragg moved forward, O'Brien, limping on one leg, helped his gunners load canister and fire at point-blank range, then hobbled to safety. Mexican infantry swarmed over the two guns, cut the harness loose from the dead and dying horses, and rolled the prizes to the rear.[54]

Bragg's field pieces now blasted away, supported by Sherman. Wool rode up, bringing Davis's Mississippians and Lane's Indianans onto the field at trail arms. They halted, formed in firing order, and swept the Mexican advance rushing toward Bragg. Wool galloped from place to place in the heat of the battle, shouting encouragement, exhorting men to fight on. When the enemy forces on Taylor's left suddenly faltered, then fell back to the gorge, the general sent May's dragoons up a ravine toward the mountain to circle and harass the crumpling Mexican flank. But Santa Anna had seen enough. While smoke hung over the field "like a veil," Carleton wrote, Mexican officers started pulling back their regiments, and by five o'clock, most of the firing had ceased. Lane's Indianans and Weatherford's Illinois infantry moved to the left and camped, Wool sent mounted pickets to roam near the enemy lines. At dusk, a heavy rain squall bathed the valley for half an hour before a deathly silence settled over the valley of the dead.[55]

As dazed, battle-weary soldiers sought their respective regiments, wagons rumbled up the ravines to collect the dead and wounded. Medical details found several dead Americans robbed, stripped, and mutilated. Starving Mexican soldiers, among those who had had been provided with proper provisions or uniforms, had rifled haversacks and donned American clothing to fight off the winter cold. The battlefield presented a grisly scene. An estimated 750 Americans had been killed or wounded. The bodies of Hardin, Yell, McKee, Lincoln, Henry Clay Jr., and numerous other officers were carried to Saltillo and interred the next day near Webster's redoubt. Enlisted men were buried in large pits dug in the rear of the pass. Teamsters took supply wagons loaded with bread, coffee, meat, and water to each camp. Rations were also handed out to 750 Mexican prisoners. Surgeons established a field hospital at Buena Vista and by candlelight they began to amputate arms and legs, the standard recourse for shattered limbs. The cold was intense, but no fires were allowed.[56]

In his tent that night, Taylor discussed plans with Wool to meet what was expected to be a renewed Mexican attack the next day. Less than 2,500 badly fatigued men bivouacked on the field that night, but fresh troops—infantry and artillery—were en route from Monterrey and Rinconada Pass. Most of the fighting men in Saltillo had started south. These men would boost Taylor's army to the number he had that morning. The officers debated whether to withdraw to Saltillo or even Monterrey or risk another battle the next day. General Miñón had again appeared on the plain southeast of Saltillo that afternoon and sent two thousand lancers to within two miles of the city. Webster's artillery fired on the horsemen, who retired toward the mountains. But they were still hovering near Palomas Pass. One officer urged Taylor to go to Buena Vista and demand that the seven hundred able-bodied soldiers camped there rejoin their regiments. The general and his staff officers rode to the place and pleaded for their service. They promised—but then hurried to Saltillo after he left.[57]

After the battle, Taylor reportedly said that Wool and Churchill advised a full retreat that evening to Saltillo. This is doubtful. To collect and move an exhausted army during the night would have been virtually impossible; the effect on morale would have been devastating. Knowing that fresh troops were on their way, Wool was optimistic. The enemy was also exhausted, hungry, and demoralized, and desertions were soaring. Buena Vista was Wool's battlefield: he selected it, fought on it, and held the enemy at bay. To retreat would be to reject his own judgment. This was his one crowning moment. His suspicion that Taylor referred to him when he spoke of those who advised retreat on the night of February 23 gnawed deeply, and in the weeks that followed the battle, he repeatedly asked Taylor to clarify the matter. Taylor, now a candidate for president, chose to avoid clarifying an issue that might tarnish his public image as the hero of Buena Vista. Whatever was said that night at Buena Vista, Taylor concluded the meeting by saying, according to an Ohio officer, "Well, gentlemen, the council is adjourned to meet after the battle."[58]

Wool shared Taylor's tent that night. Taylor ate a hearty meal and went to bed, but Wool called for his horse and, with an aide, rode out into the cloudless, moonlit night. A chain of dragoons prowled the army front. The veteran Mississippi regiment had left the battlefield, trudging north to Saltillo, with its colonel sitting in a wagon, delirious with fever from a foot wound. As Wool rode down the line, he considered shifting companies. Maj. Roger S. Dix, who accompanied him, recorded that "no persuasions or entreaties or cursing" could make the soldiers move. When an officer spoke disrespectfully and refused to order his men to relocate, Wool drew his sword and angrily whacked him with the flat of the blade—but the man still refused to rouse his weary companions. The general then rode north to the rancho, arriving about midnight. There he found a pitiful scene. Hundreds of wounded soldiers, some crying, others nearing unconsciousness and death, were crowded together in the darkened adobe buildings and corrals. Wool immediately ordered the wounded, both American and Mexican, taken that night to the spacious cathedral at Saltillo.[59]

The silence in the valley was deafening. In the distance, Lieutenant Carleton recorded, you could hear the "flapping of the wings of the fierce zapalotes [vultures]," hovering over the battlefield and the "almost human yell of the hungry wolves" gathering for their "horrible repast." Scattered over the plain were the dark forms "of what had been stalwart men and powerful steeds, some lying as if asleep, and some in strange, unnatural postures, with the moonlight resting steadily and cold on the bright points of uniforms and trappings, all still and firm as if they were belted to stone." Another young officer was equally perceptive. From the Mexican lines across the valley, where hundreds of campfires burned brightly, the rising breeze carried faint sounds of wheels creaking and men moving about. Near dawn, the rumble grew louder and was reported to Wool, who had stayed up all night. He called for his bay horse and with McDowell rode out to a hill overlooking the battlefield.[60]

As the sky purpled and streaked in the east, Wool gazed at the Mexican encampments with his spyglass. The sight was unbelievable. Santa Anna was in full retreat! With great emotion he rose in his stirrups and shouted, "Victory, Victory, Victory, the enemy has fled!" With tears streaming down powder-blackened faces, hundreds of drowsy soldiers sat up and began repeating the refrain. From regiment to regiment the cry of "victory, victory" echoed across the treeless plateau. With great emotion Wool spread the news as he dashed down to Taylor's tent, where he rushed to the general and embraced him and complimented him on his great and glorious victory. "We can't be beaten, General," Taylor blurted out, "when we all pull together."[61]

Early that morning, February 24, as burial details combed the ravines, Taylor and Wool, with a dragoon escort, crossed the battlefield and rode south toward Encantada. Santa Anna, they learned, had begun withdrawing his shattered army to Agua Nueva soon after sundown the previous evening. Faced with as many as five thousand desertions and chaos in many of his regiments, during and after the battle, Santa Anna had concluded he could not mount another major attack on Taylor's formidable position. Asserting that he had turned back the American invasion and carrying off captured flags and guns, the Mexican general retired to fight another day and began plans for defending Central Mexico. As many as fifteen hundred of his army, dead and wounded, were scattered in abandoned camps, on the battlefield, and along the road to San Luis Potosí. Wool never forgot the grisly sight on the plateau that morning: "The dead and the dying, the mutilated bodies and scattered limbs of the brave who had fallen—those with the dead horses and mules, broken muskets, swords, etc., etc. strewed for miles presented a sight which Heaven forbid I should never again behold."[62]

The casualty list was immense. Of 4,610 combatants, including officers, in Taylor's army on February 22, 746 had been killed, wounded, or were missing. No American wounded were found within Mexican lines. While there were hundreds of Santa Anna's men left wounded but living on the battlefield, yet not a single American, Wool was sure that all the Americans had been executed. Of an estimated 20,000 in Santa Anna's army, the best estimate is that 2,500 were killed or wounded. As reported later, Mexican soldiers carried away 800 of their crippled comrades from Encarnación on their backs. Over 700 were captured or surrendered. To General Churchill, the Battle of Buena Vista was San Jacinto all over again.[63]

Taylor sent Major Bliss and a dragoon attachment south to Agua Nueva under a white flag. Bliss had orders to arrange a prisoner exchange. Santa Anna agreeably released the seven American soldiers he held, plus the commands of Gaines and Borland, but he refused to send for the Mexican wounded at Saltillo. To do so, he declared bombastically, would imply he had accepted a peace. He remained determined to drive all the American forces to beyond the Nueces River. On the evening of the twenty-fifth, Lt. Daniel H. Rucker and Colonel Churchill marched three hundred Mexican prisoners to Encantada where they were exchanged. The next day the battered Mexican army began moving south for San Luis Potosí, its ranks gradually disintegrating. Of the magnificent force of 22,000 that had left that city, less than one half remained. Yet as he limped south across the desert to San Luis Potosí, Santa Anna sent couriers ahead to proclaim a great victory. He had stopped the Americans in their tracks and he had three captured cannon and three battle flags to prove it. For days, bells pealed joyously in Mexico City. On February 27, Taylor again moved his army south to Agua Nueva.[64]

Although he had gone sleepless for five days and was nearly exhausted, two days after the battle, Wool found time to write Sarah back home in Troy. He and Taylor had "fought a great battle and achieved a great victory." Santa Anna was in full retreat. Taylor was the "great man of the day," and Wool had little doubt he would be the next president of the United States. Taylor's "cool and determined bearing, strong mind, and sound judgement" was most admirable. From Camp Taylor at Agua Nueva on March 1, 1847, Wool wrote Sarah again with more details of the battle while urging her not to give his letter to the press. Although the little American army had won a great battle, he remained miffed and embarrassed that hundreds of Americans, especially the Indiana regiment, had fled the field and almost caused the Americans to lose the battle. The Hoosiers' retreat from the battlefield, which left such a dangerous gap in the American lines, was partly the result of mistaken orders, yet the imputation of cowardice hung over the Hoosier state for decades. "I presume [they] are still running in the expectation that Santa Ana [sic] and his troops are on their heels," Wool told Sarah.[65]

Even the battle-tested Taylor expressed shock at the carnage. Palo Alto, Resaca de la Palma, and Monterrey were mere "child's play" compared to Buena Vista, Taylor told Wool. "We have lost enough to put the whole land in mourning," Wool wrote Sarah. As soon as he learned that Santa Anna was in retreat, despite his fatigue, Wool had ridden over the battlefield with a small escort. Here were "men, horses, mules, pieces of wagons, broken guns, swords, pistols all mingled together, laying side by side, across and over each other," he told Sarah. In one place there was a "soldier with his head taken off, another with just his skull, another cut in two, some with arms, others with their legs off. Some shot through the head and others through the center of the body. The sight was appalling," he continued. Dead Mexicans were everywhere "from the tops of the mountains to the middle of the valley five miles below and as many miles on the plains near the mountains." On the day after the bloodletting, Wool sent orders for the alcalde at Saltillo to come to Buena Vista with a burial party and bury the Mexican dead. Hundreds of Santa Anna's wounded were found on the field, and Wool did everything he "could to relieve the wounded Mexicans" who "were treated as our own soldiers."[66]

As many as four hundred of Santa Anna's hungry and desperate men, either wounded or exhausted, were abandoned at Encarnación, forty-five miles south of Buena Vista, and all along the road leading across the desert toward San Luis Potosí. Wool ordered the alcalde of Saltillo to send twelve mules loaded with food for the Mexican wounded. If the alcalde failed to comply, he was to be jailed immediately. "We did all we could to relieve the wounded Mexicans," Wool told Sarah. Thousands of Santa Anna's men deserted. It was a depressing and appalling scene. In fact, "the whole distance was strewn with wounded, dead and dying," he told Sarah. Santa Anna had been in a "great hurry," he was sure.[67]

While companies buried the dead and couriers hurried to the Rio Grande with battle reports, Taylor's army—officers, enlisted men, and civilians—drafted official reports to superiors and wrote long letters to relatives and friends back home. They described recent experiences, repeated stories, and praised the heroes of the memorable two-day struggle. There was an outpouring of praise for Taylor as Whig newspaper editors touted him for the presidency. But others were remembered also.[68]

Writing the day after the battle, Taylor acknowledged his "great obligation" to General Wool for his "valuable services." Still later, in his lengthy official report on March 6, he was more expansive. "To Brigadier General Wool," he wrote, "my obligations are especially due. The high state of discipline and instruction of several of the volunteer regiments was attained under his command; and to his vigilance and arduous services before the action, and his gallantry and activity on the field, a large share of our success may justly be attributed." Many volunteer officers shared this view. General Wool, an Arkansas officer stated, "gained great credit" for himself in making "all the dispositions for the battle," and in exhibiting "the most quiet and unpretending bravery."[69]

In assessing the battle, Wool wisely praised his commander, but in private letters he emphasized the critical role the artillery played in holding the field. General Taylor was undoubtedly "the great man of the day," and "a great commander," he wrote Senator John Adams Dix back home in New York, but the artillery won the battle. Without the artillery, Taylor would have been overwhelmed and "easily beaten." He told Sarah the same thing, adding that each gun had fired from 100 to 250 rounds—mostly grape and canister—during the battle. Several officers singled out Braxton Bragg for his critical role during the assault on the center. Others spoke of "Paddy" O'Brien. "I heard General Bragg say," William T. Sherman later recalled, "that O'Brien at Buena Vista did more to secure a victory to our arms than he (Bragg) himself."[70]

No one doubted that Wool played a critical role in the battle of Buena Vista. He would celebrate his sixty-third birthday within a week, but the tough little veteran manifested the energy and stamina of a much younger man. For nearly sixteen hours he had been constantly in the saddle, dispatching aides to move troops to threatened salients, rallying dispirited battalions—all without regard for enemy fire. Wool freely admitted that on one occasion he despaired of holding the line. His heart sank, he said, when the left collapsed and General Torrejón's lancers came into view. But the same wild courage that drove a younger captain up the rain-drenched slopes of Queenston Heights, and emboldened him to face a host of British redcoats on Beekmentown Road thirty years before, had returned, and by great exertions he created a ragged but determined line to protect the exposed flank. Wool lacked the charisma to inspire men, but he was a fearless fighter and a superior tactician.[71]

Wool may have saved Taylor from losing the battle. Although he carefully avoided any comment that might tarnish his superior's image, several years later,

Wool admitted that Taylor had made glaring errors of judgment at Buena Vista. The general first made a mistake, he felt, on the night of February 22 when he divided his forces in the face of an overwhelming enemy. At that time, Taylor sent eight hundred men two miles to the right of the battlefield and took the elite troops, five hundred regulars, to Saltillo. Neither Napoleon nor the celebrated Denis Hart Mahan, then teaching at West Point, would have approved of this. It was agreed that the defenses of Saltillo were sufficient and the city was well defended. Wool also believed that Taylor, who knew of the skirmishing, could have reached the battlefield much earlier on February 23. Perhaps the greatest mistake was halting the battle to allow as many as two thousand trapped Mexicans to surrender. Finally, Taylor's order for O'Brien to advance without infantry support to harass on the Mexicans retreating from the gorge was premature and generated an attack on the center that would have succeeded if Wool had not rushed reinforcements to the plateau.[72]

Writing to Senator Dix, Wool modestly explained, "I ordered Sherman and Bragg's batteries to hasten to General Taylor, who was in command of the centre [*sic*], and I crossed over with the Mississippi and Third Indiana. All arrived in time to save the day." If they had arrived ten minutes later, the battle would have been lost. "It was a perfect game of chess," he wrote Sarah. With no reserves to drawn on, "every regiment and corps was compelled to change positions a dozen time in the course of the day to repel attacks made by fresh troops." When Sarah's brother, Joseph, wrote several months later to ask where Wool's headquarters had been during the battle, Wool told Sarah to "tell him mine was on horse back from the first dawn of day until dark." Wool considered Buena Vista "the greatest battle" ever fought on the North American continent. It was the "battle of battles." About 30,000 men had been involved, with only about 4,650 of them Americans. The odds had been five to one. "I trust my dear Sarah," he wrote home to Troy, "when the story is told you will have no cause to blush for your General."[73]

Despite his latent criticisms of Taylor, John Wool recognized the immense contribution Zachary Taylor had made in winning the battle. His coolness under fire and presence on the line contributed great support to wavering American soldiers. Mounted on a brown horse, "Old Zack" rode about, displaying raw courage and shouting encouragement to his tiny army amid the smoke and din of battle. Such was the role General Taylor played at Buena Vista.[74]

In the great battle at Buena Vista, Wool added fresh laurels to an already distinguished career. His crucial services, however, were drowned out by the rising clamor of the Whigs to make Taylor president. Usually outspoken in seeking credit for his services, Wool discreetly avoided statements that might adversely affect his future in the army. After Taylor's departure for Monterrey, he dutifully resumed the chore of commanding volunteer forces in the Saltillo area. Elsewhere the war raged on.

8

NOTHING BUT DUTY

Following the battle of Buena Vista, John Ellis Wool began an extended tour of occupation duty in northeastern Mexico. He spent eight months in a windswept camp at Buena Vista, where he presided over military and civil matters in the Saltillo district. Then, in December 1847, he moved to Monterrey to succeed Taylor as the commander in the three Mexican states of Coahuila, Nuevo León, and Tamaulipas. Wool instituted a rigid program to provision his regiments, curb guerrilla activity, and restart the Mexican tax system. To make his program effective, he courted wealthy *hacendados*, from whom he drew most of his supplies. At the same time, he made local and state officials accountable for Mexican acts of lawlessness. Wool had no guidelines for commanding occupation forces and disliked the assignment, but he held to a steady course and tried to maintain stability in the frontier Mexican states until peace could be declared.[1]

On February 27, 1847, four days after the bloody battle at Buena Vista, Taylor had moved his forces south to his old camp at Agua Nueva. Here officers drafted battle reports and held elections for vacant positions. Arkansas detachments patrolled the roads to the south and west, which were rapidly becoming infested with guerillas. On March 6, Taylor left for Monterrey, taking May's dragoons and Bragg's battery, with Marshall's Kentucky Cavalry and Davis's Mississippians to follow. Several days later Wool, who detested the bleak plain at Agua Nueva, brought the army back to Buena Vista. In a side canyon near a set of springs, he laid out Camp Buena Vista and established his headquarters in a tent there by a spring.[2]

Wool's first act as an occupation commander was to place Saltillo under strict military rule. He ordered Brevet Lieutenant Colonel Warren, the commandant, to round up and send to Buena Vista all able-bodied officers, soldiers, and teamsters who had no assigned duty in the city. He also sought the names of the men (especially officers) who had fled the battlefield and sought refuge there. Warren imposed a curfew and instructed his patrols to arrest everyone, American and Mexican, found on the streets after nine o'clock at night. Gambling and "tippling houses" in the city were closed. All individuals, civilian or military, must obtain a pass at the commandant's office in order to enter or leave Saltillo. Warren had difficulty enforcing the rules, having only two companies of soldiers at his disposal to act as police. Indeed, after dark, teamsters and soldiers drank, gambled, brawled, and fought over Mexican women; soldiers broke into houses of well-to-do citizens in search of money. Citizens fled and the population of the city dwindled. When a riot broke out in the camp of the Second Ohio Infantry, recently arrived from Monterrey, Warren had to call in reinforcements from Buena Vista to break it up.[3]

Wool also took a tough stand on the theft of government property. In late March, seventeen mules, four horses, and blacksmith's tools—all valued at $1,280—were stolen from the government corral. On March 29, in a second request, Warren gave Vice Governor Eduardo Gonzáles, who had returned to Saltillo, an ultimatum. Believing the robbers were Mexicans, the commandant gave Gonzáles twenty-four hours to find the culprits and return the stolen property. Otherwise, Warren would seize property in the city worth twice the value of the loss. Gonzáles immediately contacted Josiah Gregg and asked him to intercede and protest the order. Gregg's interference, which included a threat to report Warren's conduct to Washington, reached Wool. Angered, the general notified Taylor that if Gregg persisted in making trouble, he would order him out of Saltillo. Wool gave Gonzáles ten days to resolve the situation, then authorized Warren to seize Mexican property.[4]

On April 3, Gregg visited Wool at Camp Buena Vista. A courier from Colonel Alexander W. Doniphan's Missouri column in Chihuahua had brought dispatches for Taylor. Gregg wanted a pass to accompany the courier back to Chihuahua. On entering the general's tent, Wool, who had been reading newspapers, asked the doctor why he had written letters to various editors criticizing his actions. Wool's treatment of his officers and men had prompted this, Gregg replied. The general agreed that volunteer officers at first had complained about his discipline, but after the battle, many of them had confessed their error. "I have labored incessantly," Wool lectured Gregg, "to keep good order in my division: and Capt. Washington remarked to me the other day—'General, that book [laying his hand on one which was on the table—his order book], will be a guide to future armies.'" Wool kept talking. Indeed, according to the editor of Gregg's *Diary and Letters*, as Tolstoy said of Napoleon, a man "has to talk, talk, talk, merely to convince himself that he is in the right." Gregg finally stood up, and Wool responded, "I give you my hand; I buried all my disputes in the battle. All I ask is that you do me justice." The doctor left with his pass.[5]

In early April, Colonel Warren arrested José María de Ibarra, the customs collector in Saltillo, and his clerks, and confiscated his business records. A quartermaster officer accused Ibarra of being involved in the theft of some twenty government mules and horses. Ibarra's papers clearly indicated that he and Vice Governor Gonzáles had conspired to send Santa Anna military information on the eve of the battle at Buena Vista. Wool fined the collector $5,000 for the missing animals, arrested Gonzáles as a spy, and warned that if the government property were not returned he would seize livestock of comparable value on neighboring ranchos. The general forwarded translations of the incriminating letters to Taylor, recommending that the two Mexican officials be tried by court-martial. Taylor, however, counseled patience, and the two Mexicans were eventually released. Wool placed a quartermaster officer in charge of the customs house in Saltillo, and in September appointed a civilian contractor, W. J. Riddle, to serve as collector and chief of police.[6]

On March 1, Wool instituted a special tax program in Saltillo to cover property losses from robberies and to help defray occupation costs. He ordered Warren to levy a tax, in accordance with Mexican laws, upon all merchandise leaving Saltillo for San Luis Potosí and other points in the interior, and a consumption tax upon all articles, including sugar, wine, and brandy, brought into the city for sale. Warren would collect these duties, plus fines in violation of occupation orders, and after deducting expenses, he would deposit the remainder with the local army paymaster. These levies in no way interfered with the regular taxes the city collected. Wool ventured out on his own with this program, but he believed that the arrangement would meet administration approval. He felt justified when he learned in late April that Polk on March 23 had required Mexico to pay for the war either through trade concessions or by occupation duties on commerce entering Mexican ports or brought into towns in the interior.[7]

Wool adjusted his tax program in special cases. When a wealthy Manuel de Ibarra of Parras sent twenty-eight barrels of brandy and twelve barrels of flour for sale in Saltillo, the general told Warren to waive the tax and allow him to sell the goods, but only at wholesale prices. The Mexican *hacendado* "has always been our friend." On another occasion, the general cancelled the tax on a shipment of sugar when a Saltillo businessman, who was "extremely friendly to our side," complained that an army train bound for Monterrey had seized two of his mules. Wool drew on the duties, fines, and assessments not only to replace stolen animals, but to employ spies to scout enemy military movements to the south. By December 1847, the office of the commandant in Saltillo had taken in approximately $15,000 ($8,000 in taxes and the rest in license fees, fines, and seizures of cattle, mules, and corn) for debts.[8]

Wool's primary concern was to subsist his occupation forces. All his activities—scouting, escorts, dealing with the wealthy, and war on guerrillas—were tied to this endeavor. After the battle of Buena Vista, commissary officers reported that Santa Anna had drawn heavily on Coahuila to sustain his forces, and forage there was in short supply. Farmers could not make deliveries until summer crops matured. Wool could not wait until summer. "Would it not be well," he asked Taylor, "to treat them [Mexicans] as conquered people and tax them a little?" The army was in particular need of corn, "to be paid for or not according to circumstances." Taylor approved the idea, but left it to Wool to implement.[9]

The general hoped to draw on the wealthiest man in Coahuila—Jacobo Sánchez Navarro, who lived at Patos—for corn, flour, and beef. The Mexican's extensive farms and ranches could easily provide a large share of the needed provisions. In seeking an arrangement, the general was concerned with Sánchez Navarro's reported ties to Santa Anna. In March, Wool boldly asked Horace Boultbee, a Saltillo businessman employed by the *hacendado*, whether his patron had furnished arms to Santa Anna at the time of the battle. Was he still in touch with him? Boultbee seemed startled by the questions, and Wool quickly explained that he wanted to meet Santa Anna and discuss a cessation of hostilities. If he could talk to the Mexican general, he was confident that he could convince him to take "a pledge to put an end to the war." Sánchez Navarro did not take the bait. He sent Wool assurances of friendship but said nothing more. In June, an American patrol stopped a courier bearing messages from the landowner to the Mexican commander at San Luis Potosí, describing proposed American troop movements. Wool dispatched dragoons to Patos to arrest Sánchez Navarro, but he had fled. The lack of contact with the Mexican *hacendado* was no problem. Boultbee, his agent, soon began making corn and flour shipments to Wool's forces.[10]

Wool also contacted Vice Governor Gonzáles about the supply of grain and forage. He reminded him that the inhabitants of Santa Rosa, Monclova, Parras, and Saltillo had promised to remain neutral, yet during the recent hostilities, they had joined the Aguirres, Blancos, and others—large influential families that were in reality political factions—in taking up arms against the Americans. For this "gross ingratitude," Wool felt obliged to demand "an atonement" in the form of forage and foodstuffs. If brought forward promptly, he would pay liberally. He sent Gonzáles a list of farms and haciendas, compiled from a recent tour of the Saltillo district by Lieutenant Carleton and other officers, stating the quantity of corn, flour, and barley he expected from each. Quotas varied from 300 to 2,000 fanegas (fanega equals 1.58 bushels).[11]

Mexican farmers resisted the requisitions. Manuel de Ibarra, writing from Parras, branded Wool's requests oppressive. The general disagreed. He required only two thousand fanegas from that quarter, and presumed city authorities would furnish one half and Governor Aguirre the remaining half. If he knew the names of Aguirre's supporters, he would levy them directly. How could the people of Parras cry oppression when the American army paid for every fanega? But there were other protests. A farmer, Lorenzo Cino, came to Wool's headquarters at Buena Vista seeking relief. He had supplied 125 fanegas of corn out of 300 called for, but needed the rest for his family and laborers. Also, the soldiers loading the corn had threatened him and damaged his house. Wool reduced the quota. In May, as supplies grew short, detachments began searching a seventy-mile radius of Saltillo for stored grain and quickly located 4,000 bushels of corn and 100 bushels of barley. "By giving a little money," Wool reported to Taylor, "it was pointed out to us."[12]

Wool's requisitions affected market prices. He placed a ceiling of $3.00 per fanega on corn, but army demands caused civilian prices to soar. Boultbee ignored the posted schedule and retailed corn in the public market at $3.37 per fanega. When a quartermaster officer suggested seizing his stock, Wool hesitated. He was unsure about interfering with the business of a foreigner. He avoided a confrontation by raising the ceiling to meet the competition. In July, Boultbee and his partner Edward Chapman tried to corner the corn and flour market at Parras, and warned Mexican farmers that selling to the army made them American sympathizers. Wool ignored the matter. If he closed down the merchants, they might later demand that the United States pay an inflated figure to cover their losses.[13]

As summer crops matured, Wool sent mounted detachments into the countryside to assure that the Mexicans who threshed their grain were routing it to the army depot at Buena Vista. Patrols circled to the south to intercept carts and pack trains loaded with corn and barley heading for San Luis Potosí. Commissary officers employed soldiers to help drive beef herds to Camp Buena Vista from as far away as Parras. With these measures, Wool kept his troops supplied with provisions and forage through the summer.[14]

Wool strove to keep the men occupied until their enlistments expired. They drilled by companies each morning and by battalions in the afternoon. He encouraged the regiments to compete in military exercises and sports. They dressed as they chose. "Nothing is more original than the present condition of our army," an Illinois soldier recorded. "One is reminded of Fallstaff's [*sic*] soldiers, some are wearing hats, others caps, jackets, dress coats, etc. There are no two uniforms alike in the company." Wool was lenient about dress, but demanded that arms be operable. Colonel Churchill held periodic inspections and set aside entire days for officers and men to clean, oil, and repair muskets and pistols.[15]

Wool also showed a personal interest in the enlisted men. He regularly visited guardposts, chatted with groups in their camps, and spoke words of praise at afternoon parades. When two Illinois soldiers found an abandoned print shop in Saltillo and asked permission to start a weekly army newspaper, Wool was enthusiastic. The first issue of the *Picket Guard* appeared on April 5 and ran through seven numbers. As expected, the paper was highly complimentary of the general. It extolled his patience amid the curses hurled at him during the march into Mexico, and described how the curses changed to compliments after the battle of Buena Vista. Wool sent a copy to his wife. "The Regiments under my command," he wrote, "are willing to go anywhere with me. The officers say I was very cool. I know I was active and never dismounted my horse for 16 hours except for about ten minutes." Soldiers also aired their gripes in the newspaper. Those bivouacked in Saltillo complained of Mexican night watchmen blowing whistles on street corners. Everyone criticized the mail service. The *Picket Guard* also recalled the February 10 massacre near Agua Nueva, and stressed that Wool had urged clemency in the matter. "Although I would not in the slightest degree justify the acts of those who perpetrated the murders in question," he wrote Taylor on April 8, "yet I would under the circumstances, believing the officers more to blame than the men." Taylor rescinded his disciplinary action.[16]

During the spring, Wool mounted a campaign to win the coveted brevet of major general. Taylor had assured him there would be no problem, but Wool preferred to take no chances. In early March, he wrote George Gibson, commissary general and an old friend, in Washington, praising Taylor and emphasizing their perfect agreement on battle arrangements. He asked Gibson to hold his letter for publication later. Wool also mailed Sarah a long letter dated March 22, with specific instructions: "If my [battle] report should not be published in the course of a week or ten days after you receive this, you may permit the paragraphs 1 to 9 to be published, having them so altered as to place me in the third person, that is, to have it so worded as to appear coming from another person. Take pains to have it carefully done. There must be no blunder." He sent Albany politician J. A. Spencer a similar letter for circulation to mutual friends in New York State. Finally, on March 25, Wool handed Col. Jefferson Davis a copy of his letter to Gibson when the Mississippian departed Saltillo, requesting that he place it before the public back in the United States. Within thirty days, Wool's letters began appearing in newspapers back home.[17]

Wool grew nervous over the brevet. The New Orleans *Picayune* on March 26 had published a letter from an unnamed source, quoting Taylor as saying that his determination to fight at Buena Vista was "not seconded by the officers next in command." Then, on April 14, the same newspaper printed a second letter from Taylor to Col. E. G. W. Butler dated March 4. "For several hours," Taylor wrote, "the fate of the day was extremely doubtful, so much so, that I was urged by some of the most experienced officers to fall back and take up a new position. This I knew it would never do to attempt with volunteers and at once declined it." Wool on April 8, and again on the 26th, asked Taylor to clarify these statements. On April 28, Taylor replied: "The ridiculous letters referred to by you, many of which are entirely incorrect, in regard to Buena Vista, no matter who wrote them, are to be very much regretted."[18]

Why did Taylor say these things? On the fateful morning of February 23, Wool, with Taylor's permission, indeed had ordered Washington to prepare to pull guns from the barricade at the pass if necessary to protect the wagon train. When one gun was prematurely rolled back, Taylor countermanded the order. In the confusion of battle, such an act could easily have been interpreted to mean a retreat was in the offing. However, Wool wrote Taylor that he "never ever dreamed of abandoning the pass." He may not have known that when Taylor arrived, Bliss had expressed great alarm over the crumbling American line. Taylor knew such remarks would damage Bliss's chances for battlefield honors, and in writing Colonel Butler, he may have gauged his letter to enhance his own military image—and to cover for Bliss. In speaking in generalities, Taylor may also have purposely garbled the proceedings of his council on the night of the 23rd when several senior officers advised a retreat to Saltillo—and even Monterrey.[19]

Whatever prompted Taylor's remarks, Wool sat down on May 7 and penned another letter to his superior. Would Taylor explain his statement to Butler in a letter for public use? "I have not sought extraordinary applause for my conduct in battle," Wool said, "knowing that you would do me ample justice." As there had been "no difference of opinion between you and myself as to when and where the battle should be fought, and as I am certain I never advised your falling back from Buena Vista pass to take a new position, I presume you will have no objections to say so to me in a letter." Taylor hedged. Wool perhaps misunderstood the letter to Butler, he admitted, which was private and not intended for the public eye. Taylor advised Wool "to let the misrepresentations and false colouring given to reports, and letters of the battle, pass unnoticed until the official reports are made public." Knowing that he might endanger his promotion and offend the man who probably would be the next president of the United States, Wool wisely dropped the matter for the time being.[20]

Complimentary letters arrived from the States. Senator Daniel Webster praised Wool's gallantry at Buena Vista. "Few have known you longer & none respected you more," Webster wrote. The senator also mentioned that his son Edward, a captain in the Massachusetts Regiment, was sick at Matamoros. Could Wool find him a place on his staff? He wanted Edward to "see service, make useful acquaintances, & be learning." Wool promised to find a more desirable assignment for young Webster. Francis Baylies, Wool's brother-in-law, also sent heartiest congratulations. The nation was "mad with admiration of 'Old Zack,'" Baylies reported. The moment that people started calling "a distinguished man *old*, you may be sure he has their affections." Wool, too, was "deep already in the hearts of the people, for no longer than yesterday I heard a fellow bawling out—'By G-d, I'm glad *old* General Wool is safe!'"[21]

The cloud soon passed. In May, Wool learned that the Troy Common Council had voted him a sword for his services at Buena Vista. In June, the New Orleans *Bulletin* announced that Taylor had contradicted the "report that his officers second in command were opposed to giving battle to Santa Anna at Buena Vista," saying it would do great injury to those gallant officers if allowed to circulate. Wool sent Sarah clippings of the article for publication in local newspapers.[22]

In early May, with their one-year enlistments ending, the volunteer regiments at Buena Vista prepared to leave Mexico. Wool was glad. The officer corps had grown lax and soldiers frequently slipped out of camp to poach on neighboring villages and ranches. There had been fist fights, duels, and deaths in the camps. Officers requested courts of inquiry to clear their names and enhance their images back home. Hoosier Gen. Joseph Lane demanded that Col. William A. Bowles, commanding the Second Indiana in his brigade, be court-martialed for cowardice. Taylor refused to issue the order but permitted the colonel a court of inquiry, if he wanted it. Bowles did not respond. Joseph Lane then obtained a court of inquiry into his own conduct and tried to get the board to accept an amended battle report stating that he did not "order" Bowles to advance, but rather "intended" for him to do so. The court cleared Lane of blame for the disastrous retreat. Bowles now asked for a hearing. The court judged Bowles poorly trained and lacking "capacity and judgement as a commander," but found no evidence of cowardice.[23]

In mid-May, Wool held a grand review for the departing regiments. The decimated Second Kentucky Infantry paraded with a supply wagon carrying lead coffins bearing the remains of McKee and Clay. "We had a peculiar feeling when we were standing in line to bid them farewell," an Illinois soldier wrote. Men who had endured "the dangers of the campaign with us were leaving and we will never see them again." The Second Ohio left, then the Third Ohio. Doniphan's First Missouri Cavalry, which had recently arrived from Chihuahua, provided a comic relief to the process. When Wool and his staff trooped the line in full dress uniforms, the Missourians broke ranks to revel at the military pomp. On May 23, Doniphan left for home.[24]

As his Indiana brigade arranged to leave, Joseph Lane praised Wool. "I cannot think of parting with you," he stated, "without expressing my high opinion of your great worth as a military man." For five months, the general had been "prompt, faithful, and vigilant," and although "a strict disciplinarian," he had commanded with "an impartiality worthy [of] a great man." Wool's heroic exertions had "won laurels and a fame that will endure as long as the traces of American history shall exist." When Lane's men passed in review, the memory of Bowles's blunder remained. "We stood in rank and file when the Indiana brigade passed by and presented arms," wrote a volunteer. "When the 2nd regiment passed all was quiet; but when the 3rd regiment passed, there resounded a thunderous hurrah."[25]

The Illinois and Arkansas troops were the last to leave. At sunrise on May 31, Wool accompanied the two Illinois regiments through Saltillo. Outside of town, on the road to Monterrey, he bid them an affectionate farewell. On horseback, in a high, shrill voice the little general thanked his "dear Illinois boys" for their long and arduous service and complimented their courage and gallantry in battle. The soldiers gave six rousing cheers. On June 5, when the Arkansas Cavalry formed to leave, Wool was indisposed and the officers went to his tent. He talked with them briefly, praised their service, and gave each man a hearty handshake. As the dust cloud marking their departure disappeared in the distance, Wool's old division was no more.[26]

New regiments were en route to Taylor's command. As early as November 1846, Congress authorized the War Department to call on nine states for volunteers to serve for the duration of war. The advance units of four regiments—one each from Massachusetts, Virginia, North Carolina, and Mississippi—arrived on the Rio Grande in March of 1847. Congress in February also approved the raising of ten new regular army regiments, three of which—the Tenth, Thirteenth, and Sixteenth Infantry—were assigned to Taylor. These seven regiments, plus part of the Third Dragoons-—about 5,800 men—replaced the thirteen regiments he formerly had. In June, Taylor divided his command into four military districts. Col. William Davenport, with headquarters at Matamoros, took charge of the District of the Lower Rio Grande; upstream at Camargo, Brig. Gen. Enos D. Hopping commanded the District of the Upper Rio Grande. At Monterrey, Taylor retained a small force of dragoons, artillery, and a mounted Texas battalion. The newly arrived Mississippi, Virginia, and North Carolina volunteers were sent to Wool in the fourth district.[27]

The new regiments reached Camp Buena Vista in a sad state. On May 30, Col. Reuben Davis's Second Mississippi marched in with haggard faces marked by a recent bout with smallpox. Two days later, Lt. Col. Thomas B. Randolph arrived with six companies of the First Virginia Infantry, dressed smartly in dark blue uniforms with white crossbelts, trailed by wagons carrying their sick. Its commander, Col. John F. Hamtramck, was left at a hospital in Monterrey. Wool was pleased to see Randolph again. Thirty-five years before, as young officers in the Thirteenth Infantry, during the War of 1812, they had crossed the stormy Niagara and assaulted Queenston Heights. Now they were together again in the deserts of Mexico. The rest of the Virginia regiment, led by Maj. Jubal Early, pitched their tents at Buena Vista on June 25. The North Carolina infantry under Robert T. Paine, also brought a host of sick men. With these three infantry regiments, plus assorted companies of artillery, dragoons, and Texas cavalry, Wool had a force of about 2,700 men.[28]

Wool made Camp Buena Vista a training school. Officers roused their men at 4:30 A.M., supervised two to three hours of instruction morning and afternoon, and held a dress parade at retreat. A touch of comfort was added to the camp when Wool permitted Sarah Bourgette, locally known as the "Great Western" because of her size, to open an officer's club in a tent at the camp. "Although not refined either in appearance or manners," Wool wrote, Bourgette "had as good a heart an any other person," and was much admired because of her bravery early in the war and her attention to the wounded following the battle of Buena Vista. When American stragglers fled to Saltillo to say that the army had been routed, that all was lost and the army was in full retreat, "she told them they were liars and cowards and turned them out of her house." On his visits to Saltillo, Wool regularly stopped at her establishment to enjoy her stories about the "refugees" from the battlefield and catch up on town gossip. Unfortunately, he soon had to close her club at Buena Vista because of illegal liquor sales. Wool also found time to dine with the Missouri trader, Samuel Magoffin, and his teenage wife, Susan, who, he reported to Sarah, was "quite handsome and agreeable."[29]

The volunteers had been in camp less than two weeks when a "stampede" occurred. On June 17, a rider dashed up to Wool's tent and reported that nine hundred Mexicans (lancers and infantry) had been seen at a rancho below Encarnación. Wool ordered Maj. Michael H. Chevallie and his mounted Texans, posted at Encantada, to investigate, and early the next day Capt. Gaston Meares and his independent Arkansas company rode toward Palomas Pass to reconnoiter. Meares raced back and claimed that a scout had seen a large party of enemy horsemen. Wool ordered another scout and instructed Col. Samuel R. Curtis, commanding the Third Ohio volunteers and the current commandant at Saltillo, to place the city in a state of defense. Curtis barricaded the streets, doubled the guard at the supply depot, and handed out arms to American civilians. Capt. James H. Prentiss, First Artillery, took charge of the cannons in Webster's fort. At nightfall, all lights were extinguished. Wool cautioned Curtis not to bother Taylor about the "emergency." After three days of waiting, it was concluded the "Mexican cavalry" was really a large drove of wild horses wandering in the valley. Wool advised Meares to select scouts in the future who could distinguish "between horses feeding and horses mounted."[30]

The volunteer regiments Wool had led south from San Antonio, whom he had helped to discipline and lead at Buena Vista, had all gone home, and new regiments were arriving. Wool found most of the new recruits "indolent, insubordinate, and uninstructed." Moreover, they were "constantly committing the greatest outrages, killing hogs, cattle, sheep, stealing ponys, mules and robbing houses." When "they cannot find Mexicans to plunder they plunder each other," he grumbled to Sarah. With the Arkansans gone, the worst were the Texians, who were composed of "everything that is bad." Hoping to avenge the Alamo and Goliad, "they rob, plunder and murder." A delegation arrived from Lampazos to say that three Texians had been murdered near their community, and a band of twenty Texians were threatening to plunder their community. The Texians and the guerrillas, Wool wrote, "give my mounted force constant employment." During the day, Mexican civilians lined up at his headquarters to complain. Never again, he promised himself, would he engage in a foreign war with volunteers. At one time, Wool was dealing with more than fifty court-martials.[31]

On July 4, 1847, a Sunday, Wool's little army celebrated Independence Day. During the morning at Camp Buena Vista, the troops formed on the plain with regimental flags flying. Suddenly, General Wool and his staff officers "came charging almost madly" onto the field, a Virginia officer recorded. Drums rolled and the soldiers presented arms to "the hero of Buena Vista." Wool checked his horse, doffed his hat, and charged "down the whole length of the line, his gray locks streaming in the wind." His performance made "the blood tingle." The general then took a position by the national colors and saluted as the regiments and units of his command passed in review. A field battery fired a salvo to conclude the event. In Saltillo, Maj. John Washington, the new commandant, marched the garrison to the main plaza where the Declaration of Independence was read. That evening, the inhabitants of the city, American and Mexican, turned out to watch the ordnance corps fire rockets into the summer sky. For a moment, occupation duty was forgotten.[32]

On July 12, Wool handed Capt. Charles W. Davis, a senior aide who was returning to the States, a package of gifts for members of the general's household. He included Mexican scarves for Sarah and Harriette, a glass goblet for John Griswold, his nephew, and a silver fork and spoon for young Chester, John's son. The items were inexpensive but unique productions by Mexican craftsmen. Two weeks later an artist, William G. Brown Jr., visited Buena Vista and made a "likeness" of the general. At Monterrey, Brown had drawn sketches of Taylor and other officers and planned to have the set engraved and offered for sale in the States. Wool paid $100 for Brown's work.[33]

Summer brought increased guerrilla activity. Santa Anna's march to Buena Vista had stimulated this sputtering warfare, and detached cavalry units led by Gen. José Urrea and others joined fast-moving civilian irregulars to harass Taylor's supply lines that stretched back to the Rio Grande. Mexican state and local officials, and even the Catholic clergy at San Luis Potosí, encouraged their operations. The guerrilla problem had escalated in early March when Urrea captured an American train on the Camargo–Monterrey road and burned 109 wagons carrying supplies worth $500,000. The raiders butchered or burned alive forty teamsters. Retribution was quick. Within weeks, a train escorted by four hundred soldiers camped near the massacre site, and a group of Texans rode at night to a ranch near Ramos and seized and shot twenty-five Mexicans.[34]

Enraged by the murders, General Taylor on March 31 issued a stern warning to the inhabitants of the north Mexican states of Tamaulipas, Nuevo León, and Coahuila. He had crossed the Rio Grande, he stated, to make war on a despotic Mexican central government, not to harm peaceful citizens, but on every road his forces were encountering "acts of hostility and plunder." To compensate for these losses, Taylor threatened an indemnification in money or "products of the country" in Nuevo León and promised to make assessments on the other states.[35]

Mexican authorities, however, stepped up the guerrilla warfare. In Tamaulipas, Gen. Antonio Canales on April 4 ordered the adjutant inspector of the state guards to declare martial law and organize cavalry squadrons to harass Taylor's supply lines. No quarter would be given; Yankee soldiers and civilians would be killed whenever found. In Mexico City, the Mexican Congress, responding to a clamor from army officers and politicians, authorized the creation of a "light corps" of national guards and summoned all able-bodied men to enroll. The central government also promised to support privately organized guerrilla groups. In early May, General Ignacio Mora y Villamil, at San Luis Potosí, wrote Taylor, condemning his management of the war. Citing the recent massacre near Ramos, he asked the American commander if he intended to conduct future military operations "according to the usages of *civilized* nations or according to the manner of the Comanches!" In a terse response, Taylor pointed to the "savage acts" by guerrillas and declared that he would meet every threat the Mexican government might make.[36]

In Coahuila, Wool had few opportunities to check guerrilla activity. He had to commit his mounted forces—an Arkansas company, three Texas units, and two of dragoons—to patrol and escort duty. Furthermore, guerrilla parties often were fifty or more strong, whose raids could not be predicted. But he kept a watchful eye on developments. In mid-July, when Governor Aguirre called the Coahuila legislature to meet in Monclova, instead of Saltillo, reportedly to enact measures to resist the Yankee regime, Wool immediately warned Miguel Lobo, prefect of Monclova, to ignore Aguirre's call. The general added that he, too, was instituting a "no quarter" policy. His commanders had orders to execute every guerrilla captured, as well as those persons aiding them. Copies of the Lobo letter were posted in the plazas of Saltillo, Parras, and Monclova. Dragoons also scoured the Parras area in an effort to arrest Aguirre, but could not find him.[37]

Parras was a critical supply point in Wool's district. His staff officers regularly checked the customs house there to see that monies collected "beyond the wants of the city" went to the army. While exacting tribute, Wool provided a measure of protection. When powerful Comanche bands crossed the Rio Grande to plunder Mexican villages and ranchos for horses and carry women and children into captivity, he sent dragoons to intercept them. The Sánchez Navarro properties at Patos and the Ibarra estate near Parras were major targets. Wool's commanders also ripped down circulars exhorting the inhabitants to defy the invaders. When guerrillas began burning crops around Parras, Wool even rushed weapons to the landowners to arm their laborers. In doing this, Wool wisely informed Jacobo Sánchez Navarro of his actions and went through the motions of asking his approval. He also urged him to move back to his town home in Saltillo, saying he wished to have him near. To maintain a peaceful occupation, Wool sought friendships—although hollow ones—with wealthy Mexicans at every opportunity.[38]

In August, the volunteers at Camp Buena Vista grew restless. The officer corps was partly to blame. In mid-July, Brig. Gen. Caleb Cushing had arrived and Wool placed him in charge of the three volunteer regiments. Cushing had resigned from the Massachusetts legislature to campaign in Mexico. He wore elegant uniforms, traveled with servants, and entertained with fine wines and silver plates—but he was no commander. He had proved inept as a garrison commander at Matamoros, and at Buena Vista he ignored the health and discipline of his men. Regimental and company officers complained of chaotic drill schedules, lax camp rules, and poor food. Venereal disease rates soared. Court-martial proceedings became farcical when officers dared Cushing to report them for unauthorized leaves, saying they would go to Washington and be restored to duty.[39]

An explosion finally came. On August 15, shortly before midnight, a mutiny erupted in the North Carolina camp. Called to the scene, Wool found Colonel Paine, the regimental commander, the focus of the disorder. Paine, a stern disciplinarian with a hair-trigger temper, had placed a "wooden horse" near his tent and threatened to tie disobedient soldiers on it. Stones had been thrown at his tent, and when he called out the guard, the detail refused to assemble. Taking a pistol, Paine went to where Company D was camped, challenged a boisterous crowd, and when they ignored his order to disband, he fired into the throng, wounding two men. At this point, soldiers came running to the scene from every direction. Wool took Paine to his quarters until midnight, then sent him back to his tent with a guard.[40]

The next morning a group of North Carolina officers petitioned Paine to resign. Lts. Josiah S. Pender and George E. B. Singletary and twenty-three other officers signed the document. The problem was not new. On July 8, men in Company C filed a complaint against Paine, but Wool declined to interfere. Next, Cushing had several officers arrested for insubordination.[41]

Wool made a decision. As an impartial court-martial could not be convened at Camp Buena Vista, he stripped Pender and Singletary of their commissions and dishonorably discharged them. The other officers withdrew their names from the petition. Pender and Singletary demanded redress, saying their dismissals were contrary to all the rules of civilized government. Their affair was a frolic, and there had been no mutiny. Wool ignored their pleas. Later in the month, when the two young officers left for Washington to present their case to the Polk administration, Wool wrote influential friends in the States and asked them to see the president. Lt. Col. John A. Fagg of the North Carolina regiment also hastened to Washington to explain the difficulty. Wool broke up the North Carolina troops, scattering companies to Arispe's Mills and to the redoubt near Saltillo.[42]

In the closing hours of the Paine affair, Wool received orders from Taylor to send Cushing and the artillery companies at Buena Vista to join Scott's forces advancing on Mexico City. Wool pleaded to keep his artillery. "It is the only reliable force, except the Virginians, in case of an attack," he declared. He also needed artillery to keep order. "Take a regiment or two if you please," Wool implored, "but leave my artillery." Only Edward Deas's company, Fourth Artillery, was allowed to remain. After dispatching four infantry regiments to Scott, Taylor had five regiments left in northeastern Mexico—the Tenth and Sixteenth Infantry and the Virginia, North Carolina, and Mississippi volunteers, plus a few companies of artillery, dragoons, and Texas cavalry. His forces reduced to 5,500 men, Taylor abandoned all hope of further campaigning.[43]

Discipline problems at Buena Vista continued. The pompous Hamtramck, Wool's second in command, was accidentally thrown on the pommel of his saddle and injured, then was attacked with an "old complaint" that prostrated him for a month. Sickness prevailed in every company and brawls were commonplace. At an election in the Second Mississippi, drunken men disrupted the voting and Wool voided the results, relieved Reuben Davis as commander, and appointed Capt. Charles Clark temporary colonel of the regiment. The Texas troops grew contentious. On the night of September 4, two lieutenants, a sergeant, and nineteen men of Chevallie's mounted battalion—the "scum" of the unit, Capt. Robert H. Taylor said—deserted, heading for Monclova and the Rio Grande. Wool notified Mexican authorities and ranchers that these men were dangerous. "I would be glad if they [Texans] would all desert," he wrote Sarah, "for without exception they are the greatest rascals I have had anything [to] do with. If they cannot be permitted to kill, murder, and destroy whatever comes in their way, they consider it the greatest of hardships." Commanding volunteers was no easy task.[44]

With the news in September that Scott had captured Mexico City, Taylor on October 4 requested a six-month leave. His operations were principally defensive against scattered Mexican guerrilla forces, and Brigadier General Wool was "present to relieve me; an officer of talents and great experience." The officer corps at Monterrey raised a howl. "No one is pleased at exchanging [Taylor] for Wool," Braxton Bragg wrote Lt. Samuel French, "as but few have any confidence in him and none respect him. We shall have a stampede every week and probably fall back on the Rio Grande someday." Taylor's request for a leave was approved.[45]

On the morning of October 27, Wool placed Colonel Hamtramck in command at Saltillo and rode northeast to Monterrey. His party included his black servant James, his aide Irvin McDowell, and Rucker's squadron of dragoons, plus several riding horses that Ibarra had given him. The general wrote Sarah that after living in a field tent for nearly thirteen months, he would feel "like a cat in a strange garret" upon taking quarters in Monterrey. On the outskirts of the city, the travelers met Col. John M. Tibbatts, the commandant, with a carriage and an escort, and the general entered the city in style. Monterrey was a luxuriant oasis compared with austere Saltillo. Smaller but better built, it sported picturesque flat-topped houses and large groves of orange and lemon trees that perfumed the air. Towering mountains loomed to the south and west.[46]

On October 31, Wool rode out four miles to Taylor's headquarters at Walnut Springs. Here, under a large tent awning in a grove of trees near a stream, Taylor gave a collation and introduced Wool to Mexican officials and prominent citizens of Monterrey. Bragg performed a fast-paced artillery exercise. On November 8, Wool and Taylor departed for the Rio Grande, accompanied by a dragoon and artillery escort. All along the road were scenes of devastation. The town of Cerralvo was largely abandoned, buildings were in ruins, and gardens and fields lay neglected. An "air of gloom" seemed to hang over the town where the "heavy hand of misfortune has left his mark," a soldier in the party recorded. In places, the road ran over open country with abundant water and grass. At other times, Wool and Taylor found themselves passing through forests of mesquite, acacia, and ebony. The entire route "abounds in positions well calculated for ambuscades," a diarist in the party noted. Shortly after sunrise every morning, the party broke camp and the artillery and dragoons were in motion. On November 12, after five days on the road, the party reaching the Rio Grande at Mier where the two generals and their staffs boarded the steamboat *Major Brown* for the river port of Camargo. Here Wool inspected the American garrison, Taylor published orders transferring command, and the two generals parted. Three days later, Taylor sailed for the States. After thirteen days, Wool was back in Monterrey.[47]

On December 9, 1847, John Ellis Wool took formal command of the American occupation forces in northeastern Mexico. His first objective, he announced in Order 133, was to place his forces "in the most efficient condition." Despite the recent victories at Vera Cruz and Mexico City, the war was not over. "Pleasure must give way to duty; our whole duty, and nothing but our duty . . . Obedience, order, discipline, and instruction must be rigidly enforced, which the interest, honor, and glory of our country imperiously demand." This was the general's personal credo—and he expected as much from his troops.[48]

Wool established his headquarters in Gen. José María Ortega's residence, a rambling one-story building of seven rooms. The spacious drawing room featured papered walls, glistening mirrors, and colored engravings. Two chandeliers, each with thirty lights, hung from the ceiling. Outside was a large courtyard with stables for six horses. The home was too ostentatious for Wool. "My dining service being my ordinary camp service," he wrote home, "makes very little show compared with the furniture in my drawing room. I dine every day in a plain way [with] from four to six officers." But on special occasions, Wool entertained in style. On Christmas Day 1847, for example, sixty guests assembled at four o'clock to dine on Muscovy ducks, legs of mutton, tongue, and eggnog and choice wines. It was a memorable day in a foreign land.[49]

Wool tackled a multitude of duties. He asked Colonel Tibbits to conduct a census of Monterrey and compile a list of men in business and professions. The general also wanted information on the local and state tax systems. He wanted security in the city tightened, and commissioned officers placed in charge of guard details. Tippling houses, fandangos, and public dances must be licensed, and horseracing stopped on downtown streets. At headquarters, Wool settled into a busy schedule. Officers and soldiers wanted furloughs, leaves, or discharges; Mexican civilians complained of outrages; and travelers requested travel permits to leave the city. Courts-martial became a weekly ritual.[50]

In the files of the command, Wool found a letter from Secretary of War Marcy condemning his summary discharge of Lieutenants Pender and Singletary at Buena Vista. Marcy said that Wool's action had no precedence in the rules and articles of war and was "repugnant to the most obvious dictates of justice." Every soldier had the right to a hearing. The secretary ordered Taylor to constitute a court of inquiry for the aggrieved officers. Wool dispatched a letter to the adjutant general in Washington, complaining of Marcy's "unjust censure." Earlier, in San Antonio, at the beginning of his campaign, he had written General Scott about dismissals from service. On August 20, 1846, Scott had advised him that commanders could discharge volunteer officers, honorably or otherwise, "upon the presentation of such circumstances as may appear to you of great interest to the officers themselves or to the public service." Furthermore, Taylor on August 19, 1847, had approved the discharges of Pender and Singletary. Restoring the two officers to duty, Wool warned, would destroy discipline in the volunteer regiments. Having expressed his views on the matter, the general promptly convened the court of inquiry.[51]

In mid-December, Wool received a sharply worded letter from Marcy on another matter. In the early fall, the secretary privately told a mutual friend, John Cashman of Troy, that he supported Wool for a brevet as major general and said the president would make the nomination when the Senate met. Informed of this by Cashman, Wool asked New York Senator John A. Dix for his "active influence" in getting an early confirmation, as he feared that a major general from Scott's army would replace Taylor. Marcy pounced on Wool for writing Dix. "Surely an intimation made to you through a common friend as to the President's future intention in regard to yourself," he scolded, "could not have been regarded by you as an official communication." Wool was in a sensitive situation. Dissident Democrats in North Carolina had seized upon the Pender-Singletary episode to discredit Polk, who was working hard to maintain party unity.[52]

Wool spat venom at the Polk regime. "I most heartily pray for peace," he wrote Sarah. "If I can get out [of] the scrape I am in, I promise never to be caught again [with] command volunteers, and certainly not under an administration like the present—the weakest and most feeble that ever presided over the destinies of our most prosperous country." The war "was got up to promote partizan interests and to encourage slavery, and prosecuted without the slightest reference to the good of the country." The coming of peace would hopefully "throw Mr. Polk overboard and disperse his partizan friends." Marcy, Wool added in a letter home on December 30, "has not independence enough to say his soul is his own. . . . He will do anything to hold on to his office, for he is aware that when he loses that, he is gone and politically forever." As for the president, "I belong to the North and the prejudices of Polk are strong, very strong against that section. . . . All his major generals are from the South and most of his brigadiers are from that section." Frequently less than objective, Wool viewed maneuvers in Washington through a political haze and knew they could be as decisive as victories on the battlefield.[53]

In taking command of the occupation forces, Wool made few changes to their command structure. At Monterrey, Tibbatts commanded six companies of the Sixteenth Infantry, Bragg's batteries, Rucker's dragoons, and a company of Texas horse. At Saltillo, Colonel Hamtramck had three volunteer regiments, Deas's artillery, and Walter P. Lane's Texans. At Matamoros, Col. Robert E. Temple commanded on the Lower Rio Grande with five companies of the Tenth Infantry and one mounted Texas company, and had artillery detachments at Brazos Island, Point Isabel, and Fort Brown. At Camargo, in the upper Rio Grande district, Col. E. G. W. Butler had five companies of the Tenth, five of the Third Dragoons, Henry J. Hunt's company of Fourth Artillery, and James B. Reed's Texas volunteers. Four companies of the Sixteenth Infantry, stationed at Cerralvo under Col. William G. Belknap, patrolled the highway from the Rio Grande to Monterrey. With these 5,500 troops, Wool protected supply lines, chased Mexican guerrillas, and enforced occupation policies.[54]

In December 1847, the general turned his full attention to the guerrilla menace. The Camino Real stretching north from Saltillo to Monclova and the Rio Grande was free of guerrillas but the route from Monterrey to Camargo was not. Virtually every community and rancho along the route had been destroyed by the volunteers. Wool remained convinced that such vandalism only served to create more guerrillas. Many of the guerrillas were little more than bandits who were just as content to rob and murder Mexicans as Americans. Cavalry patrols were constantly kept in the field. Under the blanket of martial law Wool declared in Order 11, "savage and cowardly" attacks on American citizens and soldiers must stop, and henceforth he would exact tribute from every town, village, and hacienda that harbored and supplied guerrilla bands. He demanded that Mexican municipal authorities organize police units, ferret out offenders, and bring them to the nearest army post. If they failed to do so, the army would make local officials pay for the depredations in their vicinity. Those merchants—Mexican, American, and foreigners—paying tribute to guerrilla chieftains would be declared sympathizers and their goods confiscated. By this act, the general made Mexican authorities and the wealthy share the burden for curbing guerrilla activity.[55]

Wool meant business. When Guadalupe Lesenda, a rancher living near Salinas, north of Monterrey, reportedly paid protection money to a guerrilla leader, dragoons seized the Mexican, collected his movable property, and burned his buildings. The soldiers then went to Salinas, arrested the alcalde, and levied a $500 fine, taking money, cattle, and other items as payment. When three discharged Mississippi soldiers were murdered on the Saltillo road on January 10, 1848, Wool sent Lt. Samuel Pleasanton with an interpreter and a detachment to question the alcalde of Rinconada and neighboring ranches. Pleasanton warned that he had orders to arrest the alcalde, fine the inhabitants, and burn the countryside if the murderers were not turned over to the army. The threat produced results. On January 19, Rinconada authorities brought five Mexicans to Saltillo, where they were tried by a military commission, found guilty, and as a large crowd stood silent, hanged in the main plaza.[56]

By early February, there were fewer robberies and murders on the highways. The soldier-operated Monterrey *Gazette* praised Wool's Order 11 for dispersing the hated guerrillas who had "prowled upon our steps like so many tigers." The city also was peaceful. One officer boasted that "a timid girl of sixteen may walk alone at the dead of night, from the bishop's palace to the queen's bridge, without fear of insult." Much of the praise was probably due to the Mexican police required by Wool's orders. In many towns, alcaldes revived the local constabularies, and armed with "military safeguards" (warrants) issued at Wool's headquarters, they made arrests and brought lawbreakers to headquarters.[57]

Wool did run into difficulties, however, in dealing with Mexican officials. He tried repeatedly to contact Coahuila governor José María Aguirre, who was hostile to American rule. Upon hearing that Aguirre had fled to San Luis Potosí and was encouraging guerrilla activity, the general sent soldiers to burn the Mexican's home in Parras. In Nuevo León, Wool welcomed acting governor Francisco Morales's request to convene the state legislature, but upon hearing that Morales had guerrilla connections, he directed that the group meet near his headquarters in Monterrey. Morales refused the offer, saying the legislature would become a creature of the American military. The matter was dropped.[58]

Wool also received a feeler from Gen. Antonio Canales, the guerilla chieftain in Tamaulipas. Canales had been a major figure in the border wars of Texas and in the early 1840s tried to create the Republic of the Rio Grande, to include Tamaulipas, Nuevo León, Coahuila, and Texas west of the Nueces. Canales had made overtures to Taylor in hopes of ending the "frontier war between nations," but he was ignored. In early January 1848, Canales sent Col. José María Carrasco, his cousin, to Monterrey to open communication with Wool. According to Canales, the people of Tamaulipas wanted to declare their independence from Mexico. If the United States would support them, he would halt all resistance and rid the highways of robbers. Wool replied that if the inhabitants of Tamaulipas would lay down their arms and transmit a declaration of independence authenticated "by the proper authorities," he would forward their wishes to President Polk. In the meantime, his occupation policies would continue. Canales made no reply. Forwarding the correspondence to Washington, the general dismissed the proposal as a scheme to gain relief from American rule.[59]

Wool's speech at the Governor's Palace on the anniversary of Buena Vista rekindled the debate over his role in the battle. His remarks, published in the Monterrey *Gazette,* disclaiming that he had ordered a retreat, sent a ripple through the officer corps in the city. The leading critic was Bvt. Col. Braxton Bragg. "Nothing under Heaven could have saved us there but the *prestige* of Old Zack," Bragg wrote army friend William Tecumseh Sherman. Wool "advised a retreat and he had Washington's battery on the move when Old Zack interfered and saved us. This is all denied now with solemnity and indignation, but still it's true. Old Zack had said so, and officers who heard the order still repeat it—among them Henry Whiting of the 4th Arty." No man "deserved so little credit at Buena Vista as Genl. Wool," Bragg went on to say. Wool was the "most contemptible apology for a great man" he had ever met. Bragg condemned the Monterrey *Gazette* as "a dirty, filthy, little 4 x 5 newspaper . . . printed by soldiers on extra duty, devoted . . . to puffing 'Genl. Wool—the real Hero of Buena Vista.'"[60]

Bragg's characterization was overdrawn, but Wool certainly was no saint. He rigidly followed army regulations, was thin-skinned to slights, real or imagined, brooked no questioning of his views, and catered to officers who cooperated and supported his policies. On the other hand, Wool could be engaging and pleasant. He had a firm handshake, gave parties for his officers, and possessed a certain degree of humor. Most officers, however, never felt at ease in his presence. Whether these friendly affectations were sincere or only a pose is a moot question. The general was respected for his energy, judgment, and devotion to duty, but he lacked the charisma to stir admiration. Zachary Taylor's comment that Wool was truly a "little great man" was aptly put.[61]

While wrestling with the problems of provisioning his troops and curbing the guerrilla menace, Wool sought to revive the Mexican tax system. In May of 1847 in Saltillo, he ordered municipal officials to resume the monthly collection of taxes, with the rest, after certain deductions, going to the army. By the end of the year, collections ran about $1,000 a month at Saltillo and $2,000 at Monterrey. On January 10, 1848, Wool broadened his program to include all monies regularly raised "by the laws of Mexico, or the States of Nuevo León, Coahuila, Tamaulipas, either for the Central Government, the States, or the cities, towns, or villages therein." In each of the four military districts under his command, Wool ordered Mexican authorities each month to deliver federal and state revenues to a designated army officer, who would make proper distributions. In remote towns that suffered from Indian raids, Mexican authorities would collect only consumption taxes. In accord with Polk's orders, Wool abolished all state "transit duties." Henceforth, all domestic and foreign goods taxed at ports of entry would pass freely across state lines and into the interior. Maj. David H. Vinton, Wool's chief quartermaster, took charge of coordinating the tax program in the three Mexican states.[62]

Within days of announcing his tax program, Wool received orders from General Scott touching on the same matter. On December 31, 1847, in Order 395, at Mexico City, Scott directed Mexican state authorities in all occupied districts to resume tax collections based on Mexican revenue lists of 1843–44 and set the annual amounts for each state. In Wool's jurisdiction, Coahuila should raise $5,659, Nuevo León $50,437, and Tamaulipas $71,332. Scott held Mexican governors, legislatures, and treasurers responsible "in their persons and property" for raising these monies, and authorized commanders to levy taxes on the wealthier Mexicans to meet the quotas. To force the product of the mines into specie circulation, Scott in a separate order on December 2, prohibited the export of gold and silver bullion and taxed the shipments of silver and gold bars and coin.[63]

Wool ignored Scott's orders. He interpreted War Department instructions to mean that municipal officials should also collect interior taxes, whereas Scott did not, and pronounced financial quotas as impractical. Questioned by district commanders about the differences between his program and Scott's, Wool admitted that his policies were "entirely at variance" with the general's but assured them that they reflected War Department wishes.[64]

Wool encouraged mine owners in Zacatecas to resume their *conductas* of gold and silver for export, suggesting they direct their trains through Monterrey. Convoys moving north into the American zone paid duties at the first army checkpoint or later at the port of exit. The Mexican duty was 6 percent on coined silver and 3 percent on coined or bar gold. As silver shipments ran as high as $80,000, Wool tried to keep them secret and arranged military escorts through occupied territory.[65]

Wool also introduced a rudimentary military banking system. Paymasters generally charged American merchants and soldiers a 6 percent discount to convert specie into government drafts for mailing home. This was preferable to paying duties on exported specie, which could be easily lost in transit. The army also charged 3 percent for converting incoming stateside drafts into gold coins and 6 percent for silver. The system was not a significant source of revenue, but it provided a convenience to civilian and soldiers alike.[66]

In late February 1848, Wool extended his military rule into a fourth Mexican state—Zacatecas. He ordered Colonel Hamtramck to send a column from Buena Vista into that mining area and restart tax collection. On March 1, Colonel Charles Clark marched south from Saltillo with his Second Mississippi Infantry, Meares's Arkansas horse, and a supply train. Clark established a camp at Mazapil, in the desert in northern Zacatecas state, hired agents to scout Mexican military activities, and instructed local authorities to collect taxes. He covertly furnished escorts for the *conductas* and tried to divert silver shipments north rather than south to the Mexican government mint at San Luis Potosí. Capt. Thomas B. Linnard and Lt. John Pope, topographical engineers, accompanied the column to make surveys of the area.[67]

In late February, Wool also sent puppet commandants to the major towns in Coahuila and Nuevo León. Capt. Nathaniel W. Hunter, with two dragoon companies, a quartermaster, and an interpreter, left his temporary post at Parras for Monclova. Wool ordered Hunter to impose a levy of $2,500 on the town and neighboring villages. When the captain made no progress, the general suggested that Hunter settle on a basic figure and try again; he expected to draw at least $5,000 from the region. As a last resort, Hunter should seize the equivalent value in horses and supplies.[68]

On February 25, 1848, Capt. Kenton Harper, with four Virginia companies and Lane's Texans, took station at Parras. Wool explained to Manuel de Ibarra and the alcalde that Harper's mission was not only to restart Mexican tax collection but also protect their interests from marauding Comanches and Lipan Apaches. Harper was conciliatory but firm, the townspeople treated his men kindly, and he managed to restart the tax program. From Monterrey, Wool sent Maj. Daniel H. Rucker east to initiate tax collections in the village of China and environs. A dragoon detachment was also ordered to Victoria, Tamaulipas, but was canceled by an outbreak of smallpox.[69]

As his commanders took station in western Coahuila and northern Zacatecas, Wool on February 26 issued Order 66 that declared a general amnesty for all Mexicans within his jurisdiction who had taken up arms against the United States. The amnesty was in response to petitions from displaced citizens who desired to return home and resume "cultivating their fields, tending their flocks and herds and pursuing peaceably their ordinary avocations." Wool hoped the decree would help stabilize the economy, increase farm production, and provide more tax revenue. He also wanted to encourage Mexican authorities to resume their regular political and civic functions. Above all, he sought to lure away from the guerrilla leaders, particularly Canales, the large floating population who had joined their ranks. As for Mexicans held prisoner, Wool advised his district commanders to give "due reflection" to each case before ordering executions.[70]

In mid-March 1848, Wool learned that a peace treaty was signed on February 2 at the village of Guadalupe-Hidalgo near Mexico City. Maj. Gen. William O. Butler, who had succeeded Scott as supreme commander in Mexico, declared an armistice on March 2. This act halted the programs Wool had put in place and ended military rule in occupied territory. He ordered district paymasters to return accumulated monies to Mexican authorities and recalled puppet commanders from outlying districts. By late April, Wool's forces had returned to Buena Vista from Monclova, Parras, and Mazapil, and he had begun gathering wagons to move the army to the Rio Grande.[71]

As the occupation neared an end, Wool gave thought to the brevet. In late December, Cass wrote that both Marcy and Polk were "well disposed" toward him, and not to worry about the Pender-Singletary affair. The paperwork in the War Department regarding brevets was a cumbersome yet significant task. But Wool continued to fret, and in letters to Francis Baylies, he hinted that he might resign his commission. "Do not leave the army," Baylies replied. "Watch your time—bear with some petty mortifications . . . It requires more nervous fingers than those of Corporal Marcy and his Mustangs to pluck a solitary leaf from your wreath of laurels." In March, Wool suffered another blow to his ego, when Congress voted gold medals to Scott and Taylor, and swords to two major generals and three brigadiers, but omitted his name from the list![72]

In January, or perhaps earlier, Wool had discreetly inquired among friends in Troy about the possibility of the New York legislature awarding him a sword. The Trojans had honored him in this way, and several friends served in the legislature or had influence there. To increase support, Wool wrote nearly a dozen letters. On April 10, Trojan Amos K. Hadley, Speaker of the House in the New York legislature, introduced an appropriate resolution and the lawmakers quickly voted Wool an ornate state sword. The general used the sword resolution to push the New York delegation to take an active interest in his brevet. When he informed Baylies that his campaign was successful, his brother-in-law replied: "I rather think the proceedings of the New York legislature quickened matters at Washington."[73]

While worrying about the brevet, Wool watched the court of inquiry for Pender and Singletary wind down. The president had sent the two lieutenants back to Mexico for a hearing—and punishment if justly deserved. The inquiry opened January 26 at Saltillo, then moved to Monterrey and sat for fifty-eight days. Wool testified on the thirty-fourth day. He explained the circumstances of the riot and the basis for his decision to dismiss the two troublemakers. On April 12, the court concluded that a mutiny had indeed occurred. Singletary and Pender resigned from the service soon thereafter.[74]

In May 1848, Wool fell ill and became particularly short-tempered. He pounced on Bvt. Capt. Irwin McDowell, his efficient adjutant, accusing him of mishandling dispatches. McDowell's "contumacious and insubordinate conduct," Wool wrote the adjutant general, had become unbearable. On May 20, he placed McDowell under house arrest, then banished him to Saltillo to await orders. As Wool's illness increased, he was incapacitated for several hours every day. Bvt. Maj. Oscar F. Winship and Lt. Charles J. Helm, temporary aides, shouldered the burden of paperwork involved in the evacuation.[75]

During the twenty-one months Wool spent in Mexico, his thoughts frequently drifted back to snowy Troy and his home on the banks of the Hudson. Late at night by the flicker of a candle, long after camp life had ground to a halt and reveille had sounded, he wrote Sarah the latest news from Mexico. During his time in Mexico, he would write Sarah over 250 lengthy letters of well over 1,200 pages, detailed the horrors and carnage of war, news of General Scott's advance on Mexico City, and his growing disdain for the lack of discipline in the volunteers. He carefully dictated what portions of his letters should be released to the press. He also found time to write of brief excursions into the towering majestic mountains, the first greenery of spring, and descriptions of birds and plants he had never seen back in the States. The beauty of the scenery around Saltillo and Monterrey greatly surpassed anything he had seen. Sarah responded with over two hundred letters of her own, enclosing newspaper clippings from Troy, Albany, New York City, and newspapers everywhere, or anything that seemed to glorify or tarnish her husband's reputation as the hero of the battle of Buena Vista. Because of the uncertainty of the mail from the Rio Grande, Wool would sometimes go for a month without receiving a single letter and when the mail did arrive, there would be as many as ten of Sarah's letters. He carefully arranged the letters in chronological order and spent hours and hours reading and rereading them. He carefully preserved her letters as she did his, all to the joy of historians of another era. The general signed his letters simply "Wool" without a valediction. Never did he once use the word "love." Her letters were signed simply, "Sarah Wool." In all the correspondence, there is not the least hint of any intimacy or the closeness expected in a marriage, even one of thirty-eight years. Their letters appear to reflect more of a relationship between business partners. Perhaps their inability to have children added to this coldness and emotional distance.[76]

On June 12, Wool announced to his occupation forces that the peace treaty had been ratified in Washington and Mexico City. The war was over. His troops would retire to the Rio Grande as soon as possible. Hamtramck left Saltillo for Monterrey on June 14 with the Virginia infantry, having sent the North Carolina regiment to Cerralvo a month earlier. The Mississippians, returning from Mazapil, were slow to start because of a drunken spree in the main plaza. There were few farewells when the regiment tramped out of town.[77]

In Monterrey, Wool reviewed each regiment as it passed through the city to camps at Walnut Springs. When Major Lane's Texas battalion rode in, Wool was unwell, but he dressed, downed a glass of wine, and rushed out to review the men, as Lane recalled, "buckling on his sword with one hand and wiping his mouth with the other." On June 17, Wool gave a dinner for staff and regimental officers, liquor flowed and tongues loosened. Mississippi Colonel Clark quarreled with the general, then fled down the street, but was overtaken by a guard. Clark mumbled an apology and was released from arrest.[78]

On June 24, Wool departed Monterrey in an army ambulance. Almost two years of American occupation in northeastern Mexico was at an end. At the village of Marin on June 27, Wool received official word of his brevet award, and instructions for troop dispositions. Feeling better at Matamoros on July 4, he helped celebrate the national holiday and attended a festive party. Two days later, his entourage rode overland to Brazos Island, near the mouth of the Rio Grande. Here in a tent cooled by gulf breezes, he spent three weeks regaining his health. He sent Lieutenant Helm, one of his aides, to Washington to promote his interests. On July 23, in Order 178, Wool placed Colonel Davenport in charge of the Fort Brown area, with orders to report to Bvt. Brig. Gen. John W. Brooke at New Orleans. A week later, Wool sailed on the steamship *Talleyrand* for the Crescent City. The long and arduous Mexican campaign was at last over.[79]

Two weeks of travel on the Mississippi and Ohio Rivers restored Wool's health. At dinners along the way, the general joked about his experiences in Mexico, praised the volunteers in his command, and dwelled on his accomplishments. In Washington, he visited briefly with Marcy and the heads of the army bureaus and learned that Lieutenant Helm had done a fine job of answering questions. On August 19, New York City gave Wool a warm welcome. A delegation of one hundred Trojans, accompanied by the smartly dressed Troy Citizens Corps, escorted him to the Astor House for a lavish dinner. The next morning, as a band blared "Hail to the Chief," he boarded the steamship *Hendrick Hudson* for the trip to Troy.[80]

John Wool returned from the Mexican-American War a national hero. Two years earlier, in the heat of summer, he had mustered and forwarded twelve volunteer regiments to the Rio Grande, then in San Antonio organized one of the best equipped divisions placed in the field. Diverted from invading Chihuahua by Taylor, Wool selected the battlefield at Buena Vista and played a key role in winning the greatest battle fought during the war. As commander of the American occupation forces in northeastern Mexico, he had directed his energies to supplying his troops and curbing the guerilla menace but developed no clear-cut policies for military government. Wool's services in the war with Mexico brought him enduring fame, made him one of the great military chieftains of his day, and enshrined his name forever in the annals of the republic.

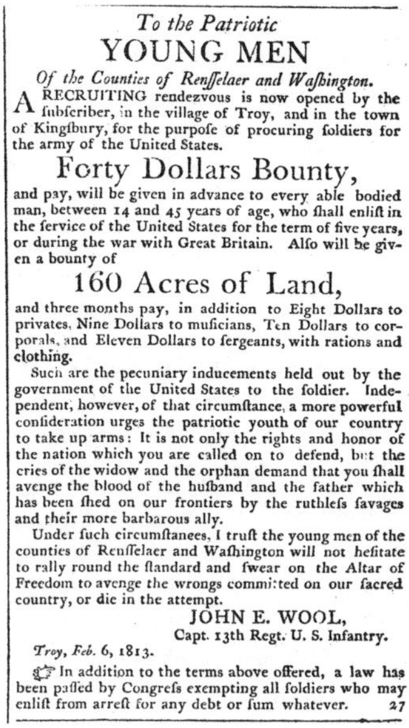

To the Patriotic

YOUNG MEN

Of the Counties of Renſſelaer and Waſhington.

A RECRUITING rendezvous is now opened by the ſubſcriber, in the village of Troy, and in the town of Kingſbury, for the purpoſe of procuring ſoldiers for the army of the United States.

Forty Dollars Bounty,

and pay, will be given in advance to every able bodied man, between 14 and 45 years of age, who ſhall enliſt in the ſervice of the United States for the term of five years, or during the war with Great Britain. Alſo will be given a bounty of

160 Acres of Land,

and three months pay, in addition to Eight Dollars to privates, Nine Dollars to muſicians, Ten Dollars to corporals, and Eleven Dollars to ſergeants, with rations and clothing.

Such are the pecuniary inducements held out by the government of the United States to the ſoldier. Independent, however, of that circumſtance, a more powerful conſideration urges the patriotic youth of our country to take up arms: It is not only the rights and honor of the nation which you are called on to defend, but the cries of the widow and the orphan demand that you ſhall avenge the blood of the huſband and the father which has been ſhed on our frontiers by the ruthleſs ſavages and their more barbarous ally.

Under ſuch circumſtances, I truſt the young men of the counties of Renſſelaer and Waſhington will not heſitate to rally round the ſtandard and ſwear on the Altar of Freedom to avenge the wrongs committed on our ſacred country, or die in the attempt.

JOHN E. WOOL,
Capt. 13th Regt. U. S. Infantry.

Troy, Feb. 6, 1813.

☞ In addition to the terms above offered, a law has been paſſed by Congreſs exempting all ſoldiers who may enliſt from arreſt for any debt or ſum whatever. 27

Capt. John E. Wool's recruiting notice in a New York newspaper at the beginning of the War of 1812. Rensselaer County Historical Society, Troy, New York.

At Queenston Heights, Upper Canada, on October 12, 1812, in the first major battle of the War of 1812, Capt. John Ellis Wool received a flesh wound in the buttocks. Wool was trying to lead soldiers of the 13th U.S. Infantry up a fisherman's path to capture the British artillery on the heights overlooking the Niagara River. American regulars and New York militia under Maj. Gen. Stephen Van Rensselaer fought British regulars, Canadian militia, and Mohawk Indians, led by Maj. Gen. Isaac Brock, who was shot in the chest and killed in the battle. The battle marked the end of a poorly managed campaign for the Americans. Today a 185-foot-tall column dedicated to General Brock stands on the heights. Wool would always take great pride in his bravery during the battle. Artist unknown, c. 1836. RiverBrink Art Museum, Queenston, Ontario, Canada.

The noted portrait painter, Francis Alexander, painted this image of General Wool in his dress uniform not long after the War of 1812. Harwood P. Hinton Collection.

Likely a painting by Francis Alexander, this is the only surviving image of Sarah Wool. No photograph has been found of her. Harwood P. Hinton Collection.

Depiction of the battle of Buena Vista on the morning of February 23, 1847, by Maj. Joseph Horace Eaton, aide-de-camp to Gen. Zachary Taylor. Although many of the geographic features are exaggerated, Eaton captured the ruggedness of the terrain as Gen. Antonio Lopez de Anna, approaching from south to north attempts to turn the American right flank. The American forces are in the foreground. Jerry Thompson Collection.

In this hand-colored lithograph of the battle of Buena Vista by the French artist Adolphe Jean-Baptiste Bayot along with German artist Carl Nebel, the American artillery is fending off the much larger Mexican army in the last attack upon the great plateau on February 23, 1847. George Wilkins Kendall and Carl Nebel, *The War Between the United States and Mexico Illustrated* (New York: D. Appleton and Company, 1851).

Samuel Chamberlain's watercolor "Gen. Wool Leading the Illinois Reg. to the Charge." San Jacinto Museum of History.

Samuel Chamberlain's watercolor "General Wool & his Entourage Scout Out Monterrey." San Jacinto Museum of History.

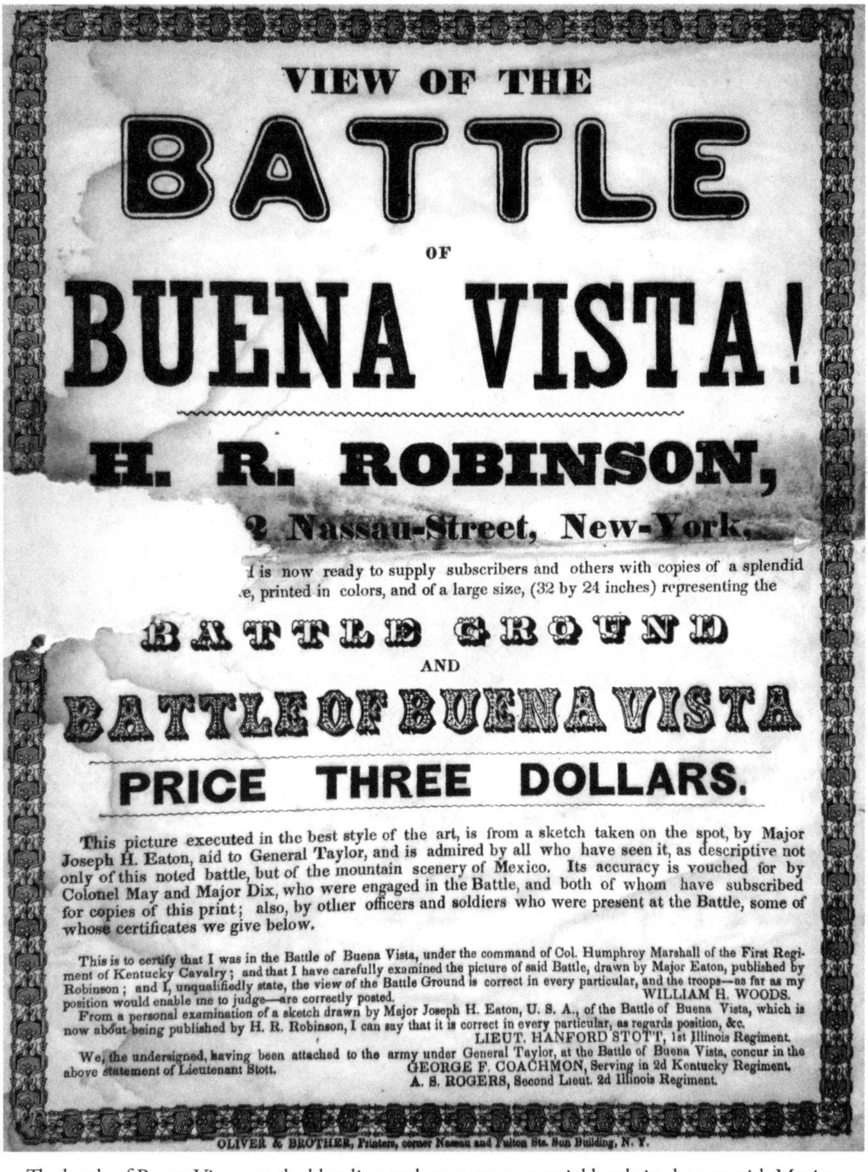

The battle of Buena Vista was the bloodiest and most consequential battle in the war with Mexico. The battle was much heralded in the United States, as this announcement of a 32-by-24-inch color print that sold for three dollars in New York. The battle helped make Zachary Taylor president of the United States. Wool Papers, New York State Library, Albany.

One of the first photographs ever taken of soldiers in war is that of General Wool (*left center*) and his staff on Calle Real in Saltillo shortly after the battle of Buena Vista.
Beinecke Library, Yale University, New Haven, CT.

Engraving by the English artist Charles Henry Jeens, "General Wool Rescues a Mexican Family." Many such images depicting American heroism in the war with Mexico were greatly exaggerated, as was this engraving. Jerry Thompson Collection.

Noted Mexican-American War historian K. Jack Bauer took this photograph of the spacious Wool House near the waterfront in Troy, New York. The residence is used today by Russell Sage College as a dormitory. Harwood P. Hinton Collection.

The diminutive five feet, four inch John Wool is shown in this pencil-on-paper lithograph silhouette by artist Auguste Edouart, alongside the six feet, five inch Winfield Scott. Hero of the war with Mexico and unsuccessful Whig candidate for president in 1852, Scott always seemed to tower over the smaller Wool, both figuratively and in national recognition. Wool was actually two years older than Scott and was the oldest general in either the Union or Confederate armies at the time of the Civil War. He outlived Scott by three years, dying in November 1869. NPG.91.126.127A. National Portrait Gallery, Smithsonian Institution.

British engraver Henry Samuel Sadd based this image of General Wool on a daguerreotype by the Virginia photographer Jesse Harrison Whitehurst. New York State Library.

This engraving of General Wool is by the lithographer and steel-plate engraver John Chester Buttre, from a photograph of Mathew Brady. Wool Papers, New York State Library.

This oil on canvas painting of Gen. John Ellis Wool was done by Alonzo Chappel a few years before the Civil War. NPG.83.159. National Portrait Gallery, Smithsonian Institution.

Three swords were presented General Wool for his heroism in Mexico. On the left is the sword presented him by the city of Troy, in the center is the sword from the State of New York, and on the right is the sword from the U.S. Congress. Catalog 401, N. Flayderman & Co., Inc., New Milford, CT. Harwood P. Hinton Collection.

At the beginning of the Civil War, General Wool was second in command to Gen. Winfield Scott. After commanding Fort Monroe, the Eastern District from Baltimore, Maryland, and the forces in the city of New York at the time of the disastrous draft riot in 1863, Wool was forcibly retired from the army. Harwood P. Hinton Collection.

This photograph of General Wool was taken at the beginning of the Civil War. National Archives.

General Wool (*seated third from left*) poses with his staff during the Civil War. Harwood P. Hinton Collection.

Artist Joseph Edward Baker made this lithograph of General Wool posed on the parapets of Fortress Monroe at the beginning of the Civil War from a photo by Matthew Brady. National Portrait Gallery. Smithsonian Institution.

Wool's self-made wealth made possible the erection of a giant monolith over his grave in Oakwood Cemetery in Troy. It cost more than $50,000 in 1869, which would be equivalent to almost $1 million today. It remains the second tallest such structure in New York State. Photograph by Jerry Thompson.

The stone for the Wool Monument at Oakwood Cemetery in Troy, New York, was quarried in Maine and taken by barge down the New England coast and up the Hudson River to Troy. Rennselaer County Historical Society, Troy, New York.

9

HUNKERS, BARNBURNERS, AND TURKEY COCKS

In the fall of 1848, Gen. John Wool resumed peacetime command. He briefly headed departments one and two in the Eastern Division under General Scott, who had been stripped of his exalted position as general-in-chief by President Polk. But in May 1849, after Taylor became president, Scott was recalled to Washington to head the army. Wool succeeded him as division commander. The scars of the war healed slowly, and as the months passed, Wool repeatedly spoke out against critics of his Mexican service. Other matters also occupied his time. His careful investments over the years in real estate, banks, and railroads had created increasing business responsibilities which demanded attention. Then, too, like other prominent military figures of his day, Wool flirted with state and national politics. Mercifully, the flirtation was brief. These were satisfying years for the veteran officer.[1]

It took nearly a year to restore the army to a peacetime posture. During the hostilities, there had been considerable shifting of commands. When Wool was ordered to war duty, General Gaines came east to head the Eastern Division. On September 7, 1848, Scott replaced Gaines, and Zachary Taylor took over the Western Division. Wool and Gaines commanded departments in the Eastern Division. On January 23, 1849, however, Taylor, now president-elect, relinquished his division responsibilities to Gaines. On May 10, Scott resumed the office of general-in-chief. Wool returned to his former assignment in the East on June 22, and, with Gaines's death on June 6, Bvt. Maj. Gen. David E. Twiggs took over in the West. This command structure remained largely unchanged for over a decade.[2]

Wool continued to reside in Troy. His stately residence, a compact, three-story brick structure at 75 First Street, stood on the southwest corner of First and Ferry Streets, only a stone's throw from the river. It overlooked a grove of trees marking the old town square, where both the general and his wife had spent many happy hours as children. At the rear of Wool's residence was a large stable, where he kept his carriage and riding horses and a spirited black pony named "Santa Anna," a gift from Manuel de Ibarra in Mexico. Wool had presented the animal to his favorite niece, Harriette Hart, an able horsewoman. As the lot sloped west down toward the

Hudson, the family enjoyed cooling breezes from the river and a panoramic view of the countryside. In these pleasant surroundings, the Wools lived comfortably with several servants and various relatives. Sarah's health was delicate, but she presided over their home in a regal manner, sponsoring teas and receptions and entertaining her husband's friends when they passed through Troy. Although they had associated with great and near great in Washington, the Wools preferred the small-town atmosphere and the nearness of family and friends.[3]

Wool's Eastern Division was a complex military jurisdiction. It included all the garrisons lying east of a line running from the western end of Lake Superior southeast across the Ohio Valley to the tip of Florida. Its four departments contained some 2,600 soldiers, out of 8,800 comprising the army. The First, Second, and Third Artillery Regiments manned the Atlantic defenses, while the Fourth Infantry was scattered from western New York to posts in the Old Northwest. Most of the regular troops were on frontier duty in Twiggs's Western Division. Wool maintained an office in Troy in a building that he owned and rented annually to the federal government. There he supervised the officers and clerks who handled routine military correspondence, reports, and administrative detail. Second Lt. Eugene E. McLean, his aide-de-camp, accompanied the general on official trips and to civic functions.[4]

Wool enjoyed the public adulation of a war hero. Admirers sent poems and composed marches in his honor. John C. Andrews, of New York City, composed and dedicated a military air entitled "United States Grand March" to Wool. Particularly gratifying was "The Buena Vista March," written by Phebe Van Schoonhover, the daughter of Troy banker James Van Schoonhover. A poem entitled "On Witnessing the Arrival and Hearty Reception of General Wool to the City," by Mrs. A. M. Nelson, appeared in the Troy *Budget* on September 16, 1848. And Francis Baylies, comparing Wool's selection of the battlefield at Buena Vista to Wellington at Waterloo, composed a set of eulogistic verses for his brother-in-law.[5]

The general was frequently a guest at special occasions around New York State. In many instances, he was escorted by the Troy Citizens Corps, a private military company he had helped organize in the fall of 1835. The group included eighty members, mostly local businessmen, who paid their own expenses and were on call to both the mayor and the governor to assist with celebrations and, if necessary, to maintain order. Like other independent companies, the Trojans were exempted from militia service and certain taxes. As interest in maintaining a militia waned during the 1830s, volunteer associations, such as the Troy Citizens Corps, did much to keep the martial spirit alive.[6]

The corps owed much to Wool. At its inception, he presented fifty copies of *Scott's Tactics* to the members and gave the first military lectures in their drill room near Washington Square. He also arranged for war hero Capt. Samuel Ringgold, stationed across the Hudson at Watervliet arsenal, to instruct the men in military arts. Whenever possible, Wool took national and state celebrities to the meetings. For example, the famous Frenchman, "Citizen" Edmund Gênet, who had settled near Albany, was occasionally a guest. The Troy Citizens Corps, smartly attired in green uniforms, white cross belts, and plumed black hats, added color and pomp to Wool's activities. They even accompanied him to the summer militia encampment held in upstate New York.[7]

By the late 1840s, the general had developed a highly remunerative portfolio of investments. He had regularly sought advice from Erastus Corning, Henry Vail, Stephen Warren, James Van Schoonhover, and other local businessmen to build his income. When investment opportunities arose, he relied on these men as brokers to buy real estate, bank stock, and railroad bonds for him. Wool also purchased town lots in Troy at sheriff's sales, made loans, and foreclosed on distressed property. Several of his town lots had buildings, one of which he rented as a store, the others as tenements. In June 1834, with money in short supply, he pledged sizeable sums to buy bank securities. Wool wrote William Baylies, Francis's brother, that many friends had applied to him for personal loans, but he hesitated to comply. The times made it difficult to collect. Two years later, on the advice of New York Senator Nathaniel P. Tallmadge, who named a son after the general, Wool purchased $4,000 in stock in the Dutchess County Bank, agreeing to pay it out in annual installments of $562.50. The bank paid an 8 percent dividend. Still later, in May 1853, the general joined several Trojans in organizing a Mutual Bank of Troy, capitalized at $200,000.[8]

Wool's business dealings were often precarious, because he depended on investment income to meet loan obligations. When a default occurred, it affected his entire finances. Fortunately, he took care of family needs first and avoided rash decisions. But occasionally his debts became worrisome. In April 1836, the general had Corning sell some railroad stock so he could meet the payments on his property in Troy.[9]

Wool was among the first in Troy to lend his name to railroad projects. Troy had long vied with Albany as a shipping point on the Hudson, and, in the late 1820s, both towns cast anxious eyes toward Massachusetts and a possible rail link with the port of Boston. A railroad would also eliminate the problem of ice interfering with winter shipping on the Hudson. It also provided a tie with the Erie Canal that ran from near Albany to Lake Erie. By the mid-1830s, when the Western Railroad and other short lines started laying track from Boston across Massachusetts, there was a scramble to bring the rails to the Hudson. The Troy & Stockbridge Railroad was chartered in May 1836 and authorized to issue $300,000 in stock. Wool was named one of eleven commissioners to promote the line. Unfortunately, the Hudson & Berkshire completed the extension first, and in December 1841, trains began running between Greenbush, across the river from Albany, via the Western Railroad to Boston. A spur eventually ran from Greenbush north to Troy.[10]

Upon his return from Mexico, Wool became involved with the Troy & Boston Railroad, which proposed laying track parallel to the Western Railroad line. The steep grade in the Berkshire Hills in western Massachusetts proved formidable and expensive, forcing the Western to charge high rates. A group organized the Troy & Greenfield to build west from Greenfield, Massachusetts, via a proposed four-mile tunnel through the Hossac Range and into southwestern Vermont. In April 1848, the Troy & Boston secured a charter to connect with this operation.[11]

In April 1850, at a stockholders' meeting in Troy, Wool urged his fellow directors to support the Troy & Boston plans. Increasing debt had dampened enthusiasm for the railroad project, and stock subscriptions were lagging. The general attacked the "debt bugbear," saying that no railroad "was ever built without a debt." He pronounced the stock a good investment. On the morning of June 10, a group of citizens, accompanied by two bands and several military companies, gathered at the courthouse in Troy and proceeded to a farm near Mt. Olympus, on the outskirts of town, for a groundbreaking ceremony. Although Wool suffered that very morning the depressing shock of a fire sweeping over his stables, he made it to the ceremony, where city officials made short addresses about the Troy & Boston—then, as prearranged, the general threw off his coat, grasped a pick, and sank it into the ground. The crowd gave three cheers. That evening townsfolk celebrated at a lavish dinner at the popular Troy House.[12]

In mid-August 1852, Wool and a group of citizens boarded an excursion train for the thirty-five-mile ride to Bennington, Vermont, on the new line. There, within view of the Revolutionary War battleground, hundreds of people picnicked, enjoyed music, and heard spirited orators. When a toast was given to the army, Wool responded. By night, the travelers were back in Troy. The Troy–Bennington branch was the only operating portion of the Troy & Boston railroad until 1875, when the Hoosac Tunnel was completed and the Bennington–Greenfield branch opened. Wool's attraction to railroads momentarily wavered in the spring of 1855. The Washington & Saratoga line, in which he held $17,000 in bonds, suffered reverses. But as late as 1863, he was a director and a major stockholder in the Albany & Vermont railroad.[13]

In his financial dealings, Wool enjoyed certain advantages. He received respectable army emoluments for his day, approximately $320 per month, owned valuable real estate, had good credit, and enjoyed reliable counsel from trusted businessmen. A conservative by nature, Wool directed his investments toward growth rather than income. Troy was a busy manufacturing center, and banks and railroads helped fuel its growth. He took pride in being a part of its development.[14]

Wool also took an active interest in advancing the fortunes of his nephew, John Griswold. When the Wools moved from Nassau to Troy in 1838, sixteen-year-old Griswold came to live with them. A personable chap, John clerked in a hardware store and kept books for a cotton firm. He regularly escorted his "Aunt Wool" to social functions, and provided family companionship when the general was away. Having no children of his own, Wool doted on his nephew and made him intimate with his business affairs. Whenever "Uncle Wool" was traveling, John wrote jocular letters commenting on the business scene, town happenings, and ladies' "tea fights." In 1843, Wool advanced his nephew the money to start his own business. With Daniel Robinson, Griswold ventured into a wholesale drug company in Troy, but shortly thereafter switched to the iron trade and banking, where he experienced great success. Griswold's future improved even more with his marriage to Elizabeth Hart, daughter of one of the wealthiest men in Troy, Richard P. Hart. In 1855, John was elected mayor of Troy. Two years later, he was president of the Troy City Bank and a major promoter of three railroads. Wool viewed with justifiable pride the role he had played in his nephew's rise in the political and business world.[15]

From time to time, Wool extended private loans to prominent people. In the early 1840s, Senator Tallmadge, whom he had known for nearly a decade, occasionally borrowed money. In early January 1842, however, when the senator needed $5,000, Wool was unable to honor the request. "You could not have applied to myself, or anyone else in this city," he wrote the senator, "in quite so bad a time for money as at the present." The United States Treasury had suspended specie payment, and local banks were in straits. No one was lending. When Tallmadge pressed again, Wool explained that $2,600, due on three loans, were in arrears and his bank stock had skipped dividends. "At this rate instead of lending," he declared, "I shall want to borrow." The next year the financial markets improved and in December 1843, Wool acquired from his brother-in-law, Joseph W. Moulton, a wealthy New York lawyer, a mortgage of $4,200 due from William Cullen Bryant, editor of the influential New York *Evening Post*. The general allowed Bryant a convenient pay schedule, and Bryant paid off the loan in February 1851 with a check for $3,093.78. In a short note, he thanked the general for the courtesy "always shown in the business relations I have had with you." It was a satisfying time for Wool, for he enjoyed a level of financial security and independence that few army officers had.[16]

Wool became absorbed not only with investments but also with state and national politics. Early in life, he had learned the value of political influence in advancing one's career, and as a young officer in the army, he had regularly sought the acquaintance of influential men in New York and in Washington. While in Mexico in 1848, Wool, perhaps inspired by Taylor's ascendancy to national prominence, apparently gave serious thought to the possibilities of entering politics, for the subject became a topic of conversation among the volunteer officers of his command. In the States, however, the sectionalism issue had fractured Democratic ranks, particularly in New York, where Martin Van Buren had espoused the Free Soil cause. Wool may have thought his non-sectional image could provide a bridge to unite Democratic ranks at both the state and national levels. Furthermore, the general was at the pinnacle of his military career, and at the age of sixty-four could not logically expect further laurels before retirement. If he ever intended to run for political office, the time was now.[17]

The movement to ease Wool toward the political arena was launched quietly in Troy by the same group that had arranged swords for him at the end of the Mexican War. The general did little publicly to encourage the idea—but, at the same time, he was careful to show interest in the proceedings. As early as March 1848, cryptic notes in letters from friends in Troy to Wool reflected a growing interest in pushing his name forward. "You will notice the maneuvers of our Politicians upon the Presidential Chess board at the present time," John P. Cashman wrote, "and congratulate yourself that you are not *yet* in the arena." A week later Cashman added that all was quiet in Troy, but "favorably moving forward."[18]

The presentation of a sword by the Trojans on August 23 boosted Wool in the public eye. The elaborate ceremony lasted an entire day. The city fathers arranged for military companies from New York City, Albany, Utica, Rochester, Schenectady, Saratoga, and Syracuse, as well as the presence of state militia officers, a governor's party, and the Whig vice-presidential nominee, Millard Fillmore. Near noon, bands marched through Troy and paused at Wool's residence, where he joined the procession to the courthouse. Here an estimated thirty thousand people had gathered in stands erected in the streets and on the public grounds. After sundry speeches, Gen. J. J. Viele presented Wool with a beautiful, two-edged, Roman-style sword with a solid silver sheath and exquisitely wrought Roman warriors on each side of the hilt. Richly engraved battle scenes of 1812 and Buena Vista covered the gold scabbard. Wool made a short speech, stressing the value of the citizen-soldier in preserving the honor and integrity of the republic, and the ceremony ended. Afterward, invited guests went to the Wool residence for a collation. Troy was proud of Wool and Wool was proud of Troy. In August 1849, the general gave a speech at a ceremony laying the corner stone of the hospital for the poor at St. Mary's Church. The establishment of such an institution long overdue in Troy, Wool told a large crowd, was for the benefit of the "sick and destitute—for the stranger and the wayfarer—for all who are unable to take care of themselves." At the asylum, Wool continued, "the sick may be healed, the hungry fed, and the naked clothed."[19]

In his speech in Troy, Wool made no references to Taylor—and Whig newspapers in New York quickly asked why. As the fall 1848 elections approached, Taylor's supporters seized every opportunity to place the "hero of Buena Vista" before the public, and play down the role of those who claimed a conspicuous role in the battle. Despite Wool's requests, Taylor still refused to clarify in writing the question of who advised a retreat during the heat of the contest. Privately, however, he named Wool.

The Whig standard-bearer seemed cavalier about the matter. "These statements as reported to you, have been reported to me," Taylor wrote Wool on July 28, just after the Whig convention, "but I have to assure you that they gave me no uneasiness whatever. I have been accustomed to hear such rumors and reports so long and so often, that I now permit them to enter one ear and go out the other."[20]

As Wool's name was frequently in the news during the early fall because of banquets and presentations, he became a frequent target for the Whig press. On October 10, the New York *Courier and Enquirer* praised Taylor's saving the day at Buena Vista, even though Wool had advised retreat. Francis Baylies, himself a Whig, branded the author of the article (Wool claimed journalist Charles King wrote it) as "stupid and malignant," and pronounced it a studied attempt "to create ill blood" between Wool and Taylor. King, Baylies asserted, was a "vain and disappointed man," a sycophant who chased every major politician. The journalist's current zeal for Taylor's reputation undoubtedly sprang from an "inherent propensity to toadyism." The publication of an article entitled "Taylor's Campaign," in the October issue of the *Democratic Review* depreciating Taylor and lauding Wool, heightened the controversy. The sniping continued for several months, but Wool refused to take the bait.[21]

In the race for the presidency in November, the New York Democracy split, with Van Buren's Free Soilers, or Barnburners, breaking away from old-line Hunker conservatives. Party leaders now sought a man and a platform to unite the factions. As the weeks passed, Wool's name surfaced. He possessed certain political assets. He was a war hero, had close ties among state politicians, and counted as friends many men of national prominence. Francis Baylies, Wool's brother-in-law, fanned the flame of politics before the general's eyes, and encouraged him to give serious thought to standing for public office. On Christmas Eve, Baylies sent a set of verses for a song he had composed, extolling Wool's distinguished career. He said the verses "might possibly do at midnight when one is genial with champagne and glory." The nation sang Gen. William Harrison into the presidency in 1840, and it might be possible to "whip up another General" in due season. "Now I say—when you are President, cherish the Poets."[22]

December 30, 1848, dawned cold and clear. At mid-morning Wool and his staff boarded sleighs carrying the Troy Citizens Corps and a host of Trojans over snowy roads to the capital at Albany. The State of New York was honoring the war services of its native son. A military band welcomed the travelers as they filed into the portico of the capital building, where a large crowd gathered. Governor John Young gave an address, then called Wool forth and in a dignified ceremony tendered him a sword of dazzling beauty. The hilt was delicately formed and gold-plated with a liberty cap at the top and figures of liberty on each side of the grip. Part of the handle was formed by an eagle "with its feet resting on pearls;" the other by a Mexican serpent "with a fine ruby in his head." Wool gave a brief gratifying response. "A government supported by citizen-soldiers," he declared, "must be the strongest in the world." As long as men could appear "as on this occasion," the nation was safe. "Let us cherish, then, this invaluable privilege" which "banishes the necessity" of large standing armies and "renders the republic invincible." The general's praise of the civilian-soldier perhaps sounded strange to some, yet he clearly gauged his remarks to appeal to the militia attending the ceremonies. A grand reception followed in Congress Hall.[23]

Wool's comments at Albany prompted the *Courier* to renew its sniping. Editor James Watson Webb, who was seeking a diplomatic appointment, bent his energies to gain Taylor's ear. The Buena Vista issue was perfect. On January 9, 1849, Webb quoted a regular army colonel who provided further "revelations" about Wool. The colonel criticized the general for tarnishing Taylor's image by speaking against him, by claiming credit due the hero of Buena Vista, and by writing letters that discredited the president-elect's battlefield honors. William Cullen Bryant immediately offered Wool space in the *Evening Post* for a rejoinder. "The attack of the *Courier & Enquirer*," the general stated, "gives me no uneasiness. On the contrary it will do me good. I cannot, however, contend with political vampires, wholesale liars or assassins." Wool pretended to overlook the Webb attack, but behind the scenes, he organized a vigorous counterattack.[24]

Baylies prepared a closely reasoned rebuttal for Wool. At Buena Vista, he stressed, Wool's troops were the best disciplined in the line and had formed the major part of the fighting force. The general had selected the battlefield, posted the regiments, and planted the batteries. During the action, he had been everywhere, rallying the fainthearted and moving troops to threatened sectors. Wool was not responsible for the rout of the Indianans; he had placed them where they could render efficient service and anticipated they would stand. How could any regular colonel accuse Wool of "military misconduct"? Let the stories "ripen," Baylies advised the general, then strike hard. The laurel wreath on his brow was "fixed too fast to be pecked off by Turkey cocks."[25]

In early 1849, Wool launched his newspaper defense. On January 22, Oliver P. Baldwin, editor of the Richmond *Republican*, attacked the *Courier*, blasting the "falsely and infamously alleged" charges against Wool. The general dispatched a copy of the article to his former military aide, Charles J. Helm, in Newport, Kentucky, who added introductory remarks and republished it in the neighboring *Covington Union*. Wool sent the enhanced *Union* clipping to the New York *Evening Post*, and slightly edited versions to the Washington *Union* and the *National Intelligencer*. He then mailed an envelope of clippings to the *Niles' Register* and asked them to publish selected items. Wool also called on prominent men for support. He wrote Webster, Dix, Cass, and other friends for copies of personal letters he sent them after the battle of Buena Vista, saying he wanted to extract his references to Taylor for publication. And once again, on February 27, 1849, about a week before the inauguration, Wool wrote Taylor. Now that his superior would be president, perhaps he would clarify the Buena Vista issue. If Taylor would respond, he promised never to trouble him again on the subject. There was no reply. Wool skipped the inauguration, but he visited the president briefly in Washington afterwards and left convinced that the matter was a dead issue. As attention turned to the scramble for patronage, the attacks on Wool ceased. The Buena Vista pounding was disagreeable, but it thrust Wool before the public and sharpened his thinking about the political arena.[26]

During the summer of 1849, Wool watched carefully the attempts to unify the New York Democratic Party. Both Van Buren's Barnburners and the conservative Hunkers, led by William L. Marcy, called for reunion. In September, at a joint convention in Syracuse, the Hunkers compromised somewhat with their opponents—but the Democrats lost the fall elections to the Whigs. As yet they had not found the right combination. Encouraged by the impasse in Democratic ranks, Wool felt the tug of politics, but he hesitated to declare himself a candidate for public office. He wrote Baylies for advice—and at the same time asked if he could enlist his pen for personal ends. The reply was an enthusiastic yes. "I am, sir, always yours," Baylies stated, "and I can say in conclusion, 'Go ahead!' I do not believe that you, like Hannibal, can melt rocks with gunpowder, but you can blow them into fragments with gunpowder!" With this reassurance, John Wool threw his hat into the political ring.[27]

In early December, the general proposed that Baylies make the initial move by delivering a lecture in Troy on Wool's Mexican War operations. He also wanted him to write a detailed history of the campaign for publication. They agreed that the project would be clothed in secrecy, that their letters make no mention of it, and that their exchange of ideas be made viva_voce. Baylies promised to deliver a lecture in January in Troy. Later in the month, there was a windfall. Bvt. Maj. George W. Hughes, who had headed the topographical engineers in Wool's column, sent him a printed copy of a lengthy memoir published by the War Department, describing the march from San Antonio to Saltillo. Straightforward and detailed, it provided Baylies valuable information for the desired essay.[28]

During the early months of 1850, while Baylies collected materials, Wool tested the political waters. Responses were mixed. John S. Roane, now governor of Arkansas, neatly sidestepped discussing Wool's role at Buena Vista, but promised support for rectifying Congress's ignoring his war service. Illinois congressman William H. Bissell showered praise. "I know not that you have any aspirations that way," Bissell wrote, "but I occasionally hear your name mentioned in connexion [*sic*] with the next presidency. And I am sure I need not add with what cheerfulness I would support you." If the Empire State "will make you its candidate in 1852," he added, "you shall be convinced that I do not overestimate your strength in the *Sucker* state." Wool also wrote his old friend Senator Lewis Cass, who held an important vote on the approval of James Watson Webb, Wool's recent adversary, for the position of charge d'affaires in Vienna. The general badgered him to make a public statement about Webb. This was a mistake. Cass reminded Wool that they had been friends for thirty years, and he had a reputation for keeping his word: he said he would vote against Webb and he did. Webb's nomination was defeated.[29]

Bryant was reluctant to wheel the New York *Evening Post* into battle for Wool. In a letter marked "private and confidential," the general spoke frankly about the two Whigs, Winfield Scott and Zachary Taylor. Scott had never been a "personal, political, or military friend," but he regretted that several books on the war, in striving to "puff" the general into the presidential chair, had grossly overdrawn his political prowess. Wool severely criticized Taylor's recommendation, in his message to Congress, that brevet pay for special assignments be abolished. Taylor had commanded an army first as a brevet brigadier general, and then as a brevet major general, and received brevet pay in both instances. Taylor would have the world believe that he was following in the footsteps of Washington, yet Washington would have "suffered his hand to have been severed from its socket" before he would have made such a recommendation as that of Taylor. There also were other subjects deserving comment. Would Bryant be interested in publishing them in the *Evening Post*? His friend advised him to postpone comments on Buena Vista, until there could be a "full and impartial discussion of the degree of credit due to the different commanders."[30]

Other friends were more responsive. In Kentucky the faithful Charles Helm, in March of 1850, placed a letter in the *Newport Daily News* promoting Wool as a presidential candidate. Helm commented briefly on the general's Mexican War service and pronounced him a war hero in the same category with Taylor and Scott. At peace, Helm said, "political considerations" had elevated one hero, depressed another, and ignored the third "with silent and almost damning praise." Wool had "no political aspirations or political enemies," but his "modest merits, his talents, his patriotism, and his public services," the Kentuckian asserted, "point him out as a future President to rule the destinies and guard the liberties of the freemen of our glorious Republic." Wool acknowledged receipt of clippings of the article, but still wavered about entering politics. "My Dear General," Helm responded, "I fully understand and appreciate your reluctance to becoming a politician," yet upon surveying the political scene, Wool's "very disinclination" to run was a factor in his favor. The Democratic aspirants had "called down upon themselves sectional opposition and jealousies by their stand on the slavery question, so the party must nominate someone whose former history "will inspire confidence" in both the North and South. Wool was a logical choice. If "the Democracy of New York" would run the general, he would receive the presidential nomination.[31]

In June 1850, Democrats from western New York approached Wool about running for governor. Party leaders in that district wanted to unite the factions behind a non-sectional figure. Wool was honored by the request, but he declined to run. He wrote to James Ames, of Rochester, that he had been "applied to by many democratic friends" to become a candidate for the high office, but had not cast his hat into the ring. The "approbation and good opinion of the people of my native state," Wool declared, tongue in cheek, were "more precious to me than office, and more than satisfies my ambition." The short-lived episode over the governorship, however, quickened his interest in the larger political scene.[32]

Within thirty days, the political picture changed. On July 9, Zachary Taylor died in Washington, D.C., of gastrointestinal complications, and Wool's friend, New Yorker Millard Fillmore, became president of the United States. Two weeks later, Fillmore invited Wool to the White House for a private dinner and chat. The general suddenly had "more friends" than ever before. "General [Sam] Houston and Senators [Henry S.] Foote, Cass, and many others have called on me," he wrote Sarah on July 24. Foote was "particularly gracious." Bissell and certain members of the House of Representatives took him to meet mutual friends. The political stage was shifting, with many "small fry" changing fronts. "I shall preserve the even tenor of my way, neither turning to the right or left," Wool said.[33]

Wool used the gubernatorial invitation to every advantage. On the eve of the state conventions in the fall, he sent copies of the Ames letter, together with articles urging him to enter politics, to newspaper editors and influential friends across the country. He even stuffed clippings in a letter to Senator Jefferson Davis, when the Mississippian requested information on Wool's dealing with Antonio Canales in Mexico. Friends added commentaries and sent the clippings of the enlarged document to other newspapers. The *Troy Family Journal* published the Ames letter and praised Wool's decision not to enter the gubernatorial contest. The editor said he was "too good a tactician to suffer his name to be mixed up in Hunker and Barnburner squabbles." The people of New York had "other and higher views" in mind for the general—"views which will be presented at the proper season." The Troy clipping was soon on its way to New York City and to papers in New England.[34]

Baylies encouraged Wool at every turn. Maj. Thomas W. Sherman, Baylies wrote on August 20, had passed through Taunton with an artillery battery en route to Boston, and he had dined with him at a hotel. The major talked freely about Buena Vista, and gave Wool "the *entire* credit" for winning the battle. But people can forget. The decorative shield in Fanueil Hall in Boston, Baylies added, carried the names of a dozen or so Mexican War heroes—Scott, Worth, Ringgold, Yell, etc.—but Wool's name was nowhere. "I would advise you," he said, "to obtain a certificate from some sergeant or corporal that you were present at the Battle of Buena Vista." Baylies complimented the general for acting discreetly in the gubernatorial matter, but advised that if his name were introduced in a state convention and *passed*, he should accept. "In future political arrangements, the Governor of New York cannot be overlooked." At the state convention, however, the Democrats squabbled and chose Horatio Seymour to run. The Whigs again swept the state in the fall 1850 elections.[35]

Wool was now definitely running to capture the favorite son nomination of the New York Democracy for the presidency. He informed friends that he was available for personal appearances, and sought out and attended important public dedications and ceremonies. In early October, Woll was welcomed to Syracuse by Mayor Alfred H. Hovey, a brass band, and a thirteen-gun salute. In his welcoming remarks, Hovey spoke of Wool's heroism at Queenston Heights, Plattsburgh, and at Buena Vista. He was later a guest of honor at a gala banquet where, following a sumptuous repast, he was given a toast: "The next President—The Agriculturalists and Mechanics of the North and West, the planters and gold diggers of the South, and the wool *growers everywhere* should rally around New York's favorite son." The *Syracuse Daily Star* applauded the general's "sterling good sense" in resisting the efforts by his friends "to make him commit himself publicly."[36]

Edwin Croswell, editor of the *Albany Argus,* privately counseled Wool against creating a groundswell at that time. A member of the old Albany Regency, Croswell was one of the most influential Democrats in New York, and his advice was valuable. It was indeed too early to name any person for 1852, Wool replied, but he noted that Cass already had been named a presidential contender in Ohio, Michigan, and twenty counties in Pennsylvania. "So far as my name has been presented in connection with the subject," Wool said, "I can truly say that it has been used without any agency whatever on my part." However, people "will say and do pretty much whatsoever they please." He could "only abide the consequences." Wool believed he stood on firm ground, and was in no "*danger of being drowned*" by a deluge of candidates who had "*to catch at straws.*"[37]

In late October, Wool went to Washington to sit on a military board. A number of officers and politicians called on him, but, as he wrote Harriette Hart, he was keenly aware that "our love and attachment are often increased, or diminished, in proportion to the benefits expected." As the board met fitfully, Wool visited with members of Congress and dined with President Fillmore and his family and with various cabinet members. On November 9, at Secretary of War Charles M. Conrad's dinner, the conversation shifted to politics. "General Scott, who it is expected by many will be the Whig nominee for the next Presidency," he told Sarah, "was quite gracious. Some, perhaps many, think that he and myself will be opposed to each other for the great prize." The Democrats must look for a man to unite the party, for no one had confidence in the "old politicians." Everyone seemed "much more attentive and civil than I have found them for several years past." Wool found himself in an embarrassing situation ten days later. While dining with General Scott, several men from Ohio called to discuss his presidential plans. Wool and a companion rose to leave, but Scott called Wool back, saying he had no secrets. Scott "begins to think he will occupy the White House," the general observed. "Very doubtful, as I think—we shall see."[38]

While in Washington, Wool sent Sarah a copy of *Stryker's American Register,* which carried Baylies's article on the general's Mexican campaign. He asked her to have the article republished in the Troy and Albany papers. As political tensions increased in 1851, Wool continued to wage a low-key campaign for New York's favorite son nomination. Considering his command responsibilities, military board meetings, and court-martial duty, he had no other course of action. Newspapers remained Wool's principal means of keeping his name before the public. Every time he mailed a clipping to an editor, he inquired about his chances in that locale. On February 10, 1851, from New York City, John A. Bryant advised that it was impossible to pick the leading Democratic contender, but he believed the general's chances were good. Because of the confusion in the national Democratic ranks, the party must nominate a man who could carry New York.[39]

While laboring over publications for Wool, Baylies suffered from gout. "This 'son of a bitch' of the gout," he wrote on April 14, "kept me in my bed nearly three weeks, but I am well now except one tender foot and much weakness and coldness." At Wool's suggestion, he was drinking Congress Water, a popular purifier, and trying to regain normal activity. Greatly disturbed over Baylies's health, Wool responded that he would "sink" without his friend's aid. Baylies chided Wool about sinking—"you who have breasted so many dangers." To walk "on the stormy waters of politics," it is necessary to have faith. "Screw your courage to the sticking point," he declared, "and you'll not fail."[40]

In early May 1851, Baylies's book, entitled *A Narrative of Major General Wool's Campaign in Mexico,* was published. A year in preparation, the slim, soft-cover work of seventy-eight pages was similar to the campaign biographies written for Taylor at the end of the Mexican War. Preparing the volume had been an ordeal for Baylies, whose illnesses repeatedly incapacitated him. Written under a cloak of secrecy, the drafts had been hand-carried back and forth from Taunton to Troy. Seventy-five of Wool's friends, principally in Troy and Albany, subsidized the *Narrative,* which was printed in Albany. In an opening statement, Baylies stated that he "had maintained an uninterrupted friendship and confidential intercourse" with the general for many years. The book was "a labor of love." A daguerreotype of Wool facing the title page depicted an urbane, kindly man attired in a major general's uniform.[41]

Written in a highly eulogistic, florid style, the *Narrative* was solidly based on official letters, documents, and reports. It focused on Wool's march into Mexico and his role in the battle of Buena Vista, both described as brilliant. Baylies also emphasized Wool's long service as inspector general—a service that "did much to prepare the army" for its achievements on the battlefields of Mexico. On his early tours, the general often had to travel "in a bark canoe, piloted by a single Indian, gliding down the long, majestic rivers of the west" en route to remote posts on the western frontier. At other times, he was a guest at banquets "with the wise, the witty, and the learned of the land." The praise marched on and on in measured cadence. Baylies also stressed Wool's qualifications for president. The general was a Union man with considerable administrative experience, indefatigable energy, and an intimate knowledge of the different parts of the nation. Baylies carefully avoided discussing the leading issues of the day—such as slavery, admission of western states, and Cuban intervention. Nor did he refer to the other presidential candidates, Democratic or Whig.[42]

Several Whig newspapers in New York criticized the praise heaped on Wool's role at Buena Vista, and cast shame for stirring controversy while the nation mourned the death of Taylor. Both the *Rochester Daily Advertiser* and the Cooperstown *Freeman's Journal* came to Wool's defense. They explained away the charges leveled at him—then proceeded to list Taylor's mistakes in the battle. Baylies requested extra copies of the *Narrative* to distribute to influential individuals around New England. He hoped that he was not taxing "the liberality of the New York Committee," and promised to hand out copies in a careful manner, "lest it should wear the appearance of electioneering prematurely." Yet seeds must be planted in due season in order to produce an abundant harvest.[43]

Baylies also published a biographical sketch of Wool in the November issue of the *Democratic Review*. Unlike the book, the article stressed the general's character, administrative ability, and military skill. He portrayed Wool as a self-made man who had acquired a wide education through reading and a commitment to learning—and played down his image as a disciplinarian and martinet. The *Troy Daily Times* commented favorably on the sketch, but found the portrait "an imperfect" rendering of the officer. The likeness failed to reflect Wool's energy and firmness, the editor said.[44]

Wool hoped to build political support first in western New York. He visited the summer militia encampments there and was feted at special dinners. In his speeches the general no longer spoke of Buena Vista, but stressed the need for a firm stand against the rising ogre of sectionalism. The nation was enjoying great prosperity, Wool told an audience in Buffalo, because of its form of government and free institutions. Yet some wanted to dissolve "this glorious union." Conciliation and harmony, a strict adherence to the constitution, and a determination to prevent discontent were needed to preserve the Union.[45]

A major contender in the race for the Democratic favorite son nomination in New York was William L. Marcy, a moderate. In September 1851, at the state convention in Syracuse, Marcy had united part of the conservative Hunkers with the liberal Barnburners. Prominent men and influential newspapers fell into line behind him. He launched a campaign to build a political machine that would win over the Hunkers, the group to which Wool leaned. A major break came when Horatio Seymour, a moderate with strength in upstate New York, swung into Marcy's camp. The action attracted much of the influence Wool had counted on in that section.[46]

In February 1852, Wool's friends in Troy met and publicly announced their support of his candidacy for the presidency. They puffed the general's character and portrayed him as a man of vision who represented New York's best choice to win the Democratic nomination. His supporters cleverly timed the announcement to fit with a carefully crafted statement by Wool denouncing the visit of the Hungarian patriot Louis Kossuth to the United States. Kossuth sought support to throw off the yoke of the Hapsburgs and secure a separate political identity for his people. When the Hapsburgs enlisted Russian aid to suppress the revolt, Congress invited Kossuth to come to America. He had arrived in early December 1851 amid great fanfare.[47]

Wool warned the nation about Kossuth. The eloquence of "the great Magyar," he wrote his friend David Stewart, a former United States senator from Maryland, was captivating the nation and exercising power over the intellect that surpassed the influence of Demosthenes or Cicero. Caution was needed, for "the silver veil which conceals this great Mokanna shall be torn away, and deep will be our wonder that we should have knelt at his altar." Those who would adopt "the principles and plans of Kossuth could eventually find themselves involved in a crusade against all the crowned heads of Europe." Many supporters urged the United States to make "a declaration of what they consider should be the law of nations." This was ridiculous, the general snorted, because experience had taught that protests without means to enforce them were worthless. Any form of intervention would mean war—and war was the greatest evil that could befall any people or nation. "It has ever been the curse of nations," Wool declared, "whether caused by fanaticism, intervention, revenge, ambition, or the acquisition of territory." War also caused oppression. "If you would guard your free, happy, and prosperous country against oppression, or oppressive taxes," he declaimed, "beware how you encourage war. Heed not the demagogue, who, to gratify his ambition, would drench his country in blood."[48]

Wool's statement represented his major effort to place his name before the nation as a presidential aspirant. The general knew that he must not only carry New York but also the Southern states, and sent David Stewart a copy of his comment on Kossuth. Stewart, who lived in Baltimore, added introductory remarks and placed it in the Annapolis *Maryland State Capitol Gazette.* "The prominent position of General Wool among the Democratic candidates for the Presidency," the commentator stated, "commands for all his opinions the attention of the country." A distinguished soldier and faithful Jacksonian, Wool was ably qualified to be the Democratic standard-bearer. A volunteer in time of war, the general had "yielded in time of peace to the urgent calls which his fellow citizens have made upon him to enter upon a new field of public service." If nominated, his election was assured.[49]

By April, Wool's letter appeared in newspapers from New England to New Orleans. Conservative editors, Democratic and Whig, found it thought-provoking and timely, while close friends declared it the reflections of an experienced statesman. The editor of the *New York Express*, a Whig sheet, characterized Wool's views as those of an honest, blunt soldier whose "straightforwardness and intelligibility of expression" reminded him of Taylor, Jackson, and Caesar. In fact, Wool had "more ideas and a better argument upon the question of American intervention in Europe" than members of Congress. The Washington *Union* thought the letter both curious and interesting. "Is it not somewhat remarkable," the paper said, "that in regard to this whole matter, the real soldiers—the men of the sword—. . . are mild and pacific in their counsel, while men of the gown, of the pulpit, and bar—and the men of peace *par eminence*—breathe nothing but war and clamor for the contest."[50]

Wool's campaign was nearing its apogee. On May 17 Robert G. Scott, a Richmond editor and delegate to the Democratic National Convention, queried the fourteen presidential contenders about the Compromise of 1850. If elected would the aspirant enforce the compromise, especially the fugitive slave provision? Wool sent Scott a curious answer. Sidestepping the question, he admitted that his name had been mentioned for high office—but stressed that it had been done "without solicitation or agency on my part." The office of president, he believed, was "neither to be sought nor declined." A number of distinguished men were seeking that exalted station, and he preferred that one of them receive the nomination rather than himself. "I assure you," he told Scott, "I have no desire to enter another and a new field, where it is probable I would be compelled to encounter all the baser passions of the human heart." If he had "answered Mr. Scott as he desired," Wool wrote David Stewart, "I would not only have appeared as seeking the office, but ready to make pledges to obtain the nomination. Such a course would not have accorded with my notions of dignity or propriety." As Stewart well knew, the general's views on the Compromise of 1850 were "unequivocal and positive" and "too much so" for Northern Free Soilers.[51]

Wool's reply to editor Scott raised eyebrows in the Democratic ranks. The general's response, the *New York Times* observed on May 31, was more remarkable for candor than courtesy. "It wasn't necessary, in withdrawing from the competition he had been engaged in with so many others for the past two or three years," the editor chided, "to attribute to politicians 'baser passions' than are called into exercise by his present profession." Wool's chances of being tapped in a contingency at the Democratic national convention were fading.[52]

Wool still believed there was a slim chance that his name might be introduced at the convention. Encouraged by the rumblings of disagreement with the "Albany clique," Wool contacted state delegates and influential individuals who planned to attend, placing in their hands letters of introduction and a commitment. The old Jacksonian, James Van Schoonhover, of Troy, and several editors and friends all agreed to represent him. Wool informed David Stewart of these arrangements and advised that several New Yorkers would call on him at the convention.[53]

On Tuesday, June 1, the Democratic National Convention opened in Baltimore. The balloting began three days later, with Lewis Cass the leading contender, followed by James Buchanan and William L. Marcy. As the days passed, and the roll was called again and again, no clear-cut choice emerged. After the thirty-third ballot, on Friday, support for Cass weakened, and Stephen A. Douglas advanced as a front-runner. The contest became heated. To break the stalemate, a Virginia delegate suddenly introduced the name of General Franklin Pierce, of New Hampshire, a dark horse. Pierce was a Mexican War veteran who fitted the need for a pliable Northern man with Southern sympathies. On the forty-ninth ballot, the exhausted delegates cast a majority vote for Pierce and the convention ended. Wool's name was never placed in nomination.[54]

Wool was unruffled by the decision at the convention. From the beginning the chance that his name would be introduced was slight—but the high stakes made the gamble worthwhile. The split in the New York Democracy provided an opportunity for an individual with a non-sectional image to attract support from both factions. He had campaigned without formally identifying with a faction, leaning on his military reputation, influential contacts, and luck. An old-line Jacksonian Democrat, Wool stood for strict construction of the Constitution, law and order, and the traditional virtues of thrift and hard work. In New York, Wool had flirted with the Hunker Democrats, which included shipping magnates and the landed aristocracy—but his equivocal nature made it difficult to place him firmly in any camp and prevented widespread support. In a sense, the general had depended on luck in winning the nomination at Baltimore—and his luck failed. Wool expressed optimism over Pierce's selection. Although "demagogues and political traders" cared for nothing beyond office spoils, he wrote Stewart, the Democratic nomination had been "conferred on one who I believe has neither begged, bribed, or intrigued for it." He saw nothing to prevent Pierce and himself from being friends. "If he is the man I believe him to be, he will not council with these political hucksters who make politics a trade." The general expressed deep gratitude to Stewart for his support in the recent contest.[55]

Wool's involvement in the presidential campaign was not over. In early September, he received orders to accompany General Scott and Surgeon Gen. Thomas Lawson on a trip west to inspect a site for a proposed military asylum—a rest home for veterans—in Kentucky. Scott had been nominated as the Whig candidate for president, and the trip quickly became a political campaign. This was also the most extended period that Wool ever spent in Scott's company during his entire military career. To many it was doubtless amusing to see the two famous generals—one of gigantic structure, the other rather diminutive in size—making public appearances. On the eve of his departure to join Scott, Wool wrote Stewart that the Whigs were trying "to make capital" out of Pierce's card playing during the Mexican War and being slapped in the face by Col. John B. Magruder. The story was false. "What passed happened at a card table," Wool declared, "but began and ended in words." At the time Pierce doubtlessly "did not anticipate" the presidential nomination. Scott's friends probably would try to use the incident in the campaign, but they should be careful. Scott, too, "has played cards."[56]

Wool hurried west via Cincinnati to meet Scott at Maysville, Kentucky, on September 18. Scott had slowed his journey to make political speeches in Pittsburgh and Cleveland. "Large bodies, and especially Presidential Candidates, move slow," he wrote Stewart on September 21. The delay had created an awkward situation for him, for acquaintances from Mexican War days had invited him to attend dinners and public gatherings. Being under orders, he had politely declined each invitation. The next day, Wool departed by stage for Blue Lick Springs. Scott and his party arrived on the twenty-fifth. Together, they surveyed the site near Harrodsburg for the veterans' home, drew up a report, and departed for Louisville.[57]

Scott turned the journey into a "grand tour." On September 28, he and Wool reached the town of Paris, where the Scott Guards, of Georgetown, escorted them with great pomp to the Bourbon County Fair. Here, before several thousand people, both generals made short speeches and were cheered. Scott was not an impressive speaker. The commanding general's "oratory or powers of speech," Wool later wrote a friend, "is very little better than my own, and not calculated to gain votes or friends. He appears wholly deficient in dogma, and his speeches contain no striking illustrations or maxims, which often supply the place of eloquence." Wool paid his respects to the aging senators John J. Crittenden in Frankfort and Henry Clay in Lexington, then received orders to return to Troy. Scott continued his "tour."[58]

On October 28, in Taunton, Massachusetts, Wool sat by the bedside of Francis Baylies and watched his dear friend pass from life to death. Baylies was sixty-nine years old. For over six months he had suffered increasing debility, and on August 21, in an almost illegible note, his brother-in-law said that his right hand was useless and he was in great pain. Attempts to dictate letters were unsatisfactory. As Baylies grew weaker, Wool had hurried to Taunton and joined the melancholy vigil which lasted nearly a week. He owed much to the ebullient Baylies, who was always clever and frank, who always had a cheery word, and who though sick provided the essential spark for Wool's recent flirtation with politics. Twenty-five years before, Wool had written that his first real friend had been Howard Moulton, Sarah Wool's father; he could rightly say that Baylies was his second. There would never be another so close. With a heavy heart the general attended Baylies's funeral and returned home.[59]

In November 1852, Franklin Pierce was elected president of the United States, and the scramble for patronage began. Wool sought a share of the spoils for several of his Hunker friends, especially David Stewart. The chances looked good, because the moderates were trying to push the New York Barnburners into the background. Wool encouraged Stewart to put in for a cabinet post. The Maryland politician stood prominently in the party, he advised. To obtain notice, Stewart "must be known as the friend of General Pierce and the friend of no one else." On January 20, 1853, the general wrote Pierce regarding possible appointments, but when the president responded he said nothing about patronage. The president was having his problems, Wool informed Stewart. Deputation after deputation had gone to Concord to dictate his choices for a cabinet. Pierce might "cry out with more propriety than Pyrrhus did, 'save me from my friends for I am afraid of none but them.'"[60]

Later in the month, when Marcy was named Secretary of State, Wool exploded. Marcy was not fitted for the office, he wrote Stewart. He was deficient "in all the higher attributes" of a statesman. He lacked knowledge "of the affairs of nations, of manners, generosity and liberality, whilst he is sordid and gives too much scope to his narrow and contracted prejudices." In a word William Marcy was "a creature of the world, a politician hanging on its favors, living on its smiles and happy or miserable in proportion to his success in obtaining the 'spoils of office.'" When Stewart applauded this masterful portrayal, Wool responded caustically that he "could draw the characters of many, who pass for patriots," but who only "work for those who pay best."[61]

Throughout the early spring of 1853, Wool relentlessly pursued an appointment for Stewart. On February 25, he arranged an interview with Pierce, but the meeting was unproductive. In March, Wool drafted additional letters in Stewart's behalf, but nothing came of the contacts. Pierce's announced policy of giving positions to both "soft" and "hardshell" Democrats compounded the situation. By July 1, Stewart grew restless. "You must have patience, my friend," Wool counseled. In early July when a district judgeship became vacant, Stewart submitted his name—then hesitated and withdrew it. Wool's efforts in his behalf had proven fruitless.[62]

On July 13, at the invitation of the president, Wool took "the cars"—as he called the train—to New York City. The first world's fair held in the United States was opening there in a beautiful new building called the Crystal Palace. Queen Victoria had sent representatives from Great Britain, and President Pierce agreed to attend. Wool appeared with the president's suite on July 14 at a reception at Castle Garden, then rode horseback through a downpour of rain in a procession to the Crystal Palace. Pierce had developed a sore throat and stumbled through his address. That evening, Wool and other officers, resplendent in dress uniforms, attended a dance in the ladies' parlor at the Astor House. On the final day of festivities, Pierce met with a number of New York Democratic politicians in his rooms. Wool talked at length with Jefferson Davis, the newly appointed Secretary of War, about patronage. The Hunkers viewed Pierce "with cold civility," but Wool was pleased at the attention the president's friends paid him.[63]

August was a busy month for the Wools in Troy. Practically every week, at the general's invitation, influential politicians dined with him and discussed politics. One week, Senator James A. Bayard, of Delaware, was a guest; the next was Taylor's attorney general, Reverdy Johnson, of Maryland, and so it went. Ill health caused Jefferson Davis to cancel a promised visit. Equally exciting was the romance that blossomed in the Wool household. John Stewart, son of the general's friend in Baltimore, had been a houseguest for several weeks, and during his stay in Troy he fell in love with Josephine Moulton, Sarah Wool's niece from New York City. The Wools were delighted. Josephine was a handsome girl, "well educated with a good mind unharkened in the ways of the world, with no desire for extravagance or for the follies of the fashionable and gay," the general wrote John Stewart's father. She would make a "kind and affectionate wife, and such a one as you and your family will be pleased with." In late September, when John Stewart returned to Troy on the eve of the wedding, the general seized every opportunity to tease the young couple, even threatening to accompany them on their wedding trip. They welcomed the day when the nuptials were held, and they departed for the southern climes.[64]

Wool's preoccupation with political and social matters suddenly ended on November 1, 1853, with the receipt of General Order 25, dated October 31. Secretary of War Davis, in his zeal to modernize the army, had reconstituted the military commands. The old Eastern-Western divisions and their satellites were replaced by five named departments. Wool would command the Department of the East, which extended west to the Mississippi River. Beyond the river were the four Departments of the West, Texas, New Mexico, and the Pacific. Department commanders would report through General-in-Chief Winfield Scott, Headquarters of the Army, in New York City. The disturbing aspect of the change was that Wool must move his headquarters from Troy to Baltimore, effective December 1.[65]

Wool hurried to New York City to confer with Scott. He had not been consulted in the changes, Scott quickly explained, and authorized Wool to recommend Troy as departmental headquarters. In Washington, the adjutant general, however, insisted to Wool that the new arrangement would stand. His mission a failure, Wool returned to Troy. Moving to Baltimore would be an unsettling experience. Sarah Wool, in frail health, could not move, and he would be separated from family and friends. However, there were compensations. Wool now commanded the largest and most prestigious jurisdiction in the nation, and his new headquarters would place him near his friend David Stewart. The assignment would also remove him from the strife-ridden political scene in New York. Whatever the pros and cons of the new assignment, Wool was first and last a soldier. He obeyed orders. He wrote Stewart on November 8 that he would soon visit Baltimore to locate an office and quarters.[66]

Following the Mexican War, Gen. John Wool had resumed command of the Eastern Division. With a staff to handle military responsibilities, he increasingly devoted time and energy to economic and political pursuits. He studied the business scene and made careful investments in real estate, railroads, and banks. Wool also was drawn into state and national politics. The New York Democratic nomination for president in 1852 captured his attention and he worked hard to create a following among the conservative Hunker faction, only to see his low-key, informal campaign flicker and fail. Wool's lack of influence in the subsequent distribution of patronage was equally disconcerting. The episode mirrored the various roles that ranking army officers often played in politics in that day. A new chapter in Wool's career began with the appointment of Jefferson Davis as secretary of war. As the general arranged to transfer his headquarters from Troy to Baltimore, Davis suddenly changed his mind. Expanding problems in the newly created Department of the Pacific required the services of an experienced and discreet commander. The secretary turned to Wool.

10

A VAST AND DISTANT LAND

In late January 1854, Wool sailed from New York City on the steamship *George Law* for Panama and California. He was to assume command of the Department of the Pacific, a distant, sprawling military jurisdiction that included the state of California and the territories of Oregon, Washington, and Utah. Wool carried instructions to preserve American neutrality, curb Indian unrest, and place the Pacific coast in a state of defense. The veteran officer was now seventy years old, but he tackled his assignment with vigor. In his zeal to accomplish his tasks, however, Wool in succeeding months clashed with Secretary of War Jefferson Davis over his methods for curbing filibustering. For nearly a year, they hurled invectives at each other in California and eastern newspapers. The sparring finally ended when Wool was forced to turn his attention to other matters in his department.[1]

Secretary Davis paid considerable attention to the far West in his annual report of December 1, 1853. The population growth in California and in the Oregon country had created the need for a transcontinental railroad and for smoothed friction between whites and American Indians over land use. Congress had voted appropriations to survey and chart railroad routes across the plains and Rockies, but the Indian problem sputtered on for lack of troops to cover this vast region. Davis had requested funds for additional troops for western service and for the construction of new posts to protect emigrant routes. The health and prosperity of the nation demanded that its remote regions be protected, united, and developed.[2]

Davis and other officials were also concerned about the recent organization of filibustering expeditions in California aimed at neighboring Mexican states. The activities of the "grey-eyed man of destiny," the lawyer, physician, and most famous of filibusters, William Walker, complicated United States negotiations with Mexico for a strip of land south of the Gila River that Davis desired for a railroad to the west coast. In the summer of 1853, the government sought to purchase the tract from Santa Anna, who had been reelected president of Mexico. James Gadsden, the American minister, was authorized to offer $55 million for the territory. The negotiations were embarrassed, however, by California filibusters, particularly Walker, who, in early December, opened a recruiting office in San Francisco to gather men, arms, and ships to seize Sonora, the large Mexican state, and establish a separate republic. Brig. Gen. Ethan A. Hitchcock, commanding the Department of the Pacific, couldn't halt these activities and asked to be relieved.[3]

In mid-December 1853, Secretary of War Davis called Wool to Washington to discuss matters in the Pacific Department. Meeting in President Pierce's office, the secretary described his plans for the military in California, the need to contain the Indian unrest in frontier districts, and the ongoing filibustering threats to Baja California and Sonora. Positive steps must be taken to curb this menace to the friendly republic of Mexico. Davis wanted Wool to replace Hitchcock. He flattered the general by speaking of his good judgment, and praised him as an officer who could handle "grave and delicate responsibilities and necessary discretionary power." In addition, the secretary said that the veteran troubleshooter would command as brevet major general—which meant a boost in pay. Wool accepted the assignment, but insisted that he have the full confidence of Pierce and Davis. Both assured him of their support. Upon leaving the White House, the general jotted down a memorandum of the conversation, which was a habit from his long years as an inspector general, though in this case, he did not trust Davis and held Pierce in low esteem. The memorandum proved valuable, for within a few months there would be conflicting interpretations of his assignment.[4]

The next few weeks were hectic. Wool studied reports from the Pacific Department and prepared a list of quartermaster and ordnance needs. He bought a second steamer trunk, ordered a new pair of boots, and had his pistols refitted with percussion caps. He wanted the extra boots because he had heard that California prices were outrageous. On January 4, 1854, Wool learned that Congress had voted him an elegant sword "for his distinguished services in the late war with Mexico," particularly for his "skill, enterprise, and courage" at the battle of Buena Vista. Wool may have helped move the sword bill through Congress. From Washington on January 7, he wrote Sarah that a friend had driven "the thanks and sword bill" through the House. James Shields "reported it to the Senate and it passed unanimously."[5]

On January 6, Wool went to the White House again. He had talked with the senators and representatives from California and learned that an expedition had sailed from San Francisco to Walker in Baja California. He hinted to Pierce and Davis that he needed "special powers" to enhance his authority, and cited Hitchcock's "special commission" from President Fillmore. Wool requested "delegated powers" from Pierce to restrain citizens from committing neutrality violations, powers greater than the secretary could bestow. The president and Davis hedged. On January 10, Wool pressed for further instructions. "I am not in possession of all your views in relation to the course that ought to be pursued," he wrote Davis. After waiting two days for a reply, the general took the train to his new departmental headquarters in Baltimore, turned over command to Col. James Bankhead, and left for Troy.[6]

A snowstorm buffeted the city when Wool boarded a train early on January 19 for New York City. A band struggled in the icy temperature to play martial airs and wish him a cheery farewell. As the train rattled north, the general fought a headache and mulled over the events of the past few days. He was unhappy that his aide-de-camp, Capt. Hamilton L. Shields, had declined to go west and asked for reassignment. News had come that the steamship *San Francisco,* bound for California with the Third Artillery Regiment, had foundered and sunk in the Atlantic with few survivors. Gadsden had consummated a treaty with Santa Anna and the document would soon reach Washington. Wool also reviewed Davis's last instructions, dated January 12. Regarding filibustering, the new commander would "use all proper means to detect the fitting out" of armed expeditions bound for Mexico, and "zealously co-operate" with the civil authorities in maintaining the neutrality laws. No "special" powers were granted. However, a week later, President Pierce issued a proclamation urging federal officers to use every effort "to arrest for trial and punishment" all persons endangering American neutrality.[7]

In New York City, Wool took lodgings in the Saint Nicholas Hotel and attended a farewell dinner hurriedly arranged by local Democrats. Former Treasury Secretary Robert J. Walker, Senator Henry S. Foote of Mississippi, and some thirty others shared the evening. The next morning, January 20, with Sarah back in Troy, Wool and Foote boarded the *George Law,* a large steamboat with accommodations for over a thousand passengers. An air of conviviality prevailed, for a number of young officers and their wives were traveling to California. At two o'clock in the afternoon, the steamship cleared her berth and headed toward the Narrows and open sea. With a heavy fog rolling in, the captain dropped anchor that night off Sandy Hook, but the following day the vessel continued south for the Caribbean.[8]

The ship touched at Kingston, on the island of Jamaica, then turned toward the port of Aspinwall or what is today Colón, on the Isthmus of Panama. In letters to Sarah, Wool described his acquaintances on board, particularly among the fair sex, and his impressions of the ports of call. He also spoke of Foote. The senator, he said, "is very much my friend and permits no opportunity [to pass] to place me and my services very prominently" before the passengers. The Southerner planned to settle in California and doubtless would become an influential politician there.

After arriving at the port of Aspinwall, or what would become Colón, on the Isthmus of Panama in February 1854, General Wool, his aides, and a party of travelers, set off for the Pacific on mules, as was the mode of travel before the completion of a railroad thirteen months later. En route, Wool's mule stumbled and fell, pinning him against an iron rail. When helped to his feet, his thigh was bruised and his knee pained him greatly, but he had no broken bones. For several weeks, the general was forced to hobble about on crutches. Halfway across the fifty-mile isthmus, the travelers were also set upon by a band of robbers. Fortunately, most of the robbers were not armed and tried simply to drag the travelers off their mules before robbing them. After a shot or two, the bandits scurried off into the jungle and the party arrived safely in Panama City, thirteen hours after departing Aspinwall. The weary travelers embarked on the *John L. Stephens,* and on February 14, they docked safely in San Francisco.[9]

Former members of the Troy Citizens Corps welcomed Wool on his arrival. They escorted him in a carriage to the Oriental Hotel, a large, fashionable establishment downtown. On February 17, the Trojans collected in the parlor and toasted the general and his exploits. Prominent citizens and city officials also paid their respects to the new department commander.[10]

San Francisco was a great commercial emporium. The city contained over fifty thousand inhabitants, or nearly one-fifth of the population of California. The bustling seaport boasted 160 hotels, nineteen banks, twelve daily newspapers, and five theaters. Consuls for twenty-seven nations resided there. Coal gas lights illuminated the main streets. Over 1,000 vessels cleared the port yearly, and in 1853, an estimated $55,000,000 worth of gold had passed from its docks to world markets. But the boom was subsiding. The year 1854 would see decreased gold production, rising unemployment, and the beginnings of depression in the Golden State.[11]

On the morning of February 16, General Hitchcock and his staff came to the Oriental, and the two generals discussed the responsibilities and problems in the Pacific command. One of the largest military jurisdictions in the nation, the department stretched from the deserts of the Mexican border north through the rain forests and snow-capped mountains of California and Oregon and Washington territories to the Canadian line, and east into Mormon country. Within this domain, 1,400 soldiers of the Third Artillery, Second and Fourth Infantry regiments, and other units, manned fifteen forts and posts. Ten installations were in California. The remote garrisons included Forts Lane and Orford, in southwestern Oregon, and, to the north Fort Steilacoom, at the southern tip of Puget Sound, in Washington Territory. To the east of Steilacoom were Forts Vancouver and Dalles, on the Columbia River. Communication between these northern posts was primarily by water. Lying two thousand miles west of the Mississippi Valley settlements, the Pacific Department was an empire unto itself.[12]

Hitchcock had taken command early in 1852 and quickly found filibustering a major headache. When he attempted to break up the expeditions being organized and outfitted in San Francisco, federal officials were reluctant to cooperate. He had recently seized the *Arrow*, which was being loaded by Walker to sail for Sonora, but United States District Attorney Samuel W. Inge had dragged his feet in examining the vessel and turning it over to the United States marshal. Walker sued Hitchcock in the state courts for return of the ship, transferred his men and arms to the *Caroline,* and departed. Hitchcock suspected that certain politicians supported the filibustering schemes. He pointed an accusing finger at California Senators William Gwin and John B. Weller, and at various local and state officials who were known expansionists.[13]

Wool assumed command of the Pacific Department on February 17, 1854. He rented a bedroom and a small parlor at the Oriental for his quarters, paying fifty dollars per week. From Hitchcock he inherited two aides-de-camp, Lt. James A. Hardie and Thomas Gardner. The assistant adjutant general was Maj. Erasmus D. Townsend, a tall, erudite Massachusetts man, who would function as his chief-of-staff. Wool quickly found his evenings filled with parties, plays, and civic events. Wherever the veteran officer appeared, the audience gave him a special welcome. He wrote Sarah that he was "quite a lion" in San Francisco.[14]

On February 25, Wool and Foote were honored at a lavish dinner in the spacious Cafe du Commerce. Governor John Bigler presided, and 150 attendees, primarily state officials and friends, attended. As introductions were made, Wool became agitated with the garbled rendition of the battle of Queenston and corrected the speaker twice. After an interlude of music, toasts were given. At the mention of Wool's name, the band struck up the spirited "Buena Vista March," and he rose and spoke briefly. The general knew the dinner was a political affair and portrayed himself as a neutral. He declared that he had "no feelings, principles, or prejudices" regarding the sectional issues disturbing the nation, saying, "I could live with as much pleasure in the South as in the North." Senator Foote then rose and presented a toast: "The Presidential Election of 1856—may it be a man with thoroughly national views." At this point, Wool and his aide quietly left the dinner. It was fortunate that he did, for the speeches quickly degenerated into barbed attacks on the Pierce administration.[15]

"Tammany [Democrats] ruled the roost at this entertainment," declared the *San Francisco Herald* the next day. The *Alta California* went further and pronounced the dinner a slap at the Gwin Democrats, who were headquartered at the federal customhouse. Tammany Democrat David C. Broderick, who badly wanted Gwin's Senate seat, had arranged the gathering to identify Wool and Foote with his following. News of the event prompted eastern papers to criticize the general for involving himself with California politics—and for not defending Pierce.[16]

Wool believed that to command effectively in the Pacific Department, he must understand the political scene. Broderick's followers were seeking to control the state legislature and local federal patronage, but there was a larger issue. San Francisco businessman Henry W. Halleck, on February 12, explained to his West Point classmate Isaac I. Stevens that California Democrats were hopelessly split. The pro-slavery, or "Chivalry" faction, led by Robert J. Walker and Gwin, were pushing for a railroad route across the southwest with a possible terminus at Guaymas, Sonora. Both James Gadsden and filibuster William Walker were working toward that same goal. Halleck predicted that Walker would fail to seize Sonora and guarantee a port at Guaymas—but Gadsden would succeed in acquiring the territory needed for a route to San Diego. Opposing the pro-southern faction were the Broderickites, or "shoulder strikers"—a conglomeration of "abolitionists, free soilers, anti-slave, spoilsmen, squatters, and true democrats all mixed up together." Halleck regarded the whole business as sordid and disgusting.[17]

Wool was appalled at the inflated prices in San Francisco. "The expenses here are about five to one in New York," he explained to Sarah. "A hack for a ride from one house to another is $5, for a day $25 to $30. A horse $10. A servant from 50 to 100 dollars. . . . Money is from two to ten percent a month. I could get ten thousand a year, good security, $3,600 and for twenty thousand $7,200." He reported to Harriette on food prices: a turkey cost $20, a chicken $2, a dozen eggs $3. Large lemons sold for seventy-five cents each, an orange for fifty cents. A glass of anything to drink was twenty-five cents. Rents were "enormously high"; the smallest cottage commanded a hundred dollars a month. No army officer could live on his regular pay in California.[18]

On the eve of the Broderick dinner, Wool had tackled the filibuster problem in the city. He was told that Walker had seized La Paz, the capital of Baja California, then sailed around the peninsula and up the Pacific coast to the town of Enseñada, seventy miles below San Diego. Here he dispatched Henry P. Watkins to San Francisco for supplies and recruits. Wool had talked with District Attorney Inge about Watkins, and found the federal official, a Southerner and close friend of Davis, questioning the need for taking action. According to Major Townsend, Inge had even asked sotto voce: "General, do you think the Administration is really intent on stopping these filibustering expeditions?" Wool replied that Watkins's activities were obvious, and he felt that local civil authorities should arrest him. Inge agreed to do so, if Wool put his "complaint" in writing. The general promptly complied, and Inge issued a warrant. Watkins was brought into court on February 23, and charged with violating federal neutrality laws. He was allowed bail and bound over for trial in April. Wool turned next to Walker. He instructed Capt. Thomas A. Dornin, commanding the U.S. sloop of war *Portsmouth*, to cruise the Mexican coast south of San Diego and ascertain Walker's movements. In mid-March came reports that the filibuster was in trouble. The *Columbus* arrived in San Francisco with Frederic Emory, Walker's so-called secretary of state, and several other men aboard. They had surrendered to Captain Dornin, who sent them north by ship to San Francisco. Emory and his cohorts were arrested, charged, released on bail, and quickly vanished into the city.[19]

On March 12, Wool stepped up the pressure. He noticed an ad in the *Alta California* announcing that the Mexican government wished to enlist three thousand colonists to settle on the northern frontier in the state of Sonora. *L'Echo du Pacifique*, a French-language newspaper, had published a similar notice. Wool wanted additional information on the matter, and asked the Mexican consul, Luis del Valle, to come to the Oriental Hotel for a conference. Gadsden had recently negotiated a treaty with Santa Anna, and the border must be kept quiet until it was ratified. Moreover, the general viewed with suspicion any colonizing effort that might be turned into a scheme to help Walker. He had learned that, two years before, Count Gaston Raoul de Raousset-Boulbon, a former French newspaper editor and politician residing in San Francisco, had launched an abortive expedition to Sonora. Boulbon had contrived a plan to develop the silver mines near the Sonoran-Arizona border. He had received the approval of Patrice Dillon, the French consul in San Francisco, and had traveled to Mexico City, where he obtained government approval. He also secured credit from Jecker, Torre, and Company, Franco-Mexican bankers. Boulbon enlisted 250 men from the floating body of French miners in San Francisco, landed at Guaymas, but found Sonoran officials hostile and suffered a military defeat. In the spring of 1853, he began organizing another expedition.[20]

Luis del Valle, an elderly man, met Wool at the Oriental on March 14. The Mexican consul explained his instructions from Mexico City regarding the colonizing venture, and assured the general that the men were colonists, not soldiers. However, it was hoped that they would also help defend the border from Apache raiders. Valle was aware of Boulbon's new scheme, which reportedly involved enlisting one thousand Frenchmen in San Francisco to support insurgents seeking to establish a separate republic in Sonora. Valle had instructions to "steal away" as many Frenchmen as possible from the count, hoping thereby to cripple his plans. French Consul Dillon had been helpful in this endeavor. Dillon had enlisted and furnished passports for some five hundred men to fill Valle's quota. The Mexican diplomat also told Wool that he had contracted with two French merchants, Edouard Cavallier and Hector Chauviteau, to charter a British vessel, the *Challenge*, to transport the colonists to Guaymas. Wool questioned Valle closely about the character of the colonists. Walker badly needed recruits, he said. Boulbon could push his men to enlist in Valle's undertaking, seize control of the group, and divert it to Walker. Wool advised the Mexican consul to cancel the ship contract and delay the project. His objective, he confided to Sarah, "was to stay the expedition in order to prevent aid to Walker, who expects to be relieved by these Frenchmen from his perilous situation."[21]

Wool and an aide now paid a visit to Consul Dillon, an Irishman long in the French diplomatic service. He told Dillon that he intended to stop the outfitting of expeditions bent on violating neutrality laws, and expressed a suspicion that Boulbon wanted control of Valle's recruits. In mid-February, the Mexican government had warned the French ministers in Mexico City and Washington about the count. Dillon found that Boulbon was indeed collecting men in San Francisco, and he had stopped giving passports. But Boulbon had come to the consulate, declared he had abandoned his plans, and was leaving for Santa Barbara. At Valle's insistence Dillon resumed issuing passports, and introduced the Mexican consul to Chauviteau and Cavallier, who arranged for him to use the *Challenge*. Wool concluded his meeting with Dillon, warning that "whether the expedition was gotten up for good or evil purposes, it was exceedingly ill-timed and . . . might lead to serious consequences." The general left convinced that Valle was being duped. The Mexican consul was being "grossly humbugged," he wrote Sarah. Boulbon was pushing his followers to join Valle's project, and on the high seas they would seize the ship, become soldiers, and grab Sonora.[22]

On March 17, a disgruntled group—Valle, Dillon, Chauviteau, and Cavallier—called on Wool at the Oriental. The *Challenge* had been denied clearance, and they demanded an explanation. The general stated that he had asked Collector Richard P. Hammond to put the vessel under "strict watch." A sea captain named Peters, formerly with Walker, had come forward and said he had been hired to join the crew and take command for Boulbon, once the *Challenge* cleared the Golden Gate. The ship was to carry powder and arms that had been stored in a house on Telegraph Hill. Wool warned his audience that the vessel must sail according to law. He then turned abruptly to Consul Dillon and boldly accused him of conspiring with Boulbon. The count was in San Francisco at that very moment, the general asserted, trying to convert the expedition into a military venture. Dillon had seen him at least twice. Incensed by the accusation, the consul jumped to his feet and stalked out of the parlor. In a terse note the next day, he denied any involvement with Boulbon. Rethinking the delicate situation and with little evidence, Wool sent a conciliatory reply, saying he accepted Dillon's disclaimer of involvement in the ill-conceived venture.[23]

Wool believed he had paralyzed Boulbon's filibustering effort by maneuvering Valle into a corner. Some thousand Frenchmen had agreed to go to Sonora as colonists, but with the Mexican consul hesitating, they could become restive and perhaps drop away. If the colonists became filibusters, the Mexican government would repudiate Valle; if he broke the contract with Cavallier and Chauviteau, he must make an expensive settlement. Wool planned to continue feeding Valle information to increase his fears. "I have got the French Consul and the Mexican Consul by the throats," he wrote home. "They are denouncing each other as the greatest scoundrels in San Francisco. When rogues fall out, honest men get their dues."[24]

On March 20, 1854, the Watkins trial began, with Foote and three other attorneys defending him. The arrest of Walker's subordinate in late February had been Wool's first move against the filibusters. An air of sympathy for the defendant pervaded the proceedings. Seventeen persons, eight of whom admitted they were filibusters, implicated Watkins, but no politician or civil official charged by rumor as accomplices was called to testify. The jury deliberated nearly twelve hours and found Watkins guilty of violating neutrality laws. Later, on April 7, the court imposed a $1,500 fine. Fred Emory, Watkins's cohort, was tried next, found guilty, and fined the same amount. Both pleaded inability to pay, and several weeks later they were released.[25]

While Watkins was on trial, Wool sought other ways to delay the *Challenge* from sailing. In so doing, he hoped that his pressure would stop enlistments, fracture the scheme, and wreck plans to reinforce Walker. Collector Hammond reported on March 20 that carpenters were adding berths in the ship, and that he was having trouble securing a passenger list. Hammond would grant clearance, but he asked Wool to station a naval vessel to overtake the *Challenge* and check for passenger violations. The law provided a penalty of five dollars for every nondisclosed passenger, with nonpayment constituting a lien against the ship. The general agreed to cooperate. On March 23, Chauviteau and Cavallier filed a passenger list at the customs office. The *Challenge* sailed from Meigs Wharf, but was stopped in San Francisco Bay by a naval cutter and escorted back. Hammond wanted a thorough inspection of the character of the passengers and freight. Five days later, Wool sent Maj. Justus McKinstry to examine the vessel. McKinstry found nothing to suggest a violation of neutrality laws and the next day, the general withdrew all objections—but suggested that Hammond should check for revenue law violations. Shortly after noon, the *Challenge* sailed again, but the revenue cutter *Frolic* hailed the captain and ordered him to return to the wharf. There, while a large crowd watched, officials impounded the ship for having too many bunks and passengers for its measurements. Two days later, Wool urged District Attorney Inge to arrest Valle for violating the Neutrality Act of 1818. The Mexican consul had been enlisting men on American soil for military duty against a friendly power. Inge hesitated, then demanded that the general put his reasons for the arrest in writing. To bolster the case, Wool got Chauviteau and Cavallier to agree to provide evidence that Valle had enlisted men to serve as soldiers in Sonora. The Mexican consul was taken into custody, charged, and released on bail.[26]

Wool was not entirely sure the expedition would become a filibustering venture. However, the way it was raised, Valle's instructions, Dillon's visits with Boulbon, and the fact that it was ill-timed and would encourage other forays convinced him that it should be stopped. He also believed that Walker was involved because of the information from Captain Peters. Peters earlier had commanded the *Republic*, which had been contracted to transport Watkins's recruits to Walker. Wool had acted on his "suspicions" in having Valle arrested, but he hoped that his behind-the-scenes maneuvers would break up the filibustering scheme. He mailed Sarah a clipping from the San Francisco *Herald* about Valle's arrest, and wrote: "I . . . did not consult anyone on the subject, nor did I ask whether it would be popular or otherwise. . . . The whole scheme of the Consul [Valle] was a nefarious one. . . . The French Consul will likely share the fate of the Mexican Consul. . . . I hope hereafter to be able to attend . . . to my appropriate duties."[27]

The detention of the *Challenge* and arrest of the Mexican consul created a furor in San Francisco. The *Herald*, in an extra edition, stated that 525 emigrants, French and German, had been enlisted, and understood they would be enrolled in the Mexican army to stop American filibustering incursions and keep "the border States of Mexico in subjection to the will of Santa Anna." Two gentlemen of the highest respectability in the city, the *Herald* reported, had furnished abundant evidence regarding the intent of the group. In promoting the venture, Valle had violated Section 2 of the Act of 1818, which forbade the enlistment of men on American soil to invade a nation with whom the United States was friendly. The *Alta California* viewed the affair with levity. It doubted that the *Challenge* could be held, for vessels sailed daily from San Francisco in violation of the revenue laws. However, the "worthy Collector" had special reasons for seizing the ship, and was now basking in the "glory of the seizure." While newspaper editors speculated over the action, carpenters removed one tier of berths, and one hundred passengers debarked. On April 3, the *Challenge* sailed with 350 men for the seaport of Guaymas.[28]

Wool's action in the *Challenge* affair provoked heated comment. The *Herald* assured its readers that the general had no part in delaying the expedition, but the French language newspapers thought otherwise. The San Francisco *Messenger* (quoted in the *Alta California*) accused Wool of acting "at the suggestion of a coterie which proposes to elevate him to the Presidency." Recent *Herald* articles approving his actions had been written by one of the staff. In response, John Nugent, editor of the *Herald*, branded the accusations "alarmingly frantic and hysterically wrathful." He added: "Everything that has appeared in this paper in the shape of an editorial in relation to the Sonora Expedition, was written by the Editor and by nobody else."[29]

Wool, meanwhile, turned many of his thoughts toward home. Contrary to his stiff exterior, the general was warm and affectionate toward relatives. In addressing Elizabeth, John Griswold's wife, he spoke with endearing terms. San Francisco, he said, was only about four years old, but it already was a "wonderful city." Business was brisk and everybody was "on the jump." He planned a trip to the mines and promised to send Elizabeth a token of his "remembrance and affection." In closing, the old soldier inquired about his little namesake, John Wool Griswold. "Johnie the young General," his father later wrote, "has this moment kissed me good night, and wishes me to ask Uncle Wool if there are any tigers in Californy and that he guesses he better come home."[30]

On April 17, the Valle trial began in district court, with Judge Ogden Hoffman presiding. Two days before, Wool tried to coach District Attorney Inge, handing him a statement summarizing the evidence and actions in the case. In his opening remarks, Inge referred to these "special instructions" and cast the general in the role of initiating the major decisions in the matter. Chauviteau testified that Wool had warned him that the Valle expedition would violate the neutrality laws, and suggested that he get the Mexican consul to cancel the contract for the *Challenge*. Valle had refused to cooperate. Cavallier echoed Chauviteau's statements, and assured the court that they had no wish to be involved in a filibustering scheme. McKinstry reported that he had found no arms on the *Challenge*. Also, Consul Dillon had assured him that the expedition was "not going to aid Walker, nor was it got up by Count Raousset-Boulbon."[31]

The next day, Valle requested that Dillon be called as a witness. The French consul refused to appear, claiming immunity under the 1853 Consular Convention between France and the United States. Judge Hoffman then fell ill and the trial was postponed. On April 25, Judge Hoffman issued a writ to arrest Dillon for contempt of court for ignoring subpoenas. Dillon and his attorney appeared and handed the judge a written protest. Which took precedence, the French consul demanded to know, the United States Constitution or a treaty? The Sixth Amendment to the Constitution granted defense counsels the power to subpoena, while Article 2 of the 1853 Convention gave foreign consuls immunity from being forced to testify in court. Having made his appearance, Dillon returned to his consulate and lowered the French flag. Hoffman dismissed the contempt charge, declaring that the treaty took precedence in the matter. The trial continued. On April 28, the jury found Valle guilty—but recommended mercy. The judge set sentencing for mid-May.[32]

The Valle affair prompted both Dillon and Wool to publish their correspondence in the newspapers. The *Herald* denounced Hoffman's release of Dillon. The decision denied Valle "the simple rights" guaranteed by the Constitution. "Let this out-raged man go free," the editor cried. The *Alta California* portrayed Dillon as much maligned and charged Wool with making a deal with Chauviteau and Cavallier. If they would sign complaints for Valle's arrest, he would let the *Challenge* sail. Wool was pleased with the outcome of the trial. On April 29, he assured Secretary Davis that he had disrupted an attempt by the French consul to land a revolutionary army in Mexico.[33]

On May 15, San Francisco suddenly forgot about Valle. On that day a government steamer arrived with the celebrated filibuster William Walker aboard. Five months earlier, at Enseñada, in Baja California, Walker had proclaimed himself president of the "Republic of Sonora." In late March, he led over one hundred men northeast across the peninsula toward Fort Yuma, on the lower Colorado River, at the Yuma Crossing, intending to turn south into Sonora. On April 8, the party reached the post in a near-starving condition. Walker and forty-five men then headed west along the international border toward San Diego. Three weeks later, at Wool's orders, Major McKinstry crossed the border near San Diego in civilian clothes and talked with Walker at the hacienda of La Tijuana, three miles to the south. A Mexican cavalry detachment hovered nearby. McKinstry urged the filibuster to surrender and promised transportation to San Francisco. On May 8, his thirtieth birthday, Walker and his tattered "army" of thirty-three men crossed the border and surrendered their arms to an army detachment. McKinstry received Walker as an emissary of the Republic of Sonora![34]

At San Francisco, McKinstry brought Walker to the Oriental Hotel to meet Wool. The general accompanied them to Inge's office, where Walker gave his parole to appear in court when called. No bail was required. The *Alta California* fumed about the outrageous "agreement" between United States representatives and the "President" of the so-called Republic of Sonora. The affair was both an insult and an injury "to our credit as a nation." Wool ignored the insinuations. As he had been requested, he had placed Valle and Walker in the hands of civil authorities. He now turned his attention to the French consul, Patrice Dillon.[35]

Wool hesitated to ask for Dillon's arrest. Several French ships of war were due to visit San Francisco in mid-May, and there was no way to predict what the disgruntled consul might do. Dillon's arrest might well blow up into an embarrassing international incident. To provide a show of force in the harbor, Wool had ordered ten heavy artillery pieces be mounted on Alcatraz Island, ten at Fort Point, and ten placed on movable siege carriages. The day that Walker arrived, Wool suddenly decided to have Dillon arrested. At the general's request, Inge filed charges against Dillon before the federal grand jury then in session. At a hearing, Chauviteau, Cavallier, and several others, testified against the consul regarding neutrality violations. The jury reported a true bill, and a warrant was issued for his arrest. Dillon, accompanied by attorneys Henry S. Foote and Edward D. Baker, came to court and posted a $10,000 bond to appear on May 22. Wool wrote David Stewart with great gusto that he had "most effortlessly vindicated the violated laws of the country." Watkins, Emory, and Valle had been tried and convicted, Walker had surrendered, and Dillon had been indicted by the grand jury. "I think filibustering in California is used up," he crowed.[36]

While assailing the filibuster community, Wool expressed concern about his public image in the East. New York would again play a major role in selecting the Democratic nominee for President in 1856, and he entertained a glimmer of hope that his name might be mentioned. A small groundswell of support was developing among friends in New York and in the Midwest. The *Advocate* of Salem, Illinois, for example, on February 23 described Wool as one of the republic's greatest soldiers, an officer who had visited with the crowned heads of Europe, and a national figure qualified to be president. Wool also tried to clear his skirts about the Broderick dinner, by assuring California Senator Gwin and others in the East that he had no idea the affair would become a political slap at Pierce. The episode had "enormously affected" the general's standing in Washington, Gwin replied, but he had tried to explain the matter to the president. Wool also thanked the editor of the Washington *Union* for responding in early April to the insinuation in the *New York Times* regarding the dinner. "As I am free from political aspiration, I stand in no need of political capital," Wool said. Even if he were available for public office, he certainly would not seek it "in the way ascribed to me" by the *Times*.[37]

The Dillon trial opened on May 23. The French consul read a lengthy protest, which the *Herald* labeled "a mass of inflated rubbish." The following day, defense attorney Baker called Cavallier to the witness stand, and when cross-examined the merchant seemed vague about the details of the *Challenge* affair. He said that Wool believed the "colonists" would join Walker, and had recommended that the contract for the *Challenge* be terminated. The general also had accused Dillon of "encouraging the expedition," but later admitted "that he had been hasty in the charge." Wool's action, Foote interjected softly with a smile, "was in accordance with the magnanimity of his character." When Inge objected to the veiled sarcasm, Judge Hoffman advised that such remarks were "only for buncombe." Baker then called William Walker to the stand. Did the witness know of a connection between Dillon and Boulbon? Walker said Boulbon's dealing with Dillon dated back more than a year, but he refused to give evidence that would implicate himself.[38]

On the third day of the trial, Inge called Wool to testify. The general traced his contacts with Dillon from March 12 forward and described his suspicions about the consul's ties with Boulbon. He had informed both consuls of the Neutrality Act of 1818 a few days after the March 17 meeting, and also warned Dillon that Boulbon would take charge of the colonizers. Wool denied that he had tried to force Dillon to turn informer against Valle. Finally, Inge introduced a letter from Valle to Collector Hammond, dated April 24. Valle stated that Dillon had written the French consul at Guaymas, promising to send 450 mercenaries to join Boulbon. They would help drive out the marauding Apaches, then prospect and open silver mines in Sonora. Wool had asked the Mexican consul to comment on the letter, but he received no reply. Defense attorney Foote suddenly moved that the case be given to the jury, but Inge objected and was sustained.[39]

On May 25, the defense strove to bolster Dillon's image. Baker introduced a copy of a letter the consul had sent to the French minister at Mexico City, assuring his superiors that he was working to frustrate Boulbon's designs. Dillon's secretary swore to its authenticity. He added that Boulbon was often at Dillon's office and home and had heard the consul warn the count: "I have a great deal of esteem for you, but we hold opinions differing in regard to Mexico, so much so I will do all in my power to prevent your plans." At this point, the defense rested its case. The jury deliberated, but could not reach a full agreement, and was discharged. Four days later, on May 29, Inge moved that the charges against Dillon be dismissed and that further proceedings against Valle be suspended, which amounted to a dismissal. The two consuls were free.[40]

The San Francisco press reviewed the Dillon trial with mixed feelings. The *Herald* stated that if the jury had been permitted to remain out until morning the outcome would have been different. It complimented Inge, however, on his "signal triumph" in the affair. He had "proved" all the charges against Dillon—which carried the moral force of a conviction. The *Alta California* blasted Inge's evidence as "remarkably lame." The newspaper labeled the trials as schemes by local federal officials to gain a pat on the back "by their overseers at Washington." Unfortunately, the paper added, these same men who "have sown the seed of discord through California" were being "disavowed at this moment" in the national capital.[41]

The assertion in the *Alta California* was true. In late May, Wool received a curt letter from Secretary Davis, dated April 14, questioning the general's loose interpretation of his instructions. Wool had gone too far in the filibustering matter. He had been ordered to aid civil authorities in apprehending those violating the neutrality laws. Under no circumstances was he supposed to "originate arrests and prosecutions for civil misdemeanors." Davis ended on a cordial note, assuring Wool that the War Department had full confidence in his handling of his command. Wool grumbled about Davis's letter, but he obeyed orders. He gave Inge a copy of the letter, and thereafter took no part in checking filibusters.[42]

While fretting over filibusters, Wool had not overlooked military matters. Soon after taking charge of the Pacific Department, he had signed contracts for the federal government to spend $12,000 on a new arsenal, thirty miles inland at Benecia, on the North Bay of San Francisco Harbor, and $7,000 on a barracks at the Presidio near the Golden Gate. He also had filed requisitions to operate the *Active*, a coast survey steamer, at $4,000 per month until the end of the fiscal year. He needed the vessel for duty in the harbor and along the coast to check on filibustering. These contracts caused trouble. On April 13, Secretary of War Davis, who was a stickler for detail, notified the general that he had overstepped spending limits on the army projects, and reminded him that congressional authority was needed to justify such large construction. The secretary wanted public property preserved, and knew that a new arsenal was needed, but he questioned Wool's ignoring regular channels in his decisions. Before he received Davis's letter in mid-May, Wool, without prior approval, had also cancelled a government contract for renting a dilapidated storage building ($2,000 a month), let bids, and drew on the San Francisco banking house of Lucas, Turner, and Company for $6,000 for a new facility. Davis and Wool were on a collision course.[43]

On May 30, Wool dispatched a stiff response to Davis's two letters. He considered the secretary's remarks on his role in curbing filibustering activities an unjust "censure." Upon reaching San Francisco, he had found the local authorities reluctant to act because of the popularity of Boulbon, Walker, and others; in fact, the district attorney would do nothing without written requests. In no instance, however, had he "originated" arrests or interfered with civil officials. Military and civil authorities had acted in perfect harmony. Wool expressed regret that Davis contested the bills for military construction, for the facilities were sorely needed. After mailing his letter to Davis, the general wrote to Senator Gwin, in Washington, and asked him to use his influence to obtain appropriations to cover the contracts in the San Francisco area. Gwin promised early attention to the matter.[44]

Rumors spread that Davis planned to transfer the departmental headquarters from San Francisco. On June 15, an order arrive that has been issued on May 18 at the headquarters of the army, instructing Wool to move his officers and staff to Benecia at an early date. In the same mail, Davis rebuked the general for threatening to retain Major Townsend, "no matter who may be sent to relieve him." The secretary hoped that, after Wool had acquainted himself more fully with the "circumstances" of his command, he would temper his language.[45]

On June 15, Wool explained his situation to General Scott, commanding the army from his headquarters in New York City. He stated that transferring his departmental headquarters inland would not only create complications but also increase expenses. All incoming military stores would have to come to the Benecia depot, then be reshipped for distribution. Supervising officers would be forced to shuttle constantly to and from San Francisco. Moreover, if he moved the two artillery companies stationed at the Presidio to Benecia, as Davis suggested, they would have to live in tents because of the shortage of barracks. Their removal would also leave San Francisco undefended and encourage filibustering. Wool hesitated to build barracks at Benecia for fear they would not be approved. If Davis's order was not promptly executed, Wool advised Scott, "it will be because it cannot be done without doing a great injury to the service."[46]

"I have lost the confidence of the Administration," the general informed David Stewart, his friend in Baltimore. He was convinced the transfer of his headquarters was punishment for attending the Broderick (anti-Gwin) dinner. He had no personal objections to the move, but he disliked the idea of his officers being "punished for my sins." And there were other reasons to question Davis's decision. Maj. Osborn Cross, department quartermaster, pronounced the shift ill-advised and expensive, while Maj. John G. Barnard, Corps of Engineers, pointed to the ongoing contest to protect the vacant parts of the military reservation at San Francisco from squatters. Civilians were poised to file claims "over every portion of this reserve," and nothing but a strong army presence could prevent them. The mayor and council of San Francisco had also protested the removal. On July 1, Wool announced that he had suspended the removal order.[47]

Wool aired his case in the East. He sent clippings (he called them "slips") commenting on the transfer to his wife and friends, and requested their aid in disseminating them to friendly editors. He enclosed copies of his suspension order, Barnard's statement, and a complimentary letter from Mayor Cornelius K. Garrison. Wool even laid his case before fellow Trojan, William L. Marcy, now Secretary of State. He had heard that the French minister had contacted Marcy, and demanded satisfaction in the Dillon matter. Wool expounded at length on the events of the past several months. He had little doubt that the filibusters would view his "banishment" to Benecia as a reprimand for his actions.[48]

Wool inquired about affairs in Troy. In March, Sarah had written that her New York-born black servant, thirty-year-old William Jackson wanted more pay. Wool explained that he paid William $14 a month the first year and promised to increase this by $1 a month each succeeding year up to $20. If William failed to serve five years, he must somehow return the increase given him over $14. There was no advantage in "being too kind to servants," the general said. It induced them to believe that "their services are of more importance than they really are." William had a comfortable position, with no exposure "to storms or cold nights." A previous servant, John Carson, had left for higher wages, and his "cold drives to Albany, night and day, soon carried him to his grave." If William sought other employment, his fate might be the same. Sarah should decide the matter. If she wished, she could dismiss the servant, sell the carriage horses, and hire transportation. Certainly, it would be cheaper.[49]

John Griswold, now mayor of Troy, wrote regularly. In March, he informed his uncle that he was keeping various properties rented and carefully watching his investments. He had found a tenant who would pay $300 annually for the building that Wool had previously leased to the government for departmental offices. Hurricane force winds had recently swept Troy, Griswold continued. Roofs had been peeled "as an orange at dinner, bricks & mortar fell in showers, & in the vicinity of the lumberyards the air was filled with boards which flew like snow flakes." Property destruction was immense. Wool's home had escaped damage. "Aunt Wool," John reported in mid-June, had finished the annual ordeal of house cleaning, and was now reading the newspapers with scissors in hand, clipping articles for the general. Still later, on August 3, Griswold wrote that Aunt Wool, a nervous person, had suffered another of "her attacks" upon hearing about the headquarters imbroglio. John was certain that the general could handle such "disagreeable emergencies." There was one consolation: a president and his cabinet lasted only four years.[50]

During his early months in San Francisco, Wool became intrigued by the high interest paid on loans. He investigated various investment possibilities, then drew on his paycheck and available credit for funds to enter the market. On April 1, he handed Mayor Garrison a government check for $2,000 to invest for him (sent to cover the general's transportation to California, plus subsistence, quarters, and three months' back pay). "I have now an income of sixty dollars per month besides my pay and emoluments," Wool wrote Sarah on April 17, and he predicted this would increase in succeeding months. On June 21, he was making $150 a month on a $5,000 loan. This "outside" income quickly moved to $180 per month and reached $240 by mid-September. At that time, his army base pay was $472.80 per month. At the end of October, the general was drawing 3 percent per month on $9,000 in short-term loans. Four months later, in February 1855, his outside income was $348 per month, and he estimated he would soon have $22,500 invested.[51]

But the investment market in San Francisco took a dive in February. Five of the fourteen banking firms in the city collapsed. Wool pulled back from the market and started sending his monthly paychecks to Sarah. As financial conditions worsened, the general sought other ways to send money home. His friend, William H. Aspinwall, owner of the Pacific Mail Steamship Company, personally carried $2,400 back to New York for him, saving Wool a 23 percent shipping cost. Wool counseled Sarah to invest the money in farm mortgages. In May, he forwarded a $10,000 draft for the same purpose. All told, in fifteen months the general sent $13,400 to Troy from California.[52]

Wool followed a varied routine during the summer of 1854. He remained in San Francisco handling routine departmental matters, but took time for social endeavors. He regularly attended the theater, occasionally played whist or poker in the Union Club downtown with his officers or club members, and went to the horse races. Practically every evening he was a guest at dinner with a wealthy family or visiting dignitary. Wool also took carriage rides into the countryside, going all the way to San Mateo with Mayor Garrison on one excursion. During these trips, he attached a veil of green gauze to the front of his hat to reduce the glare of the sun. The general also followed California politics closely. "Bribery is the order of the day," he wrote Sarah, "and the object of every man in office. The rage is to get money, no matter how it is obtained. The end justifies the means."[53]

In late August, the mail brought a copy of the Washington *Union* with comments on the transfer of Wool's headquarters. Davis's order had produced "somewhat of a sensation" in San Francisco, it said, and several newspapers there had scolded the secretary for his decision. However, Wool was not ordered west to relax in the city, but to be active and in the field. Nor had he been sent to California to suppress filibustering, for civil authorities there were perfectly capable of dealing with the problem. A large garrison was unnecessary in San Francisco, because engineers at that moment were completing fortifications to protect the city from hostile fleets. Davis's transfer order, the *Union* concluded, was meant to call Wool's attention to the public interest. The article was moderate in tone, but the general labeled it insidious. The next steamer, he wrote Stewart, would bear a "vindication" that would make Davis regret that he had censured "a veteran of forty-two years' standing."[54]

On September 8, Wool handed John Nugent, editor of the *San Francisco Herald*, a long statement for immediate publication. He admired Nugent's willingness to print controversial materials and defy local political pressures. "The war has begun between the Secretary of War and myself," Wool wrote Sarah. "We shall see who gains the victory. I did not begin the war, and therefore I will not surrender until I am compelled to lay down my arms, and that will not be very soon. I have the people of California with me and I intend to keep them so. I hope my friends will not be alarmed."[55]

The *Herald* printed Wool's statement anonymously. The epistle described how he had arrived in California bearing the confidence of the Pierce administration, and quickly learned that the most pressing matter was filibustering. The general had investigated the *Challenge* and warned civil authorities that the vessel was destined to carry men and arms to reinforce Walker in Sonora. The ship was detained, and this forced Walker to abandon his designs in Sonora. As for military matters, Wool had been anxious to tour the garrisons in his command, but he had been crippled for weeks from an accident he suffered on the isthmus. He then had two prolonged pleurisy attacks. Moreover, Inspector Gen. J. F. K. Mansfield had recently toured the Pacific Department, and reported that post commanders everywhere were vigilant. The Washington *Union*'s criticism of Wool's actions was not only unjust, the author concluded, but an "indirect" slap at the inhabitants of California. The general mailed a bundle of "slips" of the article on the next steamer.[56]

In early September, as directed Wool moved his headquarters to the military reservation at Benecia. The installation lay inland on the south shore of Carquinez Straits, and was commanded by Bvt. Lt. Col. George Nauman, Third Artillery. It included commissary and quartermaster depots, a hospital, warehouses, and a barracks for a small garrison. The wharves sat in deep water, and the Pacific Mail Steamship Company berthed vessels here for coaling and repairs. Benecia was a well-known site. The reservation had been departmental headquarters in 1852, and a small community of the same name, a mile and a half away, had served as the state capital until February 1854. Wool landed at the Benecia wharf on September 23, and established his quarters and offices in the American Hotel in town. Benecia was a quiet place and a far cry from the bustling delightful life in San Francisco. Here Wool would spend most of his duty time while in California.[57]

Before the end of the month, the general received a bristling letter from Davis. Wool's "style of complaint" on May 30, the secretary declared, was contentious, disrespectful, and bordered on insubordination. "I will here take occasion to remind you," Davis said, "that while you choose to hold the high commission of general in the army you assume an obligation to render due respect and cheerful obedience to the authority and orders of this department." The secretary of war "thinks I am made of iron," Wool confided to Stewart. He believed "that I am able to mount my horse and ride thousands of miles to examine my command comprising Utah, California, Oregon and Washington Territories." Peace and quiet prevailed throughout the department and that "was all he had a right to expect of me." Lashing out at Davis, the veteran commander fumed: "I will not permit him or anyone else to rob me of my fair fame. I am not a man of policy, I hate the word."[58]

In letters home Wool urged a wide distribution of the clippings he had sent. The *San Francisco Herald* articles should be published in "as many papers as possible," he told Sarah on September 26, "and certainly the New York *Herald*. . . . Do not fail to have it done, even if you have to pay for the publication. The ball must be kept rolling." In mid-October, the general grew more insistent. "You have enough in your possession," he exhorted his wife, to place Davis "in a very unpleasant position." She should try the *Albany Argus* and have the information "appear as a correspondence from Washington. . . . Have it attended to." Each article should be entitled "Fire to the Rear" or "The Old War Horse." The attack must continue. "You must not talk of prudence or discretion," Wool exclaimed. "It is too late for the one or other." Davis must be "rebuked."[59]

Wool's military aides, Lts. John C. Moore and James A. Hardie, encouraged him. The general had enjoyed the services of many young aides-de-camp over the years, but he rarely commented on their attributes. He described Moore, who was returning east and would visit Sarah, as amiable, entertaining, and a young bachelor without vices. "He plays cards but never bets," he said. "He is fond of smoking but never does it in my room or when walking with me." The other aide, James Hardie, was married and struggling to support a wife, child, nurse, and a horse. Like Moore, Hardie was "very capable, efficient, and faithful." He had also written articles for Wool for publication in the *Herald.* Weeks later Wool spoke with equal enthusiasm about their replacements, George Stoneman and John Bonnycastle.[60]

On October 13, Wool sent the secretary of war a carefully worded, conciliatory letter. In May, he had been greatly displeased at being accused of exceeding his instructions. He had tried to show that he had not departed from his original orders, and had obeyed the wishes set forth in Davis's April 14 letter. A long recital of his correspondence and actions concerning the filibusters followed. Wool assured Davis that he had intended no disrespect by his statements and had been "faithful in *all things* to the last degree."[61]

In October, French and British warships made separate visits to San Francisco. In the middle of the month, a French fleet anchored in the bay, and local businessmen invited Wool to attend a reception for the visiting officers. The general hesitated for fear he might compromise his stand regarding Dillon. California Senator John B. Weller and others advised him to exchange courtesies. On October 26, Wool treated the French admiral to a formal dinner and reception at the Oriental. The following day Wool, together with Weller, Garrison, Nugent, and other notables, toured the French flagship, *La Forte*. The French fired a sixteen-gun salute in Wool's honor, and, as prearranged, the American batteries on Alcatraz Island returned the courtesy gun for gun. "A strong effort was made to bring the French consul, and myself together," Wool wrote Sarah, "in order . . . to do or say something which would justify the consul in raising his flag." He had refused. Dillon was "a dishonest, hypocritical and dutiful Frenchman," generally detested in San Francisco. "I have said he was a Frenchman, he is an Irishman and his wife a[n] . . . Irish woman." On October 29, before Wool left San Francisco, the *HBM Pique*, boasting forty guns, entered the bay. A similar exchange of official visits took place over the next two days.[62]

The Wool-Davis controversy sputtered on. A copy of the Washington *Union*, dated November 1, 1854, arrived from the East. It poked fun at the occasional allusions to Wool's competence for high public office. The newspaper doubted that his prospects would "excite jealousy or alarm" on either side of the Rocky Mountains. Instead of "hunting up" evidence against the filibusters, the general should be devoting his energies to his command. On December 11, Wool responded, branding the *Union*'s assertions unjust and scurrilous. He had a clerk copy extracts from his official correspondence and various newspapers into a set of letters. He mailed copies of the set to William Cullen Bryant, of the New York *Evening Post*, former Secretary of War John Bell, and other friends. Jane Erwin Bell, wife of the former secretary, had prophesied that Jefferson Davis would cause him trouble, Wool told Bell, and her prophesy had come true.[63]

As a new year, 1855, dawned, Wool decided that his controversy with Davis must end. He was "contending with great odds," he admitted to Stewart on January 6, and could not win. Davis had patronage and power and "can put in motion those, who for pay, are ready to 'bend the suppliant hinges of the door to power.'" Others counseled the same thing. The *Alta California*, noting Wool's December 11 letter in local newspapers, regretted that the veteran soldier had descended "to a personal controversy with a hireling organ [*Union*] of an administration whose acts . . . will not bear the touchstone of purity and honesty." If it was true that "a soldier's honor is as delicate as a woman's virtue," then the *Union* "has done General Wool a 'great wrong.'" But the contest should end. James Gadsden, minister to Mexico, echoed these thoughts. Responding to Wool's letter of September 25, the diplomat doubted that Wool's zeal in combating filibustering had caused his rift with Davis. As an old soldier the general "should have known" the ageless jealousy of civil officials to control the military. The secretary was of the "civil school" and "looking . . . for higher honors."[64]

In mid-January, Wool received a fourteen-page letter from Davis, dated December 13. The secretary chided him for publishing parts of his October 13 letter in the newspapers before it had reached Washington. Davis denied that he had censured Wool; he merely reminded him that his instructions were to attend to military duties first. In the matter of filibustering, the general was to seek information for the civil authorities—and not assume the role of prosecutor or judge. Wool's correspondence clearly manifested an undue attention to matters "other than the proper duties" of his command. If Wool had lost the government's confidence, it was a "cause of regret, rather than complaint." Davis released a copy of his December 13 letter to newspapers in the East and South, after dispatching the original to California.[65]

On January 29, Wool sent another conciliatory letter to Davis. Their correspondence, he said, assumed a character which could be "of no benefit to the country or the Army." He was perplexed by his clash with the secretary. He had gone west with the friendliest of feelings toward Davis, and had endeavored to command his respect in all that he did. He admitted that he had advised strong measures to curb filibustering, but believed it a "special duty." He had contracted for the new arsenal to fulfill his instructions to "secure public property from waste or loss." Wool acknowledged that Indian unrest had developed in his department, but his garrisons were well located and alert to emergencies. In conclusion, Wool assured Davis that he had attended to every duty required of him. Here the verbal battle ended.[66]

On Washington's birthday, February 22, 1855, San Francisco honored Wool on the anniversary of Buena Vista. The general came down from Benecia with part of his staff and the Third Artillery band. In a long parade through the city, he rode in a carriage and waved to the crowds. Afterwards he reviewed the fourteen companies of the city fire department as bands blared and artillery roared a salute. A champagne party followed—then a dinner at the Metropolitan Theater. For two days, Wool "received" visitors at the Oriental Hotel, before returning to his "place of banishment" at Benecia.[67]

Writing to Stewart on March 6, Wool speculated about the presidential campaign in 1856. "I have not the vanity or presumption to say even to my best friends that I am the man," he stated. To attain that exalted position, it would have to be without any effort on his part. Wool felt he stood well with the people. In recent months, he had received over one hundred letters from friends in New York, New Jersey, Pennsylvania, Illinois, and Kentucky, urging him to become a presidential candidate. But politicians selected candidates, and he could not gain the nomination without the application of money. Printers must be paid and politicians bribed, and this he could not in good conscience do. "Give me the good opinion of my countrymen," the general said, "and I will surrender all claims or pretensions to civil office no matter how exalted the station."[68]

Wool had spent an eventful year as commander of the Department of the Pacific. Sent to suppress filibusters, start military construction, and quiet restless Indians, he found California's economy depressed, state politics in an uproar, and extra-legal expeditions a popular activity. He believed that local officials were sympathetic to filibustering, and had prodded civil authorities to interfere and prosecute the instigators. Wool felt Davis's criticism of his priorities were unwarranted and the removal of his headquarters to Benecia unnecessary, and had placed his case in the public press in both California and the East. As the verbal battle spilled toward the political arena, in the end Wool wisely backed away from the controversy. Other matters in the Pacific Department demanded his attention.

11

NATIVE AMERICAN ANNIHILATION

The most perplexing problems Wool encountered as commander of the Department of the Pacific were with Native Americans. Greedy whites seeking gold and silver, land, and trade opportunities had for years invaded and violated tribal homelands, creating friction and reducing access to traditional food sources. Indian bands retaliated by attacking emigrant parties and travelers and spreading fear into frontier settlements. Wool took the problems of Indian-white relations seriously and called on his undermanned and remote garrisons to provide what protection and security they could. Impatient governors aggravated the situation by confronting hostile Indians with undisciplined volunteer companies, some intending to exterminate a people they deemed savages. Wool denounced the unrestrained campaigns by citizen soldiers. Territorial officials, in turn, condemned the old war horse for "imbecile vacillation." The result was two wars—a war of words between federal and territorial authorities over Indian policy, and a war waged by volunteers and soldiers against a unfortunate foe.[1]

There was little doubt that the treatment of California's native population following the discovery of gold in 1848 was a great tragedy—an American genocide of epic proportions. Although Congress authorized reservations for the Native Americans, the jurisdiction over them was uncertain: they were not explicitly wards of the U.S. government, and Wool's interpretation of the California reservations' legal status denied the reservations full army protection.[2] "Until these reservations are . . . perfected," Wool later wrote, "the United States troops . . . have no right to . . . exclude the Whites from entering and occupying the reserves, or even prevent their taking from them Indians squaws and children."[3] Such practices were evil, he realized, and Congress needed to rectify the situation.

Before leaving Washington, Wool had expressed concern about Native American problems in the Pacific Department. He had requested "special powers" with such matters in mind. Indians could only be restrained by a "dedicated, steady and firm but just course," he wrote Secretary Davis. No Indian respected a civilian, preferring to negotiate instead with a military man, a warrior. This was especially true of the "roving, predatory bands" occupying the territories bordering California and

Oregon. Without special authority from the president, Wool predicted that he would be "embarrassed" by the Indian bands and thrown into conflict with the federal Indian agents west of the Rockies. His request was ignored.[4]

When Wool arrived in San Francisco, he wasted no time in questioning General Hitchcock (his predecessor) and his staff at length about the tribes in the Pacific Department. An estimated 134,000 Indian men, women, and children, one of the highest concentrations of American Indians west of the Mississippi, lived within or bordering the military jurisdiction, many of them in the interior valleys. In southern California, the former mission Indians lived in villages and worked in peonage on neighboring farms and ranches during the planting and harvesting seasons; in northern California, the Indians roamed in bands, tenaciously clinging to old haunts in the mountains and occasionally threatening travelers and settlers. To the east, the Yumas congregated around Fort Yuma, at the confluence of the Colorado and Gila Rivers, where they eked out a living from agriculture. Across the border, in southern Oregon, lay a hostile land. Along the rivers and in the dense forests, the Klamaths, Rogues, and Coquilles stole livestock, ambushed pack trains, and attacked prospectors and immigrant parties that ventured into their territories. Still farther north, in Washington Territory, Indians occupied an even larger domain. On the eastern shores of Puget Sound, in the Cowlitz Valley, and along the Columbia River, small groups of Indians subsisted on fish and roots. To the east, beyond the towering Cascades, roamed powerful tribes with cultural patterns similar to Plains Indians. Here the Klickitats and Yakimas fished for salmon; to the southeast and near the Columbia lived the Umatillas, Cayuses, and Walla Wallas.[5]

Beginning in 1851, the federal government had sought to place many of these Indians on reservations. In both California and Oregon, commissioners had concluded treaties to withdraw tribes from the proximity of settlements and paths of travel, but the results proved disheartening. Complaints over the loss of cheap Indian labor, and the suspicion that the reservations might include arable or mineral-rich land, caused the California legislature to petition the Senate to reject the treaties. The Oregon agreements met a similar fate. By 1853, Congress had placed the responsibility for negotiating treaties and creating reserves in the hands of Indian superintendents.[6]

At the time of Wool's arrival in San Francisco, Edward F. Beale, the California Indian superintendent, was attempting to establish five 25,000-acre military reservations in the state. Over $250,000 had been allocated to remove and subsist the Indians. Beale had focused his attention on tribes in southern California first. He laid out the Sebastian reserve near Tejon Pass, about sixty miles north of Los Angeles, and a farm farther north on the Fresno River. During the spring of 1854, he hoped to collect 2,500 Indians at Sebastian on 50,000 acres (two reserves at one site), put in irrigation ditches and plant 2,600 acres of wheat, barley, and corn. Surplus monies

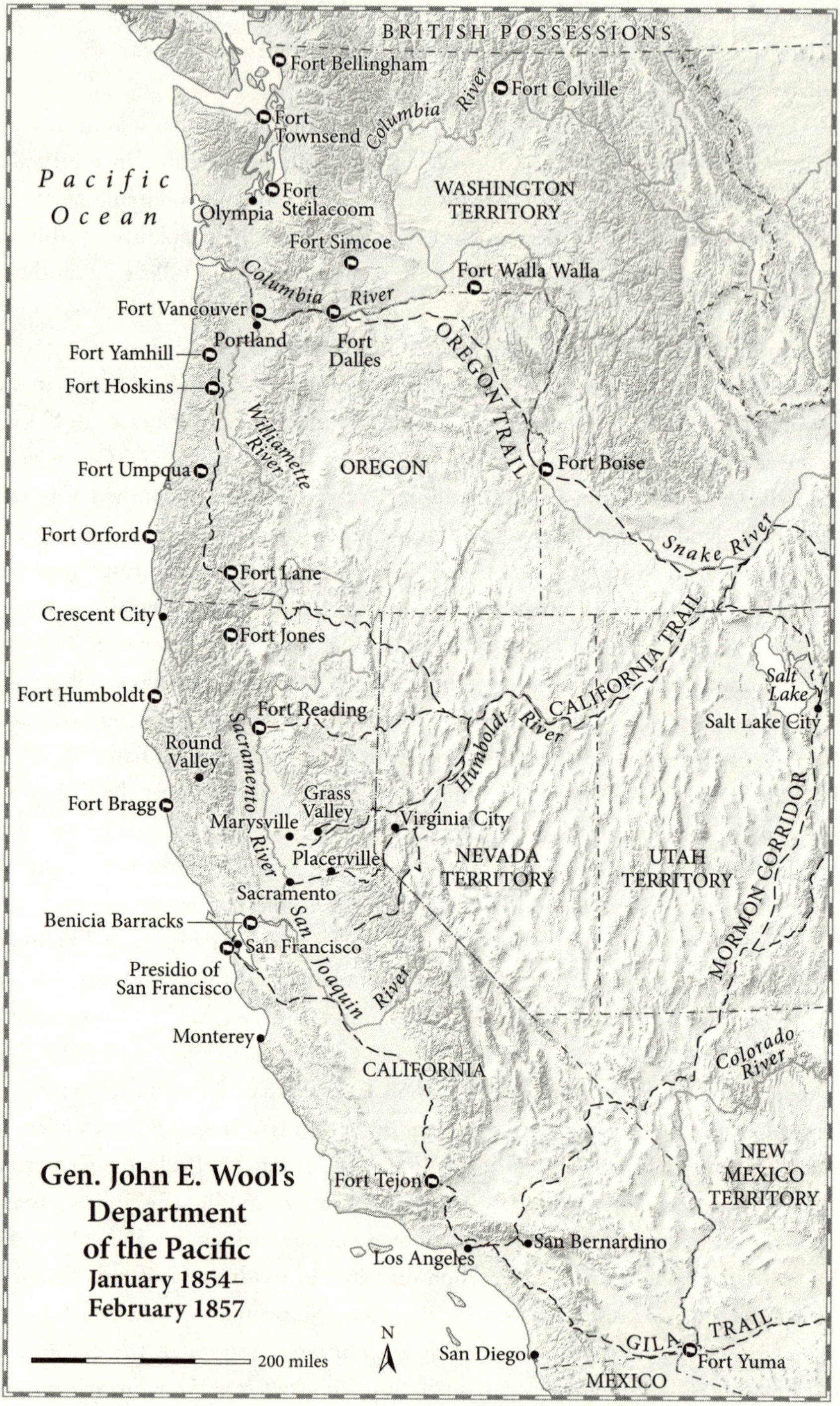

Cartography by Carol Zuber-Mallison/ZM Graphics, Inc.

from crop sales could be invested in cattle, hogs, and sheep to help make the Indians self-supporting.[7]

Wool was impressed with Beale's plans, and, in June 1854, at the superintendent's request, the general started construction of Fort Tejon, a one-company post fifteen miles southwest of the Sebastian Reservation. Inspector Gen. J. K. F. Mansfield, touring the Pacific Department that summer, complimented both Beale's work and the military site. The superintendent also planned a reserve in northern California that he tentatively referred to as the "Wool Reservation." However, Beale's tenure was cut short because of his excessive expenditures, ignoring channels of authority, and bookkeeping irregularities. In late July, Thomas J. Henley, a former California legislator and incumbent postmaster at San Francisco, succeeded Beale as California Indian superintendent.[8]

Henley seemed interested in expanding Beale's work. He visited the Sebastian and Fresno Reservations and announced plans to establish a reserve in northern California. He also proposed that the garrison at Fort Tejon rely on the neighboring Indian farm for food and forage. Wool was eager to cooperate and freely made suggestions regarding Indian affairs. In July, when he ordered the first barracks built at a sunbaked Camp Yuma, to the southeast on the Colorado River, he called Henley's attention to the Indians there. The Yumas had no reservation and were destitute. The general offered to ship Indian goods on the vessels leased by the government to transport army supplies to the mouth of the Colorado. However, Henley had to hire a private contractor to move the goods upriver to the Yumas.[9]

In early fall, Wool saw firsthand the condition of Native Americans in northern California when Henley invited him to a council near the Grass Valley community in the upper Sacramento Valley. The superintendent wanted to persuade the Indians in that vicinity to move to a reservation. On September 28, Wool and Henley boarded a steamboat in San Francisco for passage up the Sacramento River. Senator John B. Weller and his wife were also passengers. At the state capitol at Sacramento, they were entertained by the governor and shown the city. Continuing on to the head of navigation on the river, they disembarked and boarded stagecoaches for Grass Valley. At nine o'clock in the evening of September 31, Wool's stage, while on a frightful downgrade within sight of its destination, snapped its tongue and careened off the road. One frightened passenger jumped out of the stage and was seriously injured. "I was sent head over heels out of the carriage," Wool wrote Sarah, "and but for the stump which caught the carriage and held it up I would have been crushed." All the passengers were badly bruised, and the driver, who was thrown twenty feet, lay speechless with a broken collarbone. Crawling out of the wrecked stage, Wool exclaimed, "Where's my hat?" to which Senator Weller replied, "Damn your hat; look to the ladies!" A physician and a carriage were sent for to see to the battered travelers and take them into town. The general's lost hat became a running joke for the rest of the trip.[10]

At Grass Valley, Wool's party rode out to the neighboring mines, examined the placer workings, and purchased gold specimens. In town, Senator Weller and Wool spoke to a small crowd of citizens, and the general visited Lola Montez, an internationally known theatrical personality, who had taken up residence in the town. "She has faded since I first saw her," Wool wrote home. "She is thin and much emaciated. I found her exceedingly intelligent and accomplished." The travelers climbed back into a stage and traveled west to Marysville, then north through tall pines and beneath snowcapped mountains to an adobe Fort Reading located on a small creek near the Sacramento River, where they received a thirteen-gun salute upon arrival. Here Wool and his party, "four hundred miles away from civilization," were treated to a sumptuous dinner of roast pig, mutton, duck and quail, with puddings, pies, oranges, and grapes for dessert.[11]

Wool had written the commander at Fort Reading, Bvt. Lt. Col. George Wright, Fourth Infantry, asking for information on the tribes in his district. He particularly wanted Wright's views on shifting troops from Fort Jones, in the Scotts River Valley near the California-Oregon border, south to a new post in the Pitt River country. Indians and whites were constantly skirmishing near Fort Jones, and there was no Indian agent in the area. In September, north of Fort Reading, Wright had met with the chiefs and headmen of the Lower Pitt and McCloud Rivers and promised them food. Wool briefly visited the Indian families who had responded and pitched their camp near the fort.[12]

During the first week of October, the general returned to Grass Valley where he attended an Indian council held in a bull-and-bear fighting arena at Storms Ranch. Many prominent Californians were on hand, including William Gwin, James W. Denver, and Sam Brannan, a Mormon journalist who had first publicized the discovery of gold at Sutter's Mill in 1848. The visitors took seats in the stands, while twenty-five headmen, representing tribes living within a fifty-mile radius, sat on boards in the middle of the ring. With Storms interpreting, Superintendent Henley extolled the virtues of moving to the proposed Nome Lackee Reservation, to be located south of Reading in Tehama County. The federal government, Henley said, would put in crops and provide clothing until the Indians were self-sufficient. The chiefs were skeptical. Federal commissioners had made promises before, one said, but the Indians had received nothing. What about the Chinese? Why could they not be placed on reservations? The Indians had no confidence in the white man's promises. One chief asked Wool if the military would protect them. The general hesitated, then stated that if the Indians observed strict propriety in their relations with whites, he would indeed watch over them. But if they erred, he would have to chastise them. The Indians agreed to send a delegation to examine the reservation site.[13]

The council became a frolic. Senators Gwin and Weller gave spirited orations. The Indians performed a number of "exhilarating dances" with a large number of "squaws" involved, "greatly to the delight of the ladies and gentlemen present." Wool joined the merrymakers, personally directing "a war dance and a funny dance." The crowd roared when the veteran officer started jumping around, trying to imitate the natives. When one dance group appeared naked, he quickly waved them away from the arena. After the festivities ended, the visitors left for Sacramento. By October 10, Wool was back at Benecia.[14]

Wool instructed his commanders to help Henley set up new reservations. They would assist the superintendent in moving Indians and protecting them from lawless whites entering their homelands. Officers were also to maintain "a harmonious cooperation" with the Indian agents, and urge the Indians "to be guided by the views of the Agents." Recalling the discord he had faced in the Cherokee country, Wool offered wise counsel. As winter closed in, the Indians in northern California flocked to the posts for food. Wright ordered his quartermaster to feed them but advised Henley that he soon must assume the burden for their needs. The superintendent promptly replied that he had no authority to ration non-reservation bands.[15]

In early February 1855, Bvt. Lt. Col. Robert C. Buchanan, commanding at Fort Humboldt, on the northern California coast, reported an outbreak of violence to the northeast on the Klamath River. Whites living in two areas—in the vicinity of Orleans Bar and near the junction of the Klamath and Salmon Rivers, some fifty miles from Humboldt—claimed that neighboring bands were planning raids in the spring. They had attempted to make the Indians surrender their arms. When one party of whites feigned friendship, then fired into an Indian group and seized and raped several Indian women, frightened bands retaliated. Buchanan dispatched Capt. Henry P. Judah and a detachment from Fort Jones to the Klamath, and promised to send an additional fifty men as soon as possible. The presence of soldiers brought an uneasy peace in the district. Wool apprised General Scott of the outbreak: "The contest is between a party of whites—few in number—who would wantonly 'exterminate' [the Indians] after disarming them and the more right minded [citizens] who would protect them. . . . It is hard that the troops should be called upon to mediate between these contending parties, while they have also to restrain the Indians and try to protect them from destruction. Yet such is mainly their duty in California."[16]

Wool made a conscientious effort to prevent Indian unrest. He grew disenchanted with Henley, when the superintendent complained that he had no authority to employ special agents or to feed non-reservation Indians. For the time being, the general ordered his commanders to continue distributing army rations to destitute bands. When an Indian killed a white man in a fight and rushed to Fort Jones for protection, Wool told Judah to turn him over to county authorities and suggest a change of venue. There was no "Indian Territory proper" in California, he advised, and federal courts had "no jurisdiction over cases of murder committed upon Indians any more than upon whites." Perhaps the Indian could receive a fair trial in a state court in another county. The Indian population in California faced a cruel fate, "so long as the state of morals and opinions so utterly arrests the course of civil law in regard to them."[17]

During the spring, Wool's relations with Henley cooled still further. The superintendent wrote Indian Commissioner George Manypenny, in Washington, complaining about the lack of military cooperation. The general, he said, had refused to order soldiers to chase down two "Spaniards" who were indicted in Solano County for kidnapping and selling Indian children. In May, Henley became even more outspoken. He branded "a large proportion" of the army officers in California as uncooperative, and singled out Bvt. Lt. Col. Benjamin Beall, First Dragoons, commanding at Fort Tejon. Beall consistently found excuses to deny police assistance on the neighboring Sebastian Reservation.[18]

By late summer of 1855, Wool felt that Henley had become irresponsible. He had warned the bureaucrat that the Sebastian Reservation was on the "brink of failure." Then, on August 8, the general took matters into his own hands and sent Colonel Beall to investigate conditions there. A short, fat officer dubbed "Old Brilliant" because of a red nose and his addiction to liquor, Beall had served with Wool in the Mexican War and followed orders to the letter. On entering the reservation, the officer interviewed an Indian who had been an interpreter for Superintendent Beale. The man was bitter. Initially, the regular issue of clothing and food, and planned feasts and celebrations, had attracted large numbers of Indians to settle on the reserve. Now they were "like a flock of sheep without a herder." At the agency headquarters, Beall talked with Alonzo Ridley, the subagent, who was reluctant to provide information. In reporting to Wool, Beall said the number of Indians had dropped from 1,000 to less than 200.[19]

Henley protested Beall's visit. He wrote Wool a sharp letter, denouncing his "inquisitional policy." His emissary had obtained information from unauthorized persons and had made only a cursory examination of the buildings and grounds. The report was both unfair and unreliable. In the fall Major Townsend, on an inspection of military posts, also visited the Sebastian Reservation and confirmed Beall's conclusions.[20]

In October 1855, Wool's attention suddenly shifted from jousting with Henley in California to an Indian war in the Pacific Northwest. The Donation Act of 1850 had offered homesteads to settlers in Oregon and Washington Territories. To avoid friction with Indian tribes, the government sent commissioners into the wilderness to hold councils and extract treaties to move the scattered bands to reserves. While the Senate debated these agreements, the cry of gold discoveries echoed along the valleys of southwestern Oregon. A rush from California to the new diggings began. Prospecting parties suffered depredations and ambush, and they indiscriminately and without cause killed Indians. The result was war.[21]

Earlier, in the spring of 1854, while focusing on filibusters, Wool had received reports of sputtering hostilities in southern Oregon. A large group of Rogue River Indians had settled on the Table Rock Reservation at Fort Lane, near Jacksonville, but numerous bands still roamed the forests, often near settlements, and became the victims of white vengeance. In May, Joel P. Palmer, the Oregon Superintendent, reported to Wool that whites had massacred an Indian party near the mouth of the Coquille River, to the north of the Rogue, and were interfering with his efforts to move Rogues to a reserve. Local civil authorities were too weak to make arrests. Wool had shipped a detachment from San Francisco to Port Orford, to assist Palmer. However, it was obvious the military in that quarter were spread too thin. In July, Oregon governor John W. Davis made an unusual request. He wanted dragoons to escort the annual emigrant trains that passed through the Klamath-Goose Lake section of the overland route that ran from South Pass, in Wyoming, into southern Oregon and northern California. The general was unable to comply, and Davis placed an Oregon volunteer company in the field to patrol the route.[22]

Indian difficulties also erupted in another part of Wool's command. On September 1, 1854, Maj. Gabriel J. Rains, Fourth Infantry, commanding at Fort Dalles, on the Columbia River, reported an Indian attack near the Hudson's Bay Company fur post at Fort Boise, three hundred miles to the east. A mounted band of Bannock-Shoshones had swarmed over the Ward wagon train traveling the emigrant road along the Snake River. They massacred seventeen of the twenty-one members, and took the women and children captive. Rains had immediately notified his superior, Lt. Col. Benjamin L. E. Bonneville, at Fort Vancouver, sixty miles down the Columbia, of the attack. On the morning of August 30, Rains, at the request of Robert R. Thompson, Indian agent on the Umatilla, dispatched Bvt. Maj. Granville O. Haller with a surgeon, twenty-six mounted infantry, and a pack train to the massacre site. Haller had instructions to rescue the captives and punish the murderers. Three days later Thompson, Nathan Olney, Indian agent at The Dalles, and thirty-nine civilians, along with a few friendly Cayuse and Nez Perce Indians, followed the soldiers. Rains had armed the entire group. Bonneville sent an artillery company by river steamer to Fort Dalles. He promptly alerted Wool of the massacre and his measures to respond.[23]

In the meantime, at Agent Olney's urging, George L. Curry, acting overnor of Oregon since Davis's resignation in August, called out two volunteer companies at

Portland. When he applied to Bonneville for arms, the colonel replied that he had no authority to supply volunteers. He regarded Haller's force sufficient for the scout. Furthermore, the major asserted, emigration for the season was over. Cooler heads in Salem, the capital, prevailed, and Curry revoked his call.[24]

Wool complimented Bonneville and Rains on their handling of the Ward matter. Bonneville was correct in refusing to arm Oregon volunteers or muster them into federal service. There was no emergency. Upon Haller's return from the Fort Boise area, Wool wanted Rains to launch a spring 1855 scout east to the Walla Walla River. Wool thought a fort was needed in that district. He also cautioned Rains against furnishing arms and equipment to volunteers.[25]

Haller's punitive expedition accomplished little. He reached Fort Boise on October 11, buried the dead, and scouted for over two weeks. His search for the culprits and their captives proved fruitless. Olney and Thompson's civilian parties seized small groups of Indians at different places, shot five "attempting to escape," and brought several women and children back to Fort Dalles as prisoners. The two agents published their exploits in the Oregon newspapers. They were critical of Haller's operations, saying he had pushed his column too hard, worn down his horses, and found it impossible to chase the Indians.[26]

In November, Rains reported new difficulties in northeastern Oregon. Winnestas (Shoshonean) Indians reportedly had raided east into Cayuse country, driving off horses and complicating Indian relations. Furthermore, Haller had left a considerable amount of ammunition at Fort Boise, and Charles Ogden, the Hudson's Bay Company agent there, asked Rains for soldiers to protect the post, but the major had no remounts and was of little assistance. Talk about raising Oregon volunteers surfaced again. In Salem, it was announced that $75,000 in treasury drafts had arrived in the capital to compensate those who supplied the volunteers in the Cayuse War in 1851. Bills for the Rogue River War and for federal roads in Oregon were also pending in Congress. Times were hard in the Oregon country. "The people appear like Mr. Micawber," the *San Francisco Herald* observed, "constantly waiting for something to turn up."[27]

In late January 1855, Wool described the Indian problem in his department in a letter to Secretary Davis. There were two types of disturbances. The first type involved peaceful Indians acting in self-defense—or retaliating against whites who had committed outrages "upon them and their families." The second involved hostile bands striking without provocation and possibly in concert. Wool blamed most of the difficulties on "the lawlessness and brutality of a certain class of white frontiersmen, and the feeble restraint which the civil authority imposes upon them." The general felt that his garrisons were generally well located and ably commanded, but they were badly understrength. New posts were needed on the remote eastern borders of Oregon and Washington to protect emigrant routes. If forts could not be constructed, the general needed a regiment of mounted troops. "With a regiment, or even less, of well mounted Dragoons left to my discretion," Wool told Davis, "I could do much towards giving protection to emigrants, and to prevent disasters similar to the one which occurred near Fort Boise. I have now three half companies of Dragoons with broken down horses."[28]

By spring, additional troops began arriving in the Pacific Department. Bvt. Lt. Col. Edward P. Steptoe, Third Artillery, who had wintered at Salt Lake City with two artillery companies, a group of dragoon recruits, and a complement of fresh horses, arrived in California. Wool sent one company each of artillery to Forts Tejon and Yuma, and split the dragoon recruits and horses between Forts Tejon and Reading. In early May, Bvt. Capt. Christopher C. Augur and 150 recruits for the Fourth Infantry reached San Francisco by boat from the East, and immediately received orders for Forts Vancouver and Dalles. Recruiters in San Francisco actively sought men for the dragoon units.[29]

On May 18, General Wool and several staff officers sailed from San Francisco on the Pacific Mail steamer *Republic* to inspect the garrisons in Oregon and Washington Territories. Along the California coast, the vessel encountered gale winds and heavy seas. When a small fire broke out in the hold, the captain put into the harbor at Crescent City, and lay at anchor for twelve hours before the weather calmed. This drab little coastal town was the supply center for local mining districts and for the garrison at Fort Lane, Oregon, about one hundred miles inland by pack trail. As he resumed his voyage, Wool marveled at the massive forests of fir and pine along the coast. "The shores of the Pacific are without inhabitants," he wrote Sarah, "and most of the way with a dense forest of evergreen, with an extremely dangerous coast, with no safe harbours." The steamer passed the mouth of Rogue River and anchored at Port Orford. Wool went ashore, briefly inspected Lieutenant Kautz's tiny garrison, and then resumed his stormy voyage north. The vessel finally turned into the broad Columbia, and on May 24, anchored at the village of Vancouver, on the north bank of the river.[30]

At Fort Vancouver, Wool was greeted with great fanfare. Cannon boomed a thirteen-gun salute and an army band blared martial airs. The general and his staff, resplendent in dress uniforms, went ashore to meet Colonel Bonneville, who had drawn up his small garrison in ranks near the landing. A crowd of employees from the adjoining Hudson's Bay Company post was also on hand to greet the general. Vancouver was originally headquarters for the Columbia Division of the company, which controlled the fur trade in the Oregon country, and even after the Oregon Treaty in 1846, the company still occupied its old stockade and warehouses on the riverbank. In 1849, the United States Army built Fort Vancouver on high ground to the rear.[31]

Wool stayed at Fort Vancouver two days. He reminisced with Bonneville, who briefly served under him in Mexico, and Rains, who was with him in Florida and who was replacing Bonneville. As the *Republic* left to discharge cargo at Portland, six miles south, near the mouth of the Willamette River, Wool boarded the steamboat *Fashion* and discussed with his senior officers the Indian situation in Puget Sound and in the Boise country. The settlements on the sound feared an attack and had asked for protection. The general directed Capt. George Stoneman, a military aide, and Lt. William H. C. Whiting, a topographical engineer, to reconnoiter that district and prepare a plan to protect the settlers there. The most pressing matter was the Indian unrest to the east in the Boise country. Wool instructed Rains to send Haller in mid-June to the area again, and patrol the emigrant trail into Oregon for three months.[32]

On May 26, Wool boarded the *Fashion* for Portland. As the vessel docked on the west bank of the Willamette River, the band he had brought along began to play, attracting a crowd of several hundred Oregonians. Territorial delegate Joseph Lane, a veteran of Buena Vista, welcomed the general. Lane had been appointed the first territorial governor by President Polk and was seeking reelection as territorial delegate. Wool stepped down, ramrod straight, and marched with Lane and local dignitaries behind the band to the Metropolis Hotel. The distinguished general, an officer recalled, was "a small, neat man with violet colored eyes. These I noticed above all the glitter of his uniform and that of his staff. They were very sharp, like a bald eagle's." After dining, Wool spent the night on a second steamer, the *Republic*. Next morning he came ashore briefly to pose for a photographer, then, bidding a cheering crowd adieu, steamed on the *Republic* for Benecia.[33]

In late August, Wool began receiving important reports from Haller. The major had reached Fort Boise on July 15 with one hundred mounted infantry, two small howitzers, and a large amount of supplies. Agent Olney, traveling with the soldiers, called neighboring tribes to a meeting and some two hundred Indians showed up. After repeated inquiries about the Ward massacre, headmen pointed out four warriors, said to have been involved, and the soldiers seized them. Haller hastily tried the four, found three guilty, and hanged them at sundown on July 18. The fourth Indian was shot trying to escape. Haller began regular patrolling along the emigrant road for sixty miles south and east of Fort Boise.[34]

There was continued trouble near the Oregon coast. Superintendent Palmer had cleared many Indian claims, and several bands had gone to the Table Rock Reservation near Fort Lane in southern Oregon. But hostile groups continued to prowl the interior valleys. In the late summer of 1855, a band living on Applegate Creek, a tributary of the Rogue, crossed into California. Near Fort Jones, they retrieved a captive Indian woman, and murdered the white man holding her. Learning a party of angry "volunteers" was at their heels, they hurried north and rushed onto the reservation at Fort Lane. Capt. Andrew J. Smith, the commander, confronted the pursuers, warned them against trespassing, and they departed. Trouble also erupted on the coast. While Palmer was holding a council near Fort Orford, an Indian shot a white man, and the superintendent took the assailant to the post for protection. Kautz dispatched a corporal's guard in a canoe up the Rogue to deliver the prisoner to civil authorities at Jacksonville, but a party followed along the shore and in an exchange of gunfire, killed the Indian.[35]

On October 8, 1855, all semblance of peace in the Rogue River district vanished when John A. Lupton and a party of volunteers encountered twenty-five Indians, mostly women and children, making their way to the Table Rock Reservation. According to one report, Lupton spotted a woman he had kept as a mistress and called on her to tell the Indians to surrender. When they did so, Lupton's men butchered them. Captain Smith rushed to the scene to find twenty-five bodies, including eighteen women and children. When Indians at Table Rock heard of the massacre, they fled into the forests. Soon thereafter, a war party ambushed Lupton's men, wounding at least a dozen. It was said the commander was killed by his mistress. The Rogue River Valley was aflame. News of the hostilities reached Wool at Benecia at a critical juncture. In eastern Washington, the powerful Yakimas had also gone on the warpath. An Indian war on two fronts loomed.[36]

In Washington Territory, as in Oregon, the rush to profit from new gold discoveries, and the desire to settle on Indian land, had created unrest and warfare. Indian officials, hoping to avoid friction, had worked feverishly to extinguish Indian claims and concentrate tribes on reservations. Palmer had been eminently successful in negotiating treaties in Oregon, but in Washington Territory, Governor Isaac I. Stevens, who also held the office of Indian superintendent, encountered resistance. Much of the resistance was created by Stevens's inordinate haste to conclude agreements. The outburst of violence along the Rogue River in the fall of 1855 was caused by headstrong citizens taking the law into their own hands. North of the Columbia, in northern Washington, the fruits of an ill-defined treaty, and the licentious conduct of hungry prospectors, precipitated an Indian uprising of even larger proportions.[37]

Governor Stevens was the principal architect for Indian reservations in Washington. In June 1853, the thirty-five-year-old Stevens had left St. Paul, Minnesota, bearing many responsibilities on his small frame (he was just over five feet tall). He would not only be governor and Indian superintendent in the new territory, he would supervise a railroad survey from Lake Superior to Puget Sound, open a wagon road from the Walla Walla country to Fort Steilacoom on the sound, and evaluate the property claims of the Hudson's Bay Company in Washington and Oregon. He would eventually fall at the battle of Chantilly in the Civil War.[38]

In January 1855, Stevens began rapidly extinguishing Indian titles on and near Puget Sound and within five weeks, he concluded four treaties. His agents reportedly herded together Indians speaking different languages, making it difficult for interpreters to explain hurriedly prepared agreements. They encouraged subchiefs to represent the tribes, and in some instances, the agents allegedly signed for those who were reluctant. Dissatisfaction quickly developed.[39]

Stevens next turned his attention to the tribes in eastern Washington and promptly asked Wool for a military escort. The general politely advised that he had no mounted force available, but if instructed by superiors, he would do all in his power to comply. He had asked the War Department for an additional regiment and permission to erect a post in the Boise country—but no word had been received from Secretary Davis. Stevens then asked about Steptoe's command. Wool patiently explained the disposition of the fresh recruits, and the need to juggle companies to meet Indian problems. He restated his reluctance to release mounted troops for special duties.[40]

On May 21, Stevens reached Mill Creek (near the old Whitman mission) in the Walla Walla Valley. Oregon Superintendent Palmer arrived with a detachment of mounted regulars wrangled from Rains at Fort Dalles. Stevens now wrote Wool, describing his treaty plans and the need to build a post in the Walla Walla Valley. On May 29, the governor opened the council, surrounded by a tent city containing an estimated 1,800 Indians. After a week of discussions, he suggested the creation of three reservations. The Walla Wallas, Cayuses, and Umatillas should locate in Oregon south of the Columbia on a reserve watered by the Umatilla River; the Yakimas and Klickitats east of the Cascades and north of the Columbia River; and the Nez Perces farther east on a 5,000-square-mile tract that roughly coincided with their traditional homeland. The tribes had two years to settle on their reserves. On June 11, just as the council was ending, a report came that gold had been discovered near Fort Colville, in the extreme northeastern part of Washington Territory. Stevens apparently felt no need for action. He had received approval of his request to meet the Blackfeet, still farther east, near Fort Benton, and left the Walla Walla campground for the new council. Palmer and the soldiers returned to The Dalles.[41]

The Colville gold strike drew prospectors in droves. Men in San Francisco crowded aboard mail steamers and any ship they could find bound for Portland, where they purchased supplies and headed inland. In the Willamette Valley and on Puget Sound, others joined the stampede. Steamship owners, farmers, and merchants puffed the discoveries. In the following weeks, Stevens and Palmer announced in the newspapers that they had cleared Indian lands east of the Cascades for settlers. In late September, the Yakimas, angered by miners stealing horses and molesting their women, went on the warpath. Andrew J. Bolon, agent for the tribes east of the

Cascades, en route north from The Dalles to investigate the massacre of a civilian party, fell in with a group of young Yakimas. Waiting for an opportune moment, they killed him.[42]

Major Rains sent Haller into the Yakima country to search for the murderers. Haller had just returned from his summer patrol in the Walla Walla Country, but he quickly put together a column and was soon on the march. Rains also ordered Lt. William A. Slaughter, at Fort Steilacoom, near the sound, to hurry east with a detachment through Naches Pass to join Haller. Rains apprised Wool of the situation and assured him there was no need for alarm. On October 3, Haller forded the Columbia into the Yakima domain with 104 men, all recruits, with fifty riding on mules, and a pack train carrying a mountain howitzer and supplies. About sixty miles out, in the Simcoe Valley, he ran into an Indian ambush, and retreated to a hill, where he was forced to camp for thirty hours without water. The major then buried his dead—three enlisted men—cached his howitzer, and, traveling by night, finally straggled into Fort Dalles on October 10. Slaughter, learning of Haller's "defeat," had turned back.[43]

Wool heard of Haller's retreat on November 1 and began shifting units. He ordered an infantry company at Fort Reading to Fort Lane, in southern Oregon, so a dragoon detachment there could go to The Dalles. Erasmus D. Keyes's company, stationed at the Presidio at San Francisco, packed its gear for field duty and prepared to march. The general instructed Colonel Buchanan, at Fort Humboldt, to prepare a plan for establishing a camp along the Rogue. Quartermaster officers readied ammunition, stores, thirty days' rations for one thousand men, and several hundred horses and mules for shipment north. In letters to Senators Lane and Weller, in Washington, Wool again pleaded for an additional regiment.[44]

At high noon on November 6, Wool and his military suite sailed from the Vallejo Street wharf in San Francisco on the *California*, a large coal-burning steamer. The heavily laden ship passed through the Golden Gate, and turned north for Oregon only to run into a storm. At Fort Humboldt, Wool planned to take aboard a company, but could not because of the heavy seas. On November 9, at Crescent City, he received reports of a recent Indian fight with regulars at Grave Creek, north of the Rogue. After the Lupton massacre, hostile bands had boldly attacked travelers, prospectors, and settlers. At Fort Lane, Captain Smith, with some ninety dragoons and a volunteer unit, had taken the field to scout. Forty-five miles north of the fort, Smith spotted a large body of Indians on the hills near Grave Creek and attacked, only to be repulsed. Smith withdrew, threw up defensive works, and retreated to Fort Lane. He lost four killed and seven wounded, and among the volunteers, seven killed and twenty wounded. The Grave Creek fight convinced Wool that he had to mount a full-scale campaign to end the Rogue River troubles.[45]

On November 12, in pounding hail and rain, the *California* reached the mouth of the broad Columbia. Capt. C. C. Dall throttled back the engines and waited for several hours for a favorable tide before entering the south channel. While the vessel was in the breakers, one of its flues suddenly burst and the furnace blew up, shooting flames into the sky and steam and burning coals across the ship. Soldiers raced about, pulling burned men to safety and fighting the fire. Although the ship was enveloped in smoke, Dall coolly held the side-wheeler steady until a wave broke over the port quarter and threw the vessel across the bar and into the main channel. The vessel limped upstream with the fire still raging, and dropped anchor for repair. Landfall was three miles away.[46]

During the excitement, an aide wakened Wool and quietly advised that if he wished "to save any little things which he could put in his writing case, he had better pack them and be ready to go in a small boat as the ship was on fire." The general got up, hurriedly dressed, and, taking his sword and writing case, went on deck. The ship was at anchor, but he ordered it lightened by throwing several barrels of gunpowder overboard. Drawn by a strong ebb tide, the ship suddenly snapped her chain and careened toward the bar. The captain quickly threw out another anchor, and stoked the engines with a hogshead of bacon to build steam pressure. The *California* held her own until the flood tide brought relief. That evening at dinner, Wool soothed jangled nerves by passing around a bottle of champagne, and toasted the captain, his gallant crew, and the officers and men who helped save the ship. Afterward, when officers accused the old general of being the "Jonah" on the ship, he replied: "No, Sir, it was I [who] saved you. Don't you know you carry Caesar and his fortunes!"[47]

At noon on November 16, Wool went ashore at Fort Vancouver in a driving rain. The afternoon was spent unloading mules and military supplies. As he quickly learned, the Indian situation had grown worse. News of Haller's defeat caused Rains to call on acting governor Charles Mason of Washington Territory for two companies of mounted volunteers to support his regulars. Mason promptly furnished the men, and they were mustered into federal service. The call for volunteers alarmed the Indians along Puget Sound. Lieutenant Slaughter, reconnoitering with regulars and volunteers, collided with a large band of hostiles on the White River north of Puyallup Creek. As a problem loomed on the sound, Wool studied the survey and proposals that Stoneman and Whiting had made for defending the settlements there. He designated the area a subdistrict and placed Captain Keyes in charge. As the rainy season prevented an overland march, Keyes's company, after several false starts, sailed on the *California* with stores, a howitzer, rifles, and ammunition for Fort Steilacoom. Wool gave Keyes blank forms for enrolling volunteers, but cautioned that he had no authority to muster them. If an emergency arose, there would be a record when Congress reviewed claims.[48]

Wool inquired about Rains's recent foray into the Yakima country. In early October, following the Haller debacle, Rains had called on both Washington and Oregon for four mounted companies each. Governor Mason complied, but Oregon governor George L. Curry raised an entire regiment and readied the Oregonians to cross the Columbia and campaign independently in eastern Washington. Thus, during October two separate armies—regulars and volunteers—had taken the field against the Yakimas.[49]

On October 31, Major Rains left Fort Dalles with 350 regulars and a long pack train carrying howitzers, ammunition, and supplies. Lt. Philip H. Sheridan (of Civil War fame) and a dragoon detachment led the advance along the north bank of the Columbia. Col. James W. Nesmith trailed behind with six Oregon companies. At Union Gap, about seventy miles out, Rains struck an Indian camp and destroyed caches of dried salmon, huckleberries, and camas roots. As the column moved on, Yakimas frequently appeared, beating drums and yelling obscenities. After a sharp skirmish at Twin Buttes, and reports that the Yakimas were fleeing north beyond the mountains, Rains turned south and camped at the deserted Jesuit mission of St. Joseph, on Ahtanum Creek. By design or chance, the volunteers burned the mission to the ground. With heavy snow falling, Rains tramped back to Fort Dalles. The major had marched nearly three hundred miles in a show of force and destroyed a large quantity of Indian food. Wool, however, boldly pronounced the expedition a senseless operation.[50]

Rains advised the general that the danger spot was the Walla Walla country in northeastern Oregon. Hostile bands had plundered the old fur post at Fort Walla Walla and the cattle ranches in the vicinity. A majority of the settlers had fled to Fort Dalles. Rains learned that Governor Curry had sent Maj. Mark A. Chinn and four mounted Oregon companies to the Walla Walla Valley. Rains had no doubt the Oregonians would precipitate a general Indian war in that region. With Rains's report, Wool dispatched Major Townsend, his trusted aide, upriver by boat to inspect the troops at Fort Dalles and assess the possibility for a winter campaign.[51]

On November 28, Townsend reported on his trip. The garrison at Fort Dalles—two companies of artillery, one of infantry, and a dragoon detachment—wore threadbare uniforms and lacked shoes. Rains had lost over fifty mules on his expedition, and the remainder were lame. Winter operations were impossible. Townsend thought the Yakimas and Walla Wallas, although well mounted, would not venture out in freezing weather. Moreover, there were no settlers to rescue. The major offered suggestions for spring operations, nevertheless. The troops at Fort Dalles should establish two posts in the Indian country: one in the Simcoe Valley, near Haller's battleground, to control access to Yakima winter and summer grazing lands and fisheries; and a second post near Blue Mountain, in northeastern Oregon, to protect the emigrant trail. With rain and snow blanketing the Pacific Northwest, Wool dropped the idea of a winter campaign.[52]

The general remained at Fort Vancouver for several weeks. Klickitat chiefs came to the post to describe the unrest among the tribes in northeastern Oregon. It rained for days on end. Major Rains gave parties to break the monotony, and staff officers occasionally went duck hunting. Wool fell ill. Townsend later wrote Sarah Wool that her husband suffered from a complaint "contracted in Mexico"—perhaps dysentery—and that he had to take morphine to obtain rest. Then, in late December, Vancouver was icebound for three weeks, with no steamer traffic to California.[53]

The day after Keyes arrived at Fort Steilacoom, a party of Indians surrounded Lieutenant Slaughter's blockhouse on the Puyallup, twenty miles distant, and ran off thirty-two animals. Keyes and a detachment gave chase, but the natives vanished into the dense forests. On December 5, on the prairie between the confluence of the Green and White Rivers, Indians crept up to Slaughter's camp at night and shot and killed him and two of his men as they stood near a fire. Keyes withdrew the picket there to Steilacoom where he sent mounted regulars, accompanied by volunteers drawn from four Washington companies, to scout the upper Nisqually and Des Chutes Rivers. They found no hostile bands, but destroyed a large cache of wheat, flour, salmon, berries, and potatoes. With snow covering the countryside, regulars and volunteers sought quarters in blockhouses.[54]

Wool wrote numerous letters while ice-bound at Fort Vancouver. He approved a proposal by Capt. Thomas J. Cram, his chief topographical engineer, to build or improve four public roads in Washington Territory, several near The Dalles, at an estimated cost of $95,000. These highways would provide ready access to the valleys and fisheries in eastern Washington. Wool wrote General Scott pleading for another infantry regiment. Indian troubles had flared at various points in the Pacific Department, and he had great difficulty shifting troops, dispersed in small commands over 1,600 miles of territory, to meet emergencies. Secretary Davis had refused to grant him the authority to raise volunteers, but Wool now believed the need was imperative. He hoped that Scott's endorsement might carry weight in Washington. Wool sent similar letters to Joseph Lane and John Weller in Congress. "I hope you will not forget me," he told Weller. "Do not make the old and common saying good, 'out of sight, out of mind.' Although Banquo may be dead, 'Florence lives!'"[55]

The veteran officer criticized Oregon governor Curry. The governor had launched a private war against the Indians and was pursuing "an extraordinary course," he wrote Scott. On the pretense of need, he had raised two small armies. To sustain them he made large purchases of animals and supplies, paying double and triple their value in scrip. Local prices soared, forcing Wool to buy horses, mules, and forage in California and have them shipped to army posts in Oregon and Washington. The situation had political overtones. Curry, he wrote Judge R. A. Thompson, at San Francisco, was "playing a political game to trip up the heels of General Lane. To do this he must have a war and an Indian war, no matter what it costs." Political demagogues in Oregon, Wool warned Representative Howell Cobb, would soon be knocking on the doors of Congress for money to pay scrip holders and settle Indian depredation claims. The Hudson's Bay Company, Governor Stevens, and ranchers who had stored goods at Fort Walla Walla also would cry out for relief. "You will be called on by Oregon to pay two millions," the general warned.[56]

While at Fort Vancouver, Wool put to rest a wild rumor. Nesmith and his Oregon volunteers, on returning from the Yakima country with the Rains expedition, had spread the word that the mission ledger found there showed the Jesuit missionaries were supplying guns and ammunition to the Indians. To quiet the matter, Wool sent the book to the Reverend J. B. A. Brouillet, vicar general, Diocese of Nisqually (Oregon and Washington), at Vancouver. He asked him to translate the entries from French into English that allegedly involved firearms, powder, and ball. Brouillet promptly complied. During the years 1852–1854, he reported, the missionaries occasionally had purchased a few arms, but they mostly bought ammunition from the Hudson's Bay Company to barter with Indians for food (principally salmon) and to give presents to the chiefs. Brouillet calculated the total distribution as twelve pounds of powder, 239 loads of shot, 338 caps, 147 balls, one rifle, and one pistol. The vicar "rejoiced" that the ledger was in public hands. It showed that the missionaries had "nothing in view but the real welfare of the Indians; that they are *there* for the Indians alone and not for themselves." Wool thanked Brouillet for his services and attached no further importance to the matter.[57]

In late December 1855, Wool learned that the Oregon volunteers had attacked peaceful Indians in the Walla Walla area. Col. Thomas Cornelius, who had replaced Nesmith, had taken additional mounted companies to the region and, finding no hostile bands, moved north to Touchet Creek in Washington Territory. On December 5 Cornelius met Chief Peopeomoxmox and forty Walla Walla warriors bearing a white flag. The chief admitted that his braves had pillaged Fort Walla Walla and promised to pay for the damages. He also gave the volunteers several beeves for food. The Oregonians seized the chief and several others as hostages and demanded the Indians surrender their arms. In a running fight the next day with the "Waller Wallers," as Wool called them, the volunteers shot the chief, scalped him, and cut off his ears for souvenirs. On Christmas Day, Wool reported the incident to Scott and gloomily predicted that Peopeomoxmox's murder would "unite all the tribes in that region against us."[58]

On January 11, 1856, Wool sailed on the mail steamer *Columbia* from Fort Vancouver. The newly organized Ninth Infantry Regiment, he learned, was en route from the East to the Department of the Pacific. Along the Oregon coast, he unknowingly passed a steamer carrying Colonel George Wright and eight companies of the Ninth, bound for Vancouver. On January 17, just outside the Golden Gate, the general sighted and stopped a second vessel loaded with soldiers. Lt. Col. Silas Casey, also a Florida War veteran, came aboard the *Columbia.* Wool sketched his plans for the spring with Casey. In Washington Territory he wanted Wright to undertake a prolonged campaign east of the Cascades. Casey would land two companies of the Ninth at Steilacoom, combine with the three already there, and begin active operations west of the Cascades and along Puget Sound. Wool promised details later. Artillery on Alcatraz Island saluted the returning commander when his ship entered San Francisco Bay. The general had been gone over two months.[59]

At Benecia, Wool questioned Townsend about conditions in the department. The major had returned in late December to supervise affairs at headquarters. Various tribes in California were restless. At the mission San Luis Rey, subagent Cave J. Couts, a former dragoon officer, had whipped two Indians to death and was arrested and indicted. In San Diego County, the San Gorgoña tribe resisted paying land taxes and demanded an agent. The reservations at Sebastian (Tejon), Kings River, and Kern River seethed with discontent. To the east, on the Colorado River, the Yumas had suffered crop failures and posed a threat to peace. Townsend had tried to "stir up" Superintendent Henley, urging his attention to these matters. Henley replied that he could not provide agents for every band, and he had empowered local ranchers to look after the Indians in their vicinity. Townsend told Wool that Captain Judah, at Fort Jones, in northern California, had sent Henley two "pretty severe letters" concerning the plight of the Indians in Scotts Valley. "I cannot understand," the colonel said, "how it is . . . Palmer can feed the Oregon Indians . . . [but] Henley cannot feed his."[60]

Wool now paid less attention to Henley. A year later, upon reviewing the superintendent's accomplishments, he observed that there was not one properly constituted reservation in California. Congressional laws in 1853, 1854, and 1855 authorized five military reservations, not to exceed 25,000 acres each, and approved $948,300, plus the salaries of the superintendent and three agents, to remove, colonize, subsist, and protect the California Indians. The acts also required the superintendent, in selecting reserves, to seek the commanding general's approval. Wool had been contacted only once, and that was to examine the projected Nome Lackee Reservation in the upper Sacramento Valley. He had approved it, but no survey had been made, nor had California ceded its land claim there to the federal government. Without boundaries and title clearance, Nome Lackee was no more an Indian reservation "than the city of Benecia." Wool estimated that 4,000 Indians were on reserves, but 56,000 still roamed at large. He blamed part of Henley's difficulties on his agents, several of whom should be dismissed because of brutality and fraud, but the major problem was the superintendent's inability to utilize properly the "liberal means" placed at his disposal.[61]

Wool's first act upon returning to Benecia was to review a request from California governor J. Neeley Johnson to arm a group of "volunteers" at Crescent City who were planning a campaign against Indians near the Oregon border. The general replied that he saw no need for volunteers. He admitted that some 125 hostiles roamed the forests between the Rogue River and the California border, but his commanders at Forts Jones, Humboldt, Lane, and Orford could marshal 400 soldiers to protect the district. Indiscriminate killing of Indians, good and bad, Wool told Johnson, must stop. But the governor was persistent. In March, citing the "utter want of efficiency" among federal troops, he asked the California legislature to authorize a company of fifty volunteers for three months' service in the Klamath country. Wool quickly advised Johnson that a recent War Department order specified that the raising of volunteers to act with regulars had to be approved by the department commander.[62]

As he wrestled with Johnson, Wool received shocking news from elsewhere. Governor Stevens, on January 19, 1856, had returned to Olympia from his Blackfoot council on the plains breathing fire. In returning west Stevens learned of the Yakima and Walla Walla hostilities. In early December he held a council with the Spokanes in northeastern Washington, then with a group of friendly Nez Perces, he rode south toward the Walla Walla country. At Kelly's Oregonian camp, the governor appointed Benjamin F. Shaw, a militia officer who had arrived with a Washington company to escort Stevens, to organize local whites and friendly Indians to cooperate with the Oregonians. On January 14, the governor reached Fort Vancouver, three days after Wool sailed for California. Here, for two days, he harangued Wright and Rains about a plan he thought Wool should use to end the hostilities. Both officers refused to act, and the disgruntled official traveled on to Olympia.[63]

On January 21, the diminutive Governor Stevens addressed the Washington legislature and discussed his efforts to negotiate Indian treaties. The extension of federal land laws to the territory, he stressed, required the need for treaties, and he had moved quickly "in consummating them." The Indians, however, had been unfaithful. The current difficulties were not caused by his treaties, or bad conduct of whites, the governor declared, but had "originated in the native intelligence of restless Indians" who saw destiny against them. Stevens then shifted his remarks to Wool. With deep regret, he was forced to criticize "a gallant and war-worn veteran" whose name had graced "the historic rolls of the country for nearly half a century." The general, learning that Governor Mason had planned a company to escort Stevens through hostile territory, had ordered it to remain in garrison. (Actually, Shaw had taken a company to the Walla Walla country and joined the Oregonians.) Whatever Wool's motives, the governor felt duty bound to report this act to the War Department. A breach of faith existed. Stevens announced that he planned to raise Washington volunteers at an early date to campaign independently. He would offer no treaties to the hostiles. Death was "mete punishment for their perfidy—their lives only should pay the forfeit," the little governor declared.[64]

Stevens's remarks created a furor in newspapers in California and in the East. The gloom enveloping the "territory to the north of us," the *San Francisco Herald* stated on January 27, had been dispelled by a lucky star—an Indian war had broken out. The settlers in Oregon and Washington territories stood to "realize individually larger fortunes by fighting the Indians than by toiling behind the plough, laboring at a sawmill, or undertaking long and wearisome journeys in pursuit of legendary gold mines." Territorial officials had contracted for 250,000 bushels of oats, at $3 a bushel, and for 2,000 horses, at prices ranging up to $800 each. The Indian war debt was soaring toward five million dollars.[65]

The next day, in a letter to the influential *Alta California*, an "Oregonian" acknowledged that territorial businessmen and settlers would profit from "war" contracts. But such contracts were insignificant, when compared to the army's "arrangements" with the Pacific Mail Steamship Company. The military had hired a number of company vessels, many old and unseaworthy, to transport troops and supplies to the Pacific Northwest at highly inflated costs. And what about "the old veteran" who promised to "make his headquarters in the saddle?" Wool had created "a considerable flourish," approved "fat contracts to *somebody*," then suddenly ordered his troops into comfortable winter quarters. He returned to San Francisco, "heartily tired of the rude accommodations and amusements of the north." While half-clad, poorly equipped volunteers battled the enemy in remote snowy mountains, Wool probably planned to withdraw his regulars from the Indian country—which would require another fat contract![66]

A week later, a "disinterested party" in Portland came to the general's defense. Stevens's "indefinite arrangements" with the Indians, concluded during "drunken revels of the chiefs," were being denounced by the settlers as the actual cause of the hostilities. Three armies would soon be in the field against the Indians—regulars, Oregonians, and Washingtonians—in a "triangular duel." In the smoke and confusion, "traders, dealers, jobbers, packers, contractors—and the nameless phalanx of scene shifters dancing attendance around a theatre of war"—would reap a "glorious harvest." Wool had leased five steamships to shuttle animals, soldiers, and supplies to his northern garrisons, but all were seaworthy and indispensable to the service.[67]

Stevens continued his attack on Wool. On January 29, 1856, in a sharply worded letter, he blasted the general for claiming that no Indian war existed in Washington Territory. Three days before, hostile bands had fired into the village of Seattle in broad daylight. Fortunately, they were driven into the forest by local citizens, with help from sailors and marines on the *Decatur*. The situation on Puget Sound was critical—and a winter campaign was imperative. Stevens alluded again to the escort denied him, and warned that he intended to make an issue of this. "It remains to be seen," the young official stated haughtily, "whether the Commissioner selected by the President to make treaties with Indians in the Interior of the Continent is to be ignored."[68]

Wool was hoping to be conciliatory. He assured Stevens that he had disbanded no troops raised for his protection. In fact, he first learned of the matter through Stevens's letter. With the Ninth Infantry on hand, he believed he could curb the unrest—provided the volunteers withdraw from the field. He thanked the governor for his suggestions, saying many of them were part of his plan. In closing, Wool concluded that if Stevens sent charges to Washington, he trusted the governor would be "governed by truth, and truth only."[69]

In early February 1856, San Francisco newspapers reported that Governor Curry had forwarded to President Pierce a memorial by the Oregon legislature, approved on January 30, that demanded Wool be removed from command of the Pacific Department. The general had refused to prosecute the war, the legislature declared, and had publicly condemned the governor and the citizens of Oregon for their zeal in defending their homes. He had also urged California merchants to withhold supplies from Oregonians, and boasted that he would block payment of the Oregon Indian war claims by Congress. The people of Oregon wanted the president to recall the general.[70]

On February 7, despite heavy rains, Stevens and several Washington legislators, together with Governor Curry, came to Fort Vancouver. They demanded that Colonel Wright order the Ninth Infantry into the field. The colonel stood firm. The next day Stevens and others made drunken stump speeches at the fort and at Portland. He denounced Wool in strong terms and called for three volunteer companies to "pitch into the Indians." Stevens and Curry then took a steamer up the Columbia to Fort Dalles. There, on February 15, Curry dispatched Colonel Cornelius with four hundred mounted Oregonians and a supply train to relieve the volunteers in the Walla Walla country. Cornelius also carried orders to cross the Columbia into Washington Territory and invade the Yakima domain. When Wright's regulars eventually arrived, the Oregonians would return to Fort Dalles and disband. Back at Olympia, on February 19, Stevens, in a letter to Secretary of War Davis, preferred charges against Wool. He accused the general "of utter and signal incapacity" and demanded his removal.[71]

While territorial leaders were lambasting the general for idleness, Wool completed his plans to end the Indian wars in the Pacific Northwest. During the preceding months, he had called on his scattered garrisons to protect both emigrants and settlers, as well as reservation Indians. He had reshuffled commands as hostilities flared on three fronts—southern Oregon, Puget Sound, and the Upper Columbia. As territorial officials rushed volunteer companies into the field, Wool branded their action expensive and unnecessary, and stirred up an outcry for his recall. The outcry subsided, however, as commanders organized one thousand regulars to sweep through the Indian country in southern Oregon and eastern Washington.

12

CRYING HEARTS AND VIGILANTES

On March 6, 1856, a cold day, Wool sailed aboard the *Columbia* back to Oregon and Washington to ensure that his field commanders understood their duties in the spring campaigns. East and south of Puget Sound, Col. Silas Casey was pushing his troops to crush hostile resistance and move renegade bands to reservations. On the Columbia and in southwestern Oregon, however, a majority of Wool's soldiers were still in garrison. In the weeks ahead, he planned to send expeditions sweeping into the Rogue Valley to gather Indians for removal to a coast reservation. To the north a larger force would march from Fort Dalles through the Yakima domain to induce the chiefs to make peace. The most dramatic measure Wool contemplated was to close eastern Washington to settlement until Stevens's treaties were ratified. Anxious days lay ahead.[1]

As his steamship plowed its way through the choppy waters along the coast, the general reviewed with Colonel Buchanan, who had joined him in San Francisco, his plans for ending Indian hostilities in Oregon. The situation on the Rogue required immediate attention. Superintendent Palmer's bitter comment in December on the causes of the war was fresh in Wool's mind. "The future will prove," Palmer had asserted, "that this war has been forced upon those Indians . . . by a set of reckless vagabonds for pecuniary and political objects, and sanctioned by a numerous population who regard the treasury of the United States a legitimate object of plunder." Acts of cruelty that would "disgrace the most barbarous nations of the earth" had been committed by those claiming to be citizens. The Rogue Indians had been driven to desperation. Their only hope was an early removal to the Grande Ronde Reservation Palmer had marked off on the Yamhill River west of the Willamette Valley in northwestern Oregon.[2]

Palmer had experienced tense moments in moving Indians to the Grande Ronde. In late January, he had started a small group of friendly Umpquas from a camp in the interior overland to the new reserve. The removal prompted an outcry against taking Indians through the settlements, but he reached his destination without incident. In late February, at Fort Lane, as Captain Smith readied soldiers to escort a large party of Rogues to the coast, a party of angry whites appeared at the adjoining Table Rock Reservation. They accused Indian leaders George and Limpy, and their bands, who had recently fled there, of depredations on local settlers. Smith confronted the party, threatened to open fire, and they left. On February 24, Palmer started some four hundred Indians from Table Rock for the coast, escorted by a detachment of regulars and sixty armed civilians. The day before the superintendent started, a hostile band massacred over twenty whites at Gold Beach, near the mouth of the Rogue, then swept into neighboring settlements and farms. Citizens fled to Fort Orford. Fortunately, Palmer's group reached the Grand Ronde Reservation safely several weeks later.[3]

On March 8, the *Columbia* dropped anchor at Crescent City, and Wool put Ord's company ashore. As planned, Colonel Buchanan was to launch a three-pronged thrust into the lower Rogue River Valley. From a supply base at Crescent City, six mounted companies carrying pack howitzers would march from three different stations to converge on the Rogue. On March 12, Buchanan, with Ord's regulars, would head northeast from the coast over a forest trail to the Big Bend of the Rogue. At the same time, Capt. Christopher C. Augur would move south from Fort Orford to the Rogue and turn upriver. At Fort Smith in the east, Smith, reinforced by a company from Fort Reading, would march downriver. The three columns, herding Indians before them, would meet at the confluence of the Rogue and the Illinois. Here, they hoped to force the hostile bands to surrender and submit to removal. Wool conveyed best wishes to Buchanan, and sailed on to Fort Orford, where he added a detachment to Augur's force. He continued north and reached Fort Vancouver on March 10.[4]

As Wright had already started a column for Fort Dalles, Wool decided to visit his commanders on Puget Sound. He took Maj. Charles Garnett, a former aide-de-camp, and two companies of the Ninth Infantry aboard the *Columbia*, and circled out to sea and into the sound, reaching Fort Steilacoom on March 14. Wool questioned Casey regarding conditions in the district.[5]

At his arrival in January, Casey had found the countryside in an uproar over the recent Indian attack on the village of Seattle. "These inhuman butchers and bloody fiends must be met and conquered, vanquished—yes, EXTERMINATED," the Portland *Oregonian* fumed. Governor Stevens had called out three battalions of six-month volunteers to operate in western Washington. Casey had moved regulars up the Puyallup and White Rivers to Muckleshoot Prairie, the heart of the hostile country. There he erected a blockhouse, and, on February 26, began a scout district. On Lemon's Prairie, a sentinel fired into the bushes, killing a Klickitat chief, Kanasket, whose party had attempted to crawl up and fire into the men around the campfires. On March 1, Casey sent Keyes to relieve Kautz's road detail on the White River. For nearly eight hours the soldiers fired at Indians attempting an ambush. Five days later, in a swamp near Porter's Prairie, Casey attacked an Indian camp and burned the log breastworks and thirty lodges.[6]

In late February, Governor Stevens had sent a volunteer battalion upriver to Snoqualmie Falls to build blockhouses, and dispatched a second force to scout with the regulars on Muckleshoot and Porter's Prairies. Stevens recruited friendly Indians to act as guides and scouts. To clear the district for scouting, the governor ordered all "foreign born white residents" on the prairies east and south of the sound to move to Steilacoom or to the old Hudson's Bay fort at Nisqually.[7]

Wool warned Casey not to cooperate with Stevens's volunteers, unless they were mustered into federal service. The governors of Washington and Oregon had no legal right to raise troops to operate independently of federal authority. To test the extent of Stevens's interest in cooperating with the regulars, Wool asked Casey to request two Washington companies for four months' service, and recommend that the remaining volunteers be withdrawn from the field. Stevens refused the request. Wool encouraged Casey to continue his field operations, and on March 16, he left Fort Steilacoom on the steamer *Active* for San Francisco.[8]

Shortly after reaching Benecia's barracks, Wool received another lengthy castigation from Governor Stevens. Events of the past month, the governor declared on March 20, proved that the general was at last awake to the "true conditions" of the Indian war and now sought to make amends for his "unfortunate blunders." Wool doubtless realized how much he had been misled in his views concerning the "infamous Peu-peu-mox-mox." The Walla Walla chief had been slain fairly. "I have investigated that matter on the ground," Stevens said, "having not only the testimony of the officers of the Oregon volunteers and the eyewitnesses of his death, but the testimony of the friendly Indians, both Cayuses and Nez Perce." He, of course, regretted the indignities committed on the chief's body. Wool must quit despising the opinions of those "with perhaps not very inferior abilities" to his own. Stevens then mentioned Casey's request for volunteers—and branded the call a snare. If placed under a federal officer, volunteers would be withdrawn from the field. The young governor said that he was "too old a soldier" to fall for such a scheme.[9]

This was not all. Wool had complained that territorial authorities had failed to consult with him. "Why did you not inform me of your presence in the Sound on your arrival at Steilacoom?" Stevens asked. Perhaps the general "did not know the courtesy" due territorial officials, or perhaps he preferred to avoid meeting a man "whose safety you had criminally neglected, and whose general views you have been compelled to adopt." As for Wool's claim that he knew nothing of an escort, Stevens boldly accused him of being a liar. "I warn you, sir," the little governor roared, "that unless your course be changed . . . your only salvation will be the firm and decisive policy of the two territories whose services you have ignored, whose people you have calumniated, and whose respect you have long since ceased to possess." Upon reading this vituperative statement, Wool handed it to his aide, Lt. Richard Arnold, and instructed him to return it to Stevens. He refused to place the tirade in his files.[10]

The Stevens-Wool imbroglio spilled over into the public press. Before sending his abusive letter, Stevens had needled Wool in a San Francisco newspaper. In a letter dated March 8, he claimed that the department commander lacked a sufficient force in Washington Territory to end the Indian hostilities. Because of this, he had been forced to raise volunteers to accomplish this purpose. The governor also announced he was sending an agent to San Francisco to purchase supplies and ammunition. He urged local merchants to respond. On March 24, the *Alta California* noted that a "gentleman" recently from Washington Territory was warning that its scrip was over-issued and was being refused in many quarters. He advised local businessmen to beware.[11]

On April 2, Wool handed John Nugent, editor of the *Daily Herald*, an unsigned statement concerning his forces in the field. "I think the Governor must have been drunk at the time he wrote his letter," Wool wrote Nugent. The statement appeared the next day. The writer branded Stevens's claims as gross exaggerations. On March 8, there were 1,900 regulars, not 900, in Washington and Oregon Territories; on April 1 the number was 2,000. Of the thirty-three companies in the military department, nine were in southern Oregon, seven on Puget Sound, and eleven on the Columbia. This force was more than sufficient to quiet the estimated two hundred hostiles on the Rogue and an equal number causing problems near the sound. The great fear was that volunteer forces would enlarge the war. But Stevens had supporters in San Francisco. On April 4, Nugent printed a letter from "One Who Knows," requesting the author of the April 2 statement to identify himself. This act was necessary in fairness to General Wool, "who can scarcely wish to be considered either the author or prompter of it." The next day a writer publicly denounced the commander for his actions to depreciate the value of the territorial scrip and frustrate Stevens's efforts to obtain supplies.[12]

In the meantime, Wool had written friends in the East. In a long letter to New York Senators William H. Seward and Hamilton Fish, he stated that, as the governors of Oregon and Washington had publicly denounced him and the Oregon legislature had demanded his recall, he felt a vindication was in order. In considerable detail the general tediously recounted the Haller and Rains expeditions, the killing of Bolon, and the hasty treaties by Stevens. The Ninth Infantry had arrived on the Columbia, but severe weather and difficulties in obtaining animals and supplies had forced the troops into winter quarters. The war was being extended to the Walla Walla country, Wool said. Oregon volunteers scouting there were regularly suffering losses of horses, wagons, and supplies to Indian raiders. Governor Curry had authorized funds to replace the losses at great expense. Such unauthorized and unnecessary operations had but one aim—"to plunder the Treasury of the United States to make political capital for somebody." To Oregonians the war was "a God-send to the country." He enclosed clippings for further reading.[13]

Before mailing his letters, Wool added a note the next day. He asked for support. He was six thousand miles from the capitol and "required someone to defend my character, which is dear to me." His claims on Seward and Fish, he felt, were simply "what is due to one who has honestly, zealously, and faithfully discharged every duty required of him whether in behalf of the United States or my native state of New York, of which we are all citizens." Would the two senators call for his correspondence with the governors of Oregon and Washington and with the War Department? Would they defend him, should he be assailed in the Senate?[14]

During the first week of April, Wool received distressing news. Wright's campaign against the Yakimas had been stalled by an Indian attack on the small settlement at the cascades on the Columbia, west of The Dalles. Since assigning Wright to that district in mid-January, Wool had corresponded regularly with the stout little colonel. He had instructed him to equip two columns at Fort Dalles and prepare to march when grass was available. One column would build a post in the Walla Walla country, near the emigrant trail, and the second would erect one at the Seelah fisheries, a favorite haunt on a northern tributary of the Yakima River. A smaller intermediate camp might be located on Simcoe Creek, south of the abandoned Ahtanum mission. The commander of each column would hire civilians to accompany the troops to bridge streams, build boats, and cut roads. Wool believed that if Wright could keep the Indians from their sources of food and grazing grounds, he could force their submission without bloodshed. He had forwarded a topographical map to Wright with fisheries, grazing areas, and sites for posts clearly marked.[15]

But Wright had altered Wool's plans. On March 1, the colonel wrote that instead of dispatching two expeditions, he had decided to move all his forces to the Walla Walla Valley. The change may have been due in part to Wool's February 7 letter, advising Wright, if he deemed it necessary, to drop one company at the Cayuse Reserve, on the Umatilla, where depredations had been committed. Wright planned to establish a depot on the Walla Walla, then "march to the Snake or Yakima country" and pursue the Indians to make them "see and feel our power." The plan was similar to what Stevens and Curry had earlier urged on Wright. Wool was back at Benecia when he received word that Wright had altered the general's plan.[16]

On March 26, Wright left Fort Dalles, traveling east along the south bank of the Columbia for the Walla Walla country. The site for the new fort lay over one hundred miles upriver. Oregon volunteers reportedly would soon move into the Yakima country. Large groups of Indians were assembling in that quarter, and Wright expected trouble. Five miles from The Dalles, as the little army bivouacked, an express rider rushed up with shocking news. A band of Yakimas and Klickitats had attacked the settlement at the Cascades, forty-five miles downriver.[17]

After midnight, Wright and four mounted companies boarded two riverboats, and shortly before dawn, on March 28, they reached the upper landing of the Cascades where it was found the Indians had killed thirteen men, women, and children. Wright collected nine Indian suspects living nearby, and tried, convicted, and hanged them near his camp.[18]

Shortly thereafter, Wool arrived at Fort Vancouver for the fourth time, and on April 12, he sailed upriver to view the destruction at the Cascades. He was visibly displeased with Wright for his tardiness in departing Fort Dalles and for leaving his rear unprotected. The general inspected the burned buildings at the portage, questioned Steptoe and Sheridan about the attack, then proceeded to Fort Dalles. Situated on the south side of the river, the post was bustling with activity. Both the army and the Oregon volunteers outfitted here for field operations. The fort took its name from The Dalles, a favorite fishing spot on the Columbia. The river narrowed to about 150 yards here and flowed for several miles in three channels cut in basalt rock. Indian families used scoop nets to catch salmon. During his stay, Wool inspected companies of the Ninth Infantry and again discussed plans with Wright for a spring campaign.[19]

The general spoke frankly to Wright. The colonel should abandon his plans to go to the Walla Walla country and move north at the earliest moment for the Seelah fisheries in the Yakima country. The salmon fishing season was beginning, and, if kept from this food source, many of the Indians would surrender. Also, an early movement could prevent the Yakimas from crossing the Cascades to combine with hostile bands on the sound. Wool warned Wright against permitting volunteer units to accompany him. Kamiakin and other Yakima chiefs reportedly would discuss peace, if the colonel appeared only with regulars. Kamiakin should be heard. Wright must demand that the chief bring in the murderers of Agent Bolon, and give hostages as evidence of Yakima sincerity for peace. Wool's last suggestion was bold and sweeping. At his discretion, Wright could declare eastern Washington Territory off-limits to white settlers until Stevens's treaties had been ratified.[20]

By the last of April, General Wool returned downriver to Fort Vancouver. While awaiting the mail steamer for California, he turned his attention to the Grande Ronde Reservation, in northwestern Oregon. This sprawling tract, seventy-two miles long and twenty-four wide, extended from the summit of the Cascades to the coast. Here some 1,500 Indians had been collected, many from the Rogue River Valley. On March 31, Lt. William B. Hazen, who had arrived with four hundred Rogues on the reserve, reported that settlers in the neighboring Willamette Valley feared such a large congregation of Indians near them. Anticipating trouble, Hazen had started a blockhouse on the south fork of the Yamhill River. In early April, Wool learned from Palmer, who was at Dayton, Oregon, that the Indians on the Grand Rhone were restless, and several subagents had resigned. The trouble was that the Rogues, fearing white intrusion on their new homeland, had refused to hand over their arms. Palmer did not dare disarm them. Could Wool release forty stands of arms to the civilian employees—and possibly station a detachment of regulars there? The general ordered Sheridan and a dragoon detachment to relieve Hazen. In early May, Sheridan reported that the reserve was quiet.[21]

On April 29, Wool sailed for San Francisco, and both officers and men at Fort Vancouver relaxed. The veteran had kept everyone on edge regarding military courtesy and dress. His leaving brought no regrets. "I do not think," Capt. J. J. Archer wrote home, "I ever knew a man more universally disliked—he neither has [n]or deserves to have a friend—for with all the vices I have ever heard of . . . he has only the single quality of animal courage to save him from utter contempt." The charge was not new—and it would be voiced many times before the old warrior laid aside the Union blue.[22]

On May 3, Wool returned to his quarters at Benecia and looked forward to some rest. On three fronts his commanders were vigorously pursuing the enemy with well-equipped forces. Over trails, where volunteer battalions earlier had struck swiftly and indiscriminately at Indian villages, regular infantry, accompanied by heavily laden wagons or pack trains, now drove forward. The commanders had orders to collect or capture renegades without bloodshed, if possible, and to transfer them to reservations. If attacked, the soldiers were ready to respond. Casey, Buchanan, and Wright had taken the field—and the general hoped that Indian hostilities would soon end.[23]

Wool's responsibilities increased, however. California Indian superintendent Henley continued to delay in creating reservations and appointing subagents. He still refused to feed non-reserve bands. Of an estimated 60,000 Indians in the state, only 2,000 were on reservations, and the superintendent spent his entire appropriation on this group. In the San Diego district the Indians complained that whites intruded on their lands, that local ranchers allowed their cattle to destroy their crops, and that they had suffered a food shortage.[24]

To the north, in the Tule Valley, an uprising seemed imminent. During the last week of April, Indians killed a rancher's cow, and citizens in the town of Tulare met and resolved to punish the bands camped at the head of the valley. A group started up the Tule River, but about forty miles above the crossing of the Tejon road, they encountered Indians behind breastworks shouting defiance. They quickly retreated and spread the rumor that five hundred warriors (there were only around a hundred) were on the warpath. An express raced to Governor Johnson, at Sacramento, with a petition for arms. As angry citizens went on a rampage, agents hurried their charges north to the Kings River farm and to Fort Miller. On May 1, Capt. Joseph Stewart, commanding at Fort Miller, dispatched 2nd Lt. LaRhett Loralzo Livingston and twenty-six regulars to the Tule Valley with instructions to restore order. The chiefs must hand over to civil authorities the parties who killed a cow. Livingston reached the breastwork in the road, and he, too, had to retreat.[25]

Wool grew apprehensive. Another Indian war seemed imminent. At Fort Tejon, Lt. Benjamin Allston and a dragoon detachment left for the Tule River with orders to quell the disturbance. The general also honored Governor Johnson's request for arms. Soldiers at Benecia loaded sixty rifles and five thousand cartridges into wagons, deducting the shipment from the federal quota due the state for volunteer use. On May 13, Livingston reported he had smashed the log breastworks with twelve-pound shot, killed twenty of the defenders, and burned their camp. As he rushed troops into the Tule district, Wool requested Johnson confer the rank of brigadier general of militia on E. F. Beale, the former Indian superintendent, and instruct him to collect and counsel distraught Indians. Beale went to the disturbed district and was able to persuade the Indians to accept reservation life. By late June, the Tule Valley was again peaceful.[26]

As he fretted over the Tule Valley incident, a local scandal seized all of Wool's attention. On the afternoon of May 14, James King, the flamboyant editor of the crusading San Francisco *Daily Evening Bulletin,* was shot in the street by James P. Casey, a county supervisor. King had launched a campaign to expose fraud and corruption attributed to David Broderick's political machine. In his zeal he maligned Casey, claiming he had been a convict in Sing Sing Prison in New York. King refused space for a rebuttal in the *Bulletin*. Casey met the editor in the street, challenged King, and mortally wounded him.[27]

Shortly after the shooting, Casey surrendered to authorities in San Francisco and was jailed. Newspapers and citizens quickly took sides. A "mercantile junta" seized upon the attack as an opportunity to reorder the local political scene. Front Street merchants and their friends promptly met and created an extralegal group to rectify wrongs. Several years before, in 1849 and again in 1851, when municipal corruption numbed San Francisco, powerful vigilante groups had been formed to supervise the machinery of justice. However, the committee organized in 1856 surpassed its predecessors in influencing public opinion and meting out "justice."[28]

Wool carefully watched the daily developments in San Francisco. His friend, John Nugent, editor of the *Daily Herald*, was among the first to feel the fury of the vigilantes. Nugent had been friendly to the city merchant and banking interests, but he personally disliked King and rebuked his friends for seeking revenge for the attack. He urged moderation and reliance on all constituted authorities. On May 15, he lost 212 subscribers in one day, and saw copies of his newspapers publicly burned in a street. The vigilantes quickly enlisted several thousand citizens for their cause, adopted the vigilante constitution of 1851, and appointed William T. Coleman, a member of the earlier committee, to direct their activities. They surrounded and threatened to take charge of the city jail.[29]

Mayor James Van Ness frantically telegraphed Governor Johnson for help. Johnson came down from Sacramento, found city officials powerless, and contacted banker William Tecumseh Sherman, a West Pointer and newly appointed major general in the California state militia. Together, they consulted with Coleman. If King died, Coleman said, the vigilantes would not allow the courts to decide Casey's fate. The governor backed off. On May 18, three thousand vigilantes marched on the jail, and the sheriff surrendered Casey and a fellow inmate, Charles Cora, a notorious gambler, who was accused of killing U.S. Marshal William H. Richardson after the marshal had drunkenly insulted Cora's mistress. Two days later, James King died and a frenzied mob lynched both Casey and Cora amid great fanfare from platforms extended from the second story of the vigilantes' headquarters, Fort Gunneybags, on Sacramento Street. San Francisco was nearing chaos.[30]

Wool was quickly drawn into the picture. On May 30, Johnson and Sherman arrived at the Benecia wharf and visited with the general in the American Hotel. The veteran officer listened patiently as Johnson discussed his predicament. If state authorities intervened in San Francisco, the governor asked, would the general provide assistance? Wool replied in a guarded manner, emphasizing that he had very few troops stationed in the bay area. Under ordinary circumstances, he explained, only the president could authorize such a move. However, because of the remoteness of the department, a commander might, under certain circumstances, assume the authority. Why did the civil authorities at the jail not resist the vigilantes? he asked. It had been impossible to resist, the governor replied, and intimated that Casey and Cora deserved their fate. Something must be done to halt the vigilante proceedings, Johnson stated, and asked again about arms. Wool mused that if the governor proclaimed martial law in San Francisco County, a few men could probably restore order. He then shifted the conversation. He gave a long-winded recital of how he, with a handful of troops, had quelled a mutiny during the War of 1812, then commented on his difficulties with Curry and Stevens, and, finally, picked up and read a long article he had sent to an eastern newspaper. Wool then ordered wine served and invited his weary guests to a game of whist. Johnson and Sherman retired that evening confused over the general's remarks.[31]

The following morning, Wool took his visitors on a tour of the arsenal. While on the walk, he stopped and asked the governor when he intended to issue a proclamation. Within the next day or two, was the reply. According to Johnson, Wool then promised to furnish him arms. Sherman expressed doubt regarding the promise, so Johnson broached the matter again at the wharf while waiting for the packet boat. As Johnson recalled, the general replied: "Never mind; when you want them issue your requisition on me, and merely state that they shall be deducted from the quantity which the State may be allowed by the Government, and I will attend to it." Sherman later said that Wool advised that to create grounds for martial law, the governor should obtain writs of habeas corpus for the release of the prisoners held by the vigilantes. As the vigilantes would not recognize the writs, Johnson could then declare martial law, call out the militia, and send for the arms. Both Johnson and Sherman returned to San Francisco still unsure about the fruits of their trip.[32]

Sheriff David Scannell went through the motions of serving writs, found it impossible, and Governor Johnson on June 3 declared San Francisco and San Francisco County in a state of insurrection. An unlawful organization, "styling themselves the vigilante committee," had resisted the execution of the legal processes, and he ordered it to disband. County militia companies were called immediately to duty. According to plan, the next day Johnson sent a courier to Benecia with a request for "arms, accoutrements, and ammunition" that Sherman might require. The arms would be returned, or deducted from the federal quota for California.[33]

Wool refused to honor Johnson's request. In a terse note he stated that he had reexamined the laws of Congress and found that no one but the president could release arms in the case at hand. In a recent contest in Bleeding Kansas, somewhat similar to that in San Francisco, the chief executive had refused to release arms to the governor. Wool told Johnson's emissary that certain men in San Francisco "could not be trusted or relied upon." If given arms this group might use them "against the authorities themselves."[34]

Sherman was incensed. There must be a mistake, he said. Wool had agreed, in his presence, "to issue such arms as would be required in the present emergency." His feathers ruffled, Wool responded the same day. He denied that he had made such a sweeping promise. Yes, a case could arise where he might assume the responsibility for issuing arms—and he had explained to Johnson the basis for such a case. "It never entered my mind," Wool told Sherman, "to either interfere or issue arms . . . until at least a proper demonstration had been made by the civil and military authorities of the state to enforce its laws." So far, the authorities of San Francisco County and of the state had yielded to, rather than resisted, the vigilantes.[35]

Johnson exploded. An armed mob in the city had violated the constitution and laws of California and threatened violence, he angrily wrote to Wool on June 7. Civil war was imminent. The militia had been called out, and arms were desperately needed. Johnson reminded Wool that he had promised on May 31 that, "on my order, as the Governor of the State," the general would furnish such arms as needed.

Johnson specifically wanted three thousand muskets or rifles, ammunition, two mortars, three hundred shells, and two guns of large caliber. When Wool ignored the request, Johnson and Sherman hurried to Benecia that afternoon. Several members of a "conciliation party" traveled with them.[36]

While Sherman conversed with Wool, several members of the conciliation group—Henry S. Foote, Bailey Peyton, and several others—joined the discussion. The conciliators presented a compromise from the vigilantes, who announced they would disperse after a certain date if left alone and not prosecuted. Wool sought to explain what he thought was a misunderstanding about the arms. At this point, Sherman excused himself and stepped down the street to see Johnson. The governor had refused to take lodgings in the American Hotel, and had found rooms at the Solano Hotel. Sherman found another group there—David S. Terry, Volney E. Howard, and E. D. Baker—all cursing Wool, calling him a liar, and claiming he was in league with the vigilantes. Foote's party came in, discussed the compromise, and Johnson demanded that it be put in writing. Sherman, whose sympathies leaned toward compromise, deserted the governor and wrote out his resignation, and Johnson appointed Volney Howard to succeed him as militia commander.[37]

Both groups then walked to Wool's quarters. Johnson opened the conversation, expressing regret that the general had not fulfilled his promise. Wool curtly replied that at the earlier visit he had "an imperfect recollection" of the pertinent law. Upon receiving the requisition, he had carefully reread the regulations and found that he could not comply. Should the governor persist in his demand for arms, he should apply directly to the president. A short discussion ensued and Johnson stamped out. Foote's party also stormed out.[38]

Wool remained adamant about issuing arms because he sensed confusion in Johnson's camp. The governor was trying to arm and organize the militia in the face of a growing spirit of compromise, while his followers, counseling moderation, were dropping away one-by-one. The general feared Johnson's intentions, as well as his lack of control over the militia. If the arms were released, and found their way into the wrong hands, there might be bloodshed. Hence the decision.

For days, Governor Johnson thrashed about at Sacramento. He chastised Sherman for publishing a letter that presented a slightly different version of their May 31 conversation with Wool and that attributed his resignation to a difference of opinion. He deplored the fact that Foote and other "sunshine friends" who had helped elevate him to the governorship, were now seeking to disgrace him. As for Wool, Johnson swore to Attorney General William C. Kibbe, on June 10, that he would "faithfully and truly" represent "Old Granny Wool's" duplicity and falsehood to his superiors in Washington. The governor's position, however, was fast becoming untenable. On June 19, Wool released the state's arms quota—113 muskets—to

Johnson, and two days later the vigilantes seized the schooner *Julia* carrying the shipment to San Francisco.[39]

In a letter to a relative, Sherman observed that the high-minded Johnson was "now powerless." The few militiamen that reported had deserted him, leaving the unfortunate official only the "naked, unsupported position" of his office. Johnson's petition to President Pierce, dated June 19, requesting that Wool be forced to issue federal arms, fell on deaf ears. The news that the government would not interfere reached San Francisco in August. On the eighteenth of the month, William T. Coleman dissolved the vigilante committee. Johnson, however, did not revoke his proclamation of martial law until the vigilantes released the state arms on November 3, on the eve of the fall election.[40]

Wool had the last word in his contest with Johnson. On September 20, a month after receiving approval from Washington of his action regarding the arms, the general placed a long article in the *Alta California*, rebutting the charges the governor had sent to the president. He cited quotes from letters to describe his dealings with Johnson, and accused the governor of twisting his words. Johnson snapped at the bait. On October 21, he stated in the *Herald* that he had not anticipated being the subject of the general's "notable *penchant* for newspaper letter writing." Then, in a flood of prose, Johnson accused Wool of lapses of memory, ignorance of duties and powers, and incompetence. The general's reply on September 26 was short. After addressing the question of memory, he pointed to Johnson's plight and shamed him. "To conclude this brief notice of your uncourteous letter," Wool said, "if you had exhibited the same consistency and determination to maintain the laws of the country that you have to take vengeance on myself . . . you would, no doubt, have been sustained by a generous and grateful people."[41]

Although clouds hung low over San Francisco during the late spring of 1856, Wool's spirits soon brightened. His commanders in Oregon and Washington were on the move. On Puget Sound, Casey's mounted infantry were patrolling the Puyallup and Nisqually sector in the south and scouting along the Cedar and Green Rivers to the east. On May 19, the energetic colonel predicted that Indian problems in his district were nearing an end. A detachment posted near Naches Pass blocked hostiles from going east to join the Yakimas. Casey's soldiers also began erecting fish weirs at strategic points on the Puyallup, White, and Green Rivers to prevent salmon from ascending. He hoped these traps would force the remaining hostile Indians into submission. He was readying companies to march to support Wright. In mid-June, Wool congratulated Casey on the prospect of terminating his "arduous but successful operations."[42]

The general was also pleased with Casey's firm stand during the recent legal difficulties in Washington Territory. In late March, Governor Stevens had arrested five men—mixed-race people, principally—on Muckleshoot Prairie, in Pierce County. During earlier Indian disturbances, these men had returned to their farms, violating Stevens's order to remain in the settlements. The fact that several had Indian wives, and that their farms had not been raided, made Stevens suspicious. The governor charged the men with treason against the United States. Having no jail in Olympia, he asked Casey to confine them at Fort Steilacoom until he could collect evidence and appoint a military commission to sit in judgment. Casey agreed to hold the men but urged a speedy investigation.[43]

Stevens was on tenuous grounds. On May 23, his military commission reported there was no reason to hold the mixed-breed farmers for treason. The next day, at Steilacoom, Judge Chenoweth, who earlier had issued writs for the men, asked Casey for protection, fearing trouble from Stevens's volunteers. The colonel, however, drew back, stating that the controversy was between two coordinate branches of the territorial government. Instead, he talked to the commander of the volunteer detachment at Steilacoom, and convinced him that the court must be allowed to function. Stevens now wavered. On May 25, probably believing his course might cloud Indian war debts and scrip claims, the governor revoked his proclamation and ordered Judge Edward Lander and the Canadians released. In July, Judge Lander fined Stevens fifty dollars for disobeying a court order. In a rather unique action, Stevens drew upon his powers as territorial governor and pardoned himself. His friends paid the fine.[44]

In the meantime, Wool had focused his attention on Buchanan's Indian campaign in southwestern Oregon. On March 14, Captain Augur had left Fort Orford with 102 mounted soldiers, and, proceeding southeast through the mountains, he reached the meadows at the junction of the Illinois and the Rogue to await the arrival of Buchanan and Smith. When the two columns failed to appear, Augur turned down the Rogue to its mouth and found Buchanan encamped there. The colonel had been delayed in leaving Crescent City, then found the wilderness route impassable and marched up the coast to Fort Miner, at the mouth of the Rogue. He arrived at least four days behind schedule. In the meantime, Smith had marched from Fort Lane, passed the rendezvous site at the meadows, and continued northwest to Orford. Buchanan now ordered punitive strikes up the Rogue. Captain Ord, scouting eleven miles inland, struck an Indian village, fought off an estimated sixty Indians, and killed eight. Wool read Buchanan's report and complimented him on Ord's foray—but added that Augur should have accompanied Ord. San Francisco newspapers hailed Ord's fight as the first major victory of Wool's regulars in the Rogue Valley since the beginning of hostilities.[45]

On May 2, Wool made a brief stopover at Fort Orford on his return from the sound. The general was in high spirits. Casey had predicted that Indian hostilities were ending in his district. Also, Wool reported that the War Department had approved operations, even though the governors of Oregon and Washington had demanded his recall. Torrential rains in southern Oregon complicated troop movements, but Buchanan said his officers were conducting regular forays up the Rogue. Various bands had straggled into Orford, saying their people wished to come in. Wool sailed for Benecia on May 3.[46]

On May 8, Buchanan marched up Rogue River with 350 mounted soldiers bearing, according to Lt. Rodney Glisan, "the olive branch in one hand and the sword in the other." Indian runners preceded the column with instructions to arrange a council at Oak Flats, on the right bank of the Illinois. On May 15, Buchanan met with chiefs of Indian bands from both the lower and upper Rogue. They promised to assemble their people at Big Meadows, at the Big Bend of the Rogue, and prepare to move to the Grande Ronde Reservation. Conspicuously absent was Old John's renegade band. Captain Smith and ninety dragoons with a howitzer arrived at Big Meadows to provide an escort for the Indians to Fort Lane. Waiting through heavy rain, Smith became suspicious, and drew his men back from the river to a ridge between two creeks draining into the Rogue. On May 27, the captain sent an express to Buchanan for reinforcements and Augur was sent to help.[47]

Smith's situation quickly became critical. At dawn on May 28, Old John appeared with an estimated four hundred warriors. At ten o'clock they charged up the ridge in the face of concentrated fire from Smith's short-range musketoons and howitzer. The Indians quickly realized the regulars lacked long-range weapons, and, clambering up a promontory, they poured deadly fire into Smith's camp. As darkness fell, soldiers feverishly dug rifle pits and made breastworks of camp equipage. The next day, Old John again sent his warriors up the ridge, and then, at four in the afternoon, he divided his forces to strike Smith's flanks. But as the Indians began their advance, Augur, hurrying through eighteen miles of rough country in less than five hours, burst upon the scene. Smith's men cheered and charged down the slope, pushing the Indians back to the river. The battle at Big Meadows was over. Smith had lost twenty-nine dead or wounded.[48]

Buchanan and the rest of his column arrived at the battle site on May 30. Indians began coming in and expressing a willingness to go to the coast reservation. Augur, Ord, and John F. Reynolds skirmished with hostile bands in the area for several weeks. By June 15, Superintendent Palmer had arrived and started the removal process. Buchanan escorted 700 Indians to Fort Orford, where 600 boarded the *Columbia* for Portland and the Grande Ronde. Old John also decided to take "the White Man's Road" and surrendered. After nearly ten months of hostilities, on June 24, Buchanan told Wool the Rogue River War was over.[49]

But Colonel Wright was still in the Yakima country. On Council Creek, seven miles north of the ruins of St. Joseph Mission, an Indian messenger reported that

Kamiakin and other Yakima chiefs wanted to parley. Wright agreed to meet them on the Naches River on May 9.[50]

The Naches was swollen by spring rains when Wright arrived, and it was impossible to ford the river. A large encampment of Indians stretched along the opposite bank. The colonel pitched camp, and sent an emissary across the river to contact the Indians. In an exchange of messages, Kamiakin, Skloom, Teias, Owhi, and other chiefs hesitated to hold a council, and the colonel abruptly ended the parley. Steptoe was en route from Fort Dalles with four companies, and Garnett, with two companies from Puget Sound, would soon join him, increasing his force to eleven companies. He could plan his moves with confidence.[51]

Wright remained on the Naches for nearly a month. Yakima chiefs Owhi and Teias, accompanied by Leschi, a Nisqually chief from the sound, finally came over to parley. The Indians appeared nervous and spoke in generalities. Wright stated bluntly that the Yakimas must bring in their people and surrender their arms and gave them five days to comply. The Indians suddenly broke up their camps and headed for the fisheries. On May 18, Wright crossed the Naches with 450 infantrymen on a makeshift bridge and, leaving Steptoe and three companies to guard the depot, marched north into the Kittitas Valley.[52]

On July 7, Wright, continuing north, reached the Wenatchee River. Here hundreds of Indian families were engaged in salmon fishing. Father Charles Pandosy, an oblate missionary camping with the Indians, informed the colonel that Kamiakin had fled to the Palouse country and Owhi had gone east beyond the Columbia. The Indian families on the Wenatchee wanted to surrender. Wright assembled the families, and on July 9, turned south to the Columbia, accompanied by 500 Indians—mostly Yakimas and Klickitats—and 1,000 horses. In late July, the caravan of soldiers and Indians reached Fort Dalles. After three weary months of travel, Wright's footsore infantry returned to garrison. The Yakima campaign was over.[53]

Instructions from Wool soon arrived. On August 2, the general ordered Wright to construct two posts—a three-company garrison in the Walla Walla Valley and a one-company garrison near the Ahtanum mission in the Simcoe Valley to guard the Naches Pass. The colonel would expel—by force if necessary—all volunteer forces in that region. The closing paragraph contained one of the most controversial orders Wool ever issued. The general instructed Wright to use the army to seal off the eastern section of Washington and Oregon Territories, perhaps echoing the Royal Proclamation of 1763, permitting no one to enter or settle in that "Indian country." Hudson's Bay Company people with ceded rights from the Indians and miners were exempt. Wool promised further instructions on the matter. This order soon caused an uproar in Oregon and Washington Territories.[54]

On August 19, Wright reported that Governor Stevens had passed Fort Dalles with a group of volunteers who were escorting several wagons loaded with provisions. He planned to hold a council in the Walla Walla country with the Nez Perce. Stevens learned that Wool was authorizing new posts in the Yakima country and in the Walla Walla region, and he assured Wright that he would recall his volunteers when the regulars arrived. Soon afterwards, Lieutenant Colonel Steptoe organized a construction crew and left to erect a post in the Walla Walla Valley. Major Garnett would build a smaller post in the Simcoe Valley.[55]

In early September, Steptoe's slow-moving column, burdened by building materials, reached Mill Creek, six miles from Stevens's camp. An estimated four thousand Indians had assembled to meet the governor—but the principal Yakima chiefs had not appeared. Almost immediately, Stevens sent his volunteers, except one company, back to Fort Dalles and rode over to Steptoe's camp and asked for regulars to protect him. Twice he made requests and twice he was refused.[56]

The Indian council opened on September 11. Stevens lectured the Nez Perce chiefs on accepting treaties, and pointed to the agreements he had made in that vicinity the previous year. The discussion dragged on for days. He again pressed Steptoe for a show of support. Stevens then abruptly moved the council to Steptoe's camp three days later. A rumor circulated that the governor was drinking heavily. Finally, on September 17, Stevens, sensing his efforts were useless, ended the meeting with the declaration: "Follow your hearts; those who wish to go to war go!" The next day Steptoe agreed to address the Indians, assuring them of his peaceful intentions. Stevens now collected his party and started west for Fort Dalles. But a hostile Indian party set fire to the prairies, and, three miles from the council grounds, attacked the governor's train. Steptoe sent dragoons to protect Stevens. Then, leaving a work detail to build a blockhouse on Mill Creek, the colonel and his main force escorted the governor back down the Columbia.[57]

In two letters (August 18 and September 2), Wool ordered Wright to go in person to the Walla Walla district. He instructed the colonel to parley with the tribes in eastern Washington, particularly the Nez Perce, and gauge their feelings toward the whites. He also urged the post on the Walla Walla be finished and provisioned before winter. Wright delayed answering the September letter until Steptoe returned to Fort Dalles. Intuition told him he was in trouble at headquarters.[58]

In October, at Walla Walla, Colonel Wright held talks with Cayuse and Nez Perce chiefs. Howlish-Wampum, a Cayuse, orated at length. "I came up here, I found the Commissioners [Stevens and Palmer] in Council with the Nez Perces—subsequently the Cayuses were invited to come in—Beef was killed and presents offered. We would accept nothing. The Cayuses did not want to sell their land; but when we wished to speak, the Nez Perces forbid us. It was Lawyer [Nez Perce] and his people who sold the country. Our hearts have been crying ever since." Other chiefs also spoke. Eagle-from-the-Light, a Nez Perce, blamed Stevens's 1855 treaty for the first spilling of blood. He asked if the "bloody cloth" could be washed, made white, and the past forgotten. Wright assured him that indeed "the Bloody Cloth should be washed; not a spot should be left on it." The "Great Spirit" that had created both the white and red man, the colonel declared, had commanded them "to love one another." On October 31, from the Walla Walla encampment, Wright reported "all the chiefs in this and the Yakima Country" violently opposed Stevens's 1855 treaty. He hoped it would not be confirmed.[59]

In early November, Wool sent a harsh reprimand to Wright. In July, he had instructed the colonel to "have nothing to do with Stevens, then ordered that he personally visit the Walla Walla country." The colonel not only had tarried, but had permitted Stevens to enter the region. "Were you not aware," Wool stated, "that when hostilities had begun and the troops been sent to suppress them, that the duties of an Indian agent (tho' a Governor) ceased; that the power of regulating the Indians then passed from the civil to the military?" Why did Wright allow "the Agent" to precede him? Why did he send Steptoe "to attend on" Stevens, to wait his movements and enforce treaties that had led to war with the Yakimas? In conclusion, Wool hoped "that the annoyance thus given to him" would be the greatest cause of regret "either you or he may have from the past."[60]

Wright was stunned. "I have no regret," he replied on November 15, "that General Wool should have deemed it necessary to dictate such a letter to me. The high respect which I have ever had for the General forbids my answering that communication in the same tone and spirit. I . . . beg to assure the General that I shall always take great pleasure in executing his orders and carrying out his views."[61]

Wool's reprimand reflected the feelings of a man who was exhausted in both mind and body. Through the preceding spring, while pushing his commanders to take the field, he had simultaneously thrown his energy into battling those who questioned his judgment, abilities, and authority in conducting an Indian war. In lengthy epistles to Washington, D.C., Baltimore, and New York newspapers, he had boldly indicted territorial officials in Oregon and Washington for prolonging Indian outbreaks to stimulate local economies and provide platforms for political gain. The veteran commander had also lashed out at the volunteer armies that complicated his military operations. He fumed when Stevens, whom he called a "drunken sot," dared condemn him publicly. The vigilante troubles further taxed his endurance.[62]

By early July 1856, Wool was sick and sought the healing atmosphere at the resort at Napa Springs. He had lost twenty pounds and looked thin and emaciated. Even at the spa, Wool continued his verbal battles. Oregon Delegate Joseph Lane had introduced a bill in the House to provide $300,000 to meet the expenses of the Indian hostilities in Oregon and Washington. The general dispatched letters to friends in the east to set the record straight. On July 3 and 4 he wrote optimistically to William H. Seward and Russell Sage, of New York, and David Stewart, of Baltimore. Despite "misrepresentations of my incapacity and inability to conduct an Indian war," he told Seward, the hostilities near Puget Sound and in southern Oregon were nearing an end. Intelligent and humane commanders had made this possible. As for Lane's claim of being a "good Indian fighter," Wool asserted he could give the boastful politician "some useful lessons in conducting an Indian war, at least in humanity if nothing else." In other letters to Stewart and Sage, Wool stressed that his plans had produced victories in the field with only four months of campaigning. In making decisions, he followed simple rules: "I never take advice from anyone. I never have shields for bad Generalship. Whatever I do is dictated by my own sense or judgment of right and wrong."[63]

In late August, Wool heard from Russell Sage. In the House of Representatives, he had read the general's July 3 letter into the record. Lane responded. He declared that he was "tired" of Wool's meddling in Oregon. He had no wish to "pluck one laurel" from the crown of his former commander in Mexico, but he believed that the general's brilliant career had been marred by his recent Indian campaigns. Wool was "a tactician after the fashion of the military fogies of Europe, who manifested all the faults of the old system." The army, Lane asserted, was the nation's greatest curse. On September 3, Wool thanked Sage for his aid. "I have not done with those gentlemen," he assured his fellow Trojan. "By the time Congress meets in December, I will give you a statement that will make them wince." Other news arrived regarding the Indian claims. In August, Congress enacted legislation to audit Oregon and Washington Indian war debts, but made no provision for payment. Capt. A. J. Smith at Fort Lane and Capt. Rufus Ingalls quartermaster at Fort Vancouver, along with Lafayette Grover, a civilian living at Salem, Oregon, were appointed to examine the claims.[64]

By the late fall of 1856, Indian hostilities in the Pacific Northwest subsided. One by one the sources of friction faded. After Wright took the field in May, Curry withdrew the Oregon volunteers from the Walla Walla country. The Oregonians returned east and disbanded in July. By late August, the Washington volunteers in Puget Sound were discharged and the blockhouses abandoned. On October 30, at Olympia, Stevens discharged the troops who had been sent to the Walla Walla Valley. "Historians will present the fact with credit and honor to the volunteer force," he declared, "that during the six months of active service of one thousand of the citizens of Washington Territory, not a single friendly Indian has been harmed in a volunteer camp or scout—no Indian has been plundered or molested." The year 1856 had been "disastrous" to "material prosperity," but it had been rich in honorable achievements.

Stevens was already eyeing the office of territorial delegate, and promising close attention to the Indian war debts, if elected.[65]

With his commanders reporting their districts quiet, Wool reorganized his garrisons. On Puget Sound he sent Colonel Casey to distribute five companies in his command to the three posts of Steilacoom, Bellingham Bay, and Port Townsend. Wright would maintain garrisons at four forts in his district—Vancouver, Dalles, Simcoe in the Yakima country, and Walla Walla. In southern Oregon, Wool broke up the posts at Crescent City and Orford. He projected a new fort on the Siuslaw River, above the mouth of the Umpqua, near the southern boundary of the new Siletz River Reservation. Soldiers also established one-company posts to the north on the eastern boundary of the Grande Ronde Coast Reserve—one on the Yamhill west of Dayton and the other west of Corvallis.[66]

Wool's boldest action was to close eastern Washington and Oregon to non-Indian settlement. This was a domain that sprawled from the Cascades east to the Snake River country—a tract of nearly forty million acres. In a letter to Gen. Winfield Scott, he explained his reasons for the order. This region should be left in Indian hands, Wool said, until Stevens's treaties were ratified. The tribes resented the treaties and were in no mood to tolerate settlers. By military fiat he hoped to prevent collisions and warfare. Wool also doubted the region was worth the expense of clearing its title. It was a mountainous region "with valleys that could perhaps be advantageously used for raising stock, but not for cultivation."[67]

On October 22, Stevens attacked Wool's ban. In a letter to Interior Secretary Robert B. McClelland, he argued that the Donation Act of 1850, plus additional legislation in 1853 and 1854, had opened all the public lands in Washington Territory. He urged they remain available to freeholders. Could Wool "legally exercise an authority which abrogates a statute of the United States, and deprives citizens of vested rights?" For the time being, however, the government took no action, and the general's edict was allowed to stand.[68]

In September 1856, San Francisco and Oregon newspapers hinted that John Wool would soon be reassigned. An Oregon paper late in the month stated that citizens of Oregon City, Salem, and other towns in the upper Willamette Valley, upon hearing a rumor of the recall, had lighted giant bonfires, fired cannon, and denounced the general's "imbecile course" in the Indian war and his "unwarranted public abuse." The ladies contemplated making the veteran officer "a silk petticoat and nightcap, trimmed with gold lace," emblems he "richly" merited for his services in declaring there was no war—when Indians for months had been murdering women and children in cold blood.[69]

Wool's thoughts indeed had turned east. In early October, when he wrote David Stewart about his stay at White Sulphur Springs in Napa Valley, he wandered into other topics. It was too late in the day, Wool said, to think of politics. His political fever of the early 1850s had subsided. "I like my profession," the general said, "although for the last 18 months my position has been anything but pleasant." There were personal and financial matters now demanding his attention, and he hoped he could soon return home. As for the sword voted him by Congress in 1854, and never sent to him, he preferred to let the matter lie until the next administration took office.[70]

On December 4, in a letter to Adjutant Gen. Samuel Cooper, Wool officially asked to be reassigned. He had been in California nearly three years, and in recent months his responsibilities had been "multifarious, arduous, and sometimes difficult of execution." Moreover, his health was poor. "The department is well organized," the general stated, "and the posts, I believe, are judiciously located, especially in Oregon and Washington Territory with reference to the protection of the white inhabitants and to control the Indians." Having understood from the secretary of war and the president that his former command would be reserved for him, he respectfully asked to be posted in the East.[71]

In his waning months in California, Wool was invited to Sacramento to the state capital where admiring senators gathered around the old general to shake his hand, pat him on the back, and "give him their cordial personal greetings." His command of the military in California and the West Coast, the senators insisted, had been "exemplary and highly satisfactory." Wool had "won for himself the profound respect and affection of the people of California." From the state senate, he was escorted to the lower house, the assembly, where he received a standing ovation and was proclaimed a "faithful and efficient servant of the Republic." On the occasion, one California newspaper touted him as "gallant, brave and honorable, with sterling worth, and strong ability . . . a model soldier of the old school." The senate commissioned a portrait of Wool to be painted by the noted artist, William Smith Jewett, and displayed in the chamber beside that of the legendary Californian, John A. Sutter, but funds were never appropriated and the portrait never painted.[72]

In early February 1857, the anticipated orders arrived. On the nineteenth Wool informed his commanders that he was leaving the Pacific Department. He complimented his officers and men on their intelligence, energy, and zeal during a trying period. "By this union," he said, "Indian wars have sometimes been prevented, and always brought to a speedy close." He extended his thanks, commendations, and best wishes for their future welfare. He declined a dinner in his honor in San Francisco and on February 20, the seventy-two-year-old veteran temporarily turned over command to Col. Thomas T. Fauntleroy and sailed without fanfare for New York.[73]

Wool's three years in the Pacific Department had been arduous and turbulent. His overzealous actions to curb filibustering, the removal of his headquarters to

Benecia, and rumors of his presidential aspirations brought him into conflict with Secretary of War Davis. Even more exasperating had been his involvement in the thorny problems of Indian affairs. Confronted with sputtering wars in Oregon and Washington, he had placed a large force in the field in the spring of 1856 and, despite interference by volunteer armies, successfully curbed hostilities within four months. Wool's bold accusations that impatient treaty makers caused the hostilities, which politicians and speculators encouraged, aroused a hornet's nest. In the midst of the conflict, civil disorders momentarily erupted, testing severely his powers of discretion and decision. In his contests with state and territorial authorities, Wool carefully defined his position and stoutly defended the federal prerogative. He left California for home with no regrets.

13

RUSHING TO THE COLORS

The persistent clatter of a telegraph key at Wool's headquarters in Troy on Saturday afternoon, April 13, 1861, indicated great peril on the southern horizon. When the keys fell silent, the clerk hurried to Wool's home with a startling dispatch. At 1:30 that afternoon, after a thirty-three-hour bombardment by secessionist troops, Fort Sumter, in Charleston Harbor, had capitulated. Maj. Robert Anderson, the commander and a loyal Kentuckian, had lowered the Stars and Stripes and was embarking his battered garrison for New York City. No further news came by wire that night, but the Sunday morning newspapers carried bold headlines announcing the surrender. The fall of Fort Sumter had far-reaching consequences. For Wool it ended four placid years of routine command duties and signaled the coming of a bloody civil war—a war in which the old warrior, despite his advanced age, rushed to the colors.[1]

John Wool was seventy-three years old when he returned from California in the spring of 1857 and resumed command of the Department of the East. As usual, he established his headquarters in Troy. The department stretched from Maine to the Mississippi, but it was a relatively inactive jurisdiction, with less than one thousand regulars manning some ten garrisons. Three-fourths of these troops were in the South, stationed at one-company posts along the Atlantic and Gulf coasts; the largest installation was Fort Monroe, Virginia, with nearly four hundred men. The great bulk of the regular army, which totaled approximately sixteen thousand, was on duty in the Indian country west of the Mississippi. Unlike former times, Wool made few inspection tours, but he regularly visited Washington on official trips, where he renewed acquaintances and caught up on news at the War Department. He studied the reports crossing his desk in Troy and took a conscientious interest in resolving the problems within his command.[2]

Wool enjoyed public life. He appeared at patriotic and civil functions and reviewed troops at summer militia encampments. The general particularly enjoyed society affairs in the national capital, reporting faithfully to Sarah, who was home-bound, on the highlights of the evening. On April 7, he attended Senator William Gwin's "fancy ball," where everyone dressed in a costume that ranged from king and queen to beggar. "I went in my uniform as Major General Wool," he said. Many ladies asked to be remembered to Sarah. Elizabeth Moss Crittenden, wife of Kentucky senator John J. Crittenden, spoke of Sarah, Wool reported, as "the most elegant, intelligent, and agreeable lady she had ever met at Washington." There were unpleasant times, too, for the friends of yesteryear were passing. In July 1857, Wool marched as grand marshal of a long funeral cortege bearing the remains of fellow Trojan and American statesman William Learned Marcy. The pallbearers included such prominent figures as former president Pierce, Senator Seward, and Governor Horatio Seymour. Three years later, at Nassau, Wool stood by the graveside of his brother-in-law, Chester Griswold, with whom he had spent many happy days. Historians Henry B. Dawson and Benjamin Lossing visited the general to seek information for volumes that covered the War of 1812 and the Mexican War. Wool talked freely, and when proof sheets came, he spent long hours making corrections and drafting explanatory notes. The general was also pleased that he was included among the thirty-four prominent Americans in John Savage's *Our Living Representative Men*, a set of sketches of those mentioned as presidential possibilities in 1860.[3]

Wool maintained a large personal correspondence. The spirit and vinegar of former days still marked his utterances, and he remained tenacious in seeking to right injustices as he saw them. Single-minded, he insisted on old-fashioned virtues, behavior which many saw as vain, petty, and spiteful. As always, he relished the heat and clamor of battle, whether waged with sword or pen. This was apparent in his brief foray against Jefferson Davis in 1857, and in his sustained attempt to discredit the Oregon and Washington Indian war claims before Congress. In each case he won only a token victory, but enjoyed the contest.

In August 1859, Wool received an invitation from the New York Mechanics' Institute to give a speech to the workingmen of New York City. Declining the invitation because of ill health and official duties, the general did draft a long letter as tribute to the workingmen of America. As inspiration, the general recalled the life of Benjamin Franklin, who "played with the forked lightning as with a tame snake"; Roger Sherman, who had once been a shoemaker; George Walton, who had been a humble carpenter and twice became governor of Georgia; Eli Whitney, who had manufactured nails; and the bard himself, William Shakespeare, who had been a wool comber.[4]

Few men stirred Wool to wrath as did Jefferson Davis. Their heated exchange in 1854 over Wool's instructions regarding filibustering and military construction in California had made front page news for months. Wool had seen to that. The general regarded the war secretary as an overbearing, disrespectful bureaucrat whose sharp tongue proved his undoing. In April 1857, he wrote Lt. James A. Hardie, a former aide stationed in California, that Jefferson Davis had been no friend of the army. Davis had constantly sought avenues to gratify petty jealousies and seek revenge for imaginary injuries by army subordinates. Davis was incompetent to run the War Office. His order for a large-scale redeployment of troops in Oregon and Washington during the spring of 1857 clearly showed a lack of capacity to manage military affairs. Wool had warned General Scott that the operation would cost over a million dollars and could reopen the Indian wars. After Davis's term ended on March 4, Scott countermanded the secretary's order. "I have not seen an officer," Wool declared to Hardie, "who has not condemned the course and conduct of the late Secretary."[5]

A brief epilogue to the Wool-Davis controversy occurred in the summer and fall of 1857. In late May, the general wrote John B. Floyd, the new secretary of war, inquiring about the sword that Congress voted for his services at Buena Vista. The sword had been boxed and ready for delivery in mid-1855, but Davis had found excuses for not sending it to California. Floyd admitted the sword was stored in Davis's office. In June, the general's aide, Capt. Hamilton L. Shields, picked it up for Wool. Wool's anger reached Davis, now a senator from Mississippi, and he wrote Floyd on July 12, accusing Wool of perpetrating "a palpable and pitiable falsehood" regarding the shipment of the sword. Davis's response quickly appeared in print. Meanwhile, a new element surfaced to fuel their feud. Filibuster William Walker had arrived in Washington for an audience with President James Buchanan. He wanted to test the waters about launching an expedition to Nicaragua. Walker placed a letter in the New York newspapers that implied the federal civil and military authorities in California had done little to interfere with his earlier activities. The publication of the Davis and Walker letters raised Wool's dander.[6]

Wool was sick much of June, but he rose to the challenge. On July 23, he described at length his command experience in California. He recited his instructions, his efforts to block Walker, and Davis's censure. Thereafter, he had hesitated to act. In mid-August, Davis denounced Wool in the Jackson *Mississippian*. In early December, Wool responded in the Jackson *Flag of the Union*, chiding Davis for using "Billingsgate language" to defend himself. Such an action, he said, degraded his senatorial robes. The Mississippian was unworthy to be war secretary, for he had "neither respected truth, honor, or courtesy," while in office. Davis fired the final salvo on December 23 in the *New York Times*. He openly accused Wool of slandering his name in the newspapers and in official correspondence, and of maliciously misrepresenting his acts. Davis said his record was clearly stated in War Office files, and it was a waste of time to spar with Wool any further. At this point the contest ended.[7]

Wool also challenged the Oregon and Washington Indian war claims before Congress. Oregon claimed $4,500,000 and Washington $1,500,000, with additional property claims estimated at $1,000,000. Soon after returning from California, Wool went to Washington on pay matters and sought to gauge opinion on the debts. Oregon Delegate Joseph Lane, he wrote Lieutenant Hardie in April 1857, had "pretty much used himself up" in getting a bill before Congress to pay the war expenses. "He, nor all Oregon and Washington to back him, can influence Congress to go against myself or any statement I have made in regard to the Indian War in those Territories," Wool asserted.[8]

Early in 1858, when Joseph Lane and Isaac Stevens, now territorial delegate from Washington, brought up the Indian claims again, the general was ready. He followed the debate closely, and regularly fed Representative Abraham B. Olin, a fellow Trojan, and other congressmen heavily documented attacks on the bill. At Wool's request, Olin, a member of the Committee on Expenditures, also introduced Capt. Thomas J. Cram's 126-page "Military Topographical Memoir and Report on the Department of the Pacific" into the debate. Cram detailed Wool's efforts to contain the Indian problems in Oregon and Washington and described the obstructions that the volunteer troops caused. Stevens and Lane branded the essay a "voluntary" memoir and an unofficial piece of propaganda. House members Samuel Curtis and Francis P. Blair came to Wool's defense, showing conclusively that it was an official document. The House referred the claims bill to a subcommittee, which asked the third auditor of the Treasury to examine the vouchers. Wool continued to write letters to derail the bill. By the spring of 1860, the third auditor recommended payment of $2,714,808 to settle the combined claims—about one half of the amount requested. Congressional concern in "Bleeding Kansas" and rising debate over the expansion of slavery into the western territories probably did more to delay passage of the Indian war debt bill than Wool's sniping. However, he undoubtedly believed that his letters substantially influenced decisions in the matter.[9]

In 1860, John Wool threw his energies into the most important campaign of his career—the campaign to save his beloved Union. Few army officers were as vocal in demanding government action toward the restless South. On January 20, three months after John Brown's attack on the Harpers Ferry Arsenal, the general wrote to William Baylies, brother of the lamented Francis, expressing disgust at southerners' alarm. "How absurd and ridiculous is the conduct of the would-be chivalry of the South," he said. "Frightened almost out of their senses by John Brown, his seventeen white men, and five blacks. If this number of mad men could produce so great an alarm, what would be the effect of five thousand entering the Southern states?" The wounds "inflicted" by Brown and his party should be healed, and the South sustained "in all its rights and privileges" under the "National Compact." Conciliation and harmony were essential to the nation's prosperity. "I would put an end, if possible," Wool added, "to the Negro controversy, which interferes with sound intercourse, with trade, and with legislation, National as well as State. At the same time, I would let the Southern Chivalry know that their abuse and denunciations should no longer control the affairs of the Country."[10]

In April, Wool wrote Senator James H. Hammond, of South Carolina, who was less radical than other southerners relative to the John Brown episode. The slavery question must be settled soon. The "shuttlecock game of hard words" between northern and southern extremists was producing "great injury" to the nation. "For myself," Wool stated, "I can truly say I am wholly national in my feelings. I have no prejudices which would prevent me from residing with as much pleasure in the South as in the North. Indeed I feel as though I ought to be counted as much as a citizen of the South as of the North, for I have been forty and fifty years fighting, or being ready to fight, for the Union."[11]

In November 1860, with the election of Abraham Lincoln, Wool became more concerned about the rush toward disunion. In a letter to Gen. Leslie Coombs, in Lexington, Kentucky, he again denounced the extremists. "It is the *retort courteous* that creates all the trouble on the nigger question. We can no more control Mr. [Henry Ward] Beecher from talking on the subject of slavery than you can the secessionists." South Carolina extremists had purposely split the Democratic Convention to ensure the election of Lincoln, knowing this would arouse the rest of the South. The old idea of a great confederacy to include the South, the West Indies, and Central America was being discussed again. Agitation for this scheme reached back to 1832, and it had been a factor in the filibustering expeditions in the 1850s. Wool viewed South Carolina's cry for disunion as a pretext to induce her sister states to join in this grand scheme.[12]

On December 6, with South Carolina hurling insults and threatening to secede, Wool wrote his old friend Lewis Cass, a general in the War of 1812 and now the secretary of state, urging him to take action. The letter appeared in the *New York Times* and was widely cited. It reflected the feelings of a hard-nosed, Jacksonian Democrat who was perplexed at his country's reluctance to fight to preserve its union and dignity:

> Old associations and former friendship induce me to venture to address to you a few words on the state of the country.
>
> I have read the President's Message. South Carolina says she intends to leave the Union. Her Representatives in Congress say she has already left the Union. It would seem that she is neither to be conciliated [n]or comforted. I command the Eastern Department, which includes South Carolina, Georgia, Florida, Alabama, and Mississippi. You know me well. I have ever been a firm, decided, faithful, and devoted friend of my country. If I can aid the President to preserve the Union, I hope he will command my services. It will never do for him or you to leave Washington without every star in this Union in its place. Therefore no time should be lost in adopting measures to defeat

> those who are conspiring against the Union. Hesitancy or delay may be no less fatal to the Union than to the President, or your own high standing as a Statesman.
>
> It seems to me that troops should be sent to Charleston to man the Forts in the Harbor. You have eight companies at Fort Monroe, Va. Three or four of these companies should be sent without a moment's delay to Fort Moultrie. It will save the Union, and the President much trouble. It is said that to send at this time troops to that harbor would produce great excitement among the people. That is nonsense, when the people are as much excited as they can be, and the leaders are determined to execute their long-meditated purpose of separating the state from the Union. So long as you command the entrance to the City of Charleston, South Carolina cannot separate herself from the Union. Do not leave the Forts in the harbor in a condition to induce an attempt to take possession of them. It might easily be done at this time.
>
> The Union can be preserved, but it requires firm, decided, prompt and energetic measures on the part of the President. He has only to exert the power conferred on him by the Constitution and Laws of Congress and all will be safe, and he will prevent a Civil War, which never fails to call forth all the baser passions of the human heart. If a separation should take place, you may rest assured, blood would flow in torrents, followed by pestilence, famine, and desolation. . . . A separation of the States will bring with it the desolation of the Cotton States, which are unprepared for war. Their weakness will be found in the number of their Slaves, with but few of the essentials to carry on war, while the Free States have all the elements and materials for war, and to a greater extent than any other people on the face of the Globe.
>
> Think of these things, my dear General, and save the country, and save the prosperous South. . . . Peaceable secession is not to be thought of. Even if it should take place, in three months we would have a bloody war on our hands.[13]

A reporter, discussing the letter with Wool, asked whether the army would divide if secession came. With great animation, the general replied: "Do you think, sir, the army is going to fail the country at the moment it is needed? No, sir. Furthermore, I allow no officer or man under my command to admit to the possibility of disunion, and if I hear that anyone has spoken in favor of it, I will court martial him with all possible expedition; and General Scott feels as I do, sir!" As newspapers applauded Wool's call for action, the *Boston Atlas* cited the Cass letter and quipped: "Such soldier talk assures the land. It isn't wholly bursted. Our *Wool* against their cotton. And secession schemes are *worsted*."[14]

Wool became increasingly troubled over the fate of the nation. South Carolina was having another "political spasmodic convulsion," he wrote Congressman Olin on December 10, 1860, and was prepared to leave the Union. The federal government must act. An "energetic execution of the powers conferred under the constitution and congressional acts," with "a judicious application" of military force, would rescue the country from dissolution. "Can a parallel case be cited of a government destroying itself?" Wool mused. "Imbecility and timidity, if not treason in high places," he wrote Thomas Vail, a Troy banker, was threatening to dissolve the Union and precipitate a civil war. "Woe unto those who shall be the authors of as great a calamity, or shall be the cause of the destruction of the only free government on the face of the globe, the last hope of the oppressed of the world."[15]

In Washington, Wool's plea fell on deaf ears. On December 13, Secretary Cass pressed President Buchanan to reinforce the forts guarding Charleston Harbor, but Buchanan refused. The secretary then brought Generals Scott and Wool and Attorney General Jeremiah Black to a meeting with Buchanan. The president again refused to act. Cass resigned from the cabinet. On the December 20, the day South Carolina passed an ordinance of secession, he penned a letter to Wool. "We have indeed fallen upon evil times," Cass said, and he was "unwilling to remain and share in the responsibility" for what must follow. Cass recited the reasons for his decision, and closed the letter with a tribute to his friend of over forty years: "And now, my friend, farewell. You have been a gallant soldier, and by your noble deeds have inscribed your name upon the rolls of your country. May the evening of your days be without a cloud, though I fear they will not be."[16]

When secessionists drove out of Charleston harbor the *Star of the West*, loaded with provisions for Fort Sumter, Wool felt spurred to pledge his sword to the president-elect. On January 11, 1861, he wrote Abraham Lincoln, enclosing clippings of his recent letters to Cass and Olin. "Presuming that I am not altogether unknown to you," Wool began, "I have taken the liberty to transmit herewith two printed letters which indicate in part my views on the state of the Country." The preservation of the Union was paramount to him, and he offered his assistance in seeing Lincoln "placed in the Presidential Chair" on March 4. Citizens in eight states had responded to his letters and expressed "in the loftiest tone of patriotism" their determination to preserve the Union. "Any number of men and any amount of money" were available to sustain the government. Wool assured Lincoln that he was no partisan, "but a dedicated, firm, uncompromising and devoted friend of the Union, the whole Union, and nothing but the Union."[17]

Lincoln thanked Wool for his "patriotic and generous letter," and spoke knowingly of the general's military career and exploits. He had given "little attention to the military department of government," but in making future decisions he would have to rely on Generals Scott and Wool. "It affords me the profoundest satisfaction to know," Lincoln said, "that with both of you, judgment and feeling go heartily with your sense of professional and official duty, to the work."[18]

Wool doubtlessly hoped to direct the nation's armies if a crisis came. Only the enfeebled Scott stood between him and such a command. The general-in-chief was two years younger than Wool, but Scott was so obese he could not mount a horse, so rotund that he moved only with great difficulty. On the other hand, Wool, spare and alert at seventy-six, had disciplined himself in his habits and routine. Moderation was Wool's watchword. He believed that his military experience was equal to Scott's and that his knowledge of the army, gained from twenty-five years as an inspector general, probably surpassed that of his superior. He also knew the capabilities of as many young officers as Scott did, a factor that could be crucial if hostilities came. On February 2, 1861, Wool wrote Col. Lorenzo Thomas, a member of Scott's staff in Washington, saying he was anxious "to be with the general, to perform any services he may think proper to require of me."[19]

Momentarily, the eyes of the nation turned to a conference in Washington that sought to halt the drift toward war. Seven states had already passed secession ordinances and had chosen representatives to meet in Montgomery, Alabama, to create a confederacy. In the midst of the confusion, Virginia, on January 9, invited all states, "whether slaveholding or non-slaveholding," to send delegates to a conference in Washington on February 4 for the purpose of adjusting the "present unhappy controversies." Twenty-one states sent 132 delegates to what Horace Greeley, editor of the *New York Tribune*, called the "Old Gentlemen's Convention." It was a gathering of "political fossils who would not have been again disinterred but for the shock . . . [of] the secession movement." The New York legislature selected eleven delegates, and when one declined to serve, Wool was contacted and he agreed to fill the vacancy. A Democratic paper, surveying the Republican majority in the New York delegation, characterized them as "a deputation of weak-minded fanatics more fit to represent the whimsies of a Women's Rights Convention, than to confer with statesmen about matters of public moment."[20]

Wool reached Washington on February 7 and found that the conference had been in session for two days in the dance hall attached to Willard's Hotel. Former president John Tyler, of Virginia, had been chosen presiding officer, rules had been adopted, and a subcommittee of twenty-one—one representative from each delegation—was deliberating a peace proposal. David Dudley Field, an attorney and a Republican, represented New York. He and other radicals sought to delay the deliberations, anticipating a free hand in making policy after Lincoln's inauguration. While the subcommittee hammered out a draft in secrecy, the other convention members sought diversions in the city. Some of the delegates visited General Scott and talked with him about army matters; others paid their respects to John Tyler. A round of parties and receptions dominated the social scene, as the Democratic administration prepared to leave office.[21]

Wool regularly reported to Sarah on events in the capital. Convention members, he wrote on February 11, generally "appear to be conciliatory and anxious" to preserve the Union. Many delegates from the border, and a few southern states, felt that if the question were left to them, they could settle it in a few hours. The next day he attended Buchanan's last public reception, then went to Senator Stephen A. Douglas's party. Here the atmosphere was more relaxed and the crowd smaller. With time on his hands, Wool sat in the gallery of the House of Representatives on the thirteenth and witnessed the counting of electoral votes making Lincoln the new president. That afternoon, he noted, convention delegate John C. Wright, of Ohio, "died of a fit of some kind."[22]

On the morning of February 16, the subcommittee presented its proposals and debate began. There was "much political intrigue in and out of the convention," Wool wrote Sarah. "The Republicans were not united. We have a Seward and an anti-Seward party. We also have Democrats and anti-Democrats, all struggling for power . . . Between all these conflicting interests the Union may be lost." Commodore Robert F. Stockton had called and told Wool that he was in an enviable position—he was associated with no party and could vote independently. "I do not care whether he was sincere or not," the general quipped. "He put me in a good humor with myself."[23]

Within a few days, Wool became sick. The dampness of a Washington winter, overheated rooms, and irregular hours took their toll. Tyler, Alexander Doniphan, William C. Rives, and others also fell ill with lung congestion. For several days, Wool lay in bed at Willard's Hotel, his body racked by a deep-seated cough. A host of friends came by to see him, including Tyler, Governor John A. King, Attorney General Edwin M. Stanton, the New York delegates, and several ladies. "I am at least worth a dozen dead men. An old soldier is not so easily got rid of," he wrote Sarah on February 22. It was Washington's birthday and the anniversary of the battle of Buena Vista, but only a modest military parade trooped down Pennsylvania Avenue. The next morning, the president-elect arrived in Washington "very quietly and without noise, pomp, or circumstance," and checked into Willard's Hotel. The atmosphere in the capital was gray and somber. "How the times have changed," Wool said.[24]

On February 25, the delegates assembled to vote on the amended majority report and stayed in session until past midnight. By the next afternoon, amid much confusion, the chair had the roll called of the nineteen states still in attendance. Southern states' righters joined Republican radicals and voted eleven to eight to defeat the first of the seven proposals. There was a deadening silence. Then came a barrage of rebukes and insults. Several border state delegates wept like children. The meeting was quickly adjourned.[25]

The convention ended on February 27. Field left the conference to argue a case before the United States Supreme Court. The New York delegation was hopelessly divided 5–5, and the chair voided its vote. When Illinois shifted its vote to yes, the convention approved proposals appeasing the upper South and the border states. They were put together as the thirteenth amendment to the Constitution and carried to Congress. Tyler adjourned the "Old Gentlemen's Convention" sine die. "The result was satisfactory to all the conservatives of the South," Wool wrote Sarah, "and [the convention] was broke up in a good humor rejoicing at the result supposedly obtained." But in the chaos of the closing hours of Congress, the proposed amendment was all but ignored. Secessionists returned to their respective states, branding the convention an attempt to deceive the South.[26]

At General Scott's request, Wool stayed in Washington for Lincoln's inaugural. On the eve of the ceremonies, the general-in-chief introduced Wool and fourteen other ranking officers to the president-elect at Willard's. Lincoln shook hands and chatted briefly and shared a collation with them. On Monday, March 4, with riflemen lining the roofs of buildings along Pennsylvania Avenue, Wool rode to the capitol grounds in a carriage and helped place several batteries of light artillery in positions to cover the crowd gathering in the east park. The day was gray and cloudy with a threat of rain, but the skies cleared and the sun peeped through. Shortly after noon the official party arrived. Scott and Wool stationed themselves near two batteries at the north entrance to the capitol grounds, and remained there during the ceremony. The wind was cold and blew in gusts, and only occasionally could they hear Lincoln's high, shrill voice. When the president finished his address, the batteries fired a salute, signaling the end of the inauguration ceremonies. The next day Wool returned to Troy and resumed his departmental duties.[27]

In the meantime, the nation had divided. In late February, the Confederate States of America had been organized at Montgomery, Alabama, with Jefferson Davis as president. On March 1, Davis appointed P. G. T. Beauregard, removed by Scott as superintendent at West Point, a brigadier general, and sent him to Charleston Harbor. Confederate artillerists soon began firing practice salvos in the direction of Fort Sumter. In Washington, dozens of army officers, mostly in the lower grades, resigned staff and line positions to join the Confederate cause. Several southerners on Wool's staff packed up and left Troy for rebel service.[28]

On March 9, at his first cabinet meeting, Lincoln requested information on the situation at Fort Sumter. Could it be relieved? General Scott declared that a strong fleet bearing twenty thousand men was necessary to sustain the fort. Lincoln was appalled at the suggestion, and a few days later several newspapers, nudged by Secretary of

State Seward, who wanted no military confrontation, hinted that Sumter would be evacuated. Radical Republicans immediately cried out against such cowardice. Wool warned Henry Wilson, chairman of the Senate Military Affairs Committee, that evacuating Sumter would encourage disunionists to make further demands. The Confederacy was raising an army, while Washington did nothing but collect revenue in the southern states. "All is energy, activity, and efficiency on the one hand," the general declared, "and nothing but submission on the other."[29]

Finally, on April 1, the *New York Tribune* announced: "Fort Sumter to be Reinforced." A Union fleet loaded with provisions would be sent to the beleaguered federal garrison in Charleston Harbor. A second expedition would reinforce Fort Pickens on the Florida coast. By a week later, both flotillas were on the high seas. The next day, Wool watched military developments closely. On April 9, General Scott began preparations to protect the capital and secure neighboring districts. To implement his plans, he began slicing off parts of Wool's Eastern Department. He first severed the District of Columbia and the state of Maryland—two powder kegs of divided sentiment. By the thirteenth, he had deployed about one thousand regulars and marines and fifteen militia companies around the capital. Two days later, with word that reinforcements had reached Fort Pickens, Scott detached Florida from Wool's command and gave it a separate military status. With most of the southern sisters in rebellion, the old Eastern Department barely resembled its former self.[30]

On Sunday, April 14, the streets of Troy echoed with the news that Fort Sumter had surrendered the day before. Newspapers reported that waves of anger and indignation were sweeping New York and New England. Noisy crowds thronged railroad stations, anxious for news from incoming trains; there were calls for mass meetings; and militia commanders alerted their companies. By late afternoon, the city fathers of Troy had conferred with Wool and called a public meeting.[31]

On Tuesday at Troy, townspeople gathered at the Union Depot to hear patriotic addresses by John A. Griswold, Wool's nephew and a prominent businessman, Wool, the mayor, and others. Then by a voice vote the meeting requested the common council to raise a Trojan regiment. Afterwards, a group adjourned to Wool's residence on Ferry Street where the old warrior appeared and gave a short speech. Pointing to the Stars and Stripes flying over his headquarters, Wool, his eyes flashing fire, shouted with emotion: "Will you permit that flag to be desecrated and trampled in the dust by traitors? Will you permit our noble Government to be destroyed by rebels in order that they may advance their schemes of political ambition and extend the area of slavery? . . . My friends, that flag must be lifted up from the dust into which it has been trampled, placed in its proper position, and again set floating in triumph to the breeze. I pledge to you my heart, my hand, all my energies to the cause. The Union shall be maintained." The crowd cheered loudly.

Two days later, at a second "war meeting," the organizers announced that the council had voted $10,000 to fund a volunteer regiment. To stimulate enlistments, the city opened a recruiting office, sold cockades for men's hats, and encouraged churches and businesses to fly flags.[32]

Across the Hudson and downriver at Albany, Governor Edwin Morgan met with his staff and the military and finance committees of the legislature. The next morning, April 15, he began receiving telegrams from the War Department. Lincoln had issued a call for 75,000 militia for three months federal service. New York was asked to furnish the largest number, seventeen regiments, or about 13,000 men. To prevent clashes in the border state of Maryland, Governor Morgan was to send the New Yorkers to Washington by water transport, instead of by rail.[33]

On Saturday, April 20, newspapers reported more violence. The tiny federal garrison at Harpers Ferry, menaced by rebel troops, had destroyed the arsenal and retreated across the Potomac River. At the Norfolk navy yard in Virginia, the commander had scuttled several ships and evacuated the installation. On Friday, an angry mob in Baltimore attacked the train carrying the Sixth Massachusetts on its way to Washington. To avoid further bloodshed, Baltimore authorities sent civilian crews to destroy railroad bridges on the lines north to Harrisburg and Philadelphia. This severed all rail communication with New York. Wool's jurisdiction was whittled again—Scott added Pennsylvania and Delaware to the Military District of Washington.[34]

At Governor Morgan's request, Wool hurried to Albany. Morgan was besieged with requests, orders, and complaints. Secretary of War Simon Cameron had advised him to ignore military channels in procuring arms for the New York regiments. New York City businessmen demanded that Morgan speed up the process of raising troops, saying agents from other states were placing large orders in the port city. Morgan was making headway. The Seventh New York had sailed from New York City for Washington on Friday, and three other regiments were en route to Manhattan by train. But he needed Wool's assistance. The general had received no instructions regarding the emergency, but he was eager to help. Morgan had already wired the superintendent at the Springfield Arsenal to ship muskets to the state rendezvous at Elmira, Albany, and New York City. Wool now advised his departmental quartermaster and commissary officers in New York City to provision and arrange water transportation for the New York regiments arriving there.[35]

Wool spent most of Sunday, April 21, at his headquarters in Troy, sending telegrams to federal arsenals, armories, and clothing depots in the Eastern Department, inquiring about their inventories. State governors, he quickly learned, were ignoring military channels and making direct requisitions for muskets, ammunition, and blankets and uniforms. Confusion loomed everywhere. As Wool sat at his headquarters, a group of businessmen were holding a mass rally in Union Square in New

York City to honor the return of Major Anderson and his men from Fort Sumter. They also organized a Union Defense Committee (UDC) to spur the war effort. Maj. Amos B. Eaton, commissary officer in the city, telegraphed Wool for assistance. "We are laboring under a great disadvantage here," he said, "for want of an erstwhile and common military head to give force and efficiency to all the military operations of this point. . . . Someone to take the responsibility is wanted—somebody with a history—somebody who will be obeyed." Would Wool come to New York? He notified Morgan that he was ready "to assume any responsibility" to arm and provision the New York regiments and he sent similar telegrams to the governors of Massachusetts and Pennsylvania. On Monday morning, Wool and his aide, Lt. Richard Arnold, left on the train for New York City.[36]

Wool took quarters at the St. Nicholas Hotel. The city of New York, with a population of over one million, was swarming with soldiers. Tents and makeshift barracks covered every park, and a mountain of supplies and equipment lined the wharves. Soon after Wool's arrival, Thurlow Weed, a former editor of the *Albany Evening Journal*, and several members of the UDC paid him a visit. Weed, a prominent Republican, urged the general to move his lodgings to the Astor Hotel, where the UDC had its offices. The general declined, explaining he had directed incoming dispatches, letters, and telegrams to the St. Nicholas. The general expected messages hourly and wanted no interruptions. During the evening, Wool and Arnold and several clerks sorted requests from nine state governors. Governor Andrew Curtin wanted arms and ammunition for his Pennsylvania troops and for Ohio Valley volunteers arriving daily in Harrisburg. Wool dispatched telegrams to several federal depots. Within hours hundreds of crates bearing 10,000 stands of arms and 400,000 cartridges were moving by rail from New York to Pennsylvania.[37]

On Tuesday morning, April 23, Wool's quarters at the St. Nicholas was bustling with activity. In the East, the governor of New Jersey voiced alarm over the defense of Fort Delaware, and Wool advised him to order out two companies of militia or volunteers to occupy it. He sent the same instructions to the governors of Massachusetts, New Hampshire, and Rhode Island, when they requested permission to use federal army and naval installations. The general even approved a plan by the mayor and common council of New Bedford to build new defensive works at Clark's Point. The works would be turned over to the federal government on demand. Wool also telegraphed the governors in the western states. He requested Governor Richard Yates of Illinois to occupy the St. Louis Arsenal—and ship 5,000 muskets to Ohio and 3,000 to the governor of Wisconsin, keeping the rest for his own troops. Indiana, New Jersey, Vermont, and New Hampshire also received arms in the course of the next few days. In all, Wool sought to protect federal installations and encourage eleven northern states to arm for war.[38]

Events were transpiring at a lightning pace. On the afternoon of April 23, the executive board of the UDC visited Wool at the St. Nicholas. They represented the businessmen, bankers, and politicians who had met a week earlier and organized to make New York City a center for government contracting, and to place the state on a war footing. The twenty-odd organizers included the Wall Street clique of Richard N. Blatchford, Moses H. Grinnell, and William Evarts, who, along with Thurlow Weed, had been Seward delegates in the 1860 Republican convention. The UDC had ignited the fires of patriotism. The common council responded to the influence of the UDC and appropriated one million dollars for its use. The funds would be underwritten by short-term city bonds bearing 7 percent interest. The UDC also informed President Lincoln of its creation. They requested that the departments of war, navy, and treasury send agents to New York to expedite the war effort. They were needed to purchase and charter ships, procure munitions and supplies, and forward troops. The UDC also sought Wool's cooperation in their endeavors.[39]

The general found the UDC executive board gracious, respectful, and flattering. Several members were old friends. Dix, Draper, and others were gravely concerned as to the predicament of the national capital. The War Department had authorized Governor Morgan, Evarts, Blatchford, and Grinnell to advise the Navy on purchasing steamships, and had directed Morgan and Alexander Cummings, publisher of the *New York World*, to work with the army in moving troops to Washington. The War Department had also placed $2 million in the hands of Dix, Mayor George Opdyke, and Blatchford for purchases and contracts. The UDC board wanted Wool, by virtue of "his military position," to approve all their acts. Dix handed the general a letter of understanding, whereby he would endorse UDC contracts to procure provisions, clothing and equipment, and to obtain vessels to transport soldiers to Washington and elsewhere in his military department. As he signed the letter "in behalf of the Government of the United States," Wool remarked that he had assumed "a fearful responsibility" and probably "would be the only victim." The general also agreed to meet regularly with the board to advise them on military matters and to consider contracts.[40]

There was one last item. The large Cunard liner *Kedar* had arrived from Liverpool the previous day and discharged her cargo. Moses Grinnell and other UDC members had approached her owner and was able to charter the ship for twenty days at $2,500 per day to carry supplies and troops. The UDC would assume the expense. Would General Wool approve the charter-party? Wool agreed and after a brief discussion about the need for other steamships, the committee departed.[41]

That evening, editor Cummings came to see Wool. A close friend of Secretary of War Cameron, Cummings had authority from the secretary to act with the army in purchasing and shipping supplies from New York City to Washington. He showed the general his instructions and asked him to endorse them. At the bottom of the paper, Wool penned that Cummings would confer with his commissary and quartermaster officers for "instructions as will enable him to carry out the intentions of the Secretary of War." Cummings also would work with the UDC "in the discharge of the duties" that the secretary might require. That night, Wool sent a letter by special courier to General Scott, indicating in some detail his actions.[42]

On Wednesday, April 24, at an early hour, several wealthy businessmen, sporting militia commissions, presented themselves to Wool as volunteer aides. All had ties with the UDC. Included were George Schuyler, William Jay, William P. Jones, Alexander Hamilton Jr., and LeGrand B. Cannon. In the days to come, Wool would become particularly attached to Cannon. The son of an iron manufacturer in Troy, his daughter had married into the Griswold family, and had been involved in organizing the UDC. An amiable, precise, little man with an inexhaustible repertoire of stories, Cannon was an able conversationalist and pleasant companion. Wool eventually placed the fellow Trojan on his regular staff.[43]

As expected, problems developed. Transports carrying New York and Massachusetts regiments faced unruly crowds in landing troops at Annapolis. The navy called on the old frigate *Constitution,* now a training ship, to cover the debarkation. Fortunately, aid was in the offing. The UDC found two ships—the *Monticello* and the *Mount Vernon*—and requested Commodore Samuel L. Breese, commanding the Brooklyn navy yard, to charter and arm them for convoy and blockade duty. Wool arranged for the *Monticello* to escort the *Kill von Kull,* bound for Annapolis, with steel rails, workmen, and animals—all provided by the UDC. The men were to repair the railroad tracks near Baltimore. The general also telegraphed Maj. Gen. Robert Patterson, head of the Pennsylvania militia, to send troops to guard Perryville, an alternate landing place to Annapolis.[44]

On April 24, a rumor circulated in the city that the Confederates had fitted out two privateers in Hampton Roads to prey on Union shipping. The UDC immediately informed Wool that the schooner *Quaker City*, loading for Havana, was available. He promptly signed an agreement securing the vessel for thirty days at $1,000 per day with the right to purchase her. The *Quaker City* sailed several days later with two thirty-two-pounder smooth-bore guns and two six-pounders on her decks. The vessel would accompany a convoy with troops to Annapolis, then proceed to Hampton Roads in Virginia and patrol the entrance to the Chesapeake. Wool authorized the captain of the *Quaker City* to seize every vessel entering the bay without a pass or clearance papers. The captain also had permission to take Confederate prizes. Wool was now part of a novel and potentially embarrassing operation. He had approved charters for a small fleet of merchant ships, armed and commissioned by a private party supposedly for national purposes. He was not sure of his authority to do so. The activities of the *Quaker City* soon caused Wool sleepless nights.[45]

On the evening of April 25, the general wrote Scott again, describing his actions and advised that his commissary was shipping thirty thousand rations daily to Washington via Annapolis—and would continue to do so until ordered to cease. Wool also wrote Cameron explaining the responsibilities he had assumed and added that he had received no directions from Scott. "I am exceedingly anxious," the general declared, "to know the views of the Administration and what it desires. I am running without rudder or compass." He was executing "high and important functions without orders," but felt that the emergency justified his exertions. Wool had cause for apprehension. Rumors were circulating that prominent politicians were speculating and committing possible fraud in government contracts. He sent one of his aides, George Schuyler, scurrying to Washington to call on Scott, Cameron, and Lincoln and determine where he stood in the matter.[46]

On Monday, April 29, telegraph communication between New York and Washington had been restored. Secretary Cameron immediately wired Wool to cancel a shipment of 500 boxes containing 10,000 muskets en route from the Springfield armory to Ohio, and redirect them to Governor Curtin of Pennsylvania. Ordnance officers and military storekeepers notified the general that they had suspended his instructions because they conflicted with orders from Washington. When Illinois governor Yates requested heavy guns to defend the town of Cairo, the general referred him to the War Department.[47]

That same afternoon, Wool joined a large crowd on Canal Street as Col. Elmer Ellsworth's celebrated regiment of Fire Zouaves marched past en route to the wharf. Smartly dressed in red caps and shirts, gray breeches and jackets, the unit carried rifles and Bowie knives and colorful silk banners. An escort of five thousand firemen accompanied them. As the procession approached, a courier rushed up to Maj. Gen. Charles W. Sandford, commanding the New York state militia, with instructions from Governor Morgan to halt the men. The regiment was over strength. Sandford handed the note to Wool, standing nearby. The general took a quick look at the message, and sang out: "Go on, it don't make any difference if you've got 1,100 men!" At the wharf the regiment boarded the steamship *Baltic* bound for Washington.[48]

On Tuesday morning, April 30, Wool learned unofficially he was being ordered back to Troy. Schuyler reported that the administration considered the emergency over. General Scott was in full control of military matters. That evening the UDC met and expressed their gratitude to the general for the "promptness and readiness with which he has yielded to their wishes and assumed great and heavy responsibilities." The old warrior had indeed exercised unprecedented authority. As one commentator observed, Wool had "chartered vessels, forwarded supplies, purchased ammunition, garrisoned forts, directed the movement of troops, ordered the occupation of navy depots and army arsenals from Portsmouth to St. Louis, supplied arms and ammunition of war to the Western governors." In a word, Wool had set in motion "the entire military force of the North." It had been an exciting and eventful week.[49]

On the evening of May 1, Wool received a formal letter, dated April 28, from Scott's office, instructing him to cease ordering supplies and return to Troy. The UDC would work thereafter with local bureau chiefs. Scott assumed that Wool was too "feeble" for an active command and told him to resume his ordinary department routine. Wool sputtered over the word "feeble," knowing no sick or infirm person could have performed the tasks he recently completed in New York City.[50]

On May 3 in New York City, Wool and Arnold attended a formal dinner at the home of millionaire John Jacob Astor. Key UDC members, Vice President Hannibal Hamlin who had spent the week in the city assisting the UDC, prominent journalists, and various friends were present. Although the dinner was to honor Wool, the after-dinner conversation quickly centered on the state of the Union. It was generally agreed that a naval blockade of the southern ports would prostrate the infant Confederacy, and that one massive rebel thrust at Washington would probably exhaust its energy and cause collapse. There seemed little doubt everyone would be home by Christmas, if not sooner. Wool, who often dominated conversations, said little. His thoughts doubtless were on obtaining an active command—and he knew that he held a claim on the men present for support in that endeavor. That afternoon he bundled up his files and returned to Troy.[51]

His warrior instincts at a boil, Wool was desperate for active duty. He kept in constant contact with his erstwhile aides—Cannon, Hamilton, Schuyler, and Jones—whom he asked to remain in New York City to work with the UDC. Moses Grinnell and several UDC members went to Washington to plead Wool's case. They contacted the New York delegation and other prominent politicians and informed them of the general's desires. They deplored Wool's recall and the administration's failure to recognize his recent services. Speaker of the House Galusha A. Grow of Pennsylvania, notified Cameron of the rumblings, and the Secretary of the War dashed off a short letter to Wool. Cameron appreciated the general's "long, able, and faithful services to the Government," and applauded his zeal and loyalty in the recent emergency. Wool had been asked to return to Troy in order to reduce confusion over orders and troop movements.[52]

In mid-May, Wool received exciting news. Cannon wrote that General Scott was considering sending the general to command Fort Monroe, the nation's largest military installation, at the entrance to the Chesapeake. Another volunteer aide, William Jones, confirmed this, citing Alexander Cummings, the government agent, as his source. The excitement, however, quickly ended. On May 25, iron-fisted, balding

Brig. Gen. Benjamin Butler, who had expedited the transportation of troops through Maryland, received the assignment. A week later, Jones wrote Wool that Scott had ordered Wool to Monroe, but Secretary Cameron refused to approve it, because of a rumor that he had suffered a paralytic attack. The general must immediately set the record straight in the newspapers, and, if possible, come to Washington. He must speak up or the politicians "will override every officer in the Army." Sensing pressure on a weak flank, Cameron on June 7 again sent Wool a conciliatory letter, thanking him for his epistle in May but promised nothing.[53]

In late June, Wool's chances for an active command improved. Jones reported that Vice President Hamlin had introduced him to influential congressmen, many of whom would support Wool for a command. Hamlin and Senator John Sherman of Ohio "will *do* something," he said. "They are both down on Old Abe's Cabinet." Two weeks later, Schuyler, a key aide, indicated that the War Department was dissatisfied with Butler, who could not control his troops. Generals Dix and Fremont were hovering about Scott's office, but there was a strong feeling against citizen-generals. Wool's friends could capitalize on Butler's problems, but they must "attack *the administration as a whole,"* and not single out the War Secretary. Cameron was "an obstinate man, and as long as he only is called to account, his colleagues do not care to interfere," Schuyler added.[54]

Wool's campaign for active duty now took a curious turn. On July 10, Wool sent Cannon a long "vindication" of his association with the UDC, with copies going to Hamlin and others in Washington. He opened the statement by saying, "I have frequently been asked why I am not in the field battling against the traitors of the United States." Cannon orchestrated the publication of the letter.[55]

On July 13, the Washington *National Republican* commented on the *Cataline* affair. This vessel, the paper declared, had been chartered by General Wool "in those days in April" when communication with Washington was cut off. On July 25, Wool joined the fray. He handed the newspapers a revision of his May 9 letter to Secretary Cameron. The *New York Times* summarized Wool's lengthy epistle and blasted Cameron and his "creatures," Weed and Cummings, for seeking to profit from government contracts. "The people will judge between General Wool and his persecutors," the editor stated. "We sincerely trust that the force of public opinion will compel the great contract plunderers to do justice in this most flagrant case of misuse of political power." In distant San Francisco, the *Evening Bulletin* echoed these sentiments. Speculators felt the general was interfering with their plans for fat government contracts, and this had influenced Cameron and Scott to shelve him.[56]

Wool won his campaign for an active command. Butler's fiasco at the battle of Big Bethel in Virginia on June 10, followed by Brig. Gen. Irvin McDowell's disastrous and embarrassing defeat at Bull Run on July 21, prompted a call for better leadership.

Brig. Gen. George B. McClellan, who had been successful in western Virginia, was brought to Washington to reorganize and command McDowell's army. McClellan was bold, brash, and full of ambition.

On the thirty-first, the New York delegation caucused and telegraphed Governor Morgan to urge that Wool be placed in "active service" at once. On August 5, with the *New York Times* and other newspapers supporting Wool's call to duty, Morgan asked Lincoln to send Wool to Fort Monroe. The president approved the request.[57]

On August 8, General Scott wired Wool, asking if his health would permit him to take command of the Department of Virginia. "I am ready and never in better health" was the enthusiastic response. A week later, at Troy, the general bid his family farewell, and he and Lieutenant Arnold took the train for New York City. "Despite his age," a New York reporter said, the veteran officer "looked full of health and vigor." Down in Virginia, Judity Page Rivers, wife of a Confederate congressman, who had known the veteran for many years, quickly passed judgment on the appointment. "If anybody asks you about General Wool, tell them on my authority that he is a conceited goose," she wrote. "He has, I suppose, some acquaintance with routine, but an acquaintance with him forty years' standing has never brought out one idea on his side."[58]

Fort Sumter had opened a new chapter in Wool's long military career. After three hectic and exasperating years in California, he had returned home expecting less vexatious duties. A close observer of the political scene, he became keenly aware of the rising specter of sectionalism, but he placed faith in his generation to compromise and settle matters. By the late 1850s, as the nation wallowed in indecision, apathy, and extremism, Wool called for direction and action in this sea of troubles. Few in government would listen and none would act. Once the Rubicon was crossed, he sprang to the defense of the Union, yearning for active field duty. Reverses at Bull Run and elsewhere brought pressure for a stiffer military stance—and provided an opportunity for the old general to be given an active command. His tenure at Fort Monroe, Virginia, which sat on the ramparts between union and disunion, placed him in the most challenging assignment of his long military career.

14

EPAULETTED GRANNIES AND THE CONCEITED GOOSE

Shortly after dawn on August 17, 1861, a small steamship emerged from the mist in Chesapeake Bay and steered for the engineer wharf at Fort Monroe, Virginia. As the boat docked, cannon on the ramparts of the sprawling stone edifice roared a salute. Gen. John Ellis Wool, the new commander of the Department of Southeastern Virginia, had arrived. Here at Fort Monroe, for nearly ten months, Wool would supervise the busiest military installation in the country. This was the major contact point between the Union and the Confederacy. Truce boats daily shuttled thousands of letters and dozens of civilian travelers across Hampton Roads to and from Confederate Norfolk. Here, Union fleets bound for the southern capes took on provisions and fuel from the depot outside the fort. Here, in the spring of 1862, McClellan established a base for his drive up the peninsula toward Richmond—and in the waters just offshore, with thousands of soldiers watching, the *Monitor* fought its historic duel with the *Merrimac*. From the wharves at Monroe, Wool sent troops to occupy Norfolk and Suffolk and open a road to Richmond. Wool's command of Fort Monroe was a complex and perplexing assignment.[1]

Fort Monroe was the largest coastal installation in the country. Named for President James Monroe, it sat on a narrow neck of land (Old Point Comfort) at the southern tip of the Virginia peninsula. Massive granite walls—twenty feet high and thirty-five feet thick—enclosed a seven-acre compound. A man-made moat eight feet deep and sixty feet wide encircled the walls. The compound contained barracks, a hospital, a chapel, and a tree-lined parade ground. The headquarters, where Wool spent many hours, was a two-story wooden structure, which sat in a grove of live oak trees on the east side inside the walls. Three of the seven fronts of the fort had casemated rooms that served as quarters and storage. Above, on the ramparts, over one hundred large antiquated cannon pointed east into the Chesapeake and south across Hampton Roads.[2]

Maj. Gen. Benjamin Butler welcomed Wool at the wharf. Wool had known the Massachusetts politician for many years, and, despite Butler's stoutness and a "strong obliquity of vision" (that is, cross-eyed), he was a vigorous man. On entering the compound, Butler, who knew of Wool's interest in horses, promptly handed him the reins to a sturdy gray. The aged officer mounted and wheeled about under the live oak trees with the dexterity of a younger man. The two generals toured the grounds, then crossed a drawbridge to see the warehouses and lighthouse on the beach and visit the stately Hygeia Hotel, a famous health resort. It was all familiar territory to Wool.[3]

Butler had reason for his graciousness: his command was in shambles. The rooms and halls of the Hygeia Hotel overflowed with wounded soldiers from the recent disastrous battle with Confederates at Big Bethel, nine miles to the northwest. Volunteer companies were rowdy and defiant. At Camp Hamilton, on the mainland near the village of Hampton, and at Camp Butler, to the southwest at Newport News on the James River, both officers and men questioned their terms of enlistments and clamored for their pay. One regiment had stacked its arms and mutinied. Butler arrested the officers and sent them to the artillery installation on the Rip Raps, a rocky shoal one mile out at the mouth of the James River. Then there was Butler's personal humiliation of being replaced without receiving another assignment.[4]

On August 20, 1861, Wool took command of the Department of Southern Virginia. His forces included about ten thousand men, mostly volunteers, whose principal commitment was to protect the fortress. Confederate lines lay forty miles to the north at Yorktown, where Brig. Gen. John B. Magruder had scattered nine thousand men and artillery batteries across the peninsula. Four miles south of the fortress, across Hampton Roads, was Confederate Norfolk, commanded by Brig. Gen. Benjamin Huger, with 7,500 men. Long-range rebel guns on neighboring Sewall's Point protected the entrance to the Norfolk harbor. Wool's jurisdiction encompassed less than sixty square miles, but the government considered it a strategic staging area for land and naval operations against the Confederacy.[5]

As was his history, Wool quickly tackled the problems at hand. He placed Butler in command of the troops at Camps Hamilton and Butler, and turned to personnel problems. In General Order 4, the general sternly warned soldiers on pass against plundering private citizens, saying they could be court-martialed and "punished with death." He and Butler then confronted the mutinous regiment at Hamilton—and found, to his embarrassment and chagrin, that the unit was the Second Troy Infantry. Wool lectured his fellow Trojans at length, offering to overlook the mutiny if they would swear to serve their country. The men gave their word, and the general ordered them paid and returned to duty. He did court-martial the regimental officers and discharged them from the service, however.[6]

Outside the fort, a small armada of ships rode at anchor in Hampton Roads. These vessels, Butler informed Wool, were to transport an expedition to capture the Confederate forts at Hatteras Inlet, 150 miles down the North Carolina coast. Privateers used the inlet as a base to prey on coastal shipping, and sleek, fast blockade runners brought in arms, ammunition, and clothing. Two forts made of logs and sand—Hatteras and Clark—guarded the entrance. In early August, Commodore Silas H. Stringham, chief of the Atlantic Blockading Squadron, based at Hampton Roads, had received orders to close the North Carolina inlets by sinking stone-laden hulks there. Butler obtained permission to join his troops with Stringham's naval forces. Wool sought to broaden the scope of the mission. The Hatteras undertaking, he wrote Scott on August 24, should be part of a larger plan to force the southern coastal states to withdraw their forces from Virginia to protect their coastal waters. With naval operations and 25,000 soldiers, Wool offered to make strategic landings to gauge the effectiveness of the idea. His suggestion was ignored.[7]

On Monday, August 26, Wool and Butler watched 860 men from Camps Hamilton and Butler file aboard the troop transports *George Peabody* and *Adelaide.* The expedition included Col. Max Weber's Twentieth New York, 200 men from Col. Rush C. Hawkins's Ninth New York Zouaves, 100 Coast Guardsmen, and Company B, Second Artillery. Wool placed Butler in command of the troops, with orders to return to Monroe as soon as he accomplished the object of the operation. Shortly after noon, Stringham's flagship, the *Minnesota,* weighed anchor and led a flotilla of eight ships out of the roads. After stinging defeats at Bull Run and Big Bethel, the Lincoln administration needed a victory.[8]

On the twenty-seventh, Stringham's ships reached the western end of Hatteras Island at dusk and anchored. The next morning, under a naval bombardment, Butler landed his Union soldiers in heavy surf and quickly overran Fort Clark. Artillerymen set up howitzers and a rifled cannon on the beach and pounded Fort Hatteras. Two days later, Commodore Samuel Barron, the Confederate commander, surrendered. Stringham loaded 715 rebel prisoners on his ships and sailed for Monroe. On August 31, in General Order 8, Wool announced news of the victory. Butler had captured thirty-one cannon, a brig loaded with cotton, a sloop carrying provisions, five stands of colors, and 150 bags of coffee! "This will do for one day," the old general wrote Sarah that night. Newspapers proclaimed the capture of Hatteras the first Union victory of the war.[9]

Contrary to Wool's instructions, Butler left a garrison at Hatteras. Upon his return to Monroe, he insisted that it remain, and Wool gave him permission to present his case to Secretary of War Cameron in Washington. The administration approved the idea, but Butler did not return to Monroe. He accepted the command of the newly created Department of New England. On September 3, Wool dispatched a vessel to the inlet with rations, artillery shells, and fresh troops to replace Weber's Twentieth New York. Brig. Gen. Joseph J. Reynolds went along to build a wharf and storehouse. But interest in Hatteras waned. Colonel Hawkins, commanding there, pushed the Twentieth Indiana into contact with rebel troops and suffered reverses.

Brig. Gen. J. F. K. Mansfield visited the site in mid-October, and reported that maintaining the beachhead there would be difficult. By December, Hatteras was a lonely Union outpost on the Carolina coast.[10]

Wool presided over a large staff at Monroe. Capts. Charles C. Churchill and William F. Raynolds, stationed at the fort, became his aides-de-camp. Volunteer aides LeGrand Cannon, Alexander Hamilton Jr., William Jay, and William P. Jones arrived from New York. Cannon and Hamilton were commissioned majors and Jay and Jones captains. Wool appointed Col. Thomas J. Cram, who had been with him in California, his topographical officer and chief of staff. Jones became provost marshal, while Cannon directed the processing of mail and interviewed persons passing through the lines. Thirteen orderlies assisted the officers; five were clerks and eight acted as couriers. Wool wrote Secretary Seward that he had more assistants at headquarters than he would need to direct an army in the field.[11]

In his daily notes to Sarah, Wool described his accommodations and routine. He had purchased Butler's furniture for $900 and designated one wing of the headquarters building as quarters for himself and his staff. The clerks and couriers lived in the other. Wool assured his Sarah that his health was excellent and that he had become "a temperance man" and drank nothing but coffee, tea, and water. He and his staff lived well and always finished their meals "with finger bowls." Much of his time was consumed by endless guests; government officials, businessmen, and friends, all came to visit.[12]

A mass of mail flowed through Monroe every day. Morning and afternoon, a steam tug flying a Union flag met its Confederate counterpart at a buoy in Hampton Roads, and returned with mail, light freight, and passengers. Clerks dumped letter sacks—some bearing 500 to 1,000 items—on a long table in the aides' room and began the tedious process of opening envelopes and packages. Letters with money, bank drafts, and correspondence with military information went to the general's desk. In turn, Wool routed to the State Department all large drafts on northern banks intended for imprisoned Confederates and all mail from foreigners in the South addressed to European cities. Mail and packages bound for the Confederacy were also examined. On each southbound letter, a clerk pasted a slip of paper over a five-cent piece, required by the Confederacy for delivery. The mail to and from Norfolk was continuous and unending.[13]

Wool received many letters addressed to him personally. Distraught mothers and wives in the North sought help to locate a brother, husband, or father in a southern prison. Students in northern schools requested passes to return home. Petitioners wanted to visit sick or aged parents or relatives in the Confederate states. Then there were special requests. Would Wool transmit a property deed through the lines, would he permit persons to go south to pay off debts, collect rent, or sell property? Even General Scott asked for a favor. In mid-September, Scott advised that a young bride had left her wardrobe in Richmond. Could Wool secure her trunk and ship it to Baltimore? "[W]e are both too old to sympathize with young people, who in a hurry and flurry of bridal excursions forget to take their necessary effects with them," Scott wrote. But "what are the interests of belligerents in their embargoes, blockades, and stoppage of mails compared with the joys of marriage."[14]

Every morning after breakfast, Wool interviewed individuals who wanted passes. A staff officer asked northbound persons from Norfolk to declare their allegiance to the United States and to sign a statement that they carried no war contraband. Each traveler and his baggage was searched for restricted articles, such as money, jewelry, and firearms. At first, Wool advised against searching women coming from Norfolk, but after inspectors at Baltimore discovered that several parties had pinned letters and money inside their clothing, he said nothing further. On October 9, the government restricted travel into the Confederacy, requiring authority from a department in Washington for a pass. But violations continued. At Monroe, officers found a key to a military cipher in the baggage of a woman carrying a pass from General Scott. An Episcopal minister arrived at the fort with his family and eighteen trunks and presented a letter from Secretary Seward. Each of his trunks contained contraband articles.[15]

At dusk on October 3, General Wool left Monroe on a hurried trip to Washington. Rumors were flying that he would replace Maj. Gen. John C. Frémont, commanding the Department of the West, at St. Louis. Newspapers hinted that Frémont faced a court-martial for fraud in his jurisdiction. The next morning, Wool attended a cabinet meeting, where Lincoln discussed the western command, its importance, and the need to investigate and correct problems there. Would Wool go west and straighten out the mess? The general agreed to go to St. Louis, but he asked for "full powers" to make decisions—an arrangement he enjoyed at Fort Monroe. Both Secretary Seward and Attorney General Edward Bates saw no problem, but Lincoln hesitated. He wanted the veteran officer to clean house at St. Louis but not to take full command. Wool would not accept these conditions and returned to Fort Monroe.[16]

The appointment "turned upon Frémont's remaining under my command with all his rats to plunder the government," Wool wrote Sarah on October 15. Lincoln wanted him "to correct the monstrous *errors* and plunder of men about Frémont, but wished to save the head." Wool had no wish to enter "the hornet's nest with the head remaining." The Lincoln administration, he felt, lacked the moral courage to contend with the rogues around Frémont. A week later, Wool delivered a judgment on Lincoln: "It would indeed be a god send if we had a man at the helm of state capable of directing affairs of state at this important crisis. I believe Lincoln's intentions are good and they say he is honest, but his limited knowledge necessarily subjects him to be the instrument of others." It was not a war to put down rebellion, the general grumbled, but a war to satisfy politicians. Maj. Gen. David Hunter, Wool's troublesome paymaster in Mexico, took over the Western Department.[17]

Throughout the fall of 1861, Wool clamored for resources to bolster the defenses of Fort Monroe. It was the most convenient place on the Atlantic to launch naval expeditions to seize southern ports or to undertake land operations against Richmond. Butler had recognized this and tried to strengthen the approaches to the fort. At the ashen ruins of Hampton, about eight miles to the north, he had soldiers build a line of fortified trenches; to the southwest, at Newport News, he installed a long-range Sawyer gun to harass Confederate shipping on the James River. On the Rip Raps, in Hampton Roads, the army had tested a high velocity twelve-inch rifled Sawyer in hope of reaching the rebel batteries guarding Norfolk. On the beach at Monroe, Butler also had tried to mount the Floyd Gun on a firing platform. Supposedly the largest piece of ordnance in the world, this monster cannon weighed over twenty-four tons, was fourteen feet long with a fifteen-inch bore, and could hurl a 420-pound ball nearly five miles. It lay in the sand near the lighthouse. Near Hampton, an observation balloon had been raised to spy on the Confederate lines, with an operator sending messages over a telegraph wire. A telegraphic network tied Monroe with Hamilton and Butler.[18]

Wool feared that a determined rebel assault could overrun Camp Hamilton and reach the fort. The main powder magazines, which were located inside the north wall, were unprotected. The general's first step was to build up the artillery support. He increased the number of light batteries at Camp Hamilton facing the Confederate defenses, asked the War Department for experienced artillerymen to operate the big guns at Monroe, and ordered the battery at Newport News to begin practice firing. Confederate ironclads constructed upriver near Richmond must be intercepted, if they attempted to descend the James. Wool also prescribed more drill and training to toughen the volunteer infantry. Almost daily, he and an aide rode out to watch the exercises at Hamilton, and occasionally he took newspapermen along. General Wool, wrote William H. Stiner, of the *New York Herald*, "invited me to ride out with him, and he is such a queer genius that had I declined the distinguished honor, he would have considered himself highly insulted." Wool pushed the training program hard, for he had no cavalry and doubted that the volunteer infantry would stand if attacked. To reduce the element of surprise, he ordered Colonel Cram to clear the terrain north of Hamilton—an area of a dense forest, tangled underbrush and small creeks. He had soldiers build outposts and cut roads for defending troops to strike the flanks of any enemy penetration.[19]

On his visit to Washington regarding the Frémont matter, Wool had warned Lincoln and his cabinet about the defenses of Fort Monroe. He also commented on the rebel ironclad under construction at Norfolk. The Confederates had raised the hull of the steam frigate *Merrimac*, and were covering it with iron plates capable of resisting cannon shot. When completed the vessel possibly could escort rebel steamers out to sea, and, even more disturbing, destroy shipping in the roads and paralyze Monroe as a military depot. Wool may have timed his comment on the *Merrimac* for effect, for the next day, October 5, the government signed a contract with a group of businessmen to deliver within one hundred days "a floating battery" to attack the Confederate ironclad. The group included his nephew, John Griswold, a banker and ironmaster of Troy. The previous August, Congress, in special session, had appropriated $1.5 million to build one or more "steel clad steamships or floating steam batteries." Griswold and his associates had promoted an experimental vessel, designed by inventor John Ericsson, which had a revolving turret and was touted as unsinkable. In mid-September, a navy board had studied a pasteboard model of the craft, and Lincoln approved its construction. The contract was the first the government made with the Griswold group, but they eventually constructed six more "monitors" for the navy.[20]

On November 3, Wool was stunned by the news that President Lincoln had appointed George B. McClellan, a thirty-four-year-old major general of volunteers, to succeed the retiring Winfield Scott as supreme army commander. Wool was the second ranking general line officer in the regular army, and probably assumed that he would succeed Scott. He wrote Sarah on November 4 (misdated October 4) in deep depression. "The news that reached me yesterday," he said, "has determined me to resign. It is utterly impossible for me to remain in service after the gross treatment I have received by the present administration." Close friends expressed concern. Colonel Cram's wife penned a poem entitled "A Nation's Ingratitude" and presented it to him. John Griswold and several New Yorkers hurried to Fort Monroe to smooth the old warrior's feathers.[21]

New York senator Ira Harris and Congressman John Jay had warned Lincoln that Wool would resign if a younger officer were placed over him. The general's patriotism was unshakable, they said, and, although elderly, he commanded with decision, energy, and good judgment. Moreover, Wool was a national symbol, the hero of two wars who could not be ignored or disgraced. Lincoln reflected on this and privately instructed McClellan on November 1 to let "Wool's command be excepted" from his control. The young general sent Wool a courteous request for information about the Monroe salient—and the crisis passed. However, as long as Wool was stationed at Fort Monroe, McClellan never exercised complete control over all the Union forces there.[22]

In the early fall of 1861, Wool had turned his attention to the six or more thousand black refugees clustered in shacks at Hampton and around Camps Hamilton and Butler. A majority were slave families who had fled into the Union lines when Confederate forces occupied the Yorktown area. Butler had drawn on the Confiscation Act, which permitted generals to seize enemy property, and classified the blacks as "contrabands." He set up a program of "protection for work." Pvt. Edward L. Pierce, an attorney and abolitionist serving in the Third Massachusetts, became the supervisor. Pierce divided the men into details, assigned jobs, and distributed food and clothing from the army commissary. The blacks labored on breastworks at Hamilton, served as stevedores on the wharves at Monroe, and became personal servants to officers and civil officials.[23]

Wool expanded Butler's program. He assigned contrabands to the Hatteras expedition to work as cooks, firemen, and gunners' assistants. In early September, he welcomed the American Missionary Association's efforts to open a day school for black children at the old Chesapeake Female Seminary near Hampton. But as the number of blacks fleeing Virginia increased, Wool faced the dilemma of overcrowding around the army camps. In mid-September, he complained to the War Department and asked for relief. The government ordered a large number of able-bodied blacks and their families shipped to Washington to work on military defenses there. It also recruited one thousand blacks as service personnel to accompany the Port Royal Expedition being outfitted in Hampton Roads.[24]

In mid-October Wool instituted a support program for the contraband families. Army officers and civilian personnel employing black men and women had to subsist them and contribute eight dollars a month for males and four dollars for females to a special fund. The quartermaster drew on these monies to provide clothing and other needs, and used the remainder for the sick, dependent, and aged. On November 1, Wool again altered the program. He divided the contrabands into two groups: all able-bodied men over age eighteen; and all the dependents, the sickly, and the aged. The army provided the first group a daily ration and deposited $10 per month in a special fund for allowances and clothing; the second group also received one daily ration but only $5 per month. But there was another incentive. For good behavior, each able-bodied worker could draw $2 per month for his own use, and those in the dependent category $1. Men doing heavy work received "incentive wages." Wool viewed the program as an opportunity for the blacks to prove themselves responsible and deserving of freedom.[25]

Occasionally, a sensitive situation arose. One day, a Maryland planter came to the fort and demanded a black girl he claimed to own. He said several soldiers in an Illinois regiment recently transferred from Maryland to Monroe had abducted her for purposes of prostitution. The planter presented a letter from Gen. John A. Dix, commanding the Middle Department, at Baltimore, urging Wool to surrender the girl. Maryland must be kept quiet, Dix warned, and loyal citizens guaranteed their property. Wool refused to honor the request. Dix complained to Secretary of War Cameron, who issued the slave owner an order for her release. When Wool again refused to consider the matter, Colonel Cannon took the planter aside and sent him to the Illinois commander. When the Marylander presented his case at regimental headquarters, the colonel and his officers immediately challenged him for the insult—and the planter fled. A government official later asked why Wool refused to obey the War Department order, and Cannon said that the general refused to use the army to return slaves.[26]

The final chapter in Wool's contraband policy was written in the spring of 1862. In response to a House resolution requesting information on blacks in his department, he appointed Colonel Cram to head a commission to assess the program. In late March, Cram reported that approximately 1,500 blacks were in the Monroe district, with about 600 employed as laborers and living in barracks. The men needed clothing, and some complained of overwork, harsh treatment, and unfair pay. The Cram commission recommended that a civilian superintendent take charge of the contrabands. They should be paid according to skill and industry, and the army quartermaster should continue providing rations and housing. Wool endorsed the proposals and on March 18, shifted the contraband program to civilian control. The general wrote Sarah that he had no intention of liberating slaves: "My object is simply to prevent him from being a tax on the government. Here I require them to work in order to support themselves, leaving the question of freeing them or otherwise to Congress."[27]

Visitors to Fort Monroe in the fall of 1861 occasionally viewed the old general as an anachronism. Some saw an aged, hard-crusted little man, petty and conceited, a relic from another age who quoted the rulebook and fussed over his department like a mother hen. Others found the veteran officer cordial, gracious, and thoughtful, a man who possessed a phenomenal memory for names, faces, and facts, who spoke often of family and friends, and of his love for the Union. Stiner, the reporter for the New York *Herald,* in a letter to his wife, drew a sharp sketch of the general. Wool's character, he wrote, "is a conglomeration of oddity, vain conceit and a huge contempt for troops who are not of the Regular Army." In Wool's eyes, "an officer who has not graduated from West Point [was] . . . not fit to command." The journalist labeled Wool an eccentric and a martinet.[28]

Naval officers occasionally grumbled about Wool. In late October, the Port Royal Expedition—a fleet of fifty-five vessels, the largest amphibious force ever assembled by the United States—lay at anchor in Hampton Roads, waiting for clear weather to sail. Both army and naval officers found the general convivial and eager to entertain. But as the days dragged on and supplies dwindled, Wool balked at furnishing rations for Brig. Gen. Thomas W. Sherman's 17,000 troops. He complained to Secretary

Cameron about the requisitions and labeled the expedition "the worst-managed" operation he had ever seen. A deserter, indeed, had just jumped ship with the signal book and a batch of important papers. The naval commander of the expedition, Commodore Samuel F. Dupont, felt harassed by Wool, and asked his superiors in Washington to have the "old goose" removed from command. On October 29, the fleet left the roads for the southern capes.[29]

In December, cold weather engulfed the Virginia coast. Sarah Wool mailed a shawl and scarves and lectured her husband about the drafts in his quarters. The old soldier, however, paid little attention to the chilly weather. He rose as usual before dawn, called his orderly to build a fire, and by the time "the musicians" had finished reveille, he was dressed and out for a walk. After breakfast he spent the morning in his office. Around noon he and an aide took a horseback ride, and ate lunch at two o'clock with guests. He spent the afternoon at his desk, in the camps, or showing dignitaries around the fort. In the evening, Wool took walks alone around the fort. The "slim, bent form" of the general, Charles Cowton recalled, was a familiar sight to the sentinels on the ramparts. Early in the morning, or at sunset, he made his rounds, wearing a close-buttoned frock coat and a glazed black cap of Mexican War vintage. In the evening, using a kerosene lamp for illumination, Wool studied reports and wrote letters before retiring at ten o'clock. It was a rigorous schedule for a man nearing eighty.[30]

On the long winter evenings, Wool thought of friends and family in Troy. He wrote the Reverend L. W. Kennedy about McClellan, "the rising star with six hundred and sixty thousand men" under his command. At the time of McClellan's appointment, he had given serious thoughts to resigning, to throwing his commission "in the face of the incubus that hung so long" over the army. But he had changed his mind. "I am content, although I may be made to suffer for being too loyal to my God and my country," Wool confided. In letters to relatives, he commented on the progress of the war. The government, he wrote his niece Harriette, had 250,000 men camped in and about Washington "doing nothing." Elsewhere, Confederate and Union armies were standing still "looking at each other." What a comment this was "on the military genius of our country."[31]

Early in 1862, Wool tried to initiate a prisoner of war exchange. The Lincoln administration had no formal policy on war prisoners, so generals in the field made exchanges as they could. The situation became complicated in the fall of 1861 when the Union navy captured a Confederate privateer, declared its captain, Walter W. Smith, and his crew pirates, and condemned them to death. The Confederate government reacted immediately. Six Union colonels captured at Bull Run were made to draw numbers, and Michael Corcoran, the popular Irish commander of the Sixty-ninth New York Militia, was declared a hostage for Smith. If Smith was hanged, Corcoran would die also. The Confederates demanded that privateer crews be considered regular war prisoners.[32]

On January 13, at the request of Secretary of State Seward, Wool asked General Huger, commanding at Norfolk, whether Smith could be exchanged for Corcoran. Huger replied that his superiors at Richmond would honor no exchanges until the Union changed its views on the status of privateers. In early February, Wool tried again. Methodist Bishop E. R. Ames and Hamilton Fish, a former senator from New York, arrived at Fort Monroe. They carried Lincoln's authorization to proceed to Richmond and seek arrangements to send supplies to Union prisoners. Irish groups, Tammany Hall politicians, and others wanting Corcoran released, may have influenced their unofficial trip. Wool notified Huger of the "humane and merciful mission" of these "honorable gentlemen"—and added that he also wanted to discuss prisoner of war exchanges. Huger replied that two Confederate commissioners would meet Ames and Fish at Monroe, sparing them the necessity of traveling into the South. As for exchanging prisoners, he reiterated the Confederate demand regarding privateers. Their errand of mercy blocked, Ames and Fish returned to Washington.[33]

On February 11, 1862, Secretary of War Edwin M. Stanton, who had replaced Cameron, instructed Wool to seek a formal prisoner exchange on a man-for-man and grade-for-grade basis. The rest of the prisoners would be paroled to their own homeland until exchanged. Confederate privateers, he declared, would be considered as regular prisoners. With this shift in Union policy, the Confederates agreed to discuss exchange possibilities. At noon on Sunday, February 23, Wool, Cram, and Cannon met three rebel commissioners—Huger, Howell Cobb, and Col. Ortho R. Singleton—at the mail buoy and dined aboard their tug. They drew up guidelines for a general prisoner exchange and parted.[34]

Wool forwarded the plans to Stanton. The general questioned several provisions. Cobb had recommended that all prisoners "be discharged or paroled within ten days after their capture" and be delivered to "the frontier of their own country." Wool objected to the use of the word "frontier." Accepting the word, he believed, would recognize the Confederacy as a separate nation—and negate the official view that the South was in rebellion. Regarding the delivery of prisoners, Wool said there was an imbalance in the number of prisoners held, the Union forces having recently captured 13,000 at Fort Donelson. Wool felt the exchange should apply to prisoners thereafter taken. Stanton shared Wool's objections and advised him to restrict exchanges to a one-to-one basis.[35]

On the morning of March 1, Wool met Cobb again in Hampton Roads. He informed the Confederates that their insistence on the use of the word "frontier," plus the prisoner imbalance, precluded his accepting a general exchange arrangement at that time. The privateer crew had been released from confinement and could be exchanged on a one-to-one basis. With their negotiations at an impasse, the general invited his guests to dine—sandwiches, cheese, whiskey, and claret—and everyone parted in a "very agreeable state." In the weeks that followed, Wool tried to arrange one-to-one officer exchanges with Huger, but had no luck.[36]

On February 16, the steamer *Planet* docked at Fort Monroe loaded with large spools of submarine cable. The government was making a major effort to open telegraphic communication between Washington and the fort. McClellan planned to use Fort Monroe as a base for a large-scale campaign against Richmond. Crews had laid a cable from Wilmington, Delaware, down to a station at Cherrystone Inlet near Cape Charles, which lay across the Chesapeake from Monroe; a line also stretched from Wool's headquarters up the beach about a mile. A link across the bay was needed. It took three hours to send dispatches by packet boat to Cherrystone for transmission to Washington. Wool viewed the cable activity with great interest, for he had stressed repeatedly that Fort Monroe was the proper starting point for striking the Confederate capital at Richmond.[37]

Soon after taking command at Fort Monroe in August 1861, Wool had urged an early attack on Richmond. He suggested landing troops on the west side of Hampton Roads, seizing the railroad junction at Suffolk, and marching north toward the rebel capital. He believed he could capture Richmond with 25,000 men. The idea may have originated with Butler, who earlier suggested taking Suffolk, which would cut the railroad link between Norfolk and Richmond and menace the Weldon Road, the principal highway from eastern Virginia south into the Carolinas. News of the *Merrimac* caused the general to shift his attention to the capture of Norfolk and the destruction of the ironclad. Naval officers supported his views. On November 11, Capt. Thomas O. Selfridge, commanding the *Cumberland*, urged his superiors to consider a joint army-navy attack on Norfolk, and calculated the firepower required to silence the rebel batteries. Commodore Louis Goldsborough, commanding in the roads, pushed the idea in February 1862 as a way of destroying the Confederate threat to Union shipping. Several members of Congress also voiced interest in clearing the Norfolk salient. For the moment, however, the government looked to Gen. George B. McClellan for plans and prospects.[38]

During the early winter of 1861, McClellan had concentrated on raising and training a large army. Then in December, he fell ill with typhoid. On January 10, 1862, Lincoln, feeling pressure within government and party circles, called a series of policy meetings. McClellan attended the fourth session, but was vague and evasive as to his plans. Finally, in late January Lincoln ordered the Union land and naval forces to prepare for "a general movement" against the rebels on February 22. He instructed McClellan to provide for the defense of Washington, seize the railroad near Manassas Junction, and march on Richmond. The young general immediately argued for delay.[39]

Secretary Stanton requested information from Wool on the Yorktown-Norfolk vicinity. Colonel Cram went to Washington and laid a set of maps before the cabinet. During the discussion the veteran engineer said that there was a better way of reaching Richmond than by marching up the peninsula. He introduced Wool's plan to reduce Norfolk and advance via Suffolk and Petersburg. This route avoided the vast Chickahominy Swamps north and east of Richmond. After the meeting McClellan asked Cram to explain Wool's plan to Brig. Gen. John G. Barnard, his chief engineer. Cram spent three hours with Barnard, but felt he made no impression. However, in mid-February Barnard asked the Navy Department for more information on Norfolk.[40]

On February 20, Wool dispatched Colonel Cannon to Washington with alarming news. That morning, a man landed from the truce boat, ripped open his coat sleeve, and pulled a note from the lining. A workman in Norfolk reported that the *Merrimac* had been launched, and within five days the ironclad would attack the Union warships anchored off Newport News. Simultaneously, Confederate General Magruder would move south from Yorktown and strike Camp Butler at Newport News. In Washington, Cannon warned the cabinet of the danger, and cited Wool's plea that additional warships and troops be sent to Hampton Roads. Stanton passed the information to the Navy Department and to General McClellan. On February 23, Cram hurried back to Washington with additional maps and plans. But the government was not ready to act.[41]

With this indecision, Wool feverishly prepared Fort Monroe and its environs for defense against the *Merrimac*. His principal concern was the fort. As Cannon later wrote: "The garrison was entirely composed of infantry volunteers, the armament was old-fashioned and of small caliber . . . and our batteries were as useless as musket-balls against the ironclad." Quartermaster and commissary stores covered the parade ground, while outside the walls the navy stacked immense quantities of ammunition for the coastal fleets, "all utterly unprotected, and with no means of removal." The twelve-inch Sawyer gun had been emplaced on the beach near the lighthouse, but it was unpredictable. The monster Floyd gun still lay in the sand. The batteries at Newport News, eleven miles to the southwest, had also proved ineffective. The two six-inch rifles and several eight-inch Rodmans there made little impression on armored river steamers. Wool feared that the rebels would use the heavy guns of the *Merrimac* to cover a landing at the News, in conjunction with General Magruder's attack on Camp Butler. If the Confederates overran the encampments, the *Merrimac* could shell the fort.[42]

The only hope was to ram the rebel ironclad. In January, Commodore Goldsborough had assured Wool that when the rebel vessel appeared, his warships would lower their anchors to "ready slung" and drop them on her and board. On February 28, Wool asked Stanton to press Secretary of Navy Gideon Welles for gunboats. Welles replied that Goldsborough had dispatched all available warships to North Carolina waters, but Ericsson's ironclad, now called the *Monitor,* had been launched, and was being towed south to Hampton Roads. She had never fired her two eleven-inch Dahlgren guns nor had she gone through a trial run. The capabilities of the vessel were in doubt.[43]

Wool placed Fort Monroe on high alert. Sentinels on the ramparts periodically scanned the horizon with telescopes, while telegraphers stood ready to flash orders to Camp Hamilton and Newport News. Workmen finished laying a cable across the Chesapeake. On Friday, March 7, the tension increased when foreign naval officers arrived at Fort Monroe by truce boat from Norfolk, and prepared their vessels to sail. They reported that the *Merrimac* had hoisted her flag and was ready for combat. Wool believed the ironclad would attack the ships and shore batteries at Newport News first. He advised the captains of the *Roanoke* and *Minnesota*, both 44-gun steam frigates, to move and join the two warships anchored near the News—the 50-gun *Congress* and the 24-gun sloop of war *Cumberland.* He instructed Gen. Max Weber, at Camp Hamilton, to ready his troops to march for Newport News. At dusk, the shipping in the roads withdrew one or two miles to the north and east.[44]

Saturday, March 8, dawned raw and cold. About noon, John O'Brien, a junior telegrapher scanning the choppy waters with a telescope, suddenly saw smoke on the horizon and shouted "It's the *Merrimac*!" Officers, reporters, and visitors scrambled to the ramparts. An alarm gun was fired and drummers summoned the Tenth New York to duty stations inside the fort. Wool telegraphed General Mansfield, at Camp Butler, to prepare for battle, and ordered Weber to start infantry companies from Hamilton to support him. The *Minnesota* and *Roanoke* frantically weighed anchor. The *Minnesota* got under way—but ran aground two miles from Newport News; the *Roanoke* lumbered into the channel and also grounded. In the meantime, the *Merrimac,* her engine wheezing and straining to produce power, pulled away from two armed consorts. Shortly before two o'clock, she lowered her ram and headed for the *Congress* and the *Cumberland,* both anchored about one thousand yards from shore. Union frigates, gunboats, and shore batteries threw a torrent of metal at the ironclad. Wool stayed by the chattering telegraph key at Fort Monroe, receiving messages every few minutes from Newport News.[45]

A *New York Times* reporter at Camp Butler described the ensuing holocaust: "A trap-door opens in her [*Merrimac*'s] plated roof . . . and a bellow of white smoke rolls up; then the roar and the crash of the 100-pound shell in the wooden wall of the frigate [*Congress*]. . . . Now she nears the *Cumberland* sloop-of-war, silent and still . . . from the sides of both pour out a living tide of fire and smoke. . . . Now the ram has taken her position bow on, and slowly she moves . . . upon the doomed vessel. Like a rhinoceros she sinks down her head and frightful horn, and with a dead, soul-rendering crunch, she pierces her [*Cumberland*] on starboard bow. . . . The gallant ship, her bow sinking gradually, finally gives a lurch to port, and with a shudder . . . goes down . . . carrying dead, living, and wounded with her."[46]

The *Merrimac* now backed away and turned east toward the *Congress*, which lay helpless in shallow water. His ship raked by a galling fire, the captain struck his colors, and two Confederate steamers—the *Yorktown* and the *Jamestown*—came alongside and prize crews swarmed aboard. Union sailors jumped into the water and started swimming ashore. Mansfield rushed infantry to the beach to fire into the enemy gunboats and drive the Confederates off the burning vessels. They drew back when the ironclad, with a well-placed shot, demolished Mansfield's headquarters. Setting the stricken *Congress* afire with incendiary shells, the *Merrimac* next steamed for the grounded *Minnesota*. But the ebb tide was running, the frigate lay in shallow water, and the day was ending. The ironclad hauled off and with her escorts headed south toward Norfolk, leaving behind a fearful wreckage.[47]

During the early evening of the eighth, Wool sent a succession of dispatches to the War Department (received next morning because the cable across the Chesapeake had snapped). He briefly described the highlights of the battle and assessed the damage. He also rushed a wagon to the News loaded with blankets for the sailors from the stricken ships, and sent caissons racing west with shells for the large guns there. Wool feared the ironclad would bombard Fort Monroe the next day, and ordered the wharves cleared. At nine that night, the Navy towed the *Monitor* into Hampton Roads. Colonel Cannon boarded her and briefed the captain on the day's events. Wool transmitted a telegram: "The iron-clad Ericsson battery *Monitor* has arrived. Will proceed to take care of the *Merrimac* in the morning." The little ironclad anchored alongside the towering *Minnesota*. At midnight the stricken *Congress* exploded. "Pieces of burning timbers, exploding shells . . . grenades and rockets filled the air . . . in all directions," an officer on the *Monitor* recorded. "We were about two miles from the wreck and the dull heavy explosion seemed almost to lift us out of the water."[48]

At daylight on Sunday, March 9, Wool and several officers rode to Newport News and took a position on a bluff. The morning dawned calm, cloudless, and warm. In the distance, tugboats hovered near the stranded *Minnesota*, their crews retrieving barrels of rice, flour, beans and other supplies thrown overboard to lighten the vessel. The *Monitor* got up steam. At seven o'clock, the *Merrimac*, accompanied by two steamers and two tugs, appeared on the horizon, slowly heading again for the News. The *Monitor* left the shadow of the *Minnesota* and steamed into view. The Confederate consorts fled.[49]

The rebel ironclad opened the battle by sending a shell arching over its new adversary. The *Monitor* replied with solid shot. A ferocious exchange of broadsides followed. The *Merrimac* kept maneuvering in an attempt to ram its opponent, but the smaller vessel was too nimble. By noon the *Monitor* had fired forty-one rounds, in many instances at a point-blank range of twenty feet. At one point, shrapnel burst near the pilot house and wounded Lt. John L. Worden, the Union commander, and the vessel drew back into shallow water for nearly a half hour. Then, its engines belching smoke, it returned to the fray—but the *Merrimac*, listing by her stern, retreated with her consorts, sending a parting shot shrieking overhead. The *Monitor* did not pursue. Along the shores that day, thousands of soldiers, sailors, and civilians had watched one of the most significant naval battles of the century.[50]

That evening, Wool sent messages to Washington, to Sarah, and to his nephew John Griswold. "The Monitor is a noble boat," he told John, one of the builders. She not only had saved the grounded naval vessels, but also "all the public property inside and outside the Fort." In messages to Stanton and McClellan, the general recited the events of the day, adding that the Confederate ironclad had departed in a sinking condition. He predicted that she would go into dry dock for repairs. It would be several weeks before she could return to the roads. The little *Monitor* was the hero of the hour.[51]

During the naval battle, rebel cavalry had been seen two miles north of Newport News, apparently to report on the outcome of the *Merrimac*'s attack. Wool had anticipated the Confederate reconnaissance. He increased Mansfield's forces to 8,000 men, leaving 2,000 at Hamilton and Monroe. He had also asked McClellan for two additional light batteries. McClellan ignored the request and advised the general to evacuate the News and fall back to Monroe. The safety of the fort, "I need not say to so brave an officer," was paramount. The young general quickly explained that these were suggestions only. But the presence of the *Merrimac*, McClellan added, "may very probably change my whole plan of campaign."[52]

On March 12, McClellan informed Wool that he was establishing a base of operations at Fort Monroe. He was no longer in supreme command of the army, having been demoted by Lincoln on March 1 to head the Army of the Potomac. Wool worried whether he would have to submit to McClellan. Around midnight, he reminded Secretary Stanton by telegraph that he would outrank McClellan by date of brevet, if he made his headquarters at Monroe. Stanton tactfully asked Wool to cooperate with the general. To soothe Wool's ego, he added that the military installation on the Rip Raps (formerly Fort Calhoun) had been renamed Fort Wool in his honor. A few days later, the general received more gratifying news. A military bill before Congress to reduce brevet pay for major generals in the regular army (Wool was the only one) and force certain senior officers into retirement had been amended to exclude his name. For several weeks Wool had waged a well-focused writing campaign. He could now relax.[53]

In mid-March, a variety of transports began disgorging troops, artillery, stores, wagons, and mules at Monroe. "Today, over 10,000 troops have arrived, and tomorrow about 4,000 more will come," correspondent Stiner reported on March 19: "Where they are going to I don't know, but the probability is that the whole force will move from here on to Richmond." Wool sent staff and quartermaster officers to prepare camps near Camp Hamilton and Camp Hampton for incoming regiments. As the build-up continued, McClellan again asked for control over Wool's troops. Secretary Stanton telegraphed the general to have Mansfield organize the forces into a division for service under McClellan, but he carefully avoided asking Wool to subordinate himself to the Potomac commander. Wool agreed to cooperate.[54]

While McClellan slowly assembled a massive army, Wool, per Stanton's orders, clamped down on news reporters at Monroe. "General Wool tonight," wrote Stiner, "has put the crowning shield on his atrocious, fossile, imbecile, & incompetent career" with his order that correspondents "*must submit their correspondence to him for approval.*" He would see the old general "doubly d d first," Stiner chirped to an aide, before he would submit a line to him. McClellan's officers cursed Wool, too. As rain showers drenched supplies and complicated unloading, the general diverted troop transports from landing at Hamilton to the sturdier wharf at Hampton. He explained to McClellan that the shift saved a three-mile march through knee-deep mud to reach their camps.[55]

At midmorning on March 23, Gen. Samuel Peter Heintzelman arrived at Fort Monroe with the Third Corps and the vanguard of the Army of the Potomac. Wool was on the wharf to greet him, his wife, Margaret, and their teenage son, Charles, and invite them to dine with him that evening. Heintzelman greatly admired Wool, who took the family on an inspection of the *Monitor,* or what Heintzelman and the southern newspapers were calling a "Yankee cheese box on a raft." Walking onboard, one could clearly see the indentations in the ship's revolving turret made by shot from the *Merrimac* less than two weeks earlier. "She appears to be perfectly invulnerable," Heintzelman noted.[56]

McClellan's preparations attracted a host of visitors to Monroe. Vice President Hannibal Hamlin brought a party from Washington to see the sights. Wool escorted them aboard the *Monitor,* where an officer handed out fragments from the *Merrimac*'s shells. Warships in the harbor fired salutes. The Hamlin party also scrutinized a large observation balloon floating near Hampton to study the Confederate lines. After Hamlin left, the English war steamer *Rinaldo* paid a visit. On making the rounds with Wool, the captain pointed to the *Monitor* and asked if it was used to raise wrecks. No, the general replied, the vessel was used for "making them." McClellan's officers made social calls. Wool told one group: "Gentlemen, you will have an easy march on Richmond; you will encounter no serious interruptions; the enemy will fall back as you advance." The general's only fear was that the rebels would retreat beyond Richmond, forcing McClellan to maintain a highly vulnerable supply line. "This old martinet talks at random," a colonel said as they returned to camp. "God help us if we have to look for guidance to such epauletted grannies."[57]

On April 2, the atmosphere at Monroe became tense. McClellan arrived on the steamship *Commodore*, and Wool invited him to dine the next afternoon at the fort. That night the general penned fretful letters to influential New York congressmen. He described how he had helped place McClellan's vast army of 75,000 men in camp and tried to untangle monumental supply problems. The Lincoln administration demanded that he defer to the young commander. He would cooperate, but he absolutely refused to be "commanded" by him.[58]

On April 3, Wool formally greeted McClellan and his staff. There was a forty-four-year difference in their ages, but the two men had some things in common. Both were short in stature, hardy in physique, careful of attire, and courtly in manner. Both were expert horsemen. Both could be haughty, impetuous, and exasperating, yet beneath the soldier there was warmth for family and friends—and there was burning ambition. There were differences, too. Wool felt that McClellan was a poor logistician, that he lacked the ability to direct a large field staff, make decisions, and handle supply problems. He adjusted his plans slowly, waiting for an extra gun, an extra regiment, or extra bit of information before giving orders. He sought excuses and created scapegoats as needed. McClellan viewed the precise old general as a relic from the past and a serious obstacle to his launching the Peninsula Campaign. The dinner was, nevertheless, a success. Wool rambled on and on about his military exploits, while McClellan enjoyed a cigar. They then walked along the ramparts together and agreed to meet for breakfast. The next morning, McClellan and Wool briefly discussed Stanton's order, just received, formally detaching Wool's forces from the Army of the Potomac. The general assured McClellan of support when his forces marched on Richmond, which lay only one hundred miles to the northwest.[59]

On April 4, with abandoned peach orchards glowing pink with the first blossoms of spring, McClellan's grand army pressed forward. "On to Richmond" was joyously shouted from one regiment to another. The advance, about 58,000 men with 100 pieces of artillery, moved in two columns. General Heintzelman led three divisions north on the old Yorktown road, while Bvt. Brig. Gen. Erasmus D. Keyes led two divisions up the Warwick road from Newport News. Long lines of wagons, guns, and ambulances lumbered behind. By nightfall, a cold, driving rain turned the countryside into a quagmire. The next day the Union right wing entered the swampy fields before Yorktown. Through the mist and rain, they saw Confederate cannons peering from behind extensive earthworks. Magruder had spread 11,000 men along a thirteen-mile front. Some 3,000 men were posted at the point between Yorktown and Gloucester on the York River, and the same number were to the west on the James River, in the salient between Warwick Court House and Mulberry Island. Between Yorktown and Warwick, 5,000 Confederates manned incomplete earthworks. On the Warwick road, Keyes unexpectedly struck a rebel concentration and halted. McClellan called for a siege train to pound the Yorktown line.[60]

Wool reported regularly on McClellan's progress. Steady rains, he informed Stanton on April 8, created transportation nightmares. The Union troops had discarded tons of baggage and equipment. Three days later, Keyes was still stalled near Warwick Courthouse, and rebels were on their way down the James to reinforce Magruder. On April 23, Wool urged McClellan to ask McDowell, lying at Fredericksburg, to make a feint toward Richmond. "Such a movement would help you," he said. He also offered to create a diversion by landing a small force and capturing Norfolk. But the impasse continued.[61]

While McClellan sat in the rain-soaked marshes before Yorktown, the *Merrimac* reappeared in Hampton Roads. On the morning of April 11, the rebel ironclad emerged from the fog with five consorts. She dueled briefly with the Union battery at Fort Wool, then anchored in the roads midway between Sewall's Point and Newport News. The *Monitor* and other warships had orders not to engage her. Commodore Goldsborough feared that McClellan's supply base at Monroe was an inviting target. He asked Wool to blacken the glass on the lighthouse at the fort and darken Fort Wool at night. The commander promised to set off fireworks if enemy gunboats made a run for the Chesapeake at night. The vigil continued into early May. Finally, on May 4, Wool sent Sarah a short note: "The bird has flown. Major General McClellan is in possession of Yorktown. The rebels abandoned their works last night and are running away as fast as they can. *I told you so.*"[62]

Within hours after McClellan occupied Yorktown and turned toward Richmond, Wool received a curious message from Secretary Stanton. "The President," he said, "desires to know whether your force is in condition for a sudden movement, if one should be ordered for your command. Please have it in readiness." The general became excited. What did the message mean? After a hasty conference with his staff, Wool telegraphed that his infantry and artillery, with ammunition and provisions, could move immediately if the operation were by sea. If by land, he needed two days to collect wagons and teams.[63]

Shortly before nine o'clock, in the evening of May 6, the revenue cutter *Miami* docked at Fort Monroe with a distinguished group of passengers. On board were President Lincoln, Secretary of War Stanton, Treasury Secretary Salmon P. Chase, and Brig. Gen. Egbert L. Viele. Wool boarded the ship, and in a brief conference,

Lincoln said he wanted to launch a joint naval-army operation to capture Norfolk and destroy the *Merrimac*. McClellan must have free access to the James River for his gunboats and supply ships. Wool was delighted. For months he had urged the capture of the rebel city, but the irascible Goldsborough would not cooperate. By tug Wool and Lincoln proceeded to the *Minnesota* to see the commodore. Goldsborough, a junior officer wrote, was "a huge mass of inert animal matter," who was "coarse, rough, vulgar, & profane" in his speech, and "fawning and obsequious" to superiors. Lincoln questioned the naval commander about an assault on Norfolk. The officer suggested that the navy try to draw the *Merrimac* into battle and ram her. Lincoln liked the idea, and asked Goldsborough to make the attempt the next day. After breakfast, Wool took the president to view the *Monitor* and out to the artillery outpost at Fort Wool. Naval warships soon commenced a heavy bombardment of the Confederate batteries at Sewall's Point, over three miles to the south. The *Merrimac* then came out, and the Union vessels, apparently lacking a plan to try a ramming attempt, withdrew. That afternoon, Wool took the Lincoln party to the mainland on a tour of the deserted village of Hampton. On returning, the president, bareheaded, reviewed the regiments at Camp Hamilton.[64]

On the morning of May 8, Wool discussed his plans for taking Norfolk with Lincoln. During the night he, Cannon, and Cram had studied maps and estimated the men and transports needed for a landing. The discussion was suddenly interrupted by an orderly with a message. A rebel tug had surrendered at Newport News, Wool announced, and the crew reported that Huger was evacuating Norfolk, moving his troops to Richmond. The *Merrimac* had orders to make a run for the James or York rivers.[65]

Lincoln asked Wool to organize a move against Norfolk that day. The general immediately sent orders to Camp Hamilton, and within hours, infantry began boarding barges, tugs, steamers, and other craft. At noon, Goldsborough ordered another bombardment of Sewall's Point—a possible landing place. Again, the *Merrimac* steamed out and anchored near the installation. By late afternoon, the assault was cancelled. A direct assault on Sewall's Point was deemed impossible. Another landing site was needed.[66]

On the morning of May 9, Wool, Cram, and Chase sailed on the *Miami* along the Virginia shore east of Norfolk to a summer resort called Ocean View. Cram took soundings and advised that troops could land there on a boat bridge. Norfolk was only nine miles away. In the meantime, Lincoln had studied maps and wanted to check on another site, a few miles from Ocean View. At dusk, Wool sailed with Lincoln and Stanton to the site, and the president went ashore and walked briefly along the beach in the darkness. On their return to Monroe, Lincoln questioned Wool about details of an expedition. How many men would comprise his force? About ten thousand was Wool's reply. Were General Huger's forces larger? "Well, possibly," the general said, "but that is of no consequence. Huger will not fight. He will run if I land." What about Wool's lack of cavalry and artillery and reliance on untried troops? "Mr. President," Wool stiffly responded, "you are not a military man and do not understand the situation. If you stay here forty-eight hours, I will present Norfolk to you." Lincoln instructed Wool to prepare that night for a landing at Ocean View.[67]

In the evening, a bright moon and hundreds of lights danced on the water. Officers hurried blue-coated soldiers, a small contingent of horses and mules, and several artillery pieces aboard barges, schooners, and ocean steamers at the wharf. At 11:30 P.M. the tug *Lioness,* with Cram and Weber aboard, hoisted a red light and led the flotilla out into the night. By dawn at Ocean View, a tug pushed a line of empty barges, roped together, onto the beach, and engineers laid planks for a bridge and pier. Soldiers filed ashore. A Confederate picket lurking in woods fled. General Weber formed his men into a column and started for Norfolk. The *Kansas* arrived with Wool, Mansfield, Chase, and Viele. Wool sent Mansfield, Viele, and Chase on horseback with an escort to join Weber.[68]

Within an hour, Wool followed with a small mounted force and a section of light artillery. At a crossroads, he saw an astounding sight. Hundreds of soldiers were resting in the shade. Secretary Chase was stamping about, cursing the "two cackling old hens" and demanding action. Union skirmishers had run into rebel pickets, and Weber had orders to halt if he met resistance. Weber and Mansfield argued heatedly over what to do next, causing Chase to fume. Wool pulled Mansfield aside and sent him back to Monroe for reinforcements. He divided the troops into two commands, one under Viele and the other under Weber. The column moved forward again. Scouts reported that Sewall's Point had been abandoned.[69]

Wool's column passed through vacant rebel entrenchments, and soon came in sight of the church spires in Norfolk. A civilian party, waving a truce flag, approached on the road, and the general trotted forward to meet them. Mayor William W. Lamb declared that Norfolk was an open city—and asked that no Union soldiers enter it. Wool ordered the men to pitch camp. He and Chase, with a mounted bodyguard, climbed into a carriage furnished by the mayor and rode toward Norfolk. At five o'clock, on the steps of city hall, one of Wool's aides read General Order 1 to a small crowd of townsfolk. The general announced he was taking possession of the Confederate seaport, and reassured its citizens that they would be protected "in all of their rights and civil privileges." General Viele was named military governor and Wool and Chase left for Monroe.[70]

Near midnight, at Wool's headquarters, Lincoln, who had stayed up to read, heard a sentry's challenge. Wool soon burst into the president's room, exclaiming "Norfolk is ours!" Burly Stanton, dressed in his nightshirt, rushed in and grabbed the little general, hugging him and lifting him off the floor. According to Cannon, Lincoln roared with laughter and warned: "Look out Mars. If you don't the general will throw you."[71]

On the morning of May 11, Lincoln, Wool, and an official party sailed on the steamer *Baltimore* to Norfolk. Earlier, around five o'clock, there had been a tremendous explosion near Craney Island. The *Merrimac* crew had found it impossible to move the Confederate ironclad and set it afire. The blast ended her short career. The *Baltimore* steered for the site and passed over the floating wreckage. It was Sunday morning and the church bells in Norfolk were ringing. The *Monitor,* the first Union ship into the harbor, rode at anchor. That evening, Lincoln left for Washington. The destruction of the *Merrimac* removed forever the Confederate threat to Union operations in Hampton Roads. The James River was now open to gunboats to protect McClellan's left flank during his thrust toward Richmond.[72]

With Stanton's permission, Wool the next day started troops from Norfolk to occupy Suffolk, a strategic railroad junction. He again proposed an advance to Petersburg and Richmond. Gen. Ambrose Burnside, who had captured Roanoke Island, to the south, and was poised to strike Albemarle Sound, possibly could cooperate in a joint operation. Stanton relayed Wool's plan to Burnside. The commander expressed interest in the idea, but preferred to defer to McClellan's progress. McClellan soon faced formidable opposition and bitter reverses before Richmond.[73]

May 16 was a memorable day. During the morning, Wool received a telegram bearing the president's praise for the general's recent "skillful and gallant" campaign. The surrender of Norfolk and the destruction of the *Merrimac* were among "the most important successes" of the war. Then, shortly after noon came news that Lincoln had nominated Wool for a major generalship in the regular army. "The Senate suspended the rules and unanimously confirmed you at five o'clock P.M.," a friend reported. With "a grateful heart," the veteran officer promptly acknowledged the honors the government "so generously" had conferred on him.[74]

But unhappy days lay ahead. In late March, General Huger reopened the prisoner exchange issue with Wool, offering to trade officers on a one-man, equal-rank basis. On April 29, the general urged a general exchange, and the rebel commander seemed to agree. But on May 25, came a demand that all Confederate privateers in Union hands be delivered before an exchange could be made. Wool brought to Monroe eighty-five privateers from Fort Lafayette, in New York Harbor, and on June 1, sent them on a boat flying a truce flag up the James River to City Point. Huger, however, had changed his mind. He did not intend to exchange hostages for privateers in groups, but on a rank equivalency basis. The truce boat brought the privateers back, the mission a failure. Two months later, after Wool had left Monroe, Colonel Corcoran and other officers were finally exchanged.[75]

Equally unpleasant was Wool's clash with Commodore Goldsborough over the Gosport Navy Yard at Norfolk. On May 22, Goldsborough, citing Navy Department instructions, started transferring naval stores from the beach at Monroe to the Gosport installation and announced that he would take charge there. Wool snapped back that he had captured the Norfolk facility and would hold it until the president or Secretary Stanton ordered otherwise. "Do for gracious sake have this nonsense knocked out of him," Goldsborough wrote his superiors. "He needs combing." On May 24, Stanton instructed Wool to release the yard to the navy. Goldsborough soon was fuming again. Before releasing the yard, Wool had let contracts to remove the wreckage of the *Merrimac* and other sunken vessels from the harbor. When the commodore tried to halt the salvage work, Wool declared that the *Merrimac* no longer belonged to the navy, having been made into an ironclad. Goldsborough reported this outburst to the Navy Department, calling Wool narrow-minded and childish.[76]

The greatest outcry against Wool occurred in Norfolk. Since instituting military government there on May 10, the general had imposed de facto martial law on the population of 15,000 people. He hoped to force the officials and townsfolk to swear allegiance to the Union. He closed the port to shipping, stopped the sale of newspapers, and restricted travel into town. On May 15, Wool appeared before the mayor and the select and common councils. He promised to restore civil government and open the port if the officials would pledge their loyalty to the Union. The officials hedged and a lull followed. Several stores conducted business, and the United States post office reopened. A few people came to headquarters and affirmed their loyalty, but a majority held back, believing that McClellan would be defeated at Richmond.[77]

On May 22, in an effort to bring the people of Norfolk "to their senses," Wool warned that they must take the oath or suffer "strict martial law." As the food supply dwindled because of the closed port, citizens held protest meetings and accused the general of trying to starve the town into submission. The *Richmond Enquirer* was outraged at "the savage barbarity, the demon cruelty of this hoary-headed old man." Strange things began to happen. A French frigate seized a Union merchantman off Sewall's Point, its captain announcing that he was helping the United States enforce its blockade of Norfolk. The general's stranglehold on the city was ridiculous.[78]

At noon on June 1, Wool received orders transferring him to Baltimore to command the Middle Department. John A. Dix would succeed him at Fort Monroe. "I am unable to give any reasons for the change," Wool wrote Sarah. "It is said that the government wants me near them. I am perfectly satisfied because I believe the authorities have confidence in me." This decision resolved a number of problems. In reassigning Wool, Lincoln merged the Department of Virginia with McClellan's command, and by shifting Dix to Monroe, he paved the way to reopen the port of Norfolk to trade. Dix arrived on June 1, but Wool remained at the fort for several days to collect his papers and ship his furniture to Troy. After reviewed the garrison on June 7, the general left for Baltimore.[79]

John Wool had commanded Fort Monroe during a critical period in the war. Ten months earlier, he arrived at this strategic fortification at a time when the Union army was reeling from defeats at Bull Run and Big Bethel. Gathering the reins of a large responsibility, Wool had shown remarkable energy in dealing with the tasks of his unique command. He created an efficient system for handling mail and expediting travel through the lines, expanded the work program for contrabands, negotiated for prisoner exchanges, supplied provisions for naval expeditions—and entertained an unending stream of guests (six hundred, he estimated) at the fort. Wool had fretted over command and supply problems during McClellan's Peninsula Campaign—and there was great trepidation with the *Merrimac*. Upon occupying Norfolk, the general tried to impose a hardline program reminiscent of what he had used in northern Mexico nearly twenty years earlier. When his policies created deep hostility, a merciful government transferred the old general to another military theater.

15

KNOW NOTHINGS AND PLUG UGLIES

On June 8, 1862, the steamer *Georgeana* arrived from Fort Monroe and docked at Baltimore. General Wool and several staff officers debarked, received a cordial welcome from Brig. Gen. Horace Montgomery, and boarded carriages for a ride to the fashionable Eutaw House. After breakfast, the general enjoyed a rousing salute by the Seventh New York Infantry Band, called down from Fort Federal Hill in the center of the teeming metropolis. By noon, Wool was on a train to Washington to discuss his new assignment with Secretary of War Stanton.[1]

In March 1862, the War Department had created the Middle Department which included Maryland, Pennsylvania, New Jersey, and Delaware, and the eastern shore of Virginia. The headquarters were at Baltimore, the third largest city in the nation, thirty-five miles northeast of Washington, D.C. The command contained some 15,000 men, with 4,300 stationed in and about the city. General Dix, Wool's predecessor, had renovated and converted old Forts McHenry and Delaware into federal prisons, and placed heavy artillery batteries on Federal Hill and Murray Hill, which overlooked the city. Dix had also scattered detachments of soldiers to strategic bridges and depots along the Baltimore & Ohio Railroad (B&O), extending west to Harpers Ferry and beyond. As most of the fighting had been in Virginia, outside his jurisdiction, Dix had spent his time contending with southern fire-eaters in Baltimore and the repeated attempts by the Maryland legislature to pass a secession ordinance. Wool inherited all of Dix's problems.[2]

Secretary Stanton instructed the general to continue Dix's policies. He also asked Wool to establish a camp of instruction near Annapolis to train infantry, cavalry, and artillery recruits. Security along the B&O had to be tightened and local regiments kept in readiness to defend Washington. The war was going badly. McClellan had recently fought a bloody battle at Fair Oaks, seven miles from Richmond, that left the entire Army of the Potomac was stalled and on the defensive before the Confederate capital. In the Shenandoah Valley Union forces were retreating from a fast-moving rebel army under Gen. Thomas J. "Stonewall" Jackson. The Lincoln administration was greatly alarmed. If McClellan continued to suffer reverses in Virginia, the Middle Department could easily face a rebel invasion.[3]

Wool established his headquarters at the Eutaw House. Only the faithful Cram and Capt. William P. Jones remained from his Fort Monroe staff. Colonel Cannon, who had lightened the general's responsibilities for many months, had resigned and returned to civilian life. Cram continued as Wool's chief engineer, while Jones became provost marshal. Capt. George Christiansen was named senior aide-de-camp, and Lt. Col. William D. Whipple, assistant adjutant general. Wool set Cram to work studying the topography around Baltimore and along the railroad network in Maryland. He planned to increase the number of pickets along the B&O as soon as possible.[4]

On June 13, Wool and several officers went to Annapolis by train to select a site for a training camp. The War Department planned a facility large enough to handle fifty thousand men—cavalry, artillery, and infantry. Here the general would superintend the training of raw recruits, equip and brigade them, and form a "Reserve Corps d'Armé." The trip was a strenuous exercise. After studying the open terrain by horseback most of the day, the party concluded that the facility should be located on the railroad near Annapolis Junction, between Baltimore and Washington. The War Department approved the site and construction began in August.[5]

On June 15, Wool traveled west by train to inspect the Union garrison at Harpers Ferry, Virginia, sixty miles from Washington. Facing east on a peninsula at the junction of the Potomac and Shenandoah Rivers, the outpost was picturesque, but the conditions there appalled the general. Col. Dixon S. Miles, a veteran regular officer, commanded several regiments, mostly New York militia. There were no supporting fortifications on the hills across the Potomac to the north, no horses for the six hundred cavalrymen, and no gunners to man the artillery pieces. At best, Miles could muster about four hundred men to defend the bastion.[6] Harpers Ferry was indefensible, Wool advised Stanton upon his return to Baltimore. At least four regiments should be sent there immediately.

In the Shenandoah Valley, the Confederates were succeeding. General Jackson, a "determined, enterprising" commander, was hovering near Front Royal, Virginia. The Union generals in that region—Nathaniel P. Banks, John C. Frémont, and James Shields—were neglecting their depots. Banks had already lost valuable supplies and property to rebel raiders. On June 17, Stanton extended Wool's jurisdiction west of Harpers Ferry to Cumberland, Maryland, and south to the Union outpost at Winchester, Virginia. On June 20, two infantry regiments and two artillery companies boarded a train at Baltimore to join Miles at Harpers Ferry.[7] Two days later, Stanton informed Wool that McClellan had asked for more troops—at least another regiment. The general protested the order. He had sent one regiment to guard $1.5 million in supplies and animals at Frémont's depot at New Creek, and hourly expected Banks, at Middletown, to request troops to meet Jackson. Five days later Stanton again extended Wool's jurisdiction, this time to include the B&O west to Wheeling, Virginia. On the evening of July 1, Wool learned by telegraph that McClellan had fought a desperate battle with Gen. Robert E. Lee at Malvern Hill and was withdrawing his army to Harrison's Landing on the James River, his generals fuming in disgust. The campaign against Richmond had ended.[8]

On July 1, Maj. Gen. John Pope—the Saltillo captain who had led the siege and capture of Island No. 10 in the Mississippi River in April—wrote to Wool. A division commander under Frémont, in Missouri, the dashing Pope had been placed in charge of organizing the Army of Virginia, created from the forces of Banks, Frémont, and McDowell. As the units of his army lay within Wool's jurisdiction, the young general contacted him. Pope suggested that the small commands south of the Potomac be stationed in larger units along critical rail lines, turnpikes, and roads. Wool concurred, but advised Pope that before he launched a campaign, he should strengthen his forces at Winchester, Romney, and Leesburg in Virginia. These towns controlled the major roads leading north to the B&O system. All commanders should also try to keep the population in their districts as quiet as possible.[9]

Pope replied that he had strengthened the defenses at Winchester, but had no spare force for Romney. There was a fear in Washington that Lee might march north, and he was charged with protecting the capital. "I will be greatly obliged to you," Pope wrote almost as a student to his teacher, "if you can find time to give me your views in relation to my own operations here & what you think I had best do & how to dispose the forces under my command. I have great confidence in your judgments and shall be very much indebted to you for any suggestions, even if you have only time to put them in the shape of memoranda."[10]

Having increased military protection along the B&O, Wool turned his attention to the highly charged political situation in Baltimore. During the early months of the war, the Lincoln administration had authorized strong steps to keep the critical border state of Maryland from seceding. Union generals commanding in Baltimore—Butler, Banks, and Dix—had instructions to suppress all manifestations of disloyalty. To curb disorder, they had declared martial law in the state, suspended habeas corpus proceedings, and arrested and imprisoned citizens suspected of rebel sympathies. At the point of a bayonet, newspapers and journals expressing anti-Union views were also suppressed. In the midst of these harsh measures, a militant Unionist party sprang to life. Its leaders applauded and encouraged military coercion and sought to seize political control of the city and state governments. The Unionists, or "Plug Uglies" as Wool called them, hired informers to ferret out disloyal persons in Baltimore and neighboring counties, and demanded they be arrested.[11]

Many citizens were being arrested under these conditions, but Wool ameliorated the situation somewhat on July 3. A soldier detail had arrested three persons for circulating a broadside declaring that McClellan had been "utterly routed" at Richmond and was in the process of surrendering to Lee. The rumor had caused great excitement in the city, and newspapers reported that a number of investors sold large amounts of government stocks "at ruinous rates." The soldiers had hurried the agitators to old Fort McHenry, where the military lodged civil prisoners. Several days later, to relieve crowded conditions, Wool shipped eighteen prisoners to Fort Lafayette, in New York Harbor, most of whom were glad to escape harsh treatment from the commander, Brig. Gen. William W. "Black Bill" Morris. Old Fort Delaware, located on Pea Patch Island in the Delaware River, where three thousand rebels were incarcerated, was also overcrowded. When several Confederates escaped from that dreaded camp in mid-July, Wool tightened the guard and requisitioned an armed steamer to patrol the river. He also authorized the release of several hundred sick and wounded prisoners to the Union Relief Association, managed by a group of Baltimore women. The association had complained to Lincoln of conditions on Pea Patch Island, and the president approved of the men being placed in private homes to recuperate.[12]

Later that month, a federal draft for more soldiers ratcheted up the political tensions in Baltimore, presenting even sharper problems to Wool. McClellan's reverses before Richmond caused anxiety in Washington, and when the federal government, in May, required state governors to send more troops, not enough came. On July 2, Lincoln called on the governors for 300,000 volunteers to serve three years. The quota for Maryland was 8,532 men. State officials looked to Baltimore for one-third of the quota. Each volunteer would receive a federal bounty and advance pay. Substitutes were allowed. To stimulate enlistments, patriotic organizations held war meetings in many northern cities, businessmen and wealthy citizens pledged bonuses, and state legislatures, cities, counties, and townships voted appropriations to attract enlistments. The rush to the colors in the Midwest was gratifying, but Maryland lacked the volunteer spirit.[13]

Civil officials in Maryland viewed the quota with mixed feelings. On July 17, Governor Augustus W. Bradford, a strong Union man, appointed a committee of fifty to study ways to boost enlistments. They recommended that all cities and towns in the state vote funds for bounties. Baltimore Unionists urged the city council to approve $300,000 to help raise the four or five regiments required in the city, a proposal which split the city government. In a special session, the mayor and the first branch of the council favored the idea, but the second branch balked. The members said they only dealt with local issues, and since the quota involved a claim on the state, the legislature should take action. On July 23, the council met again—and the second branch again refused to act. A Unionist mob gathered outside city hall to denounce and threaten the recalcitrant members. Wool was on an inspection trip to Wheeling, and Col. William Whipple, his adjutant, telegraphed Secretary of State Seward for advice. The colonel was directed to promise prompt federal attention to the impasse. The officer informed the protesters of these instructions and assigned one hundred policemen to escort the councilmen home.[14]

On July 24, Wool arrived back in Baltimore and found several Unionist leaders waiting for him. He refused their demand to use troops to coerce the council to vote, saying such measures were "highhanded." He did agree to seek a settlement. The general called in two members of the second branch and gave them a stern lecture. The federal government needed soldiers, and Baltimore must meet its obligation. He suggested they seek bounty money by private subscription, and they agreed to try, but the next day, the councilmen reported no luck. Wool declared that for him to keep order in the city, the second branch members must resign. That afternoon, they complied and Wool telegraphed Secretary Stanton of the decision. The Union party could now fill the vacant seats and vote money for the Baltimore regiments. He hoped the secretary would approve his actions. "If any man told you I am not satisfied with your management of the middle department he lies," came the reply. "I am not satisfied with some of your subordinates, but I have no doubt they will improve under your instruction. You know I believe in you, and am ready to 'tie up' to you any time."[15]

The Unionists moved swiftly. The local chapter of the Union League, an organization active in numerous northern states, joined with the Unionists City Convention in calling a mass meeting in Monument Square on July 28. The sponsors told Wool that the object of the assembly was to stimulate volunteering. He approved of the event and agreed to attend. On the appointed day, the general sat on the grandstand and looked out over a crowd estimated at twenty thousand, probably the largest public gathering ever held in Baltimore to that time. Governor Bradford gave an exhortative address, to bursts of applause. Fourth on the agenda, Wool arose and in a high, shrill voice briefly explained his assignment in Baltimore. Then, as other speakers droned on, he left the platform and returned to headquarters at the Eutaw House.[16]

The next morning, Wool read the newspapers in great disgust. The Unionist meeting had approved a set of inflammatory resolutions. One resolution condemned the Lincoln administration for patronizing officials of the B&O Railroad and the Bay Line Steamers, whom it insinuated were disloyal. Another asked the president to instruct Wool to order all male citizens in Baltimore over eighteen to take a loyalty oath, with those who refuse expelled to the Confederacy. The resolutions especially infuriated the general because he had recently been traveling with the B&O president, John W. Garrett, and the steamboat operator, Moore N. Falls, and considered both men loyal and reputable. Before they adjourned, the Unionists created a committee to investigate disloyalty and government corruption in the city. Thoughts of the San Francisco Vigilance Committee of 1856 doubtless entered the general's mind.[17]

Wisely, Wool did not respond in public to the resolutions. His principal mission as a military commander was to keep the peace and promote and protect the interests of the governments in his jurisdiction. Although he felt strongly about the divided loyalties around him, he refused to view all Democrats and the wealthy as disloyal, as the Unionists did. However, he wisely heeded the sense of the meeting. To quiet the clamor and head off the work of the ad hoc committee, he tightened military control in Baltimore.

Wool arrested more men. In the preceding weeks, the city police had already been investigating every rumor, let alone act, of disloyalty. They had seized a cache of muskets in a downtown store and arrested its owner, a former Maryland militia officer, who had just returned from the South. They took into custody the composer and publisher of a patriotic southern march, the "Stonewall Quickstep." Individuals with quilts, clothing, or articles with Confederate emblems were also arrested, as were those, even drunks, hurrahing in public for Jeff Davis. Police were checking incoming trains and boats, and on one steamer, they discovered a large black woman who carried in her bosom a dozen letters that implicated other passengers on board as secessionists. To leave no doubt as to their loyalties, officers of the B&O and the Bay Line steamers came to headquarters to swear allegiance to the Union. Fort McHenry now overflowed with civilian prisoners, and Wool shipped some inmates south to Fort Monroe and another group north to Fort Lafayette.[18]

On August 1, the Unionists swept to victory in Baltimore in a special election to fill vacant council seats. The full body promptly met and approved $350,000 in city bonds for bounties to those who volunteered for three years of military service. The next week they raised the mayor's salary and voted $30,000 to the city militia. The councilmen also moved into other spheres. They recommended that all citizens of Baltimore be required to take a loyalty oath immediately and demanded that city employees especially, including teachers, take it. They petitioned the government to move all regulars in the city "to the seat of the war" and replace them with "loyal volunteers." Wool sought a middle ground. A large rebel army was reportedly gathering below the Potomac, possibly to strike north. If he coerced the citizens, he predicted that at least twenty thousand men would join the enemy. In a token gesture, the general ordered his officers to require the oath only of those persons leaving Baltimore by steamer.[19]

On August 4, amid the growing tension in Baltimore, President Lincoln suddenly ordered the enrollment of 300,000 state militia for nine months' duty. As the response to his request for volunteers had been poor, he set a deadline of August 15 to meet the militia quota. Governors also could channel militiamen to fill the call for volunteers. On August 9, the day the militia draft reached Baltimore, the War Department forbade all able-bodied men ages eighteen to forty-five to travel. As county assessors sent militia rolls to the governor, police swarmed through train depots, driving out men attempting to flee the city, many bound for Canada. In Philadelphia, a crowd attacked and severely beat young men trying to board trains. On August 10, as Baltimore seethed, Secretary Stanton further paralyzed travel in the Middle Department when he required everyone to have military passes to leave their counties of residence or states. Men and women quickly lined up at Wool's headquarters for permits.[20]

The general moved quickly to avert a crisis. On August 11, without consulting Stanton, he relaxed the travel restrictions. He announced that farmers and businessmen in the county, non-residents over age forty-five, foreigners with passports, and females, could pass freely to and from Baltimore. With jails bulging and Fort McHenry overcrowded, Wool ordered that henceforth no person within his jurisdiction would be arrested for disloyalty or treasonable practices, unless the charges were "submitted in writing, and the truth of the same attested under oath by the person preferring them." His order ran for nearly a week in the newspapers. Wool also released the prisoners at McHenry who took the oath or gave bond to appear for the draft or furnish a substitute. On August 14, the militia enrollment began in Baltimore without incident.[21]

Since early August, Wool had increasingly focused his attention on the threat of a Confederate invasion of Maryland. Reports were that a large rebel army was gathering in Virginia, ready to march north—and possibly menace Washington. In late July, while McClellan's battered veterans of the Peninsula Campaign recuperated and sweltered in the heat below Richmond, and Pope struggled to mold the new Army of Virginia, Wool urged the Lincoln administration to "be up and doing." "Coming events," he wrote Stanton, "cast their shadow before them." The Confederates, now seeking recognition and aid from Great Britain and France, would "do all in their power" to keep McClellan immobilized where summer fevers and desertion thinned his ranks. Union generals as a group, Wool said, had failed to seek information on rebel strengths and movements, knew little about war stratagems, and had shown poor judgment in protecting their supplies. Timidity, rather than boldness, marked their efforts. The government must shake off its lethargy, take the offensive, and put down the infamous rebellion.[22]

In mid-July, hoping to better coordinate war efforts, Lincoln brought Maj. Gen. Henry W. Halleck, a protégé of Winfield Scott's, from the western theater and appointed him general-in-chief of the Union armies. Halleck was a pedantic, fussy officer. He was an able critic of battle plans, but lacked expertise in organizing and directing military operations. Halleck suffered constantly from hay fever, seemed indecisive, plodding, and inert. His primary role was to act as a chief information officer to the president and coordinate military efforts wherever needed. Halleck took command on July 22, and on that same day the War Department created a system of army corps within the various departments to speed the organization and movement of troops. Wool was placed in command of the Eighth Corps.[23]

In a letter home to Sarah, the general commented on his activities. His recent inspection of the troops within his command had been exhausting: "I reviewed and inspected 18 thousand men stationed in some twenty places. It was somewhat a fatiguing two days. The horses I rode at the reviews were not broken and I was much troubled to manage them well." And there was news from Washington. "Halleck and [Ambrose] Burnside had gone to visit McClellan. The latter has shown himself no general . . . I would not trust [him] with the Command of [a] Regiment." McClellan "was a great pet of Davis! They corresponded on the subject of a command offered him in the Confederate army. . . . The Richmond Enquirer threatened to publish the correspondence."[24]

In late August, Wool received orders to proceed to Harrisburg, Pennsylvania, to supervise the muster, organization, and equipping of the volunteers arriving there, and forward the men to Washington as soon as possible. McClellan, per Halleck's orders, was withdrawing his army from the James River to the town of Alexandria on the Potomac and needed new levies. Furthermore, a dozen or so militia regiments called up for three months were completing their terms and clamoring to go home. Pennsylvania authorities momentarily complicated the federal muster by refusing to furnish state arms, while colonels vied with each other for recruits. Wool and his aides quickly imposed order around Harrisburg and hustled new units aboard trains for the national capital. After five days, the general traveled on to Philadelphia to perform similar duties. By August 22, fourteen Pennsylvania regiments were on their way to Washington. Their arrival was timely. Pope had thrust his army into Virginia and suffered reverses in a second bloody battle at Bull Run on August 28–30. In a telegram to Stanton, Wool pointed to "an error which I cautioned him against, that is, of leaving his rear and supplies unprotected." Young generals never seemed to learn.[25]

Wool soon became preoccupied with rebel activity in the Shenandoah Valley. Daily he requested news from his commanders in Harpers Ferry, Winchester, and Martinsburg at the northern end of the valley. Also reporting were Brig. Gen. Benjamin F. Kelley, commanding the detachments along the B&O in the so-called "railroad district," and Brig. Gen. Jacob D. Cox, in charge of the Kanawha district around Charleston in western Virginia. Union troops in Hagerstown, Williamsport, and Frederick, Maryland answered to Colonel Miles at Harpers Ferry.[26]

Wool worried about Harpers Ferry. Colonel Cram, his chief engineer, had inspected the salient in July and advised that the artillery positions there were the key to its defense. Strong batteries, supported by infantry, should be placed on the heights north, east, and west of the village. Wool already had shuttled artillery and infantry companies to Miles. In early August, while visiting the garrison, the general pointed to the towering Maryland Heights across the Potomac to the north, and gave verbal instructions to construct a blockhouse there. He also concluded that entrenchments were needed to the west, on neighboring Bolivar Heights, and an abatis should be placed across Camp Hill. But Colonel Miles, the veteran who had been court-martialed for drunkenness following the first battle of Bull Run, lacked industry. When rebel activity increased near Winchester, Wool rushed a Maryland regiment from Baltimore by train to complete the fortifications. Miles discontinued the work.[27]

On the evening of September 2, Wool telegraphed Stanton that Miles's pickets had clashed with Stonewall Jackson's scouts near Leesburg, south of the Potomac and about twenty miles southeast of Harpers Ferry. The general was dispatching infantry companies by train to strengthen the outpost at Point of Rocks and watch enemy movements. Also, two New York regiments were riding west to Harpers Ferry to replace the militia there whose three-month enlistments were expiring. Wool deployed other troops farther west at Martinsburg and New Creek, where in an emergency they could support Miles.[28]

Wool calculated that if the rebels, thought to be under Gen. Lee, who had turned back McClellan before Richmond and smashed Pope at Second Bull Run, crossed the Potomac, they would strike Harpers Ferry, the only sizeable Union bastion in western Maryland. He believed Lee would then head northeast for the B&O Railroad at Frederick. Moving swiftly the Confederate column could then turn southeast and threaten Washington before McClellan's army could move. Wool's primary objective was to delay Lee.[29]

Tensions mounted on September 3. Miles telegraphed Wool that Brig. Gen. Julius White had abandoned Winchester and brought his forces north to Harpers Ferry. Jackson's rebel pickets were active along the Potomac, while the bulk of his force of twelve thousand men lay in camp near Leesburg. Paroled soldiers from Union outposts began straggling into Point of Rocks, some ten miles southeast of Harpers Ferry. The situation was fast becoming critical. From Baltimore Wool tried to stiffen Miles's resolve: "I must leave the course you ought to pursue to your own sound discretion," he telegraphed. "Take care of your position and not expose it to surprise. Watchfulness, vigilance, and a sound discretion must be your guide at the present moment." After dark, Miles telegraphed with alarm that a New York militia regiment, its term expired, was demanding to go home. Reports on the rebel buildup continued.[30]

Wool sought to protect the railroad bridges at Monocacy Creek, northeast of Harpers Ferry, and downriver at Point of Rocks, on the Potomac. Near midnight of the third, he sent a special train loaded with a light artillery battery speeding west. Early next morning, Cram arrived and located the guns and a regiment at the Monocacy Bridge, then went on to Point of Rocks. Rebels had burned the bridge there, but the river was fordable. He urged the soldiers manning two twelve-pounder cannons to remain alert. The outposts at both Monocacy and Point of Rocks were makeshift, but time was growing short.[31]

Wool kept in constant touch with Miles. On the fourth, in a flurry of telegrams, the general ordered all paroled prisoners cleared out of Harpers Ferry, and sent west to Cumberland. He instructed White to remain in command at Martinsburg, northwest of Harpers Ferry. He advised Miles to retain the restless New York militia regiment whose enlistment had expired. The men would be branded as cowards if they left at this critical time. When the colonel protested, Wool promised to discharge them on the sixth. At ten o'clock, on the night of September 4, the report came that Lee's Confederates were splashing across the Potomac at a ford several miles below Point of Rocks and invading Maryland.[32]

In the early morning hours of September 5, Cram and two officers raced west by train to investigate. At dawn, the colonel paused briefly at the Monocacy bridge, sent a picket to observe the rebel column still crossing, then hurried on. At Point of Rocks, he scanned the countryside with a glass for signs of enemy forces. From scouts, he learned that Lee's cavalry had passed to the east and was advancing north toward the town of Frederick. Cram attached the cars on the siding, and headed back to Monocacy, hoping to cut the enemy column with the train. Near Adamstown, he narrowly escaped an ambush. At noon he telegraphed Wool that Lee was in Maryland with thirty thousand men, advancing in detached columns, with more men coming. Cram loaded the battery and infantry at Monocacy bridge, and dropped them off farther east. At dusk the exhausted officer arrived in Baltimore. Wool wired the particulars of Cram's report to Halleck.[33]

An attack on Harpers Ferry was imminent. As Lee moved into Maryland, he considered the Union garrison there a threat to his communications and planned to capture it. On September 5, Wool urged Miles to defend his position and shoot every man, officer or soldier, who abandoned his post. He reminded him to deploy artillery on the heights to annoy and delay the enemy, if attacked. The garrison must be defended "to the last extremity." Wool sent similar instructions to White at Martinsburg with a note to retire to Harpers Ferry, if necessary. A disturbing message in cipher arrived from Halleck. "I find it impossible," he informed Wool, "to get this [McClellan's] army into the field again in large force for a day or two." If Harpers Ferry were attacked, Union forces in the vicinity should be moved to Maryland Heights. But this was only a suggestion. Halleck left all dispositions to Wool's "experience and local knowledge."[34]

On the evening of September 7, Lincoln wired Wool for information. What about Harpers Ferry? Lee had thirty thousand men at Frederick, and his army was still crossing the Potomac, was the reply. "I think Harpers Ferry will be defended," Wool assured the president. By September 8, McClellan entered the picture. He advised Wool that his army was massed west of Washington at Rockville. The young general asked for cooperation—and "any suggestion that your extended military experience may dictate."[35]

As a Confederate army maneuvered for battle in Maryland, Wool encountered sharp criticism in Baltimore. During August he had cooperated with the Committee on Disloyalty, organized following the July 28 meeting, which had employed spies and used soldiers to arrest officials lacking the patriotic spirit. When the Unionists demanded more, the general drew back and sought to distance himself from their activities. On September 1, he appointed City Marshal William A. Van Nostrand to the position of civil provost marshal of the Eighth Army Corps, and made him responsible for political prisoners. Van Nostrand would cooperate with Major Jones, the military provost. With Lee's invasion, Wool tightened control over Baltimore. He ordered soldiers without passes arrested, imposed a curfew, and assigned cavalry detachments to patrol the city streets. He located five regiments a short distance west and north of the city, and sent pickets to scout all roads running west. On September 9, the state militia draft was postponed. Political prisoners who took the loyalty oath were released. But the militant Unionists wanted more.[36]

Wool wrote Sarah that the "old Know Nothings," as he called the radical Unionists, were yelping at his heels. On the tenth, the *Baltimore American* launched an attack on the general, warning that "a corporal's guard" could seize the city. Wool's "leniency and lethargy" were causing "universal dissatisfaction." Why did the government keep commanders "in positions of such extraordinary responsibility after they have proven themselves flagrantly incapable?" The old general had also surrounded himself with secessionists. "We want a man who can command our confidence," the newspaper declared, "and who cannot be hoodwinked by Secessionists putting on the guise of Unionism." That same day, a group of citizens petitioned Stanton to remove Wool from command. The secretary asked the general to come to Washington. Apparently, the plan was to transfer him to Philadelphia. Wool refused to leave Baltimore. "Influential friends of the Administration," he responded, urged him to stay in the city, and he wished to remain. Stanton cancelled the trip.[37]

All eyes now turned toward Harpers Ferry. On September 9, at McClellan's request, Wool reported that Lee and a large part of his army was camped at Frederick. Several highways into Pennsylvania lay open to him. Lee could march north to Gettysburg, or he could swing northwest through Hagerstown toward Chambersburg. Wool ruled out a thrust on Baltimore. He urged McClellan to join forces with Burnside and Franz Sigel, who were in the vicinity. Wool's communication with Miles had been cut on September 6, but he was aware that the colonel continued to report to Halleck in Washington through lines running via Wheeling and east from Pittsburgh.[38]

On September 12, Wool became involved in a telegraphic exchange between Halleck and his commanders. McClellan suggested that Miles abandon Harpers Ferry and retreat east to join him. Halleck said this was impossible, but he instructed the colonel to obey orders from McClellan. On the same day, Halleck asked Wool to release his troops to McClellan. "You can put any of my troops under McClellan's command," the general replied.[39]

The defense of Harpers Ferry was badly managed. On September 7, Lee, by proclamation, exhorted the people of Maryland to join the Confederate cause. Then, while resting his troops before striking into Pennsylvania, the Confederate commander divided his army, sending three columns under Jackson to capture Harpers Ferry. By the morning of September 13, these units began encircling the Union bastion.[40]

Colonel Miles had placed artillery and infantry in a makeshift fashion across the Potomac on Maryland Heights, which Wool considered the key defensive position. Union soldiers also occupied Bolivar Heights, west of the river, but Laudon Heights, to the south, was left undefended. On September 13, repeated rebel assaults caused green infantry on Maryland Heights to panic. Despite reinforcements and Miles's order to stand fast, the commander, wounded and unable to rally his men, spiked his guns and retreated down to the Potomac and crossed to Harpers Ferry. During the afternoon of the fourteenth, the garrison heard the rumble of heavy guns to the east toward Frederick. They anxiously watched for a Union relief force, but there was none. After dark, Miles allowed Col. Benjamin F. Davis and 1,500 cavalry to make a break across a pontoon bridge to the Maryland shore. Riding at full gallop, they escaped to the north on the Sharpsburg road. When infantry officers suggested evacuation, Miles, according to one observer, roared: "I am ordered by General Wool to hold this place, and God damn my soul to hell if I don't hold it against the enemy."[41]

At dawn on September 14, McClellan ordered Gen. W. B. Franklin's corps to cross Crampton's Gap and try to relieve the beleaguered garrison. After a hotly contested battle at the gap, at dusk Franklin pushed into the valley beyond and camped within seven miles of Maryland Heights. At dawn, a day later, Gen. Lafayette McLaws's Confederates lined up facing him. In the distance a terrific cannonade could be heard. Then suddenly, about eight in the morning, all firing ceased. Franklin remarked to his staff that Miles had surrendered—which was true.[42]

At daylight on September 15, Miles had watched rebel batteries unleash a terrific bombardment on his troops on Bolivar Heights. With his ammunition running low, he consulted his officers, who despaired of McClellan's arrival, and agreed to capitulate. Miles, who was drinking heavily, raised a white flag, and with General White, commanding on Bolivar Heights, he started on foot down the slope. Desultory firing continued and a stray artillery shell exploded behind them, blowing the calf off Miles's left leg. White promptly surrendered the garrison of 11,200 Union soldiers to Jackson, the largest number of U.S. soldiers surrendered until the battle for Bataan in World War II. Jackson paroled them and marched away to rejoin Lee. Miles died the next afternoon. Wool gloomily wrote Sarah that if Miles could have held out only a few hours, he would have been reinforced. The colonel "had not my confidence," he said. Yet the defense of Harpers Ferry had bought time for McClellan, who now prepared to strike a deadly blow at Lee.[43]

After capturing Harpers Ferry, Lee planned to concentrate his divisions near Boonsboro and invade Pennsylvania—and possibly march on the state capital at Harrisburg. The Confederate government in Richmond speculated that such an audacious campaign would show the impotence of the Lincoln administration, and bring British and French recognition. Lee's plans, however, went awry. At an abandoned rebel campground at a farm near Frederick, a Union soldier picked up three cigars wrapped in paper laying in the grass. The wrapper was a copy of Lee's Special Order 191 revealing the movement of his entire army and was rushed to McClellan. Lee heard of the discovery and drew several divisions back to engage the Union army. He fought a battle at South Mountain and turned west toward Sharpsburg and Antietam Creek, near the Potomac. As McClellan marched to meet Lee, he telegraphed Halleck for every available regiment and large amounts of ammunition and supplies. These requests went to Wool at Baltimore, with instructions to seize the railroads, if necessary, to reinforce McClellan.[44]

Wool had few troops to spare. Two days earlier, he had dispatched two regiments from Baltimore to General Banks, who commanded a force on the road to Washington. He had also sent detachments along the B&O line to collect straggling parolees from Harpers Ferry, and march them overland to a camp near Annapolis. Wool did make an effort to help. He recalled two Maryland regiments from guard duty, reclaimed another from Banks and sent the three west at midnight on September 15. The following evening came the glorious news that McClellan had fought Lee to a standstill on Antietam Creek, the bloodiest single day in American military history. Lee's battered rebel army was limping back across the Potomac into Virginia. A wave of relief swept the North. Wool hurried to Washington, where Secretary Stanton "warmly embraced" the general for helping block Lee's invasion.[45]

Wool could not long enjoy the relief of Antietam, for his responsibilities in Baltimore became increasingly disagreeable. "We have two parties," he wrote Sarah on September 23, "the Democrats & Know Nothings, their hatred toward each other is intense. To destroy each other is the determination of both parties. If the Democrats had been for the Union, the Know Nothings would have joined the rebels. . . . These men joined the Union party soon after their success in Kentucky and Tennessee—and would now exterminate those whom they joined . . . they spare neither age [n]or sex." In practicing reason toward rebel sympathizers, Wool had enraged the Know Nothings. They were making "great efforts" to get him removed.[46]

The general also explained his predicament to his favorite niece, Harriette. "The day of modesty has passed," he said. "Nothing but fulsome adulation will answer at the present time. I have no one to puff me into position. It is of a great advantage to have someone always ready to puff a man into notoriety." Wool viewed the national scene with disgust. "The President is a joker. He delights in relating smutty stories. He has his pets and they have all failed." McClellan was claiming a great victory, but had nothing to show for it and was again idle. A newspaper controversy had developed over Harpers Ferry, and Wool was being blamed for the loss. This was not true. Miles's forces had been placed under McClellan, and Wool had been ordered to obey him.[47]

On Sunday evening, September 28, after completing his report on Harpers Ferry, Wool turned again to his private correspondence. "I am heartily sick of the manner in which this war is carried on," he wrote Sarah. "The North has poured out its soldiers and wealth like water, and what have they gained—nothing but disaster and the destruction of these brave and patriotic men. We have a joker at the head of government without the first qualification to preserve a great people." The actions of Mary Lincoln were also strange. Recently, "she called at Willards," Wool said, "and waited sometime for that unprincipled Charles Wycoff [Wyckliffe, a Kentucky Democrat], who detained her to put on his gloves and then joined madam in her carriage and rode off with him." Many interesting stories "are told of this 'Lady.'" Wool had met Mary Todd Lincoln only once, in June 1862 at the White House: "I treated her as I would anyone occupying her position. She was so much pleased she declared that she had never been treated in so agreeable a manner." Soon afterwards, the first lady asked him to recommend a young friend of hers who was a watchman at the White House for a position with the army. The general promptly obliged.[48]

Shortly before midnight on October 10, Wool was notified that a large force of Rebel cavalry had crossed the Potomac into Maryland. Racing north, they had reached the vicinity of Chambersburg, Pennsylvania. Gen. Jeb Stuart, the commander, had some two thousand horsemen and a light field battery. Lee had ordered Stuart to tear up railroad lines, seize hostages for exchange, and create panic. The invaders had circled to the west of McClellan's army, which sprawled in a dozen encampments from Harpers Ferry through Sharpsburg to Hagerstown. Halleck promptly telegraphed McClellan to intercept the raiders, but the general hesitated. He wanted to determine Stuart's objectives and possible return route to the Potomac.

In Baltimore, at dawn on October 11, Wool, responding to a frantic plea from Pennsylvania governor Andrew Gregg Curtin, loaded an infantry brigade and six artillery pieces on a train that sped north to Harrisburg. In the meantime, Stuart had entered Chambersburg in a rainstorm, seized clothing, horses, and supplies, destroyed the railroad depot, and struck out to the east.[49]

Wool spent most of the day on the train. When he rolled into Harrisburg, Curtin excitedly reported that Carlisle, to the southwest, was in danger and asked Wool to take the train there. Shortly after the general left, the governor telegraphed him to forget about Carlisle—and go directly south to Hanover Junction. Exhausted, Wool reached the junction in the predawn darkness of the twelfth, and met another train with Colonel Cram and two more regiments on board. Stuart was reported approaching Gettysburg, about eight miles west of Hanover. Wool wired McClellan of his intentions and instructed Cram to intercept the raiders. Stuart, however, made only a feint at Gettysburg, then turned south via Emmetsburg into Maryland. In the meantime, Wool had gone southwest toward Monocacy, stopping here and there to check on Stuart and alert detachments guarding the railroad. The colonel of the 140th Pennsylvania Infantry remembered the "little old white headed man, very quick in his movements" who stopped briefly at his station. Wool had asked questions, then laughed and joked about the situation and departed. Later, Cram halted his train at Monocacy and kept steam up, ready to jump east or west to intercept Stuart. The rebel raiders crossed the railroad five miles to the east that day, skirmished with Union cavalry, and by night had forded the Potomac and was safely back in Virginia. In four days, Stuart had circled McClellan's entire army! Wool returned to Baltimore on Sunday afternoon, exhausted. He had spent two days and a night jolting across the countryside on a train trying to intercept an elusive enemy.[50]

The last two weeks of October were also hectic. Lottery drawings for the state militia draft spawned an uproar in Maryland and Pennsylvania. In some counties, armed men tried to block trains loaded with draftees or sought to disrupt induction proceedings. Although Wool privately opposed the draft, he dared take no stand on the matter. Only when Stanton ordered him to aid Governor Curtin did the general respond. Quotas proved hard to fill, however, and with anti-draft demonstrations in northern states and governors protesting, Secretary Stanton suspended the militia draft.[51]

In Baltimore, Wool felt increased pressure from the Unionists. With Wool's troops protecting the polls, they had won the city elections on October 9. They now wanted another military commander. Less than two weeks later, a committee complained to Lincoln that military authority was too lax. Straggling, half-sick soldiers filled the streets of Baltimore, claiming that hospitals refused to admit them. Surgeon Gen. William Hammond dismissed the complaint, attributing the problem to soldiers refusing to report for medical care. Hearing that the committee planned to visit Lincoln, Wool dispatched a letter to the president and several cabinet members, branding the group a Know Nothing tool sent to remove him. "They came back with a flea in their ear," he told Sarah.[52]

A week later, the pro-Unionist *Baltimore American* reprinted a letter from the *Harrisburg Telegraph* that questioned Wool's loyalties. The writer, the Reverend Charles A. Hay, a Lutheran minister, had visited Baltimore. There he met "a lady of well-known secession proclivities" who boasted that Wool had permitted her to remove four wounded Confederate prisoners from Fort McHenry. Were the men now in the city hospitals? the minister asked. "No, they are in the hands of our friends," she replied. "A dozen ladies scrambled for them, but I had already promised them to others, and they are well cared for." Wool promptly had Hay arrested in Harrisburg and brought to Baltimore. When he interviewed the minister, he was highly agitated, pacing up and down and calling the reverend's statements "a pack of lies." The general then stopped, picked up General Morris's report book from the fort, and read aloud. Reverend Hay immediately saw that the lady meant Morris, instead of Wool, but he still held the commanding general responsible. Released from arrest, Hay clarified his statement in the *Baltimore American* the next day.[53]

Wool now turned on his tormentors. He obtained a copy of a petition to Lincoln which questioned his "physical and mental competency" and blistered the air with invectives. He branded the statement as insubordinate to military authority. On October 28, he heard that a group planned to meet that night at the Temperance Temple to denounce him and he sent a cavalry detachment to arrest them. At eight-thirty, Provost Marshal Jones entered the building, seized several men, and collected their papers. He charged four men with conspiring to overthrow the military authorities of the Middle Department and placed them under arrest. Their papers revealed that the Unionists had collected ninety-six affidavits bearing evidence of disloyalty among city officials, and agreed to demand that the Lincoln administration remove them. But in Wool's eyes, he was the principal focus of the conspiracy.[54]

The next morning, the general sent the four prisoners to Fort Delaware and boarded a train for Washington. Shortly after noon, he saw the president, explained the situation in Baltimore, and was assured of Lincoln's support. Later in the day, when Governor Bradford and several irate Marylanders arrived, Lincoln declared he had taken care of the matter and terminated the interview. Johns Hopkins and several prominent Baltimore merchants also saw Lincoln and urged him to ignore the pleas for Wool's removal. The peace and tranquility of the city was due in large measure to the general's judgment and discretion. On October 30, Wool ordered the four prisoners released and their papers restored.[55]

Wool publicly attacked the radical element in Baltimore. In the Baltimore *Sun* and friendly New York newspapers, he defended his military policies. He denounced the attempts by "the Plug Uglies or the old Know Nothings" to overthrow his authority and "crush and disarm everyone suspected of disloyalty." This group, although professing Union loyalty, had organized a witch hunt and had falsely accused many peaceable and loyal citizens of secessionist leanings. The battle was now joined.[56]

Unionist spokesmen responded. All Union men "high and low" in the city were dissatisfied with Wool, the *Baltimore American* declared. Wealthy secessionists had entertained the general, given him gifts, and prevailed on his good graces for favors. "Super sensitiveness and martinetism" marked Wool's every act. When "dissatisfied citizens" had petitioned for his recall, the old general had pronounced the act as insubordinate and ordered arrests. It was strange that a commander in a city considered loyal "denies the right of petition, refuses to allow his conduct or qualifications to be criticized, and summarily consigns to prison those who are peacefully engaged in exercising the dearest rights guaranteed to them by free institutions." What would become of those who had violently assailed McClellan and the president, if such a rule were encouraged? "Loyal men grieve at these unfortunate exhibitions," a commentator moaned.[57]

While Baltimore Unionists stormed at Wool, he received orders to supervise the November election in Delaware. Democratic strength in the lower counties of Sussex and Kent posed a threat to the newly organized Union Party. It was rumored that southern sympathizers from the adjoining district in Maryland, the eastern shore of Virginia, and from Philadelphia would interfere with the voting. William Cannon and George F. Fisher, Unionist candidates for governor and congressman, respectively, without consulting Delaware governor William Burton, asked the War Department to send troops to maintain order. At dusk on November 2, a Sunday, General Wool sailed from Baltimore with three steamboats loaded with cavalry, infantry, and artillery detachments. Crossing the bay during the night, the flotilla reached Seaford, in Sussex County, shortly after noon on Monday. A crowd had gathered at the dock and after the soldiers filed ashore, local Unionists made speeches. Wool was cheered when he spoke and a group of women presented him with bouquets of flowers. That evening detachments of soldiers, accompanied by provost marshals, proceeded to designated points in Kent and Sussex counties. Maryland and Delaware militia that Cannon had privately requested took station in other counties.[58]

On Tuesday, November 4, the voters of Delaware cast their ballots. At several polling places, the citizens had to pass through lines of soldiers with drawn swords to reach the voting windows. In other places, they filed by troops with bayonets at ready. According to Democratic observers, many voters were intimidated and harassed, and in some instances, individuals had to take a loyalty oath to cast their ballots. Cannon, the Unionist candidate, bested his Democratic opponent and won the governorship by a mere 111 votes, but the Democrats captured the congressional seat and both houses of the state legislature. On his return to Baltimore, the *Sun* complimented Wool on his handling of an "arduous and delicate duty." This was the last act the general performed for the Unionist cause.[59]

Wool became increasingly critical of Lincoln's handling of the war. One reason was the changing political scene. Despite the use of soldiers, the administration suffered serious reverses at the polls in the fall of 1862, the Democrats scoring significant gains throughout the North. To Wool's great joy, his nephew John Griswold, in Troy, running on a Democratic ticket, won a seat in Congress. Wool had advised Griswold against running two years before, but he needed John's influence now in Washington.[60]

On November 11, a new issue burst into the news: the report of the military commission investigating the fall of Harpers Ferry. Ordered by the secretary of war, the commission opened proceedings on September 29, and, sitting as a grand jury, interrogated a dozen or so officers involved in the affair. As early as October 25, Wool turned to the press to counter insinuations that he had been responsible for the surrender. The garrison, he repeated, had been under McClellan's command at the time. After compiling nine hundred pages of testimony, the commission announced its findings. The board cleared most of the senior officers involved in the disaster, convicted Miles, who was deceased, of incompetence and criminal neglect, and censured McClellan for lack of energy in sending relief to Miles. It reserved a special judgment for Wool: "This commission would not have dwelt upon this painful subject were it not for the fact that the officer who placed this incapable [Miles] in command should share the responsibility." It was their opinion that Wool was "guilty to this extent of a grave disaster, and should be censured for his conduct."[61]

The decision revolved largely around Wool's response to questions about Halleck's September 5 telegram. In this communication, the general-in-chief stated that he was having trouble getting McClellan moving, and as Harpers Ferry faced attack Wool might want to concentrate Miles's forces on Maryland Heights—but Halleck left the decision to Wool. The general could do nothing. The rebels cut the telegraph line east from Harpers Ferry on the sixth. Furthermore, on September 12, Halleck placed Miles under McClellan. The fall of Maryland Heights had no effect on the defense of the Union garrison, Wool explained, for rebel guns placed there could not be depressed to reach Harpers Ferry. He reiterated that Miles could have held until McClellan reached him. But there were other imponderables. Before Harpers Ferry fell, Wool knew that Miles had not constructed the defenses he had requested. Why did he keep him in command? Despite all the finger pointing, the immediate cause of Miles's surrender might be traced to Col. Thomas H. Ford's fistula. Ford commanded the Union forces on Maryland Heights, and was in excruciating pain during the rebel bombardment. It was he who precipitously ordered his guns spiked and his men to withdraw from the heights, causing panic. Add to this Franklin's indecisiveness—and the garrison was lost.[62]

The commission's finding cut to the quick. During his long career, Wool had faced courts of inquiry before, but never under such trying circumstances. Nor had he ever been censured by a military tribunal for incompetency. As he rightly discerned, politics swirled about the commission. A majority of the officers were Union radicals, especially David Hunter, the president. The commission functioned under the aegis of the Committee on the Conduct of the War, called into being by radical Unionists to review battle disasters and dictate policy to Union generals. Only McClellan, Wool, and a few others refused to be intimidated. Although he understood the political overtones of the judgment, the general nevertheless smarted at the administration for allowing this to happen. It was bitter gall for the old warrior.[63]

But Wool refused to concede defeat. On November 11, from a sickbed, he dispatched a short "defense" to the Baltimore and New York papers. In terse language, he commented on the commission report and labeled the censure as pure fiction. He had not placed Miles in command at Harpers Ferry; the colonel already was there when he took over the department the previous June. At a future date, Wool promised additional attention to the matter. In a letter to Sarah on November 12, he blasted the Union radicals, saying, "I am not afraid of any of them, no, not even the President."[64]

By November 17, Wool was out of his sickbed and pouring out his emotions to Sarah. The Lincoln administration had treated him in a shabby manner, keeping him back because he was a Democrat and had popular support "in the free states." First in New York City, and later at Fort Monroe, he had been forced aside. When Lincoln had 236,000 men assembled around Washington guarding the capital, he argued, the Confederates had only 35,000 men in the Richmond vicinity. "I sent a spy who counted the [rebel] regiments," Wool said, and, upon his return, he was dispatched to Washington to convince the administration of the practicability of taking Richmond. There was no interest. Wool had also made other proposals. One involved the capture of Suffolk, at the west end of Hampton Roads. This would have isolated Norfolk and the *Merrimac,* and he could have moved directly along the south side of the James River by turnpike and railroad to the Confederate citadel. This suggestion also fell on deaf ears.[65]

In a carefully worded statement, dated November 20 and published in the *Philadelphia Inquirer,* Wool denounced the radical Unionists in Maryland. This group, he stated, had repeatedly importuned the president to remove him from command of the Middle Department. The position was an important one, but it was impossible to give satisfaction "with a population differing, as it does, on the great questions of the day, and divided into irreconcilable parts, who, because of local inclinations, have lost sight of the preservation of the Union." In a long military career, Wool had discovered "that kindness tempered with justice, accomplished more than the sword." In discharging his duties in Baltimore, he had "responded to the dictates" of his heart and believed that he had been successful. He then addressed the assertions of Baltimore Unionists that he favored secessionists, and boldly questioned the nature of their loyalty. He saw their love of the Union revolving around lucrative contracts, taking over the B&O and Bay Line steamboats, and gaining increased political patronage. In their greed for money and power, they had exterminated "the real and substantial Union men of the Country."

The *Baltimore American* republished the general's statement and added commentary. If the president needed "additional reasons" for removing Wool, the editor declared, he should read the general's blasphemous letter. In his sweeping denunciation, Wool had included "every leading Unionist" in Maryland, from the governor on down. At the same time, he courted "those who have never, by any public word or deed, showed their sympathy with the Government . . . who, in fact, are profuse in their denunciation of every act of the administration, and only have words of compromise and conciliation for traitors." The administration should remove the aged general who "has proved himself utterly incompetent here."[66]

As the clamor for his removal increased, Wool was stricken with an intense pain in his side, possibly a kidney infection or gallstones. For five days, Major Christensen, his chief aide, sent "bulletins" to John Griswold on the general's condition. Wool continually moved from bed to rocking chair and back, night and day, seeking relief. His aides kept all military business from him, as well as newspapers. A doctor prescribed large doses of opium to produce sleep. Christensen asked Griswold to get relatives and friends to write and cheer up the patient. Sarah wrote daily and wanted to come to his side. Tell Mrs. Wool, the aide advised Griswold, that "I will tend the General as faithfully as if he were my own father." Wool's illness was reported in the newspapers, but there was no official concern. Few visitors came. Only Maj. Gen. Irvin McDowell, his military aide in Mexico and the ill-fated commander at First Bull Run, came by. Taking the old general's hand, McDowell apologized for not calling sooner. On the morning of November 27, when Wool awoke early "and commenced quoting Shakespeare," the aides knew the crisis had passed. That afternoon he wrote a short note to Sarah. "Every little attack only answers to re-invigorate me," he remarked, adding, "I shall outlive all my enemies."[67]

The veteran fretted about being removed from command in Baltimore. Such an act, he confided to Sarah, would be disgraceful "to an old officer whose only fault is that he has been too loyal and too faithful to his Country." He planned to see Lincoln. "I care not how he decides," the general said. "If I am removed without a hearing, there will be a 'muss' in Congress." Lincoln used the word "muss" a great deal. "In truth everything he does ends in a muss," Wool continued. "Of all the Presidents we have had, he is the least qualified for the position."[68]

In Washington on December 10, Secretary of War Stanton told Wool he was being replaced. What assignment would the general like to have? Wool said the decision was Stanton's, not his. The secretary suggested dividing the Middle Department, but Wool quickly added that he could not accept a smaller command because of his long service and rank. And if the president sent him back to Troy, there would be trouble. "I have many friends in Congress," he stated, "who are disgusted with the conduct of the President." If he received no assignment, they would immediately request an investigation of Wool's conduct in Maryland. Lincoln would regret this. Stanton was well aware of the influential New York delegation and promised to resolve the general's situation.[69]

On December 17, Wool learned that Burnside had lost the battle of Fredericksburg. At first the reports were only that the Army of the Potomac had been turned back, then it became evident that the Federals has suffered a resounding defeat. More than twelve thousand Union soldiers had been killed or wounded as Burnside hurled assault after assault against Lee's Fredericksburg defenses, before swaggering back across the Rappahannock River. Desertions in the demoralized Army of the Potomac reached two hundred a day. "The Generals throw all the blame on the President," Wool wrote Sarah, "who is wholly and totally deficient in the art of war. He advises but will not order what he wishes done . . . politicians control, and we had an abundance of these in the army, all Lincoln men who voted and spent their money for him. They must be paid with Brigadier and Major General commissions." Wool felt humiliated. "Allow me to ask why I am treated worse than I would treat the commonest soldier. What have I done that I should be used as a shuttlecock mainly to accomodate [sic] politicians because they have been partisans of Mr. Lincoln, when they know less [of] the art of war than James, our faithful servant . . . One army after another have been lost, when if they had been properly directed would have long since ended this great struggle."[70]

The anxious hours of waiting ended on December 17. Wool learned that Maj. Gen. Robert C. Schenck would replace him in Baltimore. He was granted a leave "for such a period as you desire" before reassignment. The following day, Stanton telegraphed: "If it becomes necessary to organize a department, including New York and the New England states, would such a command be agreeable to you?" The arrangement would be fine was the quick reply. On December 22, Wool turned over command of the Middle Department to Schenck, a veteran lawyer and radical Unionist from Ohio. The next day he and several aides boarded a train for New York City and home. His long travail in Maryland was over.[71]

During his six months in Baltimore, John Wool had sat on a powder keg. In his duties, which had principally been administrative, he had sought a conciliatory course in dealing with the Unionists, but he stubbornly refused to support their programs to suppress secessionists. With Lee's invasion of Maryland, Wool had been momentarily thrown into the cockpit of maneuvering Union regiments to meet the Rebel threat. He viewed with disgust the changing military scene with incompetent generals waging war and losing battles. Throughout these hectic days, Secretary Stanton supported the old general. Wool was a rigid old soldier, but he was also loyal, industrious, and predictable—invaluable qualities in war time. Of all the commanders of the Middle Department, John Wool doubtless was the most controversial—yet during his tenure, he diligently strove to maintain order and keep a crucial border state from political wreckage.

16

COPPERHEADS AND THE NEW YORK DRAFT RIOTS

During the chilly morning of January 12, 1863, a group of officers wearing heavy overcoats entered the lobby of the fashionable St. Nicholas Hotel on Fifth Avenue in lower Manhattan, followed by an array of porters carrying steamer trunks and valises. Leading the entourage was Maj. Gen. John Wool, who had arrived to set up headquarters for the newly created Department of the East. To some observers, the new department seemed little more than a housekeeping operation: the war was hundreds of miles away and there were few troops to command. In Wool's eyes, however, the northeastern states required special attention. Stragglers and deserters thronged the larger cities, busy harbors were easy prey for Confederate sea raiders, and public interest in the war effort was lagging. Moreover, clouds of civil disorder loomed on the horizon that would make New York City the scene of the largest riot in the nation's history. On the streets of this great city, where he had played as a boy, the old soldier waged the final battle in his long and eventful career.[1]

While on leave in Troy, Wool had received a private note, dated January 3, from Col. Edward D. Townsend, the assistant adjutant general of the army, who had been his chief staff officer in California. Townsend said that he had suggested to Stanton the value of placing the general over a department to include New York and New England, and the secretary had approved the arrangement. "I hope you will not be *hard on me*," Townsend added, "for thinking you cannot at this juncture be spared to wait orders long." On January 11, the orders came, and Wool alerted his staff officers and aides—Cram, Frothingham, Christensen, Carncross, and Clinton—to collect their baggage and join him on the train that night from Troy to New York City, designated as headquarters for the Department of the East.[2]

Wool located his military offices in a spacious parlor of the St. Nicholas. Under the direction of the genial Colonel Cram, his chief of staff and longtime associate, workmen installed a line to the downtown office of the United States Military Telegraph, and aides and clerks set up furniture and organized their desks. Wool's first order of business was to call on the governors in the new department as well as the garrison commanders scattered through the Eastern Department. His command included some four thousand officers and men, stationed at twelve forts along the coast; the largest concentrations being in New York Harbor (four installations of 1,400 men) and in the vicinity of Boston. In both places, the army maintained prisons for rebel captives and political malcontents. Wool's jurisdiction also included the busy navy yards at Brooklyn, Charleston, and Portsmouth, where workmen labored over ironclads for service on the western rivers. The major activity was at the state militia rendezvous, where new regiments were organized, equipped, trained as home guards, and for the battlefield. In the weeks ahead, the general planned to tour the coastal fortifications in his jurisdiction and place them on a war footing.[3]

Wool gave first priority to the apprehension of deserters and officers on unauthorized leave. After the bloody battle of Antietam, thousands of soldiers had fled their regiments and sought anonymity and refuge in northeastern cities. Many were foreign-born soldiers who quickly vanished into friendly districts in manufacturing towns, particularly in eastern New York, New Jersey, Connecticut, and New Hampshire. Desertion was so prevalent that Lincoln compared the task of filling up the army to shoveling fleas. In January 1863, upon taking command of the Army of the Potomac, Gen. Joseph Hooker reported that 25 percent of his men were absent. To cope with the growing problem, Secretary Stanton, in September 1862, created the Provost Marshal General's Bureau, and appointed Simon Draper, a wealthy and influential New Yorker, to head its operations. Draper supervised a large corps of assistant marshals, one or more in each state, who searched for deserters and sought military assistance in making arrests. Draper's marshals were effective, but a War Department investigation in January 1863, showed that the bureau kept few records and lacked personnel.[4]

Wool stepped up the search for deserters in his department. Garrison commanders were to provide "every facility" to the marshals, even allowing them access to records on those in confinement. In New York City, the general also called on private citizens to turn in deserters and set up barracks on Broome Street and at Park Row to hold them for trial. A War Department order allowed deserters to return to their units by April 1 without punishment. Wool also questioned army leave policy. In July 1862, the War Department granted leaves only to officers disabled by wounds or disease, but he had found that Generals Heintzelman, Hooker, and others flagrantly violated this regulation, claiming delegated authority from the War Department. Wool asked Stanton for a clarification of the matter, and, upon receiving none, ordered his subordinates to tighten the rules on officer leaves.[5]

Wool surveyed the ordnance and military stores of his department. State governors were asked to report on the holdings in their arsenals, armories, and depots. New York governor Horatio Seymour was among the first to reply. Examining the return, Wool advised that New York should have in reserve at least 200 field guns and

150,000 stands of small arms, with ammunition, carriages, and necessary implements. "The great state of New York," he wrote, "should at all times be prepared to take care of herself." Similar advice went to Governor John A. Andrew of Massachusetts. "I consider Boston and Charles Town with the Navy Depot of more importance than a regiment of cavalry," Wool stated. He urged the governor to increase the military presence in his state.[6]

In mid-February 1863, the general bolstered the defenses of the "great emporium" of New York. He conferred with Col. Richard Delafield, commanding the Corps of Engineers in the harbor, and proposed placing cannon and troops at the entrance. He also wanted to build gun emplacements on Sandy Hook, off the New Jersey shore, and at two locations near the Narrows. The New York Chamber of Commerce applauded Wool's efforts and appointed a harbor defense committee to cooperate with him. On February 16, in a long letter to Stanton, the general reported he had 1,475 soldiers operating the four forts in the harbor. This force was entirely inadequate to repel a serious attack from the sea, or to keep order in New York, a city of over 800,000 people. He predicted trouble since a large number of its inhabitants were southern sympathizers. "They are doing all they can," he said, "to make the administration odious," and he urged the secretary to call up new levies—for the duration of the war or three years—to protect the harbor and city. Wool also wanted a warship and several gunboats to patrol the bay between Sandy Hook and the Narrows. Rebel privateers and ocean raiders, especially the much-feared *Alabama*, could easily slip into New York Harbor, seize merchant vessels, and shell the business district.[7]

Early on Monday morning, February 23, the general left New York City on a special train to tour army and navy installations in New England. He wanted a clearer idea of the coastal and harbor defenses, recruiting problems, and civilian support for the war. Traveling with him were Colonel Cannon, the prissy little businessman, and two military aides. The weather was cold and blustery, but newspapers had announced his coming, and townsfolk, militia units, and bands gathered at the major towns along the route to welcome the old veteran of three wars. At New Haven, Wool stood on the train platform muffled in a blue army greatcoat and waved at the crowd, but did not speak. At Hartford and Springfield, he delivered short patriotic speeches in a high sonorous voice, denouncing those who compromised with the Confederacy, and exhorting his listeners to support a "vigorous, united, and unremitting prosecution" of the war. At dusk with snowflakes in the air, Wool's train rolled into Boston to confront an anti-war demonstration. Ignoring the insults, he spoke briefly, urging support for the government and the war. In the evening, Wool visited Governor Andrew, and attended a Washington Day dinner sponsored by the Boston Light Infantry Association.[8]

The next day was equally eventful. At midmorning, the general went to the Charles Town Navy Yard, where a salute was fired in his honor. He inspected two large ironclads under construction, visited the old frigate *Niagara,* recently altered with iron plates and reinforced to carry thirty-five eleven-inch Dahlgren guns. Nearly three thousand workers swarmed about. Wool next toured the Pemberton Square Hospital, where he shook hands and tried to cheer the patients. In full dress uniform that evening, he dined with Gov. John Albion Andrew at the Parker House. Wool spoke in a "terse and soldierly style" on the duties of a citizen to his country in an hour of peril. On Wednesday morning with Andrew and Governor Nathaniel S. Berry of New Hampshire, he toured the fortifications in Boston Harbor. The next day, the special train headed south to New Bedford, where Wool inspected a new fort, and spoke to a gathering at the city hall. On Friday, February 27, he appeared before the Massachusetts legislature in Boston, where he gave a lengthy address "full of soldierly dignity and pathos," an aide recorded.[9]

On Saturday morning, Wool started for Portland, Maine. His aides murmured about the pace, but the old general relished every adulation he received. He gave short speeches to the crowds at the railroad depots at Salem, Lynn, Newburyport, and in New Hampshire, at Concord and Portsmouth. "It is my privilege to serve in the evening as in the morning of life," Wool later wrote the governor of Maine, "under a flag to which all Americans owe allegiance—and I rejoice to know that your Granite Hills do not stand more firmly than do the sons of New England in sustaining that standard of Liberty and fraternity." In Portland in the wintry darkness, Wool was escorted to the city hall to address a large crowd. Afterwards, the Seventeenth Infantry Band serenaded him at his hotel. The following day, a Sunday, Wool attended services at the Unitarian Church. Paying a short visit to Fort Preble, he returned down the coast to Portsmouth. At dinner, he introduced a new topic—the pro-Confederate "Copperhead" party in Maine.[10]

Providence, Rhode Island, on March 5, gave the general a rousing welcome. From the train platform, he "called to mind the sad condition of the country, and the danger of losing our power as a nationality." That afternoon, he stood before the Rhode Island legislature and warned against compromise. Separation would turn the nation into thirty-four bickering, warring principalities and certain ruin. Hurrying on to Hartford, Connecticut, the general made yet another official stop before heading back to New York City. In his New England tour, Wool not only gained a good idea of the defensive needs in his department, but he was also able to generated support for the government.[11]

Returning to New York City late at night on March 6, Wool missed a meeting that evening at the Cooper Institute to organize a branch of the Loyal Union League. Considering his clashes with Union radicals in Baltimore in the fall of 1862, it is interesting that on the engraved announcements, mailed on March 4, Wool's name headed the list of distinguished Union generals invited to attend. Mayor George Opdyke presided and newspapermen William Cullen Bryant and Henry J. Raymond, jurist David Dudley Field, as well as a number of other dignitaries, made speeches denouncing the "peace men." William Seward, Montgomery Blair, Ambrose Burnside, and various prominent Republicans sent letters of support. Before adjourning, the meeting gave verbal approval to create a "Loyal Union League of the Citizens of New York."[12]

Wool did attend the March 14 meeting of the league at the Academy of Music. Unlike the previous gathering, admission was by ticket, and New York's social elite predominated, with a large number of women attending. Honored guests included Senator Andrew Johnson of Tennessee, General Wool, and a half dozen prominent New York businessmen and philanthropists. Secretaries Gideon Welles and Salmon P. Chase occupied side boxes in the theater. Wool was introduced as the army's "senior" major general. "It is very cheering to see so many patriotic faces here," he said, "and more especially the patriotic faces of the ladies . . . I rely as much on their patriotism as I do upon that of the gentlemen, and perhaps a little more—for I have known some traitors among the gentlemen of the North; but I have not found any among the ladies. Their efforts have been felt and experienced throughout the army, most effectively, and my only surprise is that, after all their efforts, there are so many deserters from the army." Wool was interrupted frequently by laughter and applause. When the general concluded, the Union Glee Club sang two stanzas from the "Star Spangled Banner," and the chairman announced that Gen. Winfield Scott had been chosen as the president of the New York branch of the Loyal League. Andrew Johnson delivered the major address. Wool's appearance at the academy was a curious decision and was politically inspired. In Baltimore, he had tangled with the radical Unionists and knew their bent. In New York City he again found himself in their midst and doubtless paid lip service to avoid conflict.[13]

Unemployed and an avid radical, General Butler invited Wool to be an honored guest at an address he planned to give on April 2 at the academy. Butler told Colonel Cannon that he wanted Wool's "presence more than any man in the United States. I know he doesn't like me, but I have my reasons for wanting his support." At first Wool declined, snorting, "Why should I give my countenance to a man who has no military qualities?" But later at dinner with his nephew Congressman Griswold and several officers, Wool flared up at discourteous remarks about Butler. "General Butler is a Major General in the service of the United States," he declared, "and no man must speak disrespectfully of him in my presence!" The next day he agreed to attend Butler's speech.[14]

Butler placed Wool and his staff on center stage at the academy. The audience, a journalist wrote, "fairly blazed with the beauty and fashion of the City . . . accented by the waving of plumes, the ruddy ribbons, and the glittering jewels of New York's fairest ladies." In a flood of oratory, the gotched-eyed Butler covered a broad spectrum of topics that ranged from ideas for reconstruction of the South after the rebellion to an attack on British inconsistency on foreign policy concerning the Union. At the close, Butler crossed the stage and took Wool by the hand. The old soldier stood up and declared his endorsement of Butler. Butler needed Wool's presence to legitimize his address; Wool in no way supported Butler's radicalism but enjoyed the public adulation. He had played the game many times.[15]

Despite his advanced age, Wool enjoyed an active social life in New York City. Military organizations, politicians, and friends sent invitations. "I called to see if you would do my daughter and myself the favor to dine with us today at 6 o'clock," John Van Buren wrote on February 7, 1863. "We can give you a bit of venison and a bottle of red Madeira that her grandfather Judge Vanderport bought a year ago." In late April, the general wrote Sarah that he had attended a bridal party. "We had a fine supper and plenty of wine at 12 o'clock," he said. "The ladies were well made up with stylish materials and hair dressed as in the days of Louis the 14th. Some of the ladies wore their hair knotted back very becomingly with curls or ringlets down each side of their necks." Wool was always available to tour New York Harbor with dignitaries and friends. In late April, he took a large party that included Secretary Chase and his daughter, Katherine Jane, to visit the forts. That evening they dined with Mayor Opdyke and others. Friends and relatives from Troy also dropped by the St. Nicholas. Almost daily Wool performed ceremonial tasks that exhausted his aides.[16]

At the same time, Wool worked hard to curb the clandestine trade in New York City with the Confederacy. Provost Marshal Robert Nugent, whose "detectives" reported on rebel activities, informed the general in early April that the New York Customs House was a particularly sensitive place. Nugent brought James S. Walker, a customs employee, to Wool. Walker said that an individual named Morris T. Gudeman and others were in the city making purchases for the Confederacy with intentions of running the goods through the blockade. Moreover, Walker also said Gudeman had friends in the customs house who were falsifying papers to make them appear legitimate.[17]

With Walker's information, Wool on April 23 seized the steamer *Tubal Cain*, loading in New York for the Mexican port of Matamoros. The cargo included clothing, pistols, whiskey, quinine, plus letters indicating destinations for the various items. New York City was supplying both the Union and Confederate armies, the general wrote Sarah. "We are penny wise and pound foolish. No country has been better supplied with men and means to carry on war than the United States, and no country ever accomplished so little with the same means. Two thousand men would put an end to the nefarious traffic with the Rebel states through Texas but the government does not perceive it. Ships loaded with supplies for the Rebel Government are sent almost daily to Matamoros, and no efforts on the part of the government are made to stop them." Gudeman and several of his associates were arrested and imprisoned and the case turned over to the local courts. Customs house officials, Wool advised Stanton, were "far from being efficient" in discharging their duties.[18]

Despite the bustle of military business, Wool took time to fuss over domestic matters. Each month he sent a large part of his salary (averaging about $570) to Sarah for deposit in the Troy City Bank. He also reminded Sarah to draw the forage allowance for his two horses at the Watervliet arsenal in West Troy. She dutifully sent their servant William with a wagon across the Hudson by ferry to get the forage. "You will please make a memorandum of it," the general advised, "and tell William to draw the amount within a month or you may lose it." In late May, Wool purchased a light carriage for Sarah, one with low steps that would present "no terror" for her. On the evening of June 6, he arrived at Troy on the steam packet with the carriage on board and found William waiting with a team. The general remained at home several days, transacting private business and visiting friends, before returning to New York City.[19]

On June 15, 1863, New York newspapers announced that Gen. Robert E. Lee had launched another invasion of the North. Advance units of a large 65,000-man Confederate army had crossed the Potomac northwest of Harpers Ferry at Williamsport Crossing and were heading toward Chambersburg. What was Lee's objective? The War Department immediately asked Union commanders to report garrison strengths. Wool and his staff checked the personnel, ordnance, and stores at the forts in New York Harbor. "This running up and down the ramparts . . . is by no means light work," Wool wrote Sarah. "Those younger than myself . . . complained of the fatigue. . . . Every day I have been occupied from morning until late at night. Four nights I did not get to bed until 12 o'clock." Pennsylvanians, and the "powers that be" at Washington, "have had a 'big scare,'" and there were wild speculations about Lee's designs. If the rebels launched raids in Western Virginia, Ohio, Pennsylvania, and Maryland, "it will be godsend to the North," for they would excite the hearts of the patriots. "A raid or two in New York," Wool added, "would put down the rebellion in six months."[20]

On June 27, the telegraph key chattered incessantly at Wool's headquarters. A large-scale movement of Union troops to meet the rebel invasion was underway. In mid-June, at Stanton's call, Governor Seymour instructed Maj. Gen. Charles W. Sandford, commanding the First Division of the New State National Guard, to rush all available regiments, including those in or near New York City, by rail to Harrisburg, Pennsylvania. A week later, Navy Secretary Welles alerted the warship *Roanoke* in New York Harbor to prepare for sea duty. A cry of protest went up. Wool, Senator Edward D. Morgan, and Mayor Opdyke all pressed Welles to reconsider his order. The *Roanoke* was needed to protect shipping in the harbor. The navy had "important work" for its ships elsewhere, Welles curtly replied, and said that the ironclad *Passaic*, in the Brooklyn Navy Yard, would soon be ready for action. New York City was in no danger, Welles confided to his diary, adding that the ancient General Wool "feeds on panic and fosters excitement."[21]

Wool resisted Halleck's call for trained artillery companies stationed in the harbor forts. "They cannot be spared," he protested on June 27, explaining that they garrisoned the forts and their removal would create "great excitement" in the city. Three days later, Adjutant Gen. Lorenzo Thomas demanded that the two artillery companies at Fort Hamilton (which had no guns) be sent to the front. Wool again refused. On June 30, he informed Governor Seymour that he lacked men to operate his harbor artillery and warned that the "Alabama, or any other vessel of her class, might, without fear of injury, enter our harbor and in a few hours destroy one hundred millions of property." As late as July 3, despite repeated War Department calls, Wool held on to the artillery companies while sending hastily raised militia artillerists to Pennsylvania. Finally, he parted with the regulars, reducing his harbor command to four hundred men at nine installations. With the forts undermanned, Wool shipped the rebel prisoners to Fort Warren in Boston. All eyes now turned to Pennsylvania, where Maj. Gen. George G. Meade had taken command of the Army of the Potomac and was rushing to intercept Lee. A great battle was in the offing.[22]

On Saturday, July 4, Wool and his staff stayed at the St. Nicholas, awaiting news from the battlefield at Gettysburg. During the day, Governor Seymour gave an oration at the Academy of Music, and fireworks celebrating the national Independence Day blazed that night at Central Park. It was also Sarah's birthday. "I congratulate on your birthday the Independence of these United States, not very independent at this moment," the general wrote. Two great armies were locked in battle. "I presume it will depend on the brains of the two generals," he continued. "If Providence is on our side, as you seem to think, certainly with so great an ally we must succeed."[23]

On July 5, news came that Meade had repulsed Lee's Army of Northern Virginia, and the rebel army, battered and defeated, was retiring toward the Potomac. General Meade "covered himself with laurels," Wool wrote home. This was the first time the Army of the Potomac had "done anything worthy to be recorded in history." If the Union general could capture "the greater part of Lee's Army it will be the beginning of the end." The battle should place the anti-administration element "at a discount," and with more victories, "we will hear no more of the copperheads."[24]

Equally exciting news reached New York from the West. The seemingly impregnable Confederate fortress of Vicksburg, Mississippi, had fallen to a resolute Gen.

Ulysses S. Grant in one of the most successful campaigns of the war. Across the North, church bells rang and guns boomed a triumphant salute. It was only a matter of time before Port Hudson, Louisiana, the last Confederate stronghold on the Mississippi River, surrendered. After two bloody years of war, Gettysburg and Vicksburg represented a turning of the tide. From here on, Wool hoped, it would be downhill for the Confederacy.

As Lee withdrew back across the Blue Ridge Mountains into Virginia, the federal government started the machinery for a nationwide draft. On March 3, 1863, with a manpower crisis looming, President Lincoln signed a conscription act which required men ages 20 to 45 to enroll for two years' service in the Union army. A half million men were under arms at the end of 1862, but many of these were short-term enlistments and an estimated 100,000 were absent without leave. Under the act, the government set draft quotas for each state, based on population, and sent them to the provost marshals in the congressional districts. Draft requirements were flexible. A man could obtain a substitute, pay $300 and be released, or apply for a number of exemptions. Single men ages 20–35 were called first. In late May in Washington, Col. James B. Fry, who had replaced Simon Draper as provost marshal general, ordered the enrollment to begin. By July 1, district clerks were copying the rolls onto cards for lottery selection at provost marshal offices. Federal authorities set the date to start the operation. In New York City, the drawing was to begin on Saturday, July 11, with a quota of 12,500 in Manhattan and 5,000 in Brooklyn.[25]

On July 8, Wool received orders to dispatch his regulars to police the draft rendezvous in Buffalo, Elmira, and Rikers Island. He refused the request and asked Governor Seymour, then in the city, for permission to assign militia to the draft rendezvous instead. Wool also requested a heavy artillery regiment expected to arrive from Gettysburg, ordered to the harbor installations. As the general searched for militia companies, a new danger loomed. The USS *Ericsson* docked in the harbor on July 10 and reported that a large rebel steamer fitted with ten guns had fired at her near Nantucket. Wool instructed his commanders at the harbor entrance to load their long-range cannons, and stop and examine every vessel of size approaching the Narrows. Seymour ordered out militia companies for Wool to use, but on July 12, Wool suddenly cancelled his request! Always one to follow the rulebook, the general had consulted War Department regulations and learned that he could not use unorganized units for "special or qualified purposes." He would regret his decision.[26]

Saturday morning, July 11, dawned hot and steamy. At the draft offices around Manhattan, names were drawn and posted. Large crowds gathered and scanned the rosters. Rumors reached the general that a gang of Copperheads and deserters were planning to disrupt the drawing and even attack the Seventh Regiment's armory and seize arms to stop the draft, but nothing happened. The next day, Sunday, probably at

Wool's urging, Governor Seymour, accompanied by Bvt. Brig. Gen. Harvey Brown, commanding the few regulars in the harbor, toured the army and navy installations. The great fear was that rebel ironclads or ocean raiders would steam through the Narrows and turn their guns on the city. At every fort, the visitors found only a skeleton force on duty. As the governor pointed to the deficiencies, Brown reportedly grumbled about his assignment and Wool rambled on about his Mexican War experiences. A short meeting afterwards with city officials resolved nothing.[27]

In July 1863, New York was a fertile ground for agitators. The city ran north to Forty-Second Street, with the main business district lying south of Twenty-Third Street. Factories dotted the east side, while slaughterhouses, breweries, lumberyards, and other businesses clustered on the west side along the Hudson River. The well-to-do and rich lived in large stately mansions along lower Fifth Avenue. Rows of tenements crowded with recently-arrived European immigrants sprawled along the east side. Most of the inhabitants were day laborers, but this section of the city also harbored army deserters and sympathizers with the South. Here were large numbers of Irish who disliked the Lincoln administration's promoting blacks to compete for their jobs. They were furthered angered by companies using blacks as strikebreakers. A majority of New York's teeming masses had no roots to excite patriotism and lacked financial means to avoid the draft. In scanning the draft lists in the city newspapers on Sunday, July 12, many a heart sank. Outside, on the streets, groups circulated handbills, and here and there, speakers mounted soapboxes in public places to denounce not only the draft but draft exemptions and substitutions as well as anyone who would deprive citizens of their liberties. The stage was set to erupt.[28]

On Monday morning, July 13, Wool learned that a mob had attacked the Ninth District draft office near Third Avenue and Forty-Sixth Street soon after it opened. He and several aides went to the central police headquarters and called on Col. Robert Nugent, the provost marshal of the city. Nugent told Wool not to worry, that the police would take care of the disturbance. By the time Wool returned to the St. Nicholas, Mayor Opdyke had more details and was greatly alarmed. The mob on Third Avenue had set the draft office on fire and driven off the police guard. The mob had then easily overwhelmed a detachment of the semi-disabled veterans of the Invalid Corps ordered there by Nugent. The soldiers fired blanks then used ball cartridges. Furious, the crowd rushed the soldiers and beat two of them to death. Draft officials in the Eighth District closed their offices and fled with boxes of records. In their frenzy, the rioters seized John A. Kennedy, the city superintendent of police, who was in the area although off duty, and beat him severely. Flames from the burning Ninth District draft office quickly spread to adjoining tenements and stores, and great columns of black smoke spiraled skyward. Nugent reported that the riot was spreading and Mayor Opdyke asked Wool for help.[29]

Contrary to later reports, General Wool moved swiftly that Monday to meet the emergency. At noon he issued a call for "veteran volunteers" and concerned citizens to assemble on Tuesday morning at the Seventh Avenue Arsenal and receive arms and assignments. Wool also telegraphed marching orders to an invalid company in Newark, New Jersey, and a regular company at West Point, and sent an urgent request to five state governors in his department for militia. Orders also went to the commander at Fort Hamilton, in New York Harbor, to dispatch eighty reinforcements from the Twelfth Infantry to Manhattan. Wool asked Rear Admiral Hiram Paulding, at the Brooklyn Navy Yard, for marines to guard public property in the city. He also wanted an armed steamer to protect the arsenal at Governors Island in the harbor. At Albany, State Adjutant General John T. Sprague wired General Sandford to protect the Seventh Avenue arsenal at all costs, and promised to send two hundred soldiers by train the next morning. Early on Monday, Sandford mustered a fresh regiment, the Tenth New York, and dispatched the untrained men to Manhattan. Wool designated the downtown arsenal as the general rendezvous for the military. He placed Colonel Nugent in command of the army detachments gathering there and instructed him to cooperate with Sandford. The soldiers were to guard public buildings and arsenals and avoid contact with the mob. The general predicted that it would take at least twelve to fifteen hours to assemble his forces.[30]

As rioters swept along Third Avenue, Wool, at mid-afternoon on Monday, was besieged with requests at the St. Nicholas. Opdyke had moved his office to the hotel, and the lobbies swarmed with excited businessmen and politicians. Prominent citizens yelled at the general for action. Judge Dudley Field, Horace Greeley of the *Tribune*, and an editor for the *Evening Post*, demanded he declare martial law in the city. Wool agreed, but quickly added that he had no troops to enforce it. Opdyke then called him aside and suggested that a command be given to General Frémont, who was living in the city. At the time, the ill-fated Frémont, plus McClellan and Don Carlos Buell, were "unassigned generals" on detached service in New York City with their staffs. Wool turned away. "I had no command for a major general & certainly not one under my command who had been ignored by the President," he later wrote. Greeley wanted troops to protect the *Tribune* printing plant. Again, Wool had no troops to send, but ordered that a stack of muskets and ammunition at the Governors Island arsenal be sent to the newspaper office. "To each applicant for aid, I said the best protection is to put down the riot," the general said.[31]

The mob was immense. During the hot, steamy July afternoon, angry crowds, estimated as large as thirty thousand, roamed the East Side, from Forty-Sixth to Twenty-Eighth Streets. Shouting men and women drove a police guard from the state armory on Second Avenue; reinforced police units wielding heavy nightsticks arrived to find the building on fire and looters fleeing with weapons. Gangs swept through adjoining neighborhoods, plundering and looting stores and residences. Many of the rioters, particularly the Irish, vented their hatred on blacks. One group set fire to the Colored Orphan Asylum at Lexington and Forty-Third, then fought with the firemen who sought to evacuate the children. Elsewhere in the district, gangs of men caught blacks and beat them to death. Telegraph lines and street railways were wrecked. At dusk rioters smashed windows at the *Tribune* office and threatened destruction, until a stout police detail dispersed them. Edward S. Sanford, in charge of the U.S. Military Telegraph Office, wired Secretary Stanton at midnight on Monday that New York City was "at the mercy of a mob, whether organized or improvised, I am unable to say," and added, "It is to be hoped that tomorrow will open with a brighter prospect."[32]

By early evening, soldiers began arriving in the city from the forts in the harbor. A company of marines from the Brooklyn Navy Yard landed with three small howitzers and marched to the Seventh Avenue arsenal. A gunboat moved into the East River, anchored, and trained its guns to protect Wall Street. General Brown had left his headquarters on Governors Island and came to the St. Nicholas. Wool held Brown, a hot-tempered, crusty veteran, in low esteem. A week earlier, he had advised Colonel Townsend in the adjutant general's office in Washington that Brown had done a poor job of activating the artillery in the harbor, and did not take "interest in the affairs of the Country which the times require." Probably anticipating a hassle over his call for regulars, and wishing to avoid involving Brown in a "defensive assignment," Wool had earlier bypassed the harbor commander, and sent a troop request directly to Fort Hamilton. When Brown signed orders for the movement, he went to see Wool. In the midst of the hubbub at headquarters, Brown urged the general to call in all the military in the harbor. Wool agreed, and Brown spent the afternoon loading men onto steamers, and by evening returned to the St. Nicholas. Wool then instructed Brown to report to Sandford, at the Seventh Avenue arsenal, and take command of the regulars in place of Nugent. Miffed at being subordinated to a militia officer, Brown established himself at police headquarters instead.[33]

When Sandford reported that "a lack of harmony" existed between himself and Brown, Wool tersely addressed both generals: "Gentlemen—It is indispensable to collect your troops not stationed, and have them divided into suitable parties, with a due proportion of the police to each; and to patrol in such parts of the city as may be in the greatest danger from the rioters." Brown interpreted the instructions to mean separate commands, and Sandford again complained. Disgusted by the bickering, Wool now placed the senior officer—Sandford—in command of all the troops—militia and regulars—in the city. About nine o'clock, Brown rushed into Wool's headquarters and asked to be relieved. A heated verbal exchange ensued. The general pressed him to reconsider, but Brown flatly refused. Nugent again took charge of the regulars in the city, which by midnight had grown to four hundred men. A thunderstorm mercifully swept the streets, drowning several of the fires burning on the Upper East Side.[34]

During the night, detachments of soldiers tramped through the wet streets to designated posts. Two infantry companies from the harbor landed at Spring Street, and marched to the St. Nicholas. A section of horse-drawn artillery splashed its way to the Seventh Avenue arsenal, and in the darkness, the gunners stationed their pieces to sweep the streets. At headquarters, Wool, Cram, and other officers studied troop locations in the city. First and foremost, they were determined to protect public property. Guards and barricades were needed to secure 200,000 stands of arms deposited around Manhattan at the arsenal and armories, and at the sub-treasury, the customs house, and the post office. Equally important were city hall, arms factories, banks, gas works, and shipyards. Above all, strong measures had to be employed to check the mob. The New York police had valiantly borne the brunt of fighting that day, but Wool hoped that federal and state troops might provide support on the morrow.[35]

Tuesday, July 14, dawned hot and sultry. Uptown, many shops were closed and police patrolled the streets. About eight o'clock, Brown, his temper cooled, came to the St. Nicholas and asked that he be restored to command, saying he would serve under Sandford. Wool welcomed the veteran officer and sent him to police headquarters to cooperate with Commissioner Thomas Acton, emphasizing that the regulars must act as support for, not independently of, civil authority. As Wool later reported, Brown ignored Sandford, who had orders from Adjutant General Sprague to use available militia to protect the Seventh Avenue arsenal. As it developed, Wool soon excluded Sandford, who traveled about in civilian clothes, from his decisions, and allowed Brown a wide latitude in commanding the regulars in the city.[36]

Tuesday was a critical day in the riot. Upon restoring Brown to duty that morning, Wool instructed him to strike the rioters in a vigorous manner. "To-day," he stated, "there must be no child's play." Wool kept the telegraph busy in an effort to help quash the riot. Could the state inspector general station a militia detachment at the state arsenal at Brooklyn? Would the captain of the gunboat *Tulip* anchor and train its guns on Pine or Wall Streets? Telegrams again flashed to the governors of New York, Massachusetts, Connecticut, and New Jersey pleading for soldiers. Wool again placed ads in the city newspapers calling for "loyal citizens" to perform temporary guard duty. At midmorning, Governor Seymour arrived at the St. Nicholas. At noon, standing on the steps of City Hall behind a file of infantry with fixed bayonets, the governor, whom Gideon Welles labeled "Sir Forcible Feeble," addressed a crowd of several thousand people. Seymour stressed that he was their friend, that on Saturday he had sent his adjutant general to Washington to confer with the authorities and to ask that the draft in New York be suspended. He urged the citizens to disperse and stop destroying property. Back at the hotel, on the application of the sheriff, Seymour declared the city and county in a state of insurrection. In a separate proclamation, he invited all concerned citizens to assemble at the Seventh Avenue arsenal and other designated places in the city for volunteer duty. Over four hundred responded. But the rioting continued, and the radical press, particularly the *World* and the *Daily News*, fanned the flames of disorder.[37]

Fire bells rang across town all day long as police and soldiers battled fires and rioters. In the morning, two hundred patrolmen, traveling uptown in wagons and omnibuses, assailed a mob on Second Avenue, driving it north to Thirty-Second Street. Here the cry went up: Soldiers! Soldiers! Col. Henry J. O'Brien, leading two companies of the newly organized Eleventh New York Volunteers, supported by a detachment of regulars and two six-pounders, marched onto the scene. Apparently with Wool's permission, O'Brien had gone to Brown and obtained command of the recruits and the regular unit. While the troops fired at the mob, gunners unlimbered and sent six rounds pointblank into the shrieking masses, dispersing them. On Pitt Street, 130 regulars with bayonets charged a mob, killing and wounding twelve.[38]

In the afternoon, Brown sent regulars to help the police clear Ninth Avenue above Thirty-Fourth Street. When the blue-coated patrolmen fell back, the troops deployed as skirmishers and poured a galling fire into the yelling humanity. The police then hacked their way through a maze of barriers and cleared the avenue. On east Twenty-First Street, an infantry platoon joined police in a house-to-house battle with rioters and looters. In some instances, the soldiers fared poorly. General Sandford sent a militia company and four thirty-two-pounder howitzers to Allerton's West Side Hotel, but the rioters overwhelmed them and the soldiers raced back to the arsenal. Sandford asked for help and Brown sent a force to drive off the mob. As Tuesday afternoon wore on, the contest remained undecided. The police still bore the brunt of dealing with the disorder, but Brown's soldiers fought coolly and tenaciously. Unfortunately, Brown lacked the manpower to make a permanent impression as rioting flared simultaneously in a half-dozen places.[39]

By nightfall, the telegraph lines to Washington hummed with activity. Wool was under fire. A battery of complaints, mostly from radical Unionists, portrayed the general as fumbling and senile. The ancient soldier was "too far advanced in life and too infirm to endure the fatigue and labor incident to such an emergency," one businessman complained. "Those in charge of the civil and military administration are undecided, slow, and without capacity," said another. An "active, energetic, and intelligent soldier" was badly needed, it was said. Provost Marshal Nugent gloomily reported that the mob seemed more formidable on Tuesday than on the previous day. But help was on the way. During the afternoon, Secretary Stanton had detached several New York regiments from the Army of the Potomac, and they were soon speeding by special train to the strife-torn city.[40]

On Wednesday, July 15, the tide in the bloodshed and turmoil turned. Given free reign, Brown shuttled detachments from his little 800-man army here and there during the day to aid 2,000 city police. Sandford continued to operate independently. By late afternoon, seasoned troops were pouring into the city. The Sixty-Fifth New York State Militia arrived from Maryland with four howitzers and bivouacked at Center Market. Brown spent the day posting soldiers around the city. That evening, additional soldiers landed, enlarging Wool's forces to 1,400 men. Shortly after midnight, in a telegram to Halleck, he was confident: "I think we shall put it down to-morrow." Wool's tenure in command was crumbling, however. During the day, radical politicians, claiming he hesitated to use force, telegraphed Lincoln and cabinet members to replace the aged general. Such orders were promptly issued. General Dix would replace Wool.[41]

The devastating riots were ending. On Thursday morning, July 16, the newspapers announced that the draft had been temporarily suspended in New York, and that the city council had voted $2.5 million in bounties for volunteers. Buses and rail cars resumed operations in Manhattan. The heavy hand of the military lay over the city, as cavalry units and infantry with bayonets tramped the streets. The only serious outbreak was at dusk, when soldiers smashed a group of looters near Gramercy Park. That evening, Mayor Opdyke wired Secretary Stanton: "We had but little disturbance in the city last night, and none this morning. I think the riot is at an end."[42]

The next morning, July 17, with four regiments bivouacked in city parks and armories and more on the way, Wool reported that New York City was quiet. Before noon, Brig. Gen. Edward Richard Sprigg Canby arrived, reported to Wool, and relieved Brown as the federal commander in the city and harbor. The next day, Wool ordered Canby to begin withdrawing troops to their regular stations. The toll from the riot had been great. Over 120 people had been killed or were missing, and the property damage ran over $1.5 million, an astronomical amount of money at the time. The draft riots in New York City, coming only days after the great watershed victories at Gettysburg and Vicksburg, represented a tragic and embarrassing episode in the ugly racial, ethnic, and economic divisions in the North.[43]

Wool advised Sarah on July 17 that General Dix would relieve him the next day. "I shall not regret it, for it is anything but a pleasant command," he said. He viewed the change as primarily "political," and aimed more at Governor Seymour, a Peace Democrat, than himself. Both Seymour and Dix had presidential ambitions, and each would now have to walk with care. On July 18, Wool transferred his command to Dix, and requested Secretary Stanton send him to Troy, with a part of his staff, "there to await orders." With Dix's permission, the general stayed in the city for a few days to complete his report on the riots and pack his papers. On July 24, he took the train to Troy. Two days before, New York newspapers announced that on August 1 the army would retire John E. Wool, Harvey Brown, William S. Harney, and other aged officers.[44]

There was a bitter aftermath. As early as July 17, the day Canby replaced Brown in New York, Sandford had issued a general order which contained statements criticizing Brown for disobeying Wool's instructions on the first day of the riot. In his official report on July 20, published in the press six days later, Wool briefly described Brown's unwillingness to serve under Sandford, but added that he otherwise had obeyed Wool's orders to the letter throughout the riot. He never accused Brown of insubordination, but rather of "unsoldierly conduct." Brown, smarting from being retired with a blemish on his record, sought to defend himself. On July 30, the veteran published a lengthy defense in the *New York Herald*. He appended a supportive letter from Police Commissioner Acton and testimonials by Brown's subordinates and by Major Christensen, one of Wool's staff officers, now in disfavor. Brown recounted his actions during the hectic days in detail, and claimed that the troubles started with his misunderstanding of Wool's vague order to cooperate with Sandford.[45]

On July 31, the *Herald* injected politics into the controversy. The newspaper accused Brown of being a tool of the radical Unionists of New York City, who saw in the riot an opportunity to discredit Governor Seymour. "The riot was a purely local affair," it stated, "and the duty and power of putting it down rested exclusively in the hands of local and state authorities." Wool had taken this position from the first and had consulted regularly with Seymour and local civil officials. His successor, General Dix, had followed the same course. The bickering was also aired in the *Troy Times*, with Brown publishing a card on August 1 condemning all allegations against him as wicked and unfounded. Wool made no reply. Unfortunately, this exchange clouded for posterity the respective roles the three generals—Wool, Sandford, and Brown—had played during four turbulent days in July 1863.[46]

During the draft riots, Wool, who always followed army rules and knew well the critical line between state and federal authority, had sought to play a supporting rather than a commanding role in dealing with the emergency. He saw as his first duty the protection of public and private property, then, as his forces grew, to make troops available to assist the police. His position called for defense, rather than offense. As the commanding general of a large military department, he did not feel it his duty to quell a local civil disturbance. Wool was keenly aware of the growing outcry against him during the riots, but blamed it on politically motivated extremists who demanded harsh measures to crush draft opposition in the city. For several months they had courted him, and he had cooperated, but in the crisis the veteran suddenly adopted an independent course which placed him apart from their counsel. As on many past occasions and in various assignments, Wool carefully read the political winds and acted in a consistent manner of being inconsistent. When he left New York City for Troy, in late July 1863, the general was seventy-nine years old. It was altogether fitting that his last command had been in the Empire State, where fifty-two years before, as a young captain, he had pledged his sword to the defense of the republic.

17

NOBLE DEFENDER OF THE UNION

In the fall of 1863, the bustling river port of Troy extended a warm welcome to the old general when he settled there in retirement. The mercantile and industrial center of forty thousand people on the west bank of the Hudson River, seven miles above Albany, had always held him in great esteem and stood in awe and respect of his achievements. He was their most famous living citizen. Wool's stately brick residence at the corner of First and Ferry Streets was a well-known landmark in the city. Here, before the war, the general and Sarah entertained friends, relatives, and distinguished guests with sumptuous dinners, graced with fine wines and elegant silver settings. On New Year's Day, the Wools always honored the old tradition of an open house by greeting a host of townsfolk. But the bustle and clamor of former days were now gone; nephews and nieces were grown, married, and scattered, and many old friends had passed away. Although there were fewer visitors, Wool remained active. He daily scanned the newspapers for war news, and labored for hours, despite a lame right hand, over letters to public officials and friends. He volunteered with fund-raising and occasionally traveled by train to distant towns and cities to speak for the war effort. When hostilities ended in April 1865, the gray years followed as the sound of battle grew fainter and the old soldier was forced to march to the beat of a different drummer.[1]

Following his return to Troy in August 1863, Wool seized every opportunity to urge his fellow citizens to support the Lincoln administration and help end the war. At public functions, in letters to friends, and in short speeches to newly recruited companies who stopped at his house to salute him, the old general spoke with deep sincerity about preserving the Union. He also drafted letters for political purposes. On October 31, 1863, as New Yorkers prepared to go to the polls to choose a new state legislature, he published a letter in the *Troy Weekly Times* he had written to his nephew Congressman John A. Griswold. Ostensibly a reply to the question of his July removal from command in New York City, the general, after a token comment, launched a verbal blast at the Peace Democrats and anyone opposing the Lincoln administration. He pointed to the fake patriotism of those who "crook the pregnant hinges of the knee where thrift may follow fawning." These were the government speculators who fed on the war. Army generals had the men to win the war, he argued, but were held back by such vultures. He compared the Copperheads, who were clamoring for compromise, with the old Federalists, who, during the early years of the republic, embarrassed the Madison administration by calling the Hartford Convention to protest the War of 1812. The current Democratic faction in supporting the Peace Democrats was obstructing the war effort, Wool said, and prolonging the hostilities and the bloodshed. All Democrats must unite, stand by the flag, and avoid political suicide. They must put country above party.[2]

In New York, Wool's letter was widely cited by the Unionists, or Republicans, who conducted an all-out campaign to carry the state in the fall elections. When the voting was over in early November, the Union party had won. Although stump speakers did more to guarantee that Republicans sweep the New York elections, kind words were tendered the old general for his thoughts.[3]

Wool continued to speak out for the Union at every opportunity. In the fall of 1863, patriotic women in several northern cities organized fairs to raise money for the United States Sanitary Commission. Created by private citizens in June of 1861, the commission sought to stir enthusiasm for the Union and supplement the needs of soldiers. For the Cincinnati fair, in December 1863, the managers sold autographs, letters, photographs, and mementos from famous personages in military and civilian life. The idea spread. By early 1864, Wool began receiving endless requests for photographs, letters, or both. He responded to each request with pleasure and would frequently inserted patriotic statements denouncing "unprincipled and ambitious" southern demagogues, and encouraging enlistments to fill Union ranks. When Ellen McClellan, wife of Gen. George B. McClellan, made a request, Wool put aside his ill feelings towards her husband and sent a gracious, appreciative letter. Invited by a committee to attend the Sanitary Fair at Albany on Washington's Birthday, he wrote that he would be out of town on the specified day, but extended his reply so the letter might be used. Quoting the Roman historian Tacitus, Wool wrote that the patriot who protected and defended his country would be "remembered in history as worthy of a place among the gods." Wool's letters to fair managers frequently appeared in newspapers, providing an even wider airing of his patriotic sentiments.[4]

Early in 1864, with casualty lists growing and no end of the conflict in sight, Wool grew anxious about the continuance of the war. From Washington in late January, John Griswold sent a copy of the *Congressional Globe* carrying a speech he had made in the House of Representatives against authorizing commissions to negotiate with the rebels. Griswold's remarks struck a responsive chord. In a long letter on January 27, Wool sounded dire warnings. The North was carrying a heavy tax burden, voting millions in bounties to stimulate recruiting, and pouring hundreds of thousands of soldiers into the field. With the right leadership, its armies should soon end the hostilities. The rebels were searching frantically for alternatives. "They are willing to submit to any conditions which any European government may impose on them," Wool said, "rather than again unite with the North." However, a peace, short of reunion, would be disastrous, for it would encourage dissension among the states. Prolonging the war was equally dangerous, as it could lead to a dictatorship. "When the people become tired of a civil war," Wool observed, "a dictator follows to a certainty." Writing to New York representative Abram B. Olin the same day, Wool repeated his warnings and criticized the over-cautious Halleck. General Halleck was holding the Union forces back, fearful of another Confederate invasion of the North. Lincoln should not tolerate such dilatoriness. The sooner the president sent Halleck back to California, the better.[5]

On March 4, 1864, Wool left Troy for Washington, D.C. A new general-in-chief had been appointed to direct the Union armies, and Lincoln had invited a select group of major generals to the White House to meet him. Congress had approved the elevation of Ulysses S. Grant to the exalted rank of lieutenant general—held previously only by George Washington and Winfield Scott. Wool liked Grant. This hard-fighting western commander, he wrote Griswold in January, was "the only general we have who has the confidence of the Army and of the people." Grant arrived in the capital on the eighth, received his commission on the ninth, and suddenly left for Brandy Station to confer with Gen. George Gordon Meade, commanding the Army of the Potomac. On Grant's return to Washington to brief Lincoln and Halleck, Wool spoke with him. There is no record of their conversation, but certainly the old soldier, as he was known to do, volunteered advice. On the evening of March 12, Wool dined at the White House with Lincoln and his military guests (Grant did not appear), then the next morning joined the group that escorted Grant the to the train depot. Wool left for Troy, stopping to visit friends in Philadelphia and New York City on his way home.[6]

The welcome days of spring arrived as Grant prepared to lead the Army of the Potomac against Lee in Virginia. Wool followed the war news closely, appeared at local military functions, helped collect money for the Troy Orphan Asylum, and continued his lively correspondence. In a letter to Lincoln on April 24, he commented at length on the nation's military leadership. Wool believed that the rumored Union move on Richmond—a two-pronged attack, one south from Washington and one north from Fort Monroe—was unwise. The armies would be too far apart to unite with certainty, and Lee might repulse each individually. Also, armies should move with a minimum of baggage. Two years before, during the Peninsula Campaign in the spring of 1862, McClellan had been hampered by supply trains, his staff had been inefficient, and his army poorly organized. If the newspapers were correct, McClellan had been twenty-three days marching fifty miles. Moreover, Little Mac "did not know the value of time or the advantages of celerity of movement." Grant, Wool wrote a friend in May, was not "out of the woods" in his invasion of Virginia, but he had confidence in Grant and believed he would succeed. Success, however, "does not depend so much on numbers as [on] Generalship." A great commander understood strategy and tactics—how to maneuver troops on the battlefield. "These united with sleepless vigilance and energy will accomplish much more than numbers," Wool asserted. Unlike McClellan, whose headquarters were four to eight miles in the rear of his army, a great commander "placed himself where he could overlook the field" and, if necessary, led his soldiers into battle.[7]

Wool took a particular interest in the 1864 presidential campaign. On St. Patrick's Day, March 17, at an enormous rally in New York City, General McClellan announced his candidacy for the Democratic nomination for president. In August, newspaper editors, aware of Wool's strong feelings toward the Peace Democrats, requested statements from him. To the editor of the *Troy Times*, Wool expressed doubt that "under the state of the public mind" his comments would help check the "machinations" of rebel sympathizers in the northern states. Public apathy was widespread. The Republicans, he said, were doing nothing "to encourage the President, the Army, or the Navy." They should call meetings to support Lincoln. "Such meetings would do more to silence rebel sympathizers and Presidential factions than anything that you or I could do in relation to rebel peacemakers."[8]

In late August 1864, Wool pledged his pen to defeat McClellan. When Amos K. Hadley, editor of the *Troy Whig*, asked the general for a statement to use against the McClellan Democrats, Wool handed him copies of several letters he had previously published. In selecting extracts for publication, he asked Hadley to say nothing to "disparage General Grant. . . . Do not say or intimate that he adopted my plan. All I know on the subject is that he and myself thought alike on the same subjects." When the Democratic National Convention met in Chicago, on August 31, McClellan supporters in Troy, much to Wool's disgust, staged a large-scale demonstration, with bonfires, street processions, and bands. Democratic politicians delivered speeches on the courthouse steps, and a crowd moving through the downtown area cheered each illuminated residence, including the Wool's. The general passed up no opportunity to lash out at McClellan. On September 9, when a group of army recruits arrived from Plattsburgh and marched to Wool's house, he appeared on the stoop to give a short talk, praising their appearance and lambasting the schemes of the "traitors" assembled at Chicago.[9]

Wool applauded the *New York Times* for its stand against McClellan's candidacy. He asked George F. Noyes, an outspoken War Democrat in New York City, to hand-deliver his comments to the editor. Noyes thanked Wool for his letter and assured him that his views "belonged to the country," and would be "quoted far and wide and greatly strengthen the Union cause." McClellan's election as president, the general feared, would prove disastrous to the nation. It would mean, he said, "the trailing of our flag in the dust before its enemies, the entire subservience of the North to the South," and its eventual surrender to Jeff Davis and his cadre of traitors. A widespread conspiracy of peacemakers, with headquarters in Canada, extended over both the North and South, Wool warned. The Union was in deep peril. Through their secret associations, the conspirators used every means to "alarm and frighten." In exhorting the rank-and-file to elect McClellan, they were demoralizing both the army and navy. "It was not the sword of CAESAR," Wool warned, "that destroyed the liberty of Rome, but the demagogues that thronged the forum with souls dead to their country's honor."[10]

Wool's statement provoked a heated response. The *New York World*, a pro-McClellan organ, assailed the old general in strong language. It reopened the matter of Wool's command at Fort Monroe, saying the separation of his garrison from McClellan's forces had deprived him of "proper military control over his base of operations." Wool had demanded to retain his forces, stating that McClellan did not need them. He would encounter little or no resistance on his march to Richmond. But the old general was wrong. The editor regretted that Wool had been part of the intrigues and jealousies which hampered the Army of the Potomac. He also regretted that, on the eve of the 1864 election, the Lincoln administration should not have "dragged" Wool into writing a letter in which he calumniated McClellan. Equally shameful was the fact that the administration had recalled to duty, "in the field of partisan politics," an officer who had been forced to retire from active service.[11]

Wool reported to the *Troy Times* on a political poll he had conducted. On September 28, 1864, while returning on a special train with Governor Horatio Seymour and a group of militia officers from a military funeral at Salem, Massachusetts, the general went through the cars and asked his companions to vote on presidential aspirants said to be peacemakers. Upon tabulating the results, he announced that Lincoln received 211 votes and McClellan 60. Seymour, claiming ill health, read a newspaper and kept his eyes closed without commenting.[12]

On October 4, Wool also responded to the *World*'s accusations in a letter to his nephew Griswold that appeared the next day in the *Troy Times*. In a long, rambling discourse, the general recalled the march toward rebellion, denounced James Buchanan and his cabinet as weaklings, while turning on the Peace Democrats in the North. The northern peacemakers, he asserted, had joined with "steadfast friends" of Jefferson Davis in promoting McClellan's nomination at the Chicago Convention. The cognomen "Democrat," however, would avail McClellan no more in his race for the presidency than the appendage "Napoleon" had aided him on the peninsula. "In the latter case," Wool said, "the compliment, if such it may be called, did not even inspire him . . . if his officers are to be believed, as to induce him to place himself under fire to watch the operations of his different corps." Was there a Democrat who supported Stephen Douglas for president in 1860 who would vote for a candidate "who accepts a nomination from a convention that sympathizes with the rebels?"[13]

Newspapers in New York State reprinted Wool's October letter. At Buffalo, a McClellan stronghold, a Union Party committee paid $100 to have Wool's letter published in the local *Courier*. The Washington *Intelligencer* ran the letter and the major New York City newspapers carried it. Wool himself mailed clippings to friends near and far. "As I addressed to you in my first letter on the subject of the rebellion," he wrote Lewis Cass, "I venture to transmit to you another, and perhaps my last on the subject of the rebellion and its authors. As you have been my friend and I hope remain so still, I transmit the record to show that I have been for more than fifty-two years a steadfast and constant friend of my country and the Union." Wool even mailed a copy of his letter to Secretary of War Edwin M. Stanton, with the hope that it would meet "your approval as well as that of the President."[14]

The *New York World* attacked Wool savagely. On October 10, under the heading "Hessian Slanderer," it portrayed the general as slandering McClellan out of professional jealousy. The paper also linked Wool's outbursts with his nephew's campaign for reelection. Formerly a War Democrat, Griswold was now an "ostentatious" Republican Democrat for Lincoln. He had switched camps because the government had released him from certain unremunerated contracts. Two days later, the *World* aimed lower. Wool had developed a new avocation, the newspaper asserted. Having no young lieutenants about him "with spare dollars and inexperience in the game of poker," Wool had "taken himself to writing letters on political topics." In western New York, the Buffalo *Courier* echoed this sentiment. The paper accused the general of "robbing and impoverishing junior officers while in the service by practicing the arts of 'an accomplished blackleg.'"[15]

Wool responded to the article in the *World* with a letter to the *Troy Times* on October 12: "The writer is too much in the habit of lying to claim notice, further than that you will say that the article referring to myself *is utterly and wantonly false*. It is not the first time that the writer, who favors conspiracy and treason, has published similar articles concerning me. I will give these Copperheads something more to chew over in a day or two."[16]

On October 15, Wool fired another salvo. Instead of focusing on McClellan, he blasted the young general's supporters—the Peace Democrats. If the Copperheads won the election, they would place the United States at the mercy of Jefferson Davis and his traitors. Evidence of this had appeared in both northern and southern newspapers, as well as foreign journals, particularly those supporting Napoleon III and his

Mexican adventures as well as the aristocracy in England, "our old and never-ceasing enemy." The English, to prevent a reunion of the states—and the rise of the United States as a major commercial rival—had furnished the rebels with money, ships, and arms and now favored the election of McClellan, believing he would recognize southern independence. In their campaign strategy, McClellan's supporters were promoting the spread of secret associations, generally called the "Sons of Liberty" that was said to have 335,000 members all the way from New York to Missouri. Wool was certain their attempts would fail. There was enough "patriotism, or love of country, still remaining in the Free States, to put down this dangerous and widespread conspiracy, and save their country and their Government." The general urged citizens to vote for principles instead of men. In closing, he warned against the peacemakers: "Like the three monsters of Paris—Danton, Marat, and Robespierre—they would leave their country a howling wilderness for the want of more victims to gratify their peace propensities."[17]

The general's letters in the newspapers were not unrewarded. In late October, Secretary Stanton called Wool to Washington for a conference. Rumors of Copperhead plots to stuff ballot boxes, and disrupt the November election in New York City, largely a figment of Republican imagination, was causing local businessmen great anxiety. Troops were needed to police the voting districts. The record is not clear, but Stanton probably asked Wool to supervise the election in New York City. Writing Stanton later, the general referred to his interview, which was held on October 27 or 28: "I was invited by you to come to Washington. On my arrival . . . you offered me a command, which I was willing to accept and to perform . . . but remarked that you need not give yourself any trouble about myself, for I was then engaged in a service . . . to prevent the election of the ungrateful Major General McClellan." When Wool declined the offer, Gen. Benjamin Butler, who was visiting New York, performed the election duty along with five thousand troops ordered to the city.[18]

Taking into consideration the chaotic wartime atmosphere in the country at the time, it is remarkable that the 1864 election took place at all. When the polls closed on November 8, 1864, Old Abe, largely on the back of the soldier vote, was reelected president. Lincoln swept the North and the far West with McClellan only carrying the border states of Kentucky and Delaware and his home state of New Jersey. For Wool, the victory was even sweeter when the returns showed that his nephew, John Griswold, had won another term in Congress. Several individuals wrote to thank Wool for his help in the campaign. "If I have in the smallest degree contributed to achieve the great victory of the 8 November, 1864," Wool told one correspondent, "I am more than satisfied."[19]

With Gen. William T. Sherman having completed his devastating march through Georgia and now headed into the Carolinas, Gen. Grant's Army of the Potomac pounding away at Lee from the trenches around Petersburg, and the war dragging into 1865, the general spent long hours at his writing desk in his library, slowly composing letters. With the end of the war on the horizon, visitors became more and more infrequent and in the snowy New York winter, correspondence provided his principal contact with the outside world. Most of his letters dealt with personal matters. On January 8, Wool thanked Prosper M. Wetmore, in New York City, for sending him a copy of the recently printed Union Defense Committee report, with a supplement carrying the general's correspondence. He was pleased with the account of his work with the committee in April 1861, and ordered an extra one hundred copies of the supplement. When they arrived, he inquired about the costs of publishing in book form his letters on the rebellion. He was hoping to distribute copies to his friends.[20]

Wool's inquiry about his letters reached the newspapers in a garbled form. The *New York Herald* reported the old general was in failing health—and was preparing an autobiography. Dozens of friends promptly wrote, expressing alarm. In late January 1863, the general diligently replied to each. The reporter who commented on his health, he told a former staff officer, Col. William P. Jones, must have been a "penny a liner" who was short of funds. He assured Jones that he was "neither declining in health nor engaged in writing my autobiography. . . . My vanity is not such as to induce me to follow the example of several distinguished military chieftains" who had done so and had seen their military fame diminish. "Barring accidents, my friends may rest assured that some years will have passed before they will be called upon to mourn my departure to that undiscovered country, from whose bosom no traveler returns," he said.[21]

With snow blanketing the hillsides in the early months of the year, Wool spent much of his time indoors managing his business affairs. It was a time of accounting and planning for necessary outlays. His investments in bank, railroad, and canal stocks, as well as in mortgages, were lucrative, and even at an advanced age, he kept purchasing additional securities. He was always careful about details and watched every penny—and yet was an extremely generous man. Discussing book buying with historian Henry B. Dawson, on February 28, 1865, Wool commented on his financial obligations. Because of his retirement, he was living on a reduced income, although he continued to make substantial "quarterly donations" to various relatives. "At least five families, besides my own," he said, "depend on me for the means of living. . . . I however have only one relation of my own that depends on me. A sister who is very old and one of the best of women. She has the privilege of calling for whatever she desires."[22]

No personal records have survived to indicate which relatives Wool helped financially, but he certainly gave support to the Baylies family in Taunton, Massachusetts. Of all the men and women Wool befriended, his brother-in-law, Francis Baylies, had always been the closest. Harriette Baylies Moulton, Francis's daughter, was now caring for her aged mother and her uncle, William Baylies, who was suffering with dementia. Harriette sent admiring letters to Wool. "This day is the fourth anniversary of the Fall of Sumter," she wrote on April 12, and what "different emotions now swell the hearts of the people than in 1861." She rejoiced over Lincoln's reelection and the prospect of peace once again. "Your portrait, decorated with two small flags (placed above it at each side)," Harriette reminded her uncle, "still hangs in company with the Empress Eugenie; from the same peg—which association pleased you as I remember." The little banners were placed "in bright array to wave over the head of one of the Noblest Defenders of the Union."[23]

On Saturday morning, April 15, heartbreaking news arrived on the telegraph from Washington. President Lincoln was dead at the hands of a twenty-seven-year-old actor, pro-Confederate fanatic, and recreant assassin John Wilkes Booth. Within hours, Troy, like the rest of the Union, was in mourning. Shops and businesses closed, church bells that had so gleefully tolled Lee's surrender at Appomattox Court House only days earlier, now rang out in somber mourning. Storefronts and homes, including the Wool residence on Ferry Street, were draped in black crape and flags flew at half-mast. On Sunday, while cannon boomed regularly on the half hour from sunrise to sunset, people went to church, prayed, and heard eulogies of the departed president. On Monday, at a special meeting, the common council voted resolutions of sorrow. Wool attended the council meeting and asked to make a statement, which read in part: "The virtues and excellencies, the patriotism and conscientiousness, the honesty and ability of Abraham Lincoln are known to you all, and will be remembered so long as this nation shall last or men shall recognize the highest qualities of his race." The general advised against military display or outdoor pageantry, saying the suspension of business and solemn church services were appropriate expressions of the city's sorrow and respect.

As huge bonfires, torches, and flambeaus lit the way from New York City, Wool was in Albany when the Lincoln funeral train, pulled by a locomotive named *Union*, arrived on the Hudson River Railroad. Joining city officials of Troy and wearing a badge of mourning, Wool crossed the Hudson to join sixty thousand mourners, including delegations from Vermont and Massachusetts, as the president's casket was taken in somber procession to the assembly chamber of the state capitol. All through the afternoon and into the night as many as four thousand grieving citizens pushed and shoved passed Lincoln's open casket. On the morning of April 26, the funeral train departed for the fifteen-hour, night-time journey across western New York to Buffalo. The Civil War had ended, but its wounds would fester for decades.[24]

During the summer of 1865, Wool devoted considerable thought and energy to six lawsuits filed against him in Baltimore in December 1862 and January 1863.

Three involved outspoken secessionist politicians whom military authorities at Baltimore had sent to Fort Monroe for detention while Wool was in command. Each man claimed he had been falsely accused and imprisoned, and each sought $20,000 in damages. Three other men brought suits when they were arrested by the provost marshal in Baltimore in late October 1862, and charged with conspiracy against Wool's authority, and incarcerated at Fort Delaware. Each of these men complained of "assault and false imprisonment" and asked damages of $10,000. In the latter case, the plaintiffs retained Henry Winter Davis, an attorney and radical Unionist, as counsel. Wool hired Col. William L. Schley, a highly respected Baltimore barrister, to represent him in all six suits.[25]

In preparing for the fall court in Baltimore in 1863, Wool was forced to post $15,000 in bonds. The general had signed the bonds himself and returned them, saying he was "abundantly able" to pay the amount. One plaintiff, S. Teackle Wallis, was particularly aggrieved, claiming that he and his companions had been harshly treated at Fort Monroe. Wool disputed the allegations. The prisoners had occupied quarters in the casements of the fort like those of his officers, and the manager of the Hygeia Hotel had furnished their table with the best food. "Those whose business it was to see that they were properly attended to," he admitted, "may have connived at treating them badly or harshly, but certainly not by my order." In November 1863, Wool became ill and the cases were bound to early 1865—then postponed again.[26]

With the termination of hostilities in the spring of 1865, Wool, at Schley's suggestion, sent a letter to the plaintiffs offering a settlement. Assuming that attorney Davis and his three clients had agreed to an arrangement, the general paid Schley $500 in attorney fees. But this did not end the matter. Davis could not get his clients to agree, so the suits were continued. Wool was not greatly alarmed. If all the facts were presented, he was certain a jury would give the plaintiffs little "more than minimal damages." The opposition would seek heavy damages, Schley warned, because it was widely thought the general no longer enjoyed the confidence of the administration. Wool was certain they were making a mistake.[27]

By 1865, Wool's influence in Washington had diminished greatly. He wrote a congratulatory letter to President Andrew Johnson on June 6, 1865, but received no response. In early July, he approached the administration through his nephew Congressman Griswold, who wrote Stanton with rumors that Gen. John Adams Dix was being transferred or retired from the Department of the East, and urgently requested that Wool be appointed as his successor, even if temporarily. The act would "satisfy several purposes and be gratifying to his friends." More to the point, several persons in Baltimore were suing the general and expected to recover heavy damages. Such persecutions "visited on officers for official acts in their line of duty were shameful." Again, there was no response.[28]

Wool now wrote directly to both Stanton and Grant. He reminded Stanton of his patriotic service during the war, as well as their close personal friendship. With the wartime cases pending against him, the general needed a sign of administrative support. A short tour of duty should do the trick. On July 6, 1865, Wool explained to Grant his predicament and asked that he be assigned to active duty. The plaintiffs were "under the impression that I am not sustained by the Secretary . . . if I could show the impression entertained as false and without foundation, the suits would be withdrawn." If assigned to active duty, he would "willingly resign" the position whenever Grant or Stanton wished. In a follow-up letter on July 10, Wool recalled in detail his Civil War services and again asked for special consideration. His letters were never answered.[29]

In early August 1865, Schley reported that two of the plaintiffs—Thomas Sewall and Thomas Gardiner—had withdrawn their suits. In October, as the fall session of the Baltimore court neared, Wool went to Washington and talked with the third auditor in the Treasury Department about the cases. He also asked the auditor to hand-deliver a letter to President Johnson. His earlier letter had apparently not been received. Several weeks later, when the trials opened in Baltimore in November, Wool was not present and again the cases were carried over to the next term of the court. In March 1866, the general sent a request directly to Stanton's office, asking that the government pay Schley's attorney fees and bonds. When he heard nothing, he asked Griswold to make an appointment with Stanton and withdraw the request. "If the $10,000 should never be returned to me, I assure you it will cause not the slightest uneasiness on my part. I will with much larger sums charge it to my patriotic efforts to save the Union." In November 1866, the suits were withdrawn.[30]

Like other public figures of his day, Wool expressed strong feelings about the government program for reconstructing the South. Part of this grew out of his aversion to political extremism and from a view that the wayward states be given a chance to redeem themselves. He also favored a policy of gradualism in bringing the freedmen into American society. Wool expressed admiration for Andrew Johnson and his reconstruction policies. "We now have a man at the helm in whom I have confidence," the general told a Missouri friend in the fall of 1865. "He unites honesty with mercy and efficiency." In January 1866, Wool applauded Johnson's veto of the Freedmen's Bureau bill. If the bill did not cause a civil war, he told historian Benjamin Lossing, it would cause "something else that would have been worse, a moral degradation from which might cause oceans of blood to flow. Opinions and prejudices which have existed for centuries cannot be changed in this generation, much less in a day. The Caucasian or Saxon race will never consent to be placed on an equality with the negro, either politically, socially, or by amalgamation. It is a subject too revolting to [be] thought of."[31]

The general lectured his nephew, John Griswold, on the reconstruction issue. The Radical Republicans, he was certain, were endangering the peace of the nation by trying to force the Caucasian race to accept blacks as equals. They should wait "until it is ascertained whether the four millions of slaves, four fifths of whom are as ignorant of the institutions of the country as the mules they drive, are capable of appreciating the great boon which the Union has so generously bestowed upon them," he wrote. "Before the Saxon race will submit to be placed on equality with the Negro, they must be brought down to the standards of the latter. When that takes place, they will have become what the Negroes have been, slaves." To bring the southern states back into the Union, "it would be much better to conciliate than to violate them" and stir old animosities. "The conqueror should be magnanimous," the old general continued. "Justice tempered with mercy often accomplishes more than the sword." Griswold, however, was drifting toward the Radical Republicans. In February 1866, he voted for the Freedmen's Bureau bill and the Civil Rights Act in the opening salvo of the showdown between President Johnson and the 39th Congress that would lead to the Fourteenth Amendment. As a politician on the rise, he was supporting the party in power. That fall he won a third term in Congress.[32]

During the congressional campaign of 1866, Wool accepted an invitation to attend the pro-Johnson Soldiers and Sailors Convention in Cleveland, Ohio. President Johnson had incurred the wrath of the Radical Republicans in Congress by consistently vetoing their policies and by offering his own reconstruction program. To influence the fall elections, he made a two-week tour in late August from New York City to St. Louis, but his extemporaneous, tactless speeches produced little more than ridicule and humiliation and his efforts were largely wasted. At the same time, in August, Johnson supporters held a National Union Convention in Philadelphia. They condemned radical reconstruction policies, urged a prompt return of the South to the Union, and endorsed Johnson's policies. To secure further support, the Johnson forces organized a Soldiers and Sailors Convention to meet in Cleveland in mid-September, and invited Union officers of the army and navy, retired and active, living in the eastern and midwestern states, to attend. Since Winfield Scott had died in May, the managers asked Wool, now the senior general, to be their honored guest. The old soldier perhaps symbolized the spirit of union that had prevailed from the early days of the republic, a spirit now sadly lacking in the nation.

Wool arrived by train in Cleveland in a rainstorm on September 17. Members of the New York delegation met him at the train station and provided an escort to the fashionable Kennard House. Scattered in hotels about the city were one thousand blue-coated men, wearing badges of different states, talking, smoking, and drinking. In the lobbies of the hotels, bands played martial music. In the public square, a tented pavilion capable of holding as many as five thousand veterans, was constructed and colorfully festooned for the occasion. Circulating among the crowds, newspapermen were struck by the number of federal officeholders along with those aspiring to federal office. Certain individuals attracted attention, the most conspicuous being the flamboyant Gen. George A. Custer, described as "a man with a good deal of hair but very little brains."[33]

With a cannon shot on the afternoon of September 18, state delegates assembled and filed into the tented pavilion. Tumults of cheers rose when General Wool entered at the head of the New York delegation. He leaned heavily on the arm of Kentucky governor A. M. Bramlette, but smiled broadly as he made his way to the speaker's platform. To bring order, Bramlette instructed the band to play the "Star Spangled Banner." The governor then came forward and nominated Wool as the interim chairman. "For the purpose of temporary organization," he said, "I move that the oldest living general in the army, and perhaps the oldest in the world, Maj. Gen. John E. Wool, be called to the chair." A rousing, roaring approval followed.[34]

Assisted to the platform where civil and military dignitaries were seated, Wool moved slowly to the podium. He unfolded several sheets of paper, looked out over a sea of faces, and in a high, deliberate voice remarked that the occasion was the "most precious" of his long military career. He was honored to address such a large assembly of patriots and heroes. Putting on his spectacles, Wool then read a short address on the policies of reconstruction. There was much fear and apprehension in the land, he said, caused largely by Congress's reluctance to restore the southern states to the Union. The sooner that Congress recognized these states, the sooner the fears would end. For thirty years, a war of words between "the National Radical Abolitionists" and the southern slaveholders had raged. The slaveholders were now defeated, but the radicals, led by "inflammatory orators and aspiring demagogues," were threatening to disrupt the government. Should this course continue, he was sure, there would be another civil war. By uniting behind President Johnson, who had proved himself a bold and loyal senator, governor and then president, there was hope of averting another conflict. "War is a great evil," the elderly general declared, "and the greatest that can befall any country or people. The loss of liberty commences with oppression and oppression follows war." On this note, he concluded his address and again the crowd cheered.[35]

Wool was present for two of the three days of the convention. Escorted to and from the pavilion by Henry Wilson, a volunteer "aide" from Ohio, he watched the delegates organize, hear an array of speakers, and vote on resolutions. Each day, when he and other generals appeared, there was cheering and bands played. At the end of the second day, Wool announced that he was leaving for home. The convention rose to its feet and gave "three genuine camp cheers," while a band blared "Hail to the Chief." On September 19, he left Cleveland by train for Troy.[36]

Radical spokesmen played down the convention, saying it was little more than a forum for office seekers, that it was poorly attended, and criticized its feeble pronouncements. Republican James G. Blaine recalled later: "The venerable General Wool of the regular army, the oldest major general in the United States at that time, was made president of the convention, and his selection was significant in the proceedings. He had been all his life a soldier and nothing but a soldier. . . . He denounced the Abolitionists . . . [and] thought the convention had been called to protest another war, which he was sure the Abolitionists were determined to force on the country." Another observer claimed that Wool prated too much about "the Union and the constitution as our fathers gave them to us. This would include a flag with only 13 stars." Wool indeed had fumbled on the platform; he alluded to Lincoln's plan (when he meant Johnson's) and portrayed the Radical Republicans as abolitionists. He was from another era, another time, and his views on race were on the wrong side of history. Much of what he said at Cleveland seemed irrelevant and outdated.[37]

Yet, in calling for moderation and conciliation, Wool voiced the opinions of an important segment of American society. Writing to a convention delegate late in September, the general hoped that the Cleveland proceedings might "stay a revengeful and vindictive spirit." Southerners were a brave people. They had fought "as men never fought," and they should not be forced "into a state of desperation." The general told Lossing that he had enjoyed the convention: "If I had not gone to the convention, I should forever have regretted it. It was composed of three thousand officers of the army. . . . There was not a radical, I mean an abolition radical, among them. No Butler panting for more plunder, no [W. G.] Brownlow ready to lay waste the rebel states . . . no [Thaddeus] Stevens to desolate the Country then sell the land to pay the National debt." The radical party had "niger [*sic*] on the brain," and was "the most dangerous faction that ever existed in the Country."[38]

In the months that followed, Wool watched the expansion of the radical reconstruction program into the South. In letters to friends, he commented on the threat to the Union. "There can be no doubt," he wrote New York congressman William E. Dodge, in February 1867, "if the measures proposed should be forced upon the rebel states and the impeachment of President Johnson should be seriously pressed, we shall have another civil war." The radicals, Wool warned a friend in Louisiana, in October, regarded the Constitution as "a rope of sand, to be destroyed if they cannot force the South to place the Negro . . . on an equality with the white man." Historian Henry B. Dawson quoted Wool as saying that, "previous to 1861 we were a great and prosperous people. . . . How is it now? We find the Union dissolved and ten states governed by military satraps. . . . We have no statesmen. Demagogues alone rule and govern. My only hope is in the people, and that they will rise in their majesty in 1868, and overthrow the Dantons, Marats & Robespierres of the Union."[39]

Wool grew concerned over his image in history, precipitated, to a large degree, by the publication of Winfield Scott's two-volume *Memoirs* in October 1865. As Scott's portrayal of Wool's role at the battle of Queenston in 1812 was inaccurate, the general countered with his version in the *New York Herald*. John A. Dix chided him, saying, "I am sure Genl. Scott did not intentionally misrepresent your participation in the Battle of Queenstown. But his mistake shows how difficult it is for any man to write contemporaneous history—even his own." Scott made no reply. When solicited two years later for a donation to a Scott memorial, Wool replied that he would contribute nothing for a man who "had no regard for the truth."[40]

In August 1867, the Fenians, an Irish fraternal organization dedicated to the establishment of an independent Irish republic, invited the old general to speak at a picnic they were holding at Green Island, across the Hudson River from Troy. Although Wool declined the invitation, he wrote a lengthy letter to the Fenians praising their efforts and their cause. No people had suffered more than the Irish—"the down trodden of Europe"—and no people were more deserving of freedom. No one merited more admiration that the Irish immigrants who come from a "land of oppression to the land of freedom."[41]

Wool courted historians Lossing and Henry Dawson, doubtless hoping one would undertake his biography. He prepared sketches of certain episodes in his career, although it was painful for him to write. Lossing agreed that he would describe Wool's accomplishments in his new history of the rebellion. The general expressed great appreciation for the honor, and added, "If I am thus presented in your immortal history of the rebellion, I will live forever in the history of fame." He cooperated generously with Lossing and Dawson, furnishing them printed documents and reading proofs of their writings. Editors of biographical dictionaries also found the general highly receptive to requests for information on his army exploits. A movement was started in Troy for a statue of Wool, but the idea proved stillborn.[42]

During the winter of 1867, Wool withdrew from public life. He read to Sarah, now stricken with paralysis, arranged and rearranged his personal papers, and attended to financial obligations. He rarely appeared downtown. "This is Sunday, the better day the better deed," he wrote Dawson, on December 8. "During the winter months, I do not go to church, and for the reason that I seldom escape a severe cold owing to the church not being properly warmed in the morning. A person of my age should guard against severe colds." He had lost interest in writing. "To be frank with you," Wool wrote gloomily, "I find myself in a position so different from what I had anticipated a year since that I have no heart or inclination to write anything beyond a commonplace." Wool wrote even fewer letters in 1868. Pressed by Dawson to prepare a statement on his role in the battle of Plattsburgh, the general delayed while complaining of aches and pains.[43]

With an uneven hand in January 1869, Wool wrote Dawson that his afflictions "come and go when least expected." Spring weather brought brighter days. When an occasional friend or visitor came by, the enfeebled soldier showed them his extensive library, his presentation swords and other military souvenirs, and then took them for a short stroll in his well-kept flower garden. At commencement in June, Williams College, at Williamstown, Massachusetts, conferred an honorary Doctor of Laws degree on the old warrior. Militia bands from Albany and Troy frequently stopped in the street by his home to serenade him.[44]

In early August, Wool apologized to Henry Dawson for his delay in writing. It had been a long time, he said, since he had written a letter to "either friend or enemy." Infirmities of old age and constant attention to Sarah had turned him into a recluse in his own home. After fifty years of active life, his circumstances were depressing and unbearable. "My confinement was never anticipated, it almost unnerves me," the general told his friend. "My only resource is in my library, yet it does not supply the place of my wanted activity." His future seemed hopeless.[45]

On Monday, November 1, the *Troy Times* reported the old soldier had fallen at his home on Saturday and was in serious condition. He had ventured out onto his piazza to enjoy the genial sunshine warming the brisk autumn day and he had tripped and seriously injured himself. James, his faithful mulatto servant, and others carried him to his chambers and summoned a physician. A host of friends came to visit and cheer him. He repeatedly asked about Sarah and her health. Although assured he would recover, Wool saw no hope. "No," he replied, "this is the last flickering of a lamp that has long been burning." Relatives arrived to keep a vigil—the Griswolds, the Harts, and others. Being unable to take nourishment, he slowly sank into unconsciousness. Shortly after midnight on November 10, the eighty-five-year-old soldier breathed his last and passed into eternity. There was no struggle, but "an easy, gradual sinking away, into the last long sleep of death.[46]

In General Order 75, the commanding general-of-the-army, William T. Sherman, announced Wool's death to the army. It was with "profound regret" that "one of the very few remaining veterans of the War of 1812, Maj. Gen. John E. Wool," was dead. He received a ceremonial burial befitting a war hero. Thirteen guns boomed up and down the Hudson River every thirty minutes from Watervliet arsenal, across the Hudson from Troy, commencing as the funeral procession moved toward the cemetery. Garrisoned posts throughout the Department of the East lowered their flags to half-mast. Gen. Irvin McDowell, commanding the Department of the East, sent various units and regimental bands to Troy to participate in the ceremonies.[47]

On Saturday, November 13, the city of Troy was in mourning. All business houses closed. Despite the bitterly cold weather, an estimated fifty thousand people crowded the streets. Newspapers in Troy, Albany, and other cities printed eulogies and tributes by state and local officials and friends. It was rumored the old general had died a wealthy man, leaving an estate of over $650,000, with sizeable bequests to nieces and nephews, orphanages, and former staff officers. During the morning, troops wearing overcoats and white gloves arrived by train and ferry, together with Governor John T. Hoffman, Generals McDowell and Meade and their staffs, and other dignitaries.[48]

The funeral was at noon in the newly completed St. Paul's Episcopal Church. On the lid of the coffin lay Wool's chapeau, swords, and epaulets; below them was a plate with his name, rank, and date of birth and death. When the eulogies ended, the pallbearers placed the richly embellished coffin on a hearse drawn by six black horses, attended by four black grooms, and a long military procession began. Cannon boomed at regular intervals. Winding through downtown Troy, the column headed toward Oakwood Cemetery as six bands played "Home Sweet Home," Wool's favorite melody. At the hillside grave, near an old Mohawk trail, appropriate rites were recited, a militia detachment fired a volley of farewell, and the remains were lowered into the earth.[49]

A decade later, with money provided in Wool's will, a granite obelisk towering seventy-five feet high, carved from a quarry in Maine, was hauled up the Hudson River from Maine on a barge and placed over the grave of the general and his faithful wife, who had survived him by three and a half years. His long-time friend, William Cullen Bryant, penned the inscription cut into the monument: "This stone is erected to Maj. General John Ellis Wool, the gallant soldier, the able commander, and patriotic citizen; distinguished in many battles; and to Sarah Moulton, his excellent and worthy consort." It was a fitting memorial for a brave soldier who had dedicated his life to his country.[50]

ABBREVIATIONS

AET and CN	Army of East Tennessee and Cherokee Nation
AG	Adjutant General
AGCRP	Adjutant General, Canadian Rebellion Papers
AGO	Adjutant General's Office
ANC	*Army and Navy Chronicle*
ASP:MA	American State Papers: Military Affairs
ChiHS	Chicago Historical Society
CHS	California Historical Society
CU	Columbia University
GO	general orders
HED	House Executive Document
IGIR	Records of the Office of the Inspector General, Inspection Reports
JISHS	*Journal of Illinois State Historical Society*
LC	Library of Congress
LRAG	Letters Received, Adjutant General
LRHA	Letters Received, Headquarters of the Army
LRTB	Letters Received, Topographical Bureau
LSAG	Letters Sent, Adjutant General
MxWO	Mexican War Orders
NA	National Archives
NARA	National Archives and Records Administration
NYHS	New York Historical Society
NYSL	New York State Library
OCHS	Old Colonial Historical Society
OR	*The War of the Rebellion: A Compilation of the Official Records of the Rebellion*
ORN	Official Records of the Union and Confederate Navies in the War of the Rebellion
RCHS	Rensselaer County Historical Society
RG	Record Group
SED	Senate Executive Document
SHC	Southern Historical Collections
SHSW	State Historical Society of Wisconsin
SO	special orders

SW	Secretary of War
SWLS	Secretary of War, Letters Sent
UMi	University of Michigan
UNC	University of North Carolina
VMHB	*Virginia Magazine of History and Biography*
VR	Recollections by Solomon Van Rensselaer in Catharina Van Rensselaer Bonney's book
WP	John Ellis Wool Papers

NOTES

PREFACE

1. Mary McAdow, interview by Jerry Thompson, September 7, 2019, transcript in author files. Hinton donated an extensive collection of papers and sound recordings from his and his family's lives dating back to 1874 to the Briscoe Center for American History at the University of Texas–Austin (hereafter cited as Hinton Papers). "A Guide to the Harwood Hinton Collection, 1874–1995," accessed August 24, 2019, http://www.lib.utexas.edu/taro/utcah00419/cah-00419.html.

2. Diana Davids Hinton to Jerry Thompson, August 1, 2019, author files; 16th Census (1940), Dallas County, Texas, National Archives, Washington, DC.

3. Harwood P. Hinton Jr., "John Simpson Chisum, 1877–84," *New Mexico Historical Review* 31–32 (July 1956–January 1957).

4. Diana Hinton to Thompson, August 1, 2019, author files. While in Madison, Ann was able to complete a master's degree in library science.

5. A large portion of the Wool papers were on microfilm at the time, but the papers were found to be in such disorder, the microfilm was destroyed and few rolls survive today. The Wool papers, amounting to fifty cubic feet, have to be one of the largest collections of personal and official records kept by a nineteenth-century American military figure. For an inventory of the papers, see John Ellis Wool Papers, 1810–1869, New York State Library, last updated April 19, 2019, http://www.nysl.nysed.gov/msscfa/sc15361.htm.

6. Diana Hinton to Thompson, August 1, 2019, author files. Upon learning that Harwood had dated Nance's sister while the two were at the University of Texas, Nance was cordial and respectful.

7. Savoie Lottinville to Hinton, June 29, 1961, Hinton Papers.

8. Frank Vandiver to Hinton, May 31, 1961, Hinton Papers.

9. Bruce Dinges, interview by Jerry Thompson, July 22, 2019, transcript in author files.

10. "All historians do is steal from each other," another student remembered Hinton saying. Dawn Moore Santiago to Thompson, July 17, 2019, author files.

11. Diana Hinton to Thompson, August 1, 2019, author files. Hinton also became a life member of the Texas State Historical Association and was active in the Organization of American Historians, the Western History Association, the Arizona Historical Society, and the Historical Society of New Mexico.

12. Hinton to Lottinville, May 3, 1962, Hinton Papers. Hinton also approached Paul W. Galleher at the Arthur H. Clark Company, who replied that he was very interested in General Wool but was "over-taxed and far behind" (Galleher to Hinton, November 7, 1962, Hinton

Papers). Arthur H. Clark Jr. wrote in March 1963 offering to publish 1,500 copies of Wool's biography but wanted Harwood to cut the manuscript by 20 percent (Arthur H. Clark Jr. to Hinton, March 14, 1963, Hinton Papers).

13. [Frank Vandiver?], Reader's Report, n.d., Hinton Papers.

14. Lottinville to Hinton, October 31, 1962; Hinton to Lottinville, November 13, 1861, both in Hinton Papers.

15. Hinton to Lottinville, November 28, 1962, Hinton Papers.

16. Glen Sample Ely to Thompson, July 25, 2019, author files.

17. Edwin A. Shaw to Hinton, June 22, 1967, Hinton Papers. Even after Lottinville left the directorship of the press, he continued to communicate with Hinton, writing in September 1967 that their friendship was "one of the pleasant, most constructive things of my tenure." Lottinville would be as "proud as a new father the minute the Wool book is done. . . . By gad, we'll pull the Wool over their eyes yet!" Lottinville to Hinton, September 4, 1967, Hinton Papers.

18. Hinton to Shaw, June 19, 1967, Hinton Papers.

19. Ely to Thompson, July 25, 2019, Thompson Papers.

20. Ron Tyler to Thompson, July 24, 2019, Thompson files. Hinton found time to edit John S. Spratt's *Thurber, Texas: Life and Death of a Coal Company Town* (Austin: University of Texas Press, 1986) and Stephen Powers's 1872 epic *Afoot and Alone: A Walk from Sea to Sea by the Southern Route* (Austin: Book Club of Texas, 1995), and publish *History of the Cattlemen of Texas: A Brief Resume of the Live Stock Industry of the Southwest* (Austin: Texas State Historical Association, 1991). Both John and his mother were buried in the Hinton family plot in Laurel Land Cemetery in Dallas.

21. Hinton to Dear Jack, March 5, 2000, John P. Wilson Papers.

22. Hinton to Dear John, August 17, 2007, Wilson Papers.

23. Hinton to Dear Jack, August 22, 2009, Wilson Papers.

24. Dinges, interview with Thompson, July 22, 2019; Mary McAdow, interview with Thompson, September 7, 2019; both in author files.

25. Hinton to Dear John, June 1, 2012, Wilson Papers.

26. *Dallas Morning News*, September 11, 2016; *Midland Reporter-Telegram*, September 11, 2016; *Arizona Daily Star*, September 11, 2016.

CHAPTER I. OFF TO WAR WITH THE JOLLY SNORTERS

1. John Savage, *Our Living Representative Men: From Official and Original Sources* (Philadelphia: Childs and Peterson, 1860), 500; *Troy Times*, November 10, 1869.

2. Conklin Mann, "The Wool Family of New York," *New York Genealogical and Biographical Record* 72 (October 1941): 295–300.

3. *Troy Northern Budget*, July 15, 1805. Rensselaer County regiments are in Edward B. O'Callaghan and Berthold Fernow, eds., *Documents Relative to the Colonial History of the State of New York* (Albany: Weed, Parsons, 1856–1887), 15: 266, 272, 521, 530–40, 546. They are mentioned in Horatio G. Spafford, *A Gazetteer of the State of New York* (Albany: H. C. Southwick, 1813), 293; *Troy Family Journal*, August 30, 1852; Arthur J. Weise, *Troy's One Hundred*

Years (Troy, NY: W. H. Young, 1891), 18; and in Mann, "Wool Family," *New York Genealogical and Biological Record* 72: 165, 231, 300–304. James Wool Jr. at age 15 fought with a militia company in the battle of Bennington, Vermont, on June 6, 1777.

4. *Troy Times,* November 10, 1869; Edward M. Ruttenber, *History of the Town of Newburgh* (Newburgh, NY: E. M. Ruttenber, 1859), 43n, 60, 90–94, 100; Mann, "Wool Family," *New York Genealogical and Biological Record* 72: 304, 306; and Richard H. Kohn, *Eagle and Sword: The Federalists and the Creation of the Military Establishment in America, 1783–1802* (New York: Free Press, 1975), 17–41. Wool's baptism, recorded on August 29, 1784, in the First Presbyterian Church, New York City, listed his birth as January 31, 1784. Wool claimed February 29, 1784, however, as his birthday—and February 29, 1784, is on his monument in Oakwood Cemetery at Troy.

5. David Franks, *The New York Directory for 1786,* 2nd ed. (New York: H. J. Sachs and Co., 1905), 5, 7, 20, 22, 76, 86, 102; [Edward F. de Laney et al., comps.] "The Burghers of New Amsterdam and the Freemen of New York, 1675–1866," New York Historical Society [NYHS]; *Collections for the Year 1885* 18 (1886): ix–xii, 165, 190, 221, 284; Mann, "Wool Family," *New York Genealogical and Biological Record* 72: 304.

6. *Troy Northern Budget,* July 15, 1805; *Troy Family Journal,* August 30, 1852; Harriette Griswold Hart, "Memoir" (1863–1865), John W. G. Tenney Papers, New York City; Mann, "Wool Family," *New York Genealogical and Biological Record* 72: 300–301, 304, 306. Three weeks after her husband's death, Ann Wool gave birth to James, her eighth child (August 7, 1790–September 6, 1791). She managed a boarding house at 67 Broadway, and on June 1, 1794, married William Hutchins.

7. Spafford, *A Gazetteer,* 313–14; *Troy Family Journal,* August 13, 1852; John Woodworth, *Reminiscences of Troy, from Its Settlement in 1790 to 1807* (Albany, NY: J. Munsell, 1860), 22n, 23n, 27n, 28, 40, 45n, 46; Arthur J. Weise, *History of the City of Troy* (Troy: W. H. Young, 1876), 20–48; Weise, *Troy's One Hundred Years,* 22–39, 51; Rachel D. Bliven et al., *Resourceful People: A Pictorial History of Rensselaer County,* ed. Valerie Von Weich (Norfolk, VA: The Donning Co., 1987).

8. Hart, "Memoir," Tenney Papers; Woodworth, *Reminiscences,* 57–58, 70; Weise, *History of Troy,* 45–46, 50; Irene D. Neu, *Erastus Corning: Merchant and Financier, 1784–1872* (Ithaca, NY: Cornell University Press, 2010), 5.

9. *Troy Gazette* (Lansingburg-Troy), March 15, 1803; John E. Wool to Frances P. Baylies, November 10, 1829, in [Frances P. Baylies], "Baylies Papers," Massachusetts Historical Society *Proceedings* 46 (February 1913): 333–34; Hart, "Memoir," Tenney Papers; *Troy Weekly Times,* May 10, 1873; Henry W. Moulton, *Moulton Annals,* ed. Claribel Moulton (Chicago: Claypool, 1906), 76–77, 141–42.

10. *Troy Northern Budget,* June 11, September 17, 1805, October 27, 1807; Weise, *Troy's One Hundred Years,* 66. The 1805 census reported 79 slaves and 89 free blacks in Troy.

11. *Troy Times,* November 10, 1869; Weise, *History of Troy,* 85–88; Ray W. Irwin, *Daniel D. Tompkins: Governor of New York and Vice President of the United States* (New York: New York Historical Society, 1968), 34–44; Ivor D. Spencer, *The Victor and the Spoils: A Life of William L. Marcy* (Providence: Brown University Press, 1959), 13–18.

12. General Orders [GO], April 17, 1809, Headquarters, Albany, GO, May 6, 1809, Headquarters, New York City, in Daniel D. Tompkins, *Papers of Daniel D. Tompkins, Governor of New York, 1807–1817* (New York: Wyncoop, Hallenbeck, Crawford Co., 1898–1902), 1: 152–55, 209, 213, 220; Irwin, *Tompkins,* 61–76, 129–30.

13. Hart, "Memoir," Tenney Papers.

14. *Troy State Gazette,* October 3, 1809; *Troy Weekly Times,* May 10, 1873; Hart, "Memoir," Tenney Papers; Moulton, *Moulton Annals,* 142–43, 411; Harwood P. Hinton, "John Agustus Griswold," in John T. Hubbell and James W. Geary, eds., *Biographical Dictionary of the Union: Northern Leaders of the Civil War* (Westport: Greenwood Press, 1995), 217–18. Wool and his wife, Sarah (July 4, 1787–May 7, 1873), reared John and Harriette Griswold, the children of her sister Abby Moulton Griswold, who died in 1823 in Nassau, New York.

15. Troy *Northern Budget,* December 5, 1809; Troy *Gazette,* March 20, 27, 1810; Weise, *Troy's One Hundred Years,* 50.

16. Wool to William P. Van Ness, January 14, 1811, excerpt in *The (New York) Collector* 58 (August–September 1945): 160; Wool to Hezekiah Munsell, Spring, 1811, John W. Taylor Papers, NYHS; "Minutes," June 5, 1811, in Hugh Hastings, comp. and ed., *Military Minutes of the Council of Appointment of the State of New York, 1783–1821,* (Albany: J. B. Lyon, 1901–1902), 2: 1266–68; Benson J. Lossing, *Pictorial Field-book of the War of 1812* (New York: Harper and Brothers, 1868), 369n4; Alvin Kass, *Politics in New York State, 1800–1830* (Syracuse: Syracuse University Press, 1965), 9–20; Spencer, *Marcy,* 16–18.

17. Reginald Horsman, *The Causes of the War of 1812* (Philadelphia: University of Pennsylvania Press, 1962); John C. A. Stagg, *Mr. Madison's War: Politics, Diplomacy and Warfare in the Early Republic, 1813–1830* (Princeton: Princeton University Press, 1983), 3–4.

18. Lossing, *War of 1812,* 217–18; Francis B. Heitman, *Historical Register and Dictionary of the United States Army* (Washington, DC: Government Printing Office, 1903), 2: 281; Marvin A. Kreidberg and Merton G. Henry, *History of Military Mobilization in the United States Army, 1775–1945,* Pamphlet No. 20-212 (Washington, DC: Department of the Army, June 1955), 43. Heitman reported 6,686 officers and men in the regular army in July of 1812.

19. *Niles' Weekly Register* (Baltimore), April 25, 1812: 130; Hart, "Memoir," Tenney Papers; Heitman, *Historical Register* 1:106 (Thirteenth Infantry), 1:1059 (Wool); U. G. Alexander, comp., *History of the Thirteenth Regiment* (n.p.: Regimental Press, 1905), 198; Hugh C. McBarron Jr., "American Military Dress in the War of 1812, Part III: Regular Infantry," *Journal of the American Military Institute* 4 (Fall 1940): 186–89; Stagg, *Mr. Madison's War,* 169–71, 232. *Niles' Register* included the word "*Weekly*" and "*National*" in its masthead over the years. Cited hereafter as *Niles' Register.* Wool was not included among the six hundred officers the Senate confirmed on March 12, 1812.

20. GO, June 18, 23, 1812, Headquarters, Albany, in Tompkins, *Public Papers* 1:337, 352; Lossing, *War of 1812,* 366n; Stagg, *Mr. Madison's War,* 230–31, 239–41. For an excellent study of the war, see Robert S. Quimby, *The U. S. Army in the War of 1812: An Operational and Command Study* (East Lansing: Michigan State University Press, 1998).

21. James Mann, *Medical Sketches of the Campaigns of 1812, 13, 14* (Dedham, MA: H. Mann and Co., 1816), 11–15, 179; John J. Demers and James P. Sweeney, "Rise and Fall of

the Greenbush Cantonment," *Journal of the War of 1812 and the Era 1800 to 1840* 2 (Spring 1997): 11–13; Alexander, *Thirteenth Regiment,* 261–64.

22. Solomon Van Rensselaer recollections [henceforth VR], in Catharina V[an] R[ensselaer] Bonney, comp., *A Legacy of Historical Gleanings,* (Albany: J. Munsell, 1875), 1:210, 216, 225; Lossing, *War of 1812,* 292–93, 383n2; Henry Dawson, *Battles of the United States,* 2 vols., (New York: Johnson, Fry, and Co., 1858–1860) 2:141–43.

23. Alexander Smyth to Stephen, VR, September 29, 1812, in Bonney, *Legacy* 1: 239; *Niles' Register,* November 14, 1812, 169–70; Isaac Brock, *The Life and Correspondence of Major-General Sir Isaac Brock, K. B.* (London: Simpkin, Marshall and Co., 1845), 311–12; Lossing, *War of 1812,* 390–91; Stagg, *Mr. Madison's War,* 248–49. Army strength on the Niagara varied. *Niles' Register* cited 5,800 (regulars and militia) in the American forces and 2,800 in the British command.

24. *The War* (New York), September 26, 1812, 62; John Chrystie to Thomas H. Cushing, February 22, 1813 (cites Chrystie's report to John R. Fenwick, October 10, 1812) in John Armstrong, *Notices of the War of 1812* (New York: Wiley and Putnam, 1840), 95; Wool to William Simmons, July 2, 1813, Camp near Fort George, War of 1812 Manuscripts; *Niles' Register,* February 26, 1814, with Supplement to vol. 5:62–63; Thurlow Weed, *Life of Thurlow Weed,* eds. Harriet Weed and Thurlow Weed Barnes, vol. 1 (Boston: Houghton Mifflin and Co., 1883–84), 24; Lossing, *War of 1812,* 392. Chrystie, educated at Princeton and Columbia universities, had been an aide to the controversial Gen. James Wilkinson at New Orleans.

25. Stephen Van Rensselaer to Henry Dearborn, October 14, 1812, in Solomon Van Rensselaer, *A Narrative of the Affair of Queenston in the War of 1812* (New York: Leavitt, Lord, and Co., 1836), 64–65; Chrystie to Cushing, February 22, 1813, in Armstrong, *Notices* 1: 96–97; Robert Malcomson, *The Battle of Queenston Heights* (n. p.: Peninsula Press, 1994).

26. Stephen Van Rensselaer to Dearborn, October 14, 1812, in Rensselaer, *Narrative,* 65; *Niles' Register,* November 14, 1812, 169–70; Chrystie to Cushing, February 22, 1813, in Armstrong, *Notices* 1: 97–98; Lossing, *War of 1812,* 395.

27. Stephen Rensselaer to Dearborn, October 14, 1812, in Rensselaer, *Narrative,* 65; *Niles' Register,* November 14, 1812, 169–70; Solomon recollections, VR, in Bonney, comp., *Legacy,* 1: 254–55; Wool to W[illiam] L. Stone, September 13, 1838, J. Pierpont-Fogg Papers; Lossing, *War of 1812,* 395–96.

28. *Niles' Register,* November 14, 1812: 169; Wool to Stone, September 13, 1838, J. Pierpont-Fogg Papers; Solomon VR, February 23, 1846, to *Albany Argus,* undated clip, John E. Wool Papers [WP]; Wool, November 30, 1865, to *New York Herald,* undated clip in *The Historical Magazine* (Boston) 12 (November 1867): 283–85; Lossing, *War of 1812,* 396.

29. Wool to Solomon, October 23, 1812, VR, in Bonney, comp., *Legacy* 1:272–73; *Niles' Register,* November 14, 1812: 169; Solomon, February 23, 1846, VR, to *Argus,* undated clip, WP; David Eaton account, in Andrew W. Young, *History of Chautauqua County, New York* (Buffalo: Matthews and Warren, 1875), 174; Brock, *Brock,* 321.

30. Wool to Solomon, October 23, 1812, VR, in Bonney, *Legacy* 1:272–73; *Niles' Register,* November 14, 1812, 169; Nathan Ranney account in *Knoxville Register,* October 4, 1837; Lossing, *War of 1812,* 398.

31. Wool to Solomon, October 23, 1812, VR, in Bonney, *Legacy* 1:272–73; Wool, November 30, 1865, to *New York Herald,* in *History Magazine* 12: 285; *Chicago Tribune,* November 26, 1880; Brock, *Brock,* 322; Lossing, *War of 1812,* 398–99.

32. Wool to Solomon October 23, 1812, VR, in Bonney, *Legacy,* 1:272–73; *Niles' Register,* November 14, 1812: 170; Wool, November 30, 1865, to *New York Herald* in *History Magazine* 12: 285; Isaac Roach, "Journal of Major Isaac Roach, 1812–1824," contr. Mary Roach Archer, *Pennsylvania Magazine of History and Biography* 17 (1893): 138; Lossing, *War of 1812,* 400–403; Charles W. Elliott, *Winfield Scott: The Soldier and the Man* (New York: Macmillan, 1937), 62–64; Alden Hatch, *The Wadsworths Man* (New York: Cowan-McCann, 1959), 61–63.

33. *Niles' Register,* November 14, 1812, 170; May 4, 1816, 154; Wool to Roger Jones [adjutant general], September 16, 1850, WP; Brock, *Brock,* 322–24; Lossing, *War of 1812,* 403–4. Van Rensselaer losses included 90 killed, 100 wounded, and about 600 prisoners of war or missing—an estimated 1,000 men. The British reported a loss of some 150 killed. In 1850 Wool sent Jones a copy of his Company I, Thirteenth Infantry muster roll, dated October 31, 1812, reporting officers and men killed at Queenston.

34. Roger Sheaffe to Stephen, October 13, 16, 1812, VR, in Roger Hale Shaffee, "Letter-Book of Gen. Sir Roger Sheaffe," Buffalo Historic Society *Publications* 17 (1913): 277–78, 281–82; Smyth to William Eustis, October 20, 1812, Smyth to Dearborn, October 24, November 9, 1812, in Frank H. Severance, ed., "The Case of Brig. Gen. Alexander Smyth," Buffalo Historical Society *Publications* 18 (1914): 220–24; *Niles' Register,* November 21, 1812, 191; *Albany Argus,* April 13, 1813; Lossing, *War of 1812,* 407, 410–11; Irwin, *Tompkins,* 158; and David Clary and Joseph W. A. Whitehorne, *Inspectors General of the United States Army, 1777–1903* (Washington, DC: Office of the Inspector General and Center for Military History, 1987), 93–94.

35. Smyth to Eustis, October 20, 1812, Smyth to Dearborn, October 24, November 9, 1812 in "Smyth," Buffalo Historical Society *Publications* 18: 220–24; *Niles' Register,* November 28, 1812, 203; Lossing, *War of 1812,* 410–11, 427–28.

36. GO, November 25, 1812, Banks of the Niagara [Black Rock]; William H. Winder to Smyth, December 7, 1812, in Ernest A. Cruikshank, ed., *The Documentary History of the Campaign upon the Niagara Frontier in the Year 1812* (Welland, Ontario: Lundy's Lane Historical Society, 1900), 237, 260–62; Smyth to Eustis, November 29, 1812, in "Smyth," Buffalo Historical Society *Publications* 18: 234–35; *Albany Gazette,* December 14, 1812; *The War,* December 19, 1812, 111–12; Wool to Armstrong, April 27, 1813, WP; Lossing, *War of 1812,* 427–31. Wool left few records of his duty with Smyth. He told the *Troy Gazette* that he was a "volunteer with Colonel Winder," and said to Armstrong: "I . . . crossed [the Niagara] at Black Rock with Colonel Winder in his unsuccessful attempt on the opposite shore."

37. Wool to *New York Evening Post,* November 3, 1812; Thomas B. Randolph et al. to Wool, November 11, 1812; Stephen to Wool, December 24, 1812, VR, and P[eter] Ogilvie Jr., December 27, 1812, to *Evening Post,* December [?], 1812, in Cruikshank, ed., *Niagara Frontier,* 156–57; *Niles' Register,* November 14, 1812, 170; Chrystie to Wool, December 21, 1812, WP; David Thomas to Eustis, December 24, 1812, Griswold Papers, Rensselaer County Historical Society [RCHS], Troy, New York.

38. Stagg, *Mr. Madison's War,* 268, 283–86; C. Edward Skeen, *John Armstrong, Jr., 1758–1843: A Biography* (Syracuse, NY: Syracuse University Press, 1981), 127, 145–48.

39. Wool, "War of 1812" (draft), WP; *The War,* February 2, 1813, 137–38; *Niles' Register,* March 13, April 17, 1813, 29, 115; *Troy Post,* March 23, 1813.

40. Wool, "War of 1812," Wool to John Armstrong, April 27, 1813, and Wool to Jonathan Fish, May 18, 1813, WP; Wool to Armstrong, May 18, 1813, Letters Received, Adjutant General [LRAG], and Adjutant General [AG] to Wool, May 26, 1813, Letters Sent, Adjutant General [LSAG], Records of the Adjutant General, Record Group [RG] 94, National Archives and Records Administration [NARA]. Washington, DC; "Pay and Allowances . . . 1812, 1824, 1838 [and 1846], March 24, 1846," Senate Executive Document [SED] 246, 29-1, Serial 474, 5; Heitman, *Historical Register* 1:1067 (G. D. Young); J. Mackay Hitsman, *The Incredible War of 1812: A Military History* (Toronto: University of Toronto Press, 1965), 130–31. Wool confided to Congressman Fish that he wanted to avoid contact with certain individuals who served with him earlier in the Troy Invincibles. He asked Fish to keep the matter "entirely out of view." Wool's monthly pay and allowances increased from $71.84 (captain) to $111.68 (major).

41. *Troy Farmers' Register,* July [n.d.], 1813, cited in Joseph W. Moulton, "Sketch of the Life of General John E. Wool, USA" (circa 1864), Tenney Papers; Hitsman, *War of 1812,* 138. Moulton was Wool's nephew.

42. Wool, "War of 1812"; Dearborn to Wool, July 8, 1813; Officers of the Fifteenth Regiment to Wool, August 16, 1813, all in WP; *Niles' Register,* June 26, 1813, 27–72; AG to Wool, July 31, 1813, LSAG; *The War* August 10, 1813, 32–35; Elliot, *Scott,* 107–14; Erasmus D. Keys, *Fifty Years' Observation of Men and Events* (New York: Charles Scribner's Sons, 1884), 7–11, 48.

43. Lossing, *War of 1812,* 629–630; Skeen, *Armstrong,* 157–58; Allan S. Everest, *The War of 1812 in Champlain Valley* (Syracuse: Syracuse University Press, 1981), 124–26; Charles Ingersol, *Historical Sketch of the Second War Between the United States of America and Great Britain,* (Philadelphia: Lea and Blanchard, 1845–1849), 1:295.

44. (Philadelphia) *American Weekly Messenger,* October 9, 1813, 45; *Niles' Register,* March 19, 1814, 52; Everest, *Champlain Valley,* 127.

45. *Niles' Register,* March 19, 1814, 53; Armstrong, *Notices* 2: 189; Robert Sellar, *The U. S. Campaign of 1813 to Capture Montreal* (Huntingdon, Quebec: Gleaner Ales Print, 1913), 4–5; Everest, *Champlain Valley,* 127, 130.

46. *American Weekly Messenger,* November 20, 1813, 143; *Niles' Register,* March 19, 1814, 54; Journal, October 17–23, 1813, in George Izard, "The War of 1812 in Northern New York: General George Izard's Journal of the Chateauguay Campaign," ed. John C. Fredriksen, *New York History* 76 (April 1995): 176, 180, 186–87; Moulton, "Wool Sketch," Tenney Papers; Lossing, *War of 1812,* 647; Sellar, *Campaign of 1813,* 130–31.

47. [Journal], October 21, 27–28, 1813, in Izard, "Chateauguay Campaign," *New York History* 76: 177, 187–90; *Niles' Register,* March 19, 1814, 54; April 9, 1814: 89; Wool to Henry Dawson, March 28, 1860, Taylor Papers, NYHS; Lossing, *War of 1812,* 647–48; Sellar, *Campaign of 1813,* 8–10; Elliot, *Scott,* 127–35.

48. Wool, "War of 1812," WP; *Niles' Register,* February 1814, 380; Peter S. Palmer, *History of Lake Champlain . . .* (Plattsburgh: J. W. Tuttle, 1853), 173–74; James R. Jacobs, *Tarnished*

Warrior: Major General James Wilkinson (New York: Macmillian, 1938), 5, 12, 294, 317; Andro Linklater, *An Artist in Treason: The Extraordinary Double Life of General James Wilkinson* (New York: Walker, 2009).

49. Henry Atkinson to Charles K. Gardner, January 30, 1814, Charles K. Gardner Papers, NYSL; *Niles' Register,* March 12, 1814, 37; Jacobs, *Tarnished Warrior,* 302.

50. Wool, "War of 1812," WP; *Niles' Register,* March 26, 1814, 66.

51. [Journal], October 2–8, 1813, in Izard, "Chateauguay Campaign," *New York History* 76: 183; Atkinson to Wool, March 12, 1814; Mann P. Lomax to Wool, March 15, 1814; Wool to Atkinson, March 15, 1814, and Wool comment on duel, no date, WP; Roger L. Nichols, *Henry Atkinson: A Western Military Career* (Norman: University of Oklahoma Press, 1963), 41–43; Heitman, *Historical Register,* 1:174 (Atkinson), 639 (Lomax), and 687 (Manigault).

52. George Izard to Armstrong, May 7, June 1, 25, August 11, 23, 1814, in George Izard, *Official Correspondence . . . Relative to Military Operations of . . . Major General Izard . . . in the Years 1814 and 1815* (Philadelphia: Thomas, Dobson, 1816), 2–3, 21, 36, 65, 72–74; Wool to Sarah Wool, February 18, 1838, WP; Lossing, *War of 1812,* 857–58; Everest, *Champlain Valley,* 146, 155–56, 161.

53. Eleazar Williams Journal, August 26–27, 1814, in John H. Hanson, *The Lost Prince . . . Eleazar Williams* (New York: G. P. Putnam and Co., 1854), 260–61; *Niles' Register,* October 6, 1814, 60; (Burlington) *Vermont Gazette,* August 11, 1815; George H. Richards, *Memoir of Alexander Macomb* (New York: McElrath, Bangs, 1833), 77; Lossing, *War of 1812,* 859–60; Everest, *Champlain Valley,* 146, 155–56, 158, 161–64; Allen S. Everest, *The Military Career of Alexander Macomb and Alexander Macomb at Plattsburg* (Plattsburgh: Wild Publications, 1989). Richards was an artillery officer at Plattsburgh.

54. *Niles' Register,* October 6, 1814, 60; Wool to Dawson, March 28, 1860, Taylor Papers, NYHS; Richards, *Macomb,* 79–80; and Lossing *War of 1812,* 861.

55. *Niles' Register,* October 6, 1814, 60; Wool to Dawson, March 28, 1860, Taylor Papers, NYHS; *Troy Whig* (New York), February 7, 1866; W. Lansing and Son, eds., *Plattsburgh N. Y.* (Plattsburgh: W. Lansing and Son, 1844), 23 (Amasa C. Moore); Jeptha R. Simms, *Trappers of New York: Or a Biography of Nicholas Stoner and Nathaniel Foster* (Albany, 1851), 101–2. Both Moore and Stoner were in the battle.

56. *Washington Union,* August 28, 1857; Wool to Dawson, March 28, 1860, Taylor Papers, NYHS; Simms, *Trappers,* 103–4 (Stoner); Lossing *War of 1812,* 862.

57. *Niles' Register,* October 6, 15, 27, 1814, 61, 69, 111; Wool to Jeptha Simms, January 8, 1850, in *History Magazine* 22 (July-December 1873): 243; *Washington Union,* January 12, 1855 (St. John B. L. Skinner), and ibid., August 28, 1857 (Ranney); Wool to Phillip B. Roberts, January 6, 1859, WP; *Troy Whig,* February 7, 1866; Simms, *Trappers,* 104–5 (Stoner); Lossing, *War of 1812,* 862–64. At this point, the British had lost over 200 men killed or wounded, while the American casualties (regulars) were 45.

58. *Niles' Register,* October 6, 15, 1814, 61, 69; "Note on McGlassin," in *Troy Whig,* September 10, 1854, news clip, WP; Wool to Dawson, March 28, 1860, Taylor Papers, NYHS; Richards, *Macomb,* 87; Lossing *War of 1812,* 864–65; Everest, *Champlain Valley,* 167, 176.

59. *Niles' Register,* October 6, 15, 1814, 61, 69; Lossing, *War of 1812,* 864–70; David G. Fitz-Enz, *The Final Invasion: Plattsburgh, the War of 1812's Most Decisive Battle,* ed. John R. Elting (New York: Cooper Square Press, 2000).

60. *Niles' Register,* October 6, 15, 1814, 61, 69; Wool to Dawson, March 28, 1860, Taylor Papers, NYHS; Lossing *War of 1812,* 870, 873–74.

61. *Niles' Register,* October 6, 1814, 61; Wool to Dawson, March 28, 1860, Taylor Papers, NYHS; *Troy Whig,* February 7, 1866.

62. Simms, *Trappers,* 108–9 (Stoner); *Niles' Register,* May 4, 1816, 154; Dawson, *Battles,* 1: 89.

63. *Niles' Register,* May 4, 1816, 154; *Albany Argus,* September 21, 1843; Simms, *Trappers,* 108–9 (Stoner); Lossing, *War of 1812,* 879–80; Fitz-Enz, *Plattsburgh,* 116–17. Wool wrote Dawson that "much" of Macomb's official battle reports (September 6, 15, 1814) were "apocryphal." Years later, on September 11, 1843, Brigadier General Wool, commanding the Army's Eastern Division, was honored in Plattsburgh where he dedicated a plain marble monument to the American and British officers who fell in the Battle of Plattsburgh. The army had moved the remains of the British officers buried along Beekmentown Road to the local Riverside Cemetery. At a lavish dinner at the Fourget Hotel in town, Wool pronounced the anniversary "a healing balm" to veterans and friends alike. He then led a tour along Beekmentown road, pointing out where he met the British advance, on September 11, 1814.

64. Benjamine Mooers to Tompkins, November 8, 1814, in Plattsburgh Centenary Commission, *The Battle of Plattsburgh: What Historians Say About It . . .* (Albany: J. B. Lyon Co., 1914), 57–58; and *Niles' Register,* February 4, 1815, 354.

65. *Niles' Register,* October 15, 1814, 70; Melancton Smith (Twenty-ninth Infantry) to Secretary of War [SW] (James Monroe), January 9, 1815, (endorsed by Macomb); Tompkins to Monroe, February 5, 1815; Wool to Monroe, February 8, 1815, and David Brearley (Fifteenth Infantry) to Monroe, February 9, 1815, in Wool File, 1815, LRAG; "Records of Men Enlisted in the United States Army Prior to the Peace Establishment, May 17, 1815," 26: 3632–33; "Register of Enlistments in the United States Army, 1789–1914," Adjutant General's Office [AGO]; Elliot, *Scott,* 191.

CHAPTER 2. FEISTY LITTLE COLONEL ON INSPECTION

1. Wool, "War of 1812," WP, NYSL.

2. *Niles' Register,* May 27, 1815, 223–31; Clary and Whitehorne, *Inspectors General,* 112–13; Edward M. Coffman, *The Old Army: A Portrait of the American Army in Peacetime, 1784–1898* (New York: Oxford University Press, 1986), 43. The Northern Division contained five military departments, while the Southern Division had four. Each division had four infantry regiments (two brigades) and four artillery battalions. The Northern Division also had a light artillery regiment, and the Southern Division had a rifle regiment.

3. Wool, "War of 1812," WP, NYSL. *Niles' Register,* May 27, 1815, 223–31; Wool to D[aniel] Parker, June 3, 1815, Camp Plattsburg[h], LRAG; *Washington Intelligencer,* June 13, 1815; Heitman, *Historical Register,* 1:92 (Sixth Infantry). The Sixth Infantry, organized May 17,

1815, contained remnants of the Eleventh, Twenty-fifth, Twenty-seventh, Twenty-ninth, and Thirty-seventh wartime regiments.

4. "Organization of the Staff of the Army . . . , February 6, 1816," in *American State Papers: Military Affairs* [*ASP:MA*], (Washington, DC: Gales and Seaton, 1832–1861) 1:636; Wool to John W. Taylor, April 6, 1816, John W. Taylor Papers, NYHS; *Washington Intelligencer*, May 3, 6, 1816; Wool to William H. Crawford, June 21, 1816, LRAG; "Statement of the Sums of Money Paid Since the Peace Establishment . . . to the General Officers and Their Staff . . . March 15, 1820," House Executive Document [HED] 103, 16-1, Serial 37, Chart A, No. 15; Wool to Albert G. Harris, April 4, 1836, WP, NYSL; Heitman, *Historical Register*, 1:39 (Inspectors General); Clary and Whitehorne, *Inspectors General*, 115–17; K. Jack Bauer, *Zachary Taylor: Soldier, Planter, Statesman of the Old Southwest* (Baton Rouge: Louisiana State University Press, 1985), 30. Wool drew $50 per month as a major, plus allowances, which included four rations, forage, quarters, employment of two servants, and free shipping of baggage (500 pounds maximum). As a colonel, he drew $75 as monthly base pay.

5. Mann, *Medical Sketches*, 56; *Niles' Register*, May 18, 1816, 188–89; Spafford, *A Gazetteer*, 65–66; Lossing, *War of 1812*, 617–18; John D. Morris, *Sword of the Border: Major General Jacob Jennings Brown, 1775–1828* (Kent, OH: Kent State University Press, 2000), 2–5, 13–17, 179.

6. "Register, and Rules and Regulations of the Army for 1813 . . . , December 29, 1813," in *ASP:MA* 1:427–28; *Niles' Register*, May 27, 1815, 225 and February 1, 1817, 376. "Report of the SW . . . , January 12, 1819," SED 58, 15-2, Serial 14, Chart: Division of the North; Clary and Whitehorne, *Inspectors General*, chapters 1–8; and Morris, *Brown*, 11.

7. "Regulations of the Army, December 29, 1813," in *ASP:MA* 1:427–28; Wool to Parker, July 24, 1816, LRAG; "Money Paid to the General Officers and their Staff, March 15, 1820," HED 103, 16-1, Chart A, No. 15; J[oseph] P. Sanger, "The Inspector General's Department," *Journal of the Military Service Institution of the United States* 16 (1895): 432–33; Clary and Whitehorne, *Inspectors General*, 115–20; Heitman, *Historical Register*, 1:109 (Belton) and 1:687 (Manigault).

8. "Regulations of the Army, December 29, 1813," in *ASP:MA* 1:427; *Niles' Register*, May 27, 1815, 223–28, May 18, 1816, 188–89, and February 15, 1817, 410; Wool to Moses Porter, June 15, 1816; Wool to Jacob Brown, November 9, 1823, Letters Received, Headquarters of the Army [LRHA], RG 108, NARA; Wool to Parker, July 24, 1816, LRAG; Parker to Wool, August 1, 1816, LSAG; Wool to Jacob Brown, October 6, 1817, WP, NYSL.

9. Brown to Macomb, July 29, 1816, in Jacob Brown, Letter Book, 3 vols. (1816–1828), 2:37, Library of Congress [LC], Washington, DC. "Money Paid to the General Officers . . . , March 15, 1820," HED 103, 16-1, Chart A, No. 15; Francis Paul Prucha, *The Sword of the Republic: The United States Army on the Frontier, 1783–1846* (New York: Macmillan Co., 1969), 123–27; Everest, *Macomb*, 1–24; Frank Woodford, *Lewis Cass: The Last Jeffersonian* (New Brunswick, NJ: Rutgers University Press, 1950), 32, 116–18, 290.

10. Wool to Parker, September 10, 1816; "Statement of Account—1816," in Wool to Parker, May 18, 1817, LRAG; Macomb to Brown, September 19, 1816, in Brown, Letter Book 2:9, LC; Parker to Wool, October 5, 1816, LSAG.

11. Wool to Parker, July 24, 1816, WP, LRAG; Parker to Wool, August 1, 1816, LSAG; Wool to Josiah N. Snelling, October 13, 1816, Army Papers, Missouri Historical Society, St. Louis; Wool to Henry Leavenworth, December 22, 1816, WP, NYSL.

12. Wool to Brown, December 17, 1816, Wool to Frances S. Belton, July 24, 1817, LRAG; Wool to Leavenworth, December 22, 1816, WP, NYSL; *Niles' Register,* January 18, 1817, 351.

13. Wool to G[eorge] Graham, March 6, 1817, Letters Received, Secretary of War, Records of the Office of the Secretary of War, RG 107, NARA; Wool to Parker, April 13, 1817, WP, NYSL; *Niles' Register,* April 19, 1817, 128.

14. Wool to Parker, April 13, July 8, 12, 1817; Wool to Josiah H. Vose, December 24, 1817, WP, NYSL; Parker to Wool, April 26, 1817, LSAG; Heitman, *Historical Register* 1:381 (Douglas). Douglas served under Wool until 1821.

15. Wool to Belton, July 24, December 10, 1817, LRAG; Wool to Belton, December 14, 1817, Andrew Jackson Papers, LC.

16. *Niles' Register,* August 9, 23, 1817, 374, 415; "Miltary Review by the President, and Presentation of a Sword to Gen. Macomb [August 14, 1817]," in James Monroe, *The Papers of James Monroe: A Documentary History of the Presidential Tours of James Monroe, 1817, 1818, 1819,* ed. Daniel Preston (Westport, CT: Greenwood Press, 2003) 1:432–34; Wool to Macomb, August 15, 1817 (Macomb apology), WP, NYSL.

17. Wool to Parker, July 8, December 16, 1817 and Wool to Brown, November 27, 1817, both in WP, NYSL; Wool to Parker, November 23, 1817, LRAG; "A General Return of the Army . . . by Corps and Regiments . . . , December 1, 1817," in *ASP:MA* 1:670–71; Washington *Intelligencer,* January 10, 1818, LSAG.

18. John C. Calhoun, *The Papers of John C. Calhoun,* ed. Robert L. Meriwether, et al., (Columbia: University of South Carolina Press, 1959–2003) 2:xxxv-xl, liii-lxvii; John C. Calhoun to Brown, December 17, 1817, in ibid. 2:22; Wool to Brown, October 6, 1817, Wool to Harris, April 4, 1835, and Wool to Harris, April 4, 1836, all in WP, NYSL; Clary and Whitehorne, *Inspectors General,* 121–22.

19. Hart, "Memoir," Tenney Papers.

20. *Detroit Gazette,* July 31, 1818; Zachary Taylor to Thomas S. Jesup, August 4, 1818, Zachary Taylor Papers, LC; Abram Edwards, "A Western Reminiscence," ed. Lyman C. Draper, in State Historical Society of Wisconsin [SHSW] *Collections* (1907) 5:158–60; Walter Havighurst, *Three Flags at the Straits: The Forts of Mackinac* (Englewood Cliffs, NJ: Prentice Hall, 1966), 97–98; Robert Wooster, *The American Military Frontiers: The United States Army in the West, 1783–1900* (Albuquerque: University of New Mexico Press, 2009), 52.

21. Wool to Calhoun, August 9, 1818, in Calhoun, *Papers* 3:19; Heitman, *Historical Register,* 1:582 (Jones).

22. John A. Dix to Wool, May 23, 1819, Griswold Papers, RCHS; John A. Dix, *Memoirs of John Adams Dix,* comp. Morgan Dix (New York: Harper and Brothers, 1883), 1:56–57, and 2:264–268; Heitman, *Historical Register,* 1:375 (Dix).

23. Christopher Vandeventer to Sylvanus Thayer, May 4, 1819, in Calhoun, *Calhoun Papers* 4:52; "Report of Board of Visitors, July 1, 1819," in ibid. 4:128–29; Wool to Calhoun,

December 12, 1819, Misc. Mss., United States Military Academy Library, West Point, NY; Wool to Parker, December 12, 1819, LRAG; Stephen E. Ambrose, *Duty, Honor, Country: A History of West Point* (Baltimore: Johns Hopkins University Press, 1966), 67–68, 79–80, 89–90; Theodore J. Crackel, *West Point: A Bicentennial History* (Lawrence: University Press of Kansas, 2002), ch. 4.

24. Wool to Calhoun, December 12, 1819 and Wool to Brown, February 8, 1820, both in LRAG; "Report of SW on a Plan for the Reduction of the Army . . . December 12, 1820," HED 21, 16-2, Serial 48, 1–21; Roger J. Spiller, "Calhoun's Expansible Army: The History of a Military Idea," *South Atlantic Quarterly* 79 (Spring 1980): 189–203. In December 1819, Wool called Calhoun's attention to another problem: laxity and confusion regarding administration in General Macomb's western command.

25. Wool to Calhoun, January 5, 1819, WP, NYSL; Wool to Parker, November 12, 1819; March 6, October 4, 1820, LRAG. At Atkinson's appointment to brigadier in October of 1820, Wool, expressing concern over pending army reductions, requested a regular colonelcy.

26. Wool to Parker, March 6, October 4, 1820, LRAG; Wool, et al., to Brown, March 7, 1820, WP, NYSL; *Niles' Register,* July 29, 1820, 391; Heitman, *Historical Register* 1:92 (Sixth Infantry) and 1:1059 (Wool). Wool held the line rank of lieutenant colonel, Sixth Infantry, from February 10, 1818 to June 1, 1821.

27. Brown to Calhoun, November 13, 1820, in Calhoun, *Papers* 5:436, and references in ibid.: Officer statements (293–94, 317–19, 334, 377, 393, 653); medals (445); economy, (500–2); and army regulations (507); "Reduction of the Army, December 12, 1820," HED 21, 16-2; *Niles' Register,* May 26, 1821, 196–202; Clary and Whitehorne, *Inspectors General,* 126–28.

28. Calhoun, *Papers* 4:xviii-xx.

29. Calhoun to Generals Brown, Scott, and Edmund P. Gaines, March 10, 1821, in Calhoun, *Papers* 5:669–70; Brown to Wool, March 16, 1821, WP, NYSL; *Niles' Register,* May 26, 1821, 196–202 and August 31, 1822, 421–22; Dix to Wool, June 9, 1821, Griswold Papers, RCHS; Clary and Whitehorne, *Inspectors General,* 131–34; and Heitman, *Historical Register* 1:168 (Archer) and 441 (Gadsden). Daniel Parker, chief clerk of the War Department, was elevated on November 22, 1814, to adjutant general of the army, with the rank of brigadier. James Gadsden replaced Parker on October 1, 1820.

30. *Niles' Register,* November 3, 1821, 159; Wool to Brown, December 21, 1821, LRAG.

31. Wool to Brown, December 21, 25, 1821, LRAG; John Quincy Adams, *The Memoirs of John Quincy Adams Comprising Portions of his Diary from 1795 to 1848,* ed. Charles Francis Adams (Philadelphia: J. B. Lippincott and Co., 1875–1877), 5:489–90 (April 14, 1822) and 510–12 (May 1, 1822); *Niles' Register,* May 11, August 31, 1822, 174–75, 422; Grace F. Webster to Daniel Webster. January 14, [1825], in Daniel Webster, *The Papers of Daniel Webster: Correspondence*, eds. Charles M. Wiltse, et al., vol. 2, *1825–1829* (Hanover, NH: University Press of New England, 1976) 10; and Hart, "Memoir," Tenney Papers. Hariette Hart said her aunt, Sarah Wool, arrived in Washington with one trunk, but the number soon increased to seventeen! Wool sought closer ties in army circles. In late April 1822, he volunteered to deliver two notes (one a challenge) from General Winfield Scott to Representative John B. Floyd

(Virginia). Floyd accused Scott of altering the new army regulations before they were printed. Wool learned that Alexander Smyth, from Virginia, chair of the House Military Committee, admitted to meddling with the regulations.

32. Eliza Haywood to John Haywood, April 8, 26, 1822 and Sarah Wool to Eliza Haywood, July 16, December 25, 1822, Ernest Haywood Papers, Southern Historical Collections [SHC], University of North Carolina [UNC]; Hart, "Memoir," Tenney Papers.

33. "Report of the SW for 1822, November 27, 1822," in HED 2, 17-2, Serial 76: 24, 26, 38–39, Charts A-D; "Pay and Emoluments of Certain General Officers . . . , April 12, 1824," in *ASP:MA* 2:674, 677; Clary and Whitehorne, *Inspectors General,* 136–37.

34. Wool to John Salisbury, September 30, 1822, John E. Wool, Misc., NYHS; Mann, "Wool Family," *New York Genealogical and Biological Record* 72:303; *Longworth's American Almanac, New York Register, and City Directory, for the Forty-eighth Year of American Independence: Containing a List of Banks, Insurance Companies, Post-office Establishments, etc.* (New York: Thomas Longworth, 1823), 370. Salisbury was a relative of Wool's and New York City merchant.

35. Wool to Calhoun, June 20, 1822, in Calhoun, *Papers* 7:172–73; Wool to Salisbury, September 30, 1822, Wool, Misc., NYHS; "Report of SW, November 27, 1822," HED 2, 17-2, 24, 26, Charts C-D. Sarah Wool to Eliza Haywood, December 4, 1822, Haywood Papers, SHC, UNC; F. Clever Bald, *Michigan in Four Centuries* (New York: Harper and Row, 1954), 152; Prucha, *Sword,* 177–78. The *Superior* replaced the first lake steamer, *Walk-in-the-Water,* which was built in 1818 and wrecked in 1821 near Buffalo.

36. Wool to Salisbury, September 30, 1822, Wool, Misc., NYHS; "Report of the SW for 1822, November 27, 1822," in HED 2, 17-2, Serial 76: 24, 26, Charts A–D; Sarah Wool to Eliza Haywood, December 4, 1822, Haywood Papers, SHC, UNC; Prucha, *Sword,* 175–77.

37. Wool to Salisbury, September 30, 1822, Wool, Misc., NYHS; Wool to Calhoun, November 1, 1822, in Calhoun, *Papers* 7:326; Wool to Alex R. Thompson, July 11, 1867, WP, NYSL; Sarah Wool to Eliza Haywood December 4, 1822, Haywood Papers, SHC, UNC; "Pay of Certain Officers . . . April 12, 1824," in *ASP:MA* 2:674, 677; Joseph B. Thoburn, ed., "Letters of Cassandra Sawyer Lockwood: Dwight Mission, 1834," *Chronicles of Oklahoma* 33 (Summer 1955): 224n12. The United Missionary Society established the outpost in 1820 to minister to the Choctaw Indians. Wool made five more western inspection tours—1823, 1824, 1825, 1826, and 1839.

38. Sarah Wool to Eliza Haywood, March 5, 1823, Haywood Papers, SHC, UNC; Hart, "Memoirs," Tenney Papers; Grantor Deed Books 17, 23, 53, 63: Grantee Deed Books 12, 16, 17, 62, County Clerk's Office, County Courthouse, Rensselaer County, Troy, NY; Stafford, *A Gazetteer* (1824), 336; *Troy Times,* November 1, 1872. Wool's property dealings at Nassau with Chester Griswold, his brother-in-law, spanned the years 1824 to 1840. In 1837, the Wools moved from Nassau to Troy. They sent Hariette to Emma Williard's Female Institute (opened in Troy in 1821), and steered John into a highly successful career in business and politics.

39. Wool to Sarah Wool, December 13, 1825, WP, NYSL; Hart, "Memoir," Tenney Papers; and Nathaniel B. Sylvester, *History of Rensselaer Co., New York: With Illustrations and*

Biographical Sketches of Its Prominent Men and Pioneers (Philadelphia: Everts and Peck, 1880), 167, 423–24.

40. Wool to Benjamin Smith, October 2, 1817, Griswold Papers, RCHS; "Money Paid to General Officers and their Staff, March 15, 1820 . . . ," HED 103, 16-1, Chart A, No. 15; Wool to Sarah Wool, November 3, December 13, 1825, and Wool to Harris, April 4, 1836, all in WP, NYSL; "Pay Allowances . . . 1812, 1824, 1838, [and 1846], March 24, 1846," SD 246, 29-1, 6; Morris, *Brown,* 260.

41. Wool to Sarah Wool, November 3, 1825 and Wool to Hugh Wilson, May 16, 1828, both in WP, NYSL. Wool reminded Sarah that in the next eight months, she would receive about $1,100 for her needs: Troy Farmers Bank stock ($480), Captain Edmund Kirby note ($158), Troy Bank stock ($584), four mortgages ($258). This did not include income from rents. Wool charged Griswold $100 per year in store rent but exchanged house rent for board. Each spring, as time permitted, Wool checked fences and inspected crops. His instructions to Wilson, who was hired in May 1828, resembled military orders. The manager would mend fences, plant corn and oats on designated plots, and harvest crops promptly.

42. Wool to Calhoun, February 15, 1825, in Calhoun, *Papers* 9:565–66; *Niles' Register,* March 19, 1825, 37; Dix, *Memoirs* 1:103–5; 2: 212–13; Kass, *Politics in New York State,* 28–36; Bauer, *Zachary Taylor,* 16n4. Congress created the brevet on July 6, 1812, to reward meritorious service. The award carried no increases in pay, except when on special assignments. In 1818, Congress also granted the brevet for ten years in grade with merit.

43. Karl Bernhard, *Travels through North America by His Highness, Bernhard, Duke of Saxe-Weimar Eisenach, 1825 and 1826* (Philadelphia: Carey, Lea and Carey, 1828), 2:3–15.

44. Bernhard, *Travels through North America,* 2:15–16.

45. Ibid., 18–19.

46. For the rise and fall of the controversial William McIntosh, the son of a Creek woman and a Scotsman, see "The Rise and Fall of Chief William McIntosh," Georgia Public Broadcasting, accessed December 24, 2018, http://www.gpb.org/georgiastories/stories/story_of_chief_william_mcintosh. He was executed by his own people in February 1825. Also, Benjamin W. Griffith Jr., *McIntosh and Weatherford: Creek Indian Leaders* (Tuscaloosa: University of Alabama Press, 1988).

47. Bernhard, *Travels through North America,* 2:36.

48. Ibid., 2:52–53.

49. Ibid., 2:58–59.

50. Jedediah Morse to Calhoun, May 18, June 22, 1820, in Calhoun, *Papers* 5:127, 203–4; Wool to AG, November 10, 1826, LRAG; Bernhard, *Travels through North America,* 2:13–15, 64, 134–37. In the early summer of 1820, Jedediah Morse, the noted geographer, and his son accompanied Wool to the Great Lakes region. Morse wrote Calhoun on June 22, that the inspector was an "intelligent, active and accomplished officer—a man of dispatch, not afraid to do his duty."

51. "Report of the SW for 1826, November 28, 1826," HED 2, 19-2, Serial 148, 177; *Niles' Register,* December 30, 1826, 278–79 and March 24, 1827, 75–76; Adams, *J. Q. Adams Memoirs* 7:256 (April 9, 1827); Clary and Whitehorne, *Inspectors General,* 145–18. Wool queried

President Adams about receiving regular brigadier pay, citing his arduous duties, and the fact that Colonel Macomb, chief of the engineer corps, drew a regular brigadier's pay.

52. Charles Francis Adams, *Diary of Charles Francis Adams,* eds. Aida DiPace Donald and David Donald (Cambridge, MA: Harvard University Press, 1964), 2:3 (July [?], 1825, 97 (January 2, 1827), 110 (March 4, 1827), 118 (April 9, 1827), 120 (April 12, 1827), 396 (June 30, 1829—quote), and 3:xxv (September 3, 1829); Spencer, *Marcy,* 27–40. The Wools entertained Charles Francis Adams, the president's son and a recent Harvard graduate. Adams played a game of whist with Wool and declared the inspector "too precious by half." The Wools also encouraged Adams's courtship with Abigail Brooks, the daughter of the wealthy Peter G. Brooks. Charles and Abigail were married September 3, 1829.

53. Hart, "Memoir," Tenney Papers; [Francis Baylies], "Letters from a Massachusetts Federalist [Baylies] to a New York Democrat [Wool], 1823–1839," ed. Samuel Rezneck, *New York History* 48 (July 1967): 255–57 (sketch); Wool to Baylies, June 3, 1827, ibid.: 265–66; Kass, *Politics in New York,* 80, 2: 7-8; Spencer, *Marcy,* 27–44; and "Francis Baylies," in Allen Johnson and Dumas Malone, eds., *The Dictionary of American Biography,* 20 vols. (New York: Charles Scribner's Son, 1928–1936), 2:75–76. Wool and Baylies (1783–1853) married sisters, Sarah N. and Elizabeth Moulton.

54. Baylies to Wool, November 5, 1827; Baylies to Andrew Jackson, November 17, 1829; both in WP, NYSL; William Coleman to Baylies, June 2, 1828, in [Baylies], "Letters of Francis Baylies, 1827–1834," in Massachusetts Historical Society *Proceedings* 46: 321–23; W[illiam] C. Rives to Wool, June 9, 1828, Griswold Papers, RCHS; Hart, "Memoir," Tenney Papers. Baylies served (January 3–September 3, 1832) as chargé d'affaires in Argentina, where he tried to mediate a dispute over the seizure of an American vessel in the Falkland Islands.

55. Wool to Baylies, August 27, October 26, 1829, Baylies Family Papers, Old Colonial Historical Society [OCHS], Taunton, MA; Wool to I[saac] B. Hart, April 4, 1835, WP, NYSL; Hart, "Memoir," Tenney Papers; Wool to Baylies, August 29, 1827, Baylies Papers, OCHS; and John F. Marszalek, *The Petticoat Affair: Manners, Mutiny, and Sex in Andrew Jackson's White House* (New York: Free Press, 1997). Wool sensed confusion in the Jackson ranks. Regulations were composed without reflection, appointments were made without proper consideration, and "men fawn and play the part of sycophants." Admitting he was writing "freely," Wool advised Baylies to burn the letter. On another occasion, Wool commented on the "plight" of Secretary of State Van Buren, a widower, who often had to "gallant" Peggy Eaton to parties. "How miserable that man must be who is obliged to descend so low."

56. Wool to Baylies, August 27, October 26, 1829, Baylies Papers, OCHS; Hart, "Memoir," Tenney Papers.

57. *Niles' Register,* March 1, 15, May 3, 31, June 7, 1828, 1, 39–40, 153, 219, 241–43; Wool to James Barbour, April 12, 1828, LRAG; Adams, *J. Q. Adams Memoirs* 7:527 (May 2, 1828).

58. Macomb to Wool, November 25, 1828; Macomb to Wool and George Croghan, May 16, 1829, Headquarters of the Army, Letters Sent, RG 108, NARA; George Croghan, *Army Life on the Western Frontier: Selections from the Official Reports Made Between 1826 and 1845 by Colonel George Croghan,* ed. Francis Paul Prucha (Norman: University of Oklahoma Press, 1958), xxiv-xxvi; Clary and Whitehorne, *Inspectors General,* 152–54; John K. Mahon,

History of the Second Seminole War, 1835–1842 (Gainesville: University of Florida Press, 1967), 255.

59. Parker to Calhoun, January 7, 1818, in Calhoun, *Papers* 3:474; Wool to Macomb, November 10, 11, 1829, Records of the Office of the Inspector General, Inspection Reports [IGIR], RG 159, NARA; Clary and Whitehorne, *Inspectors General,* 152–54.

60. Calhoun to Brown, July 29, August 25, 1818, in Calhoun, *Calhoun Papers* 2:435 and 3:68; Brown to Calhoun, August 12, 1818, in ibid., 3:26; Wool to Macomb, November 10, 11, 1829; October 24, 1831, IGIR; Coffman, *The Old Army,* 151–54, 191–92; Prucha, *Sword,* 324–25. Sutlers encouraged liquor sales. In stores within garrison walls, they made liquor "their chief object of speculation," and readily extended credit to customers. Controlling sutlering was difficult, because the privileges were farmed out. "The man who farms the privilege," Wool explained, "must be remunerated," so the subcontractor had to sell his grade "proportionately high" to clear a profit.

61. *Niles' Register,* January 8, 1831, 341; Wool to Macomb, October 24, 1831, IGIR; Wool to Macomb, June 5, 1833, LRHA; Coffman, *Old Army,* 151, 154, 191–95. Corporal punishment orders were cancelled in December 1829.

62. *Niles' Register,* December 18, 1830, 286; Wool to Macomb, October 24, 1831, IGIR; Prucha, *Sword,* 325–26; Coffman, *Old Army,* 151–52, 193–96.

63. Baylies to Wool, December 2, 1826, Wool to Macomb, June 22, 1839, and Wool to Croghan, September 17, 1839, all in WP, NYSL; Wool to Joel Poinsett, July 26, 1839, Letters Received, Secretary of War; Wool to Macomb, February 22, 1841, LRHA; Wool to Brown, October 23, 1824, LRHA; "Report of the SW, November 24, 1828," HED 2, 20-2, Serial 184, 19; Wool to Macomb, November 10, 1829, October 24, 31, 1831, IGIR; Horatio A. Wilson to Wool, January 28, 1830, Griswold Papers, RCHS; Heitman, *Historical Register,* 1:1046 (Wilson). The officer corps was also in disarray. In January 1830, Wool's nephew, Second Lt. Horatio A. Wilson, Fourth Artillery, stationed at Fort Columbus, reported that the artillery corps was packed with infantry and ordnance officers and West Point graduates, making promotion difficult.

64. "Reduction of Officers of the Army, January 21, 1831," HED 61, 21-2, Serial 208, 1–5; Wilson to Wool, February 14, 1830, Griswold Papers, RCHS; Robert V. Remini, *Andrew Jackson* (New York: Twayne Publishers, 1966), 124.

CHAPTER 3. CASTING ASIDE A COLONIAL PAST

1. Wool, "Trip to Europe," draft, WP, NYSL; Stanley L. Falk, "Artillery for the Land Service: The Development of a System," *Military Affairs* 28 (Winter 1964): 97–102.

2. Wool to Cass, November 7, 1831, Lewis Cass Papers, Clements Library, University of Michigan, Ann Arbor, Michigan [UMi]; Woodford, *Cass,* 172.

3. Wool to Abram R. Woolley, December 20, 1816, WP, NYSL; Wool to Brown, June 13, 1820, Jacob Brown Collection, Clements Library, UMi; [Decius Wadsworth] to Military Storekeepers, October 24, 1818, in Calhoun, *Calhoun Papers* 3:231, Wadsworth to Calhoun, August 28, 1819, in ibid., 4:281; Wool to Macomb, November 4, 1828, IGIR; Falk, "Artillery," *Military Affairs* 28: 98–99; Heitman, *Historical Register* 1:43–44 (ordnance).

4. AG to Wool, March 14, 1823, LSAG; Wool to AG, August 14, 1827, LRAG; Wool to Brown, October 23, 1824, LRHA; Wool to Macomb, October 23, 1824, October 24, 1831, IGIR; Clary and Whitehorne, *Inspectors General,* 139–42, 151; Heitman, *Historical Register* 1:228–29 (Bomford).

5. Wool to Brown, November 16, 1827, IGIR; "Report of the SW for 1828, November 28, 1828," in HED 2, 20-2, 17; Richard P. Weinert Jr. and Robert Arthur, *Defender of the Chesapeake: The Story of Fort Monroe* (Shippensburg, PA: White Mane Publishing Co., 1989), 31–35, 47–51, 59–61; Robert Arthur, *The Coast Artillery School, 1824–1927* (Fort Monroe, VA: Coast Artillery School Press, 1928), 1–112; William B. Skelton, *An American Profession of Arms: The Army Officer Corps, 1784–1861* (Lawrence: University Press of Kansas, 1992), 248–57. The Artillery School for Instruction (also known as the School of Artillery Practice) was authorized on April 4, 1824, by GO 18, Adjutant General's Office [AGO]. From 1827 to 1834, Wool repeatedly criticized its management and lack of government support. The *Army Register* in 1831 no longer mentioned the school. GO 31, April 19, 1834, AGO, closed its operations.

6. Wool to Macomb, October 31, November 10, 1829, IGIR; "Reduction of Officers, January 11, 1831," HED 61, 21-2, 11–12.

7. Wool to Macomb, October 24, 1831, IGIR; Wool to Cass, November 7, 1831, Cass Papers, UMi; William E. Birkhimer, *Historical Sketch of the Organization, Administration, Materiel and Tactics of the Artillery Units, United States Army* (New York: Greenwood Press, 1968), 243. The Ordnance Board was established by GO 74, December 24, 1831, Headquarters of the Army [HA].

8. Birkhimer, *Artillery,* 239–43; Falk, "Artillery," *Military Affairs* 28: 99–100; Skelton, *American Profession,* 240. Tyler returned from Europe not only with a treatise on French weaponry and its use—which he translated and printed—but also with classified information on new French designs and testing.

9. Wool to Baylies, December 8, 1824, Baylies Papers, Massachusetts Historical Society; Falk, "Artillery," *Military Affairs* 28: 99–100. To some degree, Wool owed his European tour to the spoils system. Following Jackson's election, he discreetly mentioned the idea of a tour abroad as a reward for helping organize support in the state of New York for the Tennessean. On December 8, 1824, Wool wrote Baylies that several friends had informed him that the administration probably favored a European trip.

10. George Bomford to Wool, April 16, 1832, Bureau of Ordnance, Letters Sent, RG 156, NARA.

11. Wool, "Trip to Europe," WP, NYHS; Wool to Jesup, May 7, 28, 1832; Wool to Macomb, May 14, 1832; Wool to Cashier, Branch Bank of USA, NY, May 24, 1832; Wool to Edward Everett, May 28, 1832, WP, NYSL. "Citizen" Edmond Gênet, of diplomatic fame and a resident of East Greenbush, New York, gave Wool a letter of introduction to his nieces in France. Wool makes no mention of meeting the duke abroad in his diary.

12. Bomford to Wool, May 24, 31, 1832, Bureau of Ordnance, Letters Sent; European Diary, June 5–6, 1832, WP, NYSL.

13. Macomb to Wool, May 18, 1832, Headquarters of the Army, Letters Sent; European Diary, June 8–9, 1832, WP, NYSL.

14. European Diary, June 10–11, 1832, WP, NYSL; Wool to Cass, July 8, 1832, Cass Papers, UMi.

15. European Diary, July 10, 1832, WP, NYSL; Journal, October 1, 1832 in James Fenimore Cooper, *The Letters and Journals of James Fenimore Cooper,* ed. James F. Beard, 6 vols. (Cambridge, MA: Harvard University Press, 1960–1968) 2:345; Monroe Price, *The Perilous Crown: France Between Revolutions, 1814–1848* (London: MacMillan, 2007), 231–32. The cholera morbus reached Paris in the spring of 1832 and raged for six months.

16. European Diary, July 11–18, 1832, Wool to Rives, July 13, 1832, and Wool to Macomb, July 18, 1832, all in WP, NYSL; Woodford, *Cass,* 93, 97, 195; Michael O'Brien, *A Character of Hugh Legaré* (Knoxville: University of Tennessee Press, 1985), 187.

17. Wool to [Cass?], July 19, 1832, WP, NYSL; Wool to Jesup, October 30, 1832, Jesup Papers, LC; *Virginia Advocate* (Charlottesville), undated clip [1840s?], William C. Rives Papers, Duke University Library, Durham, North Carolina. Rives's papers can also be found at the Library of Congress and at the University of Virginia.

18. *New York Courier and Enquirer,* September 4, 1832; *Virginia Advocate,* clip [1840s], Rives Papers, Duke University Library; Price, *Crown,* 16–41.

19. European Diary, July 24–29, 1832, WP, NYSL; *New York Courier and Enquirer,* September 4, 1832.

20. Wool, "Trip to Europe;" European Diary, July 30–August 2, 1832, WP, NYSL; Wool to Macomb, September 13, 1832, LRHA; Sarah Wool to Wool, September 26, 1832, Joseph W. Burden Papers, NYC.

21. European Diary, August 4–13, September 2, 1832, Wool to Jones, November 30, 1832, WP, NYSL; Heitman, *Historical Register* 1:254 (T. B. Brown); Price, *Crown,* 58, 114, 161, 163, 209, 212, 226–27. LaFayette helped Louis-Phillipe gain the French throne in August 1830. Sidelined as prime minister, he briefly commanded the National Guards (citizen militia) in Paris and became a leader of the liberal republican element in the city. He died two years later in 1834. Wool had a bizarre experience in Paris. Lt. Theopholis B. Brown, "on furlough" from the Corps of Artillery, came to Wool's hotel and offered his services. As the lieutenant talked, Wool sensed that he was "a perfect madman" and quickly dismissed him. A few weeks later, Brown was taken to a Paris hospital for the insane where he died in 1834. The episode provides an interesting commentary on army "arrangements" of that day.

22. Wool to Macomb, 17, 1832, European Diary, August 18–25, 1832, Wool to Jean J. Pelet, August 27, 1832, all in WP, NYSL; Donald D. Howard, "Jean-Jacques Pelet: Warrior of the Sword and Pen," *Journal of Military History* 53 (June 1989): 1–22.

23. European Diary, August 29–30, September 1, 1832, Wool to Bomford, August 29, 1832, Wool to Rives, August 30, 1832, all in WP, NYSL; Wool to Macomb, August 30, 1832, LRHA.

24. European Diary, September 3–7, 1832, WP, NYSL; Wool to Macomb, September 13, 1832, LRHA.

25. European Diary, September 16–18, 1832, WP, NYSL; O'Brien, *Legaré,* 6–7.

26. European Diary, September 20, 22, 24–28, 1832, WP, NYSL; Wool to Macomb, September 26, 1832, LRHA; Wool to Jesup, October 30, 1832, Jesup Papers, LC; O'Brien, *Legaré,*

190–91; Price, *Crown,* 215, 220–22, 230, 240; and R. Ernest Dupuy and Trevor N. Dupuy, *The Encyclopedia of Military History: From 3500 B.C. to the Present* (New York: Harper and Row, 1977), 771. The Congress of Vienna (1814–15), following the Napoleonic era, sought to curb further French expansion by creating buffer states on the frontiers. Belgium, annexed to France, was added to Dutch territory to form a new Holland. With the rise of Louis Phillipe, Belgium declared its independence on October 4, 1830, and selected Prince Leopold of Saxe-Coburg-Saalfeld, age 41 and son-in-law of Louis Phillipe, to be its ruler. In August 1832, the Dutch attempted to reconquer Belgium, but France and England forced a withdrawal. A Dutch garrison, however, remained in Antwerp.

27. European Diary, September 29-October 1, 1832, WP, NYSL.

28. Wool to Macomb, September 26, 1832, LRHA; Wool to Jesup, October 30, 1832, Jesup Papers, LC.

29. European Diary, October 6, 1832, Wool to Cass, October 18, 1832, both in WP, NYSL; Wool to Macomb, October 17, 1832, LRHA; Cooper, *Letters and Journals,* 2:269n2. Rives left France in early October.

30. Wool to Macomb, October 17, 1832, LRHA; Wool to Jesup, October 30, 1832, Jesup Papers, LC.

31. Wool to [Thomas Aspinwall], October 15, 1832, European Diary, October 20–23, 1832, Wool to A[aron] Vail, October 25, 1832, all in WP, NYSL.

32. European Diary, October 24-November 5, 1832, WP, NYSL; Wool to Macomb, October 30, November 5, 1832, LRHA; *Army and Navy Chronicle* [*ANC*], February 14, 1842: 99.

33. European Diary, October 31, 1832, WP, NYSL; Wool to Macomb, November 5, 1832, LRHA.

34. European Diary, November 1–6, 1832, WP, NYSL; Wool to Macomb, November 5, 1832, LRHA.

35. Wool to Bomford, October [30], November 12, 1832, WP, NYSL; Wool to Macomb, November 5, 12, 19, 1832, LRHA.

36. Wool to Macomb, November 6, 12, 1832, LRHA.

37. Wool Diary, October 24, 29, November 5, 12–17, 1832, WP, NYSL; Wool to Macomb, November 12, 19, 1832, LRHA.

38. James Fenimore Cooper to Linus W. Stevens, et al., November 22, 1831, in Cooper, *Letters and Journals* 2:363, 365n (Barnet); European Diary, November 30, December 1–7, 1832, WP, NYSL; Wool to Macomb, December 6, 1832, LRHA; Price, *Crown,* 241–42. In August 1832, the Dutch attempted to reclaim Belgium. The French army (with international approval) in November laid siege to the Dutch garrison in Antwerp, and on December 23, the Dutch evacuated the citadel.

39. European Diary, November 22, 27, 1832, WP, NYSL; Cooper to Stevens, et al., November 22, 1832, in Cooper, *Letters and Journals* 2:363–64.

40. European Diary, December 10–27, 1832, WP, NYSL; Wool to Macomb, February 12, 1832, LRHA; Price, *Crown,* 241. The Belgium question dragged on for five years. The Treaty of London, April 18, 1839, guaranteed Belgium independence.

41. European Diary, February 13–28, 1833, Cass to Wool, March 19, 1833, both in WP, NYSL; Falk, "Artillery," *Military Affairs* 28: 100.

42. Wool to Macomb, November 23, 1832, LRHA; Falk, "Artillery," *Military Affairs* 28: 100–1; Birkhimer, *Artillery*, 245, 248, 262, 280.

43. Wool to John H. Eaton, May 26, 1829, IGIR; Cass to Wool, June 5, 1833, WP, NYSL; Merritt R. Smith, *Harpers Ferry Armory and the New Technology* (Ithaca, NY: Cornell University Press, 1977), 142–81; Clary and Whitehorne, *Inspectors General*, 155; James B. Whisker, *United States Armory at Springfield, 1795–1865* (Lewiston, NY: Edwin Mellon Press, 1997), passim. Whisker discusses the personalities and politics at Springfield Armory.

44. Felicia J. Deyrup, *Arms Makers of the Connecticut Valley* (Northampton, MA: Smith College Studies in History, 1948), 33:160–72.

45. Cass to Wool, June 5, 1833, Wool to [Cass], June 20, 1833, WP, NYSL; Wool to Superintendent [Roswell Lee], Springfield Armory, June 14, 20, 1833, Bureau of Ordnance, Springfield Army Records, RG 156, NARA; *ANC*, October 12, 1837, 231, and October 15, 1840, 251–52; Bernhard, *Travels* 1:56.

46. Wool to [Macomb], June 24, 25, 1833, LRHA, Wool to [Macomb], June 26, 1833, both in WP, NYSL.

47. Wool to [Macomb], June 24, 1833, LRHA; Wool to J[ohn] Robb, June 25, July 5, 1833, Wool to [Macomb], June 26, 1833, Wool Ms., NYSL.

48. Wool to [Joseph Weatherford], June 28, July 27, 1833, Wool to Robb, July 14, WP, NYSL; Wool to Superintendent [Weatherford], July 12, 1833, Bureau of Ordnance, Springfield Army Records; Deyrup, *Arms Makers*, 165, 172.

49. Wool to Acting Superintendent [Weatherford], Inspectors, and Paymaster, July 15, 1833, WP, NYSL.

50. Wool to Robb, July 9, 28, 1833, Wool to My Dear General [Macomb], July 24, 1833, both in WP, NYSL.

51. Wool to Cass, September 24, 1834, WP, NYSL; Skelton, "United States Army," 61–72, 91–100, 222–34; Skelton, "Commanding General," *Military Affairs* 34:119–20; and Clary and Whitehorne, *Inspectors General*, 157–58.

52. Macomb to Wool, August 6, 1831, Headquarters of the Army, Letters Sent; Wool to Macomb, October 24, 1831, IGIR; Wool to Cass, September 24, 1834, WP, NYSL; Skelton, "United States Army," 32–34, 236–38.

53. Weinert and Arthur, *Defender*, 65–66; Skelton, "United States Army," 217, 223; and William B. Skelton, "Officers and Politicians: The Origins of Army Politics in the United States before the Civil War," *Armed Forces and Society* 6 (Fall 1979): 34–35.

54. Macomb to Wool, July 7, 1834, Headquarters of the Army, Letters Sent; Cass to Wool, July 10, 1834, Secretary of War, Letters Sent [SWLS]; R[obert] E. Lee to A[ndrew] Talcott, July 26, November 1, 1834, in Robert E. Lee, "Lieutenant Lee Reports to Captain Talcott on Fort Calhoun's Construction on the Rip Raps," *Virginia Magazine of History and Biography* [*VMHB*] 60 (July 1952): 471, 476; Wool to Macomb, October 8, 1834, WP, NYSL; Weinert and Arthur, *Defender*, 68–69; Douglas S. Freeman, *R. E. Lee: A Biography*, 4 vols. (New York: Charles Scribner's Sons, 1934–35) 1:102–3, 124–25. The pile of rocks that Wool visited was

made an artillery bastion and named Fort Calhoun. During the Civil War in May 1862, the site was renamed Fort Wool. In April 1834, Monroe was declared a regular "fort" and no longer called a "fortress."

55. Lee to Talcott, July 26, November 1, 1834, in Lee, "Lee Reports," *VMHB* 60: 471, 476; Wool to Macomb, September 23, 1834, LRHA; Skelton, "United States Army," 242–43.

56. Wool to Macomb, September 23, 1834, LRHA; Wool to Cass, September 24, 1834, WP, NYSL.

57. Wool to Macomb, September 23, 1834, October 8, 1834, WP, NYSL; Lee to Talcott, November 22, 1834, in Lee, "Lee Reports," *VMHB* 60: 478; Weinert and Arthur, *Defender,* 70; Skelton, "United States Army," 224.

58. Wool to Macomb, October 24, 1831, LRHA; Prucha, *Sword,* 245.

59. Wool to Cass, April 24, 30, 1833, LRHA; James W. Silver, *Edmund Pendleton Gaines: Frontier General* (Baton Rouge: Louisiana State University Press, 1949), 216–22. Commanding the sprawling Western Department, General Gaines echoed Wool's views, but recommended the building of five posts, instead of three.

CHAPTER 4. NO RESTING PLACE WHERE WHITE MEN TREAD

1. *ANC,* March 24, June 23, 1836: 181, 399; AG to Wool, June 20, 1836, ALS; Wool to AG, June 20, 1836, LRAG; Charles J. Kappler, comp. and ed., *Indian Affairs: Laws and Treaties, 1778–1883,* 2 vols. (Washington, DC: Government Printing Office, 1903–1904), 2:439–47; James F. Corn, "Conscience or Duty: General John E. Wool's Dilemma with Cherokee Removal," *Journal of Cherokee Studies* 3 (Winter 1978): 35–39; Lawrence M. Hauptman, "General John E. Wool in Cherokee Country, 1836–37: A Reintrepretation," *Georgia Historical Quarterly* 85 (Spring 2001): 1–26. For recent and exceptional scholarship, see Samuel J. Watson, *Peacekeepers and Conquerors: The Army Officer Corps on the American Frontier, 1821–1846* (Lawrence: University of Kansas Press, 2013), 141–77.

2. Henry T. Malone, *Cherokees of the Old South* (Athens: University of Georgia Press, 1956), xi, 1–3, 171–82; John R. Finger, *Eastern Band of Cherokees, 1819–1900* (Knoxville: University of Tennessee Press, 1984), 1–16; David Williams, *The Georgia Gold Rush: Twenty-Niners, Cherokees, and Gold Fever* (Columbia: University of South Carolina Press, 1993), 21, 24–28, 57.

3. Thurman Wilkins, *Cherokee Tragedy: The Ridge Family and the Decimation of a People* (Norman: University of Oklahoma Press, 1986), 242–49, 257–58; Carl J. Vipperman, "The Bungled Treaty of New Echota: The Failure of Cherokee Removal, 1836–1838," *Georgia Historical Quarterly* 73 (Fall 1989): 540–58.

4. Wool to SW [Cass], June 30, July 1, 1836, LRAG; Rufus L. Baker to Wool, July 14, 1836, Wool to Macomb, October 12, 1836, WP, NYSL.

5. Wool to AG, July 5, 1836, Newton Cannon to Wool, July 9, 1836, (2 letters), all in LRAG; AG to Wool, July 9, 1836, LSAG; Jackson to Wool, August 23, 1838, Jackson Papers, LC; Wool to Macomb, October 12, 1836, WP, NYSL.

6. *ANC,* June 23, 1836: 399; GO 1, July 4, 1836, Athens (Tennessee), Army of East Tennessee and Cherokee Nation [AET and CN], in Black Hawk War, 1832, Creek War, 1836, Cherokee Campaign, 1836–37, and Northern and Vermont Frontiers, 1838, in Orders and Special

Orders 13: 459–604 (Cherokees), AGO; Wool to AG, July 5, 1836, Wool to Matthew M. Payne, July 8, 1836, LRAG; Wool to Thomas G. Lyon, July 10, 1836; Wool to Charles M. Hitchcock, July 17, 1836; Wool to Macomb, October 12, 1836; Wool to Benjamin F. Butler, November 6, 1836; all in WP, NYSL; Heitman, *Historical Register* 1:777 (M. M. Payne).

7. Cannon to Wool, July 9, 1836, LRAG; GO 2, 9, July 10, 12, 1836, Athens, AET and CN, Orders, AGO; Wool to Nathan Towson, July 15, 1836; Wool to Macomb, October 12, 1836; Wool to Butler, November 6, 1836, all in WP, NYSL; Carolyn Hyman, "Richard G. Dunlap," in Ron Tyler, ed., *The New Handbook of Texas*, 6 vols. (Austin: Texas State Historical Association, 1996), 2:729.

8. Wool to Scott, July 12, 1836, WP, NYSL; Wool to Jesup, July 25, 1836, Jesup Papers, LC; Elliott, *Scott,* 310–12, 320, 324.

9. Wool to SW [Cass], June 30, 1836; GO 6, 11, July 11, 12, 1836, Athens, AET and CN, Orders, AGO; Wool to Joseph Byrd, July 22, 1836; all in LRAG; Wool to Chileab S. Howe, July 23, 1836; Wool to Macomb, October 12, 1836; Wool to Mrs. Butler, November 24, 1836; all in WP, NYSL; Heitman, *Historical Register* 1:347; and Chileab S. Howe Papers, SHC, UNC. Wool leaned heavily on Howe, an 1825 West Point graduate, to supply his small army.

10. Wool to William Schley, July 13, 1836; Wool to Matthew M. Payne, July 16, 25, 1836; Wool to Butler, November 6, 1836; all in WP, NYSL; Wool to James Morrow, July 16, 1836; Wool to Thomas Vernon, July 23, 1836 (two letters); Wool to Commanding Officer, Georgia Militia/Volunteers, July 5, 1836; all in LRAG.

11. GO 13, 23, July 14, 21, 1836, Athens, AET and CN, Orders, AGO; Wool to Cunningham, July 18, 21, 1836; Wool to Preston Harvill, July 21, 1836; all in WP, NYSL.

12. Wool to Cass, July 5, 1836, LRAG; Wool to A. R. S. Hunter, July 15, 21, 1836; Wool to Howe, July 23, 1836; both in WP, NYSL.

13. Cass to Wool, July 9, 1836; Wool to Payne, July 23, 1836; both in WP, NYSL; GO 25, July 24, 1836, Athens, AET and CN, Orders, AGO; Theda Perdue, ed., *Cherokee Editor: The Writings of Elias Boudinot* (Knoxville: University of Tennessee Press, 1983), 22, 151n72.

14. Wool to Howe, July 24, 1836, Chileab S. Howe Papers, SHC, UNC; Wool to AG, August 8, 1836, LRAG; Wool to Macomb, October 12, 1836, WP, NYSL; Wool to Mrs. [Nathan] Warren, November 21, 1836, Personal Papers, John E. Wool, LC; Samuel Rezneck, *Profiles Out of the Past of Troy, New York, Since 1789* (Troy, NY: Greater Troy Chamber of Commerce, 1970), 34, 38, 157–59; Malone, *Cherokees,* 107–9, 135; Finger, *Eastern Band of Cherokees,* 13–14.

15. Wool to AG, July 30, 1836, LRAG.

16. Wool to AG, August 8, 1836, LRAG; GO 37, August 13, 1836, Valley Town, AET and CN, Orders, AGO; Wool to Macomb, October 12, 1836, WP, NYSL; Wool to Mrs. [Nathan] Warren, November 21, 1836, Wool, LC; Duane H. King, "The Origin of the Eastern Cherokees as a Social and Political Entity," in Duane H. King, ed., *The Cherokee Indian Nation: A Troubled History* (Knoxville: University of Tennessee Press, 1979), 169.

17. *ANC,* July 7, 1836: 9; Wool to Cary A. Harris, August 15, 1836, LRAG; Wool to Jackson, August 16, 1836, Jackson Papers, LC; Wool to Macomb, October 12, 1836, WP, NYSL; Ronald W. Satz, "Carey Allen Harris, 1836–1838," in Robert M. Kvasnicka and Herman J.

Viola, eds., *The Commissioners of Indian Affairs, 1824–1977* (Lincoln: University of Nebraska Press, 1979), 17–22.

18. Wool to AG, July 30, August 8, 1836; Wool to Harris, August 15, 1836; all in LRAG; Wool to J. H. Hook, August 16, 1836; Wool to Macomb, October 12, 1836; both in WP, NYSL; *ANC*, September 15, 1836: 174.

19. Wool to Jackson, August 30, 1836, Jackson Papers, LC; Wool to Nathaniel Tallmadge, October 6, 1836, Nathaniel Pitcher Tallmadge Papers, SHSW; John Ross, *Letter from John Ross, The Principal Chief of the Cherokee Nation to a Gentleman of Philadelphia* [May 6, 1837] (Philadelphia: n. p., 1837), 10–12; Gary E. Moulton, *John Ross: Cherokee Chief,* (Athens: University of Georgia Press, 1978), 5–53, 79; William R. Snell, "The Council at Red Clay Council Grounds, Bradley County, Tennessee, 1832–1837," *Journal of Cherokee Studies* 2 (Fall 1977): 344–45, 350.

20. Harris to Wool, July 30, August 1, 2, 13, 1836; Cass to Wool, September 3, 1836; both in SWLS; Wool to Cass, August 20, 1836, Letters Received, Secretary of War.

21. Wool to Richard G. Dunlap, August 4, 1836, LRAG; Wool to Macomb, October 12, 1836, WP, NYSL; Wilkins, *Cherokee Tragedy,* 192, 196; John Ehle, *Trail of Tears: The Rise and Fall of the Cherokee Nation* (New York: Anchor Books-Doubleday, 1988), 182–83.

22. John Ross, et al., "To the Senate and House of Representatives, June 21, 1836," in John Ross, *The Papers of John Ross,* ed. Gary E. Moulton, 2 vols. (Norman: University of Oklahoma Press, 1984), 1:432; GO 43, September 4, 1836, New Echota, AET and CN, Orders, AGO; Wool to Schley, September 4, 1836; Wool to Macomb, October 12, 1836, WP, NYSL; Wool to Harris, September 30, 1836, LRAG; Hyman, "Dunlap," in Tyler, et al., eds., *Handbook of Texas,* 2:729. Governor Schley's version of the Bishop-Vernon clash appeared in the *Niles' Register,* November 26, 1836, 205.

23. Jackson to Wool, August 7, 23, 1836; Wool to Jackson, August [15], 1836; both in Jackson Papers, LC; Wool to Charles H. Nelson, August 27, 1836; Wool to Jesup, August 31, 1836, both in WP, NYSL.

24. Wool to Jackson, August 30, 1836, Jackson Papers, LC; GO 42, September 7, 1836, New Echota, AET and CN, Orders, AGO; Wool to Butler, November 6, 1836, LRAG.

25. Cass to Wool, August 23, 1835, SWLS; Wool to Cass, September 10, 1836, LRAG.

26. Wool to Cass, September 10, 1836, LRAG; Wilson Lumpkin, *The Removal of the Cherokee Indians from Georgia,* 2 vols., (New York: Dodd, Mead and Co., 1907) 2:7, 9; Carl J. Vipperman, "The Particular Mission of Wilson Lumpkin," *Georgia Historical Quarterly* 66 (Fall 1982): 295, 313–14.

27. Wool to Cass, September 12, 1836, LRAG; Lumpkin, *Cherokee Indians* 2:60–62.

28. GO 42, September 1, 1836, New Echota, and GO 49, September 14, 1836, Red Clay, AET and CN, Orders, AGO; Cass to Wool, September 3, 1836, SWLS; Jackson to Wool, September 7, 1836, Jackson Papers, LC; Wool to Cass, September 18, 1836, LRAG; John M. Wooten, *Red Clay in History* (Cleveland, TN: n. p., 1935), 5–6; Moulton, *Ross,* 83–84; Wilkins, *Cherokee Tragedy,* 242–43; Snell, "Red Clay," *Journal of Cherokee Studies* 2: 344–45, 350.

29. Wool to Cass, September 18, 1836, LRAG.

30. Wool to Cherokee Committee, September 9, 1836, Wool to Daniel Larkson, September 19, 1836, Wool to Albert S. Lenoir, September 19, 1836, WP, NYSL.

31. [Wool], "To the Cherokee People, September 19, 1836," WP, NYSL; Wool to Cass, September 25, 1836, Wool to AG, October 6, 1836, LRAG; *Athens Republican* (Tennessee), November [10], 1836. clip, Howe Papers, SHC, UNC; Ross, *Letter from John Ross,* 11–12, 21–25; Finger, *Eastern Cherokees,* 14; Wilkins, *Cherokee Tragedy,* 242; Snell, "Red Clay," *Journal of Cherokee Studies* 2: 351.

32. Lumpkin, *Cherokee Indians* 2:46–47.

33. GO 58, October 6, 1836, New Echota, AET and CN, Orders, AGO; Lumpkin, *Cherokee Indians* 2:9–10, 43–45, 57–63.

34. Harris to Wool, October 12, 17, 1836, SWLS.

35. GO 55, September 28, 1836, Red Clay, SO 68, October 29, 1836, New Echota, and GO 74, November 3, 1836, Fort Cass, AET and CN, Orders, AGO; Wool to Howe, October 19, 1836, Howe Papers, SHC, UNC; *ANC,* November 24, December 22, 1836: 335–36, 389; Wool to John C. Spencer, September 7, 1842, WP, NYSL; Lumpkin, *Cherokee Indians* 2:55. By December 1, 1836, Wool had reduced the Tennessee (on and off duty) troops from 2,450 to 361 on active duty.

36. Wool to Harris, November 2, 1836, Wool to Butler, November 6, 1836, LRAG.

37. GO 69, 70, 75, November 1, 2, 21, 1836, Fort Cass, AET and CN, Orders, AGO.

38. Wool to Butler, November 15, 1836, LRAG; Wool to S[tephen] Warren, November 21, 1836, WP, NYSL; Wool to Mrs. [Nathan] Warren, November 21, 1836, Wool, Misc., LC.

39. Wool to Dunlap, August 12, 1836, Wool to John H. Garrett, August 30, 1836, Wool to Nelson, September 19, 1836, WP, NYSL; GO 46 and 47, September 11, 12, 1836, New Echota, AET and CN, Orders, AGO; Lumpkin, *Cherokee Indians* 2:43; Wilkins, *Cherokee Tragedy,* 283–84.

40. Lumpkin, *Cherokee Indians* 2:67–70.

41. *Athens Republican,* November [16], 1836, clip, Howe Papers, SHC, UNC; *Athens Republican,* November 23, 1836, quoted in Wool to Butler, November 28, 1836, LRAG; Wool to Mrs. B. F. Butler, November 24, 1836, WP, NYSL; Wool to Tallmadge, November 25, 1836, Tallmadge Papers, SHSW; Wool to Butler, November 28, 1836, LRAG; Butler to Wool, December 24, 1836, SWLS; Kenneth L. Valliere, "Benjamin Currey, Tennessean Among the Cherokees: A Study of the Removal Policy of Andrew Jackson, Part II," *Tennessee Historical Quarterly* 41 (Fall 1982): 140–58. Harris sent copies of his Wool letters to Currey while acting secretary of war.

42. Wool to Tallmadge, November 25, 1836, Tallmadge Papers, SHSW.

43. Butler to Wool, November 16, 1836, SWLS; Wool to Tallmadge, December 19, 1836, Tallmadge Papers, SHSW; Lumpkin, *Cherokee Indians* 2:70–72.

44. Wool to Howe, December 8, 1836, Howe Papers, SHC, UNC; SO 89, 90, both on December 8, 1836, New Echota, AET and CN, Orders, AGO; Wool to Tallmadge, January 7, 1837, Tallmadge Papers, SHSW; Lumpkin, *Cherokee Indians* 2:72–73; Vipperman, "Bungled Treaty," *Georgia Historical Quarterly* 73: 550–51.

45. Lumpkin, *Cherokee Indians* 2:78–80; Ross, *Ross Papers* 1:489–90.

46. Wool to Miss [Sarah] Warren, December 20, 1836, WP, NYSL.

47. Wilkins, *Cherokee Tragedy,* 298–99.

48. Wool to AG, January 11, 1837, LRAG; Lewis Ross to Brother [John Ross], January 16, 1837, in Ross, *Ross Papers* 1:467.

49. Wool to S[tephen] Warren, November 21, 1836, January 23, March 3, April 22, 1837; Wool to SW, March 18, 1837; Wool to President, Bank of Troy, May 13, 1837; Wool to Poinsett, November 3, 1838, Wool to William R. Lewis, November 15, 1838, WP, NYSL; Lumpkin, *Cherokee Indians* 2:102–5; Wilkins, *Cherokee Tragedy,* 304. By the spring of 1837, Wool had drawn only one third from his government fund of $72,000 for needy Cherokees, since few applied. As Lumpkin sought access to the account for other purposes, Wool moved funds from the Bank of Maryland to the Bank of Troy. In the fall of 1838, he presented drafts ($12,181.82 and $4,382.62) to settle his government accounts.

50. Wool to AG, February 18, 1837, LRAG; Lewis Ross to Brother, February 18, 1837, in Ross, *Ross Papers* 1:468–69; Wool to Miss [Sarah] Warren, March 3, 1837 (2 letters), WP, NYSL. After the Cherokees voted, Wool invited several Indian leaders to his tent. He repeated parts of his speech and offered White Path, an elderly Cherokee, a blanket. The man rejected the offer, saying he was getting old and already had enough luggage to carry. Would you take it to your wife? the general asked. No, was the reply.

51. [Wool], "Cherokees," March 22, 1837, Howe Papers, SHC, UNC. In the week that followed, detachments posted copies of the general's proclamations in various Cherokee settlements.

52. Wool to Howe, March 25, 1837, Howe Papers, SHC, UNC; Wool to William Derrick, March 23, 1837, Wool to C. C. Clay, March 24, 1837, Wool to Edward Deas, March 30, 1837, Wool to John R. Delany, March 30, 1837, Wool to SW, March 31, 1837, LRAG; GO 12, 15, March 25, April 3, 1837, New Echota, AET and CN, Orders, AGO; Grant Foreman, *Indian Removal: The Emigration of the Five Civilized Tribes of Indians* (Norman: University of Oklahoma Press, 1972), 141–52, 188.

53. Wool to Howe, March 25, 1837, May 1, 5, 1837, Howe Papers, SHC, UNC; Wool to Delany, March 30, 1837, LRAG; Wool to Stephen Warren, April 22, 1837, WP, NYSL; Foreman, *Indian Removal,* 188–89. Wool's last contact with the North Carolina Cherokees was in May 1837, when he sent Lieutenant Howe to check on rumors of arms shipments from Salem into the region. The rumor was unfounded.

54. GO 30, August 8, 1836, Valley Town, GO 78, November 29, 1836, New Echota; and GO 18, April 22, 1837, New Echota, AET and CN, Orders, AGO; Poinsett to Wool, March 23, 1837, SWLS; Wool to Howe, March 25, May 1, 5, 1837, Howe Papers, SHC, UNC. Wool ordered the soldiers to pay for the bacon they destroyed.

55. *ANC,* December 29, 1836, 410; *Niles' Register,* January 7, 1837, 290; Clay to Poinsett, April 17, 1837 (encl. Lyon to Morrow, March 22, 1837, Morrow to Clay, April 3, 1837, Clay to Morrow, April 6, 1837), Letters Received, Secretary of War; Wool to Clay, April 21, 1837, LRAG; Poinsett to Wool, April 25, 1837, SWLS.

56. Poinsett to Wool, April 21, 25, 1837, SWLS; *ANC,* April 27, July 20, 1837: 264, 43; Wool to Derrick and Officers of the Georgia Volunteers, June 26, 1837, Wool to G. R. Grossman, et al., June 26, 1837, and Wool to J. W. Lide and John S. Young, June 29, 1837, WP, NYSL; Lumpkin, *Cherokee Indians* 2:114–15. *Niles' Register,* July 29, 1837, 339; Elliott, *Scott,* 346–55. On May 8, 1838, Gen. Winfield Scott arrived at the Cherokee Agency at Calhoun, Tennessee, to take charge of Cherokee emigration. Within a month, he dispatched three groups numbering 3,000 for points west, and by fall contracted with the Cherokee chiefs to transport the remaining population (13,000) to their new homes. In December 1838, the Cherokee removal was complete.

57. *Tennessee Journal* (Athens), June 10, 1837; Wool to Poinsett, July 1, 1837, Wool to Cass, January 1, 1838, WP, NYSL; *Troy (NY) Whig,* July 6, 1837; Macomb to Wool, July 17, 1837, Headquarters of the Army, Letters Sent; Wool to Poinsett, July 19, August 6 (has Poinsett endorsement of August 11), 1837, LRHA; Poinsett to Wool, July 27, 1837, SWLS; "Proceedings of a Court of Inquiry Relating to Transactions of Brevet Brigadier General John E. Wool, and Those Under His Command in the Cherokee Country, in Alabama, July 26, 1837 [October 9, 1837]," in *ASP:MA* 7: 532–71.

58. Wool to William C. DeHart, Wool to Jones [AG] both on August 10, 1837, WP, NYSL; *Niles' Register,* September 23, November 4, 1837, 40, 152; "Proceedings" *ASP:MA* 7: 532–71; Keyes, *Fifty Years' Observation,* 4; Elliott, *Scott,* 325–31.

59. "Proceedings," *ASP:MA* 7: 533, 567–68.

60. Wool to Morrow, June 3, 1837, WP, NYSL; "Proceedings [October 9, 1837]," in *ASP:MA* 7: 533–38, 345; *Niles' Register,* November 4, 1837, 152; Kappler, comp. and ed., *Indian Affairs* 2:446 (1835 treaty).

61. "Proceedings [October 9, 1837]," in *ASP:MA* 7: 533–39, 548; *Niles' Register,* November 4, 1837, 152. Following Riddle's testimony, DeHart asked several volunteer officers who had served with Wool to comment on the general's attitude and demeanor during his sojourn in the Cherokee country. They emphasized that Wool had pursued a mild and conciliatory course and a willingness to cooperate with state authorities in all matters. The Gunter case had not been resolved when Wool completed his assignment.

62. "Proceedings [October 9, 1837]," in *ASP:MA* 7: 767–71; Scott to Leslie Combs, September 12, 1837, Winfield Scott Papers, Special Collections, University of Arizona; *ANC,* October 5, 1837, 216–17; *Niles' Register,* November 4, 1837, 152.

CHAPTER 5. DEFENDING THE CANADIAN BORDER

1. Wool to E[dwin] Croswell, December 19, 1837, WP, NYSL.

2. Albert B. Corey, *The Crisis of 1830–1842 in Canadian-American Relations* (New Haven, CT: Yale University Press, 1942), 1–5, 25–29, 70; Howard Jones and Donald A. Rakestraw, *Prologue to Manifest Destiny: Anglo-American Relations in the 1840s* (Wilmington, DE: Scholarly Resources, 1997), 21–23; Kenneth R. Stevens, *Border Diplomacy: The Caroline and McLeod Affairs in Anglo-American Relations, 1837–1842* (Tuscaloosa: University of Alabama Press, 1989); Samuel J. Watson, "Army Officers Fight the 'Patriot War': Reactions to Filibustering on

the Canadian Border, 1837–1839," *Journal of the Early Republic* 18 (Fall 1998): 485–519. Also: Watson, *Peacekeepers and Conquerors,* 249–56.

3. F[rancis] B. Head to Henry S. Fox, January 8, 1838, in James D. Richardson, comp., *A Compilation of the Messages and Papers of the Presidents, 1789–1897,* 10 vols. (Washington, DC: Government Printing Office, 1896–99) 4:1678–79; N. Gagnon to Martin Van Buren, December 28, 1838, in ibid., 4:1616–17; and H. W. Rogers to Van Buren, December 30, 1838, in ibid., 4:1618–19; Corey, *Crisis,* 30, 34–35, 66; Jones and Rakestraw, *Prologue,* 24–26.

4. Rogers to Van Buren, December 30, 1837, in Richardson, comp., *Messages* 4:1618–19; Cory, *Crisis,* 36–37; Jones and Rakestraw, *Prologue* 31–33.

5. *Vermont Argus and Free Press* (Middlebury), January 2, 1838; AG to Wool, January 3, 1838 (encloses copy of Poinsett to Macomb, January 3, 1838), LSAG; Elliott, *Scott,* 337; Corey, *Crisis,* 47, 57. The *Argus* published Secretary of State John Forsyth's letters to the governors of Michigan, New York, and Vermont.

6. Van Buren's Proclamation, January 3, 1838, in Richardson, comp., *Messages* 4:1616, and Poinsett to Scott, January 5, 1838, in ibid., 4:1620; Cory, *Crisis,* 50, 63–64; Elliot, *Scott,* 338.

7. Wool to AG, January 9, 1838, Adjutant General, Canadian Rebellion Papers [AGCRP]; Wool to Erastus Corning, January 13, 1838, Simon Gratz Autograph Collection, SHSW; Wool to Sarah Wool, January 14, 1838, and Wool to J. W. Taylor, January 15, 1838, WP, NYSL.

8. Wool to J. W. Taylor, January 16, 1838, WP, NYSL; Joseph W. Moulton, "The Canadian Rebellion: General Wool on the Frontiers," (c. 1863), Burden Papers; Elliott, *Scott,* 339.

9. Wool to Sarah Wool, January 14, 1838, and Wool to J. W. Taylor, January 16, 1838, WP, NYSL; *ANC* 6 (January 15, 1838): 61–62; Moulton, "Canadian Rebellion," Burden Papers; Jones and Rakestraw, *Prologue,* 39; Elliott, *Scott,* 339. Van Rensselaer, MacKenzie, and others were later indicted at Albany. After fourteen months in jail, MacKenzie was pardoned by Van Buren.

10. *Buffalo Commercial Advertiser*, January 15, 1838, quoted in *Troy Whig,* January 19, 1838; Keyes, *Fifty Years' Observation,* 323; Elliott, *Scott,* 339–41; Jones and Rakestraw, *Prologue,* 39.

11. Abby Maria Hemenway, ed., *The Vermont Historical Gazetteer: A Magazine Embracing a History of Each Town, Civil, Ecclesiastical, Biographical and Military,* 6 vols. (Ludlow, VT: A. M. Hemenway, 1860–1863) 1:504–6; 4:1071, 1073; Cory, *Crisis,* 63–64; Elliott, *Scott,* 342. For operations against patriots in Michigan, see Prucha, *Sword,* 312–18.

12. Scott to Wool, January 17, 1838 (encloses copy of Silas H. Jenison, January 17, 1838), Wool to Scott, January 26, 1838, AGCRP; Wool to Sarah Wool, January 27, 1838, and Wool to AG, June 11, 1838, WP, NYSL; The Neutrality Act of 1818 is in 3 U.S.C. (1818); *ANC* February 20, 1840, 128; Heitman, *Historical Register* 1:439 (Smith/Fraser) and 1:711 (Miller). Scott asked the governors of New York and Vermont to place ten militia companies each (two battalions of five companies) on standby for three months' duty.

13. Wool to Scott, January 26, 1838, AGCRP; Wool to Sarah, January 27, 1838, Wool Mss., NYSL.

14. Wool to Scott, January 26, 1838, AGCRP; *Troy Whig,* February 5, 1838; William Smith to Wool, December 6, 1838, WP, NYSL.

15. Wool to Scott, January 27, 1838, AGCRP.

16. Wool to Moore, Missisquoi Bay, January 29, 1838, and James Botham to Wool, January 30, 1838, AGCRP.

17. Wool to Sarah, January 30, 31, February 2, 1838, WP, NYSL.

18. Wool to Corning, February 1, 1838, Vermontiana Collection, University of Vermont, Burlington.

19. Wool to Jenison, February 5, 1838, WP, NYSL; Wool to Marcy, February 5, 1838, Marcy Papers, NYSL; Wool to Scott, February 6, 1838, AGCRP; *Vermont Chronicle* (Windsor), February 21, 1838, cites *Vermont Messenger* (St. Albans); Corey, *Crisis,* 66–68. By March 6, 1838, the British had 4,500 troops in Canada and had declared martial law.

20. Wool to Marcy, February 8, 1838, Marcy Papers, NYSL; *Albany Argus,* February 16, 1838; *Windsor Chronicle,* March 7, 1838; Wool to Scott, March 19, 1838, LRAG; Moulton, "Wool Sketch," Tenney Papers. Drs. Robert Nelson and Cyrille-Hector-Octave Côté had both attended the University of Vermont.

21. *Vermont Patriot and State Gazette* (Montpelier), February 19, 1838; *Middlebury Argus,* cited in Moulton, "Wool Sketch," Tenney Papers; Stephen Kenny, "The Canadian Rebellions and the Limits of Historical Perspective," *Vermont History* 58 (Summer 1990): 186; Jean-Paul Bernard, "Vermonters and the Lower Canadian Rebellion, 1837–1838," *Vermont History* 58 (Fall 1990): 258.

22. Wool to Scott, February 14 (2 letters), March 6, 19, 1838, and Wool to Marcy, February 18, 1838, AGCRP.

23. Wool to Legaré, March 17, 1838, WP, NYSL; Moulton, "Canada Rebellion," Tenney Papers.

24. John Colborne to Wool, February 20, 1838, Wool to Colborne, February 21, 1838, Wool to Scott, February 22, 1838, and Wool to Skinner, February 23, 1838, all in AGCRP; Wool to Richardson, comp., *Messages,* 2:99; *Vermont Chronicle* (Windsor), February 21, 1838.

25. George B. Manser to Wool, February 21, 1838, WP, NYSL; Wool to Scott, February 21, March 6, 1838, and Wool to Autos I. Bristol, February 21, 1838, AGCRP; *Windsor Chronicle,* February 21, 1838. Each company was composed of from thirty to forty mounted men.

26. Robert Nelson to J. B. Ryan, February 25, 1838, AGCRP; *Vermont Gazette* (Bennington), March 6, 1838; Kenny, "Canadian Rebellion," *Vermont History* 58: 189. Ryan also edited the *North American*, published out of Swanton, Vermont.

27. Wool to Scott, February 22, March 6, 1838, and Wool to Morris S. Miller, April 21, 1838, AGCRP; *Bennington Gazette,* March 6, 1838; Hemenway, ed., *Gazetteer* 1:508–509.

28. Wool to SW, February 27, 1838, and Wool to Scott, March 6, 1838, AGCRP; *Bennington Gazette,* March 6, 1838; Hemenway, ed., *Gazetteer* 4:1075.

29. Wool to SW, February 27, 1838, AGCRP; Wool to Sarah, March 20, 1838, WP, NYSL.

30. Wool to SW, March 2, 1838, and Wool to Scott, March 6, 1838, AGCRP; Wool to Sarah Wool, March 20, 1838, and Wool to Horace B. Sawyer, September 10, 1838, WP, NYSL; Moulton, "Wool Sketch," Tenney Papers.

31. Wool to SW, March 2, 1838, AGCRP; *Bennington Gazette,* March 6, 1838; *Windsor Chronicle,* March 7, 14, 1838; Wool to Sawyer, September 10, 1838, Wool, Mss., NYSL.

Moulton, "Wool Sketch," Tenney Papers, cites a Plattsburgh newspaper. Hemenway, ed., *Gazetteer* 4:1075.

32. Wool to Scott, March 6, 1838, AGCRP; Wool to Sarah, March 7, 1838, and Wool to Horace B. Sawyer, September 10, 1838, WP, NYSL; *Albany Argus* and *Windsor Chronicle,* March 7, 1838; William Kingsford, *The History of Canada,* 10 vols. (Toronto: Rowsell and Hutchinson, 1887–1898), 10:109.

33. Wool to Scott, March 1, 6, 19, 1838, and Wool to Miller, April 21, 1838, AGCRP; *Albany Argus,* March 7, 1838; Moulton "Wool Sketch," Tenney Papers; Hemenway, ed., *Gazette,* 4:1060.

34. Wool to Scott, March 6, 19, 1838, AGCRP; Wool to Sarah Wool, March 7, 1838, WP, NYSL; *Windsor Chronicle,* March 14, 1838.

35. SO, March 4, 1838, Champlain [Wool], and "Abstract of Ordnance and Ordnance Stores Captured by Brig. Gen. John E. Wool, etc. and received March 5–9 [1838]," Alexander Catlin Papers, University of Vermont; Wool to Scott, March 6, 1838, AGCRP; *Troy Whig,* March 9, 1838; Moulton, "Wool Sketch," Tenney Papers.

36. Wool to Miller, March 4, 1838, Vermontiana Collection, University of Vermont; *Windsor Chronicle,* March 7, 1838; Wool to AG, March 9, 1838, and Wool to Scott, March 28, 1838, April 18, 1838, AGCRP; Wool to Sarah Wool, March 16, 1838, WP, NYSL.

37. Wool's orders: GO 5, 8, March 5, 18, 1838, Champlain [New York], GO 14, March 14, 1838, Plattsburgh; Wool to Scott, March 6, 11, 1838, and Wool to AG, March 9, 1838, AGCRP; Wool to Sarah Wool, March 20, 1838, J. W. R. Bromley to Wool, April 17, 1838, and Smith to Wool, April 30, 1838, WP, NYSL; Wool to Miller, April 21, 1838, LRAG; *ANC* 6 (April 26, 1838): 263. Wool was especially disappointed with Lt. Morris S. Miller, his quartermaster. He wrote Sarah that the officer was "wholly unacquainted" with his duties. He had "no head, no judgment, no forecast." Miller saw "nothing and permits himself to be duped by everybody."

38. Wool to James Platt, March 12, 13, 14, 1838, GO 8, March 18, 1838, Champlain, and Wool to Scott, March 19, 1838, AGCRP; Wool to Sarah Wool, March 20, 1838, and Wool to Sawyer, September 10, 1838, WP, NYSL.

39. Wool to Colborne, March 13, 1838, Colborne to Wool, March 19, 1838, and Wool to Scott, March 22, 1838, AGCRP.

40. *Plattsburgh Whig Extra,* March 3 1838; Wool to Sarah Wool, March 14, 20, 1838, WP, NYSL; *Vermont Patriot* (Montpelier), March 12, 1838.

41. Wool to Sarah Wool, March 12, 20, 1838, Wool to Croswell, March 16, 1838, and Wool to J. C. Moore, March 19, 1838, WP, NYSL; *ANC* 6 (April 19, 1838): 246, cites *Plattsburgh Republican;* Wool to Tallmadge, April 22, 1838, Tallmadge Papers, SHSW; Moulton, "Wool Sketch," Tenney Papers.

42. Wool to Bromley, Alexander Cummings, and Major General Cross, all on March 21, 1838, Bromley to Wool, April 2, 1838, and Wool to Scott, April 2, 1838, AGCRP; Cummings to Wool, March 29, 1838, WP, NYSL; Lossing, *War of 1812,* 662n.

43. Neutrality Act of 1838 (March 10, 1838) in 5 U.S.C (1838); Wool to Scott, April 2, 1838 (encloses Cummings to Wool, March 29, 1838), with Scott's endorsements, AGCRP; Legaré to Wool, April 2, 1838, WP, NYSL; Wool to Legaré, April 13, 1838, Fogg Collection,

Maine Historical Society, Portland; Moulton, "Wool Sketch," Tenney Papers; Moulton, "Canadian Rebellion," Burden Papers; Jones and Rakestraw, *Prologue,* 35. The Neutrality Act of March 10, 1838, authorized revenue officers to seize all vessels, vehicles, arms, and munitions along the border that were designated for the invasion of any nation at peace with the United States. On March 1, Wool had acted under a "liberal interpretation" of his duty, standing on the law of nations, treaties, and neutrality acts for his authority, according to Moulton, "Wool Sketch." Moulton, "Canadian Rebellion," says Wool acted "under the expressed or implied sanctions of the Authorities, and by a latitudinarian interpretation of existing laws."

44. Wool to AG, May 2, 18, 1838, LRAG; SO 2, May 18, 1838, Burlington, AGCRP; *Windsor Chronicle,* May 22, 1838; *Montpelier Patriot,* June 5, 1838.

45. *Albany Argus,* June 4, 1838; *ANC,* June 14, July 5,1838, 381, 12; Smith to Wool, December 6, 1838, and Miller to Wool, December 8, 1838, WP, NYSL. At Wool's request, Miller and Smith, six months later, commented on Nelson's charges. They agreed that the general occasionally spoke to patriot groups in "conciliatory, complimentary" terms. Smith recalled that Wool once even said that he might consider resigning and coming to "live among them." If war broke out with Great Britain, he would be pleased to command such men! On another occasion, Smith added, Wool had mused that if "a military officer of rank, experience, and reputation—one in whom the American people could confide in—would come forward and erect his standard, he might march into Canada at the head of a very large and formidable force."

46. *ANC* June 14, 1838, 381; *Albany Argus,* June 15, 1838; Wool to Sawyer, September 10, 1838, Jenison to Wool, November 28, 1838, Smith to Wool, December 6, 1838, and Miller to Wool, December 8, 1838, Mss., NYSL. During the summer of 1838, Sawyer wrote Wool that Vermont newspapers were stirring up trouble again. The general advised that in response to the "pious, church-going" people of St. Albans and Swanton, Sawyer would "come [in] second best." In November, Wool changed his mind and asked Jenison, Smith, and Miller to draft supportive letters for his use. The journalistic sputtering soon faded.

47. Wool to AG, May 2, 1838 (includes Macomb endorsement [May 12]), and Wool to Macomb, May 28, 1838, AGRL; AG to Wool, May 14, 1838, LSAG; Macomb to Wool, June 2, 1838, Headquarters of the Army, Letters Sent; Wool to Macomb, June 7, 1838, LRHA; *ANC* July 5, 1838, 13–14; Moulton, "Wool Sketch," Tenney Papers; Lossing, *War of 1812,* 662n.1; Jones and Rakestraw, *Prologue,* 40. Johnston, a Canadian living in Clayton, New York, and a patriot sympathizer, was hired by an anti-British group to capture and destroy the *Sir Robert Peel,* a passenger steamboat on the St. Lawrence River. Governor Marcy of New York declared Johnston's party outlaws and offered a reward for their capture. Johnston took refuge in the Thousand Islands in the river, but in the fall he surrendered to local authorities, was tried in Syracuse, and acquitted.

48. Wool to Sarah Wool, June 8, 1838, Wool to AG, June 11, 1838, and Wool to [B. C.] Howard and [G. W.] Kemble, July 2, 1838, WP, NYSL.

49. Wool to Sarah Wool, February 20, 1838, Wool Papers, NYSL.

50. Van Buren to House of Representatives, September 26, 1837, in Richardson, comp., *Messages,* 4:1564–66, and Edward Kent to Van Buren, April 28, 1838, in ibid. 4:1687–90;

Poinsett to Wool, June 16, 1838, SWLS; *Niles' Register,* June 30, 1838, 273; Wool to Howard and Kimble, July 2, 1838, and Wool to Poinsett, October 30, 1838, WP, NYSL; *Albany Argus,* July 9, 1838; Henry S. Burrage, *Maine in the Northeastern Boundary Controversy* (Portland: Printed for the State, 1919), 116–124, 175–80, 224–27; Heitman, *Historical Register* 1:468 (James D. Graham) and 1:578 (J. E. Johnston); Jones and Rakestraw, *Prologue,* 1–8; Poinsett to Wool, June 14, 1838, SWLS; *Portland Advertiser,* quoted in *Niles' Register,* June 30, 1838, 273; Wool to Howard and Kemble, July 2, 1838, Wool to Poinsett, October 30, 1838, WP, NYSL; *Albany Argus,* July 9, 1838.

51. Wool to Howard and Kemble, July 2, 1838; Wool to Poinsett, October 30, 1838, WP, NYSL; Poinsett to Wool, June 16, 1838, SWLS; *Portland Advertiser,* quoted in *Niles' Register,* June 30, 1838: 273; *Albany Argus,* July 9, 1838; Heitman, *Historical Register* 1:468 (Graham) and 1:578 (Johnston).

52. *Bangor Whig,* July 18, 1838; Wool to Harriette Hart, July 25, 1838, Wool to Poinsett, October 30, 1838, WP, NYSL. Governor Kent asked Wool to recommend the building of a fort on the coast south of Bangor at Bucksport.

53. Wool to Poinsett, October 30, 1838, WP, NYSL; *Bangor Whig,* July 18, 1838.

54. Wool to Poinsett, August 24, 1838, LRAG; Wool to Poinsett, October 30, 1838, WP, NYSL; James D. Graham to Wool, November 10, 1838, in SD 35, 25-3, 2–16; *ANC* November 1, 1838, 131–36; Daniel Webster, "Defense of the Treaty of Washington, April 6–7, 1846," in Daniel Webster, *The Papers of Daniel Webster; Speeches and Formal Writings,* eds. Charles M. Wiltse, et al., vol. 2, *1834–1852,* (Hanover, NH: University Press of New England, 1988), 361–78, 389–97; Howard Jones, *To the Webster-Ashburton Treaty: A Study in Anglo-American Relations, 1783–1843* (Chapel Hill: University of North Carolina Press, 1977).

55. Wool to Poinsett, August 24, 1838, LRAG; Wool to Poinsett, October 20, November 10, 1838, WP, NYSL; *ANC* November 1, 1838, 131–36; Daniel Webster, "Defense of the Treaty of Washington," 2:364–97; James D. Graham to Wool, November 1, 8, 1838, in SD 35, 25-3, Serial 339, 2–16.

56. DeWitt Bloodgood to Wool, November 21, 1838, Griswold Papers, RCHS; James and Ann E. Van Brokle to Wool, May 15, 1835, in Grantee Book 35: 413, Rensselaer County Court House, Troy; Wool to Sarah Wool, January 9, 1837, and February 18, April 2, June 22, 1838, WP, NYSL.

57. Wool to I. B. Hart, May 3, 1839, WP, NYSL; Prucha, *Sword,* 333–34; Clary and Whitehorne, *Inspector General,* 166–74. Wool unburdened himself in his letters to Hart, his nephew by marriage. "For two months I witnessed little else than a continued struggle for political power . . . I became disgusted and was glad to fly a city where intreague [sic], profligacy, and corruption is the order of the day. We have certainly seen and experienced the best of days of the republic . . . The days of free government are numbered."

58. *ANC* 8 (March 14, 1839): 168, ibid., 8 (April 4, 1839): 217, ibid., 8 (May 16, 1839): 314, and ibid., 8 (June 13, 1839): 382; Wool to A. G. Moore, March 21, 1839, in the *New York Collector* 58 (August–September 1945): 160 (excerpt); Wool to I. B. Hart, May 3, 4, 5, 1839, WP, NYSL; Wool to AG, May 6, 1839; Wool to Macomb, October 18, 1839, LRAG.

59. Wool to Macomb, October 18, 1839, LRAG.

60. Wool to Macomb, October 18, 1839, LRAG; "Report of the SW for 1839, November 30, 1839" in SD 1, 26-1, Serial 354, 41–60.

61. "Report of the SW, November 50, 1839," in SD 1, 26-1, 44–48, 55–56; Wool to Poinsett, March 15, 1840, Chicago Historical Society [ChiHS]; *Niles' Register* 58 (April 25, 1840): 115–16, ibid., 58 (May 22, 1840): 79, and ibid., 58 (October 17, 1840): 97; Prucha, *Sword,* 298 (map); Bauer, *Taylor,* 75–95; Mahon, *Second Seminole War,* 245–75.

62. Wool to Z. Taylor, February 10, 1840, and Wool to [Mary] Warren, February 14, 1840, WP, NYSL. In early 1840, the army briefly considered using bloodhounds to track Florida Indians. A kennel of thirty-three dogs with five handlers were imported from Cuba and attached to Twiggs's command at Fort Heileman in northern Florida. The experiment was not successful.

63. Wool to Macomb, February 18, 1840, and Wool to Mrs. B[enjamin] F. Butler, March 2, 1840, WP, NYSL; Wool to Macomb, March 12, 1840, Isadore M. Fixman Collection, Rensselaer Polytechnic Institute, Troy, New York; Prucha, *Sword,* 297; Bauer, *Taylor,* 88–94; Mahon, *Second Seminole War,* 247; Joseph I. Lambert, *One Hundred Years with the Second Cavalry* (Fort Riley, KS: Capper Printing Co., 1939), 16. Wool concluded that Taylor's outposts were useless. Each station had less than a dozen men, and when they confronted thirty or forty hostile Indians, there could but retreat. The general needed a strike force that could stay in the field and move quickly.

64. Wool to Mrs. B. F. Butler, March 2, 1840; Wool to James P. Preston, March 15, 1840, WP, NYSL; Wool to Poinsett, March 15, 1840, ChiHS; Heitman, *Historical Register* 2:558; Bauer, *Taylor,* 94. A site on the Suwannee River, twelve miles from its mouth near Fort Fanning, was designated Camp (Fort) Wool in March 1840. Wool made no mention in his report of seeing Taylor, who had been ill.

65. Wool to Poinsett, March 15, 1840, ChiHS; Bauer, *Taylor,* 93; *ANC* 10 (April 2, 1840): 20.

66. *Niles' Register,* May 2, 9, 30, 1840, 133, 145, 193; Prucha, *Sword,* 297–300; Bayer, *Taylor,* 94; Mahon, *Second Seminole War,* 275–87. Bvt. Brig. Gen. Walker K. Armistead served only one year before he was succeeded by Col. William J. Worth.

67. Wool to John Bell, June 29, 1841, and Letters of Recommendation Submitted by Wool . . . , June 29, July 27, August 6, 1841, LRAG; *Niles' Register,* July 10, 1841, 291; Elliott, *Scott,* 399–400; Heitman, *Historical Register,* 1:39 (inspectors general department); Clary and Whitehorne, *Inspectors General,* 171–75.

68. Wool to Bell, June 29, 1841, LRAG; Nichols, *Atkinson,* 207, 219–21; Heitman, *Historical Register* 1:239 (Brady). Brady entered the army in 1792.

69. Wool to Bell, June 30, 1841, LRAG; Harriette Hart to Wool, July 11, 1841; Wool to Sarah Wool, August 16, 20, 23, 1841, WP, NYSL.

70. Wool to Sarah Wool, August 16, 20, 23, 1841, WP, NYSL. Wool claimed he could count on at least six hundred people for support!

71. AG to Wool, September 1, 1841, LSAG; *New York Military Magazine* (Philadelphia), September 4, 1841, 1:202; September 15, 1841, in Hitchcock, *Fifty Years,* 135; Z. Taylor to Ethan Allen Hitchcock, November 3, 1841, Taylor Papers, LC; Bauer, *Taylor,* 99.

72. Hemenway, ed., *Gazetteer,* 1:499–500, 509–10, and 4:1077; Cory, *Crisis,* 120, 130–33, 152; Jones and Rakestraw, *Prologue,* 43–44, 47–48, 50, 53.

73. Wool to Scott, September 24, October 11, 1841, LRAG; *Niles' Register,* September 25, 1841, 56; Henry Underwood to Wool, September 26, 1841, and Fortune C. White to Wool, September 28, 1841, William H. Seward Papers, University of Rochester; Robert Anderson to [Horace Brooks], September 30, 1841, Robert Anderson Papers, LC; Heitman, *Historical Register,* 1:164 (Anderson), and 249 (Brooks); Corey, *Crisis,* 143, 151–54; Jones and Rakestraw, *Prologue,* 62–67.

74. *Niles' Register,* October 9, 16, 23, 1841, 90, 104–8, 119–25; Wool to Scott, October 11, 18, 1841, LRAG; AG to Wool, October 13, 1841, LSAG; Stevens, *Border Diplomacy,* 155; Jones and Rakestraw, *Prologue,* 48.

75. Wool to J[oshua] Spencer, February 22, 1842, WP, NYSL.

CHAPTER 6. ACROSS THE RIO GRANDE WITH OLD FUSSY

1. May 26, 28, 1846, in James K. Polk, *The Diary of James K. Polk,* ed. Milo M. Quaife, 4 vols. (Chicago: A. C. McClurg and Co., 1910), 1:429, 434; Moulton, "Wool Sketch," Tenney Papers; Spencer, *Marcy,* 153–54; Justin Smith, *The War with Mexico,* 2 vols. (New York: Macmillan Co., 1919), 1:181–83, 190–92. An excellent overview of the war is John S. D. Eisenhower, *So Far from God: The U.S. War with Mexico, 1846–1848* (New York: Random House, 1989). Also see: Irving W. Levinson, *War within War: Mexican Guerrillas, Domestic Elites, and the United States of America, 1846–1848* (Fort Worth: Texas Christian University Press, 2005); Pedro Santoni, *Mexicans at Arms: Puro Federalists and the Politics of War, 1845–1848* (Fort Worth: Texas Christian University Press, 1996); James M. McCaffrey, *Army of Manifest Destiny: The American Soldier in the Mexican War, 1846–1848* (New York: New York University Press, 1992); and James C. Pinheiro, *Manifest Ambition: James K. Polk and Civil-Military Relations during the Mexican War* (Westport, CT: Praeger International, 2007).

2. "Military Forces in Mexican War, January 3, 1850," HED 24, 31-1, Serial 576, 2–3; Smith, *War with Mexico* 1: chs. 3, 4, 7, 9; K. Jack Bauer, *The Mexican War, 1846–1848* (New York: Macmillan and Co., 1974), 3–48, 66–72; Upton, *Military Policy,* 203–4; George W. Smith and Charles Judah, eds., *Chronicles of the Gringos* (Albuquerque: University of New Mexico Press, 1968), 465n71, 467n85.

3. Wool to Sarah Wool, May 21, 23, 24, June 7, 1846, WP, NYSL; May 22, 1846, in Polk, *Diary* 1:417–18; Wool to Taylor, November 20, 1846, LRAG; Moulton, "Wool Sketch," Tenney Papers; Smith, *War with Mexico* 1:198–200; Spencer, *Marcy,* 154–56; Bauer, *Mexican War,* 73–75.

4. AG to Wool, May 28, 30, 1846, LSAG; Wool to Marcy, June 5, 7, 13, 1846, William L. Marcy Papers, LC; *Missouri Reporter* (St. Louis), June 9, 13, 1846; Moulton, "Wool Sketch," Tenney Papers; Bauer, *Mexican War,* 71–72.

5. Wool to Marcy, June 10, 13, 1846, Marcy Papers, LC; Smith, *War with Mexico* 1:195.

6. July 1, 1846, in [anon.], "Sketches of a Campaign in Coahuila," *American Whig Review* 16 (November 1852): 455–56; Samuel E. Chamberlain, *My Confession,* ed. William H. Goetzmann (Austin: Texas State Historical Association, 1996), 47, 50, 52; Wool to Marcy, June 25,

1846, Marcy Papers, LC; Wool to AG, June 24, 1846, LRAG; M. Margaret Jean Kelly, *The Career of Joseph Lane, Frontier Politician* (Washington, DC: Catholic University of America Press, 1947), 32.

7. Wool to AG, July 1, 1846, LRAG; AG to Wool, June 11, 1846, LSAG; Francis Baylies, *A Narrative of Major General Wool's Campaign in Mexico, in the Years 1846, 1847, and 1848* (Albany, NY: Little and Co., 1851), 9–10.

8. AG to Wool, June 11, July 1, 3, 1846, and Marcy to Taylor, June 8, 1846, LSAG; *Missouri Reporter,* July 7, 1846.

9. Wool to AG, July 16, 17, 1846, LRAG; Harriette Hart to Wool, July 26, 1846, WP, NYSL; Chamberlain, *My Confession,* 55; Moulton, "Wool Sketch," Tenney Papers. Edmund Schriver, Samuel P. Heintzelman, and William Wall all requested reassignment.

10. July 18, 23, 1846, in [anon.], "Sketches," *American Whig Review* 16: 457–59; GO, July 23, 1846, New Orleans, WP, NYSL; Adolph Engelmann to Parents, July 28, 1846, in Adolph Engelmann, "The Second Illinois in the Mexican War: Mexican War Letters of Adolph Engelmann, 1846–1847," ed. and trans. Otto B. Engelmann, *Journal of Illinois State Historical Society* [*JISHS*] 26 (January 1934): 362.

11. Wool to Sarah Wool, July 29, August 19, 1846, and George Talcott to Wool, May 29, June 5, 1846, WP, NYSL; July 28, 1846, in [anon.], "Sketches," *American Whig Review* 16: 459; Engelmann to Parents, July 28, 1846, in Engelmann, "Letters," *JISHS* 26: 363; Letter from Gen. Wallace dated July 24, 1846, in Isabel Wallace, *Life and Letters of General W. H. L. Wallace* (Chicago: R. R. Donnelley and Sons, 1909), 17–18; Henry Whiting to Jesup, November 30, 1846, in "Mexican War Correspondence, April 28, 1848," HED 60, 30-1, Serial 520, 685–86.

12. July 30–31, Aug; 4, 6, 1846, in [anon.], "Sketches," *American Whig Review* 16: 459–62; Jesup to Thomas F. Hunt, July 19, 1846, in Smith and Judah, eds., *Chronicles,* 372.

13. GO 1, SO 2, August 2, 4, 1846, Port Lavaca, Mexican War Orders [MxWO], AGO, National Archives [NA]. All general and special orders in this group were issued by Wool, unless otherwise noted.

14. August 7–8, 1846, [John Jay Langdon], Mexican War Diary, NYHS; August 8, 1846, in [anon.], "Sketches," *American Whig Review* 16: 463; Charles Kingsbury to Wool, August 14, 1846, WP, NYSL; Moulton, "Wool Sketch," Tenney Papers; David A. Clary, *Eagles and Empire: The United States, Mexico, and the Struggle for a Continent* (New York: Bantam Books, 2009), 164–65; T. Harry Williams, *Lincoln and His Generals* (New York: Alfred A. Knopf, 1952), 19, characterizes McDowell. A brief sketch is in "William Chauncey Langdon," in Miller and Malone, eds., *Dictionary of American Biography,* 5:589. Langdon, a former government clerk in Washington, DC, had moved his family to Louisiana by 1846, and served a brief three months as an officer in the First Volunteer [Louisiana] Regiment. He traveled with Wool to Monclova, Mexico, as a private observer.

15. GO 7, August 15, 1846, San Antonio, MxWO, AGO; Wool to AG, August 15, 1846, LRAG; August 29, 1846, in Josiah Gregg, *Diary and Letters of Josiah Gregg,* ed. Maurice G. Fulton, 2 vols. (Norman: University of Oklahoma Press, 1941, 1944), 1:220–21; Wool to [William C.] Young, August 18, 1846, WP, NYSL; John T. Lee, ed., *Josiah Gregg and Dr. George*

Engelmann (Worcester, MA: American Antiquarian Society, 1932); Thomas H. Kreneck, "The North Texas Regiment in the Mexican War," *Military History of Texas and the Southwest* 12, no. 2: 109–18; Henry W. Barton, *Texas Volunteers in the Mexican War* (Wichita Falls, TX: Texian Press, 1970), 68–70. Also see: George Rollie Adams, *General William S. Harney: Prince of Dragoons* (Lincoln: University of Nebraska Press, 2001), 88, 90–93.

16. Taylor to Wool, August 2, 1846, LSAG; Albert C. Horton to Wool, August 20, 1846, and Wool to Horton, August 24, 1846, Texas State Archives, Austin. GO 22, August 29, 1846, San Antonio, MxWO, AGO; Barton, *Texas Volunteers,* 64, 68–69, 73–74, 79; Henry W. Barton, "Five Texas Frontier Companies," *Southwestern Historical Quarterly* 66 (July 1962): 17–26.

17. GO 9, August 21, 1846, San Antonio, MxWO, AGO; Wool to AG, September 2, 1846, LRAG; *Niles' Register,* September 26, 1846, 56; *Washington Union,* July 18, 1846.

18. GO 13, August 16, 1846, San Antonio, MxWO, AGO. Engelmann to Parents, August 26, 1846, in Engelmann, "Letters," *JISHS* 26: 377–78, describes army rations.

19. August 28, September 27, 1846, in Gregg, *Diary and Letters* 1:217, 237–39, and 245; Engelmann to Parents, August 26, 31, September 19, 1846, in Engelmann, "Letters," *JISHS* 26: 376, 380, 383–84; [Edward Everett], "A Narrative of Military Experience in Several Capacities," Illinois State Historical Society *Transactions for 1905* (Springfield: Illinois State Historical Library, 1906), 206–7; *Niles' Register,* October 24, 1846, 119.

20. Engelmann to [Parents], September [n.d.], 1847, in Engelmann, "Letters," *JISHS* 26: 330; *Arkansas Democrat* (Little Rock), October 16, 1846; *Niles' Register,* November 21, 1846, 179; *Washington Union,* September 28, 1846. Quote regarding Yell is in Walter L. Brown, "The Mexican War Experiences of Albert Pike and the 'Mounted Devils' of Arkansas," *Arkansas Historical Quarterly* 12 (Winter 1953): 305.

21. August 28, 1846, in [Langdon] Diary, NYHS; Archibald Yell to Wool, August 22, September 9, 1846, WP, NYSL; Brown, "Pike," *Arkansas Historical Quarterly* 12: 304.

22. Orders No. 20, San Antonio, August 28, 1846, WP, NYSL.

23. Young to Wool, August 22, 1846, WP, NYSL; Wool to Taylor, September 15, 1846, LRAG; *Niles' Register,* September 26, 1846, 56; Adams, *Harney,* passim; Keyes, *Fifty Years' Observation,* 287–88, describes Harney.

24. Wool to Sarah Wool, September 24, 1846, WP, NYSL; George W. Hughes, "Memoir Descriptive of the March of a Division of the United States Army, Under the Command of Brigadier General John E. Wool, from San Antonio de Bexar, in Texas, to Saltillo, in Mexico," in SED 32, 31-1, Serial 558, 10; *Niles' Register,* October 10, 1846, 89–90, and May 8, 1847, 156; *Washington Union,* November 4, 1846.

25. Charles Thomas to Wool, August 17, 19, 1846, James R. Irwin to Wool, August 30, September 20, 1846, and Wool to Thomas, August 25, 1846, WP, NYSL; *Washington Union,* November 4, 1846.

26. Stephen W. Kearny to Marcy, March 4, 1846 (copy), WP, NYSL; Taylor to AG, July 2, 1846, Taylor to Wool, August 14, 1846, Wool to AG, September 2, 1846, and Wool to Taylor, September 15, 1846, LRAG; Hughes, "Memoir," SED 32, 31-1, 6–7; W. H. L. Wallace to Father [John Wallace], November 6, 1846, in Wallace, *W. H. L. Wallace,* 22, discusses the two presidios.

27. Wool to Sarah Wool, September 24, 1846, WP, NYSL; GO 74, SO 78, both September 22, 1846, and GO 77, September 23, 1846, San Antonio, MxWO, AGO; Wool to AG, September 28, 1846, LRAG; Hughes, "Memoir," SED 32, 31-1, 5, states that Wool had 3,400 men in his division. Years later, in a letter to Abraham Lincoln (April 24, 1864), Wool praised Lee's work in Mexico, saying that as a result of the captain's "indomitable perseverance and energy, I was not detained a day," WP, NYSL.

28. Wool to Sarah Wool, September 24, 1846, WP, NYSL; GO 77, 78, 81, September 23, 24, 27, 1846, San Antonio, MxWO, AGO; September 27, 1846, in [Langdon] Diary, NYHS; Wool to AG, September 28, 1846, LRAG; "Report on General Wool's road from San Antonio de Bexar, Texas, to the Presidio de Rio Grande, Mexico," WP, NYSL; Chamberlain, *My Confession,* 68, 71; Hughes, "Memoir," SED 32, 31-1, 12–15, 17; *Niles' Register,* November 7, 1846, 152–53; SO 87, September 25, 1846, San Antonio, MxWO, AGO. Capt. John H. Connor's Texas Mounted Company was stationed at Castroville to protect the frontier from Native Americans and to escort army supply wagons to the Rio Grande. The only officer with Wool's column whose wife went along was the paymaster, Maj. David Hunter. For recent scholarship on the Battle for Monterrey, see: Christopher D. Dishman, *A Perfect Gibraltar: The Battle for Monterrey, Mexico, 1846* (Norman: University of Oklahoma Press, 2010).

29. October 8, 1846, in [Langdon] Diary, NYHS; Wool to [alcalde], October 9, 1846, WP, NYSL; Engelmann to Parents, October 9, 1846, in Engelmann, "Letters," *JISHS* 26: 392; *Arkansas Democrat,* November 27, 1846.

30. GO 88 and 89, October 9, 1846, Presidio, MxWO, AGO; Chamberlain, *My Confession,* 73; Robert E. Lee to Wife [October 9, 1846], in Fitzhugh Lee, *General Lee* (New York: D. Appleton and Co., 1894), 34; Engelmann to [Parents], October 13, 1846, in Engelmann, "Letters," *JISHS,* 26: 393.

31. Clary, *Eagles and Empire,* 225; October 9, 11, 1846, in [Langdon] Diary, NYHS; October 9, 11, 1846, in Gregg, *Diary and Letters* 1:256, 258; Wool to Sarah Wool, October 12, 1846, WP, NYSL; Wool to AG, October 14, 1846, LRAG.

32. Wool to Sarah Wool, October 12, 1846, WP, NYSL; Wool to AG, October 14, 1846, LRAG; Hughes, "Memoir," SED 32, 31-1, 17–18; James H. Carleton, *Battle of Buena Vista* (New York: Harper and Row, 1848), 162; Jonathan W. Buhoup, *Narrative of the Central Division, or Army of Chihuahua, Commanded by Brigadier General Wool* (Pittsburgh: M. P. Morse, 1847), 29; George T. M. Davis, *Autobiography of the late Col. Geo. T. M. Davis, Captain and Aid-de-camp Scott's Army of Invasion (Mexico), From Posthumous Papers* (New York: Jenkins and McCowan Press, 1891), 94, 99, 101, 105; Wallace to Father, July 19, 1846, in Wallace, *W. H. L. Wallace,* 15.

33. GO 95, October 15, 1846, MxWO, AGO; October 12, 19, 1846, in [Langdon] Diary, NYHS; October 13, 15, 1846, in Gregg, *Diary and Letters* 1:259–60; *New Orleans Picayune,* October 30, 1847, mentions Thomas H. Addicks as Wool's interpreter.

34. GO 101, October 15, 1846, Presidio, MxWO, AGO; October 16, 18, 1846, in [Langdon] Diary, NYHS; Hughes, "Memoir," SED 32, 31-1, 18–19; Carleton, *Buena Vista,* 167–68; *Arkansas Democrat,* December 4, 1846.

35. Wool to AG, October 19, 1846, and Taylor to Wool, October 3, 1846, LRAG; October 18, 1846, in [Langdon] Diary, NYHS; October 18, 1846, in Gregg, *Diary and Letters* 1:265.

36. Hughes, "Memoir," SED 32, 31-1, 24; *Arkansas Democrat,* January 1, 1847; Davis, *Autobiography,* 106–7; *Niles' Register,* December 26, 1846, 263.

37. Carleton, *Buena Vista,* 171–72; Davis, *Autobiography,* 107–8; Hughes, "Memoir," SED 32, 31-1, 40; *Arkansas Democrat,* January 1, 1847; Charles H. Harris III, *The Sánchez Navarros: A Socio-economic Study of a Coahuilan Latifundio, 1846–1853* (Chicago: Loyola University Press, 1964); Also, Charles H. Harris III, *A Mexican Family Empire: The Latifundio of the Sánchez Navarro Family, 1765–1867* (Austin: University of Texas Press, 1975), 148, 169, 212.

38. GO 115, October 28, 1846, Las Aquintas, MxWO, AGO; October 29, 1846, in John J. Hardin Notebook, John J. Hardin Papers, ChiHS. K. Jack Bauer kindly copied the Wool references in the Hardin notebook. October 29, 1846, in [Langdon] Diary, NYHS; Quote is in William S. Harney, "Charges," in Harney to William W. S. Bliss, December 3, 1846, LRAG; Adams, *Harney,* 92–93; Gustave Koerner, *Memoirs of Gustave Koerner, 1809–1896,* ed. Thomas J. McCormick, 2 vols. (Cedar Rapids, IA: Torch Press, 1909), 1:499, describes Hardin.

39. Samuel E. Chamberlain, *My Confession: Recollections of a Rogue* (New York: Harper and Brothers, 1956), 73–74. This incident is recalled in Clary, *Eagles and Empire,* 226.

40. October 31, 1846, in [Langdon], Diary, NYHS; GO 119, November 2, 1846, Monclova, MxWO, AGO; George W. Hughes to Irwin McDowell, n.d., "Description of the March of Gen. Wool's Army from Monclova to Parras, Mexico," WP, NYSL; Wool to Miguel Lobo, October 31, 1846, WP, NYSL; November 3, 18, 1846, in Gregg, *Diary and Letters* 1:272–73, 279–82; Davis, *Autobiography,* 108; *Arkansas Democrat,* December 11, 1846, and January 1, 1847; *Troy Times,* November 10, 1869.

41. Wool to Taylor, November 1, 1846, LRAG; Taylor to AG, November 12, 1846, LRAG; October 20, 1846, in Polk, *Diary* 2:199; Bauer, *Taylor,* 187–88. In November, Polk urged Scott to seize the port of Tampico or Vera Cruz, and he decided to attach Wool's troops to his army.

42. November 6, 1846, in Augustus F. Ehinger Diary, Charles F. Ward Papers, Roswell, New Mexico; November 6, 1846, in Gregg, *Diary and Letters* 1:273.

43. GO 126, November 8, 1846, Monclova, MxWO, AGO; November 15, 1846, in [Langdon] Diary, NYHS; November 7, 1846, in Hardin Notebook, Hardin Papers, ChiHS; November 21, 1846, in Gregg, *Diary and Letters* 1:285; Engelmann to Parents, November 19, 1846, in Engelmann, "Letters," *JISHS* 26: 409; Davis, *Autobiography,* 111–18; *Niles' Register,* May 8, 1847, 156; *Arkansas Democrat,* January 1, 1847.

44. November 18, 19, 1846, in [Langdon] Diary, NYHS; Wool to Taylor, November 29, 1846, LRAG; Hughes, "Memoir," SED 32, 31-1, 44–48; Hughes to J. H. Prentiss, November 12, 1846, WP, NYSL; Bauer, *Taylor,* 188, states that Taylor ended the armistice on November 15. An inspection of Wool's army while they were encamped at Monclova revealed that most of the men were healthy and well-armed except for some companies of Colonel Yell's Arkansans, who were sickly. S. Churchill, "Report of Inspection of the troops at Monclova, Mexico, under command of Brig. Gen. John E. Wool, November 12, 1846," WP, NYSL.

45. Wool to AG, November 16, 1846, and Wool to Taylor, November 20, 1846, LRAG; GO 143, November 23, 1846, Monclova, MxWO, AGO; November 25, 27, 1846, in Gregg, *Diary and Letters* 1:286–90; Buhoup, *Narrative,* 84–85; Chamberlain, *My Confession,* 115–16; Engelmann to Parents, December 1, 1846, in Engelmann, "Letters," *JISHS* 26: 412; Wallace to Father, December 8, 1846, in Wallace, *W. H. L. Wallace,* 26.

46. Bliss to Wool, November 13, 21, 23, 1846, and Taylor to AG, November 14, 1846, LRAG.

47. Wool to Taylor, December 7, 1846, LRAG; Carleton, *Buena Vista,* 173; *Niles' Register,* January 16, 1847, 309; *Arkansas Democrat,* January 29, February 19, 1847; James Hobbs, *Wild Life in the Far West: Personal Adventures of a Border Mountain Man* (Glorieta, NM: Rio Grande Press, 1969), 151–54; Wallace to Father, December 8, 1846, in Wallace, *W. H. L. Wallace,* 26–27; Harris, *Sánchez Navarros,* 21, 71; Hughes, "Memoir," SED 32, 31-1, 32–33. Ibarra quoted beef at four cents a pound and flour at nine dollars a cargo (300 pounds). Lt. Col. Henry Clay Jr. was killed while leading a charge at the battle of Buena Vista.

48. Wool to Taylor, December 7, 1846, LRAG; Wool to Taylor, December 10, 1846, WP, NYSL.

49. Bliss to Wool, December 5, 10, 1846, LRAG; SO 149, 150, both December 12, 1846, Parras, MxWO, AGO.

50. December 16, 1846, in Ehinger Diary, Ward Papers; Engelmann to Parents, December 16, 1846, in Engelmann, "Letters," *JISHS* 26: 415; Clary, *Eagles and Empire,* 164; Lewis Wallace, *Lew Wallace: An Autobiography,* 2 vols. (New York: Harper and Row, 1906) 1:163; Charles J. Peterson, *Military Heroes of the War with Mexico: With a Narrative of the War* (Philadelphia: W. A. Leary, 1848), 193.

51. Wallace to Father, December 23, 1846, in Wallace, *W. H. L. Wallace,* 28–29; *Niles' Register,* January 16, 1847, 306; Wool to AG, January 17, 1847, and Wool to Taylor, January 20, 1847, LRAG; Chamberlain, *My Confession,* 127.

52. Wool to Harriette Hart, July 1, 1847, WP, NYSL; Harris, *Sánchez Navarros,* 8–10. Wool said that his chess opponent was one of the Sánchez Navarro brothers. Baylies, *Wool's Campaign,* 21, identifies the chess player as a nephew of the *hacendado*, and the woman as the nephew's wife.

53. SO 167, December 21, 1846, Encantada, MxWO, AGO; Wool to Taylor, January 22, 1847, and Wool to AG, January 3, 1847, LRAG; Wool to Cass, January 25, 1847, Cass Papers, UMi; John B. Duncan to Alexander Wright, January 30, 1847, in Alfred J. Henderson, "A Morgan County Volunteer in the Mexican War [John B. Duncan]," *JISHS* 41 (December 1948): 395; December 12, 1846, in Gregg, *Diary and Letters,* 1:306–7, and December 14, 1846, in ibid. 2:238; Chamberlain, *My Confession,* 129; Baylies, *Wool's Campaign,* 22.

54. December 17, 1846, in Gregg, *Diary and Letters* 1:314; Wool to Cass, January 25, 1847, Cass Papers, UMi; Wool to Carleton, July 27, 1847, WP, NYSL; Chamberlain, *My Confession,* 129; Hughes, "Memoir," SED 32, 31-1, 39–40; Carleton, *Buena Vista,* 177; *Niles Register,* January 9, 1847, 290. Worth told Wool that Maj. Gen. William Butler was peeved at him for disobeying his order to halt at San Juan de la Vaquería.

55. Wool to Carleton, July 27, 1847, WP, NYSL; Introduction, in Gregg, *Diary and Letters* 2:5; Chamberlain, *My Confession,* 129–30; Walter H. Herbert, *Fighting Joe Hooker* (Indianapolis, IN: Bobbs Merrill, 1944), 28. Capt. Joseph Hooker, famous for the battle of Chancellorsville in the Civil War, was Butler's aide.

56. Wool to D. T. Vail, July 1, 1847, WP, NYSL; Carleton, *Buena Vista,* 177, 179–80; Chamberlain, *My Confession,* 130.

57. Wool to Bliss, January 22, 1847, LRAG; December 25, 1846, in Gregg, *Diary and Letters* 1:320–23; Lee to Wife, December [n.d.], 1846, in Lee, *General Lee,* 35; *Arkansas Democrat,* February 5, 1847. A Mexican employee had passed the rumor to a civilian butcher, who caused the panic.

58. William O. Butler to Bliss, December 28, 1846, and Wool to Bliss, January 22, 1847, LRAG; GO 20 (Butler), December 28, 1846, Saltillo, MxWO, AGO; Carleton, *Buena Vista,* 180–81.

59. January 4, 1847, in Ehinger Diary, Ward Papers; SO 182, 183 (courts-martial), both January 2, 1847, Encantada, MxWO, AGO; December 18, 19, 1846, in Gregg, *Diary and Letters* 1:316, 318.

60. Wool to Yell, January 4, 1847, LRAG; Yell to Wool, January 5, 1847, WP, NYSL; *Arkansas Democrat,* February 5, 1847; Harris, *Sánchez Navarros,* 4–5, 35–36; Harris, *A Mexican Family Empire,* 287. Chamberlain, at *My Confession,* 201, wrote that on New Year's Eve, in the village of Patos, a Texan with a ranger detachment, which was escorting a wagon train, became intoxicated and rode his horse into the church, roped a large wooden crucifix, ripped it from the altar, and dragged it around the plaza. Father Juan E. Berain attempted to stop the ranger but was ridden down. Horrified citizens seized the Texan, tied him to the cross, and slashed him mercilessly. The rangers heard his cries, charged into the village, and fired into the crowd. As the man screamed for relief from his misery, the rangers shot him and ended his torment.

61. Harney to Bliss, December 3, 1847; Samuel C. Ridgely to Taylor, January 18, 1847, and Lorenzo Thomas to Wool, January 5, 1847, LRAG; Adams, *Harney,* 95; Lambert, *Second Cavalry,* 34–35. Harney later refused to obey an order from Scott, was court-martialed and found guilty. President Polk set aside the verdict and restored Harney to duty.

62. Thomas to Wool, January 8, 1847, and Wool to AG, January 17, 1847, LRAG; Wool to Vail, July 1, 1847, WP, NYSL; Lee to Wife, January 17, 1847, in Clifford Dowdey, *Lee* (Boston: Little, Brown and Co., 1965), 81.

63. Wool to AG, January 17, 1847, and Wool to Yell, January 15, 1847, LRAG; Wallace to Father, January 19, 1847, in Wallace, *W. H. L. Wallace,* 33; January 4–6, 1847, in Ehinger Diary, Ward Papers.

64. Wool to AG, January 17, 1847, LRAG; Wool to Vail, July 1, 1847, WP, NYSL; Wool to Sarah Wool, January 17, 1847, WP, NYSL; January 25, 1847, in Ehinger Diary, Ward Papers; *Arkansas Democrat,* March 26, 1847; Heitman, *Historical Register,* 1:546.

65. Wool to Taylor, January 20, 1847; Joseph Hooker to Wool, January 20, 1847; Wool to Bliss, January 22, 1847, and Thomas to Wool, January 22, 1847, LRAG.

66. Wool to Taylor, January 20, 1847, LRAG; Wool to Cass, January 25, 1847, Cass Papers, UMi; Wool to Sarah Wool, February 8, 1847, WP, NYSL.

67. Wool to Bliss, April 19, 1847, and Thomas to Wool, January 22, 1847, LRAG; GO 202 (Butler), January 25, 1847, Saltillo, MxWO, AGO; Wool to Sarah Wool, January 3, 25, 1847, WP, NYSL; Duncan to Wright, January 30, 1847, in Henderson, "Morgan County Volunteer," *JISHS* 41: 394; Baylies, *Wool's Campaign,* 25.

68. Wool to Taylor, January 27, 29, 1847, LRAG; Wool to Sarah Wool, February 1, 1847, WP, NYSL; Engelmann to Parents, January 29, 30, 1847, in Engelmann, "Letters," *JISHS* 26: 432, 434; *Arkansas Democrat,* March 26, 1847; Bauer, *Taylor,* 207.

69. Wool to Taylor, January 29, 1847, LRAG; GO 6 (Taylor), January 28, 1847, Monterrey, MxWO, AGO.

70. GO 207 (Butler), January 28, 1847, Saltillo, MxWO, AGO; January 24, 1847, in Ehinger Diary, Ward Papers; Wallace to Father, January 19, 1847, in Wallace, *W. H. L. Wallace,* 33.

71. Taylor to James Buchanan, August 29, 1847, in Zachary Taylor, *Letters of Zachary Taylor from the Battle-Fields of the Mexican War,* ed. William H. Samson (Rochester, NY: Genesee Press, 1908), 182; Engelmann to Parents, February 6, 1847, in Engelmann, "Letters," *JISHS* 26: 438; Baylies, *Wool's Campaign,* 37; John Frost, *Life of Major General Zachary Taylor* (New York: D. Appleton and Co., 1847), 277; William S. Henry, *Campaign Sketches of the War with Mexico* (New York: Harper, 1847), 276; Smith, *War with Mexico* 1:141, 179; Bauer, *Taylor,* 194.

72. Bliss sketch, in Susan Shelby Magoffin, *Down the Santa Fe Trail and into Mexico: The Diary of Susan Shelby Magoffin, 1846–1847,* ed. Stella M. Drumm (New Haven, CT: Yale University Press, 1926), 252n11; Engelmann to Parents, February 6, 1847, in Engelmann, "Letters," *JISHS* 26: 438; Grady McWhiney, *Braxton Bragg and Confederate Defeat*, vol. 1, *Field Command* (New York: Columbia University Press, 1969), passim; Davis, *Davis Papers* 3:v-vii; Smith, *War with Mexico* 1:141.

73. Wool to Taylor, February 5, 1847, LRAG; GO 9 (Taylor), February 11, 1847, Agua Nueva, MxWO, AGO; Wool to Sarah Wool, February 7, 1847, WP, NYSL; Wallace to Father, February 14, 1847, in Wallace, *W. H. L. Wallace,* 38–39; Bliss to Richard H. Dana, Jr., March 8, 1848, in Richard Henry Dana, Jr., *The Journal of Richard Henry Dana, Jr.,* ed. Robert F. Lucid, 3 vols. (Cambridge, MA: Harvard University Press, 1968) 1: 344.

74. Wool to Sarah Wool, February 13, 1847, WP, NYSL; Saltillo *Picket Guard,* April 14, 1847; February 11, 1847, in Ehinger Diary, Ward Papers; February 13, 1847, in Gregg, *Diary and Letters* 2:36; Buhoup, *Narrative,* 107–8; *Arkansas Democrat,* March 26, 1847; Chamberlain, *My Confession,* 130, 132, 134. Chamberlain, who depicted the massacre in one of his paintings, said that Mexicans murdered volunteers because of outrages committed against women at Agua Nueva by the American troops on Christmas Day.

75. GO 9 (Taylor), February 11, 1847, Agua Nueva, MxWO, AGO; Bliss to Yell, February 14, 1847, George Lincoln to Yell, February 11, 1847, and Yell to Taylor, February 14, 19, 1847, LRAG; *Arkansas Democrat,* April 2, May 28, 1847; Bauer, *Mexican War,* 208.

76. February 14, 1847, in Ehinger Diary, Ward Papers; Benjamin F. Scribner, *Camp Life of a Volunteer: A Campaign in Mexico, Or a Glimpse at Life in Camp* (Philadelphia: J. Gihon, 1850),

57–58; John S. Roane to Wool, January 14, 1850, WP, NYSL; Chamberlain, *My Confession,* 132, 137–39, 141, 143; [Baylies], "Wool," *Democratic Review* 29: 449; Bauer, *Taylor,* 195.

77. Wool to Sarah Wool, February 20, 1847, WP, NYSL; February 20, 1847, in Ehinger Diary, Ward Papers; Lambert, *Second Cavalry,* 33; Bauer, *Mexican War,* 209.

78. Santa Anna's Order of March, January 28, 1847, San Luis Potosí [trans.], in Charles W. Davis to Wool, February 27, 1847, WP, NYSL; Ramón Alcaraz, *The Other Side: Or Notes for the History of the War Between Mexico and the United States,* trans. Albert C. Ramsey (New York: John Wiley, 1850), 114–18; Bauer, *Mexican War,* 205–6; Smith, *War with Mexico* 1:380.

CHAPTER 7. TORRENTS OF BLOOD

1. Carleton, *Buena Vista,* 12–19; William E. Estis [Sgt., Co. E, 1st Mississippi Rifles], account in Varina Howell Davis, *Jefferson Davis, Ex-President of the Confederate States of America: A Memoir by His Wife,* 2 vols. (New York: Belford, 1890), 1:338. Santa Anna's army was estimated at 15,142 men.

2. Roane to Wool, January 14, 1850, WP, NYSL; Wool to Dix, March 22, 1848, John Adams Dix Papers, Columbia University [CU]; Taylor to E[dward] G. W. Butler, March 4, 1847, cited in Baylies, *Wool's Campaign,* 26–27; Estis, account in V. H. Davis, *Davis* 1:338; Chamberlain, *My Confession,* 149, 152; Henry W. Benham, *Recollections of Mexico and the Battle of Buena Vista, February 22 and 23, 1847. By an Engineer officer on its twenty-fourth Anniversary* (Boston, 1871), 8; McWhiney, *Bragg,* 54.

3. Wool to Bliss, March 4, 1847, LRAG; February 21, 1847, in Gregg, *Diary and Letters* 2:44–45; Duncan to Henry C. Wright, March 6, 1847, in Henderson, "Morgan County Volunteer," *JISHS* 41: 396.

4. Wool to Dix, March 22, 1847, Dix Papers, CU; Carleton, *Buena Vista,* 24, 43; Estis, account in V. H. Davis, *Jefferson Davis* 1:338.

5. Duncan to Wright, March 6, 1847, in Henderson, "Morgan County Volunteer," *JISHS* 41: 396–97; February 22, 1847, in Gregg, *Diary and Letters* 2:46; Carleton, *Buena Vista,* 42–43.

6. Carleton, *Buena Vista,* 24–25; Buhoup, *Narrative,* 112–13; Chamberlain, *My Confession,* 152.

7. Hughes, "Memoir," SED 32, 31-1, 39; Carleton, *Buena Vista,* 7–9.

8. Carleton, *Buena Vista,* 6–9; Hughes, "Memoir," SED 32, 31-1, 31–32, 39; Adolphus Wislizenus, *Memoir of a Tour of Northern Mexico Connected with Col. Doniphan's Expedition in 1846 and 1847* (Washington, DC: Tippin and Streeper, 1848), 75; *Arkansas Democrat,* April 30, 1847.

9. James H. Lane to Joseph Lane, May 15, 1847, LRAG; Buhoup, *Narrative,* 113–14; Carleton, *Buena Vista,* 30; Ellen Hardin Walworth, "The Battle of Buena Vista," *Magazine of American History* 3 (December 1879): 719.

10. C[lary] H. Fry to Irvin McDowell, March 5, 1847; J. H. Lane to Joseph Lane, May 15, 1847; Wool to Bliss, March 4, 1847, all in LRAG.

11. Carleton, *Buena Vista,* 35; [Baylies], "Wool," *DmR* 29: 450; Walworth, "Buena Vista," *Magazine of American History* 3: 720.

12. Wool to Dix, March 22, 1848, Dix Papers, CU; Carleton, *Buena Vista,* 35; Baylies, *Wool's Campaign,* 29.

13. Carleton, *Buena Vista,* 32–33, 36; February 22, 1847, in Gregg, *Diary and Letters* 2:46; Chamberlain, *My Confession,* 155; Estis, in V. H. Davis, *Jefferson Davis* 1:340.

14. Taylor to AG, February 24, March 6, 1847, LRAG; Carleton, *Buena Vista,* 36; *Niles' Register,* April 3, 1847, 64; Wallace to George Green, March 1, 1847, in Wallace, *W. H. L. Wallace,* 41.

15. Wool to Bliss, March 4, 1847, LRAG; Carleton, *Buena Vista,* 38–40, 48, 52. Taylor's line from the road east across the plateau to the mountains, included (in order): Hardin's First Illinois, Thomas's gun, Bissell's Second Illinois, French's gun, Bowles's Second Indiana, and O'Brien's three guns.

16. Wool to Bliss, March 4, 1847, and Humphrey Marshall to Wool, March 1, 1847, LRAG. Wool to Marshall, May 12, 1849, WP, NYSL.

17. Wool to Marshall, May 12, 1849, WP, NYSL; Marshall to Wool, March 1, 1847, LRAG.

18. Wool to Bliss, March 4, 1847, and Braxton Bragg to Bliss, March 2, 1847, LRAG; Carleton, *Buena Vista,* 40–41; Engelmann to Parents, March 1, 1847, in Engelmann, "Letters," *JISHS* 26: 443; Baylies, *Wool's Campaign,* 30.

19. Wool to Dawson, May 18, 24, 1860, ChiHS; Wool's lengthy letter to Dawson, May 24, 1860, appears in K. Jack Bauer, ed., "General John E. Wool's Memoranda of the Battle of Buena Vista," *Southwestern Historical Quarterly* 72 (July 1973), 111–23; [Baylies], "Wool," *DmR* 29: 451.

20. Marshall to Wool, March 1, 1847, LRAG; Wallace to Green, March 1, 1847, in Wallace, *W. H. L. Wallace,* 43.

21. Carleton, *Buena Vista,* 43–45; Baylies, *Wool's Campaign,* 37–38; Walworth, "Buena Vista," *Magazine of American History* 3: 722.

22. Chamberlain, *My Confession,* 155, 157; Carleton, *Buena Vista,* 45–49; Walworth, "Buena Vista," *Magazine of American History* 3: 723–24.

23. Wallace, *Autobiography* 1:169–70, 184; Baylies, *Wool's Campaign,* 32; Walworth, "Buena Vista," *Magazine of American History* 3: 723–24. Baylies, "Wool," *DmR* 29: 451, estimates Wool's force at 2,815 men.

24. Wool to Bliss, March 4, 1847, LRAG; Carleton, *Buena Vista,* 49–51, 54, 59; Wallace *Autobiography* 1:170; Wallace to Green, March 1, 1847, in Wallace, *W. H. L. Wallace,* 42–44.

25. Marshall to Wool, March 1, 1847, and Braxton Bragg to Bliss, March 2, 1847, LRAG.

26. McWhiney, *Bragg,* 54, 76; Lester R. Dillon Jr., *American Artillery in the Mexican War, 1846–47* (Austin, TX: Presidial Press, 1975), 11–14, 55–57. Smith and Judah, eds., *Chronicles,* 382–84, describes the ordnance used in the war.

27. Wool to Dawson, May 24, 1860, ChiHS; Wool to Dawson, June 2, 1865, WP, NYSL; Wool to Bliss, March 4, 1847; Xerxes Trail to Wool, March [23], 1847, LRAG; Carleton, *Buena Vista,* 50–52; Thomas H. Kreneck, "From Enthusiasm to Disillusionment: The Texas Volunteer Infantry in the Mexican War," *Texana* 12 (Fall 1974): 374–77.

28. Chamberlain, *My Confession,* 157–58; Carleton, *Buena Vista,* 56; Alcaraz, *The Other Side,* 123.

29. J. H. Lane to Joseph Lane, May 15, 1847; Washington to McDowell, February 28, 1847, LRAG; Wool to Dawson, May 24, 1860, ChiHS; Carleton, *Buena Vista,* 58, 67–68.

30. Wool to Dawson, May 24, 1860, ChiHS; Wool to Dawson, June 2, 1865, WP, NYHS; Joseph Lane to Wool, February 25, 1847; John P. J. O'Brien to Washington, February 25, 1847, and William Bissell to Wool, February 28, 1847, all in LRAG; Roger S. Dix to John A. Dix, February 25, 1847, in Dix, comp., *Memoirs* 1:210–12; L. Wallace, *Autobiography,* 1:170, 184, 186; Alcaraz, *The Other Side,* 124.

31. Wool to Dawson, May 24, 1860, ChiHS; Wool to Sarah Wool, February 26, 1847, WP, NYSL; Wallace to Green, March 1, 1847, in Wallace, *W. H. L. Wallace,* 44–45.

32. Wool to Dawson, May 24, 1860, ChiHS; Wool to Dawson, June 2, 1865, NYHS; Joseph Lane to Wool, February 25, 1847; O'Brien to Washington, February 25, 1847, Wool to Bliss, March 4, 1847, all in LRAG; Carleton, *Buena Vista,* 58, 60–62; Benham, *Recollections,* 15–16. Benham attributes part of Bowles's confusion to the fact that the Indiana column saw O'Brien limber up to move forward (teams faced to the rear to hitch up), and assumed the battery was retreating. The cowardice charged to the Hoosiers was so embarrassing to the state of Indiana that when regiments from the state were formed at the beginning of the Civil War, their commander, Gen. Lew Wallace, made them kneel and swear that they would avenge the disgrace visited upon the state by the cowardice of her troops at Buena Vista.

33. Wool to Bliss, March 4, 1847; Joseph Lane to Wool, February 25, 1847; Trail to Wool, [March 23], 1847, and Marshall to Wool, March 1, 1847; all in LRAG. Sylvester Churchill to Stephen A. Douglas, [March 1847], in Koerner, *Gustav Koerner* 1:504–5; Carleton, Buena Vista, 64–67, 83; Walworth, "Buena Vista," *Magazine of American History* 3: 727–28; Robert R. Miller, *Shamrock and Sword: The Saint Patrick's Battalion in the U.S.-Mexican War* (Norman: University of Oklahoma Press, 1989), 53.

34. Wool to Bliss, March 4, 1847; William Weatherford to [Wool], February 26, 1847; and Fry to McDowell, March 5, 1847; all in LRAG.

35. Bragg to Bliss, March 2, 1847, LRAG.

36. Bissell to Wool, February 28, 1847, LRAG; Wool to Dix, March 22, 1848, Dix Papers, CU; Wool to Dawson, May 24, 1860, ChiHS; Bissell to Davis, February 22, 1850, Davis, *Davis Papers* 4:80; Baylies, *Wool's Campaign,* 33–34; Miller, *Saint Patrick's Battalion,* 53–55; David Lavender, *Climax at Buena Vista: The Decisive Battle of the Mexican-American War* (Philadelphia: University of Pennsylvania Press, 1966), 197–98; Clary, *Eagles and Empire,* 277–78.

37. Wool to Dix, March 22, 1848, Dix Papers, CU; Wool to Dawson, May 24, 1860, ChiHS; Bliss to Dana, March 8, 1848, in Lucid, ed., *Dana* 1:343; Carleton, *Buena Vista,* 72–73; Hobbs, *Wild Life,* 159; Bauer, *Mexican War,* 214. Bauer, *Taylor,* 201, says Wool advised a retreat.

38. Wool to Sarah Wool, February 26, 1847, WP, NYSL; Wool to Dawson, May 24, 1860, ChiHS; Wool to Dawson, June 2, 1865, NYHS; *Arkasnas Democrat,* April 30, 1847.

39. Wool to Dawson, May 24, 1860, ChiHS; Jeff Davis to Bliss, March 2, 1847, LRAG; Wool to Sarah Wool, June 11, 29, 1847, WP, NYSL; Chamberlain, *My Confession,* 159, 161.

40. Davis to Bliss, March 2, 1847; Charles May to Bliss, March 3, 1847; Wool to Bliss, March 2, 1847; and Joseph Lane to Wool, February 25, 1857, LRAG; Estis account, in V. H.

Davis, *Davis,* 1:342–43; Chamberlain, *My Confession*, 162; Gregg, *Diary and Letters* 2:48–49; Baylies, *Wool's Campaign*, 34.

41. Wool to Sarah Wool, June 8, 11, 1847, WP, NYSL; February 23, 1847, in Gregg, *Diary and Letters*, 2:49. Lieutenant Benham, an engineer on Taylor's staff, reported (his source was McDowell) that Wool, "in an excess of caution, and in fear of a defeat," urged Taylor to order Washington to prepare his battery to retreat. Taylor yielded and Wool sent McDowell with the order. Washington started hitching the teams to the artillery pieces and one gun actually started to the rear. Washington immediately recalled the gun and refused to move without "positive orders" from Taylor. Taylor halted the move, realizing that a retreat would create a panic. [Benham], *Recollections*, 20; Bragg to W[illiam] T. Sherman, March 1, 1848, W.T. Sherman Papers, LC. Bragg stated essentially the same thing. See also Smith, *War with Mexico* 1:558n12.

42. Marshall to Wool, March 1, 1847; Wool to Bliss, March 4, 1847; and May to Bliss, March 3, 1847; all in LRAG; Wallace to Green, March 1, 1847, in Wallace, *W. H. L. Wallace*, 45; Robert L. Duncan, *Reluctant General: The Life and Times of Albert Pike* (New York: E. P. Dutton and Co., 1961), 123–35.

43. Davis to Bliss, March 2, 1847; J. H. Lane to Joseph Lane, May 15, 1847, and Bragg to Bliss, March 2, 5, 1847; all in LRAG. Davis, *Davis Papers*, 3:147n16, n18, n21, n23, 148, 149n30, n36; Baylies, *Wool's Campaign*, 34; Bauer, *Taylor*, 203.

44. Davis to Bliss, March 2, 1847; T[homas] W. Sherman to Bliss, March 2, 1847; and J. H. Lane to Joseph Lane to Joseph Lane, May 15, 1847, LRAG; Carleton, *Buena Vista*, 98–99.

45. Bragg to Bliss, March 2, 5, 1847; Davis to Bliss, March 2, 1847, and Wool to AG, August 9, 1847; all in LRAG; Wool to Dawson, May 24, 1860, ChiHS; Grayson M. Prevost to Wool, August 3, 1847, WP, NYSL; Carleton, *Buena Vista*, 100; Baylies, *Wool's Campaign,* 34; Peterson, *Military Heroes*, 192–93.

46. Carleton, *Buena Vista*, 101–3; Chamberlain, *My Confession*, 161; Gregg, *Diary and Letters*, 2:51; Alcaraz, *The Other Side*, 127.

47. Several observers commented on the flags. Wallace to Green, March 1, 1847, in Wallace, *W. H. L. Wallace*, 46, said two Mexican officers emerged on foot with a flag from the heavy battery on the left. One was "an elderly man with a blue jacket and a fur collar." The other was "a young olive-colored Spaniard, bedecked with green cloth and gold lace." Alcaraz, *The Other Side*, 126–27, stated that a Mexican officer, José María Montoya, and an associate, apparently without Santa Anna's knowledge, crossed the battlefield. Benham labeled the incident a ruse. It appears that the Mexican column found themselves cut off and, fearing for their lives, feigned a message from Santa Anna. Unwittingly, they saved several thousand Mexican soldiers facing surrender in the cove. [Benham], *Recollections*, 17. Also, Wool to Bliss, March 4, 1847, LRAG; and Walworth, "Buena Vista," *Magazine of American History* 3: 732. For Crittenden's mission, see Bragg to Bliss, March 5, 1847, LRAG; February 23, 1847, in Gregg, *Diary and Letters*, 2:51; *Niles' Register*, 72 (April 10, 1847), 83; Wool to Dawson, May 24, 1860, ChiHS, and [Baylies], "Wool," *DmR*, 29: 452–53. Wool wrote Sarah (June 11, 1847, WP, NYSL) that his forces were poised to take prisoners, but the flag sent by Taylor, "for what purpose I never inquired," prevented this. "We ceased fire until the flag passed," he

added. The Mexicans "secured the flag" and escaped to the plateau. Neither Taylor nor Wool mentioned the Crittenden episode in their battle reports, but both the *Arkansas Democrat* and the *New Orleans Picayune* did so. Wool to Sarah Wool, June 11, 1847, WP, NYSL; Monroe et al., *Davis Papers*, 3:138n16.

48. Wool to Bliss, March 4, 1847, LRAG; Wool to Dawson, May 24, 1860, ChiHS; Gregg, *Diary and Letters*, 2:52; Alcaraz, *The Other Side*, 126–27; Baylies, *Wool's Campaign*, 34–35; Carleton, *Buena Vista*, 106; Christopher J. Einolf, *George Thomas: Virginian for the Union* (Norman: University of Oklahoma Press, 2006), 52–53.

49. Wool to Bliss, March 4, 1847; Fry to McDowell, March 5, 1847; both in LRAG; Wool to Dawson, May 24, 1860, ChiHS; February 23, 1847, in Gregg, *Diary and Letters*, 2:52. Baylies; *Wool's Campaign*, 34–35; Bauer, *Taylor*, 204.

50. Bragg to Bliss, March 2, 1847, and J. H. Lane to Joseph Lane, May 14, 1847, LRAG; Alcaraz, *The Other Side*, 127–28.

51. Wool to Dawson, May 24, 1860, ChiHS; Weatherford to [Wool], February 26, 1847, LRAG; Notes in Gregg, *Diary and Letters*, 2:71–72; Carleton, *Buena Vista*, 107–9; Wool to Sarah Wool, March 29, 1847, WP, NYSL; Wallace to Green, March 1, 1847, in Wallace, *W. H. L. Wallace*, 47–48; Walworth, "Buena Vista," *Magazine of American History* 3: 733–34.

52. Weatherford to [Wool], February 25, 1847, and J. H. Lane to Joseph Lane, May 15, 1847, LRAG; Wallace to Green, March 1, 1847, in Wallace, *W. H. L. Wallace*, 47–49; Carleton, *Buena Vista*, 111; Baylies, *Wool's Campaign*, 36–37.

53. Wool to Sarah Wool, June 11, 1847, WP, NYSL; O'Brien to Washington, February 25, 1847; Wool to Bliss, March 4, 1847; both in LRAG; Wool to Dix, March 22, 1848, Dix Papers, CU; Carleton, *Buena Vista*, 112.

54. O'Brien to Washington, February 25, 1847, and Bragg to Bliss, March 2, 1847, LRAG; Carleton, *Buena Vista*, 22–23.

55. Wool to Dix, March 2, March 22, 1848, Dix Papers, CU; Wool to Dawson, May 24, 1860, ChiHS; Wool to Bliss, March 4, 1847; Davis to Bliss, March 2, 1847; J. H. Lane to Joseph Lane, May 15, 1847, and Bragg to Bliss, March 2, 1847, LRAG; Carleton, *Buena Vista*, 117–19, 126; Wallace to Green, March 1, 1847, in Wallace, *W. H. L. Wallace*, 50; Baylies, *Wool's Campaign*, 37. Benham (*Recollections*, 24) reported that Wool nearly blundered as the battle ended when he ordered May to take his dragoons and a spy company (230 men) and attack the Mexican heavy battery at the upper edge of the plateau, guarded by over 3,000 infantry. Major Mansfield rushed up and urged him to revoke the order, saying there was no backup if the charge failed. Wool agreed.

56. Subsistence issued to Mexican prisoners at Buena Vista, "Message from the President, transmitting Reports from Secretary of State and Secretary of War . . . , March 30, 1848," HED 56, 30-1, Serial 518, 372; Carleton, *Buena Vista*, 126–27; Gregg to Van Buren *Arkansas Intelligencer*, March 22, 1847 in Gregg, *Diary and Letters* 2:65; Wool to Dix, March 2, 1847, March 22, 1848, Dix Papers, CU; *Arkansas Democrat*, April 2, 1847; Wallace to Green, March 1, 1847, in Wallace, *W. H. L. Wallace*, 50–52.

57. Samuel G. French, *Two Wars: An Autobiography of General Samuel G. French . . . Mexican War, War Between the States, a Diary: Reconstruction Period, His Experiences, Incidents,*

Reminiscences, etc. (Nashville: Confederate Veteran, 1901), 82; Carleton, *Buena Vista*, 128–29; Bliss to Dana, March 8, 1848, in Lucid, ed., *Dana* 1:343; William Warren to Wool, March 1, 1847, LRAG; February 23, 1847, in *Diary and Letters*, 2:47, 53; Baylies, *Wool's Campaign*, 37; Ohio officer [George W. Morgan, 2nd Ohio] to editor of the *Cincinnati Chronicle News-Letter*, cited in Smith and Judah, eds., *Chronicles*, 98–99.

58. "Extracts from a report made by an officer of Engineers . . . attached to staff of General Santa Anna, [February 1847]," and Wool to Vail, July 1, 1847, WP, NYSL; [Morgan] to *Cincinnati Chronicle News-Letter*, in Smith and Judah, eds., *Chronicles*, 342–43; Wool to Dix, March 27, 1848, Dix Papers, CU.

59. Roger Dix to John A. Dix, February 25, 1847, in Dix, comp., *Memoirs*, 1:1–2; Hitchcock to Thomas Lawson, March 11, 1847, in Smith and Judah, eds., *Chronicles*, 342–43; Wool to Dix, March 22, 1848, Dix Papers, CU.

60. Carleton, *Buena Vista*, 125–26; Wallace to Green, March 1, 1847 in Wallace, *W. H. L. Wallace*, 50; Wool to Dix, March 22, 1848, Dix Papers, CU; Baylies, *Wool's Campaign*, 38–39.

61. *Monter[r]ey Gazette*, February 26, 1848; *Niles' Register*, April 10, 1847; Carleton, *Buena Vista*, 129–30; Wool to Dix, March 22, 1848, Dix Papers, CU; Baylies, *Wool's Campaign*, 38–39; Wool to Dix, March 22, 1848, Dix Papers, CU.

62. Wool to Dix, March 22, 1848, Dix Papers, CU; Carleton, *Buena Vista*, 131–32; February 24, 1847, in Gregg, *Diary and Letters* 2:54–55; Alcaraz, *The Other Side*, 131; Smith, *War with Mexico*, 1:397.

63. Wool to Sarah Wool, February 26, April 6, 1847, and Wool to J. A. Spencer, et al., March 30, 1847, WP, NYSL; Wool to Bliss, March 30, 1847; LRAG; Lavender, *Climax at Buena Vista*, 211, 241n34; Churchill to Wool, February 27, 1847, WP, NYSL.

64. Taylor to AG, March 6, 22, 1847, LRAG; Churchill to Wool, February 26, 1847, WP, NYSL; Carleton, *Buena Vista*, 132–35; February 24, 1847, in Gregg, *Diary and Letters* 2:55; Baylies, *Wool's Campaign*, 40–41.

65. Wool to Sarah Wool, February 25, 26, March 1, 1847, WP, NYSL.

66. Wool to Sarah Wool, March 1, 5, 1847, WP, NYSL.

67. Wool to Sarah Wool, March 6, 21, 1847, WP, NYSL; Davis to Bliss, March 2, 1847, LRAG; Wool to Dix, March 2, 1847; March 22, 1848, Dix Papers, CU.

68. Wool to Sarah Wool, February 25, 26, March 1, 1847, WP, NYSL; Roger Dix to John A. Dix, February 25, 1847, in Dix comp., *Memoirs* 1:210–11; *Arkansas Democrat*, April 23, 30, 1847. Taylor's reports in *Niles' Register* 72 (April 3 and 24, 1847), 68, 115–16. Bauer, *Taylor*, 220–22.

69. Taylor's reports in *Niles' Register*, April 3 and 24, 1847, 68, 115–16; *Arkansas Democrat*, April 30, 1847.

70. Wool to Sarah Wool, March 21, 1847, WP, NYSL; Davis to Bliss, March 2, 1847, LRAG; Wool to Dix, March 2, 22, 1847, Dix Papers, CU. In 1848, journalist Richard Henry Dana Jr., interviewed Bliss, who spoke frankly about Bragg. Bliss dismissed as untrue such remarks as "A little more grape, Capt. Bragg," and "Never mind, Major Bliss and I will support you." Bliss emphasized that the fate of the battle hung on Bragg's timely and determined resistance. With only three guns, Bragg took an exposed position and inflicted great losses on

the enemy, and "saved the day." Bliss to Dana, March 8, 1848, in Lucid, ed., *Dana* 1:342. Daniel T. Kuehl, "Double Shot Your Guns and Give 'em Hell! Braxton Bragg and the War in Mexico," *Civil War History* 37 (March 1991): 51–65.

71. Wool to Sarah Wool, March 1, 1847, WP, NYSL; *Arkansas Democrat*, April 30, June 25, 1847.

72. Marcy diary, December 3, 1849, assessed Taylor as a commander in Thomas M. Marshall, ed., "Diary and Memoranda of William L. Marcy, 1849–1851," *American Historical Review* 24 (April 1919): 446, 455; *New York Freeman's Journal*, October 25, 1851; Smith, *War with Mexico* 1:556n7, 557n10; McWhiney, *Bragg*, 65, 71, 73; Ambrose, *West Point*, 101–2. Also see Bauer, *Taylor*, 214, and Bauer, *Mexican War*, 217.

73. Wool to Sarah Wool, March 1, May 8, September 24, 1847, WP, NYSL; Wool to Dix, March 22, 1848, Dix Papers, CU.

74. Wool to Dix, March 22, 1848, Dix Papers, CU.

CHAPTER 8. NOTHING BUT DUTY

1. Bauer, *Mexican War,* 221–24; Clary, *Eagles and Empire,* 384–89.

2. Wool to Roane, March 9, 1847, WP, NYSL; Joseph Lane, O'Brien, et al. to Wool, February 25, 1847, Taylor to AG, March 6, 14, 1847, and Wool to Bliss, March 4, 6, 12, 1847, LRAG; February 27, 1847, LRAG.

3. Wool to Warren, February 28, 1847; GO (Warren), February 27, 1847, Saltillo, and Warren to Wool, March 3, 6, 1847, WP, NYSL; Wool, SO 293, March 15, 1847, and Wool, GO 245, March 16, 1847, Buena Vista, MxWO, AGO.

4. Wool to Taylor, March 30, 1847, LRAG; Warren to Wool, March 31, 1847; Wool to Warren, April 26, 1847; Warren to Edward Gonzales, March 29, 1847, WP, NYSL; March 29, 1847, in Gregg, *Diary and Letters* 2:69.

5. Horgan introduction in Gregg, *Diary and Letters* 2:6, and April 2–3, 1847, in ibid. 2:79–84.

6. Wool to Warren, April 14, 15, 26, 1847, Wool to Churchill, April 16, 1847, Wool to Washington, July 25, 1847, Warren to Gonzales, March 29, 1847, Wool to Bliss, April 19, September 30, 1847, WP, NYSL; Wool to Bliss, April 17, 1847, LRAG; Smith and Judah, eds., *Chronicles,* 503n68.

7. Wool to Roger Jones, January 3, 1849, Wool to Warren, May 18, 1847, and Wool to Bliss, September 30, 1847, WP, NYSL; GO 245, 286, March 16 and May 8, 1847, Buena Vista, MxWO, AGO; *Niles' Register* 72 (April 10, 1847): 93–94. Smith, *War with Mexico* 2:487n22, mentions the taxes that Wool imposed.

8. Wool to Marcy, January 24, 1848, and Wool to Warren, March 30, 1847, WP, NYSL; Wool to Washington, July 19, August 8, 24, 26, 1847, and Wool to Jones, December 26, 1847, LRAG; March 22, 1847, in Gregg, *Diary and Letters* 2:210.

9. Wool to Taylor, March 7, 1847, and Bliss to Wool, March 7, 1847, LRAG; Harris, *Sánchez Navarros,* 17–18; Harris, *A Mexican Family,* 242–43.

10. Wool to Bliss, March 14, 1847, and Wool to Taylor, June 1, 1847, WP, NYSL; Horace Boultbee to Jacobo Sánchez Navarro, March 16, 1847, cited in Harris, *Sánchez Navarros,* 17–18.

11. Wool to Gonzáles, March 18, 1847, Wool to Warren, March 18, 1847, and Wool to Taylor, March 30, 1847, LRAG; Wool to Thomas Addicks, April 10, 1847, Wool to Bliss, April 2, 1847, and Wool to Gonzáles, April 9, 1847, WP, NYSL.

12. Wool to Manuel de Ybarra, April 16, 1847, Wool to James L. Donaldson, June 8, 1847, Wool to Whiting, June 30, 1847, and Wool to Addicks, April 26, 1847, WP, NYSL; Wool to Bliss, June 22, 1847, LRAG.

13. McDowell to Washington, June 27, 1847 (2 letters), WP, NYSL; Wool to Bliss, July 19, 1847, LRAG; [Wool to John F. Hamtramck], November 7, 1847, John Francis Hamtramck Papers, Duke University Library.

14. Wool to Commander, Texas Cavalry, July 7, 1847, Wool to Daniel H. Rucker, July 10, 1847, Wool to George W. Adams, July 11, 1847, Wool to Taylor, July 12, 1847, and Wool to Michael Chevallie, June 30, 1847, WP, NYSL.

15. GO 254, March 28, 1847, Buena Vista, MxWO, AGO; Wool to Bliss, April 2, 1847, WP, NYSL; March 21, 1847, in Ehinger Diary, Ward Papers.

16. Wool to Taylor, April 8, 1847, and Wool to Sarah Wool, April 17, 1847, WP, NYSL; Saltillo *Picket Guard,* April 14, 1847; *Arkansas Democrat,* May 28, 1847; March 15, 1847, in Ehinger Diary, Ward Papers; Buhoup, *Narrative,* 134–35; Dayton W. Canaday, "Voice of the Volunteer of 1847," *JISHS* 44 (Autumn 1951): 199–209.

17. Wool to Sarah Wool, March 21, 22, 28, 29, 1847, and Wool to Spencer, et al., March 30, 1847, WP, NYSL; *Niles' Register* April 10, 1847, 83; [Baylies], "Wool," *DmR* 29: 455; Davis to Wool, March 25, 1847, in Davis, *Davis Papers* 3:164. Wool also wrote Dix, Bell, Rives, Cass, Baylies, and Brigadier General Newman S. Clarke.

18. Taylor to Wool, April 28, 1847, Taylor Papers, LC; Wool to Taylor, May 7, 1847, WP, NYSL; *New Orleans Picayune* letter (dated March 4), quoted in *Niles' Register* May 1, 1847, 135.

19. Wool to Taylor, May 13, 1847, and Wool to Sarah Wool, June 29, 1847, WP, NYSL; February 23, 1847, in Gregg, *Diary and Letters* 1:48–49, 51; Benham, *Recollections,* 20; Smith, *War with Mexico* 1:558n12.

20. Wool to Taylor, May 7, 13, 1847, WP, NYSL.

21. Webster to Wool, April 7, 1847, in Webster, *Webster Papers: Correspondence,* 6:222–24; Wool to Webster, May 19, 1847, WP, NYSL; Baylies to Wool, April 4, 1847, Tenney Papers.

22. John P. Cashman to Wool, April 12, 1847, and Wool to Sarah Wool, June 29, 1847, WP, NYSL; Baylies, *Wool's Campaign,* 67–68.

23. Wool to Bliss, March 28, 1847; and Bliss to Wool, March 23, 1847, LRAG; GO 275, April 23, 1847, Buena Vista, MxWO, AGO; *Arkansas Democrat,* May 28, 1847; Also see Duncan, *Pike,* 127; Herman J. Viola, "Zachary Taylor and the Indiana Volunteers," *Southwestern Historical Quarterly* 72 (January 1969): 341–43; Willie P. Mangum speech in U. S. Senate, January 6, 1851, in Willie P. Mangum, *The Papers of Willie Person Mangum,* ed. Henry T. Shanks, 5 vols. (Raleigh: North Carolina State Department of Archives and History, 1956) 5:695–721.

24. May 14, 1847, in Ehinger Diary, Ward Papers; GO 293, May 21, 1847, Buena Vista, MxWO, AGO; William E. Connelley, *War with Mexico, 1846–1847* (Topeka, KS: Crane and Co., 1907), 454–59, 482. Wool led the Missourians to the battlefield and, sitting in a camp

chair, described the fighting. When he explained Bowles's retreat, a brawny soldier squatting at Wool's side, suddenly slapped the general on the thigh, almost overturning the chair. "Right there," the soldier roared, "is where you made a mistake, General! When they retreated, you ought to have pressed them . . . yes sir, there is where you made a d——d bad mistake!" (ibid., 484). Also see Joseph G. Dawson III, *Doniphan's Epic March: The 1st Missouri Volunteers in the Mexican War* (Lawrence: University Press of Kansas, 1999).

25. Joseph Lane statement, May 20, 1847, in Frost, *Taylor,* 297; May 26, 1847, in Ehinger Diary, Ward Papers.

26. May 31, 1847, in Ehinger Diary, Ward Papers; Buhoup, *Narrative,* 139–43.

27. *Niles' Register* June 19, July 17, 31, 1847, 250–51, 308, 352; Smith and Judah, eds., *Chronicles,* 463n28, 466n74.

28. Robert T. Paine to Wife, June 22, 1847, Robert Treat Paine Collection, SHC, UNC; *Niles' Register* July 31, 1847, 352; Lee A. Wallace Jr., "The First Regiment of Virginia Volunteers, 1846–1848," *VMHB* 70 (January 1969): 47, 54, 60, 63–65. A photographer arrived in Monterrey and Saltillo in May or June 1847, and took images on June 1 of the newly arrived First Virginia Volunteers. Photos were also taken in Monterrey of Taylor and Bliss and in Saltillo of Wool with his staff and a dragoon escort. Martha A. Sandweiss, et al., *Eyewitness to War: Prints and Daguerreotypes of the Mexican War, 1846–1848* (Fort Worth, TX: Amon Carter Museum; Washington, DC: Smithsonian Institution Press, 1989).

29. GO 326, June 22, 1847, Buena Vista, MxWO, AGO; McDowell to Reuben Davis, June 24, 1847, Wool to Mrs. [Sarah] Bourget, June 24, 1847, and Wool to Sarah Wool, June 5, 11, 1847, WP, NYSL. See Brian Sandwich, *The Great Western: Legendary Lady of the Southwest* (El Paso: Texas Western Press, 1991); and *St. Louis Reporter,* June 29, 1846.

30. Wool to Samuel R. Curtis, June 20, 21, 1847, Samuel R. Curtis Papers, Bancroft Library, University of California, Berkeley; Wool to Chevallie, June 17, 1847, Wool to Gaston Meaes, June 18, 1847; and Wool to Sarah Wool, June 26, 1847, WP, NYSL; June 20, 1847, in Magoffin, *Santa Fe Trail,* 231–33.

31. Wool to Sarah Wool, July 31, August 14, 21, October 17, December 4, 19, 23, 1847, WP, NYSL.

32. *Fredricksburg Semi-Weekly News,* August 16, 1847; July 4, 1847, in Magoffin, *Santa Fe Trail,* 236–37; GO 10 (Washington), July 3, 1847, Saltillo, MxWO, AGO; Baylies, *Wool's Campaign,* 50.

33. Wool to Sarah Wool, July 12, 31, 1847, WP, NYSL. Sandweiss, et al., *Eyewitness to War,* 60–61, 172.

34. Taylor to AG, May 23, 1847, LRAG; May 28, 1847, in Gregg, *Diary and Letters* 2:139–40; Chamberlain, *My Confession,* 175; *Niles' Register,* May 22, 29, June 19, 1847, 184, 198–99, 251; Bauer, *Mexican War,* 218–21; Smith, *War with Mexico* 2:169–70. Fourteen of the wagons destroyed by General Urrea contained clothing for the volunteers, who Wool reported were quite "ragged and ma[d]e a very shabby appearance." The contrast to the Mexican soldiers, who were sharply dressed with blue overcoats, was embarrassing. Wool to Sarah Wool, March 21, 1847, WP, NYSL.

35. *Niles' Register,* May 8, 1847, 152; Smith, *War with Mexico* 2:170; Bauer, *Taylor,* 200.

36. Taylor to Wool, May 19, 1847, WP, NYSL; *Niles' Register,* May 15, 22, 29, 1847, 169, 185, 199, and June 26, July 31, 1847, 265, 341; *Arkansas Democrat,* May 28, 1847; Smith, *War with Mexico* 2:421n3.

37. Wool to Bliss, June 5, 1847; Wool to Lobo, July 25, 1847; and Wool to McDowell, July 26, 1847; all in WP, NYSL; Wool to Taylor, August 5, 1847, LRAG; Baylies, *Wool's Campaign,* 50–51.

38. Wool to McDowell, July 26, 1847; Wool to Rucker, May 11, 1847; Wool to Ignacio Arizaba, October 6, 1847; Wool to Sánchez Navarro, August 5, 1847; Wool to Ybarra, August 7, 1847; and Wool to Hamtramck, November 7, 1847; all in WP, NYSL; *Niles' Register,* August 28, 1847, 411; Harris, *Sánchez Navarros,* 76–79.

39. Wool to Hamtramck, December 29, 1847, and Wool to Bliss, August 8, 1847, LRAG. Officers of the Second Mississippi Regiment to Wool, July 17, 1847, and Wool to Caleb Cushing, August 12, 1847, Caleb Cushing Papers, LC; GO 378, July 30, 1847, Buena Vista, MxWO, AGO; Wool to Cushing, August 6, 1847, WP, NYSL; Chamberlain, *My Confession,* 206; Claude M. Fuess, *The Life of Caleb Cushing,* 2 vols. (New York: Harcourt Brace and Co., 1922), 2:33–52.

40. Paine to Wife, August 23, 1847, Paine Collection, SHC, UNC; Smith and Judah, eds., *Chronicles,* 425–31, and Josiah S. Pender and George E. B. Singletary to Cushing, August 18, 1847, in ibid., 430–31; "A Report from the Secretary of War . . . relative to the dismissal . . . of J. S. Pender and G. E. B. Singletary . . . August 10, 1848," in HED 78, 30-1, Serial 522; Wool to Bliss, August 15, 1847, LRAG; Wallace, "First Virginia," *VMHB* 70: 66–67.

41. Wool to Jones, December 9, 1847 (with encls.), LRAG; William B. Franklin to Paine, July 8, 1847, and Wool to Bliss, August 8, 1847, WP, NYSL. Paine testimony, in "Pender and Singletary," HED 78, 30-1, 45–50, 54.

42. Wool to Bliss, August 15, 1847, Wool to Jones, December 9, 1847, and Taylor to Wool, August 19, 1847, LRAG; Franklin to Singletary, August 28, 1847, WP, NYSL; Paine to Wife, August 23, 1847, Paine Collection, SHC, UNC. Wool also gave dishonorable discharges to two privates (Jason Hunter, Co. A, North Carolina Volunteers; and Thomas King, Co. G, Virginia Volunteers) who were involved in the fracas. Wallace, "First Virginia," *VMHB* 70: 67.

43. Wool to Taylor, August 19, 1847, WP, NYSL; Wool to Taylor, August 21, 1847, LRAG; *Niles' Register,* September 18, 1847, 40–41.

44. Wool to Bliss, August 25, October 18, 1847, LRAG; GO 454, September 20, 1847, Buena Vista, MxWO, AGO; Wool to Taylor, September 22, 1847, Wool to Sarah Wool, September 5, 1847, Robert H. Taylor to Wool, September 5, 1847, and Wool to Washington, September 5, 1847, WP, NYSL; April 14, 1848, in Gregg, *Diary and Letters* 2:213–14.

45. Wool to Sarah Wool, October 8, 1847, WP, NYSL; Taylor to AG, October 4, 1847, LRAG; Bragg to Samuel G. French, October 13, 1847, quoted in McWhiney, *Bragg,* 96.

46. Wool to Sarah Wool, October 25, November 1, 1847, WP, NYSL; *Arkansas Democrat,* December 10, 1847; Harriette Hart, "Memoir," Tenney Papers. Wool brought several Mexican horses back to Troy. Monterrey is described in *Niles' Register,* April 3, 1847, 71.

47. Wool to Jones, November 14, 1847, LRAG; GO 126 (Taylor) and GO 510 (Wool), November 14, 1847, Camargo, MxWO, AGO; Wool to Sarah Wool, November 1, 14, 1847, WP, NYSL; "Journal of a March from Monter[r]ey to Camargo and back . . . between

November 8, 1847 and the 21[st] of the same Month," WP, NYSL; Taylor to My Dear Doctor [Robert C. Wood], November 17, 1847, in Taylor, *Taylor Letters*, 150–52; *Arkansas Democrat*, December 10, 1847.

48. GO 133, December 9, 1847, Monterrey, MxWO, AGO; Wool to Jones, December 7, 1847, LRAG. *Arkansas Democrat*, January 7, 1848. On December 7, Wool received GO 132 (Taylor), November 25, 1847, Brazos Island, transferring command to him.

49. Wool to Sarah Wool, November 29, December 6, 26, 1847, WP, NYSL; Paine to Wife, December 17, 1847, Paine Collection, SHC, UNC.

50. Wool to John W. Tibbatts, November 6, 1847, McDowell to Tibbatts, November 7, 22, December 20, 1847, and Wool to Sarah Wool, December 4, 5, 23, 1847, WP, NYSL.

51. Marcy to Taylor, October 18, 25, 1847, LSAG; Wool to Jones, December 7, 1847, LRAG; [Wool] to Jones, December 23, 1847, WP, NYSL.

52. Cashman to Wool, September 3, 1847; Wool to Sarah Wool, October 17, 1847; WP., NYSL; Wool to J. A. Dix, November 2, 1847, Dix Papers, CU; Marcy to Wool, November 18, 1847, Marcy Papers, NYSL. Smith and Judah, eds., *Chronicles*, 425, comments on North Carolina politics.

53. Wool to Sarah Wool, December 19, 30, 1847, WP, NYSL.

54. *Niles' Register*, September 18, 1847, 41; "Message from the President . . . , December 7, 1847," SED 1, 30-1, Serial 503, 96, (Taylor's forces);

55. Wool to Jones, December 11, 1847, Wool to Hamtranck, December 1, 18, 1847, LRAG; and GO 11, December 17, 1847, Monterrey, MxWO, AGO;

56. McDowell to Bragg, January 1, 1848, and Wool to Samuel Pleasanton, January 15, 1848, LRAG; [Wool to Eligio de Castillo], January 17, 1848, WP, NYSL; *Monter[r]ey Gazette*, February 5, 1848, in Baylies, *Wool's Campaign*, 54. Wool used GO 109 (Taylor), September 29, 1847, Monterrey, MxWO, AGO, to create military commissions to try Mexicans "who commit murder and other grave offenses" against American officers, soldiers, and civilians. The commissions were governed by GO 20 (Scott), February 19, 1847, which declared martial law in Mexico. On August 14, 1847, Wool wrote Sarah that Mexicans "high or low" could not be trusted. "The one would not hesitate to kill you for your coat, and the other would [kill] in order to get rid of you. It is a lying and treacherous race" (WP, NYSL).

57. SO 7, December 11, 1847, Monterrey, MxWO, AGO; "Safeguard," January 3, 1848, WP, NYSL; *Monter[r]ey Gazette*, February 5, 1848, in Baylies, *Wool's Campaign*, 54, and *Newport Daily News*, February [n.d.], 1850, in ibid., 61–62.

58. Wool to Jones, January 7, 1848, and Wool to Francisco Morales, December 21, 1847, LRAG; *Arkansas Democrat*, January 7, 1848; Smith, *War with Mexico* 2:418n76.

59. William Davenport to McDowell, December 27, 1847, McDowell to Davenport, December 31, 1847, encloses Antonio Canales to Taylor, December 20, 1847; Canales to Wool, January 30, 1848, and Wool to Canales, February 3, 1848, WP, NYSL; Wool to Jones, February 4, 1848, LRAG; *Arkansas Democrat*, February 11, 1848; Joseph Milton Nance, *After San Jacinto: The Texas-Mexican Frontier, 1836–1841* (Austin: University of Texas Press, 1963), 213, 252–56, 363; Baylies, *Wool's Campaign*, 55–56.

60. Bragg to James Duncan, January 13, 1848, in McWhiney, Bragg, 98; *Monter[r]ey Gazette,* February 26, 1848, in WP, NYSL; Bragg to Sherman, March 1, 1848, W. T. Sherman Papers, LC; August 31, 1847, in Magoffin, *Santa Fe Trail,* 256–57.

61. Taylor to Robert C. Wood, February 28, 1848, in Taylor, *Letters,* 157.

62. GO 11, January 10, 1848, Monterrey, MxWO, AGO; Wool to Marcy, January 24, 1848; Wool to Hunter, March 16, 1848; and Wool to David H. Vinton, March 12, 1848, WP, NYSL; *Niles' Register,* December 18, 1847, 256; Smith, *War with Mexico* 2:265, 407; and ibid., 487n22 (Wool's policies); Thomas M. Davies Jr., "Assessments during the Mexican War; An Exercise in Futility," *New Mexico Historical Review* 41 (July 1966): 197–98. On March 31, 1847, Polk approved military levies in occupied Mexico.

63. GO 376 (Scott), December 15, 1847, Mexico City, in Smith and Judah, eds., *Chronicles,* 416–17; *Niles' Register,* January 29, 1848, 340; Smith, *War with Mexico* 2:262–67, and ibid., 487n22; Elliott, *Scott,* 562; Davies, "Assessments," *New Mexico Historical Review* 41: 198–206.

64. Wool to Marcy, January 24, 1848, and Wool to Davenport, February 1, 20, 1848, WP, NYSL.

65. McDowell to Hamtramck, February 1, 1848, LRAG; McDowell to Ralph G. Norvell, February 26, 1848, McDowell to E. G. W. Butler (and Henry L. Webb), March 9, 1848, WP, NYSL; and *Niles' Register* December 18, 1847, 256.

66. GO 19 (Wool), January 17, 1848, Monterrey, MxWO, AGO; Wool to Davenport, March 17, 1848, and Wool to Marcy, March 29, 1848, WP, NYSL.

67. McDowell to Hamtramck, Feb, 21, March 20, 1848, and Wool to Jones, February 1, 1848, LRAG; Wool to Sarah Wool, January 3, 1848, and Wool to Hamtramck, March 15, 1848, WP, NYSL; Bragg to French, October 13, 1847, in McWhiney, *Bragg,* 96. The shift of the Second Mississippi was timely. Col. Charles Clark had recently been released from arrest for interfering with the chain of command. Linnard and Pope had tried Wool's patience. According to Bragg, the two officers had kept two Mexican girls, one fourteen years old, for "carnal purposes," and had paraded them through Monterrey in an open carriage acquired from the quartermaster pool. Pope was transferred to Saltillo, but his mistress followed him. The girls' mothers demanded that Wool intervene, but every time the girls were sent home, they ran back to Pope and Linnard. By assigning the lieutenants to the expedition, Wool hoped to resolve the matter. Wool to Sarah Wool, January 3, 1848, and Wool to Hamtramck, March 15, April 12, 1848, WP, NYSL. Bragg to French, October 13, 1848, in McWhiney, *Bragg,* 96.

68. Wool to Hunter, February 20, March 5, 16, 1848, WP, NYSL; Wool to Jones, March 2, 1848, LRAG.

69. Wool to Ibarra, February 23, 1848; Wool to Rucker, March 18, 1848; and Wool to Sarah Wool, March 2, 1848; all in WP, NYSL; Wool to Jones, March 2, 1848, LRAG; Wallace, "First Virginia," *VMHB* 70: 73–74.

70. GO 66, (Wool), February 26, 1848, Monterrey, MxWO, AGO; Wool to Jones, March 2, 1848, LRAG; and Wool to E. G. W. Butler, March 13, 17, 1848, WP, NYSL.

71. Wool to AG, March 21, 1848, McDowell to Hamtramck, March 23, 1848, and McDowell to Hunter, March 24, 1848, LRAG; GO 18 (Butler), March 6, 1848, Mexico City, MXWO, *Niles' Register*, July 5, 1848, 4; Bauer, *Mexican War*, 384–85. The armistice was signed on March 2, 1848. Smith, *War with Mexico* 2:470n14.

72. Wool to J. A. Dix, December 30, 1847, March 22, 1848, Dix Papers, CU; Cass to Wool, December 26, 1847, WP, NYSL; Baylies to Wool, March 31, 1848, Baylies Papers, OCHS; *Niles' Register* February 12, 1848, 373. In early March 1848, Congress voted medals to Scott and Taylor and swords to W. O. Butler, T. L. Hamer, J. P. Henderson, J. A. Quitman, D. E. Twiggs, and W. J. Worth. Wool was ignored. Heitman, *Register* 1:46–47.

73. Wool to Washington Hunt, et al., February 16, 1848; Cashman to Wool, March 17, 1848; and William Hart to Wool, February 16, 1849, WP, NYSL; Baylies to Wool, March 12, May 15, 1848, Baylies Papers, OCHS; Baylies, *Wool's Campaign*, 68, 73. There was a claim, which Wool never refuted, that he drafted the House resolution himself at Monterrey. William Hart to Wool, February 16, 1848, WP, NYSL.

74. William G. Freeman to Pender, May 10, 1847, WP, NYSL; Marcy to Wool, January 17, 1848, Marcy Papers, LC; "Pender and Singletary," HED 78, 30-1, 210–12. Wool's testimony is in ibid., 189–99. Lieutenant J. B. Pender resigned from the army on May 8, 1848. William G. Freeman to Pender, May 10, 1847, WP, NYSL; and Smith and Judah, eds., *Chronicles*, 425, report Polk pardoned the two officers.

75. SO 112, April 9, 1848, Monterrey, MxWO, AGO; Wool to Hamtramck, June 11, 1848, Wool to Butler, March 13, 17, April 3, 1848, and Charles J. Helm to McDowell, June 2, 1848, WP, NYSL. Wool to Jones, April 12, May 28, 1848, and Wool to Scott, September 9, 1848, LRAG. Wool's flap with McDowell, his assistant adjutant general, developed in March, when the staff officer mailed Colonel Butler, at Mier, a copy of Wool's amnesty, together with an order to stay the execution of one of Canales's lieutenants, a guerilla named Gonzales. Butler immediately queried whether Wool had an "understanding" with Canales.

76. Wool to Sarah Wool, January 3, 25, 1847, WP, NYSL.

77. GO 156, June 12, 1848, Monterrey, MxWO, AGO; Wool to Jones, June 8, 1848, LRAG; "Memo of Money Collected under Wool's Orders in 1847–1848," WP, NYSL; June 14, 1848, in Gregg, *Diary and Letters* 2:218–19; Smith, *War with Mexico* 2:251.

78. GO 160, June 16, 1848, Monterrey, MxWO, AGO; Helm to Hamtramck, June 16, 1848, LRAG; Helm to Charles Clark, June 17, 1848, WP, NYSL; Walter P. Lane, *The Adventures and Recollections of General Walter P. Lane, A San Jacinto Veteran* (Austin: Jenkins Publishing Co., 1970), 69–70; *Troy Times*, June 8, 10, 1865.

79. Jones to Wool, June 2, 1848, WP, NYSL; AG to Wool, June 7, 1848, LSAG; Wool to Marcy, July 4, 8, 1848, Wool to AG, July 6, 27, 1848, and Wool to Davenport, July 23, 1848, LRAG; GO 178, July 23, 1848, Brazos Island, MxWO, AGO; Baylies, *Wool's Campaign*, 66.

80. Helm to Wool, July 25, 29, 1848, WP, NYSL; Baylies, *Wool's Campaign*, 66–67; Harry P. Judson, *A History of the Troy Citizens Corps, Troy, New York* (Troy, NY: Troy Times Printing House, 1884), 34–35; and Savage, *Our Living Representative Men*, 500.

CHAPTER 9. HUNKERS, BARNBURNERS, AND TURKEY COCKS

1. Wool to Cass, January 14, 1849, and Helm to Wool, June 19, 1850, WP, NYSL; *Troy Family Journal,* May 3, 1850, and May 20, 1853; *Niles' Register,* October 11, 1848, 226–27, and May 16, 1849, 305.

2. *Niles' Register,* October 11, 1848, 226–27, and February 7, May 16, 1849, 82 and 305. Wool to George Gould, August 24, 1849, WP, NYSL; Heitman, *Historical Register* 1:442; Raphel P. Thian, comp., *Notes Illustrating the Military Geography of the United States* (Washington, DC: Government Printing Office, 1881), 20.

3. Grantee Deed Book 35: 413, Rensselaer County Court House, Troy, New York; Wool to Scott, September 9, 1848, LRAG; Hart, "Memoir," Tenney Collection.

4. Wool to Scott, September 9, 1848, LRAG; Wool to Churchill, June 30, 1849, and Wool to Sarah Wool, March 1, 1847, WP, NYSL; *Niles' Register,* August 2, 9, October 11, 1848, 65, 82, and 226–27, January 17, 1849, 33. Bvt. Maj. George Winship was division adjutant general and Bvt. Brigadier General Sylvester Churchill, inspector general. Wool's office is mentioned in "Names and Number of the Major Generals . . . number of officers and soldiers to their staff, and the rent of the buildings occupied by them as officers, March 17, 1862," SED 3, 37-2, Serial 1122, 7.

5. Wool to Gustave Blessner, August 1, 1849, and Poem and Clipping File, WP, NYSL; Baylies, *Wool's Campaign,* 77; "Buena Vista March" (dedicated to Wool), copy in Samuel Peter Heintzelman Papers, Library of Congress.

6. Judson, *Troy Citizens Corps,* 7–24; John K. Mahon, *History of the Militia and the National Guard* (New York: Macmillan, 1983), 79–85.

7. Judson, *Troy Citizens Corps,* 10–26; Bliven, et al., *Rensselaer County,* 19.

8. Wool's numerous land transactions (1835–67) are in Rensselaer County deed books, Troy, New York. See in particular: Grantee 59: 312; 78: 365, and 104: 207, 409. Also Grantor 83: 377; 105: 476; 113: 253, 281; 117: 150; 123: 356, and 131: 300. Wool to E. Heisburg, May 12, 1840, NYHS. Wool to Corning, May 12, 1828, and June 12, 1833; Wool to Stephen Warren, March 18, 1837; Tallmadge to Wool, May 15, 1838; Wool to [?], January 7, 1841; Wool to I. B. Hart, May 6, 1839, and Wool to Sarah Wool, March 10, 1846, WP, NYSL. Wool to William Baylies, June 15, 1834, Baylies Papers, Massachusetts Historical Society. Sarah Wool to Tallmadge, September 12, 1836, and Wool to Tallmadge, March 4, 1842, Tallmadge Papers, SHSW; *Troy Family Journal,* May 20, 1853. In the late 1830s, Wool owned stock in at least six banks.

9. Wool to Corning, April 11, 1836, Winfield Scott Papers, Special Collections, University of Arizona Library.

10. Weise, *History of Troy,* 166; Salsbury, *Boston and Albany,* 24–30, 52–53, 90–93, 151, 172.

11. Weise, *History of Troy,* 206; Salsbury, *Boston and Albany,* 43, 173, 280–81.

12. *Troy Family Journal,* May 3, June 11, 1850; Hart, "Memoir," Tenney Collection.

13. *Troy Family Journal,* August 20, October 8, 1852; *Troy Times,* August 11, 1863; Salsbury, *Boston and Albany,* 280–81. Sometime in the 1850s, Wool headed a group of New York and Canadian businessmen who studied a possible canal link between Lake Champlain and

the St. Lawrence. Wool to Sarah Wool, April 24, 1855, and Wool to Bloodgood, June 18, 1863, WP, NYSL.

14. A brigadier general received per month: $104.00 pay, $72.00 rations, $24.00 forage, and $46.50 to hire servants.

15. John Griswold to Wool, July 10, 1839, Griswold Papers, RCHS; Griswold to Wool, March 8, 1840, and February 16, 1841, Burden Collection; Wool to Tallmadge, February 25, 1842, Tallmadge Papers, SHSW; *Troy Times* and *Troy Whig,* November 1, 1872; Rezneck, *Profiles,* 101–4.

16. Wool to Tallmadge, January 20, March 4, 1842, Tallmadge, SHSW; Wool to William Cullen Bryant, December 30, 1843, William C. Bryant Papers, NYPL; W. C. Bryant to Frances F. Bryant, July 27, 1849, in William C. Bryant, *The Letters of William Cullen Bryant,* ed. William Cullen Bryant II and Thomas G. Voss, 6 vols. (New York: Fordham University Press, 1975–92) 3:77; Bryant to Wool, February 25, 1851, WP, NYSL.

17. Woodford, *Cass,* 255–59.

18. Cashman to Wool, March 10, 17, 1848, WP, NYSL; Weise, *History of Troy,* 201.

19. *Troy Whig,* August 24, 1848; Richard Arnold, comp., *Ceremonies on Occasion of the Presentation of the Swords voted Major General John E. Wool by the Common Council of the City of Troy, the Legislature of New York, and the Congress of the United States* (Troy, NY: A. W. Scribner and Co., 1860), 5–23; Judson, *Troy Citizens Corps,* 36–38; Baylies, *Wool's Campaign,* 67–72; Miscellaneous newspaper clipping, n.d., WP, NYSL. In addition to the sword with a sheath of solid silver presented by the citizens of Troy, Wool received two other swords as a result of his heroism during the Mexican-American War. A remarkable jeweled sword, said to be one of the finest examples of any American sword ever made, was given Wool by the State of New York on December 30, 1848. The hilt and sheath were covered with engravings in exquisite detail depicting the New York State seal and scenes of infantry, artillery, and cavalry in action, while the hilt displayed full sculptured nude figures supporting both the grips and the pommel. An American eagle at the center of the knuckle bow had a pearl in its talons surmounted with four very large faceted emeralds. Congress, following a resolution in January 1854, presented to Wool a finely finished sword designed by Capt. J. G. Benton of the U. S. Ordnance Corps, with the unique hilt in the design of an ear of corn surmounted with an exquisitely detailed American eagle having diamonds inset for eyes and surmounted by four very large emeralds. In the 1890s, the Griswold family allowed the swords to be displayed at the prestigious Metropolitan Museum of Art in New York City, where they were among only a handful of American weapons of sufficiently artistic merit to be worth public exhibition. In 1977, the three swords were offered for sale by the N. Flayderman and Company of New Milford, Connecticut. Harwood Hinton's note in the margin on the page describing the swords indicated an asking price of $175,000 (*N. Flayderman & Co., Inc., Catalog* [1977], Item no. 1508). Featured on the cover of the catalogue, the swords were among the finest ever offered for sale in the United States.

20. Taylor to Wool, July 28, 1848, WP, NYSL. Rufus R. Wilson, in *Washington: The Capital City,* 2 vols. (Philadelphia: J. B. Lippincott, 1902) 2:64, says that Taylor told South Carolina Senator A. P. Butler that Wool was the first officer he met. Wool said all was lost!

21. Baylies to Wool, October 21, 1848, Baylies Papers, OCHS; Wool to Cass, January 14, 1849, WP, NYSL; *New York Courier and Enquirer,* October 10, 1848; [anon.], "Taylor's Campaign," *DmR* 23 (October 1848): 305–16. By the 1850s, members of the officer corps occasionally commented on Wool's proclivity toward poker and games of chance. A regular who served in Mexico stated that the general was "excessively addicted" to gambling, and in a single season won over $40,000 (*Boston Commonwealth,* undated clipping, WP, Duke University Library). Wool's correspondence mentions no large amounts of money sent home, but the charge echoed through the years. D[avid] S. Stanley, *Personal Memoirs of Major-General D. S. Stanley, USA* (Cambridge, MA: Harvard University Press, 1917), 34, portrayed Wool as a notorious gambler who won a great deal of money from young lieutenants.

22. Wool to Cooper, December 8, 1848, Cooper Papers, Yale University; Baylies to Wool, December 24, 1848, Baylies Papers, OCHS; Dix, *Memoirs,* 1:259–66; Spencer, *Marcy,* 185–90; Baylies, *Wool's Campaign,* 77.

23. *New York State Republican* (Troy), January 9, 1849. Arnold, comp., *Ceremonies,* 25–36. Baylies, *Wool's Campaign,* 73–76.

24. Wool to Cass, January 14, 1849, and Wool to Tallmadge, February 6, 1849, WP, NYSL; Wool to Bryant, January 14, 1849, Bryant Papers, NYPL. James Webb was a former army officer (1817–27), duelist, and muckraker. James L. Crouthamel, *James Watson Webb: A Biography* (Middletown, CT: Wesleyan University Press, 1969), 5, 11, 73–76, 96, 106–12.

25. Baylies to Wool, January 21, 1849, Baylies Papers, OCHS.

26. Oliver P. Baldwin to Wool, February 7, 1849; Helm to Wool, January 26, February 21, April 7, 1849, Wool to Cass, January 14, 1849, Roane to Wool, May 15, 1849, and Wool to Taylor, February 26, 1849, WP, NYSL; Wool to Joseph Gates, March 16, 1849, J. Pierpont Morgan Papers, NYPL; Wool to Dix, February 7, 1849, Dix Papers, CU; Baylies to Wool, March 10, 1849, Baylies Papers, OCHS; Wool to Webster, March 14, 1849, in Webster, *Webster Papers: Correspondence* 6:455; *Niles' Register,* April 18, 1849, 241–42.

27. Baylies to Wool, November 5, 1849, Baylies Papers, OCHS; Wool to Mary Spencer, September 6, 1849, WP, NYSL; Spencer, *Marcy,* 185–90. Wool remained in the public eye. In August, he laid the cornerstone for the Troy Hospital, and the next month attended the state fair in Albany. Weise, *History of Troy,* 204.

28. Baylies to Wool, December 16, 1849, Baylies Papers, OCHS; George W. Hughes to Wool, December 26, 1849, WP, NYSL.

29. Roane to Wool, January 14, 1850; Bissell to Wool, January 19, 1850, and Cass to Wool, January 23, 1850, WP, NYSL; Crouthamel, *Webb,* 112–14.

30. Wool to Bryant, January 2, 1850, Bryant Papers, NYPL; Bryant to Wool, April 15, 1850, in Bryant, *Letters* 3:125.

31. Helm to Wool, June 19, 1850, WP, NYSL. Helm letter, in the *Newport News,* [March 1850], quoted in Baylies, *Wool's* Campaign, 60–61. The *News* began publication on March 7, 1850.

32. Wool to James Ames, June 12, 1850, in *Troy Family Journal,* August 8, 1850; Wool to Davis, August 6, 1850, WP, NYSL.

33. Wool to Sarah Wool, July 24, 28, 1850, WP, NYSL. Bauer, *Taylor,* 315–16.

34. Wool to Davis, August 6, 1850, and Baldwin to Wool, August 20, 1850, WP, NYSL. *Troy Family Journal,* August 9, 1850.

35. Baylies to Wool, August 20, 1850, Baylies Papers, OCHS; Wool to Sarah Wool, November 16, 1850, WP, NYSL; Dix, *Memoirs* 1:259–60.

36. Baldwin to Wool, August 20, 1850, WP, NYSL; *Troy Family Journal,* September 6, 1850; *Syracuse Star,* October 4, 1850.

37. Wool to Croswell, October 7, 1850, Personal File–Wool, NYSL.

38. Wool to Sarah Wool, October 21, November 8, 10, 19, 1850, and Wool to Harriette Hart, November 1, 1850, WP, NYSL.

39. Wool to Sarah Wool, October 21, 1850, and John A. Bryant to Wool, February 10, 1851, WP, NYSL. Francis Baylies, "The March of the United States Troops, under the Command of General John E. Wool, from San Antonio, Texas to Saltillo, Mexico, in the Year 1846," *Stryker's American Register and Magazine* 4 (July 1850): 297–312.

40. Baylies to Wool, January 24, April 14, 20, 1851, Baylies Papers, OCHS.

41. Baylies, *Wool's Campaign,* 1–4. For several years, Wool's portrait, painted in 1851 by James Irving of Troy, was on exhibit in the Rensselaer County Historical Society in Troy but was returned to the Griswold family. Kathy Sheehan, interview by Jerry Thompson, December 14, 2018.

42. Baylies, *Wool's Campaign,* 6.

43. Baylies to Wool, June 8, 1851, Baylies Papers, OCHS; *Rochester Advertiser,* and *Buffalo American and Commercial Advertiser,* cited in *Freeman's Journal* (Cooperstown, NY), October 25, 1851.

44. [Baylies], "Wool," *DmR,* 29: 435; *Troy Daily Times,* December 2, 1851.

45. *Rochester Daily American,* August 29, 1851; [Baylies], "Wool," *DmR,* 29: 461; *Chenango Free Democrat* (Greene, NY), September 26, 1851.

46. Spencer, *Marcy,* 194–206; Samuel A. Pleasants, *Fernando Wood of New York* (New York: AMS Press, 1966), 28–29.

47. *Troy Whig,* February 13, 1852; *New York Times,* February 18, 1852; *Albany Argus,* March 4, 1852; *Troy Northern Budget,* March 1852, undated clipping, WP, NYSL; Donald S. Spencer, *Louis Kossuth and Young America: A Story of Sectionalism and Foreign Policy, 1848–1852* (Columbia: University of Missouri Press, 1977), 83–150.

48. *Troy Northern Budget,* March 1850, undated clip, WP, NYSL; "David Stewart," in James G. Wilson and John Fiske, eds., *Appleton's Cyclopaedia of American Biography,* 6 vols. (New York: D. Appleton and Co., 1887–89) 5:685.

49. *Maryland State Capitol Gazette* (Annapolis), quoted in *Albany Argus,* March 4, 1852.

50. *Albany Argus,* March 4, 1852; *New York Times,* February 18, 1852; *Washington Union,* February 18, 1852; *New Orleans Delta,* March 6, 1852; *New York Express,* February n.d., 1852, clip, WP, NYSL. Wool also mailed clips to members of Congress.

51. Wool to Robert C. Scott, May 24, 1852, and Wool to David Stewart, May 28, 1852, WP, NYSL; *Richmond Enquirer,* May 28, 1852; *New York Times,* May 31, 1852. Franklin Pierce also declined to make a public statement. Roy F. Nichols, *Franklin Pierce: Young Hickory of the Granite Hills* (Philadelphia: University of Pennsylvania Press, 1931), 201. Thirteen Democrats

replied. Wool is included in a list of fourteen Democratic aspirants at "Democratic Candidates for the Presidency," *American Whig Review* 15 (April 1852): 316.

52. *New York Times,* May 31, 1852.

53. Wool to Stewart, May 28, 1852, WP, NYSL.

54. Wool to Stewart, June 8, 1852, WP, NYSL; Dix, *Memoirs,* 1:267–69; *New York Times,* June 4–5, 1852; Spencer, *Marcy,* 208–11; Nichols, *Pierce,* 202–4.

55. Wool to Stewart, June 8, 1852, WP, NYSL.

56. Wool to Stewart, September 12, 1852, WP, NYSL; AG to Wool, September 13, 1852, LSAG; Nichols, *Pierce,* 167, 213.

57. Wool to Stewart, September 21, October 8, 1852, and Wool to Sarah Wool, September 26, 1852, WP, NYSL.

58. Wool to Stewart, October 8, 1852, WP, NYSL; Wool to R[ichard] H. Stanton, October 14, 1852, Mss., Harvard University, Cambridge, Mass. Julia S. Ardery, "The Rogers Family and Old Cane Ridge," Kentucky Historical Society *Register* 53 (July 1955): 243–44, quotes the diary (September 28–29, 1852) of William Rogers.

59. Baylies to Wool, August 21, 1852, and William Baylies to Wool, February 16, 1853, Baylies Papers, OCHS; *Troy Family Journal,* November 5, 1852.

60. Wool to Stewart, November 26, December 2, 1852, and January 20, February 5, 1853, WP, NYSL; Dix, *Memoirs,* 1:270–72.

61. Wool to Stewart, February 25, March 6, 1853, WP, NYSL; Spencer, *Marcy,* 216–20.

62. Wool to Stewart, February 25, March 6, May 19, July 9, 18, 1853, WP, NYSL.

63. Wool to Stewart, July 18, 1853, WP, NYSL; *New York Tribune,* July 15, 1853; Nichols, *Pierce,* 279–83; Ivan D. Steen, "America's First World's Fair: The Exhibition of the Industry of All Nations at New York's Crystal Palace, 1853–54," NYHS *Quarterly* 47 (July 1963): 263–70.

64. Wool to Stewart, August 29, September 18, 1853, WP, NYSL; Davis to Wool, August 30, 1853, in Davis, *Davis,* 5:244. Bryant, *Bryant Letters,* 3:400, notes that Leonice Josephine Moulton (1834–1922) married John Stewart (1826–1901), a Baltimore merchant.

65. GO 1, November 14, 1853, Eastern Division, Troy, WP, NYSL. Francis Paul Prucha discusses the command changes at *A Guide to the Military Posts of the United States, 1789–1895* (Madison: State Historical Society of Wisconsin, 1964), 149–51.

66. Wool to David Twiggs, December 15, 1853, and Wool to Stewart, November 8, 1853, WP, NYSL.

CHAPTER 10. A VAST AND DISTANT LAND

1. Wool to Sarah Wool, January 29, 1854, WP, NYSL.

2. "Report of the SW, December 1, 1853," HED 1, 33-1, Serial 711, 3–6.

3. Charles H. Brown, *Agents of Manifest Destiny: The Lives and Times of the Filibusters* (Chapel Hill: University of North Carolina Press, 1980), 185–93.

4. Wool to Davis, October 13, 1854, in "Correspondence Between the Late Secretary of War and General Wool . . . , March 25, 1858," HED 88, 35-1, Serial 956, 112–13, and Davis To Wool, December 13, 1854, ibid., 122–28. Wool to Sarah Wool, January 7, July 18, October 12, 1854, WP, NYSL. Nichols, *Pierce,* 248.

5. Wool to Sarah Wool, January 7, 1854, Wool to Jesup, December 24, 1853, and Wool to AG, December 26, 1853, WP, NYSL. McAlexander, comp., *Thirteenth Regiment,* 259.

6. Wool to Sarah Wool, January 7, 1854; GO 1, January 9, 1854, New York, and GO 1, January 12, 1854, Baltimore, Eastern Division, WP, NYSL; in "Correspondence," HED 88, 35-1, are Wool to Davis, October 13, 1854, 112–13, Davis to Wool, December 13, 1854, 122–28, and Wool to AG, January 19, 1854, 7–8. January [n.d.], 1855, in Edward D. Townsend, *The California Diary of General E. D. Townsend,* ed. Malcolm Edwards (Los Angeles: Ward Ritchie Press, 1970), 91, describes Hitchcock's "special commission" and problems.

7. Wool to AG, January 19, 1854, in "Correspondence," HED 88, 35-1, 7–8, and Davis to Wool, December 13, 1854, "Correspondence," 122–28; Hamilton L. Shields to Wool, January 17, 1854, and Wool to Sarah Wool, January 20, 1854, WP, NYSL; *Troy Family Journal,* January 20, 1854; *Washington Intelligencer,* January 20, 1854; Judson, *Troy Citizens Corps,* 41; Spencer, *Marcy,* 285–86; Brown, *Agents,* 209.

8. Wool to Sarah Wool, January 21, 1854, and *New York Herald,* January [20], 1854, WP, NYSL.

9. Miscellaneous newspaper clipping, February 1854, WP, NYS; Wool to Sarah Wool, January 29, February 2, 7, 15, 1854, WP, NYSL.

10. Wool to Sarah Wool, February 15, 1854, WP, NYSL; *Alta California* (San Francisco), February 18, 1854. The Oriental Hotel is described at "San Francisco Society: From *The Directory of* 1879," intro. Dorothy Harriet Huggins, California Historical Society [CHS] *Quarterly* 19 (September 1940): 229.

11. Theodore Hittell, *History of California,* 4 vols. (San Francisco: N. J. Stone, 1897) 3:403, 412, 414, 423–24.

12. February 16, 1854, in Hitchcock, *Fifty Years,* 407. "Report of the SW for 1853," HED 1, 33-1, 95. "Report of the SW, December 4, 1854," HED 1, 33-2, Serial 778, 6, 62. See also Durwood Ball, *Army Regulars on the Western Frontier, 1848–1861* (Norman: University of Oklahoma Press, 2001), 51, 124.

13. October 9, 1853, in Hitchcock, *Fifty Years,* 400–5; January [n.d.], 1855, in Townsend, *Diary,* 91–94; Brown, *Agents,* 192–93.

14. Wool to Sarah Wool, February 26, 1854; GO 2, February 17, 1854, San Francisco, Department of the Pacific, WP, NYSL; Townsend, *Diary,* vii.

15. Wool to Sarah Wool, February 26, 1854, and Wool to Stewart, September 1, 1854, WP, NYSL; *San Francisco Herald,* March 1, 1854; *Alta California,* February 26, 1854; *Troy Family Journal,* March 25, 1854.

16. *San Francisco Herald,* February 26, 1854; *Alta California,* February 27, 1854; Troy *Family Journal,* March 25, 1854; excerpts from Eastern presses in the *San Francisco Placter Times and Transcript,* May 18, 1854.

17. Henry W. Halleck to Isaac I. Stevens, February 12, 1854, in Isaac I. Stevens, "Letters of Governor Isaac I. Stevens, 1853–1854," ed. John S. Richards, *Pacific Northwest Quarterly* [*PNQ*] 30 (July 1939): 330–31.

18. Wool to Sarah Wool, February 26, 1854, and Wool to Harriette Hart, March 14, 1854, WP, NYSL.

19. Wool to Davis, March 1, 1854, in "Correspondence," *HED 88:* 35–1, 10–11; Wool to Thomas, February 28, 1854; ibid., 9–10, and Wool to AG, March 15, 1854, ibid., 19; *San Francisco Herald,* February 24, March 1, April 28, 1854, and February 8, 1855. January [n. d.], 1855, in Townsend, *Diary,* 96. Davis, *Davis Papers* 4: 85n; Brown, *Agents,* 194–95, 217.

20. Wool to Samuel W. Inge, April 15, 1854, WP, NYSL; *Alta California,* May 1, 1854. Filibuster interest in Sonora dated from the spring of 1851, when Joseph C. Morehead, a former state official in California, organized an expedition to seize the Mexican state. Most of his men deserted at San Diego. The central government in Mexico City then instructed its consul in San Francisco to enlist a group of Frenchmen to colonize Sonora. Rufus K. Wyllys, *The French in Sonora* (Berkeley: University of California Publications, 1932), 35–66, 69–77, 83, 107, 116, 120–57; A[braham] P. Nasatir, "Guillaume Patrice Dillon," CHS *Quarterly* 35 (December 1956): 319–20; Brown, *Agents,* 168–73.

21. Wool to Sarah Wool, March 24–26, 1854, and Wool to Inge, April 15, 1854, WP, NYSL; *Alta California,* May 1, 1854; *San Francisco Herald,* April 28, 1854. Wyllys, *French in Sonora,* 156–57, 172–75.

22. Wool to Sarah Wool, March 24–26, 1854, and Wool to Inge, April 15, 1854, WP, NYSL; *San Francisco Herald,* April 28 (quote), May 25, June 1, 1854; *Alta California,* April 28, May 1, 1854; Nasatir, "Dillon," CHS *Quarterly* 35: 309–13.

23. Wool to Richard P. Hammond, March 13, 15, 1854, in "Correspondence," HED 88, 35-1, 35–36, respectively, and Wool to Patrice Dillon, March 20, 1854, "Correspondence," 34–35; Wool to Inge, April 15, 1854, WP, NYSL; *San Francisco Herald,* April 28, May 25, June 1, 1854; *Alta California,* April 28, 1854; Nasatir, "Dillon," CHS *Quarterly* 35: 321.

24. Wool to Sarah Wool, March 24–26, 1854, WP, NYSL. The contract was complicated by del Valle's demand that the French merchants buy a large cargo of Peruvian rice at an inflated price from him. The Mexican government would pay $42 for each "emigrant"—$35 to the merchants and $7 to del Valle (Wool to Inge, April 15, 1854, WP, NYSL). Wool calculated that del Valle could ultimately pocket $12,000 from the deal.

25. *Alta California,* April 1, 1854. William D. Scroggs, *Filibusters and Financiers: The Story of William Walker and His Associates* (New York: Russell and Russell, 1969), 52–54; Brown, *Agents,* 212–13.

26. Wool to Justus McKinstry, March 28, 1854; Wool to Sarah Wool, March 24, 1854; Inge to Wool, March 30, Wool to Justus McKinstry, March 28, 1854; Wool to Sarah Wool, March 24, 1854; Inge to Wool, March 30, 1854, and Wool to Inge, April 15, 1854, WP, NYSL; Wool to William H. Ball, March 20, 1854, in "Correspondence," HED 88, 35-1, 46, and Wool to Hammond, March 31, 1854, "Correspondence," 47. *San Francisco Herald,* March 30, 31 (extra), April 1, 28, May 25, June 8, 1854, and February 8, 1855; *Alta California,* May 1, 21–22, 1854; Scroggs, *Filibusters,* 55; Hittell, *California* 3:745; Nasatir, "Dillon," CHS *Quarterly* 35: 321.

27. Wool to Sarah Wool, April 1, 1854, WP, NYSL; *San Francisco Herald,* April 15, 28, May 25, June 1, 1854.

28. *San Francisco Herald,* March 31 (extra), April 1, 2, 1854; *Alta California,* April 1, May 1, 1854.

29. *Alta California,* April 2, 1854; *San Francisco Herald,* March 30, April 5, 1854.

30. Wool to Elizabeth Griswold, April 6, 1854, Burden Collection; John Griswold to Wool, April 17, 1854, Griswold Papers, RCHS.

31. Wool to Inge, April 15, 1854, WP, NYSL; Inge speech, in Wool to Marcy, August 14, 1854, in "Correspondence between Major General Wool and the Different Departments of the Government, January 19, 1855," SED 25, 33-2, Serial 751, 8; *San Francisco Herald,* April 19, 28, 1854; *Alta California,* May 1, 1854.

32. Wool to Sarah Wool, April 17–28, 1854, WP, NYSL; *San Francisco Herald,* April 26, 28, 29, 1854; *Alta California,* May 1, 1854. Nasatir, "Dillon," CHS *Quarterly* 35: 314, 321; Scroggs, *Filibusters,* 56.

33. Wool to Davis, April 29, 1854, WP, NYSL; *San Francisco Herald,* April 28, June 1, 1854; *Alta California,* May 1, 1854.

34. Samuel P. Heintzelman to E[dward] Townsend, April 8, 1854, and Wool to McKinstry, April 29, 1854, WP, NYSL; *San Francisco Herald,* May 16, 18, 1854; Hittell, *California,* 3:765–68; Brown, *Agents,* 201, 206–8; Scroggs, *Filibusters,* 42, 46–48.

35. *San Francisco Herald,* May 16, 1854; *Alta California,* May 18, 1854; Walker is described at Thomas R. Warren, *Dust and Foam; Or, Three Oceans and Two Continents* (New York: C. Scribner, 1859), 212–13.

36. Wool to Stewart, May 16, 1854; Wool to Inge, May 15, 1854, and Wool to Sarah Wool, May 4, 1854, WP, NYSL; Wool to Scott, May 15, 1854, in "Correspondence," HED 88, 35-1, 61; *San Francisco Herald,* May 16, 17, 1854, and February 8, 1854.

37. Wool to Sarah Wool, May 4, 1854, and William Gwin to Wool, April 4, 1854, WP, NYSL; Wool to A. O. P. Nicholson, May 16, 1854, Mss., Henry E. Huntington Library, San Marino, California; *Salem Advocate* (IL), February 23, 1854.

38. *San Francisco Herald,* May 24, 25, 1854; *Alta California,* May 25, 1854. On the night of May 23, Boulbon, with a small group of men, used the pilot boat *Belle* to take a load of arms to the *Challenge,* then sailed for Guaymas, Sonora. Upon landing he assumed leadership of the French troops. After haggling with the local Mexican commandant, who had orders from Santa Anna to merge the French with Mexican troops, Boulbon attacked the garrison. On August 12, 1854, he was captured, tried, and shot (Brown, *Agents,* 214–16).

39. Wool to Cass, July 1, 1854, WP, NYSL, describes the Guaymas letter. *San Francisco Herald* and *Alta California,* May 25, 1854.

40. *San Francisco Herald* and *Alta California,* May 26, 1854.

41. *San Francisco Herald,* May 26, 1854; *Alta California,* May 27, 1854.

42. Davis to Wool, April 14, 1854, in "Correspondence," HED 88, 35-1, 52. Walker was indicted on May 24. He appeared in court on June 2 and denied that he had broken neutrality laws. His trial was postponed, and he was released on bail. Walker obtained another continuance in August, and in October 1854, he was acquitted. In February 1855, Walker brought a letter to Wool from Francisco Castillon, who had seized Nicaragua and requested Walker to raise three hundred men to aid him. Wool cited his instructions from Davis, and refused to interfere. *New York Times,* July 23, 1857; Hittell, *California* 3:770–71; Scroggs, *Filibusters,* 62–63, 65, 86–87; Wooster, *American Military Frontiers,* 132.

43. Wool to Davis, March 14, 1854, in "Correspondence," HED 88, 35-1, 11; Davis to Wool, April 13, 1854, ibid., 51, and Wool to AG, March 31, 1854, ibid., 27; Wool to Davis, April 24, 1854, and Wool to Gwin, May 31, 1854, WP, NYSL.

44. Wool to Davis, May 30, 1854, in "Correspondence," HED 88, 35-1, 66–68; Wool to Gwin, May 31, 1854, and Gwin to Wool, June 27, 1854, WP, NYSL.

45. Wool to Thomas, June 1, 14, 1854, in "Correspondence," HED 88, 35-1, 72–73 and 73–76; SO 80, May 18, 1854, San Francisco, Department of the Pacific, in "Correspondence," 64, and AG (quotes Davis) to Wool, May 17, 1854, ibid., 63. January [n.d.], 1855, in Townsend, *Diary,* 95–96.

46. Wool to Thomas, June 14, 1854, in "Correspondence," *HED* 88, 35-1, 75–76.

47. Wool to Stewart, June 15, 29, 1854; Osborn Cross to [Townsend], June [?], 1854; J[ohn] G. Barnard to Wool, June 24, 1854, and Wool to Davis, March 31, 1854, WP, NYSL; Wool to Thomas, July 1, 1854, in "Correspondence," HED 88, 35-1, 83–85, and Wool to Jesup, March 31, 1854, "Correspondence," 25–26; *Alta California,* June 29, 1854. Davis's removal order may have been due to Wool's request on March 31 for increased allowances for staff, rather than from an affront caused by the general's attending the Foote dinner or being overzealous in curbing filibustering. Davis's endorsement (May 10) on Wool's March 31 letter, advising Jesup to move Wool's headquarters to Benecia, in Davis, *Davis Papers* 5:327–28.

48. Wool to Stewart, June 29, 1854; Wool to Croswell, June 16, 1854, and Wool to Sarah Wool, June 23, 1854, WP, NYSL.

49. Wool to Sarah Wool, April 5–14, 1854, WP, NYSL; 7th Census (1850), Rensselaer County, New York, NA. A thirty-year-old, West Indies-born female servant, Ann Latsom, was also in the household at the time.

50. Griswold to Wool, March 19, April 17, June 18, August 3, 1854, Griswold Papers, RCHS.

51. Wool to Sarah Wool, April 17, June 21, July 18–29, September 6–14, October 29–30, 1854, and January 29, 1855, WP, NYSL.

52. Wool to Sarah Wool, February 26, April 10, 12, 24, May 6, 10, 1855, and Wool to I. B. Hart, April 13, 1855, WP, NYSL.

53. Wool to Sarah Wool, May 6–15, June 7–15, July 6–15, 18–29, 1854, WP, NYSL.

54. Wool to Stewart, September 1, 1854, WP, NYSL.

55. Wool to Sarah Wool, June 21, September 6–14, 1854, WP, NYSL. *San Francisco Herald,* September 11, 1854; Davis, *Davis Papers* 5:476. All of Mansfield's inspection reports can be found in LRAG, RG 94, NA.

56. *San Francisco Herald,* September 11, 1854.

57. GO 10, September 2, 1854, San Francisco, Department of the Pacific, and Wool to Sarah Wool, September 26, 1854, WP, NYSL. June 1, 1852, in Townsend, *Diary,* 47–49. Introduction, and September 3, 1854, in C. S. Winder, "Diary of a Bachelor Lieutenant at Benecia in 1854 [C. S. Winder]," eds. Alice Lloyd and Arthur T. Brice, *Pacific Historian* 14 (Spring 1970): 77, 81.

58. Wool to Stewart, September 26, 1854, WP, NYSL; Davis to Wool, August 18, 1854, in "Correspondence," HED 88, 35-1, 98.

59. Wool to Sarah Wool, September 26, October 12, 1854, WP, NYSL. Inge to Davis, October 16, 1854, in Davis, *Davis Papers* 5:89, stated that Wool had made distorted statements during the del Valle trial: "The old man is in his dotage and the monomaniacal idea that he is [a] prominent candidate [for] the Presidency has taken complete possession of him," Inge wrote.

60. Wool to Sarah Wool, June 21, 1854, and January 8, May 10, 1855, WP, NYSL.

61. Wool to Davis, October 13, 1854, in "Correspondence," HED 88, 35-1, 111–14.

62. Wool to Sarah Wool, October 20–23, 29–31, and James Hardie to Wool, October 20, 1854, WP, NYSL; *San Francisco Herald,* October 27, 28, November 1, 1854, and December 1, 1855; "Continuation of the Annals of San Francisco. [Extracted from the Daily Papers of the Time.] June 1854 (continued)," CHS *Quarterly* 15: 181. This series continues Frank Soule, et al., *Annals of San Francisco,* which appeared in *The Pioneer* magazine. A severe earthquake rocked San Francisco on October 21. Dillon raised his flag a year later, on November 30, 1855, after a second visit by a French warship. Scroggs, *Filibusters,* 61–62.

63. Wool to Bryant, December 14, 1854, and Wool to Bell, December 15, 1854, WP, NYSL. *Washington Union,* November 1, 1854, and January 14, 1855.

64. Wool to Stewart, January 6, 1855, and James Gadsden to Wool, January 4, 1855, WP, NYSL; *Alta California,* Dec, 24, 1854. *New York Times,* January 8, 1855, hinted that Jefferson Davis was considering running for president and that he viewed Wool as a rival candidate. Davis's verbal skirmish in the newspapers possibly depreciated his chances for the nomination. In California, Wool courted politicians and sought to enhance his "national" image.

65. Davis to Wool, December 13, 1854, in "Correspondence," HED 88, 35-1, 122–28. *New York Times,* January 8, 1855; *New York Herald,* February 8, 1855; *Washington Union,* January 14, 1855; *New Orleans Picayune,* January 16, 1855.

66. Wool to Davis, January 29, 1855, and Wool to Sarah Wool. January 29, 1855, WP, NYSL.

67. Wool to Sarah Wool, February 26, 1855, and Wool to I. B. Hart, April 13, 1855, WP, NYSL; *Washington Union,* November 1, 1854.

68. Wool to Stewart, March 6, 1855, WP, NYSL.

CHAPTER II. NATIVE AMERICAN ANNIHILATION

1. For an overview of Wool's involvement in Indian affairs in the Pacific Northwest, see Robert M. Utley, *Frontiersmen in Blue: The United States Army and the Indian, 1848–1865* (New York: Macmillan Co., 1967), 178–200.

2. Benjamin Madley, *An American Genocide: The United States and the California Indian Catastrophe* (New Haven, CT: Yale University Press, 2016), 170–71, 260.

3. Wool to David C. Broderick and Wm. Gwin, January 27, 1857, in Interior Department Appointment Papers, quoted in Madley, *An American Genocide,* 171.

4. Wool to Davis, January 7, 1854, in "Correspondence," HED 88, 35-1, 4–5; Davis to Wool, January 12, 1854, ibid., 6.

5. "Report of the Commissioner of Indian Affairs, November 25, 1854," HED 1, 33-2, Serial 777, 223–24, 402–31, and "Report of the SW for 1854," HED 1, 33-2, 6; Hubert H. Bancroft, *History of California,* 7 vols. (San Francisco: A. L. Bancroft, 1884–1890), 7:474–88;

Albert L. Hurtado, *Indian Survival on the California Frontier* (New Haven, CT: Yale University Press, 1988), 1–3, 100–108.

6. Joseph Ellison, *California and the Nation, 1850–1869* (Berkeley: University of California Press, 1927), 85–88, 93; Hubert H. Bancroft, *History of Oregon,* 2 vols. (San Francisco: History Co., 1886, 1888), 2:206–16, 245; Hurtado, *Indian Survival,* 132–41.

7. Edward F. Beale to Wool, May 12, 1854, WP, NYSL; Beale to George Manypenny, February 8, 1854, in "Report of the Commissioner of Indian Affairs for 1854," HED 1, 33-2, 506–7; Gerald Thompson, *Edward F. Beale and the American West* (Albuquerque: University of New Mexico Press, 1983), 46, 49, 56–58, 64–69.

8. SO 60, June 24, 1854, San Francisco, Department of the Pacific, and Mansfield to Wool, July 1, 1854, WP, NYSL; *Alta California,* July 2, 1854; Thomas J. Henley to Manypenny, September 25, 1854, Letters Received, California Superintendency, M-234, Roll 33, NARA; Wool to Thomas, September 14, 1854, in "Correspondence," HED 88, 35-1, 103. Also, Henley in Davis, *Davis Papers* 3:312n15, and Thompson, *Beale,* 71–73.

9. Henley to Manypenny, August 28, 1854, in "Report of the Commissioner of Indian Affairs for 1854," HED 1, 33-2, 508–12; Henley to Wool, July 26, August 7, 1854, Henley to Townsend, August 22, 1854, Wool to Sarah Wool, July 18–29, 1854, and Townsend to Henley, August 25, 1854, WP, NYSL.

10. Wool to Sarah Wool, October 12, 1854, WP, NYSL. *New York Herald,* November 19, 1854.

11. Wool to Sarah Wool, October 12, 1854, WP, NYSL; Miscellaneous newspaper clipping, n.d., WP, NYSL.

12. Townsend to George Wright, April 17, 1854, WP, NYSL; Wright to Townsend, September 20, 1854, in "Correspondence," HED 88, 35-1, 110–11, and Wool to Thomas, June 14, 1854, "Correspondence," 73–74. Also, Carl P. Schlicke, *General George Wright: Guardian of the Pacific Coast* (Norman: University of Oklahoma Press, 1988), 103, 105.

13. Wool to Sarah Wool, October 12, 1854, WP, NYSL; *Alta California,* October 6, 1854; *San Francisco Herald,* October 12, 1854; Fred B. Rogers, *Bear Flag Lieutenant: The Life Story of Henry L. Ford* (San Francisco: California Historical Society, 1951), 54–55; Hurtado, *Indian Survival,* 145.

14. Wool to Sarah Wool, October 12, 1854, WP, NYSL; *San Francisco Herald,* October 12, 1854.

15. Townsend to Lucien Loeser, October 14, 1854, and Townsend to Wright, December 28, 1854, WP, NYSL.

16. Wool to Thomas, January 30, February 26, April 11, 1855, and Townsend to Robert C. Buchanan, February 22, WP, NYSL; William F. Strobridge, *Regulars in the Redwoods: The U. S. Army in Northern California, 1852–1861* (Spokane, WA: Arthur H. Clark Co., 1994).

17. Wool to Townsend, August 18, 1855, and Townsend to Henry M. Judah, August 30, 1855, WP, NYSL.

18. Wool to Henley, March 5, 1855, WP, NYSL. Davis to Robert McClelland, May 23, 1855, in Jefferson Davis, *Jefferson Davis, Constitutionalist: His Letters, Papers, and Speeches,* ed. Dunbar Rowland, 10 vols. (Jackson, MS: Department of Archives and History, 1923), 2:469;

Henley to Mannypenny, September 29, 1854, and May 31, 1855, Letters Received, California Superintendency, M-234, Roll 33. Hurtado, *Indian Survival,* 145.

19. Wool to Henley, January 20, 1855, Henley to Wool, October 15, 1855, and Benjamin F. Beall to Wool, August 11, 1855, WP, NYSL.

20. Henley to Wool, October 15, 1855, WP, NYSL; October 1, 15, 1855, in Townsend, *Diary,* 96, 124–29.

21. Bancroft, *History of Oregon* 2:206–46; Stephen D. Beckham, *Requiem for a People: The Rogue Indians and the Frontiersmen* (Norman: University of Oklahoma Press, 1971), 71, 76–78, 115–26, 132–34, 143–44.

22. Joseph P. Palmer to Wool, May 12, 1854, and John W. Davis to Wool, July 17, 1854, WP, NYSL; *Alta California,* June 4, 1854; Beckham, *Requiem,* 132–34; *Oregon Statesman* (Salem), July 25, 1854; James E. Hendricksen, *Joe Lane of Oregon: Machine Politics and the Sectional Crisis, 1849–1861* (New Haven, CT: Yale University Press, 1967), 120.

23. Gabriel J. Rains to Townsend, September 1, 1854, and Wool to J. W. Davis, January 29, 1855, WP, NYSL; Wool to Thomas, September 14, 1854, in "Correspondence," HED 88, 35-1, 104–5, and Granville O. Haller, Field Return, September 30, 1854, "Correspondence," 118–21; Terence O'Donnell, *An Arrow in the Earth: General Joel Palmer and the Indians of Oregon* (Portland: Oregon Historical Society, 1991); Stanley S. Spaid, "Joel Palmer and Indian Affairs in Oregon," (PhD diss., University of Oregon, 1950), 144, 159; Hendricksen, *Lane,* 96–97.

24. *Oregon Statesman,* September 26, October 17, 1854; Robert H. Ruby and John A Brown, at *The Cayuse Indians: Imperial Tribesmen of Old Oregon* (Norman: University of Oklahoma Press, 1972), 206, say the Indians attacking the Ward train were Bannock-Shoshones, and not Snakes. Figures vary concerning the number of persons lost.

25. Townsend to Benjamin L. E. Bonneville, October 2, 1854, and Townsend to Rains, October 16, 1854, WP, NYSL.

26. Haller, Field Return, September 30, 1854, in "Correspondence," HED 88, 35-1, 118–21; *Oregon Statesman,* October 24, 31, 1854.

27. *Oregon Statesman,* June 6, November 14, 28, 1854; *San Francisco Herald,* August 3, 1854.

28. Wool to Davis, January 29, 1855, WP, NYSL.

29. Townsend to Edward P. Steptoe, February 13, 1855, in "Correspondence," HED 88, 35-1, 158–59, and Townsend to Thomas, May 31, 1855, ibid., 162.

30. Wool to Sarah Wool, May 30, 1855, WP, NYSL.

31. Ibid.; *San Francisco Herald,* May 31, 1855; Theodore Winthrop, *The Canoe and the Saddle* (Tacoma, WA: J. H. Williams, 1913), 247.

32. Wool to Sarah Wool, May 30, 1855, and Wool to Rains, May 14, 1855, WP, NYSL.

33. Wool to Sarah Wool, May 30, 1855, WP, NYSL; *San Francisco Herald,* May 31, 1855. Quote in Will J. Trimble, "A Soldier of the Oregon Frontier [Joel G. Trimble]," Oregon Historical Society *Quarterly* 8 (March 1907): 45.

34. Wool to Thomas, September 4, 1855, and Wool to Rains, May 24, 1855, WP, NYSL.

35. *Oregon Statesman,* December 12, 1854; Wool to Thomas, September 4, 1855, WP, NYSL; Spaid, "Palmer," 133–39.

36. Wool to Sarah Wool, March 4, 1856, and Wool to Thomas, November 3, 1855, WP, NYSL.

37. Wool to Thomas, November 3, 1855, WP, NYSL; Spaid, "Palmer," 88–144; Kent D. Richards, *Isaac I. Stevens: Young Man in a Hurry* (Provo, UT: Brigham Young University Press, 1979), 190, 194, 197–210.

38. Richards, *Stevens,* xi–xiii, chs. 2–7; Stevens to Marcy, June 21, 1854, in "Report of Governor Stevens, Relative to the Property of the Hudson's Bay and Puget Sound Company . . . , February 7, 1855," SED 37, 33-2, Serial 752, 1–12; Richards, *Stevens,* 159–72, 174, 182.

39. Erasmus D. Keyes to Townsend, November 12, 1856, WP, NYSL; *Alta California,* February 6, 1856; Richards, *Stevens,* 197–209.

40. Wool to Stevens, February 19, 21, 1855, WP, NYSL.

41. Stevens to Wool, May 22, 1855, in "Indian Affairs on the Pacific, February 14, 1857," HED 76, 34-3, Serial 906, 237–38; *Oregon Statesman,* June 30, July 28, 1855; Spaid, "Palmer," 148–52; Richards, *Stevens,* 215–25.

42. Rodney Glisan, *A Journal of Army Life* (San Francisco: A. L. Bancroft, 1874), 234–36; Charles Stevens to [Brother Levi], August 1, 1855, in Charles Stevens, "Letters of Charles Stevens, Pt. V," ed. E. Ruth Rockwood, Oregon Historical Society *Quarterly* 38 (June 1937): 166–67; *Oregon Statesman,* August 4, 1855; *San Francisco Herald,* October 16, 1855; William N. Bischoff, "The Yakima Indian War, 1855–1856" (PhD diss., Loyola University-Chicago, 1950), 64–65, 79; Richards, *Stevens,* 212–13, 224, 236–37.

43. Wool to Thomas, November 3, December 25, 1855, and March 30, 1856, WP, NYSL; *San Francisco Herald,* November 6, 1855; Richards, *Stevens,* 239–41.

44. De Lancey Floyd-Jones to Rains, October 18, 1855; SO 89, November 1, 1855, Benecia, Department of the Pacific; Wool to Thomas, November 3, 1855, and March 30, 1856, and Wool to John B. Weller, November 18, 1855, WP, NYSL. On October 19, Capt. E. O. C. Ord and two artillery companies sailed for Fort Vancouver. Wool to Joseph Lane, November 5, 1855, Joseph Lane Mss., Indiana University.

45. *San Francisco Herald,* November 6–7, 1855; November 6, 11, in Townsend, *Diary,* 147–49; Glisan, *Journal,* 262–63; Thomas J. Cram, "Military Topographical Memoir and Report on the Department of the Pacific, March 3, 1859," HED 114, 35-2, Serial 1014, 44–47. This document has been reprinted as Thomas Jefferson Cram, *Topographical Memoir* (Fairfield, WA: Ye Galleon Press, 1977).

46. November 12, 1855, in Townsend, *Diary,* 150–52.

47. November 12–13, 1855, in Townsend, *Diary,* 152–56; C. Stevens to Brother and Sister, November 12, 1855, in Stevens, "Stevens Letters," Oregon Historical Society *Quarterly* 38: 170.

48. November 16, 1855, in Townsend, *Diary,* 157; Keyes, *Fifty Years' Observation,* 251; Wool to Thomas, July 28, 1855, enclosing Stoneman-Whiting report, dated July 5, 1855, in "Correspondence," HED 88, 35-1, 171–78; Wool to Thomas, November 17, December 13, 1855, and Townsend to Keyes, November 17, 1855, WP, NYSL; Richards, *Stevens,* 241–42, 255–56.

49. Wool to Thomas, December 13, 25, 1855, and March 30, 1856, WP, NYSL; Cram, *Topographical Memoir,* 44–45.

50. Wool to Thomas, December 25, 1855, and March 30, 1856, WP, NYSL; P[hilip] Sheridan, *Personal Memoirs,* 2 vols. (New York: Webster, 1888), 1:53–66; November 20, 1855, in Townsend, *Diary,* 160–61; Bischoff, "Yakima War," 118–27; Richards, *Stevens,* 244–45.

51. Rains to Townsend, November 20, 1855, and Wool to Thomas, December 25, 1855, WP, NYSL.

52. November 23–27, 1855, in Townsend, *Diary,* 164–70; Townsend to Wool, November 28, 1855, and Wool to Thomas, December 25, 1855, WP, NYSL.

53. Wool to Thomas, January 19, 1856, and Townsend to Sarah Wool, March 14, 1856, WP, NYSL; November 28, 1855, in Townsend, *Diary,* 170–73.

54. December 13, 1855, in Townsend, *Diary,* 174–75; Keyes to Townsend, December 21, 1855, and Wool to Thomas, December 13, 1855, WP, NYSL; Cram, *Topographical Memoir,* 101–2; Keyes, *Fifty Years' Observation,* 251–53.

55. Wool to Thomas, December 13, 1855, and Wool to Weller, December 14, 1855, WP, NYSL; Wool to Lane, Lane Mss., Indiana University.

56. Wool to Thomas, December 25, 1855; Wool to R. A. Thompson, December 26, 1855, and Wool to Howell Cobb, January 8, 1856, WP, NYSL.

57. J. B. A. Brouillet to Wool, December 5, 1855, and Wool to Brouillet, December 8, 1855, WP, NYSL; *Oregon Statesman,* December 25, 1855; November 20, 1855, in Townsend, *Diary,* 161–63; Bischoff, "Yakima War," 145–46.

58. Wool to Sarah Wool, February 20, 1856, and Wool to Thomas, December 25, 1855, WP, NYSL; December 19, 1855, in Townsend, *Diary,* 176–77; Ruby and Brown, *Cayuse Indians,* 215–19; Richards, *Stevens,* 247.

59. Wool to Thomas, January 19, 1856, and SO 6, January 19, 1856, San Francisco, Department of the Pacific, WP, NYSL; *San Francisco Herald,* February 21, 1856; Cram, *Topographical Memoir,* 106; Bischoff, "Yakima War," 145–46.

60. Townsend to Wool, January 1, 1856, and Henley to Townsend, December 31, 1855, WP, NYSL; December 18–24, 1855, in Townsend, *Diary,* 176–77.

61. Wool to David C. Broderick and Gwin, January 28, 1857, WP, NYSL. Wool cited congressional acts of March 3, 1853, July 31, 1854, and March 1, 1855, and instructions of the interior secretary, dated April 13, 1853. Hurtado, *Indian Survival,* 144–47, discusses the Nome Lackee reservation.

62. Wool to J. Neely Johnson, January 21, March 4, 1856, WP, NYSL; *San Francisco Herald,* March 7, 1856.

63. Stevens to Rains, January 17, 1856, WP, NYSL; Alvin M. Josephy Jr., *The Nez Perce Indians and the Opening of the Northwest* (New Haven, CT: Yale University Press, 1965), 343–56, 361–62; Richards, *Stevens,* 249–53, 258.

64. Stevens to Washington Legislature, January 21, 1856, in "Indian Disturbances in the Territories of Washington and Oregon, May 9, 1856," SED 66, 34-1, Serial 822, 23–27; Richards, *Stevens,* 258.

65. *San Francisco Herald,* January 27, 1856.

66. *Alta California,* January 28, 1856.

67. Ibid., February 6, 1856.

68. Stevens to Wool, January 29, 1856, enclosing letter of December 23, 1855, WP, NYSL; Richards, *Stevens,* 260.

69. Wool to Stevens, February 12, 1856, WP, NYSL.

70. Oregon Memorial to the President, January 30, 1856, in "Indian Hostilities in Oregon and Washington Territories, July 8, 1856," in HED 118, 34-1, Serial 859, 31–32; *San Francisco Herald* and *Alta California,* February 15–17, 1856.

71. Wright to Wool, February 10, 1856, WP, NYSL; George L. Curry to Thomas R. Cornelius, February 15, 1856, in "Indian Hostilities," HED 118, 34-1, 22–24; Stevens to Davis, February 19, 1856, in "Indian Disturbances in Washington and Oregon," SED 66, 34-1, 3–9; *Alta California,* February 22, 1856; *Washington Republican* (Steilacoom), June 5, 1857. Richards, *Stevens,* 289, mention Stevens's drinking.

CHAPTER 12. CRYING HEARTS AND VIGILANTES

1. Wool to Thomas, March 5, 1856, WP, NYSL; Cram, *Topographical Memoir,* 48–49.

2. Palmer to Wool, December 1, 1855, in "Indian Disturbances in California, February 21, 1856," SED 26, 34-1, Serial 819, 37–38; Beckham, *Requiem,* 163, 166; Marvin E. Kroeker, *Great Plains Command: William B. Hazen in the Frontier West* (Norman: University of Oklahoma Press, 1976), 10–11.

3. Palmer to Wool, February 12, 1856; A[ndrew] J. Smith to Floyd-Jones, February 23, 1856, and William B. Hazen to Floyd-Jones, March 31, 1856, WP, NYSL; *San Francisco Herald,* March 5, 1856; Spaid, "Palmer," 188–89, 193, 204; Beckham, *Requiem,* 163–66, 174.

4. George Crook, *George Crook: His Autobiography,* ed. Martin F. Schmitt (Norman: University of Oklahoma Press, 1953), 9–10; Cram, *Topographical Memoir,* 49; John C. Bonnycastle to Buchanan, March 7, 1856, and Wool to Wright, March 11, 1856, WP, NYSL; Glisan, *Journal,* 291.

5. Wool to Wright, March 11, 1856; Wright to Floyd-Jones, March 12, 1856; and Wool to Sarah Wool, March 19, 1856, WP, NYSL.

6. Silas Casey to Townsend, February 4, 1856, and Casey to Wool, March 4, 6, 9, 1856, WP, NYSL; Utley, *Frontiersmen in Blue,* 175–82 (quote); Wooster, *American Military Frontiers,* 139–40; Keyes, *Fifty Years' Observation,* 254–60; Cram, *Topographical Memoir,* 197–198; Richards, *Stevens,* 259.

7. Stevens to Davis, March 9, 1856, in "Indian Disturbances," SED 66, 34-1, 68–69; James Tilton to William F. Tolmie, March 2, 1856, and Tolmie to Dugal Mackintosh, March 15, 1856, in Clarence B. Bagley, "Attitude of the Hudson's Bay Company during the Indian War of 1855–1856," *Washington Historical Quarterly* 8 (October 1917): 301, 303; Richards, *Stevens,* 274–75.

8. Wool to Casey, March 14, 1856, and Casey to Wool, June 20, 1856, WP, NYSL; Cram, *Topographical Memoir,* 111; *San Francisco Herald,* March 20, 1856; Richards, *Stevens,* 265.

9. Stevens to Wool, March 20, 1856, in *Washington Intelligencer,* May 5, 1856.

10. Stevens to Wool, March 20, 1856, in *Washington Intelligencer,* May 5, 1856; Wool to Townsend, June 18, 1856, WP, NYSL.

11. *San Francisco Herald,* March 20, April 3, 1856; *Alta California,* March 24, 1856.

12. Wool to Nugent, April 2, 1856, WP, NYSL. *San Francisco Herald,* April 3–5, 1856.

13. Wool to Hamilton Fish and William H. Seward, April 2, 1856, Hamilton Fish Papers, LC. Wool also wrote the editor of the *Washington Intelligencer.* His letter appeared in the *Congressional Globe* 34-1, 1135–36.

14. Wool to Fish and Seward, April 3, 1856, Fish Papers, LC.

15. Wool to Wright, January 19, 1856, and Wool to Townsend, May 17, 1856, WP, NYSL; Cram, *Topographical Memoir,* 108–9.

16. Wool to Townsend, May 17, 1856, Wright to Floyd-Jones, March 1, 1856, and Wool to Palmer, March 7, 1856, WP, NYSL; Cram, *Topographical Memoir,* 110.

17. J. J. Archer to Sister Nannie, April 11, 1856, J. J. Archer Papers, Maryland Historical Society, Annapolis; Wright to Floyd-Jones, March 25, April 4, 1856, WP, NYSL; Cram, *Topographical Memoir,* 112.

18. Wright to Floyd-Jones, April 4, 5, 1856, in "Indian Hostilities," HED 118, 34-1, 8–9; Cram, *Topographical Memoir,* 112; Sheridan, *Personal Memoirs* 1:73–74, 80–82.

19. November 24–26, 1855, in Townsend, *Diary,* 167–70; Winthrop, *Canoe and the Saddle,* 251; Wool to Townsend, May 17, 1856, WP, NYSL; Bischoff, "Yakima War," 172.

20. Wool to Wright, April 23, 24, 1856, WP, NYSL; R. R. Thompson to Wright, April 20, 1856, in "Indian Hostilities," HED 118, 34-1, 18–19.

21. Hazen to Floyd-Jones, March 31, 1856, Sheridan to Floyd-Jones, May 6, 1856, and Wool to Palmer, April 19, 1856, WP, NYSL; Palmer to Wool, April 13, 1856, in "Indian Hostilities," HED 118, 34-1, 13; Cram, *Topographical Memoir,* 54.

22. Archer to Mother, April 30, 1856, Archer-Mitchell-Stump-Williams Family Papers, Maryland Historical Society, Annapolis.

23. Wool to Thomas, May 4, 1856, WP, NYSL.

24. William A. Winder to Henry S. Burton, April 29, 1856, and W[illiam] W. Mackall to Henley, August 5, 1856, WP, NYSL.

25. John Stewart to Floyd-Jones, May 1, 1856, Stewart to LaRhett L. Livingston, May 1, 1856, and Wool to Thomas, May, 1856, WP, NYSL.

26. Stewart to Floyd-Jones, May 16, 1856, in "Indian Hostilities," HED 118, 34-1, 21; Stewart to Floyd-Jones, June 13, 1856, and Wool to Thomas, May 17, 20, 1856, WP, NYSL; Wool to Beale, September 21, 1858, Decatur House Papers, LC; Madley, *An American Genocide,* 245–46.

27. Robert M. Senkewicz, *Vigilantes in Gold Rush San Francisco* (Palo Alto, CA: Stanford University Press, 1985), 156–67; Richard M. Brown, *Strain of Violence: Historical Studies of American Violence and Vigilantism* (New York: Oxford University Press, 1975), 134–43.

28. Senkewicz, *Vigilantes,* 168–71; John Caughey, *California: A Remarkable State's Life History* (Englewood Cliffs, NJ: Prentice Hall, 1970), 228–30.

29. *San Francisco Herald,* May 15–16, 1856; Senkewicz, *Vigilantes,* 171; Hittell, *California* 3:488–94.

30. *Alta California,* May 21, October 15, 1856; Senkewicz, *Vigilantes,* 171–72; Hittell, *California* 3:496–514, 528–30.

31. Johnson to Wool, October 17, 1856, in *San Francisco Herald,* October 21, 1856; Wool to Johnson, September 17, 1856, in *Alta California,* September 20, 1856; W[illiam] T. Sherman, *Memoirs of Gen. W. T. Sherman, Written by Himself,* 2 vols. (New York: C. L. Webster and Co., 1891), 1:153.

32. Johnson to Wool, October 17, 1856, in *San Francisco Herald,* October 21, 1856; Sherman, *Memoirs* 1:154–55.

33. Proclamation of Governor, June 3, 1856, in "Correspondence," HED 88, 35-1, 187–88, and Johnson to Wool, June 4, 1856, ibid., 186–87; Sherman, *Memoirs* 1:155.

34. Wool to Johnson, June 5, 1856, in "Correspondence," HED 88, 35-1, 188; E. A. Rowe to Johnson, October 9, 1856, in *San Francisco Herald,* October 22, 1856.

35. Sherman to Wool, June 6, 1856, in J. Neeley Johnson, "The Law and Order View of the San Francisco Vigilance Committee of 1856: Taken from the Correspondence of Governor J. Neeley Johnson [Pt. I]," arranged by Herbert G. Florcken, CHS *Quarterly* 14 (December 1935): 362; Wool to Sherman, June 6, 1856, Sherman Papers, LC; Sherman, *Memoirs* 1:157.

36. Johnson to Wool, June 7, 1856, in "Correspondence," HED 88, 35-1, 188–89; Sherman Memorandum of June 7, in Johnson, "Vigilance Committee," CHS *Quarterly* 14: 364–65.

37. Sherman Memo, in Johnson, "Vigilance Committee," CHS *Quarterly* 14: 364–66; Sherman, *Memoirs* 1:157–58; Hittell, *California* 3:537–39.

38. Sherman Memo, in Johnson, "Vigilance Committee," CHS *Quarterly* 14: 366; Rowe to Johnson, October 9, 1856, in *San Francisco Herald,* October 22, 1856; Wool to Johnson, September 17, 1856, in *Alta California,* September 20, 1856; Johnson to Wool, October 17, 1856, in *San Francisco Herald,* October 21, 1856.

39. Johnson to Sherman, June 10, 1856, Sherman Papers, LC; Johnson to William C. Kibbe, June 10, 1856, in Johnson, "Vigilance Committee," CHS *Quarterly* 15 (March 1936): 71; *Alta California,* October 15, 1856.

40. Sherman to Thomas Ewing, June 16, 1856, in Johnson, "Vigilance Committee," CHS *Quarterly* 14: 368–69; Johnson to Franklin Pierce, June 19, 1856, CHS *Quarterly* 15: 80–83; Kibbe to Johnson, August 14, 1856, CHS *Quarterly* 15: 252; Proclamation, November 3, 1856, CHS *Quarterly* 15: 263, and Sherman to Johnson, October 29, 1856, CHS *Quarterly* 15: 260; Senkewicz, *Vigilantes,* 177.

41. *Alta California,* September 20, October 26, 1856; *San Francisco Herald,* October 21, 1856.

42. Casey to Wool, April 15, May 19, 1856, and Wool to Casey, June 16, 1856, WP, NYSL.

43. Stevens to Casey, March 31, 1856, in "Indian Hostilities," HED 118, 34-1, 47–48, and Casey to Stevens, March 31, 1856, ibid., 48; Richards, *Stevens,* 274–76. Also see Roy Lokken, "The Martial Law Controversy in Washington Territory, 1856," *PNQ* 43 (April 1952): 91–119; Casey to Stevens, April 3, 1856, in "Indian Hostilities," HED 118, 34-1, 49; and Richards, *Stevens,* 277–82.

44. Casey to Francis A. Chenoweth, May 24, 1856, in "Indian Hostilities," HED 118, 34-1, 53, and Casey to Wool, May 24, 1856, ibid., 54; Samuel F. Cohn, "Martial Law in Washington Territory," *PNQ* 27 (October 1936): 207–10; Richards, *Stevens,* 282–86.

45. E. O. C. Ord to Buchanan, March 27, 1856, and Wool to Buchanan, April 11, 1856, WP, NYSL; *San Francisco Herald,* April 18, 1856; Glisan, *Journal,* 293–308; Beckham, *Requiem,* 181–82.

46. Buchanan to Floyd-Jones, May 1, 1856, WP, NYSL; Glisan, *Journal,* 319–21; *San Francisco Herald,* May 4, 1856.

47. Wool to Thomas, June 17, 1856, and Buchanan to Floyd-Jones, May 1, 1856, WP, NYSL; Cram, *Topographical Memoir,* 50–51; Glisan, *Journal,* 324, 328; Beckham, *Requiem,* 185–86.

48. Wool to Thomas, June 17, 1856, WP, NYSL; Cram, *Topographical Memoir,* 52–53; Beckham, *Requiem,* 186–87.

49. Wool to Thomas, June 17, 1856, WP, NYSL; Wool to Seward, July 4, 1856, Seward Papers, University of Rochester; Cram, *Topographical Memoir,* 53; Glisan, *Journal,* 342–49; Beckham, *Requiem,* 187–89.

50. Wright to Wool, May 1, 6, 8, 9, 1856, WP, NYSL; Richards, *Stevens,* 293–94.

51. Wright to Wool, May 9, 1856, WP, NYSL; Wool to Samuel Cooper, June 3, 1856, in "Indian Hostilities," HED 118, 34-1, 54.

52. Wright to Wool, June 11, 20, 25, 1856, WP, NYSL; Cram, *Topographical Memoir,* 113; Richards, *Stevens,* 294–95.

53. Wright to Floyd-Jones, July 7, 9, 1856, and Wright to Mackall, July 18 (2 letters), 25, 27, 1856, WP, NYSL.

54. Mackall to Wright, August 2, 1856, WP, NYSL; *Oregon Statesman,* September 9, 1856, published Wool's closure order (dated August 20); N[ewman] S. Clarke to Thomas, June 29, 1857, in "Indian Affairs in Oregon and Washington Territories, May 10, 1858," in HED 112, 35-1, Serial 958, 2; Wool to Wright, April 24, 1856, WP, NYSL. Also, Ball, *Army Regulars on the Western Frontier,* 64–65,

55. Wright to Mackall, August 17, 19, 1856, WP, NYSL; Richards, *Stevens,* 302–3.

56. Steptoe to Wright, November 20, 1856, WP, NYSL; Cram, *Topographical Memoir,* 115–16; Josephy, *Nez Perce,* 373–74; Richards, *Stevens,* 303–4.

57. Steptoe to Wright, November 20, 1856, WP, NYSL; Cram, *Topographical Memoir,* 116; Richards, *Stevens,* 304–6; Josephy, *Nez Perce,* 374–76.

58. Mackall to Wright, October 19, 1856, WP, NYSL; Josephy, *Nez Perce,* 377.

59. Wright to Wool, October 31, 1856, WP, NYSL; Cram, *Topographical Memoir,* 117–18.

60. Mackall to Wright, October 19, 1856, WP, NYSL.

61. Wright to Mackhall, November 15, 1856, WP, NYSL.

62. *Washington Intelligencer,* May 3, 1856; *New York Herald,* May 6, 1856; *New York Tribune,* March 31, 1856; *Baltimore Republican,* May 11, 1856; Wool to Townsend, May 30, June 18, 1856, and Wool to Stewart [October 8], 1856, WP, NYSL.

63. Wool to Seward, July 4, 1856, Seward Papers, University of Rochester; SO 68, July 16, 1856, Benecia, Department of the Pacific; Wool to Russell Sage, July 3, 1856, and Wool to Stewart, July 4, 1856, WP, NYSL; Hendricksen, *Lane,* 129–30.

64. Wool to Sage, September 3, 1856, WP, NYSL; *Oregon Statesman,* September 30, October 14, 1856; Hendricksen, *Lane,* 130; Richards, *Stevens,* 333–35, 342. In 1861, Congress approved claims for Oregon and Washington for $2,714,808.55.

65. Casey to Wool, August 15, 1856, WP, NYSL; GO 7 (Stevens), October 30, 1856, Isaac I. Stevens, in *Message of the Governor of Washington Territory* (Olympia, WA: Edward Furst, 1857), 47–48; Spaid, "Palmer," 243; Richards, *Stevens,* 330.

66. Mackall to Cross, July 19, 1856, and Mackall to Casey, Aug 2, 1856, WP, NYSL.

67. Wool to Thomas, November 1, 1856, WP, NYSL; Bischoff, "Yakima War," 13, 305; Robert Newell to Arnold, January 16, February 1, 1857, WP, NYSL; Wool to Brouillet, October 20, 1856, J. B. A. Brouillet File, Archdiocese of Seattle Archives, Seattle, Washington.

68. Stevens to McClelland, October 22, 1856, in *Papers of the Governor,* 59–60; Clarke to Thomas, June 29, 1857, in "Indian Affairs," HED 112, 35-1, 2–3; Richards, *Stevens,* 307.

69. *San Francisco Sun,* cited in *Oregon Statesman,* Sept 23, 1856; *Oregon City Times* [n.d.] quoted in *San Francisco Herald,* October 1, 1856.

70. Wool to Stewart [October 8], 1856, WP, NYSL.

71. Wool to Cooper, December 4, 1856, in "Correspondence," HED 88, 35-1, 207–8. In November 1856, General Scott pressed for Wool's reassignment, but Secretary of War Davis ignored the request. Townsend to Sarah Wool, December 10, 1856, WP, NYSL. Wool's last week in Benecia was fraught with problems caused by an earthquake on January 9–10, which destroyed part of Fort Tejon. Beall to Wool, January 8, 1857, WP, NYSL.

72. Miscellaneous newspaper clippings, n.d., WP, NYSL. The clipping from the *San Francisco Evening Post* announcing the commissioning of a portrait is dated Thursday, May 24, [1855]. Also, *Journal of the Sixth Session of the Legislature of the State of California* (Sacramento, CA: B. B. Redding, 1855), 293–94, 726–27; Koren Benoit to Jerry Thompson, February 5, 6, 2019, email in author's files.

73. GO 2, February 19, 1857, Benecia, Department of the Pacific, WP, NYSL; *Alta California,* February 20, 1857.

CHAPTER 13. RUSHING TO THE COLORS

1. W. A. Swanberg, *First Blood: The Story of Fort Sumter* (New York: Charles Scribner's Sons, 1957), 320; Allan Nevins, *The War for the Union,* 4 vols. (New York: Charles Scribner's Sons, 1959–71), 1:88–89.

2. "Report of the SW, December 3, 1860," SED 1, 36-2, Serial 1079, 189–226; Wool to Sarah Wool, April 22, 1857, and April 11, 1858, WP, NYSL.

3. *The New York Military Gazette,* March 1, 1859, 66; *Troy Arena,* September 19, 1860; Wool to Dawson, May 16, 1860, Mss., NYHS; Wool to Dawson, May 21, 1860, ChiHS; Wool to Dawson, September 5, 1859, and Wool to Sarah Wool, Apr 11, 1858, WP, NYSL; Wool to Lossing, April 24, 1860, NYPL; *New York Times,* July 7, 9, 1857; Savage, *Our Living Representative Men,* 493–503.

4. Miscellaneous newspaper clipping, August 24, 1859, NP, NYSL.

5. Wool to Hardie, April 5, May 4, 1857, James A. Hardie Papers, LC; Wool to John Griswold, January 22, 1856, WP, NYSL. Jefferson Davis's recollections of army pay, February 15,

1859, are in Davis, *Jefferson Davis,* 3:540–53. In 1856, Wool believed that Davis was dragging his feet in approving extra pay and allowances promised for his duty in California as a brevet major general. In 1859, as a regular brigadier, Wool drew over $8,000 per year, an amount larger than that of a cabinet member or the chief justice of the U.S. Supreme Court.

6. Wool to John B. Floyd, May 20, June 6, 1857, and Floyd to Wool, May 30, 1857, WP, NYSL; Davis-Wool correspondence, in *New York Times,* July 23, 1857; *New York Herald,* December 7, 1857, and *Washington Intelligencer,* June 17, 1857; Brown, *Agents,* 409–12.

7. *Troy Whig,* June 24, 1857; *New York Times,* July 23, December 23, 1857; *New York Herald,* December 7, 1857. Wool also resented that his January 29, 1855, reply to Davis's censuring letter (December 13, 1854) was omitted from the Davis-Wool correspondence, published in "Instructions and Correspondence between the Government and Major General Wool . . . January 3, 1855," SED 16, 33-2, Serial 751. He asked Representative Abraham B. Olin (from Troy) to see if the president would allow the letter to be published as a separate government document. Olin had no luck (Wool to Abraham B. Olin, Dec 16, 1857, WP, NYSL).

8. Wool to Hardie, April 5, 1857, Hardie Papers, LC. Wool to Olin, December [n.d.], 1859, WP, NYSL; Richards, *Stevens,* 333–35.

9. Wool to Curtis, June 7, 1858, Curtis Papers, Bancroft Library, University of California, Berkeley; Wool to Olin, February 4, April 23, 1858, December [n.d.], 1859, and March 24, June 8, 1860, WP, NYSL; Cram, *Topographical Memoir,* 113. At Wool's order, Cram, on June 20, 1855, started the memoir, drawing heavily on departmental orders and correspondence. The Indian war debts bill finally passed in 1861, providing $2,714,808. Richards, *Stevens,* 336–42; Hendricksen, *Lane,* 178, 201, 245. Payment was slow. See "Report . . . in Relation to the Indian war claims in Oregon and Washington Territories, May 2, 1862," SED 46, 37-2, Serial 1122, 1, 2, 11.

10. Wool to William Baylies, January 20, 1860, Baylies Papers, OCHS.

11. Wool to James H. Hammond, April 27, 1860, James H. Hammond Papers, LC.

12. Wool to Combs, November 23, 1860, WP, NYSL.

13. Wool to Cass, December 6, 1860, Cass Papers, UMi.

14. *San Francisco Evening Bulletin,* January 25, 1861, cites news from the *New York Herald* and the *New York Tribune. Boston Atlas,* undated, cited in Frank Moore, ed., *Rebellion Record,* vol. 1, *Poetry* (New York: Arno Press, 1977), 20.

15. Wool to Olin, December 10, 1860, in *Albany Evening Journal,* January 14, 1861; Wool to D. T. Vail, December 17, 1860, WP, NYSL.

16. Cass reply, December 20, 1860, Cass Papers, UMi; Woodford, *Lewis Cass,* 325–29.

17. Wool to Lincoln, January 11, 1861, Robert T. Lincoln Papers, LC. Wool regularly wrote to old friends.

18. Lincoln to Wool, January 14, 1861, in Abraham Lincoln, *Collected Works of Abraham Lincoln,* ed. Roy P. Basler, 9 vols. (New Brunswick, NJ: Rutgers University Press, 1953–55) 4:175.

19. Wool to Thomas, February 2, 1861, in *The War of the Rebellion: A Compilation of the Official Records of the Rebellion* [hereafter referred to as *OR* and cited by series, volume, and part], 128 vols. (Washington, DC: Government Printing Office, 1888–89), I, 51, Pt. 1, 313.

Information on Wool is derived from his letters to Sarah Wool, August 1861-December 1862, WP, NYSL. LeGrand B. Cannon, *Personal Reminiscences of the Rebellion, 1861–1866* (Freeport, NY: Books for Libraries Press, 1971), and *Troy Times,* November 11, 1869; Elliott, *Scott* 2:695.

20. William W. Hoppin Jr., *Peace Conference of 1861 at Washington, D.C.* (Providence, RI: Standard Printing Co., 1891). Hoppin provides an eyewitness account of the proceedings. Robert G. Gunderson, "The Washington Peace Conference of 1861: Selection of Delegates," *Journal of Southern History* 24 (August 1958): 347, 353, and Robert T. Gunderson, *Old Gentlemen's Convention: The Washington Peace Conference of 1861* (Madison: University of Wisconsin Press, 1961), preface, 3–6, 10, 12, 105.

21. Wool to Sarah Wool, February 13, 1861, WP, NYSL; Lucius E. Crittenden, *A Report of the Debates and Proceedings in the Secret Sessions of the Conference Convention for Proposing Amendments* (New York: D. Appleton and Co., 1864), 9–28; Gunderson, *Old Gentlemen's Convention,* 43–50, 54–55.

22. Wool to Sarah Wool, February 11, 13, 1861, WP, NYSL.

23. Wool to Sarah Wool, February 16, 1861, WP, NYSL.

24. Wool to Sarah Wool, February 21–23, 1861, WP, NYSL; Gunderson, *Old Gentlemen's Convention,* 58; Benjamin F. Cooling, *Symbol, Sword, and Shield: Defending Washington during the Civil War* (New York: Archon Books, 1975), 25.

25. Wool to Sarah Wool, February 26–27, 1861, WP, NYSL; Gunderson, *Old Gentlemen's Convention,* 85–88.

26. Wool to Sarah Wool, February 27, March 1, 1861, WP, NYSL; Gunderson, *Old Gentlemen's Convention,* 89–91, 93–95. On March 3, the Senate voted 28 to 7 to kill the Crittenden proposal.

27. Keyes to Wool, March 5, 1861, and Wool to Sarah Wool, February 27, 1861, WP, NYSL; Washington *Intelligencer,* March 5, 1861; Albert Gallatin Riddle, *Recollections of War Times; Reminiscences of Men and Events in Washington, 1860–1865* (New York: G. P. Putnam Sons, 1895), 11, 13–15; Margaret Leach, *Reveille in Washington* (New York: Harper and Brothers, 1941), 41–44.

28. Cannon, *Reminiscences,* 21; Nevins, *War for the Union* 1:17, 28, 30–31; Arthur P. Wade, "Roads to the Top—An Analysis of General Officer Selection in the United States Army, 1789–1898," *Military Affairs* 40 (December 1976): 160; Coffman, *Old Army,* 95–97. For example, former Wool aide Eugene E. McLean, Assistant Quartermaster, resigned April 25, 1861, to join the Confederacy. Heitman, *Historical Register* 1:675.

29. Wool to Henry Wilson, March 14, 1861, WP, NYSL; Elliot, *Scott,* 701–4.

30. Thian, comp., *Notes,* 59; Nevins, *War for the Union* 1:59–60, 65, 78–79; Cooling, *Symbol,* 31–32.

31. Lucius E. Crittenden, *Recollections of President Lincoln and his Administration* (New York: Harpers Brothers, 1891), 107; Rawley, *Morgan,* 134–35; Swanberg, *First Blood,* 320.

32. *New York Times,* April 17, 1861; *Troy Weekly Times,* November 9, 1872; Weise, *History of Troy,* 229–30; Benson J. Lossing, *Pictorial History of the Civil War,* 3 vols. (Philadelphia: G. W. Childs, 1866–68), 1:357.

33. [Simon Cameron] to Edward D. Morgan, April 15, 1861 (tel.), Edward D. Morgan Papers, NYSL; Rawley, *Morgan,* 134–35.

34. James S. Wadsworth to Wool, April 19, 1861 (tel.), WP, NYSL; Nevins, *War for the Union* 1:80–83, 87. Thian, comp., *Notes,* 59, indicates that Wool's formal command of the Department of the East ended on April 9, 1861.

35. George D. Morgan to E. D. Morgan, (2 tel.), Simon Draper to E. D. Morgan, (tel.), Cameron to Gilbert C. Davidson, Wool to A. B. Eaton (commissary), and Daniel D. Tompkins (quartermaster), all April 20, 1861, Morgan Papers, NYSL; Wool to Scott, April 23, 1861, *OR* III, 1, 106; *Union Defence Committee of the City of New York* (New York: Union Defence Committee, 1885), 9; Rawley, *Morgan,* 136, 139–41.

36. Wool to Springfield armory (Massachusetts), Kennebec arsenal (Maine), and to Chief, Clothing Department (Philadelphia), tel., all on April 21, 1861; Superintendent, Springfield Armory to Wool, C. Thomas (Philadelphia) to Wool, April 21, 1861, and Eaton to Wool, April 20, 1861 (tel.), WP, NYSL; Wool to Scott, April 23, 1861, *OR* III, 1, 106; Wool to E. D. Morgan, April 21, 1861, Morgan Papers, NYSL; *Union Defence Committee,* 3–8; Ernest A. McKay, *The Civil War and New York City* (Syracuse, NY: Syracuse University Press, 1990), 62–64.

37. Thurlow Weed to Wool (tel.), April 21, 22, 1861, Andrew Curtin to Wool, Wool to Watervliet arsenal, William Dennison to Wool, and Wool to Commanding Officer, Watertown arsenal, all on April 22, 1861, WP, NYSL; Wool to Scott, April 23, 1861, *OR,* III, 1, 106; *Troy Times,* July 27, 1861; Nevins, *War for the Union* 1:80; Glydon G. Van Deusen, *Thurlow Weed: Wizard of the Lobby* (Boston: Little, Brown, and Co., 1947), 81, 213–14.

38. Wool to Scott, April 23, 25, 1861, *OR* III, 1, 106, 114; and Wool to Cameron, May 9, 1861, ibid., III 1, 179; William B. Hesseltine, *Lincoln and the War Governors* (New York: Alfred A. Knopf, 1948), 156.

39. Cannon, *Reminiscences,* 14–16; *Union Defence Committee,* 3–4, 10–11, 57–66; Glyndon G. Van Deusen, *William Henry Seward* (New York: Oxford University Press, 1967), 58, 222, 288.

40. Wool to Cameron, May 9, 1861, *OR* III, 1, 179; Dix to Wool, April 23, 1861, WP, NYSL; Lincoln to Senate and House, May 26, 1862, in Lincoln, *Works* 5:241–42; "Report on Government Contracts, December 17, 1861," House Report 2, 37-2, Ser. 1142, Pt. 1, 55–58; *Troy Times,* July 27, 1861.

41. Wool to Cameron, May 9, 1861, *OR* III, 1, 179; Cameron to Wool, May 10, 1861, WP, NYSL; William M. Robinson Jr., *The Confederate Privateers* (New Haven, CT: Yale University Press, 1928), 304.

42. Wool to Scott, April 23, 1861, *OR* III, 1, 106; *Troy Times,* July 27, 1861; Van Deusen, *Weed,* 249, 251, 284.

43. Wool to William P. Jones, January 31, 1865, WP, NYSL; *Troy Whig,* November 1, 1872; Cannon, *Reminiscences,* 17, 21, 201, 215, 218; Heitman, *Historical Register* 1:280, 492–93, 571, 583.

44. Samuel M. Felton to William Sprague, April 23, 1861, WP, NYSL; Wool to Scott, April 25, 1861, *OR* III, 1, 114; *Troy Times,* July 27, 1861; Samuel L. Breese to Gideon Welles,

April 24, 1861, in *Official Records of the Union and Confederate Navies in the War of the Rebellion* [*ORN*], 30 vols. (Washington, DC: Government Printing Office, 1894–1922), I, 4, 321; *Union Defence Committee,* 17–18, 124; Robinson, *Confederate Privateers,* 304.

45. Wool to Scott, April 25, 1861, *OR* III, 1, 114; and Wool to Cameron, May 9, 1861, ibid., III, 1, 179; *Union Defence Committee,* 18, 138–39; Robinson, *Confederate Privateers,* 304–6.

46. Wool to Scott, April 25, 1861, *OR* III, 1, 114, and Wool to Cameron, May 9, 1861, ibid., III, 1, 179; *Troy Times,* April 27, July 27, 1861.

47. Seward to Draper, April 29, 1861, Tompkins to Wool, April 25, 1861, Cameron to Wool, April 29, 1861, Military Storekeeper, Springfield, to Wool, April 29, 1861, and Richard Yates to Wool, April 29, 1861, (all tels.) WP, NYSL; Wool to Assistant Adjutant General, May 3, 1861, *OR* III, 1, 146.

48. *Troy Times,* July 27, 1861; Ruth P. Randall, *Colonel Elmer Ellsworth* (Boston: Little, Brown and Co., 1960), 232–36.

49. *Troy Times,* July 27, 1861; *Union Defence Committee,* 21–22, 69, 153–56.

50. Townsend to Wool, April 28, 1861, *OR,* III, 1, 134; and Wool to Townsend, May 3, 1861 in ibid., III, 1, 1466; *Troy Times,* July 27, 1861; *Union Defence Committee,* 21.

51. May 3, 1861, in George Templeton Strong, *The Diary of George Templeton Strong,* eds. Allan Nevins and Milton H. Thomas, 4 vols. (New York: Macmillan, 1952) 3:139; H. Draper Hunt, *Hannibal Hamlin of Maine* (Syracuse, NY: Syracuse University Press, 1969), 152.

52. Wool to Cannon, May 4, 1861, in Cannon, *Reminiscences,* 23; Jones to Wool, May 8, 1861, WP, NYSL; Galusha A. Grow to Cameron, May 5, 1861, *OR* III, 1, 160, and Cameron to Wool, May 6, 1861, ibid., III, 1, 161.

53. Cannon to Wool, May 14, 1861, and Jones to Wool, May 15, 25, June 2, 7, 1861, WP, NYSL; *Troy Times,* July 27, 1861.

54. Jones to Arnold, June 20, 1861, and George Schuyler to Wool, July 4, 1861, WP, NYSL.

55. Cannon to Wool, July 8, 13, 1861, WP, NYSL; Wool to Cannon, July 10, 1861, in Cannon, *Reminiscences,* 24; Hunt, *Hamlin.*

56. *Washington National Republican,* cited in Schuyler to Wool, July 16, 1861, WP, NYSL; *New York Times,* July 26, 1861; *Troy Times,* July 27, 1861; *San Francisco Evening Bulletin,* July 30, 1861.

57. *New York Times,* August 1, 1861; *San Francisco Evening Bulletin,* August 12, 1861; E. D. Morgan to Lincoln, August 5, 1861, in Lincoln, *Works* 4:478n, and Lincoln to Scott, August 7, 1861, *Works,* 4:478; Nevins, *War for the Union* 1:211–12, 217–18, 224–26.

58. Scott to Wool, and Wool to Scott, August 8, 1861, WP, NYSL; Mrs. W. C. Rives to daughter, May 22, 1861, Rives Papers, Duke University Library; *Leslie's,* August 15, 1861, 234.

CHAPTER 14. EPAULETTED GRANNIES AND THE CONCEITED GOOSE

1. Henry L. Graves, *A Confederate Marine: A Sketch of Henry Lea Graves with Excerpts from the Graves Family Correspondence,* ed. Richard Harwell (Tuscaloosa, AL: Confederate Publishing Co., 1963), 35–36.

2. *Leslie's,* April 13, 1861, 328; July 14, 1861, in William H. Russell, *My Diary North and South,* 2 vols. (Boston: T. O. H. P. Hurnham, 1863), 2:161, 165; Lossing, *Civil War* 1:499; Weinert and Arthur, *Defender,* 27–29, 102.

3. July 14, 1861, in Russell, *My Diary* 2:162; Wool to Sarah Wool, August 17, 18, 1861, WP, NYSL; Richard S. West, *Lincoln's Scapegoat General: A Life of Benjamin F. Butler, 1818–1893* (Boston: Houghton Mifflin, 1965), 106; and Weinert and Arthur, *Defender,* 75–78, 97.

4. July 14, 1861, in Russell, *My Diary* 2:160, 167; Benjamin F. Butler to F[ranklin] Scott, August 13, 16, 1861, *OR* I, 51–1, 447–48, and 449–50, respectively; West, *Scapegoat General,* 101; Howard P. Nash Jr., *Stormy Petrel: The Life and Times of General Benjamin F. Butler, 1818–1893* (Rutherford, NJ: Fairleigh Dickinson University Press, 1969), 118; and Weinert and Arthur, *Defender,* 29–30, 90–93.

5. "Report of the SW, July 1, 1861," SED 1, 37-1, Serial 1112, 56–57; Weinert and Arthur, *Defender,* 87–88, 104–5.

6. SO 9, August 21, 1861, and GO 4, August 24, 1861, Fort Monroe, Department of Virginia, *OR* I, 4, 602–3; Wool to Sarah Wool, August 24, 1861, WP, NYSL.

7. Townsend to Wool, August 13, 21, 1861, *ORN* I, 6, 82, 106; Wool to Scott, August 24, 1861, *OR* I, 4, 602; Richard S. West, *Mr. Lincoln's Navy* (New York: Longmans, Green and Co., 1957), 75–76; James M. Merrill, *The Rebel Shore: The Story of Union Sea Power in the Civil War* (Boston: Little, Brown and Co., 1957), 17–18; Lossing, *Civil War* 2:105.

8. SO 13, August 25, 1861, Fort Monroe, Department of Virginia, *ORN,* I, 6, 112; Rush C. Hawkins, "Early Coast Operations in North Carolina," in Robert U. Johnson and Clarence C. Buel, eds., *Battles and Leaders of the Civil War,* 4 vols., (New York: Thomas Yoseloff, 1956), 1:632, 633n; Lossing, *Civil War* 2:105.

9. Wool to Sarah Wool, August 31, 1861, WP, NYSL; Wool to Scott, September 2, 1861, *OR* I, 4, 580–81; Lossing, *Civil War* 2:106; Nash, *Stormy Petrel,* 118–23.

10. Wool to Cameron, September 3, 1861, *OR* I, 4, 604; Townsend to Wool, September 4, 1861, ibid., I, 4, 606; Wool to Rush C. Hawkins, September 10, 1861, ibid., I, 4, 605; Wool to Scott, September 13, 1861, ibid., I, 4, 607, and Mansfield to Scott, October 14, 1861, ibid., I, 4, 626–27; Hawkins, "Early Coast Operations," in Johnson and Buel, eds., *Battles and Leaders* 1:635–40. Rowena Reed, *Combined Operations in the Civil War* (Annapolis, MD: Naval Institute Press, 1978), 12–19, regards the Hatteras Expedition as a tactical failure. Lincoln felt holding Hatteras would interfere with his blockade policy. E[varette] B. Long, *The Civil War Day by Day: An Almanac, 1861–1865* (Garden City, NJ: Doubleday and Co., 1971), 123.

11. Wool to Cameron, September 22, 1861, *OR* I, 4, 616, and Wool to Scott, August 24, 1861, ibid., I, 4, 602–3. Wool to Seward, October 28, 1861, Seward Papers, Univeristy of Rochester; Wool to Thomas, December 21, 1861, in "Names and Numbers of Major Generals [and] . . . officers and soldiers to their staff," SED 33, 37-2, 5; Heitman, *Historical Register* 1:280, 301, 335, 819; Baron Ernest Von Vegesack, a Swede, served as a volunteer aide on Wool's staff, and later as a field commander under McClellan (ibid., 1:989–90).

12. Wool to Sarah Wool, August 27, September 10, 30, 1861, WP, NYSL.

13. Wool to Seward, November 1, 27, 1861, Seward Papers, University of Rochester; Benjamin Huger to Wool, November 9, 1861, *OR* II, 3, 130; William D. Whipple to Huger, November 29, 1861, *OR* II, 3, 149, and Thomas A. Scott to Wool, December 24, 1861, *OR* II, 3, 169; Cannon, *Reminiscences,* 120–24.

14. Ellen Jettison to Wool, December 12, 1861, Charles Carter to Wool, December 19, 1861, Ella C. Weimar to Wool, December 10, 1861, James N. Cameron to Wool, December 11, 1861, Diana Jordan to Wool, December 16, 1861, and Winfield Scott to Wool, September 11, 1861, all in WP, NYSL.

15. Wool to Seward, October 10, 1861, Seward Papers, University of Rochester; Cannon, *Reminiscences,* 126–35; Welles to Louis Goldsborough, October 9, 1861; *ORN* I, 6, 300–1.

16. Wool to Sarah Wool, October 7, 9, 1861, WP, NYSL; *San Francisco Evening Bulletin,* October 9, 14, 15, 1861.

17. Wool to Sarah Wool, October 15, 21, 1861, WP, NYSL; Long, *Civil War,* 134.

18. Wool to Corning, December 11, 1861, Erastus Corning Papers, Brown University, Providence, RI; Wool to Welles, September 4, 1861, *ORN* I, 6, 168; *Leslie's,* April 13, July 20, and August 31, 1861, 328, 147, 247; July 14, 1861, in Russell, *My Diary* 2:166–67, 170, 174, 178; Weinert and Arthur, *Defender,* 89, 97–101; Lossing, *Civil War* 1:502.

19. William H. Stiner to Wife, December 14, 1861, Misc. Stiner Papers, NYHS; Thomas J. Cram to Stephen H. Long, June 20, 1861 to October [n.d.], 1862, Letters Received, Topographical Bureau [LRTB], Office of the Chief of Engineers, Microcopy 506, Roll 17 (January 1860–October 1865), NA; *Leslie's,* April 13, 1861, 246; *San Francisco Evening Bulletin,* October 5, 1861.

20. Wool to Scott, October 6, 1861, *OR* I, 4, 620–21. Quote is from *Troy Whig,* November 1, 1872, which also describes the arrangements to build the *Monitor.* John Niven, *Gideon Welles: Lincoln's Secretary of the Navy* (New York: Oxford University Press, 1973), 365–69; William C. Church, *The Life of John Ericsson,* 2 vols. (New York: Charles Scribner's Sons, 1890), 1: 242–59; Neu, *Corning,* 53–55; William N. Still, *Monitor Builders: A Historical Study of the Principal Firms and Individuals Involved in the Construction of the USS Monitor* (Washington, DC: National Park Service, 1988).

21. Lincoln to George B. McClellan, November 1, 1861, in Lincoln, *Works* 5:9–10; Wool to Sarah Wool, October [November] 4, November 5, 13, 1861, and Mrs. T. J. Cram, "A Nation's Ingratitude," (poem), December [November] 5, 1861, WP, NYSL.

22. Ira Harris to Lincoln, November 1, 1861, John Jay to Lincoln, November 2, 1861, and Lincoln to McClellan, November 1, 1861, all in Lincoln, *Works* 5:9–10; McClellan to Wool, November 6, 1861, *OR* I, 4, 628.

23. July 14, 1861, in Russell, *My Diary* 2:173–74; Tinsley L. Spraggins, "Mobilization of Negro Labor for the Department of Virginia and North Carolina, 1861–1865," *North Carolina Historical Review* 24 (April 1947): 161, 163, 177–78, 181; Benjamin Quarles, *The Negro in the Civil War* (Boston: Little, Brown, 1953), 61, 94; Fred Shannon, "The Federal Government and the Negro Soldier, 1861–1865," *Journal of Negro History* 11 (October 1926): 567; Louis S. Gerteis, *From Contraband to Freedman: Federal Policy toward Southern Blacks, 1861–65* (Westport, CT: Greenwood Press, 1973), 11–19.

24. Wool to Cameron, September 18, 1861, *OR* II, 1, 770–71; Cameron to Wool, September 20, 1861, ibid., II, 1, 771, and T. A. Scott to Wool, October 5, 1861, ibid., I, 6, 175; Quarles, *Negro in the Civil War,* 61; Oliver Otis Howard, *Autobiography of Oliver Otis Howard,* 2 vols. (New York: Baker and Taylor Co., 1907), 2:174–75.

25. SO 72, October 14, 1861, and GO 34, November 1, 1861, both at Fort Monroe, Department of Virginia, *OR* II, 1, 774–75; Cannon, *Reminiscences,* 54–57; Shannon, "Negro Soldier," *Journal of Negro History* 11: 581; Gerteis, *Contraband,* 19–20.

26. Cannon, *Reminiscences,* 48–53.

27. Cram to Wool, March 20, 1862, in "Africans in Fort Monroe Military District . . . , March 25, 1862," HED 85, 37-2, Serial 1135, 3–14; Wool to Edwin M. Stanton, March 22, 1862, *OR* II, 1, 812; Cannon, *Reminiscences,* 55–73. Wool to Sarah Wool, April 20, 1862, WP, NYSL; Gerteis, *Contraband,* 20–21.

28. [William H. Stiner], "Description of Character of Brevet Major General John E. Wool in the War of the Rebellion," [Summer 1862], Misc. Stiner, NYHS. Also, Charles W. Cowtan, *Services of the Tenth New York Volunteers (National Zouaves),* (New York: Charles H. Ludwig, 1882), 54–57.

29. Wool to Cameron, October 28, 1861, *OR* I, 6, 184; Samuel F. Dupont to Gustavus Fox, October 28, 1861, in Gustavus Vasa Fox, *Confidential Correspondence of Gustavus Vasa Fox: Assistant Secretary of the Navy, 1861–1865,* eds. Robert M. Thompson and Richard Wainwright, 2 vols. (New York: Naval History Society, 1920) 1:62–64; West, *Mr. Lincoln's Navy,* 83; Lossing, *Civil War* 2:115–16.

30. Wool to Sarah Wool, December 3, 16, 1861, WP, NYSL; Cowtan, *Tenth New York,* 55–56.

31. Wool to L. W. Kennedy, December 16, 1861, ChiHS; Wool to Sarah Wool, December 22, 1861, and Wool to Harriette Hart, December 29, 1861, WP, NYSL.

32. John G. Nicolay and John Hay, *Abraham Lincoln: A History,* 10 vols. (New York: Century Co., 1890), 7:447–48; Judah P. Benjamin to Davis, March 17, 1862, *OR* II, 3, 820, and Benjamin to John H. Winder, November 10, 1861, *OR* II, 3, 131–32; William F. Keeler, *Aboard the USS Monitor, 1862: The Letters of Acting Paymaster William Frederick Keeler, U. S. Navy, to His Wife Ann,* ed. Robert W. Daly (Annapolis, MD: United States Naval Institute, 1964), 144n.

33. Seward to McClellan, January 13, 1862, *OR* II, 3, 191–92; Huger to Wool, January 18, 27, February 9, 1862, ibid., II, 3, 197, 217, 248, C. P. Daly to Stanton, February 16, 1862, ibid., II, 3, 265, and Wool to Huger, February 4, 1862, ibid., II, 3, 235; Nicolay and Hay, *Lincoln* 7: 449.

34. [Stanton] to Wool, February 11, 1862, draft, Seward Papers, University of Rochester. Seward apparently drafted the February 11 instructions to Wool and Stanton sent them. Wool to Huger, February 13, 21, 1862, *OR* II, 3, 259–60, 296, and Wool to Stanton, February 24, 1862, *OR* II, 3, 310; Howell Cobb to Wife, February 25, 1862, in Ulrich B. Phillips, ed., "The Correspondence of Robert Toombs, Alexander H. Stephens, and Howell Cobb," in American Historical Association *Annual Report for 1911,* 2 vols. (Washington, DC: American Historical Society, 1913) 2:589; William F. Keeler to Ann, April 29, 1862, in Keeler, *USS Monitor,* 91;

Cannon, *Reminiscences,* 116–18; Horace Montgomery, *Howell Cobb's Confederate Career* (Tuscaloosa, AL: Confederate Publishing Co., 1959), 14.

35. Wool to Stanton, February 23, 1862, *OR* II, 3, 301–302, and Stanton to Wool, February 26, 1862, ibid., II, 3, 322; Nicolay and Hay, *Lincoln* 7:449–50.

36. Wool to Stanton, March 2, 1862, *OR* II, 3, 341; Stanton to Wool, February 26, 1862, ibid., II, 3, 322; Wool to Cobb, March 5, 1862, ibid., II, 3, 347–48; Cobb to Benjamin, March 4, 1862, ibid., II, 3, 812–13, and Wool to Huger, March 24, 1862, ibid., II, 3, 402; Wool to Sarah Wool, March 1, 1862, WP, NYSL; Nicolay and Hay, *Lincoln* 7:450–51.

37. Wool to Scott, October 6, 1861, *OR* I, 4, 620, and Charles C. Fulton to Fox, February 16, 1862, *ORN* I, 6, 650; David H. Bates, *Lincoln in the Telegraph Office* (New York: Century Co., 1907), 115–17; Weinert and Arthur, *Defender,* 125–26.

38. Thomas Cram, "Military Memoir on Taking Norfolk and Richmond, November 28, 1862," LRTB M-506, Roll 17; Thomas C. Selfridge to Fox, November 11, 1862, in Fox, *Correspondence* 1:397–99, and Goldsborough to Fox, February 23, 1862, ibid. 1: 243–44; Wool to Scott, August 24, 1861, *OR* I, 4, 602; Wool to U[lysses] S. Grant, July 10, 1865, WP, NYSL; July 14, 1861, in Russell, *My Diary* 2:177–78; Nevins, *War for the Union* 1:303, 371–72; Lossing, *Civil War* 1:502; Cobb to Wife, February 22, 1862, in Phillips, ed., "Correspondence," American Historical Association *Report for 1911* 2: 588.

39. Lossing, *Civil War* 2:354–56; Nevins, *War for the Union* 1:404–7 and 2:41–42.

40. Wool to Grant, July 10, 1865, WP, NYSL; Cram, "Norfolk," LRTB, M-506, Roll 17; Barnard to Fox, Feb 12, 1862, in Fox, *Correspondence* 1:419–22.

41. Jones to McClellan, February 20, 1862, in Fox, *Correspondence* 1:427–28; Wool to McClellan, February 22, 1862, WP, NYSL. Stanton to Wool, February 22, 1862, *OR* I, 9, 16, and Wool to Stanton, February 23, 1862, *OR* I, 9, 17: Cannon, *Reminiscences,* 76–79. Wool told Stanton that with fifty thousand men he could have taken Richmond at any time during the previous three months.

42. T. G. Baylor to J[ames] W. Ripley, March 11, 1862, *ORN* I, 7, 93; Cram, "Norfolk," LRTB, M-506, roll 17; Cannon, *Reminiscences,* 83–86, 100; Weinert and Arthur, *Defender,* 94.

43. Wool to Stanton, February 28, 1862, *ORN* I, 6, 676–77, and Welles to Stanton, March 5, 1862, *ORN* I, 6, 677; Cram, "Norfolk," LRTB, M-506, Roll 17; Keeler to [Anna], March 6, 1862, in Keeler, *USS Monitor,* 6, 7n, 27 (letter).

44. Wool to Mansfield, March 7, 1862, WP; Cram, "Norfolk," LRTB, M- 506, Roll 17; Cannon, *Reminiscences,* 81–82; Stiner's report, in *New York Herald,* Mar. [n.d.], 1862, Misc. Stiner Papers, NYHS; Louis M. Starr, *Bohemian Brigade: Civil War Newsmen in Action* (New York: Alfred A. Knopf, 1954), 91; John E. O'Brien, *Telegraphing in Battle* (Scranton, PA: Raeder Press, 1910), 92.

45. Mansfield to Wool, March 8, 1862 (8 tel.), *ORN* I, 7, 3–4; Cram, "Norfolk," LRTB, M-506, Roll 17. O'Brien quote, in *Army Times: A History of the U. S. Signal Corps* (New York: G. P. Putnam's Sons, 1961), 23–24; Cannon, *Reminiscences,* 81–82; Adolph A. Hoehling, *Thunder at Hampton Roads* (Englewood Cliffs, NJ: Prentice Hall, 1976), 126.

46. *New York Times,* March 14, 1862, quoted in J. Cutler Andrews, *The North Reports the Civil War* (Pittsburgh: University of Pittsburgh Press, 1955), 227–28.

47. *New York Times,* March 14, 1862, 228; Cannon, *Reminiscences,* 83–85.

48. Mansfield to Wool, March 8, 1852 (4 tel.), and Wool to Stanton, March 9 [8], 1862 (2 disp.), *ORN* I, 7, 4–5. Cannon, *Reminiscences,* 86–87. Keeler to [Anna], March 6, 1862, in Keeler, *USS Monitor,* 31–32, 40. Quote on *Monitor,* in Bates, *Telegraph Office,* 115–17; Hoehling, *Thunder,* 128–30.

49. Cannon, *Reminiscences,* 87–88; Keeler to [Anna], March 6, 1862, in Keeler, *USS Monitor,* 32–33; Weinert and Arthur, *Defender,* 113.

50. Fox to Welles, March 9, 1862 (tel., 6:45 p. m.), in Fox, *Correspondence* 1:434; Keeler to Wife and Children, March 9, 1862, and Keeler to [Anna], March 6, in Keeler, *USS Monitor,* 26, 34–39; Cannon, *Reminiscences,* 88–89. An excellent account of the battle is William C. Davis, *Duel Between the First Ironclads* (Baton Rouge: Louisiana State University Press, 1981).

51. Wool to John Griswold, March 9, 1862, and Wool to Sarah Wool, March 9, 1862, WP, NYSL; Wool to Stanton [and McClellan], March 9, 1862, Robert T. Lincoln Papers, LC; Wool to McClellan, March 9, 1862, *ORN* I, 7, 34.

52. Mansfield to Wool, March 9, 1862, in *ORN* I, 7, 79; Wool to McClellan, March 9, 1862, ibid., I, 7, 34, and McClellan to Wool, March 9, 1862, ibid. I, 7, 74–75; Randolph B. Marcy to Wool, March 9, 1862, ibid., I, 7, 77.

53. Wool to Stanton, March 13, 1862 (tel.), *OR* I, 9, 29; Stanton to Wool, March 18, 1862, ibid. I, 11–3, 13, and Wool to Stanton, March 18, 1862, ibid. I, 11–3, 14; Wool to Sarah Wool, March 21, 1862, Wool to Olin, February 3, 21, 26, 1862, Wool to Corning, February 26, 1862, and Wool to Harris, March 2, 1862, all in WP, NYHS. By GO 3, March 11, 1862, AGO, Washington, DC, *OR* I, 5, 54.

54. Stiner to Wife, March 19, 1862, Misc. Stiner Papers, NYHS; McClellan to Stanton, March 19, 1862, *OR* I, 11–3, 18; Wool to Stanton, March 21, 1862, *OR* I, 11–3, 27–28, and Daniel D. Woodbury to McClellan, March 19, 1862, *OR* I, 11–3, 22; Cram to Long, June 20, 1861 to October [n.d.], 1862, LRTB, M-506, Roll 17. McClellan shuttled 110,000 men, 14,500 animals, and 44 artillery batteries to the Fort Monroe area between March 17 and April 6. James A. Huston, "Logistical Support of Federal Armies in the Field," *Civil War History* 7 (March 1961): 39.

55. Stanton to Wool, March 14, 1862, *OR* I, 9, 31, and William F. Smith to McClellan, March 25, 1862, ibid. I, 11–3, 38; Wool to McClellan, March 26, 1862, WP, NYSL. Stanton to Wool, March 26, 1862, *OR* I, 11–3, 38–39, citing Lincoln's instructions, ordered Wool "to waive exercise of your authority in his [McClellan's] favor pending the expedition." Stiner to Wife, March 19, 1862, Misc. Stiner Papers, NYHS.

56. Samuel Peter Heintzelman Journal, March 24, 1862, Library of Congress, Washington, DC; Jerry Thompson, *Civil War to the Bloody End: The Life and Times of Major General Samuel P. Heintzelman* (College Station: Texas A&M University Press, 2006), 155.

57. Thaddeus S. C. Lowe to Wool, March 13, 1862, *OR* III, 3, 272; Keeler to Wife and Children, March 11, 31, 1862, and Keeler to Anna, March 30, 1862, in Keeler, *USS Monitor,* 48, 65–67; Charles C. Bombaugh, "Extracts from a Journal Kept during the Earlier Campaigns of the Army of the Potomac," *Maryland Historical Magazine* 5 (December 1910): 11; Hunt, *Hamlin,* 167.

58. McClellan to Mary Ellen McClellan, April 3, 1862, in Stephen W. Sears, *The Civil War Papers of George B. McClellan: Selected Correspondence, 1860–1865* (New York: Ticknor and Fields, 1989), 225. Wool to Preston King, et al., April 2, 1862, WP, NYSL. Cannon, *Reminiscences,* 146–51, describes the maneuvering in Washington to arrange the Wool-McClellan meeting. Andrews, *North Reports,* 195. Also, see: Ethan S. Rafuse, *McClellan's War: The Failure of Moderation in the Struggle for the Union* (Bloomington: University of Indiana Press, 2011).

59. Wool to Sarah Wool, April 3, May 27, 1862, Wool to Harriette Hart, April 5, 1862, and Wool to Stanton, April 4, 6, 1862, WP, NYSL; Thomas to McClellan, April 3, 1862, *OR* I, 11–3, 65, and McClellan Report, August 4, 1863, ibid. I, 11–1, 8; Cannon, *Reminiscences,* 151–52; Nevins, *War for the Union* 1:269–73. For a study of McClellan's performance as a general, see Kenneth P. Williams, *Lincoln Finds a General: A Military Study of the Civil War,* 5 vols. (New York: Macmillan, 1950), 1:105, 112–13, 141, 145, 147, 159–65, 230–32, 357–58, and 2:479. Williams, *Lincoln and His Generals,* 25–32, 133,168, 174, 178; Stephen W. Sears, *George B. McClellan: The Young Napoleon* (New York: Ticknor and Fields, 1988).

60. Keyes, *Fifty Years' Observation*, 442; McClellan Report, August 4, 1863, *OR* I, 11–1, 7–10.

61. Wool to Stanton, April 11, 1862, *ORN* I, 7, 219–20; Wool to Peter H. Watson, April 8, 1862; Wool to McClellan, April 23, 27, 1862, WP, NYSL.

62. Wool to Sarah Wool, May 4, 1862, WP, NYSL; Goldsborough to Wool, April 20, 1862, *ORN* I, 7, 251; Keeler to Anna, April 11, 1862, in Keeler, *USS Monitor,* 73–75; John T. Wood, "The First Fight of the Iron-Clads," in Johnson and Buel, eds., *Battles and Leaders* 1:706–7.

63. Stanton to Wool, May 4, 1862, and Wool to Stanton, May 5, 1862, both in *OR* I, 11–3, 130.

64. T[homas] J. Cram, "Upon the Taking of Norfolk, May 10, 1862," WP, NYSL; Mansfield to Wool, May 8, 1862, *ORN* I, 7, 330; *New York Herald,* May 12, 1862; Cannon, *Reminiscences,* 156.

65. T[homas] J. Cram, "Upon the Taking of Norfolk, May 10, 1862," WP, NYSL; Mansfield to Wool, May 8, 1862, *ORN* I, 7, 330; *New York Herald,* May 12, 1862; Cannon, *Reminiscences,* 156.

66. Cram, "Taking of Norfolk," WP, NYSL; S. P. Chase to Janet Chase, May 8, 1862, in Chase, *Lincoln's Cabinet,* 78–79; Keeler to Anna, May 8, 1862, in Keeler, *USS Monitor,* 110–13; Viele, "A Trip," *Scribner's Monthly* 16: 818–19; *New York Herald,* May 12, 1862; Cannon, *Reminiscences,* 155.

67. S. P. Chase to Janet Chase, May 11, 1862, in Chase, *Lincoln's Cabinet,* 80–82; Cram, "Taking of Norfolk," WP, NYSL; Viele, "A Trip," *Scribner's Monthly* 16: 819; Cannon, *Reminiscences,* 158.

68. Cram, "Taking of Norfolk," WP, NYSL; Cannon, *Reminiscences,* 159; *New York Herald,* May 12, 1862; Viele, "A Trip," *Scribner's Monthly* 16: 819, 821. Viele said that Stanton had not included Wool in the expedition. The veteran officer came down to the wharf and pleaded "with much emotion" with the secretary to allow him to command the operation. Stanton

finally agreed, remarking that "he could not inflict sorrow upon gray hairs." This was Wool's last combat experience.

69. S. P. Chase to Janet Chase, May 11, 1862, in Chase, *Lincoln's Cabinet*, 83; Cram, "Taking of Norfolk," WP, NYSL; Viele, "A Trip," *Scribner's Monthly* 16: 820–21.

70. GO 1, May 10, 1862, Norfolk, *OR* I, 51–1, 613; Cram, "Taking of Norfolk," WP, NYSL; S. P. Chase to Janet Chase, May 11, 1862, in Chase, *Lincoln's Cabinet*, 84; Stanton to Watson, May 10, 1862, *OR* I, 11–3, 162–63; Viele, "A Trip," *Scribner's Monthly* 16: 821–22; Lossing, *Civil War* 2:388; Orville J. Victor, *The History, Civil, Political, and Military, of the Southern Rebellion*, 4 vols. (New York: J. D. Torrey, [1861–1868]), 3:171.

71. S. P. Chase to Janet Chase, May 11, 1862, in Chase, *Lincoln's Cabinet*, 84; Cannon, *Reminiscences*, 161–63; Frances F. Browne, *The Everyday Life of Abraham Lincoln* (New York: G. P. Putnam's Sons, 1913), 392.

72. Cram, "Taking of Norfolk," WP, NYSL; Cannon, *Reminiscences*, 163; Keeler to Anna, May 10–11, 1862, in Keeler, *USS Monitor*, 116–21.

73. Stanton to Ambrose Burnside, May 11, 1862, *OR* I, 9, 386; Cram, "Norfolk," LRTB, M-506, Roll 17; Wool to Stanton, May 13, 1862, *OR* I, 11–3, 169, and Burnside to Stanton, May 16, 1862, ibid. I, 9, 388.

74. Watson to Wool, May 16, 1862, *OR* I, 11–1, 635; Stanton to Wool, May 16, 1862, ibid. I, 51–1, 618, and Wool to Stanton, May 17, 1862, ibid. I, 11–1, 635; Wilson to Wool, May 16, 1862, WP, NYSL.

75. Wool to Huger, March 27, April 7, 29, 1862, *OR* II, 3, 407, 430, 504–5; Huger to Wool, April 30, May 27, 1862, ibid. II, 3, 507, 601, and Wool to Stanton, June 1, 2, 6, 1862, ibid. II, 3, 618, 632, 652–53; Huger to Wool, June 5, 1862, in "Exchange of Prisoners of War . . . June 11, 1862," HED 124, 37-2, Serial 1137, 9–10; Keeler to Anna, June 3, 1862, in Keeler, *USS Monitor*, 144–45.

76. Goldsborough to Wool, May 22, 1862, *ORN* I, 7, 421; Wool to Goldsborough, May 22, 24, June 1, 1862, ibid. I, 7, 421, 424, 447, and A. Ludlow Case to Goldsborough, May 26, 1862, ibid. I, 7, 428; Goldsborough to Fox, May 22, 23, June 1, 1862, all in Fox, *Correspondence* 1:274–78; Stanton to Wool, May 24, 1862, *OR* I, 51–1, 633.

77. Wool to Stanton, May 15, 1862, *OR* I, 51–1, 617, and Norfolk Councils, Resolutions, May 16, 1862, ibid. I, 51–1, 627; Wool to Stanton, May 20, 1862, WP, NYSL; *Washington Intelligencer*, May 17, 20, June 2, 1862. By May 30, about two thousand persons had taken the oath. Lenoir Chambers, "Notes on Life in Occupied Norfolk, 1862–65," *VMHB* 73 (April 1965): 132, 135–36.

78. Wool to Sarah Wool, May 28, 1862, WP, NYSL; *Washington Intelligencer*, May 27, 30, 1862; *Richmond Enquirer*, June 4, 7, 1862; Chambers, "Notes," *VMHB* 73: 135. Military government lasted in Norfolk until June 1863. Ludwell H. Johnson III, "Blockade or Trade Monopoly? John A. Dix and the Union Occupation of Norfolk," *VMHB* 93 (January 1985): 56–77.

79. GO 57, June 2, 1862, Washington, DC, AGO, *OR* I, 11–3, 207; Wool to Sarah Wool, June 1, 1862, WP, NYSL; *Baltimore American and Commercial Advertiser*, June 9, 1862; Williams, *Lincoln Finds a General* 1:216.

CHAPTER 15. KNOW NOTHINGS AND PLUG UGLIES

1. *Baltimore American,* June 9, 1862. The *American* was a Unionist paper.

2. Wool to Stanton, June 29, 1862, *OR* I, 12–3, 443; Abstract [personnel], Middle Department, June 30, 1862, ibid. III, 2, 185, and William D. Whipple to William Hoffman, July 8, 1862, ibid. II, 4, 151; *Baltimore Sun,* October 25, 1862; Dix, *Memoirs* 2:24–28, 46; Upton, *Military Policy,* 293n; Nevins, *War for the Union* 1:80.

3. Cram to Long, June 20, 1861 to October [n.d.], 1862, LRTB, M-506, Roll 17; Nevins, *War for the Union* 2:122–29.

4. Cram to Long, June 20, 1861 to October [n.d.], 1862, LRTB, M-506, Roll 17; Whipple to Hoffman, July 8, 1862, *OR* II, 4, 151; Cannon, *Reminiscences,* 166.

5. GO 59, June 5, 1862, Washington, DC, AGO, *OR* I, 12–3, 346; *Baltimore American,* June 10, 14, 1862; Cram to Long, June 20, 1861 to October [n.d.], 1862, LRTB, M-506, Roll 17.

6. Wool to Stanton, June 15, 16, 1862, *OR* I, 12–3, 394, 397.

7. Wool to Stanton, June 15, 16, 17, 20, 1862, *OR* I, 12–3, 394, 397, 403, 415.

8. Wool to Stanton, June 22, July 16, 1862, *OR* I, 12–3, 424–25, 477–78, and Wool to John Pope, July 1, 1862, ibid. I, 51–1, 713–14; Nevins, *War for the Union* 2:131, 134–37.

9. Wool to Pope, July 1, 1862, *OR* I, 51–1, 713–14, and Wool to Stanton, July 2, 1862, ibid. I, 12–3, 449; Nevins, *War for the Union* 2:143, 151.

10. Pope to Wool, July 11, 1862, WP, NYSL.

11. *Baltimore American,* October 31, 1862; Dix, *Memoirs* 2:24–35; Hesseltine, *War Governors,* 213–15; Charles B. Clark, "Suppression and Control of Maryland, 1861–1865," *Marlyand Historical Magazine* 54 (September 1959): 243–48; Charles L. Wagandt, *The Mighty Revolution* (Baltimore: Johns Hopkins University Press, 1964), 17–33. The term "Plug Uglies" may have derived from Postmaster General Montgomery Blair's reference to Baltimore political appointments as "obnoxious plugs."

12. *Baltimore American,* July 4, 1862; Whipple to Hoffman, July 8, 1862, *OR* II, 4, 225; Lincoln to Wool, July 13, 1852, WP, NYSL; Dix, *Memoirs* 2:47–48; Nancy T. Keen, "Confederate Prisoners of War at Fort Delaware," *Delaware History* 13 (April 1968): 1–27; William W. Glenn, *Between North and South: A Maryland Journalist Views the Civil War,* eds. Bayly Ellen Marks and Mark N. Schatz (Rutherford, NJ: Fairleigh Dickinson University Press, 1976), 33–34, 68–70, 249, 315.

13. Nevins, *War for the Union* 2:143–44, 163; Charles B. Clark, "Recruitment of Union Troops in Maryland, 1861–1865," *Maryland Historical Magazine* 53 (June 1958): 156; Hesseltine, *War Governors,* 194, 198–200, 277–78.

14. *Baltimore Sun,* July 22, 23, 24, 1862; Whipple to Seward, July 23, 1862 (2 letters), *OR* II, 4, 270–71; Glenn, *Between North and South,* 319–21.

15. *Baltimore Sun,* July 24, 28, 1862; Council to Wool, July 25, 1862 (with undated Baltimore newspaper clip), and Stanton to Wool, July 26, 1862, WP, NYSL; Wool to Stanton, July 25, 1862, *OR* I, 51–1, 727; *Baltimore American,* November 24, 1862; Glenn, *Between North and South,* 322–23.

16. *Baltimore Sun,* July 29, 1862; *Baltimore American,* November 24, 1862; Wagandt, *Mighty Revolution,* 95, 97–98.

17. Wool to Stanton, June 15, 1862, *OR* I, 12–3, 394; *Baltimore Sun,* July 29, 1862; *Baltimore American,* November 24, 1862; Wagandt, *Mighty Revolution,* 95–96.

18. *Baltimore American,* July 28, 30, August 4, 6, 1862; *Baltimore Sun,* July 31, August 4, 1862; Whipple to William A. Van Nostrand, July 23, 1862, *OR* II, 4, 271; Stanton to Wool, August 1, 1862, ibid. II, 4, 321, and Wool to Thomas, August 2, 1862, ibid. II, 4, 330.

19. *Baltimore Sun,* August 2, 5–7, 1862; *Baltimore American,* August 6, 8, November 24, 1862.

20. *Baltimore American,* August 9, 11, 1862; Kreidberg and Henry, *Military Mobilization,* 103; Hesseltine, *War Governors,* 200–1, 277–78; Nevins, *War for the Union* 2:164, 316.

21. GO 22, August 10, 1862, in Jones to Stanton, August 15, 1862, *OR* II, 4, 430; *Baltimore American,* August 11–13, 1862; *Baltimore Sun,* August 14–15, 1862.

22. Wool to Stanton, July 21, 1862, *OR* I, 11–3, 330–31.

23. GO 84, July 22, 1862, Washington, DC, AGO, *OR* I, 11–3, 333; Cooling, *Symbol,* 125; Nevins, *War for the Union* 2:150–52.

24. Wool to Sarah Wool, July 27, 1862, WP, NYSL.

25. Wool to Stanton, August 15, 1862; Wool to Halleck, August 20, 1862, and Wool to [Cannon], September 6, 1865, WP, NYSL; Halleck to Wool, August 13, 1862, *OR* III, 2, 370, and Wool to Stanton, August 30, 1862, ibid. I, 51–1, 771.

26. Joseph Darr Jr., to Hoffman, August 7, 1862, *OR* II, 4, 355; Wool to Halleck, August 7, 1862, ibid. I, 12–3, 543, and SO 57, August 8, 1862, Baltimore, Middle Department, ibid. I, 19–1, 789.

27. Wool testimony, October 30, 1862 (Harpers Ferry hearings), *OR* I, 19–1, 788–94, and SO 77, August 25, 1862, Baltimore, Middle Department, ibid. I, 19–1, 789; Cram to Long, June 20, 1861 to October [n.d.] 1862, LRTB, M-506, Roll 17; Edward H. Ripley, "Memories of the Ninth Vermont at the Tragedy of Harpers Ferry, September 15, 1862," in A. Noel Blakeman, ed., *Personal Recollections of the War of the Rebellion* (New York: G. P. Putnam Sons, 1912), 134, 155–56.

28. Wool to Stanton, September 2, 1862 (two letters), *OR* I, 12–3, 806–7.

29. Cram to Long, June 20, 1861 to October [n.d.], 1862, LRTB, M-506, Roll 17.

30. Dixon Miles to Wool, and Wool to Miles, both on September 3, 1862, *OR* I, 51–1, 784, and Miles to Wool, September 3, 1862, ibid. I, 19–2, 174.

31. Cram to Long, June 20, 1861 to October [n.d.], 1862, LRTB, M-506, Roll 17.

32. Miles to Halleck and Wool, September 4, 1862 (three tel.), *OR* I, 19–2, 180; Wool to Miles and Julius White, September 4, 1862, ibid. I, 19–2, 181; Wool to Miles, September 4, 1862, ibid. I, 19–1, 790, and Miles to Wool, September 5, 1862 (two tel.), ibid. I, 19–1, 790; Cram to Long. June 20, 1861 to October [n.d.], 1862, LRTB, M-506, Roll 17.

33. Cram to Long, June 20, 1861 to October [n.d.], 1862, LRTB, M-506, Roll 17; Wool to Halleck, September 5, 1862, *OR* I, 19–2, 188–89.

34. Wool to Miles, September 5, 1862 (three tel.), *OR* I, 19–1, 790; Wool to White, September 6–7, 1862, ibid. I, 19–1, 791, and Halleck to Wool, September 5, 1862, ibid. I, 19–1, 751; Halleck to Wool, September 5, 1862, WP, NYSL.

35. Lincoln to Wool, and Wool to Lincoln, September 7, 1862, *OR* I, 19–2, 207, and McClellan to Halleck (encl. McClellan to Wool, September 8), September 8, 1862, ibid. I, 19–2, 212.

36. Wool to Halleck, August 23, 1862, and George W. Pittman to Wool, September 9, 1862, WP, NYSL; GO 30, September 1, 1862, Baltimore, Middle Department, *OR* I, 19–2, 287; Cram to Long, June 20, 1861 to October [n.d.], 1862, LRTB, M-506, Roll 17; *Baltimore American,* September 1, 6, 8, 1862; *Baltimore Sun,* September 8–10, 1862.

37. Wool to Sarah Wool, September 9, 1862, and Wool to William Louis Schley, June 22, 1865, WP, NYSL; Thomas Webster et al. to Stanton, September 10, 1862, *OR* I, 19–2, 251; Halleck to Wool, and Wool to Halleck, September 10, 1862, *OR* I, 19–2, 246, and Wool to Halleck, and Halleck to Wool, September 11, 1862, *OR* I, 19–2, 266. Wool's activities at this time hardly belies the judgment that Henry M. Flint gave to Frederic Hudson, September 10, 1862, cited in Williams, *Lincoln and His Generals,* 4n: Wool "repeated things he had said a few minutes before, his hands shook, and he had to ask his aides if he had put his hat on straight."

38. Wool to McClellan, September 9, *OR* I, 19–2, 231, and Henry M. Binney to White, September 18, 1862, *OR* I, 19–1, 534; Miles to Halleck, September 11, 1862, *OR* I, 51–1, 819.

39. McClellan to Halleck, and Halleck to McClellan, September 11, 12, 1862, *OR* I, 19–1, 758; Halleck to Miles, September 12, 1862, ibid. I, 19–1, 758, and Wool to Halleck, September 12, 1862, ibid. I, 19–2, 275.

40. Binney to White, September 18, 1862, *OR* I, 19–2, 534–36; Matthew Forney Steele, *American Campaigns* (Washington, DC: Byron S. Adams, 1901), 1:263–66; James V. Murfin, *The Gleam of Bayonets* (New York: Thomas Yoseloff, 1965), 135–40; Paul R. Teeter, *A Matter of Hours: Treason at Harpers Ferry* (Rutherford, NJ: Fairleigh Dickinson University Press, 1982), 49–50, 54–58, 90–92.

41. Wool to Halleck, September 15, 1862, *OR* I, 19–1, 759; White to Whipple, September 22, 25, 1862, ibid. I, 19–1, 525–27, 531; Binney to White, September 18, 1862, ibid. I, 19–1, 536–38, and Thomas Noakes testimony, October 19, 1862, ibid. I, 19–1, 767; Steele, *American Campaigns* 1:266.

42. Charles Russell testimony, October 16, 1862, *OR* I, 19–1, 720–21; Upton, *Military Policy,* 379–80; Steele, *American Campaigns* 1:266.

43. White to Whipple, September 22, 1862, *OR* I, 19–1, 528; Binney to White, September 18, 1862, ibid. I, 19–1, 539–40, and Wool report, September 27, 1862, ibid. I, 19–1, 518–21; Wool to Sarah Wool, September 16, 18, 1862, WP, NYSL.

44. Halleck to Wool, September 17, 1862, *OR* I, 19–2, 319; Murfin, *Bayonets,* 115, 132–33.

45. Thomas to Wool, September 17, 1862, *OR* I, 19–2, 319; Wool to Halleck, September 17, 1862, ibid. I, 19–2, 320; Halleck to Wool, and Wool to Halleck, September 18, 1862, ibid. I, 19–2, 327; Wool to Sarah Wool, September 22, 1862, WP, NYSL.

46. Wool to Sarah Wool, September 23, 1862, WP, NYSL.

47. Wool to Harriette Hart, September 24, 1862, WP, NYSL.

48. In July 1862, Mary Todd Lincoln sent a bouquet of flowers and asked Wool to recommend a friend of hers for a sutler's appointment at the camp of instruction to be set up near Annapolis. Mrs. Abraham Lincoln to Wool, July 3, 1862, in Abraham Lincoln, *The Collected Works of Abraham Lincoln: Supplement, 1832–1865,* ed. Roy P. Basler (Westport, CT: Greenwood Press, 1974), 140; Wool to Sarah Wool, September 28, 1862, WP, NYSL

49. *Baltimore Sun,* October 13, 1862; Wool to Halleck, October 14, 1862, *OR* I, 19–2, 29; John W. Thomason Jr., *Jeb Stuart* (New York: Charles Scribner's Sons, 1930), 297, 301–2.

Also, Emory M. Thomas, *Bold Dragoon; The Life of J. E. B. Stuart* (New York: Harper and Row, 1986).

50. Wool to Halleck, October 14, 1862, *OR* I, 19–2, 29–30, and Wool to McClellan, and McClellan to Wool, October 12, 1862, ibid. I, 19–2, 76; Richard P. Roberts to [Emma], October 14, 1862, Richard P. Roberts Collection, Harter Williams files, Bethesda, Maryland. *Baltimore Sun,* October 14, 1862; Thomason, *Jeb Stuart,* 309–10.

51. *Baltimore Sun,* October 16, 17, 1862; Curtin to Stanton and Stanton to Curtin, October 22, 1862, *OR* I, 19–2, 468–69, and Wool to Halleck, October 24, 1862, *OR* I, 19-2, 480; Kriedberg and Henry, *Military Mobilization,* 104; Hesseltine, *War Governors,* 201–2.

52. *Baltimore American,* October 9, 1862; Lincoln to William A. Hammond, October 18, 1862, in Lincoln, *Works* 5:467; Wool to Sarah Wool, October 20, 1862, WP, NYSL; Wagandt, *Mighty Revolution,* 79, 88–89.

53. *Baltimore American,* October 29, November 1, 1862; *Baltimore Sun,* October 29–30, 1862.

54. *Baltimore American,* October 29, November 1, 3, 1862; *Baltimore Sun,* October 29, 1862; *Baltimore Gazette,* October [29], 1862, clipping in Wool to Sarah Wool, October 29, 1862, WP, NYSL; Wagandt, *Mighty Revolution,* 96.

55. Wool to Sarah Wool, October 29, 1862, WP, NYSL; Augustus Bradford to Lincoln, October 29, 1862, *OR* II, 4, 663; Wool to Lincoln, October 29, 1862, and Johns Hopkins to Lincoln, October 30, 1862, Robert T. Lincoln Papers, LC; *Baltimore American,* October 30, 31, 1862; *Baltimore Sun,* October 30, 31, 1862; Wagandt, *Mighty Revolution,* 96.

56. *Baltimore American,* October 31, 1862, citing the *New York Evening Post.* Also, *Troy Times,* November 3, 1862.

57. *Baltimore American,* October 30, 31, November 1, 1862.

58. Cram to Long, June 20, 1861 to October [n.d.], 1862, LRTB, M-506, Roll 17; *Baltimore Sun,* November 6, 1862; Harold B. Hancock, "The Political History of Delaware during the Civil War: Part IV, Two Years of Tension," *Delaware History* 8 (March 1958): 78–79.

59. *Baltimore Sun,* November 6, 1862; Hancock, "Two Years of Tension," *Delaware History* 8: 79–81.

60. *Troy Whig,* November 1, 1862; Wool to Sarah Wool, November 5, 1862, and Wool to Griswold, November 6, 1862, WP, NYSL; Nevins, *War for the Union* 2:318–22.

61. Wool Report, September 27, 1862, *OR* I, 19–1, 518–23; Julius White report, September 16, 1862, ibid. I, 19–1, 524–31, and Harpers Ferry testimony, ibid. I, 19–1, 549–93, 720–802 (quote on 800); *Baltimore American,* October 25, November 11, 12, 1862.

62. Halleck to Wool, September 5, 1862, *OR* I, 19–1, 757; Wool testimony, October 30, 1862, ibid. I, 19-1, 788–94; Binney testimony, October 3, 1862, ibid. I, 19–1, 576–80; and George L. Willard testimony, October 6, 1862, ibid. I, 19–1, 559–66; *Baltimore American,* October 25, November 11–12, 1862. Also, Margaret Askew, "Harpers Ferry: Could It Have Been Defended?" *Virginia Cavalcade* 29 (Summer 1979): 14–21.

63. *Baltimore American,* November 12, 1862; T. Harry Williams, "The Committee on the Conduct of the War," *Journal of American Military Institutions* 3 (Fall 1939): 139–56. Williams listed Heintzelman, Keyes, Hooker, Butler, Frémont, McDowell, and Pope as pro-radical generals. Also, Teeter, *Harpers Ferry,* 213–18.

64. Wool to Sarah Wool, November 12, 1862, WP, NYSL; *Baltimore American,* November 12–13, 15, 1862. Daniel E. Sutherland, "'Altamount' of the *Tribune:* John Williamson Palmer in the Civil War," *Maryland Historical Magazine* 78 (Spring 1983): 54–66, concludes Wool was used as a scapegoat for the surrender of Harpers Ferry.

65. Wool to Sarah Wool, November 17, 1862, WP, NYSL.

66. *Baltimore American,* November 24, 1862, carried the *Inquirer* article and editorial comments.

67. Charles T. Christiansen to Griswold, November 24, 25, 26, 28, 1862, and Wool to Sarah Wool, November 28, 1862, WP, NYSL.

68. Wool to Sarah Wool, December 7, 1862, WP, NYSL.

69. Wool to Sarah Wool, December 10, 1862, WP, NYSL.

70. Wool to Sarah Wool, December 17, 1862, WP, NYSL.

71. Stanton to Wool, December 17, 1862, *OR* I, 21, 864; Stanton to Wool and Wool to Stanton, December 18, 1862, ibid. I, 21, 865, and Robert C. Schenck to Thomas, December 22, 1862, ibid. I, 51–1, 961–62; Wool to Sarah Wool, December 24, 1862, and Wool to Mrs. Gettings, December 19, 1862, WP, NYSL; Wagandt, *Mighty Revolution,* 96.

CHAPTER 16. COPPERHEADS AND THE NEW YORK DRAFT RIOTS

1. Wool to Stanton, January 11, 1863, WP, NYSL; GO 1, January 12, 1863, New York City, Department of the East, *OR* I, 21, 967–68; James McCague, *The Second Rebellion: The Story of the New York City Draft Riots of 1863* (New York: Dial Press, 1968); Laurence M. Hauptman, "John E. Wool and the New York City Draft Riots of 1863: A Reassessment," *Civil War History* 49 (December 2003): 370–87; Barnet Schecter, *The Devil's Own Work: The Civil War Draft Riots and the Fight to Reconstruct America* (New York: Walker and Co., 2005).

2. [Townsend] note to Gen. [Wool], January [3], 1863; Wool to AG, January 6, 1863; and Wool to Cannon, January 21, 1863, WP, NYSL; GO 1, January 12, 1863, New York City, Department of the East, *OR* I, 21, 967–68. New staff appointments included Lt. Col. John B. Frothingham (Assistant Adjutant General), Capt. Septimus Carncross (Assistant Adjutant General), and Capt. DeWitt Clinton (Assistant Judge Advocate General).

3. Consolidated Abstracts from Returns of the United States Army [Department of the East], January 31, 1863, *OR* III, 2, 957; and Abstracts from Returns, Department of the East, May, 1863, ibid., I, 25–2, 592; Wool to Stanton, February 16, 1863, and Wool, "Notes on Inspection Tour," February 23–March 6, 1863, WP, NYSL; July 13, 1863, in Strong, *Strong* 3:337.

4. Ella Lonn, *Desertion during the Civil War* (Gloucester, MA: Peter Smith, 1966), 138, 144–45, 151, 173, 178; James W. Geary, "Civil War Conscription in the North: A Historiographical Record," *Civil War History* 32 (September 1986): 208–28.

5. Wool to Commander, Fort Lafayette, January 24, 1863, Wool to Commander, Fort Columbus, February 10, 1863, Wool to Stanton, February 4, 16, 1863, and Stanton to Wool, February 5, 1863, WP, NYSL. Stanton added New Jersey to Wool's command. McKay, *New York City,* 185.

6. Wool to Horatio Seymour, January 29, 1863, and Wool to John A. Andrew, February 6, 1863, WP, NYSL.

7. Wool to Seymour and Wool to Stanton, February 16, 1863, and Wool to P. Pent, February 16, 18, 1863, WP, NYSL. Cannon, *Reminiscences,* 177; McCague, *Second Rebellion,* 13; Bern Anderson, "The Naval Strategy of the Civil War," *Military Affairs* 26 (Spring 1962): 18. McKay, *New York City,* 134–37. Also, Ben Anderson, *By Sea and by river: The Naval History of the Civil War* (New York: Alfred A. Knopf, 1962).

8. Wool, "Inspection Tour," February 23, 1863, WP, NYSL.

9. Ibid., February 24–27, 1863, WP, NYSL.

10. Ibid., February 28-March 1–4, 1863, and Wool to Nathaniel S. Berry, March 9, 1863, WP, NYSL.

11. Wool, "Inspection Tour," March 5–6, 1863, and Wool to Andrew and other governors, March 9, 1863, WP, NYSL; *New York Times,* March 9, 1863; Nevins, *War for the Union* 3:162–67.

12. Wool, "Inspection Tour," March 6, 1863, WP, NYSL; *Loyal Meeting of the People of New-York to Support the Government, Prosecute the War, and Maintain the Union . . . March 6, 1863* (New York: George F. Nesbitt and Co., 1863), 3–48, appendix.

13. *Loyal Meeting,* 57–62.

14. Cannon, *Reminiscences,* 177–81; West, *Scapegoat General,* 201, 212, 215.

15. Cannon, *Reminiscences,* 181; West, *Scapegoat General,* 212–14.

16. John Van Buren to Wool, February 7, 1863, Griswold Papers, RCHS; Wool to Sarah Wool, April 25, 29, May 1, 1863, WP, NYSL.

17. Wool to Barney, April 19, 1864, WP, NYSL. Wool also complained of counterfeit Confederate scrip in circulation. *Troy Times,* October 8, 13, 1863.

18. Wool to Stanton, April 23, 1863, Seward Papers, University of Rochester; Wool to Stanton, May 1, 1863, Wool to Sarah Wool, April 29, 1863, and Wool to Barney, April 19, 1864, WP, NYSL; *Troy Times,* October 8, 13, 1863.

19. Wool to Sarah Wool, May 3, 17, 27, June 4, 14, 1863, WP, NYSL. In May 1863, Wool received 744 pounds of oats and 868 pounds of hay.

20. Wool to Sarah Wool, June 20, 1863, WP, NYSL; Nevins, *War for the Union* 3:80.

21. Wool to Welles and Welles to Wool, June 27, 1863, *OR* I, 27–3, 367; Wool to Stanton, June 27, 1863, ibid., I, 27–3, 365, and Charles W. Sandford to John T. Sprague, December 30, 1863, ibid. I, 27–2, 228. Sprague to Sandford, June 16, 1863, in Horatio Seymour, *Public Record: Including Speeches, Messages, Proclamations, Official Correspondence, and other Public Utterances of Horatio Seymour,* comps. and eds. Thomas Cook and Thomas W. Cox (New York: I. W. England, 1868), 114; June 27, 1863, in Gideon Welles, *Diary of Gideon Welles,* ed. Howard K. Beale, 3 vols. (New York: W. W. Norton and Co., 1960), 1:347; Jack F. Leach, *Conscription in the United States: Historical Background* (Rutland, VT: C. E. Tuttle Publishing Co., 1952), 291–92.

22. Wool to Stanton, June 27, July 5, 1863, *OR* I, 27–3, 365, 551, and Thomas to Wool, June 30, July 3, 1863, ibid. I, 27–3, 435, 510; Wool to Seymour, June 30, 1863, in Seymour, *Public Record,* 150; Wool to Stanton, July 3, 1863, WP, NYSL.

23. Wool to Sarah Wool, July 4, 1863, WP, NYSL; Seymour speech, July 4, 1863, in Seymour, *Public Record,* 118–24; McCague, *Second Rebellion,* 10–12.

24. Wool to Sarah Wool, July 7, 1863, WP, NYSL.

25. T[homson] P. McElrath, "The Draft Riots in New York," in *Annals of the War, Written by Leading Participants North and South* (Philadelphia: Times Publishing Co., 1879), 286. First Lt. Thomas Price McElrath, 5th Artillery, was a regular army officer assigned to guard New York Harbor under Gen. Harvey Brown during the riots. Heitman, *Historical Register* 1:439; Nevins, *War for the Union* 3:119–21; Kriedberg and Henry, *Military Mobilization,* 104–5; William F. Hanna, "The Boston Draft Riot," *Civil War History* 36 (September 1990): 262–73.

26. Wool to Seymour, July 9, 1863, and Wool to Frothingham, July 10, 1863, WP, NYSL; Seymour to Lincoln, August 3, 1863, *OR* III, 3, 614, and Richard Delafield to Joseph G. Totten, July 15, 1863, *OR* I, 27–2, 922.

27. *New York Herald,* July 12, 1863; McCague, *Second Rebellion,* 53–54; Nevins, *War for the Union* 3:121; Irving Werstein, *July, 1863* (New York: Julian Messner, 1957), 98–99.

28. Strong, *Strong* 3:334n; Albon P. Man Jr., "Labor Competition and the New York Draft Riots of 1863," *Journal of Negro History* 36 (October 1951): 404; Leach, *Conscription,* 293, 304; Adrian Cook, *The Armies of the Streets: The New York Draft Riots of 1863* (Lexington: University Press of Kentucky, 1974), 3–5, 55–56; Werstein, *July, 1863,* 23. Also, Iver Bernstein, *The New York City Draft Riots: Their Significance for American Society and Politics in the Age of the Civil War* (New York: Oxford University Press, 1990), 3, 5, 8–11, 13.

29. Wool to Stanton, July 20, 1863, *OR* I, 27–2, 878, and Robert Nugent to James B. Fry, July 15, 1863, ibid. I, 27–2, 899; Wool to Seymour, July 20, 1863, in Seymour, *Public Record,* 131–32; McElrath, "Draft Riots," in *Annals,* 288–90; *New York Herald,* July 14, 1863; Nevins, *War for the Union* 3:121; Kriedberg and Henry, *Military Mobilization,* 115; Cook, *Armies,* 56–62; McCague, *Second Rebellion,* 63–68, 70, 73.

30. Wool to Stanton, July 20, 1863, *OR* I, 27–2, 878; Sprague to Sandford, July 13, 1863, ibid., I, 27–2, 913; Nugent to Fry, July 15, 1863, ibid., I, 27–2, 899; Wool to Hiram Paulding, July 13, 1863 (2 messages), ibid., I, 27–2, 882–83, and Sandford to Sprague, December 30, 1863, ibid., I, 27–2, 228; Wool to Richard Frothingham, July 15, 1863, and Wool to Schley, June 22, 1865, WP, NYSL; Wool to Seymour, July 20, 1863, in Seymour, *Public Record,* 122; McElrath, "Draft Riots," in *Annals,* 292–94; William J. Tenney, *The Military and Naval History of the Rebellion in the United States* (New York: D. Appleton and Co., 1866), 417; McCague, *Second Rebellion,* 88; Cook, *Armies,* 67–68, 84–85.

31. July 13, 1863, in Strong, *Strong* 3:336–37; Moulton, "Wool Sketch," Tenney Collection. Wool to Frothingham, July 15, 1864, and Wool to Schley, June 22, 1865, WP, NYSL; Wool to Stanton, July 3, 1865, WP, NYSL; McCague, *Second Rebellion,* 78, 109; Cook, *Armies,* 88.

32. Wool to Stanton, July 20, 1863, *OR* I, 27–2, 878, and Edward S. Sanford to Stanton, July 13, 1863 (several messages), ibid. I, 27–2, 886–87; McElrath, "Draft Riots," in *Annals,* 290–91; *New York Times,* July 14, 1863; McCague, *Second Rebellion,* 79–80; Nevins, *War for the Union* 3:122.

33. Wool to Stanton, July 20, 1863, *OR* I, 27–2, 878, and Nugent to Fry, July 14, 15, 1863, ibid. I, 27–2, 896, 899; Wool to Seymour, July 20, 1863, in Seymour, *Public Record,* 132–33; Wool to Townsend, July 10, 1863, and Wool to Schley, June 22, 1865, WP, NYSL; McElrath,

"Draft Riots," in *Annals,* 293–95; *New York Herald,* July 24, 30, 1863; Cook, *Armies,* 84; McCague, *Second Rebellion,* 87, 89–90; Werstein, *July, 1863,* 79–80.

34. *New York Herald,* July 24, 30, 1863; Sandford to Sprague, December 30, 1863, *OR* I, 27–2, 228; Wool to Stanton, July 20, 1863, ibid. I, 27–2, 878–79, Nugent to Fry, July 15, 1863, ibid. I, 27–2, 899, Wool to Harvey Brown and Sandford, July 13, 1863, ibid. I, 27–2, 879–80, and SO 13, July 13, 1863, New York City, ibid. I, 27–2, 880; Wool to Seymour, July 20, 1863, in Seymour, *Public Record,* 132–33; Wool to Schley, June 22, 1865, WP, NYSL; McElrath, "Draft Riots," in *Annals,* 293; July 13, 1863, in Strong, *Strong* 3:337; *Troy Times,* July 31, 1863; Werstein, *July, 1863,* 80–81; McCague, *Second Rebellion,* 90–91; Cook, *Armies,* 86; Nevins, *War for the Union* 3:122.

35. Wool to Seymour, July 20, 1863, in Seymour, *Public Record,* 133; Wool to Schley, June 22, 1865, WP, NYSL; Sandford to Sprague, December 30, 1863, *OR* I, 27–2, 228; McElrath, "Draft Riots," *Annals,* 295–96; Nevins, *War for the Union* 3:122.

36. Wool to Seymour, July 20, 1863, in Seymour, *Public Record,* 133–34; Wool to Stanton, July 20, 1863, *OR* I, 27–2, 880; Sprague to Sandford, July 13, 1863, ibid. I, 27–2, 913, and Nugent to Fry, July 14, 1863, ibid. I, 27–2, 897; *New York Herald,* July 30, 1863; McElrath, "Draft Riots," in *Annals,* 295–96, 303; Nevins, *War for the Union* 3:122.

37. Wool to Brown, Cram to Josiah T. Miller, and Christensen to Stephen G. Sluyter, all dated July 14, 1863, in *OR* I, 27–2, 884, and Wool to Andrew et al., July 14, 1863, ibid. I, 27–2, 885; *New York Times,* July 15, 1863; McElrath, "Draft Riots," in *Annals,* 298, 301; Nevins, *War for the Union* 3:123; McCague, *Second Rebellion,* 116–18, 119 (Sir Forcible Feeble); Lossing, *Civil War* 3:89n.

38. McElrath, "Draft Riots," in *Annals,* 297, 299; Cook, *Armies,* 101–2, 115–20; Werstein, *July, 1863,* 132–33; McCague, *Second Rebellion,* 109–13, 120.

39. Cook, *Armies,* 119–20; McCague, *Second Rebellion,* 120–21, 124–26.

40. Thomas T. Davis to Stanton, July 14, 1863, *OR* I, 27–2, 917, F. B. Cutting to Stanton, July 14, 1863, ibid. I, 27–2, 914; Nugent to Fry, July 14, 1863, ibid. I, 27–2, 897; Marshall Lefferts to Sprague, October [n.d.] 1863, ibid. I, 27–2, 250, and Watson A. Fox to Nelson Randall, September 10, 1863, ibid. I, 27–2, 277. In January 1863, radical Unionists in New York City sought to replace Wool.

41. *New York Herald,* July 15, 1863; Christensen to Brown, July 15, 1863 (several orders), *OR* I, 27–2, 885, William F. Berens [to Sprague], January 30, 1864, ibid. I, 27–2, 251–53; SO 111, July 15, 1863, New York City, Department of the East, ibid. I, 27–2, 924; Wool to Halleck, July 16, 1863, ibid. I, 27–2, 876; Nugent to Fry, July 16, 1863, ibid. I, 27–2, 901, and D[avid] D. Field to Chase, July 15, 1863, ibid. I, 27–2, 919–20. GO 217, July 15, 1863, Washington, DC, AGO, *OR* I, 27–2, 919–20 (SO 19 and SO 20 replaced Wool with Dix). Also, July 16, 1863, in Welles, *Welles* 1:373, 405.

42. Sanford to Stanton, July 16, 1863, *OR* I, 27–2, 891; Wool to Stanton, July 16, 18, 1863, ibid. I, 27–2, 876–77, and George Opdyke to Stanton, July 16, 1863, ibid. I, 27–2, 926; *New York Herald,* July 16, 1863.

43. Wool to Stanton, July 16, 1863, *OR* I, 27–2, 876; SO 313, July 15, 1863, Washington, DC., AGO, ibid. I, 27–3, 708, Wool to E. R. S. Canby, July 17, 1863, ibid. I, 27–2, 886, and SO 114 (Dix), July 18, 1863, New York City, Department of the East, ibid. I, 27–2, 928;

Nevins, *War for the Union* 3:124–25. The draft in New York City resumed on August 19, 1863. McKay, *New York City,* 212. For casualties in the riot, see McKay, *New York City,* 208–9, Cook, *Armies,* 193–96, and Bernstein, *Riots,* 5, 288, 289n8.

44. Wool to Stanton, July 18, 1863, *OR* I, 27–2, 877, and GO 64 (Dix), July 18, 1863, New York City, Department of the East, ibid. I, 27–2, 929; Wool to Sarah Wool, July 17, 18, 1863, WP, NYSL; GO 20, July 16, 1863, Washington, DC, AGO, cited in *New York Herald,* July 22, 1863.

45. McElrath, "Draft Riots," in *Annals,* 303–4; *New York Herald,* July 23, 26, 30, 1863; Wool to Stanton, July 20, 1863, *OR* I, 27–2, 880–81; *Troy Times,* July 31, 1863; *Troy Weekly Times,* August 1, 1863. McCague, *Second Rebellion,* 176, 196n.

46. *New York Herald,* July 31, 1863; *Troy Times,* July 31, 1863; *Troy Weekly Times,* August 1, 1863; Dix, *Memoirs* 2:76–77.

CHAPTER 17. NOBLE DEFENDER OF THE UNION

1. Wool to Theseus A. Cheney, October 4, 1863, Mss., UMi; *Troy Times,* January 2, 1864; *Troy Whig,* November 1, 1872; Hinton, "John Augustus Griswold," *Biographical Dictionary,* 217–18; "John A. Griswold," in Wilson and Fiske, eds., *Appleton's* 3:3; Franklin B. Hough, *Gazetteer of the State of New York* (Albany: A. Boyd, 1872), 556.

2. *Troy Times,* September 4, 14, October 21, 1863, and August 15, 17, 1864; Wool to Grant, July 6, 1865, WP, NYSL; Wool to Griswold, August 30, 1863, in *Troy Weekly Times,* October 31, 1863.

3. Wool to Grant, July 6, 1865, WP, NYSL; Hesseltine, *War Governors,* 337.

4. Wool to Miss M. S. Worth, January 7, 1864, Wool to Ellen McClellan, February 2, 1864, Wool to Griswold, February 24, 1864, and L[ewis] J. Cist to Wool, May 9, 1864, WP, NYSL; *Troy Whig,* February 20, 1864; William Y. Thompson, "Sanitary Fairs of the Civil War," *Civil War History* 4 (March 1958): 61–67.

5. Wool to [Griswold], January 27, 1864, and Wool to Olin, January 27, 1864, WP, NYSL; *Congressional Globe* 38-1, New Series No. 10, January 13, 1864, 150.

6. *New York Tribune,* March 4, 14, 1864; *New York Herald,* March 9–13, 1864; Wool to [Griswold], January 27, 1864, WP, NYSL; *Troy Times,* March 14, April 5, 1864; Nevins, *War for the Union* 4:7–8.

7. *Troy Times,* April 26, May 25, 1864; Wool to Lincoln, April 24, 1864, WP, NYSL; Wool to Cheney, May 9, 1864, Mss., UMi.

8. *New York Herald,* March 18, 1864; Wool to L. M. Francis, August 23, 1864, WP, NYSL.

9. Wool to A[mos] K. Hadley, August 29, 1864, WP, NYSL; *Troy Times,* September 1, 9, 1864. Also, Nicholas P. Kamaras, "George B. McClellan and the Election of 1864" (PhD diss., University of Delaware, 1976).

10. Wool to editor, September 12, 1864, *New York Times,* undated clip; George F. Noyes to Wool, September 12, 1864, and Wool to [Noyes], September 14, 1864, WP, NYSL.

11. *New York World,* September 14, 1864.

12. *Troy Times,* September 27–28, 1864.

13. *Troy Times,* October 5, 1864.

14. *Buffalo Courier,* October 10, 1864; A. W. [Cawfield] to Wool, November 24, 1864; Wool to Cass, October 9, 1864, and Wool to Stanton, October 5, 1864, WP, NYSL.

15. *New York World,* October 10, 12, 1864; *Troy Times,* October 11, 13, 1864.

16. *Troy Times,* October 13, 1864.

17. *Troy Times,* October 25, 1864.

18. Wool to Schley, June 22, 1864, and Wool to Sarah Wool, October 26, 1864, WP, NYSL; *Troy Times,* October 28, 1864; West, *Scapegoat General,* 274–75; T. Harry Williams, *Lincoln and the Radicals* (Madison: University of Wisconsin Press, 1941), 235. Wool wrote Schley that he had refused the appointment because his rank, experience, and services entitled him to a more responsible assignment.

19. Wool to [Dix], November 20, 25, 1864, WP, NYSL; *Troy Times,* November 8, 1864. The fact that Griswold personally financed the raising of the Twenty-first New York Cavalry in Troy in the late summer of 1864 doubtless enhanced the possibilities of his reelection to Congress. *Troy Whig,* November 1, 1872.

20. Wool to Prosper M. Wetmore, January 8, 13, 1865, WP, NYSL.

21. Wool to W[illiam] P. Jones, January 31, 1865 (two drafts), and Wool to Harriette Baylies Moulton, January 27, 1865, WP, NYSL; *Troy Times,* February 3, 1865.

22. Wool to Cannon, February 4, 1865, WP, NYSL; Wool to Dawson, February 28, 1865, Mss., NYHS; Harriette Hart, "Memoir," Tenney Collection.

23. Wool to Harriette Moulton, March 12, 1865, and Harriette Moulton to Wool, April 11, 12, 1865, WP, NYSL.

24. *A Tribute of Respect by the Citizens of Troy to the Memory of Abraham Lincoln,* ed. Benjamin Hower Hall (Troy, NY: Young and Benson, 1865), 1–8, 28–31, 93–95, 245, 249; *Troy Times,* April 25, 1865.

25. *Baltimore Sun,* December 3, 1862; *San Francisco Evening Bulletin,* January 20, 1863.

26. Wool to Schley, July 18, 1863, Wool to George H. Briggs, November 12, 1863, and Wool to Griswold, February 24, 1864, WP, NYSL.

27. Wool to Schley, June 22, 1865, WP, NYSL.

28. Wool to Andrew Johnson, June 6, 1865, Andrew Johnson Papers, LC; Griswold to Stanton, July 1, 1865, WP, NYSL.

29. Wool to Stanton, July 3, 1865, and Wool to Grant, July 6, 10, 1865, WP, NYSL.

30. Wool to Schley, August 6, 1865, Wool to Wilson, Third Auditor, October 30, 1865, Wool to Griswold, March 8, April 19, 1866, and Wool to Lossing, October 9, 1866, WP, NYSL. Wool's cases are in the *Baltimore Sun,* November 1865 and 1866.

31. Wool to Thomas M. Hite, September 28, 1865, in *New York Times,* October 22, 1865; Wool to Lossing, February 28, 1866, Mss., NYHS. Wool voiced similar sentiments in a letter to Andrew Johnson, March 31, 1866, WP, NYSL.

32. Wool to Griswold, March 5, 1866, WP, NYSL.

33. *New York Tribune* and *Cincinnati Enquirer,* September 18, 1866; *New York Herald,* September 18–19, 1866.

34. *New York Herald, New York Tribune,* and *Cincinnati Enquirer,* September 18, 1866.

35. *New York Tribune,* September 18, 1866.

36. *New York Herald,* September 18, 19, 1866.

37. *New York Tribune,* September 18, 1866; James G. Blaine, *Twenty Years of Congress: From Lincoln to Garfield,* 2 vols. (Norwich, CT: Henry Bill Publishing Co., 1884–86), 2: 228–29.

38. Wool to Gilbert E. Winters, September 29, 1866, and Wool to Lossing, October 9, 1866, WP, NYSL.

39. Wool to William E. Dodge, February 27, 1867, WP, NYSL; Wool to Dawson, December 8, 1867, Mss., NYHS; Wool to William L. Poole, October 20, 1867, in *New York Times,* November 5, 1867.

40. Wool to editor, *New York Herald,* October 19, 1865; Dix to Wool, December 9, 1865, and Wool to William Hall et al., March 6, 1867, WP, NYSL; Winfield Scott, *Memoirs of Lieut.-General Scott, L.L.D. Written by Himself* (New York: Sheldon and Co., [1864] 1865).

41. Wool to Committee of Invitation, August 12, 1867, WP, NYSL.

42. Wool to Lossing, December 10, 15, 1865, and Wool to Henry J. Morgan, Jun 23, 1864, WP, NYSL; Wool to Dawson, June 2, 1865, and Wool to Lossing, February 28, 1866, Mss., NYHS; *Troy Times,* February 13, 1865.

43. Wool to Dawson, December 8, 1867, November 18, 1868, and January 10, 1869, Mss., NYHS; Wool to Dawson, November 18, 1868m and January 10, 1869, Mss., NYSL.

44. Wool to Dawson, December 8, 1867, January 10, 1969, Mss., NYSL; "Albany Blues Visit Wool," Albany newspaper clip, WP, NYSL; Emmons Clark, *History of the Seventh Regiment of New York, 1806–1889,* 2 vols. (New York: Seventh Regiment, 1890), 2:173; Wyllie E. Wright, librarian, Williams College, to Harwood P. Hinton, April 19, 1960, Samuel Peter Heintzelman Papers, Library of Congress.

45. Wool to Dawson, August 8, 1869, Mss., NYHS.

46. *Troy Times,* November 1–3, 8, 10, 1869; Miscellaneous newspaper clippings, n.d., NP, NYSL.

47. *Troy Times,* November 12, 13, 1869.

48. *Troy Times,* November 11–13, 1869.

49. *Troy Times,* November 13, 1869. Gen. W. T. Sherman's General Order announcing Wool's death appeared in the *Army and Navy Journal,* November 20, 1869, 208. Weise, *History of Troy,* 218, 254; J[ohn]. C. Hoadley, ed., *Memorial of Henry Sanford Gansevoort* (Boston: Rand, Avery and Co., 1875), 290–91.

50. Wool's will, March 17, 1868, specified that Sarah Wool receive the homestead, $25,000 in cash, and an annual allowance of $10,000. Former military aides, orderlies, and servants received sums ranging from $1,000 to $5,000. Donations went to Williams College and three local orphanages. Friends who named sons after him, received several thousand dollars each. The general left his marble statue of Cleopatra to his niece, Harriette Hart. Swords and military accoutrements went to a grand-nephew (John Wool Griswold). Numerous relatives received sums for "friendly and kind feelings." The general also set aside $50,000 to erect a monument over his and Sarah's graves. John E. Wool, "Wills and Proofs," Surrogate Records, Book 72, pages 16–27, Rensselaer County Court House, Troy, New York; *Troy Times,* November 13, 1869. Sarah Wool died on May 10, 1873 and was buried beside her husband on the hill overlooking the Hudson River in Oakwood Cemetery. *Troy Weekly Times,* May 10, 1873. The

erection in 1879 of the towering granite obelisk proved to be a major undertaking. The monument was described at the time as the largest block of granite "ever cut in the United States" for such a purpose. It soared seventy-five feet high at completion. *Troy Press,* August 27, 1879; Moulton, *Moulton,* 140; *Army and Navy Journal,* June 14, 1879, and October 29, 1887; DeWitt Clinton, ed., *Picturesque Oakwood* (Troy, NY: n.p., 1897), 189.

BIBLIOGRAPHY

Manuscripts and Archival Collections

Archer-Mitchell-Stump-Williams Family. Papers. Maryland Historical Society, Annapolis, Maryland.

Army Papers. Missouri Historical Society, St. Louis, Missouri.

Baptismal Records. First Presbyterian Church, New York City, New York.

Baylies, Francis. Family Papers. Old Colonial Historical Society, Taunton, Massachusetts.

Brouillet, J. B. A. Papers. Archdiocese of Seattle Archives, Seattle, Washington.

Brown, Jacob. Letterbook. 3 vols. Manuscript Division, Library of Congress, Washington, DC.

Bryant, William Cullen. Papers. New York Public Library, New York, New York.

Burden, Joseph W. Papers. New York City, New York.

Cass, Lewis. Papers. Clements Library, University of Michigan, Ann Arbor, Michigan.

Catlin, Alexander. Papers. University of Vermont, Burlington, Vermont.

Corning, Erastus. Papers. Brown University, Providence, Rhode Island.

Curtis, Samuel R. Papers. Bancroft Library. University of California at Berkeley.

Cushing, Caleb. Papers. Library of Congress, Washington, DC.

Dix, John Adams. Papers. Columbia University, New York, New York.

Ehinger, Augustus F. Diary. Charles F. Ward Papers, Roswell, New Mexico.

Eighth Census (1860). National Archives, Washington, DC: Rensselaer County, New York.

Fish, Hamilton. Papers. Library of Congress, Washington, DC.

Fixman, Isadore M. Collection. Rensselaer Polytechnic Institute, Troy, New York.

Gardner, Charles K. Papers. New York State Library, Albany, New York.

Grantee Deed Books. County Clerk's Office, Rensselaer County, Troy, New York.

Griswold. Papers. Rensselaer County Historical Society, Troy, New York.

Hammond, James H. Papers. Manuscript Division, Library of Congress, Washington, DC.

Hamtramck, John Francis. Papers. Duke University Library, Durham, North Carolina.

Hardie, James A. Papers. Library of Congress, Washington, DC.

Hardin, William S. Papers. Chicago Historical Society, Chicago, Illinois.

Haywood, Ernest. Papers. Southern Historical Collection, University of North Carolina, Chapel Hill, North Carolina.

Heintzelman, Samuel Peter. Papers. Manuscript Division, Library of Congress, Washington, DC.

Howe, Chileab S. Papers. Southern Historical Collection, University of North Carolina Library, Chapel Hill, North Carolina.

Jackson, Andrew. Papers. Manuscript Division, Library of Congress, Washington, DC.

Johnson, Andrew. Papers. Manuscript Division, Library of Congress, Washington, DC.

Lane, Joseph. Papers. Indiana University, Bloomington, Indiana.

[Langdon, John Jay]. Mexican War Diary. New York Historical Society, New York, New York.

Lincoln, Abraham. Papers. Manuscript Division, Library of Congress, Washington, DC.

Lincoln, Robert T. Papers. Manuscript Division, Library of Congress, Washington, DC.

Marcy, William L. Papers. Manuscript Division, Library of Congress, Washington, DC.

Morgan, Edward D. Papers. New York State Library, Albany, New York.

Morgan, J. Pierpont. New York Public Library, New York, New York.

National Archives and Records Administration, Washington, DC.

- Adjutant General Records, Record Group 94
  - Canadian Rebellion Records
  - Letters Received
  - Letters Sent
  - Orders
- Bureau of Ordnance, Record Group 156
  - Letters Sent
  - Springfield Armory Records
- Headquarters of the Army, Record Group 108
  - Letters Sent
  - Letters Received
- Records of the Office of the Inspector General, Record Group 159
  - Inspection Reports
- Secretary of War, Record Group 107
  - Letters Received
  - Letters Sent
- Topographical Bureau
  - Letters Received

Pierpont-Fogg, J. Papers. New York Public Library, New York City, New York.

Rives, William C. Papers. Duke University Library, Durham, North Carolina.

Seventh Census (1850). National Archives, Washington, DC: Rensselaer County, New York.

Seward, William H. Papers. University of Rochester Library, Rochester, New York.

Sixth Census (1840). National Archives, Washington, DC: Rensselaer County, New York.

Stiner, William H. Papers. New York Historical Society, New York, New York.

Tallmadge, Nathaniel P. Papers. State Historical Society of Wisconsin, Madison, Wisconsin.

Taylor, John W. Papers. New York Historical Society, New York City, New York.

Taylor, Zachary. Papers. Manuscript Division, Library of Congress, Washington, DC.

Tenney, John W. G. Papers. Rensselaer County Historical Society, Troy, New York.

Vermontiana Collection. University of Vermont, Burlington, Vermont.

War of 1812 Manuscripts, Indiana University Library, Bloomington, Indiana.

Wool, John Ellis. Papers. New York State Library, Albany, New York.

Government Publications

American State Papers. *Proceedings of court of inquiry in case of Brigadier General John E. Wool and those under his command in Cherokee country, Alabama, protection of Indian land and property rights.* 25th Cong., 1st sess., 1837.

Journal of the Sixth Session of the Legislature of the State of California. Sacramento, CA: B. B. Redding, 1855.

Kreidberg, Marvin A. and Merton G. Henry, *History of Military Mobilization in the United States Army, 1775–1945*, Pamphlet No. 20–212. Washington, DC: Department of the Army, June 1955.

U.S. House Executive Document 103, *Statement of the Sums of Money Paid Since the Peace Establishment . . . to the General Officers and Their Staff . . . , March 15, 1820.* 16th Cong., 1st sess., 1820.

U.S. House Executive Document 21, *Report of Secretary of War on a Plan for the Reduction of the Army . . . December 12, 1820.* 16th Cong., 2nd sess., 1821.

U.S. House Executive Document 2, *Report of Secretary of War, November 27, 1822.* 17th Cong., 2nd sess., 1823.

U.S. House Executive Document 2, *Report of Secretary of War, November 24, 1828.* 20th Cong., 2nd sess., 1829.

U.S. House Report 143, *Petition of Brigadier General John E. Wool for double rations.* 24th Cong., 1st sess., 1838.

U.S. House Report 339, *Petition of Brigadier General John E. Wool for double rations.* 26th Cong., 1st sess., 1840.

U.S. House Executive Document 24, *Military Forces in Mexican War.* 30th Cong., 1st sess., 1848.

U.S. House Executive Document 56, *Correspondence between the Secretary of War and Generals Scott and Taylor and Between General Scott and Mr. Trist.* 30th Cong., 1st sess., 1848.

U.S. House Executive Document 56, *Message from the President transmitting Reports from Secretary of State and Secretary of War.* 30th Cong., 1st sess. 1848.

U.S. House Executive Document 60, *Mexican War Correspondence.* 30th Cong., 1st sess., 1848.

U.S. House Executive Document 78, *A Report from the Secretary of War . . . relative to the dismissal . . . of J. S. Pender and G. E. B. Singletary.* 30th Cong., 1st sess., 1848.

U.S. House Executive Document 24, *Military Forces Employed in the Mexican War.* 31st Cong., 1st sess., 1850.

U.S. House Executive Document 17, *California and New Mexico.* 31st Cong., 1st sess., 1850.

U.S. House Executive Document 1, *Report of Secretary of War.* 33rd Cong., 1st sess., 1854.

U.S. House Report 281, *Petition of Brigadier General John E. Wool for double rations.* 33rd Cong., 1st sess., 1854.

U.S. House Executive Document 65, *Affairs in Oregon.* 33rd Cong., 1st sess., 1855.

U.S. House Executive Document 118, *Indian Hostilities in Oregon and Washington Territories.* 34th Cong., 1st sess., 1856.

U.S. House Executive Document 93, *Indian Hostilities in Oregon and Washington.* 34th Cong., 1st sess., 1856.

U.S. House Executive Document 112, *Indian Affairs in Oregon and Washington Territories.* 35th Cong., 1st sess., 1858.

U.S. House Executive Document 88, *Message of President transmitting correspondence between late Secretary of War and Major General Wool.* 35th Cong., 1st sess., 1858.

U.S. House Executive Document 114, *Military Topographical Memoir and Report on the Department of the Pacific, March 3, 1859.* 35th Cong., 2nd sess., 1859

U.S. House Executive Document 2, *Report on Government Contracts, December 17, 1861.* 37th Cong., 2nd sess., 1862.

U.S. House Executive Document 124, *Case of Major General Wool on Exchange of Prisoners of War.* 37th Cong., 2nd sess., 1862.

U.S. House Executive Document 85, *Africans in Fort Monroe Military District* . . . 37th Cong., 2nd sess., 1862.

U.S. House Executive Document 124, *Exchange of Prisoners of War . . . , June 11, 1862.* 37th Cong., 2nd sess., 1862.

U.S. Senate Executive Document 58, *Report of the Secretary of War . . . , January 12, 1819.* 15th Cong., 2nd sess., 1819.

U.S. Senate Executive Document 246, ... *Pay and Allowances . . . 1812, 1824, 1838 [and 1846], March 24, 1846.* 29th Cong., 1st sess., 1846.

U.S. Senate Executive Document 1. *Message from the President . . . at the Commencement of the First Session of the Thirtieth Congress.* 30th Cong., 1st sess., 1847.

U.S. Senate Executive Document 36, *Report of the Secretary of War Showing the Number of Troops in the Service.* 30th Cong., 1st sess. 1848.

U.S. Senate Executive Document 32, *Memoir Descriptive of the March of a Division of the United States Army, Under the Command of Brigadier General John E. Wool, from San Antonio de Bexar, in Texas, to Saltillo, in Mexico.* 31st Cong., 1st sess., 1850.

U.S. Senate Executive Document 37, *Report of Governor Stevens, Relative to the Property of the Hudson's Bay and Puget Sound Company . . . February 7, 1855.* 33rd Cong., 2nd sess. 1855.

U.S. Senate Executive Document 25, *Presidential message communicating report and accompanying documents of copies of correspondence between Major General John E. Wool and the different departments of government.* 33rd Cong., 2nd sess., 1855.

U.S. Senate Executive Document 37, *Report of Governor Stevens, Relative to the Property of the Hudson's Bay and Puget Sound Company . . . February 7, 1855.* 33rd Cong., 2nd sess. 1855.

U. S. Senate Executive Document 16, *Instructions and Correspondence between the Government and Major General Wool . . . , January 3, 1855.* 33rd Cong., 2nd sess. 1855.

U.S. Senate Executive Document 66, *Indian Disturbances in the Territories of Washington and Oregon, May 9, 1856.* 34th Cong., 1st sess. 1856.

U.S. Senate Executive Document 26, *Indian Disturbances in California, February 21, 1856.* 34th Cong., 1st sess. 1856.

U. S. Senate Executive Document 1, *Report of the Secretary of War, December 3, 1861.* 36th Cong., 2nd sess. 1860.

U.S. Senate Executive Document 45, *Report . . . in Relation to the Indian war claims in Oregon and Washington Territories, May 2, 1861.* 37th Cong., 2nd sess. 1862.

U.S. Senate Executive Document 33, *Names and Numbers of Major Generals* [and] . . . *officers and soldiers to their staff.* 37th Cong., 2nd sess. 1862.

U.S. Senate Executive Document 61, *Present condition of the Military Asylum, May 29, 1862.* 37th Cong., 2nd sess. 1862

Newspapers

Albany (N.Y.) Argus
Albany Evening Journal
Albany Gazette
Albany Weekly Argus
American Weekly Messenger (Philadelphia)
Annapolis (Md.) Gazette
(Annapolis) Maryland State Capitol Gazette
Athens (Tenn.) Republican
(Athens) Tennessee Journal
Baltimore American
Baltimore American and Commercial Advertiser
Baltimore Gazette
Baltimore Republican
Baltimore Sun
Bangor (Me.) Whig
(Bennington) Vermont Gazette
Boston Atlas
Brooklyn (N.Y.) Star
Buffalo Commercial Advertiser
Buffalo Courier
(Burlington) Vermont Gazette
(Charlottesville) Virginia Advocate
Chicago Tribune
(Cincinnati) Chronicle News-Letter
Cincinnati Enquirer
Detroit Gazette
Frank Leslie's Illustrated Newspaper (New York)
(Fredericksburg, Va.) Semi-Weekly News
(Greene, N.Y.) Chenango Free Press
Knoxville (Tenn.) Register
(Little Rock) Arkansas Democrat
Liverpool Albion (UK)
(Middlebury) Vermont Argus and Free Press
(Monterrey, Calif.) Gazette

(Montpelier) Vermont Patriot and State Gazette
Nashville (Tenn.) Republican
(New Orleans) Delta
(New Orleans) Picayune
Newport (Va.) Daily News
(New York) Collector
New York Courier and Enquirer
(New York) Evening Post
New York Express
(New York) Freeman's Journal
New York Herald
(New York) Leslie's
New York Military Gazette
New York Times
New York Tribune
Niles' Weekly Register (Baltimore)
Oneida Morning Herald (Utica, N.Y.)
Pittsburgh Morning Chronicle
Plattsburgh (N.Y.) Whig
(Plattsburgh, N.Y.) Republican
Portland (Ore.) Advertiser
(Portland) Oregon Weekly Times
Richmond (Va.) Enquirer
Rochester (N.Y.) Advertiser
(Rochester, N.Y.) Daily Union
Rochester (N.Y.) Weekly Times
(St. Albans) Vermont Messenger
(St. Louis) Missouri Republican
(St. Louis) Reporter
Salem (Ill.) Advocate
(Salem, Ore.) Statesman
(San Francisco) Alta California
(San Francisco) Daily Herald
(San Francisco) Daily State Register
(San Francisco) Evening Bulletin
San Francisco Herald
San Francisco Placer Times and Transcript
(Saltillo, Mexico) Picket Guard
(Steilacoom) Washington Republican
Syracuse (N.Y.) Daily Star
Troy (N.Y.) Arena

Troy (N.Y.) Daily Times
Troy (N.Y.) Daily Whig
(Troy, N.Y.) Family Journal
(Troy, N.Y.) Farmers' Register
(Troy) New York State Republican
(Troy, N.Y.) Northern Budget
Troy (N.Y.) Post
Troy (N.Y.) State Gazette
Troy (N.Y.) Times
Troy (N.Y.) Weekly Times
Troy (N.Y.) Whig
(Van Buren) Arkansas Intelligencer
(Washington, D.C.) Army and Navy Chronicle
(Washington, D.C.) Congressional Globe
(Washington, D.C.) National Intelligencer
(Washington, D.C.) Union
Washington (D.C.) National Republican
(Windsor) Vermont Chronicle
Windsor (Vt.) Chronicle

Books

Adams, George Rollie. *General William S. Harney: Prince of Dragoons.* Lincoln: University of Nebraska Press, 2001.

Adams, Charles Francis. *Diary of Charles Francis Adams.* Edited by Aida DiPace Donald and David Donald. 3 vols. Cambridge, MA: Harvard University Press, 1964.

Adams, John Quincy. *The Memoirs of John Quincy Adams Comprising Portions of his Diary from 1795 to 1848.* Edited by Charles Francis Adams. 12 vols. Philadelphia: J. B. Lippincott and Co., 1875–1877.

Alcaraz, Ramón. *The Other Side: Or Notes for the History of the War Between Mexico and the United States.* Translated by Albert C. Ramsey. New York: John Wiley, 1850.

Alexander, U. G., comp. *History of the Thirteenth Regiment.* N. P., Regimental Press, 1905.

Ambrose, Stephen E. *Duty, Honor, Country: A History of West Point.* Baltimore: Johns Hopkins University Press, 1966.

American State Papers: Indian Affairs. 2 vols. Washington: Gales and Seaton, 1832–34.

American State Papers: Military Affairs. 7 vols. Washington: Gales and Seaton, 1832–61.

American State Papers: Miscellaneous. 2 vols. Washington: Gales and Seaton, 1834.

Andrews, J. Cutler. *The North Reports the Civil War.* Pittsburgh: University of Pittsburgh Press, 1955.

Annals of the Congress of the United States, 1789–1824. 42 vols. Washington: Gales and Seaton, 1834–56.

Armstrong, John. *Notices of the War of 1812.* 2 vols. New York: Wiley and Putnam, 1840.

Arnold, Richard, comp. *Ceremonies on Occasion of the Presentation of the Swords voted Major General John E. Wool by the Common Council of the City of Troy, the Legislature of New York, and the Congress of the United States.* Troy, NY: A. W. Scribner and Co., 1860.

Arthur, Robert. *The Coast Artillery School, 1824–1927.* Fort Monroe, VA: Coast Artillery School Press, 1928.

Bald, F. Clever. *Michigan in Four Centuries.* New York: Harper and Row, 1954.

Ball, Durwood. *Army Regulars on the Western Frontier, 1848–1861.* Norman: University of Oklahoma Press, 2001.

Bancroft, Hubert H. *History of California.* 7 vols. San Francisco: A. L. Bancroft, 1884–1890.

———. *History of Oregon.* 2 vols. San Francisco: History Co., 1886, 1888.

Barbuto, Richard V. *Niagara, 1814: America Invades Canada.* Lawrence: University of Kansas Press, 1999.

Barton, Henry W. *Texas Volunteers in the Mexican War.* Wichita Falls, TX: Texian Press, 1970.

Bates, David H. *Lincoln in the Telegraph Office.* New York: Century Co., 1907.

Bauer, K. Jack. *The Mexican War, 1846–1848.* New York: Macmillan and Co., 1974.

———. *Zachary Taylor: Soldier, Planter, Statesman of the Old Southwest.* Baton Rouge: Louisiana State University Press, 1985.

Baylies, Francis. *A Narrative of Major General Wool's Campaign in Mexico, in the Years 1846, 1847, and 1848.* Albany, NY: Little and Co., 1851.

Beckham, Stephen D. *Requiem for a People: The Rogue Indians and the Frontiersmen.* Norman: University of Oklahoma Press, 1971.

Benham, Henry W. *Recollections of Mexico and the Battle of Buena Vista, February 22 and 23, 1847. By an Engineer officer on its twenty-fourth Anniversary.* Boston: n.p., 1871.

Bernhard, Karl. *Travels through North America by His Highness, Bernhard, Duke of Saxe-Weimar Eisenach.* 2 vols. Philadelphia: Carey, Lea, and Carey, 1828.

Bernstein, Iver. *The New York City Draft Riots: Their Significance for American Society and Politics in the Age of the Civil War.* New York: Oxford University Press, 1990.

Birkhimer, William E. *Historical Sketch of the Organization, Administration, Materiel and Tactics of the Artillery, United States Army.* New York: Greenwood Press, 1968.

Blaine, James G. *Twenty Years of Congress: From Lincoln to Garfield.* 2 vols. Norwich, CT: Henry Bill Publishing Co., 1884–86.

Blakeman, A. Noel, ed. *Personal Recollections of the War of the Rebellion.* New York: G. P. Putnam Sons, 1912.

Bliven, Rachel D. et al. *Resourceful People: A Pictorial History of Rensselaer County.* Edited by Valerie Von Weich. Norfolk: Donning Co., 1987.

Bonney, Catharina Van Rensselaer, comp. *A Legacy of Historical Gleanings.* 2 vols. Albany: J. Munsell, 1875.

Brock, Isaac. *The Life and Correspondence of Major-General Sir Isaac Brock, K. B.* Edited by Ferdinand Brock Tupper. London: Simpkin, Marshall and Co., 1845.

Brooks, Nathan Covington. *A Complete History of the Mexican War, 1846–1848.* Chicago: Rio Grande Press, 1965.

Brown, Charles H. *Agents of Manifest Destiny: The Lives and Times of the Filibusters.* Chapel Hill: University of North Carolina Press, 1980.

Brown, Richard M. *Strain of Violence: Historical Studies of American Violence and Vigilantism.* New York: Oxford University Press, 1975.

Browne, Frances F. *The Everyday Life of Abraham Lincoln.* New York: G. P. Putnam's Sons, 1913.

Bryant, William C. *The Letters of William Cullen Bryant.* Edited by William Cullen Bryant II and Thomas G. Voss. 6 vols. New York: Fordham University Press, 1975–92.

Buhoup, Jonathan W. *Narrative of the Central Division, or Army of Chihuahua, Commanded by Brigadier General Wool: Embracing All the Occurrences, Incidents and Anecdotes From the Time of Its Rendezvous at San Antonio de Bexar Till Its Juncture with Gen'l Taylor, and Its Final Disbandment at Camargo—With an Account of Its Sufferings While Passing Through a Barren and Hostile Country—Together With a Description of the Battle of Buena Vista, and an Interesting Appendix.* Pittsburgh: M. P. Morse, 1847.

Burrage, Henry S. *Maine in the Northeastern Boundary Controversy.* Portland: Printed for the State, 1919.

Calhoun, John C. *The Papers of John C. Calhoun.* Edited by Robert L. Meriwether et al. 22 vols. Columbia: University of South Carolina Press, 1959–2003.

Cannon, LeGrand B. *Personal Reminiscences of the Rebellion, 1861–1866.* Freeport, NY: Books for Libraries Press, 1971.

Carleton, James H. *Battle of Buena Vista.* New York: Harper and Row, 1848.

Carpenter, John A. *Sword and Olive Branch: Oliver Otis Howard.* New York: Fordham University Press, 1999.

Caughey, John. *California: A Remarkable State's Life History.* Englewood Cliffs, NJ: Prentice Hall, 1970.

Chamberlain, Samuel E. *My Confession: Recollections of a Rogue.* New York: Harper and Brothers, 1956.

———. *My Confession.* Edited by William H. Goetzmann. Austin: Texas State Historical Association, 1996.

Church, William C. *The Life of John Ericsson.* 2 vols. New York: Charles Scribner's Sons, 1890.

Clary, David, and Joseph W. A. Whitehorne. *Inspectors General of the United States Army, 1777–1903.* Washington, DC: Office of the Inspector General and Center for Military History, 1987.

Clary, David A. *Eagles and Empire: The United States, Mexico, and the Struggle for a Continent.* New York: Bantam Books, 2009.

Clinton, DeWitt, ed. *Picturesque Oakwood.* Troy, NY: n.p., 1897.

Coffman, Edward M. *The Old Army: A Portrait of the American Army in Peacetime, 1784–1898.* New York: Oxford University Press, 1986.

Connelley, William E. *War with Mexico, 1846–1847: Doniphan's Expedition and the Conquest of New Mexico and California; Includes a Reprint of the Work of Col. John T. Hughes.* Topeka, KS: Crane and Co., 1907.

Cook, Adrian. *The Armies of the Streets: The New York Draft Riots of 1863.* Lexington: University of Kentucky Press, 1974.

Cooling, Benjamin F. *Symbol, Sword, and Shield: Defending Washington during the Civil War.* New York: Archon Books, 1975.

Cooper, James Fenimore. *The Letters and Journals of James Fenimore Cooper.* Edited by James F. Beard. 6 vols. Cambridge, MA: Harvard University Press, 1960–1968.

Corey, Albert B. *The Crisis of 1830–1842 in Canadian-American Relations.* New Haven, CT: Yale University Press, 1942.

Cowtan, Charles W. *Services of the Tenth New York Volunteers (National Zouaves).* New York: Charles H. Ludwig, 1882.

Crackel, Theodore J. *West Point: A Bicentennial History.* Lawrence: University Press of Kansas, 2002.

Cram, Thomas Jefferson. *Topographical Memoir.* Fairfield, WA: Ye Galleon Press, 1977.

Crittenden, Lucius E. *Recollections of President Lincoln and his Administration.* New York: Harpers Brothers, 1891.

———. *A Report of the Debates and Proceedings in the Secret Sessions of the Conference Convention for Proposing Amendments.* New York: D. Appleton and Co., 1864.

Croghan, George. *Army Life on the Western Frontier: Selections from the Official Reports Made Between 1826 and 1845 by Colonel George Croghan.* Edited by Francis Paul Prucha. Norman: University of Oklahoma Press, 1958.

Crook, George. *George Crook: His Autobiography.* Edited by Martin F. Schmitt. Norman: University of Oklahoma Press, 1953.

Crouthamel, James L. *James Watson Webb: A Biography.* Middletown, CT: Wesleyan University Press, 1969.

Cruikshank, Ernest A., ed. *The Documentary History of the Campaign upon the Niagara Frontier in the Year 1812.* Welland, Ontario: Lundy's Lane Historical Society, 1900.

Cunliffe, Marcus. *Soldiers and Civilians: The Martial Spirit in America, 1776–1865.* New York: Free Press, 1973.

Cutrer, Thomas W. *Ben McCulloch and the Frontier Military Tradition.* Chapel Hill: University of North Carolina Press, 1993.

Dana, Richard Henry, Jr. *The Journal of Richard Henry Dana, Jr.* Edited by Robert F. Lucid. 3 vols. Cambridge, MA: Harvard University Press, 1968.

Davis, George T. M. *Autobiography of the late Col. Geo. T. M. Davis, Captain and Aid-de-camp Scott's Army of Invasion (Mexico), From Posthumous Papers.* New York: Jenkins and McCowan Press, 1891.

Davis, Jefferson. *Jefferson Davis, Constitutionalist: His Letters, Papers, and Speeches.* Edited by Dunbar Rowland et al. 10 vols. Jackson, MS: Department of Archives and History, 1923.

Davis, Varina Howell. *Jefferson Davis, Ex-President of the Confederate States of America: A Memoir by His Wife.* 2 vols. New York: Belford, 1890.

Davis, William C. *Duel Between the First Ironclads.* Baton Rouge: Louisiana State University Press, 1981.

Dawson, Henry. *Battles of the United States.* 2 vols. New York: Johnson, Fry, and Co., 1858–1860.

Dawson, Joseph G. *Doniphan's Epic March: The 1st Missouri Volunteers in the Mexican War.* Lawrence: University Press of Kansas, 1999.

De Laney, Edward F. et al., comps. "The Burghers of New Amsterdam and the Freemen of New York, 1675–1866." New York Historical Society. New York: 1866.

DePalo, William A., Jr. *The Mexican National Army, 1822–1852.* College Station: Texas A&M University Press, 1997.

Dillon, Lester R., Jr. *American Artillery in the Mexican War, 1846–47.* Austin, TX: Presidial Press, 1975.

Dishman, Christopher D. *A Perfect Gibraltar: The Battle for Monterrey, Mexico, 1846.* Norman: University of Oklahoma Press, 2010.

Dix, John A. *Memoirs of John Adams Dix.* Compiled by Morgan Dix. 2 vols. New York: Harper and Brothers, 1883.

Donald, David Herbert. *Lincoln.* New York: Simon and Schuster, 1995.

Dowdey, Clifford. *Lee.* Boston: Little, Brown and Co., 1965.

Duncan, Robert L. *Reluctant General: The Life and Times of Albert Pike:* New York: E. P. Duncan and Co. 1961.

Dupuy, Ernest R. and Trevor N. Dupuy. *The Encyclopedia of Military History: From 3500 B.C. to the Present.* New York: Harper and Row, 1977

Ehle, John. *Trail of Tears: The Rise and Fall of the Cherokee Nation.* New York: Anchor Books-Doubleday, 1988.

Einolf, Christopher J. *George Thomas: Virginian for the Union.* Norman: University of Oklahoma Press, 2006.

Eisenhower, John S. *So Far from God: The U. S. War with Mexico, 1846–1848.* New York: Random House, 1989.

Elliott, Charles W. *Winfield Scott: The Soldier and Man.* New York: Macmillan Co., 1937.

Ellison, Joseph. *California and the Nation, 1850–1869.* Berkeley: University of California Press, 1927.

Everest, Allan S. *The War of 1812 in Champlain Valley.* Syracuse, NY: Syracuse University Press, 1981.

———. *The Military Career of Alexander Macomb and Alexander Macomb at Plattsburgh.* Plattsburgh, NY: Wild Publications, 1989.

Finger, John R. *Eastern Band of Cherokees, 1819–1900.* Knoxville: University of Tennessee Press, 1984.

Fitz-Enz, David G. *The Final Invasion: Plattsburg, the War of 1812's Most Decisive Battle.* Edited by John R. Elting. New York: Cooper Square Press, 2000.

Foreman, Grant. *Indian Removal: The Emigration of the Five Civilized Tribes of Indians.* Norman: University of Oklahoma Press, 1972.

Fox, Gustavus Vasa. *Confidential Correspondence of Gustavus Vasa Vox: Assistant Secretary of the Navy, 1861–1865.* Edited by Robert M. Thompson and Richard Wainwright. 2 vols. New York: Naval History Society, 1920.

Franks, David. *The New York Directory for 1786.* 2nd ed. New York: H. J. Sachs and Co., 1905.

Frazier, Donald S., ed. *The United States and Mexico at War: Nineteenth-Century Expansionism and Conflict.* New York: Simon and Schuster Macmillan, 1995.

French, Samuel G. *Two Wars: An Autobiography of General Samuel G. French . . . Mexican War; War Between the States, a Diary; Reconstruction Period, His Experiences, Incidents, Reminiscences; etc.* Nashville, TN: Confederate Veteran, 1901.

Frost, John. *Life of Major General Zachary Taylor; with notices of the war in New Mexico, California and in southern Mexico.* New York: Appleton and Co., 1847.

Fryer, Mary Beacock. *Volunteers, Redcoats, Rebels, and Raiders: A Military History of the Rebellion in Upper Canada.* Toronto: Dundurn Press, 1987.

Fuess, Claude M. *The Life of Caleb Cushing.* 2 vols. New York: Harcourt Brace and Co., 1922.

Gallagher, Gary W., ed. *The Richmond Campaign of 1862: The Peninsula & the Seven Days.* Chapel Hill: University of North Carolina Press, 2000.

Gerteis, Louis S. *From Contraband to Freedman: Federal Policy toward Southern Blacks, 1861–65.* Westport, CT: Greenwood Press, 1973.

Gilpin, Alec R. *The War of 1812 in the Old Northwest.* East Lansing: Michigan State University Press, 1958.

Glenn, William W. *Between North and South: A Maryland Journalist Views the Civil War.* Edited by Bayly Ellen Marks and Mark N. Schatz. Rutherford, NJ: Fairleigh Dickinson University Press, 1976.

Glisan, Rodney. *A Journal of Army Life.* San Francisco: A. L. Bancroft, 1874.

Goetzmann, William H. *Army Exploration in the American West, 1803–1863.* New Haven, CT: Yale University Press, 1959.

Goss, Thomas J. *The War within the Union High Command: Politics and Generalship during the Civil War.* Lawrence: University of Kansas Press, 2003.

Graves, Donald E. *Red Coats and Grey Jackets: The Battle of Chippawa, 1814.* Toronto: Robin Brass, 1994.

Graves, Henry L. *A Confederate Marine: A Sketch of Henry Lea Graves with Excerpts from the Graves Family Correspondence.* Edited by Richard Harwell. Tuscaloosa, AL: Confederate Publishing Co., 1963.

Greenberg, Amy S. *A Wicked War: Polk, Clay, Lincoln, and the 1845 U.S. Invasion of Mexico.* New York: Vintage Books, 2012.

Gregg, Josiah. *Diary and Letters of Josiah Gregg.* Edited by Maurice G. Fulton. 2 vols. Norman: University of Oklahoma Press, 1941, 1944.

Griffith, Benjamin W., Jr. *McIntosh and Weatherford: Creek Indian Leaders.* Tuscaloosa: University of Alabama Press, 1988.

Gunderson, Robert T. *Old Gentlemen's Convention: The Washington Peace Conference of 1861.* Madison: University of Wisconsin Press, 1961.

Hall, Benjamin Hower, ed. *A Tribute of Respect by the Citizens of Troy to the Memory of Abraham Lincoln.* Troy, NY: Young and Benson, 1865.

Hanson, John H. *The Lost Prince . . . Eleazar Williams.* New York: G. P. Putnam, 1854.

Harris III, Charles H. *A Mexican Family Empire: The Latifundio of the Sánchez Navarro Family, 1765–1867.* Austin: University of Texas Press, 1975.

———. *The Sánchez Navarros: A Socio-economic Study of a Coahuilan Latifundio, 1846–1853.* Chicago: Loyola University Press, 1964.

Hastings, Hugh, comp. and ed. *Military Minutes of the Council of Appointment of the State of New York, 1783–1821.* 3 vols. Albany, NY: J. B. Lyon, 1901–1902.

Hatch, Alden. *The Wadsworths Man.* New York: Cowan-McCann, 1959.

Havighurst, Walter. *Three Flags at the Straits: The Forts of Mackinac.* Englewood Cliffs, NJ: Prentice Hall, 1966.

Hazen, William B. *A Narrative of Military Service.* Huntington, WV: Blue Acorn, 1993.

Heidler, David S. and Jeanne T. Heidler. *The Encyclopedia of the War of 1812.* Santa Barbara, CA: AC-CLIO, 1997.

———. *Old Hickory's War: Andrew Jackson and the Quest for Empire.* Baton Rouge: Louisiana State University Press, 2003.

Heitman, Francis B. *Historical Register and Dictionary of the United States Army.* 2 vols. Washington, DC: Government Printing Office, 1903.

Hemenway, Abby Maria, ed. *The Vermont Historical Gazetteer: A Magazine Embracing a History of Each Town, Civil, Ecclesiastical, Biographical and Military.* 6 vols. Ludlow, VT: A. M. Hemenway, 1860–1863.

Henderson, Timothy J. *A Glorious Defeat: Mexico and its War with the United States.* New York: Hill and Wang, 2007.

Hendricksen, James. *Joe Lane of Oregon: Machine Politics and the Sectional Crisis, 1849–1861.* New Haven, CT: Yale University Press, 1967.

Henry, William S. *Campaign Sketches of the War with Mexico.* New York: Harper, 1847.

Herbert, Walter H. *Fighting Joe Hooker.* Indianapolis, IN: Bobbs Merrill, 1944.

Hesseltine, William B. *Lincoln and the War Governors.* New York: Alfred A. Knopf, 1948.

Hickey, Donald R. *The War of 1812: A Forgotten Conflict.* Urbana: University of Illinois Press, 1989.

Hitsman, J. Mackay. *The Incredible War of 1812: A Military History.* Toronto: University of Toronto Press, 1965.

Hittell, Thedore. *History of California.* 4 vols. San Francisco: N. J. Stone, 1897.

Hoadley, J[ohn] C., ed. *Memorial of Henry Sanford Gansevoort.* Boston: Rand, Avery and Co., 1875.

Hobbs, James. *Wild Life in the Far West: Personal Adventures of a Border Mountain Man.* Glorieta, NM: Rio Grande Press, 1969.

Hoehling, Adolph A. *Thunder at Hampton Roads.* Englewood Cliffs, NJ: Prentice Hall, 1976.

Holt, Michael F. *The Rise and Fall of the American Whig Party: Jacksonian Politics and the Onset of the Civil War.* New York: Oxford University Press, 1999.

Hoppin, William W., Jr. *Peace Conference of 1861 at Washington, D.C.* Providence, RI: Standard Printing Co., 1891.

Horsman, Reginald. *The Causes of the War of 1812.* Philadelphia: University of Pennsylvania Press, 1962.

Hough, Franklin B. *Gazetteer of the State of New York.* Albany, NY: A Boyd, 1872.

Howard, Oliver Otis. *Autobiography of Oliver Otis Howard.* 2 vols. New York: Baker and Taylor Co., 1907.

Hunt, H. Draper. *Hannibal Hamlin of Maine.* Syracuse, NY: Syracuse University Press, 1969.

Hurtado, Albert L. *Indian Survival on the California Frontier.* New Haven, CT: Yale University Press, 1988.

Ingersol, Charles. *Historical Sketch of the Second War Between the United States of America and Great Britain.* 2 vols. Philadelphia: Lea and Blanchard, 1845–1849.

Irwin, Ray W. *Daniel D. Tompkins: Governor of New York and Vice President of the United States.* New York: New York Historical Society, 1968.

Izard, George. *Official Correspondence . . . Relative to Military Operations of . . . Major General Izard . . . in the Years 1814 and 1815.* Philadelphia: Thomas, Dobson, 1816.

Jacobs, James R. *Tarnished Warrior: Major General James Wilkinson.* New York: Macmillan, 1938.

Johannsen, Robert W. *To the Halls of the Montezumas: The Mexican War in the American Imagination.* New York: Macmillan, 1974.

Johnson, Allen and Dumas Malone, eds. *The Dictionary of American Biography.* 20 vols. New York: Charles Scribner's Son, 1928–1936.

Johnson, Robert U. and Clarence C. Buel, eds. *Battles and Leaders of the Civil War.* 4 vols. New York: Thomas Yoseloff, 1956.

Johnson, Timothy D. *Winfield Scott: The Quest for Military Glory.* Lawrence: University of Kansas Press, 1998.

Jones, Howard. *To the Webster-Ashburton Treaty: A Study in Anglo-American Relations, 1783–1843.* Chapel Hill: University of North Carolina Press, 1977.

Jones, Howard and Donald A. Rakestraw. *Prologue to Manifest Destiny: Anglo American Relations in the 1840s.* Wilmington, DE: Scholarly Resources, 1997.

Josephy, Alvin M., Jr. *The Nez Perce Indians and the Opening of the Northwest.* New Haven, CT: Yale University Press, 1965.

Judson, Harry P. *A History of the Troy Citizens Corps, Troy, New York.* Troy, NY: Troy Times Publishing House, 1884.

Kappler, Charles J., ed. and comp. *Indian Affairs: Laws and Treaties, 1778–1883.* 2 vols. Washington, DC: Government Printing Office, 1903–1904.

Kass, Alvin. *Politics in New York State, 1800–1830.* Syracuse, NY: Syracuse University Press, 1965.

Keeler, William F. *Aboard the USS Monitor, 1862: The Letters of Acting Paymaster William Frederick Keeler, U. S. Navy, to His Wife Ann.* Edited by Robert W. Daly. Annapolis, MD: United States Naval Institute, 1964.

Kelly, Margaret Jean. *The Career of Joseph Lane, Frontier Politician.* Washington, DC: Catholic University of America Press, 1947.

Kendall, George Wilkins. *Dispatches from the Mexican War.* Edited by Lawrence Delbert Cress. Norman: University of Oklahoma Press, 1999.

Keys, Erasmus D. *Fifty Years' Observation of Men and Events.* New York: Scribner's, 1884.

Kieffer, Chester L. *Maligned General: The Biography of Thomas Sidney Jesup.* San Rafael, CA: Presidio Press, 1879.

King, Duane, ed. *The Cherokee Indian Nation: A Troubled History.* Knoxville: University of Tennessee Press, 1979.

Kingsford, William. *The History of Canada.* 10 vols. Toronto: Rowsell and Hutchinson, 1887–1898.

Klement, Frank L. *Copperheads in the North.* Shippensburg, PA: White Mane, 1999.

Klunder, Willard Carl. *Lewis Cass and the Politics of Moderation.* Kent, OH: Kent State University Press, 1996.

Koerner, Gustave. *Memoirs of Gustave Koerner, 1809–1896.* Edited by Thomas J. McCormick. 2 vols. Cedar Rapids, IA: Torch Press, 1909.

Kohn, Richard H. *Eagle and Sword: The Federalists and the Creation of the Military Establishment in America, 1783–1802.* New York: Free Press, 1975.

Kroeber, A. L. and C. B. Kroeber. *A Mohave War Reminiscence, 1854–1880.* New York: Dover Publications, 1994.

Kroeker, Marvin E. *Great Plains Command: William B. Hazen in the Frontier West.* Norman: University of Oklahoma Press, 1976.

Lambert, Joseph I. *One Hundred Years with the Second Cavalry.* Fort Riley, KS: Capper Printing Co., 1939.

Lansing, W., and Son, eds. *Plattsburgh N. Y.* Plattsburgh, NY: W. Lansing and Son, 1844.

Lavender, David. *Climax at Buena Vista: The Decisive Battle of the Mexican-American War.* Philadelphia: University of Pennsylvania Press, 1966.

Leach, Margaret. *Reveille in Washington.* New York: Harper and Brothers, 1941.

Lee, Fitzhugh. *General Lee.* New York: D. Appleton and Co., 1894.

Lee, John T., ed. *Josiah Gregg and Dr. George Engelmann.* Worcester, MA: American Antiquarian Society, 1932.

Leach, Jack F. *Conscription in the United States: Historical Background.* Rutland, VT: C. E. Tuttle Publishing Co., 1952.

Levinson, Irving. *War within War: Mexican Guerrillas, Domestic Elites, and the United States of America, 1846–1848.* Fort Worth: Texas Christian University Press, 1996.

Life of General Worth; to which is added a sketch of the life of Brigadier-General Wool. New York: Nafis & Cornish, 1847.

Lincoln, Abraham. *Collected Works of Abraham Lincoln.* Edited by Roy P. Basler. 9 vols. New Brunswick, NJ: Rutgers University Press, 1953–55.

Linklater, Andro. *An Artist in Treason: The Extraordinary Double Life of General James Wilkinson.* New York: Walker, 2009.

Long, E[varette] B. *The Civil War Day by Day: An Almanac, 1861–1865.* Garden City, NJ: Doubleday and Co., 1971.

Lossing, Benson J. *Pictorial Field-book of the War of 1812.* New York: Harper and Brothers, 1868.

———. *Pictorial History of the Civil War.* 3 vols. Philadelphia: G. W. Childs, 1866–68.

Loyal Meeting of the People of New York to Support the Government, Prosecute the War, and Maintain the Union . . . March 6, 1963. New York: George F. Nesbitt and Co., 1963.

Lumpkin, Wilson. *The Removal of the Cherokee Indians from Georgia.* 2 vols. New York: Dodd, Mead and Co., 1907.

McCaffrey, James M. *Army of Manifest Destiny: The American Soldier in the Mexican War, 1846–1848.* New York: New York University Press, 1992.

McCague, James. *The Second Rebellion: The Story of the New York City Draft Riots of 1863.* New York: Dial Press, 1968.

McKay, Ernest A. *The Civil War and New York City.* Syracuse, NY: Syracuse University Press, 1990.

Madley, Benjamin. *An American Genocide: The United States and the California Indian Catastrophe.* New Haven, CT: Yale University Press, 2016.

Mangum, Willie P. *The Papers of Willie Person Mangum.* Edited by Henry T. Shanks. 5 vols. Raleigh: North Carolina State Department of Archives and History, 1956.

Magoffin, Susan Shelby. *Down the Santa Fe Trail and into Mexico: The Diary of Susan Shelby Magoffin, 1846–1847.* Edited by Stella M. Drumm. New Haven, CT: Yale University Press, 1926.

Mahon, John K. *History of the Militia and the National Guard.* New York: Macmillan, 1983.

———. *History of the Second Seminole War, 1835–1842.* Gainesville: University of Florida Press, 1967.

Malcomson, Robert. *The Battle of Queenston Heights.* N.p.: Peninsula Press, 1994.

Malone, Henry T. *Cherokees of the Old South.* Athens: University of Georgia Press, 1956.

Mangum, Willie P. *The Papers of Willie Person Mangum.* Edited by Henry T. Shanks. 5 vols. Raleigh, NC: State Department of Archives and History, 1956.

Mann, James. *Medical Sketches of the Campaigns of 1812, 13, 14.* Dedham, MA: H. Mann and Co., 1816.

Marszalek, John F. *The Petticoat Affair: Manners, Mutiny, and Sex in Andrew Jackson's White House.* New York: Free Press, 1997.

May, Robert E. *Manifest Destiny's Underworld: Filibustering in Antebellum America.* Chapel Hill: University of North Carolina Press, 2002.

McWhiney, Grady. *Braxton Bragg and Confederate Defeat.* Vol. 1, *Field Command.* New York: Columbia University Press, 1969.

Merrill, James M. *The Rebel Shore: The Story of Union Sea Power in the Civil War.* Boston: Little, Brown and Co., 1957.

Merry, Robert W. *A Country of Vast Designs: James K. Polk, the Mexican War, and the Conquest of the American Continent.* New York: Simon and Schuster, 2009.

Miller, Robert R. *Shamrock and Sword: The Saint Patrick's Battalion in the U.S.-Mexican War.* Norman: University of Oklahoma Press, 1989.

Moore, Jamie W. *The Fortification Board 1816–1828 and the Definition of National Security.* Charleston, SC: The Citadel, 1981.

Monroe, James. *The Papers of James Monroe: A Documentary History of the Presidential Tours of James Monroe, 1817, 1818, 1819.* Edited by Daniel Preston. 2 vols. Westport, CT: Greenwood Press, 2003.

Montgomery, Henry. *The Life of Major General Zachary Taylor.* First Rate Publishers, n.d.

Montgomery, Horace. *Howell Cobb's Confederate Career.* Tuscaloosa, AL: Confederate Publishing Co., 1959.

Moore, Frank, ed. *Rebellion Record: A Diary of American Events.* 12 vols. New York: Arno Press, 1977.

Morris, John D. *Sword of the Border: Major General Jacob Jennings Brown, 1775–1828.* Kent, OH: Kent State University Press, 2000.

Moten, Matthew, *The Delafield Commission and the American Military Profession.* College Station: Texas A&M University Press, 2000.

Moulton, Gary E. *John Ross: Cherokee Chief.* Athens: University of Georgia Press, 1978.

Moutlon, Henry W. *Moulton Annals.* Edited by Claribel Moulton. Chicago: Claypool, 1906.

Murfin, James V. *The Gleam of Bayonets.* New York: Thomas Yoseloff, 1965.

Nance, Joseph Milton. *After San Jacinto: The Texas-Mexican Frontier, 1836–1841.* Austin: University of Texas Press, 1963.

Nash, Howard P., Jr. *Stormy Petrel: The Life and Times of General Benjamin F. Butler, 1818–1893.* Rutherford, NJ: Fairleigh Dickinson University Press, 1969.

Ness, George T., Jr. *The Regular Army on the Eve of the Civil War.* Baltimore: Toomey Press, 1982.

Nevins, Allan. *The War for the Union.* 4 vols. New York: Charles Scribner's Sons, 1959–71.

Neu, Irene D. *Erastus Corning: Merchant and Financier, 1784–1872.* Ithaca, NY: Cornell University Press, 2010.

New American State Papers: Military Affairs. Edited by Benjamin Franklin Cooling. 19 vols. Wilmington, DE: Scholarly Publications, 1979.

Nicolay, John G. and John Hay. *Abraham Lincoln: A History.* 10 vols. New York: Century Co., 1890.

Nichols, Roger L. *Henry Atkinson: A Western Military Career.* Norman: University of Oklahoma Press, 1963.

Niven, John. *Gideon Welles: Lincoln's Secretary of the Navy.* New York: Oxford University Press, 1973.

O'Brien, John E. *Telegraphing in Battle.* Scranton, PA: Raeder Press, 1910.

O'Brien, Michael. *A Character of Hugh Legaré.* Knoxville: University of Tennessee Press, 1985.

O'Callaghan, Edward B. and Berthold Fernow, eds. *Documents Relative to the Colonial History of the State of New York.* 15 vols. Albany, NY: Weed, Parsons, 1856–1887.

O'Donnell, Terence. *An Arrow in the Earth: General Joel Palmer and the Indians of Oregon.* Portland: Oregon Historical Society, 1991.

Official Records of the Union and Confederate Navies in the War of the Rebellion. 30 vols. Washington, DC: Government Printing Office, 1894–1922.

Palmer, Peter S. *History of Lake Champlain . . .* Plattsburg: J. W. Tuttle, 1853.

Perdue, Theda, ed. *Cherokee Editor: The Writings of Elias Boudinot.* Knoxville: University of Tennessee Press, 1983.

Peskin, Allan. *Winfield Scott and the Profession of Arms.* Kent, OH: Kent State University Press, 2004.

Peterson, Charles J. *Military Heroes of the War with Mexico: With a Narrative of the War.* Philadelphia: W. A. Leary, 1848.

Phillips, Ulrich B., ed. "The Correspondence of Robert Toombs, Alexander H. Stephens, and Howell Cobb." In American Historical Association *Annual Report for 1911.* 2 vols. Washington, DC: American Historical Society, 1913.

Pinheiro, James C. *Manifest Ambition: James K. Polk and Civil-Military Relations during the Mexican War.* Westport, CT: Praeger International 2007.

Plattsburgh Centenary Commission. *The Battle of Plattsburgh: What Historians Say About It . . .* Albany, NY: J. B. Lyon Co., 1914.

Pleasants, Samuel A. *Fernando Wood of New York.* New York: AMS Press, 1966.

Polk, James K. *The Diary of James K. Polk.* Edited by Milo M. Quaife. 4 vols. Chicago: A. C. McClurg and Co., 1910.

Price, Monroe. *The Perilous Crown: France Between Revolutions, 1814–1848.* London: Macmillan, 2007.

Prucha, Francis Paul. *Broadax and Bayonet: The Role of the United States Army in the Development of the Northwest, 1815–1860.* Lincoln: University of Nebraska Press, 1967.

———. *A Guide to the Military Posts of the United States, 1789–1895.* Madison: State Historical Society of Wisconsin, 1964.

———. *The Sword of the Republic: The United States Army on the Frontier, 1783–1846.* New York: Macmillan Co., 1969.

Quarles, Benjamin. *The Negro in the Civil War.* Boston: Little, Brown, 1953.

Quimby, Robert S. *The U.S. Army in the War of 1812: An Operational and Command Study.* 2 vols. East Lansing: Michigan State University Press, 1998.

Rafuse, Ethan S. *McClellan's War: The Failure of Moderation in the Struggle for the Union.* Bloomington: Indiana University Press, 2011.

Randall, Ruth P. *Colonel Elmer Ellsworth.* Boston: Little, Brown and Co., 1960.

Reed, Rowena. *Combined Operations in the Civil War.* Annapolis, MD: Naval Institute Press, 1978.

Remini, Robert V. *Andrew Jackson.* New York: Twayne Publishers, 1966.

———. *Andrew Jackson and his Indian Wars.* New York: Viking Penguin, 2001.

Rezneck, Samuel. *Profiles Out of the Past of Troy, New York, Since 1789.* Troy, NY: Greater Troy Chamber of Commerce, 1970.

Richards, George H. *Memoir of Alexander Macomb.* New York: McElrath, Bangs, 1833.

Richards, Kent D. *Isaac L. Stevens: Young Man in a Hurry.* Provo, UT: Brigham Young University Press, 1979.

Richardson, James D., comp. *A Complication of the Messages and Papers of the Presidents, 1789–1897.* 10 vols. Washington, DC: Government Printing Office, 1886–99.

Riddle, Albert Gallatin. *Recollections of War Times; Reminiscences of Men and Events in Washington, 1860–1865.* New York: G. P. Putnam Sons, 1895.

Robinson, William M., Jr. *The Confederate Privateers.* New Haven, CT: Yale University Press, 1928.

Rogers, Fred B. *Bear Flag Lieutenant: The Life Story of Henry L. Ford.* San Francisco: California Historical Society, 1951.

Ross, John. *The Papers of John Ross.* Edited by Gary E. Moulton. Norman: University of Oklahoma Press, 1984.

Ruby, Robert H., and John A. Brown. *The Cayuse Indians: Imperial Tribesmen of Old Oregon.* Norman: University of Oklahoma Press, 1972.

Russell, William H. *My Diary North and South.* 2 vols. Boston: T. O. H. P. Hurnham, 1863.

Ruttenber, Edward M. *History of the Town of Newburgh.* Newburgh, NY: E. M. Ruttenber, 1859.

Sandweiss, Martha et al. *Eyewitness to War: Prints and Daguerreotypes of the Mexican War, 1846–1848.* Fort Worth, TX: Amon Carter Museum; Washington, DC: Smithsonian Institution Press, 1989.

Sandwich, Brian. *The Great Western: Legendary Lady of the Southwest.* El Paso: Texas Western Press, 1991.

Savage, John. *Our Living Representative Men: From Official and Original Sources.* Philadelphia: Childs and Peterson, 1860.

Schecter, Barnet. *The Devil's Own Work: The Civil War Draft Riots and the Fight to Reconstruct America.* New York: Walker and Co., 2005.

Schlicke, Carl P. *General George Wright: Guardian of the Pacific Coast.* Norman: University of Oklahoma Press, 1988.

Scott, Winfield. *Memoirs of Lieut.-General Scott, L. L. D. Written by Himself.* New York: Sheldon and Co., 1865.

Scribner, Benjamin F. *Camp Life of a Volunteer: A Campaign in Mexico, Or a Glimpse at Life in Camp.* Philadelphia: J. Gihon, 1850.

Scroggs, William D. *Filibusters and Financiers: The Story of William Walker and His Associates.* New York: Russell and Russell, 1969.

Sears, Stephen W. *The Civil War Papers of George B. McClellan, Selected Correspondence, 1860–1865.* New York: Ticknor and Fields, 1989.

———. *George B. McClellan: The Young Napoleon* (New York: Ticknor and Fields, 1988).

Sellar, Robert. *The U. S. Campaign of 1813 to Capture Montreal.* Huntingdon, Quebec: Gleaner Ales Print, 1913.

Senkewicz, Robert M. *Vigilantes in Gold Rush San Francisco.* Palo Alto, CA: Stanford University Press, 1985.

Seymour, Horatio. *Public Record: Including Speeches, Messages, Proclamations, Official Correspondence, and other Public Utterances of Horatio Seymour.* Compiled and edited by Thomas Cook and Thomas W. Cox. New York: I. W. England, 1868.

Sheridan, P[hilip]. *Personal Memoirs.* 2 vols. New York: Webster, 1888.

Sherman, W. T. *Memoirs of Gen. W. T. Sherman, Written by Himself.* 2 vols. New York: C. L. Webster and Co., 1891.

Silver, James W. *Edmund Pendleton Gaines: Frontier General.* Baton Rouge: Louisiana State University Press, 1949.

Simms, Jeptha R. *Trappers of New York: Or a Biography of Nicholas Stoner and Nathaniel Foster.* Albany, NY: N.p., 1851.

Skaggs, Davis Curtis and Gerard T. Altoff. *A Signal Victory: The Lake Erie Campaign, 1812–1813.* Annapolis, MD: Naval Institute Press, 1997.

Skeen, C. Edward. *John Armstrong, Jr., 1758–1843: A Biography.* Syracuse, NY: Syracuse University Press, 1981.

Skelton, William B. *An American Profession of Arms: The Army Officer Corps, 1784–1861.* Lawrence: University of Kansas Press, 1992.

Sketch of the Life and Public Service of Maj. Gen. John E. Wool, United States Army. New York: Kettell & Moore, 1851.

Smith, George W. and Charles Judah, eds. *Chronicles of the Gringos: The U. S. Army in the Mexican War, 1846–1848, Accounts and Eyewitnesses & Combatants.* Albuquerque: University of New Mexico Press, 1968.

Smith, Justin. *The War with Mexico.* 2 vols. New York: Macmillan Co., 1919.

Smith, Merritt R. *Harpers Ferry Armory and the New Technology.* Ithaca, NY: Cornell University Press, 1977.

Spafford, Horatio G. *A Gazetteer of the State of New York.* Albany, NY: H. C. Southwick, 1813.

Spencer, Donald S. *Louis Kossuth and Young America: A Story of Sectionalism and Foreign Policy, 1848–1852.* Columbia: University of Missouri Press, 1977.

Spencer, Ivor D. *The Victor and the Spoils: A Life of William L. Marcy.* Providence, RI: Brown University Press, 1959.

Stagg, John C. A. *Mr. Madison's War: Politics, Diplomacy, and Warfare in the Early Republic, 1813–1830.* Princeton, NJ: Princeton University Press, 1983.

Starr, Louis M. *Bohemian Brigade: Civil War Newsmen in Action.* New York: Alfred A. Knopf, 1954.

Steele, Matthew Forney. *American Campaigns.* Washington, DC: Byron S. Adams, 1901.

[Stevens, Isaac I.]. *Messages of the Governor of Washington Territory, Also, The Correspondence with the Secretary of War, Gen. Wool, the Officers of the Regular army, and the Volunteer Service of the Washington Territory.* Olympia, WA: Edward Furst, 1857.

Stevens, Kenneth R. *Border Diplomacy: The Caroline and McLeod Affairs in Anglo-American Relations, 1837–1842.* Tuscaloosa: University of Alabama Press, 1989.

Still, William N. *Monitor Builders: A Historical Study of the Principal Firms and Individuals Involved in the Construction of the USS Monitor.* Washington, DC: National Park Service, 1988.

Stout, Joseph A., Jr. *The Liberators: Filibustering Expeditions into Mexico, 1848–1862, and the Last Thrust of Manifest Destiny.* Los Angeles: Westernlore Press, 1973.

Strobridge, William F. *Regulars in the Redwoods: The U. S. Army in Northern California, 1852–1861.* Spokane, WA: Arthur H. Clark Co., 1994.

Strong, George Templeton. *The Diary of George Templeton Strong.* Edited by Allan Nevins and Milton H. Thomas. 4 vols. New York: Macmillan, 1952.

Swanberg, W. A. *First Blood: The Story of Fort Sumter.* New York: Charles Scribner's Sons, 1957.

Sylvester, Nathaniel B. *History of Rensselaer Co., New York: With Illustrations and Biographical Sketches of Its Prominent Men and Pioneers.* Philadelphia: Everts and Peck, 1880.

Taylor and his Generals, a Biography of Major-General Zachary Taylor; and sketches of the lives of Generals, Worth, Wool, and Twiggs . . . New York: Burgess, Stringer & Co., 1847.

Taylor, Zachary. *Letters of Zachary Taylor from the Battle-Fields of the Mexican War.* Edited by William H. Samson. Rochester, NY: Genesee Press, 1908.

Teeter, Paul R. *A Matter of Hours: Treason at Harpers Ferry.* Rutherford, NJ: Fairleigh Dickinson University Press, 1982.

Tenney, William J. *The Military and Naval History of the Rebellion in the United States.* New York: D. Appleton and Co., 1866.

The Territorial Papers of the United States. 26 vols. Edited by Clarence Carter. Washington, DC: Government Printing Office, 1787–1934.

Thian, Raphel T., comp. *Notes Illustrating the Military Geography of the United States.* Washington, DC: Government Printing Office, 1881.

Thomas, Emory M. *Bold Dragoon; The Life of J. E. B. Stuart.* New York: Harper and Row, 1986.

Thomason, John W., Jr. *Jeb Stuart.* New York: Charles Scribner's Sons, 1930.

Thompson, Gerald. *Edward F. Beale and the American West.* Albuquerque: University of New Mexico Press, 1983.

Thompson, Jerry. *Civil War to the Bloody End: The Life and Times of Major General Samuel P. Heintzelman.* College Station: Texas A&M University Press, 2006.

Tompkins, Daniel D. *Papers of Daniel D. Tompkins, Governor of New York, 1807–1817.* 3 Vols. New York: Wyncoop, Hallenbeck, Crawford Co., 1898–1902.

Townsend, Edward D. *The California Diary of General E. D. Townsend.* Edited by Malcolm Edwards. Los Angeles: Ward Ritchie Press, 1970.

Tyler, Ron, ed. *The New Handbook of Texas.* 6 vols. Austin: Texas State Historical Association, 1996.

Union Defence Committee of the City of New York. New York: Union Defence Committee, 1885.

Utley, Robert M. *Frontiersmen in Blue: The United States Army and the Indian, 1848–1865.* New York: Macmillan Co., 1967.

———. *Indian Frontier, 1846–1890.* Albuquerque: University of New Mexico Press, 2003.

Van Deusen, Glydon G. *Thurlow Weed: Wizard of the Lobby.* Boston: Little, Brown, and Co., 1947.

———. *William Henry Seward.* New York: Oxford University Press, 1967.

Van Rensselaer, Solomon. *A Narrative of the Affair at Queenston in the War of 1812.* New York: Leavitt, Lord, and Co., 1836.

Victor, Orville J. *The History, Civil, Political, and Military, of the Southern Rebellion.* 4 vols. New York: J. D. Torrey, [1861–1868].

Wagandt, Charles L. *The Mighty Revolution.* Baltimore: Johns Hopkins University Press, 1964.

Wallace, Isabel. *Life and Letters of General W. H. L. Wallace.* Chicago: R. R. Donnelley and Sons, 1909.

Wallace, Lewis. *Lew Wallace: An Autobiography.* 2 vols. New York: Harper and Row, 1906.

War of the Rebellion: A Compilation of the Official Records of the Rebellion. 128 vols. Washington: Government Printing Office, 1888–89.

Warren, Thomas R. *Dust and Foam: Or, Three Oceans and Two Continents.* New York: C. Scribner, 1859.

Watson, Samuel. *Peacemakers and Conquerors: The Army Officer Corps on the American Frontier, 1821–1846.* Lawrence: University of Kansas Press, 2013.

———, ed. *Warfare in the USA, 1784–1861.* Burlington, VT: Ashgate Publishing Co., 2005.

Webster, Daniel. *The Papers of Daniel Webster: Correspondence.* Edited by Charles M. Wiltse et al. 7 vols. Hanover, NH: University Press of New England, 1976.

Webster, Daniel. *The Papers of Daniel Webster: Speeches and Formal Writings.* Edited by Charles M. Wiltse et al. 2 vols. Hanover, NH: University Press of New England, 1988.

Weed, Thurlow. *Life of Thurlow Weed.* Edited by Harriet Weed and Thurlow Weed Barnes. 2 vols. Boston: Houghton Mifflin and Co., 1883–84.

Weigley, Russell F. *The American Way of War: A History of United States Military Strategy and Policy.* New York: Macmillan Press, 1973.

———. *History of the United States Army.* New York: Macmillan Co., 1967.

Weinert, Richard P., Jr., and Robert Arthur. *Defender of the Chesapeake: The Story of Fort Monroe.* Shippensburg, PA: White Mane Publishing Co., 1989.

Weise, Arthur James. *History of the City of Troy.* Troy, NY: W. H. Young 1876.

———. *Troy's One Hundred Years.* Troy, NY: W. H. Young, 1891.

Werstein, Irving. *July, 1863.* New York: Julian Messner, 1957.

Wesley, Edgar B. *Guarding the Frontier: A Study of Frontier Defense from 1815 to 1825.* Westport, CT: Greenwood Press, 1970.

West, Richard S. *Mr. Lincoln's Navy.* New York: Longmans, Green and Co., 1957.

———. *Lincoln's Scapegoat General: A Life of Benjamin F. Butler, 1818–1893.* Boston: Houghton, Mifflin, 1965.

Whisker, James B. *United Stares Armory at Springfield, 1795–1865.* Lewiston, NY: Edwin Mellon Press, 1997.

Winders, Richard Bruce. *Mr. Polk's Army: The American Military Experience in the Mexican War.* College Station: Texas A&M University Press, 1997.

Wilkins, Thurman. *Cherokee Tragedy: The Ridge Family and the Decimation of a People.* Norman: University of Oklahoma Press, 1986.

Williams, David. *The Georgia Gold Rush: Twenty-Niners, Cherokees, and Gold Fever.* Columbia: University of South Carolina Press, 1993.

Williams, Kenneth P. *Lincoln Finds a General: A Military Study of the Civil War.* 5 vols. New York: Macmillan, 1950.

Williams, T. Harry. *Lincoln and His Generals.* New York: Alfred A. Knopf, 1952.

———. *Lincoln and the Radicals.* Madison: University of Wisconsin Press, 1941.

Wilson, James G. and John Fiske, eds. *Appleton's Cyclopaedia of American Biography.* 6 vols. New York: D. Appleton and Co., 1887–89.

Wilson, Rufus R. *Washington: The Capital City.* 2 vols. Philadelphia: J. B. Lippincott, 1902.

Winthrop, Theodore. *The Canoe and the Saddle.* Tacoma, WA: J. H. Williams, 1913.

Wislizenus, Adolphus. *Memoir of a Tour of Northern Mexico, Connected with Col. Doniphan's Expedition in 1846 and 1847.* Washington, DC: Tippin and Strepper, 1848.

Woodford, Frank. *Lewis Cass: The Last Jeffersonian.* New Brunswick, NJ: Rutgers University Press, 1950.

Woodworth, John. *Reminiscences of Troy, from Its Settlement in 1790 to 1807.* Albany, NY: J. Munsell, 1860.

Wooster, Robert. *The American Military Frontiers: The United States Army in the West, 1783–1900.* Albuquerque: University of New Mexico Press, 2009.

Wooten, John M. *Red Clay in History.* Cleveland, TN: n.p., 1935.

Wyllys, Rufus K. *The French in Sonora.* Berkeley: University of California Publications, 1932.

Young, Andrew W. *History of Chautauqua County, New York . . .* [with] *Biographical and Family Sketches.* Buffalo, NY: Matthews and Warren, 1875.

Articles

Ball, Durwood. "Filibusters and Regular Troops in San Francisco, 1851–1855." *Military History of the West* 28 (1998).

Bauer, K. Jack, ed. "General John E. Wool's Memoranda of the Battle of Buena Vista. *Southwestern Historical Quarterly* 72 (July 1973).

Baylies, Frances P. "Baylies Papers," *Proceedings* 46 (February 1913).

———. "Letters from a Massachusetts Federalist [Baylies] to a New York Democrat [John E. Wool], 1823–1839." Edited by Samuel Rezneck. *New York History* 48 (July 1967).

———. "The March of the United States Troops, under Command of General John E. Wool, from San Antonio, Texas to Saltillo Mexico, in the Year 1846." *Stryker's Register and Magazine* 4 (July 1850).

Beltman, Brian W. "Territorial Commands of the Army: The System Refined but Not Perfected, 1815–1821." *Journal of the Early Republic* 11 (Summer 1991).

Benham, Henry Washington. "Recollections of Mexico and the Battle of Buena Vista, Feb. 22 and 23, 1847." *Old and New* (June and July 1871).

Bernard, Jean-Paul. "Vermonters and the Lower Canadian Rebellion, 1837–1838." *Vermont History* 58 (Fall 1990).

Brown, Walter L. "The Mexican War Experiences of Albert Pike and the 'Mounted Devils' of Arkansas." *Arkansas Historical Quarterly* 12 (Winter 1953.

Canaday, Dayton W. "Voice of the Volunteer of 1847." *Journal of Illinois State Historical Society* 44 (Autumn 1951).

Clark, Charles B. "Suppression and Control of Maryland, 1861–1865." *Maryland Historical Magazine* 54 (September 1959).

Corn, James F. "Conscience or Duty: General John E. Wool's Dilemma with Cherokee Removal." *Journal of Cherokee Studies* 3 (Winter 1978).

Dawson, Joseph G. "American Civil-Military Relations and Military Government, and the Service of Colonel Alexander Doniphan in the Mexican War." *Armed Forces and Society* 22 (Summer 1996).

———. "Zealous for Annexation: Volunteer Soldiering, Military Government, and the Service of Colonel Alexander Doniphan in the Mexican-American War." *Journal of Strategic Studies* 19 (December 1996).

Demers, John J. and James P. Sweeney. "Rise and Fall of the Greenbush Cantonment." *Journal of the War of 182 and the Era 1800 to 1840* 2 (Spring 1997).

Deyrup, Felicia J. *Arms Makers of the Connecticut Valley* (Northampton, MA: Smith College Studies in History, 1948), 33:160–72

Edwards, Abram. "A Western Reminiscence." In State Historical Society of Wisconsin *Collections,* edited by Lyman C. Draper (1907) 5:158–60.

Engelmann, Adolph. "The Second Illinois in the Mexican War: Mexican War Letters of Adolph Engelmann." Edited and translated by Otto B. Engelmann. *Journal of Illinois State Historical Society* 26 (January 1934).

Fitzgerald, Michael S. "'Nature Unsubdued:' Diplomacy, Expansion and the American Military Buildup of 1815–1816." *Mid-America* 77 (1995).

———. "Rejecting Calhoun's Expansible Army Plan: The Army Reduction Act of 1821." *War in History* 3 (Summer 1976).

Gunderson, Robert G. "The Washington Peace Conference of 1861: Selection of Delegates." *Journal of Southern History* 24 (August 1958).

Hauptman, Lawrence M. "General John E. Wool in Cherokee Country, 1836–37: A Reinterpretation." *Georgia Historical Quarterly* 85 (Spring 2001)

———. "John E. Wool and the New York City Draft Riots of 1863: A Reassessment." *Civil War History* 49 December 2003.

Henderson, Alfred J. "A Morgan County Volunteer in the Mexican War [John B. Duncan]." 41 *Journal of Illinois State Historical Society* (December 1948).

Hinton, Harwood P. "John Agustus Griswold." In *Biographical Dictionary of the Union: Northern Leaders of the Civil War,* edited by John T. Hubbell and James W. Geary. Westport, CT: Greenwood Press, 1995.

———. "John Wool." In *The United States and Mexico at War: Nineteenth-Century Expansionism and Conflict,* edited by Donald S. Frazer. New York: Simon and Schuster Macmillan, 1998

Howard, Donald D. "Jean-Jacques Pelet: Warrior of the Sword and Pen." *Journal of Military History* 53 (June 1989).

Huggins, Dorthy Harriet. "San Francisco Society: From *The Directory of 1879.*" [California Historical Society] *Quarterly* 19 (September 1940).

Izard, George. "The War of 1912 in Northern New York: General George Izard's Journal of the Chateauguay Campaign." Edited by John C. Fredriksen. *New York History* 76 (April 1995).

Johnson, J. Neeley. "The Law and Order View of the San Francisco Vigilance Committee of 1856: Taken from the Correspondence of Governor J. Neeley Johnson." [California Historical Society] *Quarterly* 14 (December 1935).

Kenny, Stephen. "The Canadian Rebellions and the Limits of Historical Perspective." *Vermont History* 58 (Summer 1990)

Kimball, Jeffrey. "The Fog and Friction of Frontier War: The Role of Logistics in American Offensive Failure during the War of 1812." *Old Northwest* 5 (1979–1980).

Kreneck, Thomas H. "The North Texas Regiment in the Mexican War." *Military History of Texas and the Southwest* 12 (No. 2).

Kuehl, Daniel T. "Double Shot Your Guns and Give 'em Hell! Brazton Bragg and the War in Mexico." *Civil War History* 37 (March 1991).

Lee. Robert E. "Lt. Lee Reports to Captain Talcott on Fort Calhoun's Construction on the Rip Raps." *Virginia Magazine of History and Biography* (July 1952).

Lee, Wayne E. "Fortify, Fight, or Flee: Tuscarora and Cherokee Defensive Warfare and Military Culture Adaptation." *Journal of Military History* 68 (July 2004).

Leonard, Thomas C. "Red, White, and Army Blue: Empathy and Anger in the American West." *American Quarterly* 26 (May 1974).

Lokken, Roy. "The Martial Law Controversy in Washington Territory, 1856." *Pacific Northwest Quarterly* 43 (April 1952).

McBarron, Hugh C., Jr. "American Military Dress in the War of 1812, Part III: Regular Infantry." *Journal of the American Military Institute* 4 (Fall 1940).

McElrath, T. P. "The Draft Riots in New York." In *Annals of the War, Written by Leading Participants North and South.* Philadelphia: Times Publishing Co., 1879.

Mann, Conklin. "The Wool Family of New York." In *New York Genealogical and Biographical Record* 72 (October 1941).

Marshall, Thomas M., ed. "Diary and Memoranda of William L. Marcy, 1849–1851." *American Historical Review* 24 (April 1919.

May, Robert E. "Young American Males and Filibustering in the Age of Manifest Destiny: The United States Army as a Cultural Mirror." *Journal of American History* 78 (1991).

Nasatir, A. P. "Guillaume Patrice Dillon." [California Historical Society] *Quarterly* 35 (December 1956).

Roach, Isaac. "Journal of Major Isaac Roach, 1812–1824." Contributor, Mary Roach Archer. *Pennsylvania Magazine of History and Biography* 17 (1893).

Sanger, J. P. "The Inspector General's Department." *Journal of the Military Service Institution of the United States* 16 (1895).

Satz, Ronald W. "Carey Allen Harris, 1836–1838." In *The Commissioners of Indian Affairs, 1824–1977,* edited by Robert M. Kvasnicka and Herman J. Viola. Lincoln: University of Nebraska Press, 1979.

Sheaffe, Roger Hale. "Letter-Book of Gen. Sir Roger Sheaffe." Edited by Frank H. Severance. [Buffalo Historical Society] *Publications* 17 (1913).

Skelton, William B. "Army Officers' Attitudes Towards Indians, 1830–1860." *Pacific Northwest Quarterly* 67 (1976).

———. "High Army Leadership in the Era of the War of 1812: The Making and Remaking of the Officer Corps." *William and Mary Quarterly* 51 (1994).

———. "Officers and Politicians: The Origins of Army Politics in the United States before the Civil War." *Armed Forces and Society* (Fall 1979).

———. "Professionalization in the U. S. Army Forces and Society." *Armed Forces and Society* 1 (1975).

"Sketches of a Campaign in Coahuila." *American Whig Review* 16 (November 1852).

Stevens, Issac I. "Letters of Governor Isaac I. Stevens, 1853–1854." Edited by John S. Richards. *Pacific Northwest Quarterly* 30 (July 1939).

Thoburn, Joseph B., ed. "Letters of Cassandra Sawyer Lockwood: Dwight Mission, 1834." *Chronicles of Oklahoma* 33 (Summer 1955).

Vipperman, Carl J. "The Bungled Treaty of New Echota: The Failure of Cherokee Removal, 1836–1838." *Georgia Historical Quarterly* (Fall 1989).

———. "The Particular Mission of Wilson Lumpkin." *Georgia Historical Quarterly* 66 (Fall 1982).

Viola, Herman J. "Zachary Taylor and the Indiana Volunteers." *Southwest Historical Quarterly* 72 (January 1969).

Watson, Samuel J. "Knowledge, Interest and the Limits of Military Professionalism: The Discourse on American Coastal Defense, 1815–1860." *War in History* 5 (1998).

———. "Manifest Destiny and Military Professionalism: Junior U.S. Army Officers' Attitudes Toward War With Mexico, 1844–1846." *Southwestern Historical Quarterly* 99 (July 1996).

———. "Thomas Sidney Jesup: Soldier, Bureaucrat, Gentleman Democrat." In *The Human Tradition in the Early Republic*, edited by Michael A. Morrison. Wilmington, DE: Scholarly Resources, 2000.

———. "The Uncertain Road to Manifest Destiny: Army Officers and the Course of American Territorial Expansionism, 1815–1846." In *Manifest Destiny and Empire: Essays on Antebellum American Expansionism*, edited by Christopher Morris and Sam W. Haynes. College Station: Texas A&M University Press, 1997.

———. "United States Army Officers Fight the 'Patriot War:' Responses to Filibustering on the Canadian Border, 1837–1839." *Journal of the Early Republic* 6 (1998).

Winder, C. S. "Diary of a Bachelor Lt. at Beneica in 1854." Edited by Alice Lloyd and Arthur T. Brice. *Pacific Historian* 14 (Spring 1970).

Wooster, Robert. "Military Strategy in the Southwest, 1848–1860. *Military History of Texas and the Southwest* 15 (1979).

Dissertations and Theses

Adams, George Rollie. "General William Shelby Harney: Frontier Soldier, 1800–1889." PhD diss., University of Arizona, 1983.

Bergmann, William H. "Commerce and Arms: The Federal Government, Native Americans, and the Economy of the Old Northwest, 1783–1807." PhD diss., University of Cincinnati, 2005.

Bloom, John Porter. "With the American Army in Mexico, 1846–1848." PhD diss., Emory University, 1949.

Childress, David T. "The Army in Transition: The United States Army, 1815–1846." PhD diss., Mississippi State University, 1974.

Dillon, Lester R., Jr. "American Artillery in the Mexican War, 1846–1847." MA thesis, University of North Texas, 1969.

Hinton, Harwood Perry. "The Military Career of John Ellis Wool, 1812–1863." PhD diss., University of Wisconsin 1960.

Kamaras, Nicholas P. "George B. McClellan and the Election of 1864." PhD diss., University of Delaware, 1976.

Kretchik, Walter Edward. "Peering Through the Mist: Doctrine as a Guide for U. S. Army Operations, 1775–2000." PhD diss., University of Kansas, 2001.

Long, William Wallace. "A Biography of Major General Edwin Vose Sumner, U.S.A, 1797–1863." PhD diss., University of New Mexico, 1971.

Miller, Cynthia Ann. "The United States Army Logistics Complex, 1818–1845: A Case Study of the Northern Frontier." PhD diss., Syracuse University, 1991.

Smith, Carlton B. "The United States War Department, 1815–1842. PhD diss., University of Virginia, 1967.

Spaid, Stanley S. "Joel Palmer and Indian Affairs in Oregon." PhD diss., University of Oregon, 1950.

Steinhauer, Dale R. "'Sogers:' Enlisted Men in the U. S. Army, 1915–1860." PhD diss., University of North Carolina, 1992.

Waghelstein, John Davis. "Preparing for the Wrong War: The United States Army and Low Intensity Conflict, 1755–1890." PhD diss., Temple University, 1990.

Watson, Samuel J. "Professionalism, Social Attitudes, and Civil-Military Accountability." PhD diss., Rice University, 1996.

Westermann, Robert Paul, Jr. "'To the Public Prosperity': The United States Army and the Market Revolution, 1815–1844." PhD diss., Texas A&M University, 2001.

Wooster, Robert A. "Military Strategy in the American West, 1815–1860." MA thesis, Lamar University, 1979.

Wynn, Dennis J. "The San Patricios and the United States-Mexican War of 1846–1848." PhD diss., Loyola University of Chicago, 1982.

INDEX